GRAPHICS
GEMS
II

This is a volume in

The Graphics Gems Series

A Collection of Practical Techniques
for the Computer Graphics Programmer

Series Editor

Andrew S. Glassner
Xerox Palo Alto Research Center
Palo Alto, California

GRAPHICS GEMS II

edited by

JAMES ARVO

Program of Computer Graphics
Cornell University
Ithaca, New York

ACADEMIC PRESS, INC.
Harcourt Brace Jovanovich, Publishers
Boston   San Diego   New York
London   Sydney   Tokyo   Toronto

ACADEMIC PRESS, INC.
1250 Sixth Avenue, San Diego, CA 92101

United Kingdom Edition published by
ACADEMIC PRESS LIMITED
24-28 Oval Road, London NW1 7DX

Library of Congress Cataloging-in-Publication Data

Graphics gems II/edited by James Arvo.
      p.   cm.
    Includes bibliographical references and Index.
    ISBN 0-12-064480-0 (alk. paper)
    1. Computer graphics.   2. C (Computer program language)
I. Arvo, James. 1956– .   III. Title: Graphics gems II.
T385.G6972   1991
006.6—dc20   91-4716
                                                            CIP

Printed in the United States of America
91 92 93   9 8 7 6 5 4 3 2 1

About the Cover

The cover image is the second in the "Gems" theme that I began last year. Andrew Glassner and I bounced some ideas back and forth, and the design solidified pretty quickly. The gems themselves are the same as in last year's image.

The picture was generated at Pacific Data Images using their in-house software. All of the textures and models are procedurally generated. The sand texture, the sand surface shape, the woodgrain, the sea foam, and the starfish texture are all derived from fractal noise patterns. I spent most of my time on the water, making it look all shiny and wet and transparent, but not too transparent. The foam on the water's surface was also very time-consuming. Another challenge was to get the gems to all pile on top of each other convincingly. I wrote a program that dropped them, one at a time, and as they fell, they were rotated to the angle that moved them the furthest down without intersecting anything that was there already. This program took a couple of hours to run, but it was much faster than trying to place them by hand.

The picture was rendered with a ray-tracing program and took 50 hours on an Silicon Graphics 4D25 computer at a resolution of 2250 × 3000 pixels with four samples per pixel.

Thaddeus Beier
Silicon Graphics Computer Systems

◆

When Andrew asked if I wanted to do the cover for *Graphics Gems II*, I said "Sure . . . we can reuse the software we built last year for *Graphics Gems*." While it wasn't quite that simple, it was much easier to produce this cover than the first one. As before, the image was designed on a color monitor producing red, green and blue pixels. For printing, we needed to convert these pixels to cyan, magenta, yellow, and black pixels (printer color space). Once in this form, the image was processed commercially to produce half-toned film suitable for printing. This final step was performed at Kedie-Orent, Sunnyvale, California, on their Crosfield digital prepress system.

As was the case with the first "Gems" picture, many of the original image colors could not be exactly reproduced in print form. The colors had to be modified to map into the set of colors that can be produced by the printer, its gamut. The trick is to do the modification while maintaining the appearance of the image. In this picture, the colors in the sand, shells, and water were mostly inside the printer gamut. However, some of the gem colors, particularly the bright blue-greens, were far outside the gamut. The transformation we applied was similar to the one we designed for *Graphics Gems*; colors outside of the gamut were desaturated to colors of the same lightness while maintaining the same hue. If one color of a particular hue needed to be desaturated, all colors of the same hue would be desaturated to preserve shading detail. However, colors outside of the gamut move more than colors inside of the gamut to maintain the overall saturation.

The colors of the *Graphics Gems II* cover are lighter and more delicate than the cover of *Graphics Gems*, and much more of the image lies in the interior of the printer gamut. We tuned the transformation for this image to minimize the change to the less saturated colors, preserving the subtle shading in the sand and water.

Thanks to Bill Wallace, who wrote the original gamut mapping software for *Graphics Gems*, and to Ken Fishkin, who helped with the production of the cover this year.

Maureen Stone
Xerox Palo Alto Research Center

CONTENTS

The symbol ◇ denotes gems that have accompanying C implementations in Appendix II.

I
2D GEOMETRY AND ALGORITHMS

II
IMAGE PROCESSING

III
FRAME BUFFER TECHNIQUES

IV
3D GEOMETRY AND ALGORITHMS

V
RAY TRACING

VI
RADIOSITY

VII
MATRIX TECHNIQUES

VIII
NUMERICAL AND PROGRAMMING TECHNIQUES

IX
CURVES AND SURFACES

C
APPENDIX I:
C UTILITIES

C
APPENDIX II:
C IMPLEMENTATIONS

FOREWORD

by Andrew Glassner

Welcome to *Graphics Gems II*, a new collection of practical techniques and methods for the computer graphics programmer. This book is a collection of contributions from many people, most of whom work independently of each other. Yet through these volumes we are able to share our observations and insights with each other and our readers, and together build a communal library of graphics programming techniques.

In the preface to the original *Graphics Gems*, I wrote that "This book . . . concludes one turn of a cycle of discovery, documentation, editing, publishing, and reading, which will in turn lead to new discoveries." I am delighted that we have completed another loop around the cycle, and emerged with another strong collection of programming techniques. As with its predecessor, the articles in this book are primarily not research results; those can be found in the formal professional literature. Rather, the *Graphics Gems* books are a conduit for practical information. Much of the detailed information in these volumes would be inappropriate for a technical paper, but is invaluable to the implementor.

This volume has been edited by Jim Arvo, who is well known in the graphics community as a skilled researcher and teacher. Jim and I have taught several courses together at SIGGRAPH conferences and other venues, and I have always been impressed with his insight and eagerness to share his knowledge. The fine selection and organization of material in this volume demonstrates his abilities well.

There may be more volumes in the *Graphics Gems* series. We will continue to solicit and collect contributions, and organize them into new books, as long as the quality remains high and the results useful. Each volume will be edited by a different individual, since I believe this will help keep the results lively and fresh, and reflect the diversity that is part of what makes computer graphics such an exciting field to work in.

One quality that I believe is shared by most engineers and scientists is a desire for elegance. An elegant solution is one that is simple and direct, and often provokes an "Aha!" reaction when first encountered. Often such clean techniques depend on an insight derived from knowledge or experience from another context. Many of the techniques in this book fit this criterion for elegance, and enlarge the repertoire of tools upon which we draw for solutions to new, unexpected challenges. Each time we learn how another person solved an important problem, we grow as designers and implementors.

It is in celebration of the twin spirits of growth and sharing that we bring you this book. I hope you find it informative and useful.

PREFACE

Continuing in the spirit of the inaugural *Graphics Gems* volume, *Graphics Gems II* represents the collective expertise of a large and diverse group of people. The common thread shared by all the contributors is that each has devised or refined useful ideas which can benefit other computer graphics practitioners, and they have graciously agreed to disseminate them. The resulting amalgam has a character quite distinct from any text book on the subject, as it reflects ideas and approaches every bit as diverse and unique as the people behind them.

In the field of computer graphics, as with almost any endeavor, there is rarely a best way to do anything. Therefore, this volume shares a recurring theme with the original volume by presenting techniques for doing well-known operations faster or easier. Some present a new way of looking at an old problem while others provide useful mathematical machinery with broad application.

There are several ways to use this book. First, it can be a source of solutions to specific problems. If one of the gems in this collection addresses a particular problem of interest to you, the idea can be employed with little ado. This is facilitated by the program listings provided with many of the gems. A second way to use this book is to simply browse, learning clever solutions to problems you may not have encountered or even considered yet. Often the ideas behind the gems can be applied in contexts much broader than those shown, or they may serve as the seeds to get you thinking along new lines. In any event, there is much to be gained by looking over the shoulders of experienced graphics programmers as they apply the subtle tricks of the trade.

The overall structure, mathematical notation and pseudo-code used here are the same as in the first volume. The scope and names of some parts have been changed slightly to best accommodate this new collection of gems. In order to make this book as self-contained as possible we have included several of the important sections verbatim from the first volume for easy reference; there are the sections entitled "Mathematical Notation", "Pseudo-Code", and the listings "Graphics Gems C Header File" and "2D and 3D Vector Library" in Appendix I. The last of these contains several corrections and extensions. Only the part titled "Radiosity" has no counterpart in the first volume. This new part has been added to complement the part on ray tracing and to reflect current research trends.

The gems comprising each part all relate to some common theme. Gems that share something more fundamental are linked via the "See also" section at the end of each gem. Gems identified by gem number are contained in this volume; gems identified by page number are in the first volume of Graphics Gems. The mathematical background which is assumed in most of the gems is limited to elementary calculus and linear algebra, the staples of computer graphics.

The C programming language has been used for all the program listings in the appendix because it is widely used and is among the most portable of languages. It is also a favorite among graphics programmers because of its flexibility. These considerations made it the obvious choice. All the C code in this book is in the public domain, and is yours to study, modify, and use. As of this writing, all code listings are available via anonymous ftp transfer from the machine "weedeater.math.yale.edu" (internet address 130.132.23.17). When you connect to this machine using ftp, log in as "anonymous", and give your own last name as the password. Then use the "cd" command to move to the directory "pub/GraphicsGems". Download and read the file called README to learn about where the code is kept, and how to report bugs.

Thanks are due to the many people who made this book possible. First and foremost I'd like to thank all the gem contributors, whose expertise and insight is what this book is all about. Also, I'd like to thank Andrew Glassner for pioneering this whole adventure and for assisting in every aspect along the way. Thanks and congratulations are due to Sari Kalin for making the entire project come together with apparent ease, and to Alison Dowd for her meticulous assistance. Special thanks to Terry Lindgren for his tremendously helpful input where it was most needed, and to Greg Ward, John Francis, Paul Heckbert, and Eric Haines for their reviews, expert opinions, and helpful suggestions. Finally, I'd like to thank Craig Kolb for providing a safe haven for the public domain C code.

MATHEMATICAL NOTATION

Geometric Objects

0	the number 0, the zero vector, the point $(0, 0)$, the point $(0, 0, 0)$
a, b, c	real numbers (lower-case italics)
P, Q	points (upper-case italics)
$\mathbf{l}, \mathbf{m}$	lines (lower-case bold)
$\mathbf{A}, \mathbf{B}$	vectors (upper-case bold) (components A_i)
$\mathbf{M}$	matrix (upper-case bold)
θ, φ	angles (lower-case greek)

Derived Objects

$\mathbf{A}^\perp$	the vector perpendicular to $\mathbf{A}$ (valid only in 2D, where $\mathbf{A}^\perp = (-A_y, A_x))$
$\mathbf{M}^{-1}$	the inverse of matrix $\mathbf{M}$
$\mathbf{M}^T$	the transpose of matrix $\mathbf{M}$
$\mathbf{M}^*$	the adjoint of matrix $\mathbf{M}$ $\left(\mathbf{M}^{-1} = \dfrac{\mathbf{M}^*}{\det(\mathbf{M})}\right)$
$|\mathbf{M}|$	determinant of $\mathbf{M}$
$\det(\mathbf{M})$	same as above
$\mathbf{M}_{i,j}$	element from row i, column j of matrix $\mathbf{M}$ (top-left is $(0, 0)$)
$\mathbf{M}_{i,}$	all of row i of matrix $\mathbf{M}$

$\mathbf{M}_{,j}$ all of column j of matrix $\mathbf{M}$

$\triangle\,ABC$ triangle formed by points A, B, C

$\angle\,ABC$ angle formed by points A, B, C with vertex at B

Basic Operators

$+\,,\,-\,,\,/\,,\,*$ standard math operators

$\cdot$ the dot (or inner or scalar) product

$\times$ the cross (or outer or vector) product

Basic Expressions and Functions

$\lfloor x \rfloor$ floor of x (largest integer not greater than x)

$\lceil x \rceil$ ceiling of x (smallest integer not smaller than x)

$a\,|\,b$ modulo arithmetic; remainder of $a \div b$

$a \bmod b$ same as above

$B_i^n(t)$ Bernstein polynomial $= \binom{n}{i} t^i (1 - t)^{n-i}$, $i = 0 \cdots n$

$\binom{n}{i}$ binomial coefficient $\dfrac{n!}{(n - i)!\,i!}$

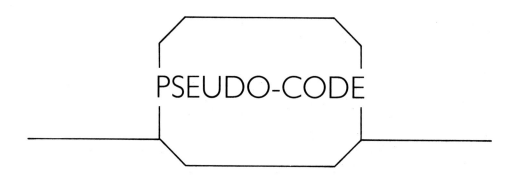

PSEUDO-CODE

Declarations (not required)

name: TYPE ← initialValue;
examples:
π:**real** ← 3.14159;
v: **array** [0..3] **of integer** ← [0, 1, 2, 3];

Primitive Data Types

array [lowerBound..upperBound] **of** TYPE;
boolean
char
integer
real
double
point
vector

matrix3
    equivalent to:
    matrix3: record [array [0..2] of array [0..2] of real;];
    example: m: Matrix3 ← [[1.0, 2.0, 3.0], [4.0, 5.0, 6.0], [7.0, 8.0, 9.0]];
    m[2][1] is 8.0
    m[0][2] ← 3.3;   assigns 3.3 to upper-right corner of matrix

matrix4

equivalent to:
matrix4: record [array [0..3] of array [0..3] of real;];
example: m: Matrix4 ← [
      [1.0, 2.0, 3.0, 4.0],
      [5.0, 6.0, 7.0, 8.0],
      [9.0, 10.0, 11.0, 12.0],
      [13.0, 14.0, 15.0, 16.0]];
m[3][1] is 14.0
m[0][3] ← 3.3;   *assigns 3.3 to upper-right corner of matrix*

Records (Structures)

Record definition:
Box: **record** [
      left, right, top, bottom: **integer**;
      ];

newBox: Box ← **new**[Box];
      dynamically allocate a new instance of Box and return a pointer to it

newBox.left ← 10;
      this same notation is appropriate whether newBox is a pointer or structure

Arrays

v: **array** [0..3] **of integer** ← [0, 1, 2, 3]; *v is a four-element array of integers*

v[2] ← 5;   *assign to third element of v*

Comments

A comment may appear anywhere – it is indicated by italics

Blocks

> **begin**
>> Statement;
>> Statement;
>> . . .
>> **end**;

Conditionals and Selections

> **if** Test
>> **then** Statement;
>> [**else** Statement];   *else clause is optional*

> result = **select** Item **from**
>> instance: Statement;
>> **endcase**: Statement;

Flow Control

> **for** ControlVariable: Type ← InitialExpr, NextExpr **do**
>> Statement;
>> **endloop**;

> **until** Test **do**
>> Statement;
>> **endloop**;

> **while** Test **do**
>> Statement;
>> **endloop**;

> **loop**; *go directly to the next endloop*

> **exit**; *go directly to the first statement after the next endloop*

> **return**[value]   *return value as the result of this function call*

Logical Connectives

or, and, not, xor

Bitwise Operators

bit-or, bit-and, bit-xor

Relations

$=, \neq, >, \geq, <, \leq$

Assignment Symbol

$\leftarrow$

(note: the test for equality is $=$)

Available Functions

These functions are defined on all data types

min(a, b)	*returns minimum of a and b*
max(a, b)	*returns maximum of a and b*
abs(a)	*returns absolute value of a*
sin(x)	*sin(x)*
cos(x)	*cos(x)*
tan(x)	*tan(x)*
arctan(y)	*arctan(y)*
arctan2(y, x)	*arctan(y/x), defined for all values of x and y*
arcsin(y)	*arcsin(y)*
arccos(y)	*arccos(y)*
rshift(x, b)	*shift x right b bits*
lshift(x, b)	*shift x left b bits*
swap(a, b)	*swap a and b*
lerp(α, l, h)	*linear interpolation:* $((1 - \alpha)*l) + (\alpha*h) = l + (\alpha*(h - l))$

clamp(v, l, h)   *return l if $v < l$, else h if $v > h$, else v: $min(h, max(l, v))$*

floor(x) or $\lfloor x \rfloor$ *round x towards 0 to first integer*

ceiling(x) or $\lceil x \rceil$ *round x away from 0 to first integer*

round(x)   *round x to nearest integer, if frac(x) = .5, round towards 0*

frac(x)   *fractional part of x*

CONTRIBUTORS

Numbers in parentheses indicate pages on which authors' gems begin.

James Arvo (264, 355, 357), *Cornell University, Program of Computer Graphics, Ithaca, New York, 14853, arvo@wisdom.graphics.cornell.edu*

Thaddeus Beier (cover), *Silicon Graphics Computer Systems, 2011 Shoreline Boulevard, Mountain View, California, 94043*

Jeffrey C. Beran-Koehn (299), *Minard 300, North Dakota State University, Fargo, North Dakota, 58105, beran-ko@plains.nodak.edu*

Hanspeter Bieri (107), *Institut für Informatik und angewandte Mathematik der Universität Bern, Langgassstrasse 51, CH-3012, Bern, Switzerland*

Rod G. Bogart (72), *Chrysler Center, Room 229, 2121 Bonisteel Boulevard, Ann Arbor, Michigan 48109, rgb@caen.engin.umich.edu*

Ronald B. Capelli (389), *IBM Corporation, Department C13, Building 703-2, P.O. Box 950, Poughkeepsie, New York 12602*

Shenchang Eric Chen (293), *Apple Computer, Inc., MS60W, 20707 Valley Green Drive, Cupertino, California 95014, chense@apple.com*

Joseph M. Cychosz (251), *Purdue University CADLAB, Potter Engineering Center, 520 Evergreen, West Lafayette, Indiana 47907, cychosz@ecn.purdue.edu*

Andrew S. Glassner (89, 179, 191), *Xerox PARC, 3333 Coyote Hill Road, Palo Alto, California 94304, glassner.pa@xerox.com*

Ronald N. Goldman (170, 324, 332, 338), *Department of Computer Science, Rice University, P.O. Box 1892, Houston, Texas 77251*

Eric Haines (247, 267), *3D/Eye, Inc., 2359 North Triphammer Road, Ithaca, New York 14850, erich@eye.com*

James Hall (138), *Prime/Computer Vision, 14 Cosby Drive, Bedford, Massachusetts, 01730*

Steve Hollasch (467), *1437 West 6th Street, Tempe, Arizona 85281-3205*

Jeff Holt (86), *Intergraph Corporation, 4515 Bonnell Drive, #25H, Huntsville, Alabama 35894-0001, UUNET!INGR!HOLT!HOLT*

David Kirk (257, 264), *CALTECH Computer Science 256-80, Pasadena, California 91125, dk@csvax.caltech.edu*

Andreas Kohler (107), *Institut für Informatik und angewandte Mathematik der Universität Bern, CH-3012 BERNE, Langgassstrasse 51, Switzerland*

Mark E. Lee (277, 283), *Amoco Production Company, Tulsa Research Center, P.O. Box 3385, Tulsa, Oklahoma 74102, zmel02@trc.amoco,com*

Terence Lindgren (138, 420), *Prime/Computer Vision, 14 Cosby Drive, Bedford, Massachusetts, 01730*

Patrick-Gilles Maillot (219), *Sun MicroSystems, Inc., 2550 Garcia Avenue, MTV 21-04, Mountain View, California 94043*

David Martindale (147), *Imax Systems Corporation, 2525 Speakman Drive, Sheridan Park, Ontario, Canada, L5K 1B1, labrea!adobe!uunet!utai!imax!dave*

Nelson Max (101), *L-301, Lawrence Livermore National Laboratory, P.O. Box 808, Livermore, California 94550, max2@llnl.gov*

Gary W. Meyer (159), *Department of Computer and Information Science, University of Oregon, Eugene, Oregon 97403, gary@cs.uoregon.edu*

Hong Tong Minh (232), *c/o Daniel Thalmann, Computer Graphics Lab., Swiss Federal Institute of Technology, CH-1015 Lausanne, Switzerland, thalmann@eldi.epfl.ch*

Claudio Montani (202), *Istituto di Elaborazione dell'Informazione, Consiglio Nazionale delle Ricerche, Via Santa Maria 46, 56126 Pisa, Italy, montani@icnucevm.cnuce.cnr.it*

Doug Moore (406), *Department of Computer Science, Rice University, P.O. Box 1892, Houston, Texas 77254, dougm@rice.edu*

Jack C. Morrison (10), *5654 South Jackpine Road, Evergreen, Colorado 80439, ncar!boulder!agcsun!jackm*

F. Ken Musgrave (25, 163), *Departments of Mathematics and Computer Science, Yale University, Box 2155 Yale Station, New Haven, Connecticut 06520, musgrave@yale.edu*

Christopher J. Musial (387, 435), *801 Leonard Drive, Rock Hill, Missouri 63119*

Alan W. Paeth (93, 143, 147, 174, 371, 381, 440), *NeuralWare, Inc., Penn Center West, Building 4, Suite 227, Pittsburgh, Pennsylvania 15276*

Mark J. Pavicic (299), *Minard 300, North Dakota State University, Fargo, North Dakota 58105, pavicic@plains.nodak.edu*

Andrew Pearce (273, 275), *Alias Research, #500, 110 Richmond Street E., Toronto, Ontario, Canada M5C 1P1, pearce@alias.UUCP*

Mukesh Prasad (7), *Meta Mind, Inc., Two Trolley Square, Suite 146, East Haven, Connecticut 06512*

Jack Ritter (392), *SHO Graphics, 1890 N. Shoreline Boulevard, Mountain View, California, 94043*

Jon Rokne (5, 14, 17, 19), *Department of Computer Science, University of Calgary, Calgary, Alberta, Canada T2N 1N4, rokne@cpsc.ucalgary.ca*

David Schilling (371), *4609 148th Avenue NE II201, Bellevue, Washington 98007*

John F. Schlag (105, 377, 417), *105-A Fairview Avenue, Capitola, California 95010*

Dale A. Schumacher (50, 57, 78), *399 Beacon Street, St. Paul, Minnesota 55104, dal@syntel.mn.org*

Roberto Scopigno (202), *Instituto CNUCE Consiglio Nazionale delle Ricerche, Via Santa Maria, 36, 56126 Pisa, Italy, scop@icnucevm.cnuce.cnr.it*

Hans-Peter Seidel (424, 428), *Department of Computer Science, University of Waterloo, Waterloo, Ontario, Canada N2L 3G1, hpseidel@watcgl.waterloo.edu*

Clifford A. Shaffer (172), *Department of Computer Science, Virginia Tech, Blacksburg, Virginia 24061, shaffer@cs.vt.edu*

Peter Shirley (306), *Computer Science Department, 101 Lindley Hall, Indiana University, Bloomington, Indiana 47405-4101, shirley@cs.indiana.edu*

Kenneth Shoemake (351, 366, 368, 394, 412), *Xerox PARC, 3333 Coyote Hill Road, Palo Alto, California 94304*

François Sillion (311), *Cornell University, Program of Computer Graphics, Ithaca, New York, 14853, fxs@fsaturn.graphics.cornell.edu*

Jonathan E. Steinhart (31), *20180 Baker Creek Road, McMinnville, Oregon 97128-8016*

Filippo Tampieri, (303), *Program of Computer Graphics, 580ETC Building, Cornell University, Ithaca, New York, 14853, fxt@graphics.cornell.edu*

Daniel Thalmann (232), *Computer Graphics Laboratory, Swiss Federal Institute of Technology, CH-1015 Lausanne, Switzerland, thalmann@ligsg2.epfl.ch*

Nadia Magnenat Thalmann (232), *MIRALab, CUI, University of Geneva, 12 rue du lac, CH 1207, Geneva, Switzerland, thalmann@uni2a.unige.ch*

Spencer W. Thomas (72, 116, 320), *EECS Department, University of Michigan, 1101 Beal Avenue, Ann Arbor, Michigan 48109-2110, spencer@eecs.umich.edu*

Samuel P. Uselton (277, 283), *NASA Ames Research Center, M/S T 045-1, Moffett Field, California 94035, uselton@nas.nasa.gov*

Douglas Voorhies (26, 257), *Apollo Systems Division, Hewlett-Packard, 300 Apollo Drive, Chelmsford, Massachusetts 01824, dougv@apollo.com*

Greg Ward (80, 396), *Lawrence Berkeley Laboratory, 1 Cyclotron Road, 90-3111, Berkeley, California, 94720, gjward@ldl.gov*

Joe Warren (406), *Department of Computer Science, Rice University, P.O. Box 1892, Houston, Texas 77254, jwarren@rice.edu*

Kevin Wu (342), *Sun MicroSystems Inc., 2550 Garcia Avenue, MTV 21-04, Mountain View, California 94043, kevin.wu@eng.sun.com*

Xiaolin Wu (126), *Department of Computer Science, University of Western Ontario, London, Ontario, Canada N6A 5B7, wu@csd.uwo.ca*

Sue-Ken Yap (84), *CSIRO Division of Information Technology, P.O. Box 664, Canberra, ACT 2601, Australia, ken@csis.dit.csiro.au*

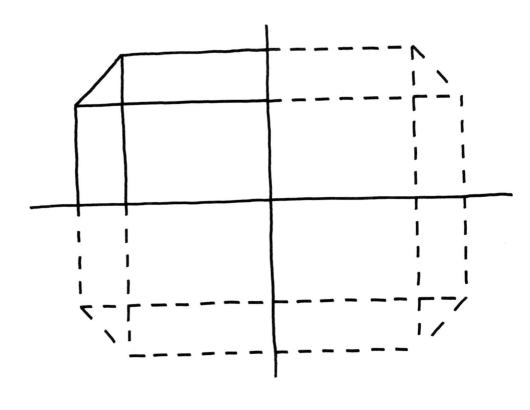

2D GEOMETRY
AND
ALGORITHMS

2D GEOMETRY AND ALGORITHMS

Two-dimensional geometry pervades computer graphics. For that reason, a graphics programmer requires tools for solving a wide variety of 2D geometrical problems efficiently. Solutions to several typical 2D problems are presented in this Part: computing the area of a planar figure, the distance from a point to a line, and finding the minimal enclosing area for some set of objects.

Problems of this type arise partly because of the inherent two-dimensional nature of the screen or surface on which graphics output is displayed. Another reason 2D geometry is important is that larger problems in three dimensions are frequently attacked by reducing them to smaller and simpler problems in one or two dimensions. This tactic of breaking a large problem into little palatable ones is perhaps nowhere more evident than in large computer programs. Graphics, in particular, tends to reduce ultimately to a large number of small 2D problems, increasing the importance of handling each one robustly and efficiently.

The first six gems of this Part address some common 2D operations that can serve as basic building blocks for more complex tasks. The next two gems deal with generating and utilizing a class of *space-filling* curves. These curves are members of an infinite family of related curves that possess an interesting property: If the steps in their constructions are carried out a sufficiently large number of times, the resulting curves will come arbitrarily close to every point in some region of space. Although this concept is equally valid in spaces of any dimension, space-filling curves are most immediately useful and accessible for computer graphics when they are in two dimensions. For instance, their convoluted paths provide an interesting order in which to generate the pixels of an image, as described in Gem number I.8. The final gem in this Part describes a uniform framework that provides many useful operations on two-dimensional figures.

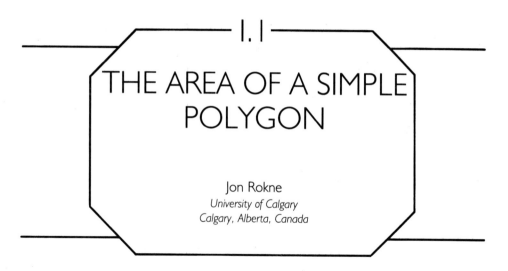

1.1

THE AREA OF A SIMPLE POLYGON

Jon Rokne
University of Calgary
Calgary, Alberta, Canada

The formula for the area of a triangle is given in "Triangles" (Goldman, 1990b). This was generalized by Stone (1986) to a formula for a simple polygon that is easy to remember.

Let $P_i = (x_i, y_i)$, $i = 1, \ldots, n$ be the counterclockwise enumeration of the vertices of the polygon as in Fig. 1.

The area of the polygon is then

$$A = \frac{1}{2} \begin{vmatrix} x_1 & x_2 & \cdots & x_n & x_1 \\ y_1 & y_2 & \cdots & y_n & y_1 \end{vmatrix},$$

where the interpretation of

$$\begin{vmatrix} x_1 & x_2 & \cdots & x_n & x_1 \\ y_1 & y_2 & \cdots & y_n & y_1 \end{vmatrix}$$

is the summing of the products of the "downwards" diagonals and subtraction of the product of the "upwards" diagonals.

A specific example serves to clarify the formula. Consider the polygon in Fig. 2.

The area of this polygon is

$$A = \frac{1}{2} \begin{vmatrix} 6 & 5 & 2 & 4 & 2 & 6 \\ 2 & 4 & 3 & 3 & 1 & 2 \end{vmatrix}$$

$$= (6 \times 4 + 5 \times 3 + 2 \times 3 + 4 \times 1 + 2 \times 2$$

$$- 5 \times 2 - 2 \times 4 - 4 \times 3 - 2 \times 3 - 6 \times 1)/2$$

$$= 7.5.$$

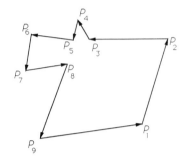

Figure 1.

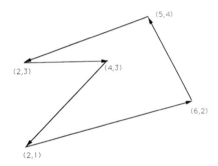

Figure 2.

See also IV.1 The Area of Planar Polygons and Volume of Polyhedra, Ronald N. Goldman

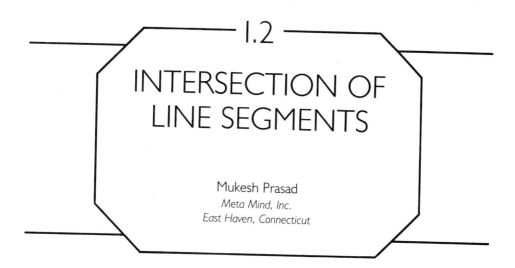

1.2

INTERSECTION OF LINE SEGMENTS

Mukesh Prasad
Meta Mind, Inc.
East Haven, Connecticut

Problem

Given two line segments in 2D space, determine whether they intersect or not. If they intersect, then determine the point of intersection.

Algorithm

The following approach is particularly efficient if the lines often do not, in fact, intersect—since it works from partial results. It also is very adaptable to integer-only computation.

Let the line **L12** connect points $(x1, y1)$ and $(x2, y2)$.

Let the line **L34** connect points $(x3, y3)$ and $(x4, y4)$.

Let the equation of **L12** be $F(x, y) = 0$, and that of **L34** be $G(x, y) = 0$. Then this approach consists of the following steps:

1. From the equation of **L12**, by substituting $x3$ and $y3$ for x and y, compute $r3 = F(x3, y3)$.

2. Compute $r4 = F(x4, y4)$.

3. If (i) $r3$ is not equal to 0, (ii) $r4$ is not equal to 0, and (iii) the signs of $r3$ and $r4$ are the same (either both positive or both negative), the lines do not intersect. Terminate algorithm.

4. From the equation of **L**34, compute $r1 = G(x1, y1)$.

5. Compute $r2 = G(x2, y2)$.

6. If (i) $r1$ is not equal to 0, (ii) $r2$ is not equal to 0, and (iii) the signs of $r1$ and $r2$ are the same, the lines do not intersect. Terminate algorithm.

7. Lines intersect (or they are collinear). Compute point of intersection

Notes

- The algorithm is determining if:
    - $(x3, y3)$ and $(x4, y4)$ *lie on the same side of* **L**12. *If they do, the line segments obviously do not intersect.*
    - $(x1, y1)$ and $(x2, y2)$ *lie on the same side of* **L**34. *If they do, the line segments obviously do not intersect.*

    Otherwise, the lines must intersect, or be collinear.

- Comparison of signs usually is very efficient. The C Implementation for this gem (Appendix 2) assumes a 2's complement number representation, and uses the XOR operation to determine efficiently whether the signs are the same or not.

- The intermediate results obtained are useful in the final step—"compute point of intersection"—improving the algorithm efficiency.

- The algorithm, obviously, will work in floating point coordinates; but if all x_i and y_i are available as integers (as is usually the case in bitmap graphics) and the result is required on an integer grid, only integer arithmetic is required. However, for integer-only arithmetic, care should be taken to guard against the possibility of overflow. The polynomial evaluations in the C Implementation (Appendix 2) are at most of degree 3; therefore, using 32-bit integers, a range of 0–1023 in both X and Y directions can be handled. For larger ranges, floating point operations may be necessary, or a rearrangement of the intersection–point computations may be necessary.

- For further efficiency, the cases of $r1$, $r2$, $r3$, or $r4$ being 0 can be handled separately. In these situations, one of the end points is the point of intersection, and need not actually be computed.

- If a collinearity check needs to be efficient, it can also be determined from the fact that both $r3$ and $r4$ (or both $r1$ and $r2$) will be 0 in this case. The lines may or may not overlap in this case, and if necessary, that can be easily determined by comparing extents.

See also (49) *A Fast 2D Point-on-Line Test, Alan W. Paeth*; (304) *Intersection of Two Lines in Three-Space, Ronald Goldman*

DISTANCE FROM A POINT TO A LINE

Jack C. Morrison
Evergreen, Colorado

This Gem gives efficient formulae for the distance d_1 between a point P and the line defined by points A and B, and the distance d_2 between P and the line segment **AB**. (See Fig. 1.) An example of this application is an interactive program searching for a displayed line segment nearest to a cursor being moved by the user. For this type of operation, coordinates usually are integers, and computationally expensive functions need to be avoided to provide rapid response. Often, finding d_1^2 or d_2^2 is sufficient.

The distance from a point to a line is the length of the segment **PQ** perpendicular to line **AB**. Start with the formula for the area of triangle $\triangle ABP$,

$$\frac{1}{2}\left| A_x B_y + B_x P_y + P_x A_y - A_y B_x - B_y P_x - P_y A_x \right|.$$

Rearranging terms to save *multiplies* gives the following formula for $a2$, twice the signed area of $\triangle ABP$:

$$a2 = (P_y - A_y)(B_x - A_x) - (P_x - A_x)(B_y - A_y).$$

Since the area of $\triangle ABP$ is also given by

$$\frac{1}{2}d_1|\mathbf{AB}|,$$

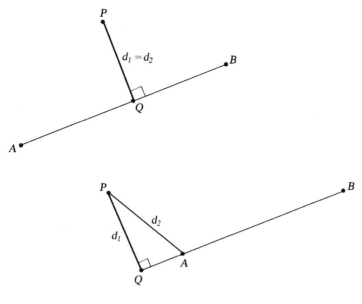

Figure 1.

the square of the desired distance can be computed as

$$d_1^2 = \frac{a2^2}{(B_x - A_x)^2 + (B_y - A_y)^2}.$$

The differences in the denominator already were computed for $a2$, so the total operation count is six *adds*, five *multiplies*, and one *divide*. If d_1 is needed directly, a square root also is necessary; but if an approximation will do, we can apply Alan Paeth's *Graphics Gem* shortcut for $|\mathbf{AB}|$ to get

$$d_1' = \frac{|a2|}{|B_x - A_x| + |B_y - A_y| - \dfrac{1}{2}\min\big(|B_x - A_x|, |B_y - A_y|\big)}$$

for an approximate distance with only two *multiplies* and one *divide*.

When the perpendicular intersection point Q is outside the segment AB, d_1 is shorter than d_2, the distance from P to the nearest point of the segment. For applications only interested in segments within some maximum distance from P, a simple bounding box test can be used to quickly reject segments that are too far away:

$$\min(A_x, B_x) - \text{margin} < P_x < \max(A_x, B_x) + \text{margin},$$

$$\min(A_y, B_y) - \text{margin} < P_y < \max(A_y, B_y) + \text{margin},$$

and then d_1 can be taken as an approximation for d_2.

To properly compute the distance d_2, note first that

$$d_2 = |\mathbf{AP}| \quad \text{if } Q \text{ is on the half-line from } A \text{ away from } B,$$

$$d_2 = d_1 \quad \text{if } Q \text{ is on the segment } \mathbf{AB},$$

$$d_2 = |\mathbf{BP}| \quad \text{if } Q \text{ is on the half-line from } B \text{ away from } A.$$

The appropriate case can be determined by using the dot product equality,

$$\mathbf{AP} \cdot \mathbf{AB} = |\mathbf{AP}||\mathbf{AB}| \cos a$$

$$= (P_x - A_x)(B_x - A_x) + (P_y - A_y)(B_y - A_y),$$

where a is the angle $\angle PAB$.

If Q is at A, then a is 90°, and $\cos a$ (and the dot product) is zero. If Q is on the same side of A as B, a is less than 90°, and the dot product is positive. This leads to the following algorithm for d_2:

```
t ← (Px − Ax)(Bx − Ax) + (Py − Ay)(By − Ay)        (dot product)
if t < 0
        then d2 ← |AP|                               Q beyond A
        else begin
                t ← (Bx − Px)(Bx − Ax) + (By − Py)(By − Ay)
                if t < 0
                        then d2 ← |BP|               Q beyond B
                        else d2 ← d1                 Q on AB
        end
```

The coordinate differences again can be reused, and an approximation for $|\mathbf{AP}|$ and $|\mathbf{BP}|$ may be sufficient.

With integer coordinates for A, B, and P, these formulae can be computed without using floating point, although care is required to prevent overflow. For example, the worst case for three points in a 512×512 region gives a value of $262{,}144$ for $a2$, whose square exceeds 32 bits.

See also (3) *Useful 2D Geometry, Andrew S. Glassner*

AN EASY BOUNDING CIRCLE

Jon Rokne
University of Calgary
Calgary, Alberta, Canada

In *Graphics Gems* (Ritter, 1990), we find a near-optimal algorithm for computing a bounding sphere for N points in 3D space. Here, we present a simple exact algorithm for computing the smallest bounding circle for N points $P_1, \ldots, P_N$ in 2D. It was devised for a numerical analysis problem by E. Grassmann, who met with a fatal climbing accident when the paper (Grassmann and Rokne, 1979) was about to be published.

We use the convention that a point P in 2D can be written as $P = (P_x, P_y)$, where P_x is the x coordinate of P and P_y is the y coordinate of P. Also, $|P - Q|$ is the Euclidean distance between P and Q.

From geometry, it follows that the smallest bounding circle is defined by two or three points of the pointset. See, for example, Rademacher and Toeplitz (1957).

Case 1. The circle is determined by two points, P and Q. The center of the circle is at $(P + Q)/2.0$ and the radius is $|(P - Q)/2.0|$.

Case 2. The circle is determined by three points, P, Q, and R, forming a triangle with acute angles.

The two cases are shown in Fig. 1.

In both cases, there may be other points of the pointset lying on the circle.

The algorithm proceeds as follows. First, determine a point P with the smallest P_y. Then find a point Q such that the angle of the line segment **PQ** with the x axis is minimal. Now find R such that the absolute value of the angle $\angle PRQ$ is minimal.

If this angle is acute, then the circle C_1 determined by P, Q, and R contains—according to elementary geometry—all the points, since there

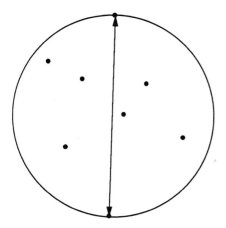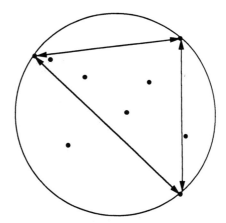

Figure 1.

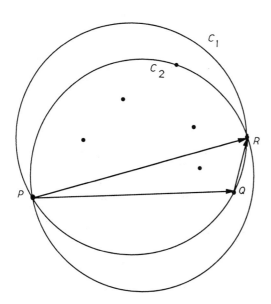

Figure 2.

are no points to the right of the directed segment **PQ**. If the triangle PQR has acute angles only, we are finished. If the angle at R is obtuse, then the center of the circle we are looking for is $(P + Q)/2.0$ and the radius is $|(P - Q)/2.0|$.

If the angle at P or Q is obtuse, say at Q, we replace Q by R and repeat to get a circle C_2. See Fig. 2.

From elementary geometry, it follows that the center of C_1 is to the left of the directed line segment **PR**, since the angle at Q otherwise would be acute. Since the radius of C_2 at most is as large as that of C_1, it follows that all the points inside C_1 that are to the right of the segment **PR** also are inside C_2. No points are lost, therefore, and C_2 contains all the points of the pointset.

We claim that after finitely many repetitions, we get the minimal circle. To show this, we only need to observe that a point to the right of the line segment **PR** stays to the right, and therefore, we have at most $N - 2$ iterations.

The algorithm has a worst-case complexity of $O(N * *2)$.

See also (*301*) *An Efficient Bounding Sphere, Jack Ritter*

I.5

THE SMALLEST CIRCLE CONTAINING THE INTERSECTION OF TWO CIRCLES

Jon Rokne
University of Calgary
Calgary, Alberta, Canada

In *Graphics Gems* (Thompson, 1990), an algorithm is given for the area of intersection of two circles. Here we give a simple pseudo-code for finding the center and radius of the smallest circle containing the intersection of two circles.

We use the convention that a point in 2D can be written as $P = (P_x, P_y)$ where P_x is the x coordinate of P and P_y is the y coordinate of P. Also, $|P - Q|$ is the Euclidean distance between P and Q.

The two circles are (P, r) and (Q, s) and the circle containing the intersection is (R, t).

In Fig. 1, we show the case of non-trivial intersection.

Let $l = |P - Q|$. Then from the geometry, we have for this case the two equations,

$$z^2 + t^2 = r^2,$$

$$(l - z)^2 + t^2 = s^2,$$

which can be solved for

$$z = (l^2 + r^2 - s^2)/(2l),$$

$$t = \sqrt{r^2 - z^2}.$$

The other cases are $(P, r) \subseteq (Q, s)$, $(Q, s) \subseteq (P, r)$, and $(P, r) \cap (Q, s) = \varnothing$.

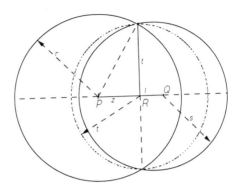

Figure 1.

Pseudo-Code

$l \leftarrow |P - Q|$;
If $l > r + s$ **then** *"intersection empty"*
    else if $l + r < s$ **then** $C \leftarrow P, t \leftarrow r$;
      else if $l + s < r$ **then** $C \leftarrow q, t \leftarrow s$;
        else begin
          $z \leftarrow (l^2 + r^2 - s) / (2l)$;
          $t \leftarrow \sqrt{r^2 - z^2}$;
          $R \leftarrow P + (P - Q)z/l$;
        end
       endif
      endif
    endif

See also I.6 Appolonius's 10th Problem, Jon Rokne

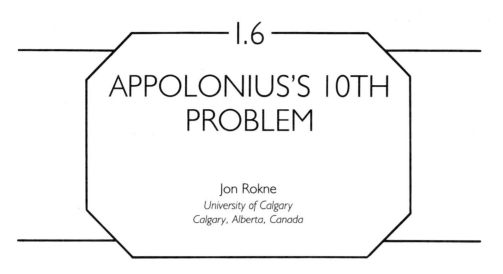

1.6

APPOLONIUS'S 10TH PROBLEM

Jon Rokne
University of Calgary
Calgary, Alberta, Canada

A problem that occurs in computer graphics and CAD is the construction of the smallest circle touching three given circles from the outside. This problem already was considered by Appolonius (c. 262–190 B.C.).

The solution given here was used in a numerical analysis problem (Grassmann and Rokne, 1979).

It should be pointed out that the problem of finding the smallest sphere containing three given spheres also is reduced to the problem of Appolonius by considering the plane passing through the centers of the spheres.

We note first that the problem may have no solution; i.e., there might not exist a circle touching the given circles from the outside. See Figs. 1 and 2.

In Fig. 1, there is no circle that touches the given circles, whereas in Fig. 2, at least one of the circles has to be outside. The decision procedure for the case in Fig. 1 is obvious, whereas the decision procedure for the case in Fig. 2 requires the computation of the outside common tangents of the largest and the smallest circle as well as for the largest and the middle circle. See Glassner (1990b).

It is convenient to use some geometric properties of complex analysis to develop the algorithm. These are not stressed in the usual courses in complex analysis in North America; hence, we refer to Behnke *et al.*, (1983), where the required formulas are given.

We identify points in the plane with complex quantities; that is, if Z is a point in 2D, then we write the x coordinate as Re Z and the y coordinate as Im Z, and we also think of it as a complex quantity, $Z = \text{Re } Z + i\,\text{Im } Z$. An overline means reflection with the real axis for a

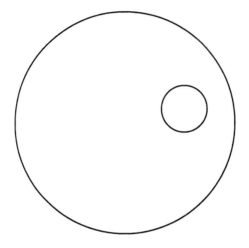
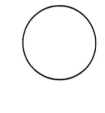

Figure 1.

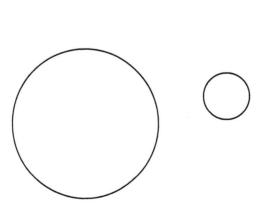
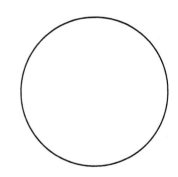

Figure 2.

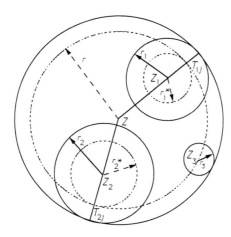

Figure 3.

point in 2D and the complex conjugate when we consider the point as a complex quantity.

Let (Z_i, r_i), $i = 1, 2, 3$ be the center and radii of the circles. First, subtract the smallest radius, say r_3, from the other two, getting $r_i^* = r_i - r_3$.

If we can find a circle (Z, r) that passes through Z_3 and touches (Z_i, r_i^*), $i = 1, 2$ from outside, then the disc $(Z, r + r_3)$ will be the solution to the original problem. The geometry of this is shown in Fig. 3.

To find this circle, we use the transformation,

$$W = \mathscr{T}(Z) = \frac{1}{Z - Z_3},$$

mapping the Z plane into a W plane.

This maps the unknown circle onto a straight line, the two other circles into circles with centers and radii (W_i, ρ_i), where (as shown by Gargantini and Henrici (1972), Eq. (2.1), or any textbook describing the Moebius transformation)

$$W_i = \frac{\overline{(Z_i - Z_3)}}{|Z_i - Z_3|^2 - (r_i^*)^2}, \qquad \rho_i = \frac{r_i^*}{|Z_i - Z_3|^2 - (r_i^*)^2},$$

$$i = 1, 2.$$

$$(1)$$

Note that $\rho_i < 0$ if Z_3 is contained in disc i, $i = 1, 2$, and that any circle through Z_3 in the Z plane is mapped into a line in the W plane.

The problem now is to find a common tangent line, l: Re $UW = c$, in the W plane. This line mapped back into the Z plane will provide the desired circle.

If l separates the centers from the origin, the corresponding circle in the Z plane will separate the centers from ∞, i.e., contain the given discs inside.

The constants U and c are determined by the following method. We can assume that $|U| = 1$. Then the distance formula gives

$$\text{Re } UW_i - c = \rho_i, \qquad i = 1, 2. \tag{2}$$

Subtracting, we get

$$\text{Re } U(W_1 - W_2) = \rho_1 - \rho_2,$$

and calling

$$\alpha = \arg U(W_1 - W_2),$$

we get

$$\cos \alpha = \frac{\rho_1 - \rho_2}{|W_1 - W_2|} \tag{3}$$

and

$$\sin \alpha = \pm\sqrt{1 - \cos^2 \alpha}, \tag{4}$$

so

$$\cos \alpha + i \sin \alpha = \frac{U(W_1 - W_2)}{|W_1 - W_2|},$$

and multiplying both sides by

$$\frac{\overline{(W_1 - W_2)}}{|W_1 - W_2|},$$

22

we get

$$U = (\cos \alpha + i \sin \alpha) \frac{\overline{(W_1 - W_2)}}{|W_1 - W_2|}. \tag{5}$$

The ambiguity of the root in Eq. (2) gives the two solutions, U_1, U_2, expected from geometry. (The geometric meaning of α is the angle between the normal of l and that of the line joining W_1 and W_2.) The fact that we have positive ρ_i has the geometric meaning that the normals $\overline{U_j}$ point towards the centers, and the line does not separate the centers.

Using the first of the equations, (2), we get the corresponding c_j,

$$c_j = \operatorname{Re} W_1 U_j - \rho_i. \tag{6}$$

The line separates the W_i from the origin if $c_j > 0$.

We shall need the points of contact as well. They are

$$T_{ij}^* = W_i - \rho_i \overline{U_j}, \qquad i = 1, 2, \quad j = 1, 2.$$

We now transform the equations, $\operatorname{Re} U_j W = c_j$, back into the Z plane and get

$$\operatorname{Re} \frac{U_j}{Z - Z_3} = \frac{1}{|Z - Z_3|^2} \operatorname{Re} U_j \overline{(Z - Z_3)} = c_j,$$

and writing $Z - Z_3 = \xi + i\eta$, $U_j = m_j + i n_j$, we get

$$m_j \xi + n_j \eta = c_j(\xi^2 + \eta^2),$$

or since, $|U_j| = 1$,

$$\left(\xi - \frac{m_j}{2c_j} \right)^2 + \left(\eta - \frac{n_j}{2c_j} \right)^2 = \frac{1}{4c_j^2},$$

i.e., the circle has center $Z = U_j/(2c_j) + Z_3$ and radius $r = 1/(2c_j)$.

We can see that we need only the line for which c_j is greater, since we are interested in the circle of minimal radius.

The points of contact are

$$T_{ij} = \frac{1}{T_{ij}^*} + Z_3.$$

The computations are quite simple as shown by the following pseudo-code.

Pseudo-Code

Compute r_1^*, r_2^*.
Compute W_1, W_2, ρ_1, ρ_2 from (1).
Compute $\cos \alpha$ from (3) and $\sin \alpha$ from (4).
Compute c_1, c_2 from (5).
Choose $c = \max(c_1, c_2)$ and corresponding U from (5).
The required circle is then $Z = U/(2c) + Z_3$ with radius $r = 1/(2c)$.

See also I.5 The Smallest Circle Containing the Intersection of Two Circles, Jon Rokne

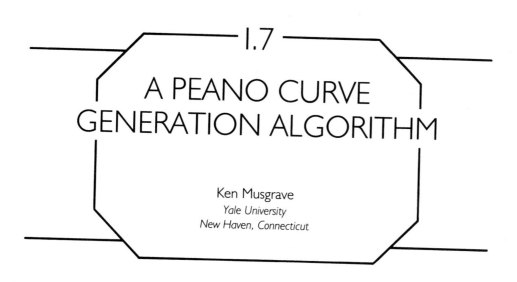

1.7

A PEANO CURVE GENERATION ALGORITHM

Ken Musgrave
Yale University
New Haven, Connecticut

One occasionally may desire a space-filling *Peano curve* in n dimensions (Peano, 1980). The Peano curve is a fractal with integer–fractal dimension. This curve provides a continuous mapping from the integers to n-space, with the properties that all points in the domain are close in the range, and most points that are close in the range are close in the domain. Applications we have found include image compression, color quantization (Stevens *et al.*, 1983; Whitten and Neal, 1982), and debugging for interactive four-dimensional rotation routines.

We have implemented Butz's algorithm (1971) for generating an n-dimensional Peano curve to m bits of precision, that is, with 2^m segments per dimension, 2^{mn} segments total. It is based on bitwise boolean operations, and is the only algorithm we have ever coded where we have had absolutely no insight into how it works. But the code's correct operation has been verified in two, three and four dimensions. See figs. 1 and 2 (color insert) for an example in 2-dimensions.

The algorithm, but not its derivation, is described in Butz (1971). Unfortunately, no insight is offered there for the logic of the algorithm.

See also I.8 Space-Filling Curves and a Measure of Coherence, Douglas Voorhies

I.8

SPACE-FILLING CURVES AND A MEASURE OF COHERENCE

Douglas Voorhies
Hewlett Packard Co.
Chelmsford, Massachusetts

Traversal

Performance of ray tracers and other rendering algorithms can be improved by altering the primary ray generation sequence. The key is to better exploit coherence.

Coherence provides opportunities to use memory more effectively. Modern memory hierarchies employ caches, translation look-aside buffers, and paging, which depend upon extreme repetition in the reference pattern. In this environment, rendering approaches that minimize churning of the working set runs considerably faster, even if the total computation is the same.

Object–space rendering (e.g., ray tracing or reverse-mapped volumetric) typically processes the screen–space pixels in scanline order, which is mediocre in its churning of the working set. An object whose screen projection is several pixels across will have several consecutive pixels that enjoy the same intersections and similar lighting experiences, but the scanline traversal sequence then leaves the object and does not return for a long time. Thus, scanline traversal exploits only one dimension of object coherence.

An ideal traversal sequence visits all the pixels in the entire area of each object before moving on to the next object, thus exploiting coherence in two dimensions. Unfortunately, there is a wide range of on-screen object sizes, and neither their size nor position is known *a priori*. Furthermore, different levels of memory hierarchies work best with repetition within working sets of different sizes. Thus, the concept of *object area* in this context may be extended to mean repetitious access at many size levels.

Two important properties for a traversal sequence which exploits coherence are that:

1. *All the pixels* in an area are visited before moving on.

2. The sequentially visited areas always are *adjacent*.

Both properties decrease the reloading of memory by minimizing the number of times an object area is exited and reentered. Assuming that the traversal sequence is fixed rather than adaptive, its selection must be based on shape alone.

Space-Filling Curves

Some space-filling curves can exploit coherence in two dimensions despite a range of object area sizes. As fractals, they are self-similar at multiple resolutions. Thus, if they do a good job of visiting all the pixels corresponding to a particular object area at one scale, then they may have

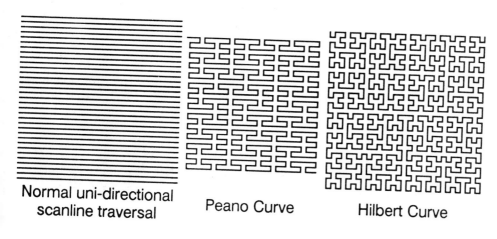

Normal uni-directional
scanline traversal

Peano Curve

Hilbert Curve

Figure 1.

this advantage for much larger or smaller object areas. As topologically continuous curves, areas visited always are adjacent. Let us look at two of them, as shown in Fig. 1.

Peano curves are recursive boustrophedonic patterns. They snake back and forth at multiple recursion levels, filling the plane. Since each pattern enters and exits from opposite rectangle corners, they implicitly use serpentines with an odd number of swaths, a minimum of three. Thus, they can be self-similar at 3×3, 9×9, 27×27, 81×81, etc. resolutions. (If squeezed in one dimension only, they can repeat as 2×3, 6×9, 18×27, 54×81, etc.)

A *Hilbert curve* is folded even more tightly. It can visit all the pixels in a 2×2, 4×4, 8×8, 16×16, etc. area before moving on, so its self-similar, area-filling patterns are more numerous and closer together in scale.

A Measure of Coherence

How can one measure the ability of a traversal sequence to exploit coherence, independent of a specific image and renderer? A pragmatic measure can be based on the notion of a memory working set. For a given object area, any traversal will consist of consecutive pixels that are within that object's screen projection and others that lie outside. Part of the working set of a renderer can be thought of as the *current object area*

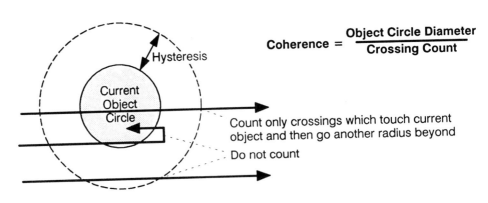

$$\text{Coherence} = \frac{\text{Object Circle Diameter}}{\text{Crossing Count}}$$

Figure 2.

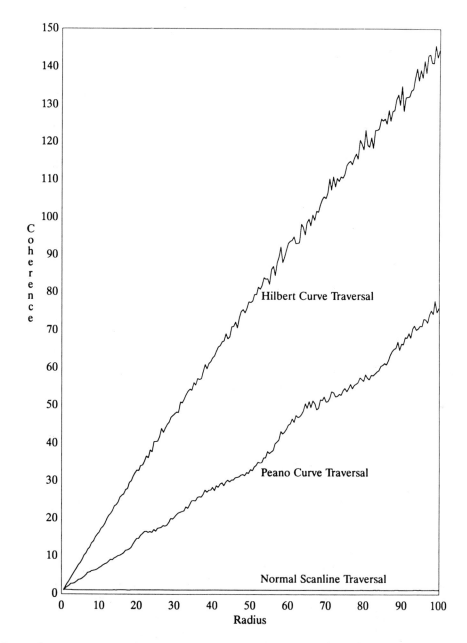

Figure 3. Average coherence of Peano and Hilbert traversal sequences for object radii of
.5 to 100.

plus the recently touched ones. In this context, *high coherence* means staying within the current object area (or nearby ones) most of the time, and venturing outside rarely, until all the current object area pixels have been visited.

To make this concrete, I assume that an imaginary object projects as a circle in screen space. Choosing a circle favors no traversal direction over another. Coherence of a traversal sequence then is the current object circle's diameter divided by the number of times the sequence exits the circle. Hysteresis is added by only counting paths that exit the object circle and then venture another radius away; this avoids penalizing small excursions beyond the circle that immediately return. See Fig. 2.

By this pragmatic measure, object areas not touching the screen edges have a coherence measure of 1.00 for normal scanline traversal, since all sequences that penetrate the circle exit and continue all the way to the screen edge and thus are counted. For Fig. 3, a 1024×1024 screen is traversed by three methods: normal scanline traversal, a Peano curve, and a Hilbert curve. (Since the Peano curve did not fit evenly into 1024×1024, it was clipped.) The coherence of 1000 circles centered at random on-screen positions is averaged for a range of radii.

Both the Peano and Hilbert curves far exceed the *coherence = 1.00* measure of conventional scanline traversal. The Hilbert curve appears superior, and is easier to generate. Better performance from a real renderer can be expected simply by choosing either of these alternative traversal sequences.

See also I.7 A Peano Curve Generation Algorithm,
Ken Musgrave

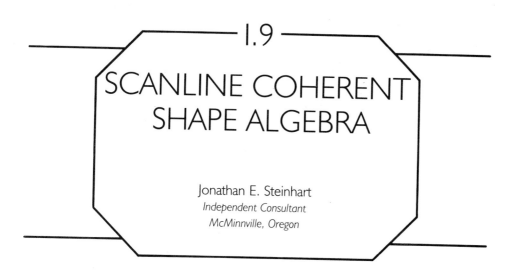

I.9

SCANLINE COHERENT SHAPE ALGEBRA

Jonathan E. Steinhart
Independent Consultant
McMinnville, Oregon

Introduction

Shape algebra has many applications in raster graphics. Window management systems use shape algebra to compute the visible regions of overlapping windows. Shape algebra can be used to implement caps and joins in fat line drawing code. POSTSCRIPT™-style (Adobe, 1985a, 1985b) clip paths are yet another application of shape algebra.

This gem details an approach to shape algebra that can be implemented efficiently as part of a raster graphics system. Routines are provided that implement the basic *union*, *intersection* and *difference* operations as shown in Fig. 1. A number of utility functions and special purpose variations also are provided, as are some example applications.

Background

Previous published work in this area falls into two categories: quadtrees (Samet, 1990a, 1990b) and the Apple™ patent (Atkinson, 1986).

Quadtrees are data structures that represent arbitrary shapes through rectangular two-dimensional binary subdivision. Although shape algebra can be performed efficiently on quadtrees, the binary subdivision technique makes it expensive to coalesce adjacent rectangles. This makes it difficult to take advantage of scanline coherence during rasterization.

The Apple™ patent uses a scanline-width bit mask to mark horizontal transitions across the region boundaries. The bit mask is updated at each vertical boundary transition. Although the Apple™ approach allows one to take advantage of scanline coherence, it has two major disadvantages.

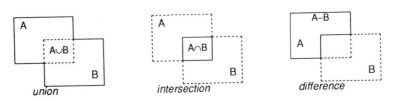

Figure 1. Basic shape algebra operations.

First, the bit mask is expensive to maintain for wide scan lines. Second, there is an unquantified legal expense involved in the utilization of this patent.

Two unpublished papers exist that describe portions of the approach presented here, Gosling (1986) and Donato and Rocchetti (1988). Earlier versions of this work appear in Steinhart *et al.* (1989, 1990).

Data Structures

Our approach is to represent arbitrary shapes as y-sorted lists of x-sorted, non-overlapping rectangles. The decomposition of an ellipse with a rectangular hole into our shape representation is shown in Fig. 2.

We store shape representations as linked lists. Although packed array formats such as the one discussed in Steinhart *et al.* (1989) are more compact, a significant amount of data copying can occur in the difference operation. Also, it is difficult to manage the amount of array space required, since the worst-case combination of a shape containing m rectangles with a shape containing n rectangles is a shape containing $m \times n$ rectangles.

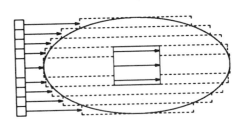

Figure 2. Sample shape decomposition.

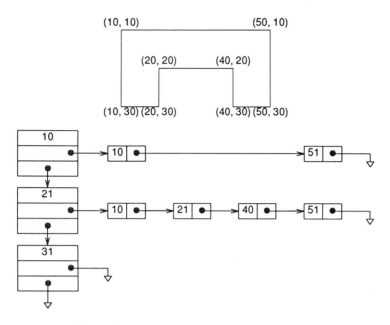

Figure 3. Representation of a sample shape.

The choice of memory management techniques used for the data structures can have a dramatic impact on the performance of the algorithms. This gem does not go into the details of memory management, since the choice of technique is very dependent on the operating environment.

A *shape* is a vertically ordered set of horizontal *spans*. Each span contains a horizontally ordered set of *segments*. The span data structure contains the y coordinate of the top of the span, a pointer to the next span, and a pointer to the segment list. Each element of the segment list contains an x coordinate and a pointer to the next segment. Figure 3 shows a sample shape and the data structures that represent it.

There are three spans in the structure. The first one describes the rectangle ((10,10),(50,20)). The second span describes the two rectangles, ((10,20),(20,30)) and ((40,20),(50,30)). The third span describes no rectangles and merely provides the upper y bound for the second span.

Note that we place the pixels between the grid lines as shown in Fig. 4a, not on the grid lines as shown in Fig. 4b.

Figure 4.   Pixel locations.

Spans and structures are constructed from instances of the *span* and *segment* data structures, defined as follows:

```
segment: record [          span: record [
    next: ↑segment;            next: ↑span;
    x: integer;                x: ↑segment;
    ];                         y: integer;
                               ];
```

We allow a NIL pointer to represent an empty shape for convenience.

The Basic Algorithm

The shape algebra routines alternately process spans in an outer loop and segments in an inner loop. Let us look at what happens with operations on two simple shapes, the rectangles ((10,10),(20,20)) and ((15,15),(25,25)), as shown in Fig. 5.

The outer loop contains two pointers, one for each span list. One pointer is advanced—or both are—each time through the loop. The span whose y value is lowest has its pointer advanced; both pointers are advanced if both spans have the same y value. The effect is to generate a new set of span y values as shown in Fig. 6.

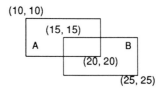

Figure 5.   Two simple shapes.

34

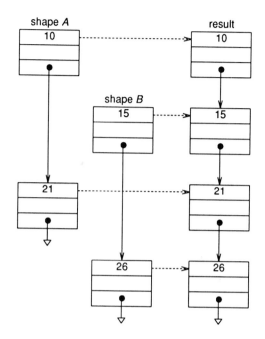

Figure 6. Span processing.

Each iteration through the outer loop produces a y coordinate and a pair of segments to be operated on by the inner loop. Note that the outer loop supplies an empty segment in cases where one shape begins or ends before the other.

The inner loop processes the segments in much the same manner as the outer loop processes the spans. A bit is used to keep track of the state of each segment. Each x value toggles this state bit. The state bits from each segment are combined into a state code as shown in Fig. 7.

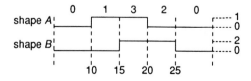

Figure 7. State code generation.

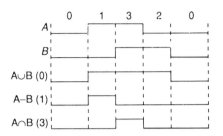

Figure 8. Shape algebra opcodes.

One segment is advanced—or both are—each time through the inner loop. The segment that ends at the lower x coordinate is advanced; both segments are advanced if they both end at the same place. The state code is monitored; x values that cause the state code to change to or from the *opcode* are added to the output. The effect of each opcode is shown in Fig. 8. Note that code 1 produces A–B; a code of 2 would produce B–A.

The x coordinates in segments come in pairs. The first coordinate in each pair is a transition from "off" to "on" for the coordinate value. The second coordinate in each pair is a transition from "on" to "off" that occurs *after* the coordinate value.

The basic shape algebra routine is presented as follows. Although a single routine could be used to implement all of the operations, a considerable amount of time can be wasted using the opcode to choose the appropriate special case handling code. Substantial performance benefits can be realized by using optimized code for each opcode. The special case handling code is discussed in the following sections.

```
procedure shape_operation(shape1, shape2, opcode)
begin
    result ← x1 ← x2 ← NIL;
    handle special cases that occur before the shapes overlap in y
    while shape1 ≠ NIL and shape2 ≠ NIL do
    begin
        test ← shape1.y − shape2.y;
        if test ≤ 0 then
            begin y ← shape1.y; x1 ← shape1.x; shape1 ← shape1.next;
            end;
```

if test ≥ 0 **then**
>   **begin** y ← shape2.y; x2 ← shape2.x; shape2 ← shape2.next;
>   **end**;

flag ← old ← 0;
segment ← NIL;
handle special cases that occur before the shapes overlap in x
p1 ← x1; p2 ← x2;
while p1 ≠ NIL **and** p2 ≠ NIL **do**
begin
>   test ← p1.x − p2.x;
>   **if** test ≤ 0 **then**
>   >   **begin** x ← p1.x; flag ← flag **bit-xor** 1; p1 ← p1.next; **end**;
>   **if** test ≥ 0 **then**
>   >   **begin** x ← p2.x; flag ← flag **bit-xor** 2; p2 ← p2.next; **end**;
>   **if** flag = opcode **or** old = opcode **then**
>   >   **begin** *append a new element to segment with value x*
>   >   **end**;
>   old ← flag;
>   **end**;

handle special cases that occur after the shapes overlap in x
if segment ≠ NIL **or** result ≠ NIL **then**
>   *append a new element to result with values y and segment*
end;

handle special cases that occur after the shapes overlap in y
return [result];
end;

Intersection

The intersection algorithm takes advantage of the fact that the result is empty if one operand is empty. Only one piece of special case code is necessary; the remaining pieces are empty.

special case code for before the shapes overlap in y
if shape1 = NIL **or** shape2 = NIL
>   **return** [NIL];

Union

Both shape operands must be traversed to the end in the union algorithm. We can get some performance improvement by avoiding the tests and handling the cases where one span or segment is empty as straightforward copies.

> *special case code for before the shapes overlap in y*
> **if** shape1 = NIL **then**
>   **begin return** [*a copy of shape2*]; **end**;
> **if** shape2 = NIL **then**
>   **begin return** [*a copy of shape1*]; **end**;
> **if** shape1.y < shape2.y **then**
> **begin**
>   *copy the span from shape1 and append it to result*
>   x1 ← shape1.x;
>   shape1 ← shape1.next;
>   **end**;
> **else if** shape2.y < shape1.y **then**
> **begin**
>   *copy the span from shape2 and append it to result*
>   x2 ← shape2.x;
>   shape2 ← shape2.next;
>   **end**;
>
> *special case code for before the shapes overlap in x*
> **if** x1 ≠ NIL **then**
>   **begin** *copy x1*; **end**;
> **else if** x2 ≠ NIL **then**
>   **begin** *copy x2*; **end**;
> **else**
>   *do the normal inner loop processing*
>
> *special case code for after the shapes overlap in x*
> **if** x1 ≠ NIL **then**
>   **begin** *copy the remainder of x1*; **end**;
> **else if** x2 ≠ NIL **then**
>   **begin** *copy the remainder of x2*; **end**;

special case code for after the shapes overlap in y
if shape1 ≠ NIL **then**
    begin *copy the remainder of shape1 to result* **end**;
else
    begin *copy the remainder of shape2 to result* **end**;

Difference

Only the first shape operand must be traversed to the end in the difference algorithm. We can get some performance improvement by avoiding the tests and handling the cases where one span or segment is empty as straightforward copies.

special case code for before the shapes overlap in y
if shape1 = NIL **then**
    return [NIL];
if shape2 = NIL **then**
    begin return [*a copy of shape1*]; **end**;
if shape1.y < shape2.y **then**
begin
    copy the span from shape1 and append it to result
    x1 ← shape1.x;
    shape1 ← shape1.next;
    end;
else if shape2.y < shape1.y **then**
    begin x2 ← shape2.x; shape2 ← shape2.next; **end**;

special case code for before the shapes overlap in x
if x1 = NIL **then**
    begin *segment is NIL*; **end**;
else if x2 = NIL **then**
    begin *copy x1*; **end**;
else
    do the normal inner loop processing

special case code for after the shapes overlap in x
if x1 ≠ NIL **then**
    begin *copy the remainder of x1*; **end**;

special case code for after the shapes overlap in y
if shape1 ≠ NIL **then**
        begin *copy the remainder of shape1 to result* **end**;

Handy Utilities

This section presents several utility functions that make working with shape descriptions easier. The first creates a shape from a description of a rectangle.

```
procedure shape_box(x, y, width, height)
begin
    result ← new[span];
    result.y ← y;
    result.next ← new[span];
    result.next.y ← y + height;
    result.next.next ← NIL.
    result.x ← new[segment];
    result.x.x = x;
    result.x.next ← new[segment];
    result.x.next.x ← x + width;
    result.x.next.next ← NIL.
    return [result];
    end;
```

A useful variant of the *shape_box* routine, *shape_tmp_box*, creates the shape in a static data area. This allows temporary shapes to be generated without memory allocation overhead.

The next utility makes a copy of a shape description.

```
procedure shape_copy(shape)
begin
    for each span in shape do
    begin
        add a span to the result with the y from the current span
```

```
        for each segment in the current span do
                add a new segment to the new span with the x from the current
                segment
        end
    return [result];
    end;
```

The third utility translates a shape by a relative x, y offset.

```
    procedure shape_translate(shape, x, y)
    begin
        for each span in shape do
        begin
            span.y ← span.y + y;
            for each segment in the current span do
                    begin segment.x ← segment.x + x; end
        end
        return;
    end;
```

The final utility deallocates the storage consumed by a shape description.

```
    procedure shape_free(shape)
    begin
        while shape ≠ NIL do
        begin
            x ← shape.x;
            while x ≠ NIL do
            begin tmpx ← x; x ← x.next; free_memory(tmpx); end
            tmpy ← shape; shape ← shape.next; free_memory(tmpy);
        end
        return;
    end;
```

Applications

Shape algebra is useful for computing and representing the visible area of
windows in window management systems. Let us assume that we have a

hierarchical window system in which descendent windows are clipped to their ancestors' boundaries. The *window* data structure shown next contains pointers to other windows in the window tree, the size and position of the window, and the visible area description.

```
window: record[
       parent: ↑window;       parent window
       child: ↑window;        highest priority (frontmost) child)
       n_sib: ↑window;        next lowest priority sibling
       p_sib: ↑window;        next highest priority sibling
       x: integer;            x coordinate of upper left corner
       y: integer;            y coordinate of upper left corner
       width: integer;        width of window
       height: integer;       height of window
       visible: ↑span;        shape that describes visible area
       ];
```

Figure 9 shows how the window pointers describe the relationship of a window with other windows in the window tree.

The visible area for each window in the tree can be computed using the following algorithm.

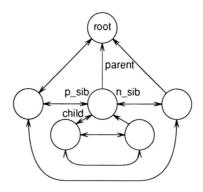

Figure 9.   Window tree.

```
procedure compute_window_area( )
begin
    root.visible ← shape_box(root.x, root.y, root.width, root.height);
    compute_subwindow_area(root);
    return
    end

procedure compute_subwindow_area(parent)
begin
    for each child in order from front to back do
    begin
        shape_free(child.visible);
        child.visible = shape_intersect(parent.visible,
        shape_tmp_box(child.x, child.y, child.width, child.height));
        tmp = parent.visible;
        parent.visible = shape_difference(parent.visible, child.visible);
        shape_free(tmp);
        compute_subwindow_area(child);
        end
    return
    end
```

Complex graphical objects such as fat curves can be generated using shape algebra. One technique for the generation of fat curves to drag a pen along the curve trajectory. An example of this technique is shown in Fig. 10. The line marks the actual trajectory; the dashed boxes show the pen shape description.

Figure 10.   Fat curve generation.

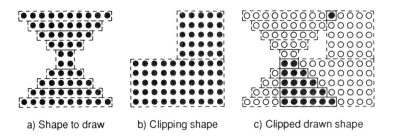

a) Shape to draw b) Clipping shape c) Clipped drawn shape

Figure 11. Complex clipping.

The following algorithm can be used to generate fat curves. Note that a special union routine that took pen offset parameters would be more efficient than the repeated translation of the pen shape description.

```
curve_shape ← NIL
for each point in the curve do
begin
    translated_pen ← shape_translate(pen, point.x, point.y);
    curve_shape = shape_union(curve_shape, translated_pen);
    shape_free(translated_shape);
end
```

Another application of shape algebra is complex clipping such as that used by POSTSCRIPT™ and by window management systems. The algorithms for the rasterization of many primitives, including polygons (Foley *et al.*, 1990) and fat curves, produce output that essentially is a y-sorted list of x-sorted rectangles. These primitives can be clipped easily to arbitrary shapes using intersection as shown in Fig. 11.

An efficient variation on the intersection routine for clipping is *intersect and fill*. This variation invokes an actual drawing function each time a new rectangle would be added to the result shape instead of building the shape.

Improvements

An examination of shape algebra applications reveals a pattern; temporary shapes are being created, used, and then destroyed. This gives memory management a real workout. The following type of operation is typical:

$$shape1 \leftarrow shape1 \ op \ shape2;$$

The amount of overlap between shape operands often is minimal when compared to the total size of the shapes in operations such as fat curve drawing. The *shape_union* and *shape_difference* routines can be modified to substantially reduce memory management overhead in such applications.

> **procedure** shape_operation(shape1, shape2, opcode)
> **begin**
> > **for any part of shape1 that comes before any part of shape2 do**
> > *detach spans from shape1 and attach them to the result*
>
> > *do the normal operation*
>
> > **for any part of shape1 that comes after any part of shape2 do**
> > *detach spans from shape1 and attach them to the result*
>
> > *free the spans in shape1 that overlapped shape2*

This is effective only for the union and difference operations as the non-overlapping parts of shapes are discarded for intersection operations.

Shape algebra operations can produce fragmented shapes in which more than the minimal number of rectangles is used to represent the shape. Such shapes can be compressed into minimal representations, although this typically consumes more time than it saves. Compression is a worthwhile optimization only in situations where a computed shape is used for a long period of time without being changed.

Acknowledgments

I would like to thank Julie Donnelly, Robert Reed, and Ken Rhodes for their proofreading, without which this gem would have been flawed.

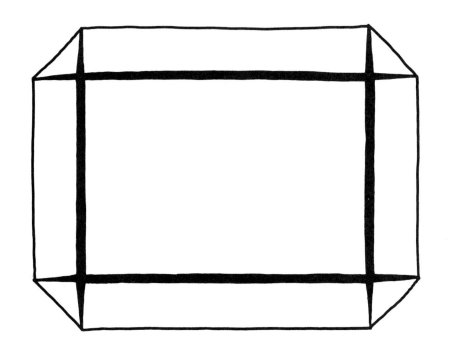

IMAGE
PROCESSING

IMAGE PROCESSING

The output of every graphics program is an *image*. Images are typically represented as a two-dimensional array of pixels, or some encoding of that information. When the input and output of a program are both images, we say the program is performing *image processing*. All the gems of this part involve some form of image transformation or change of representation. These include accurate pixel representations, scaling and sharpening, rotation, mapping an image into a nearly equivalent image with fewer colors or shades of gray, and compression.

This last topic, compression, is driven by a very common problem. A picture may be worth a thousand words, but as many a graphics programmer will attest, it frequently takes many more than a thousand words to store one. In fact, the storing of images is notorious for eating up vast amounts of secondary storage, such as disk or tape. Fortunately, most images contain a large amount of redundant information that can be squeezed out for compact storage. Two of the gems in this part present simple approaches for doing just that.

IMAGE SMOOTHING AND SHARPENING BY DISCRETE CONVOLUTION

Dale A. Schumacher
St. Paul, Minnesota

One of the reasons for capturing an image digitally is to allow us to manipulate it to better serve our needs. Often this will include trying to improve the subjective appearance of an image through smoothing of grainy features or sharpening of indistinct features. These goals sometimes can be accomplished through the use of a *discrete convolution* operation (also called *digital filtering*).

Discrete convolution determines a new value for each pixel in an image by computing some function of that pixel and its neighbors. Often this function simply is a weighted sum of pixel values in a small neighborhood of the source pixel. These weights can be represented by a small matrix that sometimes is called a *convolution kernel*. The dimensions of the matrix must be odd so there will be a central cell to represent the weight of the original value of the pixel for which we are computing a new value. The new value is computed by multiplying each pixel value in the neighborhood of the central pixel by the corresponding weight in the matrix, summing all the weighted values, and dividing by the sum of the weights in the matrix. The following pseudo-code shows this computation for a 3×3 convolution kernel.

```
input:      array [1..width] of array [1..height] of pixel;
output:     array [1..width] of array [1..height] of pixel;
kernel:     array [-1..1] of array [-1..1] of integer;
sum, ksum:  integer;
```

50

```
compute_output_value(x: integer, y: integer);
begin
        sum ← 0;
        ksum ← 0;
        for j: integer ← −1, j ← j + 1, j <= 1 do
                for i: integer ← −1, i ← i + 1, i <= 1 do
                        sum ← sum + (kernel[i][j]*input[x + i][y + j]);
                        ksum ← ksum + kernel[i][j];
                        endloop;
                endloop;
        output [x][y] = sum / ksum;
        end;
```

One of the simplest kernels is one that gives all pixels in a 3×3 neighborhood equal weight, as shown in Fig. 2. This sometimes is called a *box filter*, since the shape of the filtering function this kernel represents is a one-unit-high box three units on a side. This kernel simply computes the average pixel value over a 3×3 area and has a smoothing effect on the image, since the central pixel is made more similar to its neighbors.

The kernel shown in Fig. 3 is similar to the box filter, but ignores completely the original value of the center pixel. This produces a halo-like effect around sharp edges in the image. This filter can be thought of as computing the average of the neighborhood surrounding a pixel, a useful concept to remember for later discussion.

Figure 4 sometimes is called a *triangle* or *tent filter* because it defines a pyramid-shaped volume. This filter gives a little more weight to the center pixel, although the overall weight given to the center versus the surrounding average is still $\frac{1}{3}$ versus $\frac{2}{3}$. Notice how the stronger center-weights in this and the next filter reduce the smoothing effect.

Figure 5 shows a half-and-half balance between the pixel's current value and the value suggested by the average of the pixel's neighbors. If the diagonal neighbors were included, with weights of 1 in each corner, then the weight of the central pixel would have to be 8 to achieve the same half-and-half balance.

Another commonly used filter is an approximation of a gaussian distribution, as shown in Fig. 6. Sampling of the real world (which we assume is a continuous function) to create a discrete image often is described as a

Figure 1. Original test image.

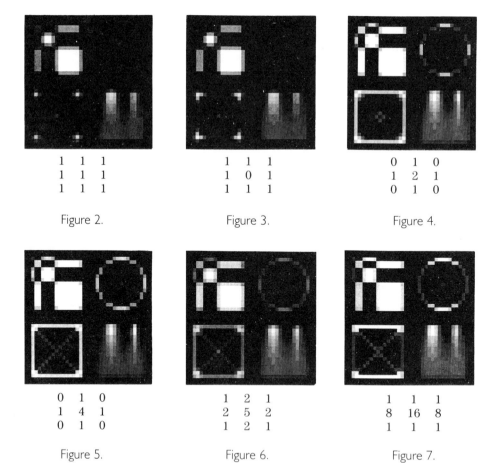

1 1 1	1 1 1	0 1 0
1 1 1	1 0 1	1 2 1
1 1 1	1 1 1	0 1 0
Figure 2.	Figure 3.	Figure 4.

0 1 0	1 2 1	1 1 1
1 4 1	2 5 2	8 16 8
0 1 0	1 2 1	1 1 1
Figure 5.	Figure 6.	Figure 7.

sequence of spatially separated gaussian-shaped samples; thus, using a gaussian weighted filter should accurately emulate such sampling.

Up to now, the filters shown have been horizontally and vertically symmetrical. Sometimes, an asymmetric filter is desired, such as for processing images taken from interlaced video. Since two fields of a video frame are spaced 1/60th of a second apart in time, the image often shows much more coherence in the horizontal direction, along the scanline, than in the vertical. The filter shown in Fig. 7 often works well on captured video. Vertical lines are smoothed, but horizontal lines stay distinct.

Smoothing reduces noise by *spreading it out* over a larger area, making it more diffuse. This also has the same effect on any sharp transitions in a source image. Some detail will be lost by smoothing, so you must take care in how you apply this operation. Smoothing works best on images where the smallest detail of interest is at least as large as the filtering kernel, such as the 3×3 pixels in the examples given thus far. Smoothing also can be used to improve the performance of some compression and dithering algorithms, by making the changes in the pixels' values more gradual.

On the other hand, there are many times when we would rather perform the inverse of smoothing to sharpen an image, attempting to bring out details that are indistinct. Interestingly enough, it is possible to do exactly that with a carefully chosen filtering kernel.

If we look at smoothing as a way of enhancing the similarity between nearby pixels, sharpening should enhance the differences. If we take a weighted average of the pixels surrounding a given pixel, excluding the central pixel (as in Fig. 3), and take that average away from the value of the central pixel, we enhance the difference between that pixel and its neighborhood. The kernel in Fig. 9, sometimes called a *discrete laplacian filter*, computes this difference. By weighting the neighboring pixels negatively, we take their value away rather than add it to the central pixel. This produces the desired edge-sharpening effect. Note that the weight of the central pixel is 1 greater than the sum of the negative weights. If this filter is applied to a large area of all the same value, the weight of the neighbors cancels four times the center value, leaving one times the center value remaining, and the pixel thus retains its original value.

If we want our sharpening filter to have a little larger radius, we need to define a larger kernel. The kernel shown in Fig. 10 is the sharpening

53

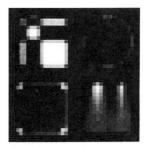

Figure 8. Smoothed test image.

$$\begin{array}{ccc} 0 & -1 & 0 \\ -1 & 5 & -1 \\ 0 & -1 & 0 \end{array}$$

Figure 9.

$$\begin{array}{ccc} -1 & -2 & -1 \\ -2 & 13 & -2 \\ -1 & -2 & -1 \end{array}$$

Figure 10.

$$\begin{array}{ccc} -1 & -2 & -1 \\ -2 & 16 & -2 \\ -1 & -2 & -1 \end{array}$$

Figure 11.

Figure 12. Ideal test image.

54

(a) Original image,   (b) processed version.

Figure 13.

counterpart of the gaussian kernel in Fig. 6. The center weight again is 1 minus the sum of the neighbor's weights.

Sometimes, the sharpening effect of the previous two kernels is a bit too harsh, and may overemphasize some high-frequency noise in the image. In that case, we want to moderate the sharpening somewhat. This can be done by weighting the center pixel higher than simply required to offset the negative weights, as shown in Fig. 11. This essentially gives a little more weight to the current pixel value versus the value derived by the edge-sharpening computation. None of these convolutions can exactly recover the ideal image (Fig. 12) from the smoothed image (Fig. 8), but they go a long way toward that goal.

Now, test images are fine and can show quite clearly how the various convolutions operate on extreme conditions, but how well does this work in practice? Figures 13 and 14 show some real-world examples of edge-sharpening convolutions. In each case, the (a) figure is the original image and the (b) figure is the processed version. Although it may seem like it, the original images are not out of focus.

The examples of convolution kernels shown here all happen to be 3×3 matrices; however, this by no means is required. Larger matrices take proportionally longer to convolve an image, and basically are extensions of the principles shown here. The primary reason to use a larger

(a) Original image,.   (b) processed version.

Figure 14.

matrix is to cause wider effects. With a 3×3 matrix, pixels two or more units away will have no effect on the current pixel.

There are a large number of useful ways to apply discrete convolution for image enhancement. I have touched on only a few of the basic building blocks. Creative combinations of these techniques, particularly conditional application of various filters, will greatly enrich your image processing capacity. Books by Gonzalez and Wintz (1987) and Pratt (1978) contain much more information about discrete image filtering and many other topics. Also, both books go into far greater depth explaining the mathematics behind these operations.

See also (*166*) *Smoothing Enlarged Monochrome Images*, *John Olsen*; (*171*) *Median Finding on a* 3×3 *Grid*, *Alan W. Paeth*

II.2

A COMPARISON OF DIGITAL HALFTONING TECHNIQUES

Dale A. Schumacher
St. Paul, Minnesota

Digital halftoning is a process that allows us to trade spatial resolution for grayscale resolution in an image. Typically, this is used to display an image with a large number of grayscale values on a device that supports significantly fewer distinct grayscale values. In many cases, such as typical printing devices, the device can represent only the two levels, *black* and *white*. On such devices, we give the illusion of differing grayscale values by producing patterns with the values available. The perceived grayscale value is proportional to the density of such patterns.

Many halftoning techniques can be generalized to thresholding an image with a *pattern mask*. This pattern mask is a matrix of threshold values that define which of two adjacent output grayscale values will be assigned to a pixel based on the position and value of that pixel. Since the thresholding matrix nearly always is much smaller than the image itself, the thresholding values are *tiled* over the image area. This is equivalent to saying that the thresholding value used for a given pixel is taken from the thresholding matrix by computing the modulo of the pixel location with the size of the matrix. The following pseudo-code shows how a thresholding matrix is applied to an image to create a black-and-white halftone.

```
input:        array [1..image_width] of array [1..image_height] of pixel;
output:       array [1..image_width] of array [1..image_height] of pixel;
threshold:    array [1..matrix_width] of array [1..matrix_height] of pixel;
t:            pixel;
i, j:         integer;
threshold_dither;                    {dither to BLACK and WHITE}
```

```
begin
        for y: integer ← 1, y ← y + 1, y <= image_height do
                j ← ((y − 1) mod matrix_height) + 1;
                for x: integer ← 1, x ← x + 1, x <= image_width do
                        i ← ((x − 1) mod matrix_width) + 1;
                        if input[x][y] > threshold[i][j] then
                                output[x][y] ← WHITE_PIXEL;
                        else
                                output[x][y] ← BLACK_PIXEL;
                        endloop;
                endloop;
        end;
```

For this discussion, we will use floating point values in the thresholding matrix, and we will assume that image data is in the range [0.0, 1.0], with black being 0.0 and white being 1.0. Many implementations will use the integer range [0, 255] for processing efficiency.

Threshold Dithering

We now can define halftones by their thresholding matrix. Let us start with a halftone so simple it usually is not even thought of as a halftone at all—the single element matrix [.44]. This "halftoning matrix" simply will apply the same threshold to all pixels in the image, resulting in an output image like Fig. 2. This is equivalent to *quantizing* the image to two levels, assigning each pixel to the nearest of the two possible output values.

Now let us take a slightly more complex matrix, as shown in Fig. 3b. This is called a *2 × 2 ordered dither*. This matrix results in five distinct grayscale patterns, thus five apparent output grayscale levels. As long as all elements of a halftone matrix are different, the number of apparent grayscale levels created is $(N * M) + 1$, where N and M define the size of the matrix.

A larger version of the ordered dither matrix is shown in Fig. 4b. Since this is a 4 × 4 matrix, it creates 17 output levels. The intent of the

Figure 1.   Original image.   Figure 2.   Single threshold.

ordered dither is to fill the matrix evenly, reducing the amount of aliasing introduced by patterns in the halftone matrix. Arbitrary sized ordered dithering matrices can be created through a simple recursive algorithm (Hawley, 1990). The actual threshold values are evenly spaced intervals between 0.0 and 1.0. The matrix in Fig. 4c represents the *fill order* of the matrix in Fig. 4b. This is the order in which pixels are *set* within the

.2 .6
.8 .4

(a)   (b)

Figure 3.   2 × 2 ordered dither.

(a)

.06	.53	.18	.65		1	9	3	11
.76	.30	.88	.41		13	5	15	7
.24	.71	.12	.59		4	12	2	10
.94	.47	.82	.35		16	8	14	6

(b)   (c)

Figure 4. 4 × 4 ordered dither.

matrix as the grayscale value of the corresponding source pixel increases. It often is useful, for analysis, to separate the fill order from the actual threshold values, although when the algorithm is implemented, we most often want to combine the two to save processing time.

As seen from the preceding, the patterns created by a halftone matrix can be defined simply by a fill order independent of the threshold values. Another halftone matrix, which shows the effects of strong patterns in the halftone matrix on the resultant image, is given by the fill-order matrix in Fig. 5b. This matrix creates strong "horizontal lines" in the output image.

On the other end of the spectrum, the matrix in Fig. 6b takes a different approach to minimizing the aliasing effect. This is a *magic-square* dither, since the fill-order values form a magic square. Since a magic

1	2	3	4
5	6	7	8
9	10	11	12
13	14	15	16

(a)   (b)

Figure 5.   4 × 4 horizontal lines.

1	7	10	16
12	14	3	5
8	2	15	9
13	11	6	4

(a)   (b)

Figure 6.   4 × 4 magic square.

30	19	13	20	31	35
18	8	5	9	21	29
12	4	1	2	10	28
17	7	3	6	14	27
26	16	11	15	22	32
34	25	24	23	33	36

(a)   (b)

Figure 7. 6 × 6 90° halftone.

15	9	17	32	22	30
7	1	3	19	35	23
13	5	11	27	26	33
31	21	29	16	10	18
20	36	24	8	2	4
28	25	34	14	6	12

(a)   (b)

Figure 8. 6 × 6 45° halftone.

square sums to equal values along all rows, columns, and diagonals, this fill order should be ideal in filling the pixels in such a way that the number of dots along any row, column, or diagonal will be approximately equal.

On many output devices, smearing, variance in dot size, blurring, and other similar effects make the use of patterns like the preceding impractical, since those patterns rely on being able to image single pixels accurately and consistently. On devices where such precision is not practical, a *clustered-dot* dither may be more appropriate. Clustered-dot dithers create patterns very similar to those created by the optical halftoning process used to print photographs in books, magazines, and newspapers.

Figures 7b and 8b give two examples of such a halftone matrix. In photographic halftoning, these patterns are created by a screen consisting of small transparent dots on an opaque field. The spacing of these dots, described in lines (of dots) per inch, and the angle along which these lines run defines by the parameters of the screen. The matrix in Fig. 7b acts like a 90-degree screen, with the lines per inch proportional to the pixels per inch in the source image. The matrix in Fig. 8b acts like the more commonly used 45-degree screen.

Contrast Adjustment during Halftoning

The perceived brightness of various halftone patterns differs, even at the same dot density. Also, all halftoning seems to reduce contrast. Due to these effects, it often is desirable to apply a contrast enhancement transform to an image while halftoning. Going back to the separation between threshold levels and fill order, we find the means to accomplish the contrast adjustment essentially "for free" while halftoning. The key is to incorporate the transform into the threshold levels. Figure 9b shows the normal case, a linear transform, with four thresholding levels, as would be required by a 2×2 matrix. Figure 9d shows the same four threshold levels as derived from a contrast-enhancement transform curve. Note that the threshold levels are nonlinearly spaced to make the transformed output levels linear.

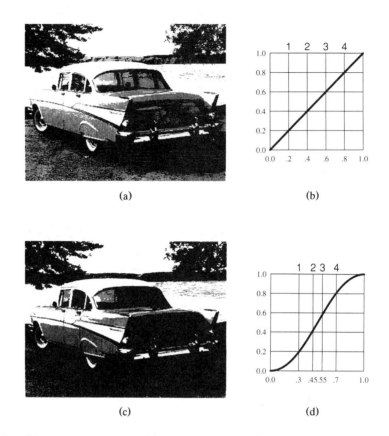

Figure 9. (a) 2×2 linear dither, (b) linear transform (c) 2×2 contrast-enhanced dither, (d) contrast enhancement transform.

Halftoning to Multiple Output Levels

Thus far, we have assumed that the output of our halftoning process was strictly black or white, which is true for a large number of output devices. However, there is considerable usefulness in halftoning to multiple output levels. Extending the various threshold methods to multiple output levels consists of first picking the nearest pair of output values for a given input, then using the threshold matrix to determine which of the two output values to use, considering the range [lower_value, higher_value] to map to the normalized [0.0, 1.0] in the threshold matrix. The following pseudocode gives the general algorithm for applying threshold dithering to multiple output levels.

```
input:       array [1..image_width] of array [1..image_height] of pixel;
output:      array [1..image_width] of array [1..image_height] of pixel;
threshold:   array [1..matrix_width] of array [1..matrix_height] of pixel;
range:       pixel;                   distance between output levels
base:        pixel;                   lower end of target range
i, j:        integer;


threshold_dither(n: integer);         dither to n output levels
begin
        n ← n − 1;                    convert number of levels to number
                                      of ranges
      range ← (1.0 / n);
      for y: integer ← 1, y ← y + 1, y < = image_height do
              j ← ((y − 1) mod matrix_height) + 1;
              for x: integer ← 1, x ← x + 1, x < = image_width do
                    i ← ((x − 1) mod matrix_width) + 1;
                    base ← floor(input[x][y] / range) * range;
                    if (input[x][y] − base) > (threshold[i][j] * range) then
                          output[x][y] ← base + range;
              else
                          output[x][y] ← base;
              endloop;
          endloop;
      end;
```

Error Diffusion Dithering

An entirely different approach to halftoning is a group of algorithms known as *error diffusion* methods. Since dithering must approximate a desired output level by creating patterns with the available output levels, there is a certain quantifiable error in the approximation at a given pixel.

Error diffusion carries that error over to bias the values of nearby pixels to balance out the error. This spreads the error out over a small area, creating a diffusion effect. The spread of the error is controlled by a weighting matrix such that a fraction of the error is applied to some number of nearby pixels. Since the image is processed in the normal left-to-right and top-to-bottom order, and pixel values are not changed once assigned, the weighting matrix can distribute the error only to *unassigned* output locations. The following pseudo-code illustrates the general algorithm. The special-case processing required to handle edges properly is omitted here for simplicity.

```
input:      array [1..image_width] of array [1..image_height] of pixel;
output:     array [1..image_width] of array [1..image_height] of pixel;
weight:     array [−filter_dx..+filter_dx] of
                 array [−filter_dy..+filter_dy] of integer;
sum:        integer;                sum of values in weighting filter
value:      pixel;                  value chosen for a pixel
error:      pixel;                  quantization error for a pixel
range:      pixel;                  distance between output levels
base:       pixel;                  lower end of target range

diffusion_dither(n: integer);       dither to n output levels
begin
        n ← n − 1;                  convert number of levels to number
                                    of ranges
     range ← (1.0/n);
     sum ← 0;
     for j: integer ← −filter_dy, j ← j + 1, j <= +filter_dy do
             for i: integer ← −filter_dx, i ← i + 1, i <= +filter_dx do
                 sum ← sum + weight[i][j];
             endloop;
        endloop;
     for y: integer ← 1, y ← y + 1, y <= image_height do
             for x: integer ← 1, x ← x + 1, x <= image_width do
                 dither_pixel(x, y);
             endloop;
        endloop;
     end;
```

```
dither_pixel (x: integer, y: integer);        determine pixel values, spread error
begin
        if (input[x][y] < 0.0) then
                value ← 0.0;
        else if (input[x][y] > 1.0) then
                value ← 1.0;
        else begin
                base ← floor(input[x][y] / range) * range;
                if (input[x][y] − base) > (0.5 * range) then
                        value ← base + range;
                else
                        value ← base;
        end;
        output[x][y] ← value;
        error ← input[x][y] − value;
        for j: integer ← −filter_dy, j ← j + 1, j <= +filter_dy do
                for i: integer ← −filter_dx, i ← i + 1, i <= +filter_dx do
                        if weight[i][j] ≠ 0 then
                                input[x + i][y + j] ← input[x + i][y + j]
                                        + (error * weight[i][j] / sum);
                endloop;
        endloop;
end;
```

The classic weighting matrix is shown in Fig. 10b (Floyd and Steinberg, 1975). Other useful filters are shown in Figs. 11b (Jarvis *et al.* 1976) and 12b (Stucki, 1981).

Ulichney (1987) presents an excellent analysis of the halftoning process and suggests several improvements to the preceding algorithm. First, some undesirable aliasing effects are produced by the raster scanning pattern inherent in this dithering process. One way to reduce this effect is to traverse the image with a *serpentine* raster pattern. Start scanning left to right on the first scanline, as usual, then reverse the scanning direction and traverse the next scanline right to left. Continue alternating scanning directions on each scanline. Remember that the weighting matrix also will need to be left/right-reversed. Figures 13 and 14 contrast normal raster and serpentine raster scanning methods.

0	0	0
0	0	7
3	5	1

(a)   (b)

Figure 10.   Floyd–Steinberg filter.

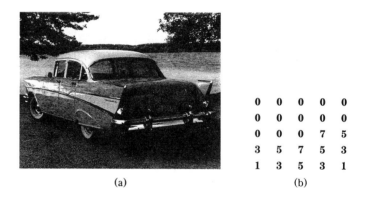

0	0	0	0	0
0	0	0	0	0
0	0	0	7	5
3	5	7	5	3
1	3	5	3	1

(a)   (b)

Figure 11.   Jarvis, Judice, and Ninke filter.

0	0	0	0	0
0	0	0	0	0
0	0	0	8	4
2	4	8	4	2
1	2	4	2	1

(a)   (b)

Figure 12. Stucki filter.

A useful suggestion from Ulichney is to introduce some random noise in the dithering process. This noise, which should have uniform probability density (white noise), can be added in any of several stages of the dithering process, and the amount of noise can be adjusted for best effect. First, the threshold value (a constant 0.5 in the pseudo-code example) can be randomly adjusted up or down. Second, the position of the diffusion weight can be chosen randomly using the filter weights to bias

Figure 13.   Normal raster.

Figure 14.   Serpentine raster.

Figure 15. Blue noise added.

the selection of a position for a single error diffusion weight. Finally, the weights themselves can be altered randomly. If noise is added to the weight values, it must be accounted for either by adjusting the filter sum, to ensure unity gain, or by adjusting two weights, with the same initial values, in equal and opposite directions. Variation of the threshold value combined with variation in weights was used to produce Fig. 15.

One final improvement to the dithering process is to account for its inherent dispersion. Since we are trading spatial resolution for grayscale resolution, it is natural that we will lose some of the high spatial fre-

Figure 16. Edge-enhanced.

quency components of the source image. It only makes sense that we could compensate somewhat by emphasizing such components before halftoning. Figure 16 was created using the same method as in Fig. 15, except that the source image had an edge-sharpening convolution applied before halftoning. This sort of processing is discussed further in the preceding gem in this book.

Conclusion

Proper use of digital halftoning methods can result in excellent reproduction of images with much higher grayscale resolution than that available on a particular display device. This gem is meant to give a practical introduction and comparative guide to some of the halftoning methods in use today. Ulichney's book (1987) is an excellent next step for those interested in further comparative analysis and discussion of digital halftoning techniques.

See also II.1 Image Smoothing and Sharpening by Discrete Convolution, Dale A. Schumacher; II.3 Color Dithering, Spencer W. Thomas, Rodney G. Bogart; III.1 Efficient Inverse Colormap Computation, Spencer W. Thomas; III.2 Efficient Statistic Computations for Optimal Color Quantization, Xiaolin Wu; (*176*) *Ordered Dithering, Stephen Hawley*; (*196*) *Useful* 1-*to-*1 *Pixel Transforms, Dale A. Schumacher*.

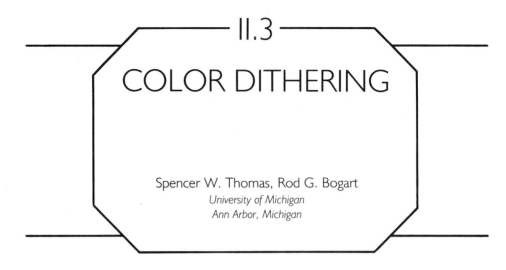

II.3

COLOR DITHERING

Spencer W. Thomas, Rod G. Bogart
University of Michigan
Ann Arbor, Michigan

Introduction

Although several sources discuss dithering to a binary image (Ulichney, 1988; Hawley, 1990), there apparently is no widely available literature on dithering to a multilevel color image. This gem discusses two color dithering techniques, a simple ordered dither and an error-propagation dither based on the Floyd–Steinberg method (Floyd and Steinberg, 1975).

Conventions

Throughout this discussion, we will assume that color values are in the range 0.0–1.0, unless it is stated explicitly otherwise. Mathematical expressions operating on colors will be written with scalar variables; however, you can assume that the operation should be applied separately and simultaneously to the red, green, and blue components of the color.

Gamma Correction

To get the proper visual effect, the dithering process assumes that the input and output values are linear in the image brightness; i.e., a number twice as large as another produces a pixel twice as bright. This is almost never true for display devices, and may not be true of input files. Thus, both the input and output values must be *gamma-corrected* (Schumacher, 1990; Hall, 1990; Foley *et al.*, 1990) for optimal visual performance. Input gamma correction maps the input values to a linear scale. Output gamma correction affects the values that are loaded into the output color table, but has no effect on the dithering process or the resulting pixel values.

If the input image has a gamma of γ_i, then each input pixel value x (in the range 0–1) must be mapped by the function $f(x) = x^{1/\gamma_i}$. Similarly, to display an image on a display with a gamma of γ_d, each value c must be mapped to the actual output value by $g(c) = c^{1/\gamma_d}$. However, for error-propagation dithering, the uncompensated output value must be used to compute the error. The discussions that follow will assume that any gamma correction necessary has been done, and therefore, will operate solely in the linear domain.

Ordered Dithering

The simplest form of dithering is *ordered dithering*. In the bilevel case, a function $d(x, y)$ is used to determine whether the output value v is a 0 or a 1 by comparing it with the pixel value c:

$$v = \begin{cases} 1 & c > d(x, y), \\ 0 & c \le d(x, y). \end{cases}$$

Usually, the function $d(x, y)$ is implemented using an $m \times n$ matrix:

$$d(x, y) = \mathbf{M}[y \bmod m][x \bmod n].$$

Dithering to a multilevel display is only slightly more complex. If the output will have $l + 1$ distinct levels (i.e., the output range is $0..l$), then the dithering function is

$$v = \text{floor}(l \cdot c) + \begin{cases} 1, & \text{frac}(l \cdot c) > d(x, y), \\ 0, & \text{frac}(l \cdot c) \le d(x, y). \end{cases}$$

If c is an integer in the range $0..cmax$, then, letting $k = cmax/l$, the floor and frac functions can be replaced by $\text{floor}(c/k)$ and

$c - \text{floor}(k \cdot \text{floor}(c/k))$. The function $d(x, y)$ should produce an integer in the range $0..(k - 1)$.[1]

What should $d(x, y)$ look like? It will be implemented as a matrix, as suggested previously. Hawley (1990) suggests one way to build such a matrix.

The code included here uses a slightly different method. It always computes a 16×16 matrix. With 256 entries in the matrix, it would be possible to get 257 output levels, certainly sufficient for any (8-bit) input image, even if the output image is bilevel. The matrix is a magic square constructed as the *outer product* of a 4×4 magic square with itself. The entries in the square are scaled into the range $0..k$ ($cmax = 255$ in the C Implementation).

The C code (Appendix 2) assumes that the input values are 8-bit unsigned integers. For efficiency, to avoid repeatedly using the *divide* and *mod* operators, arrays of 256 entries are built, such that $divN[c] = \text{floor}(c/k)$ and $modN[c] = c - \text{floor}(k \cdot div\,N[c])$. We then can write the dithering function as a macro:

```
macro dither(x, y, c)
    (divN[c] + (if mod N[c] > M[y bit-and 15][x bit-and 15]
        then 1
        else 0))
```

The only remaining task is deciding what the output color set should be. It is easiest to dither with the same number of levels of each primary color, and the resulting image will look better than if differing numbers of levels were used for the different primaries.[2] If 256 entries are available in the color table of the output device, setting $l = 5$ ($k = 51$) produces

[1]The astute reader will note that, if $d(x, y) = (k - 1)$, 1 never will be added at the pixel (x, y). This is correct. Suppose $k = 128$. Then if $c = 127$, the output value will be 1, except when $d(x, y) = 127$. If $d(x, y)$ is uniformly distributed, 127 out of 128 pixels will be 1, and the 128th will be 0, giving an average output value of $127/128$, exactly what is desired. To get all the pixels to have a value of 1, c should be 128.

[2]I have tried the vaunted "3-3-2" allocation of bits (3 to red, 3 to green, and 2 to blue). The assumption behind this is that the eye is less sensitive to blue, so not as many levels of blue are needed. However, the eye is quite sensitive to color variation in something that should be gray, and that is what you get with this setup. There are eight levels of red and green $\{0, 1/7, 2/7, 3/7, 4/7, 5/7, 6/7, 1\}$, and four levels of blue $\{0, 1/3, 2/3, 1\}$. These sets coincide only at white and black.

six output levels per primary and uses 216 entries in the color table.[3] The 40 left over can be used for other purposes (sometimes a definite advantage). If we can assign the value $(r \cdot k, g \cdot k, b \cdot k)$ (with r, g, b in the range 0..5) to the cell $36 \cdot r + 6 \cdot g + b$, the mapping from dithered color to color table index is trivial. If this is not possible (for example, if the color table belongs to an X server), then an intermediate mapping table, $T[0..5][0..5][0..5]$, must be built, such that $T[r][g][b]$ contains the appropriate color table index.

A sample image dithered with ordered dither is shown in Fig. 1 (see color insert).

Error-Propagation Dithering

The main drawback with ordered dither can be seen from the aforementioned example. The dither pattern is quite evident in the result. *Error-propagation dithering* techniques reduce the apparent patterning by making the dot placement appear more random. The basic idea is this: At each pixel, choose the *best* output color for the given input color. Then compute the error (difference) between the chosen output color and the input color. Spread the error out nearby pixels that have not yet been output. A number schemes exist for distributing the error. The Floyd–Steinberg method gives 7/16 to the next pixel to the right (assuming scanning from left to right along a scanline), 3/16 to the previous pixel on the next scanline, 5/16 to the adjacent pixel on the next scanline, and 1/16 to the next pixel on the next scanline. (See Fig. 2.) Note that the error propagation can result in color values that are out of their allowed range, so the code must be careful to clamp the values before trying to compute an output color.

An advantage of error-propagation dither over ordered dither is that it can use an arbitrary color table. The problem of choosing an output color, given an arbitrary RGB color, is solved easily by using an inverse colormap, as described in the first gem of Part III in this book, "Efficient Computation of Inverse Colormaps." Note that the inverse colormap should be computed before any output gamma compensation is applied to the color table, and the error values also should be computed from the uncompensated table. The best results will be obtained if the input colors

---

[3]The C Implementation in Appendix 2 allows any value of $l \geq 1$.

3·E/16	5·E/16	1·E/16
DONE	THIS PIXEL	7·E/16

Figure 2.   Floyd–Steinberg error propagation. Direction of processing is left to right, bottom to top.

lie within the convex hull of the color table. Otherwise, some error could be lost when out-of-range values are clamped.

Type color is equivalent to array[1..3] of real
function fsdither(thisrow, nextrow:**array**[0..511] **of color;**
                           x:**integer**):**integer;**
begin
    Current entry may have accumulated error; clamp it.
    for c ← 1 **to** 3 **do**
        thisrow[x][c] ← clamp(thisrow[x][c], 0, 1);
    Find closest representative color, get its index.
    color_index ← closest_color(thisrow[i]);
    Propagate the error.
    color_map is a global array of the output colors.
    for c ← 1 **to** 3 **do**
    begin
        err ← thisrow[index][c] − color_map[color_index][c];
        if x < 511 **then**
        begin
            thisrow[x + 1][c] ← thisrow[x + 1][c] + 7*err/16;
            nextrow[x + 1][c] ← nextrow[x + 1][c] + err/16;
        end;
        nextrow[x][c] ← nextrow[x][c] + 5*err/16;
        if x > 0 **then**
            nextrow[x − 1][c] ← nextrow[x − 1][c] + 3*err/16;

```
    end;
  return color_index;
    end;
```

A complete C Implementation of this algorithm including optional edge enhancement, is included in the freely distributed Utah Raster Toolkit. (Contact one of the authors of this gem for details.)

Figure 3 (see color insert) shows an example of the application of this dither algorithm.

See also II.2 A Comparison of Digital Halftoning Techniques, Dale A. Schumacher; III.1 Efficient Inverse Colormap Computation, Spencer W. Thomas; III.2 Efficient Statistic Computations for Optimal Color Quantization, Xiaolin Wu; *(176) Ordered Dithering, Stephen Hawley*

II.4

FAST ANAMORPHIC IMAGE SCALING

Dale A. Schumacher
St. Paul, Minnesota

There are many ways to rescale an image to the desired size. Some are considerably more accurate than others, and the more accurate methods generally are more computationally intensive. The method I will present is not particularly accurate, but it can be accomplished quite quickly and produces generally acceptable results. Better, but slower, methods exist involving filtering and are significantly more complicated.

Pixel remapping operations like stretching, rotation, skewing, and rescaling are often thought of, and thus often implemented, as mappings from positions in the source image to positions in the destination image. This approach, however, often leaves "holes" in the destination due to rounding error in the computation of the destination position or the fact that there is not a one-to-one mapping between source pixels and destination pixels.

Taking a different approach to the problem can eliminate these errors. Think of the remapping as defining which source pixel a particular destination pixel is taken *from*. This maps positions in the destination *from* positions in the source. The processing loop then is over the destination pixels rather than the source pixels, and thus, each pixel in the destination is assigned a value, even if more than one destination pixel maps from the same source pixel. This method may skip some of the source pixels, not using their value at all, but in the previous method, that would correspond to more than one source pixel mapping to the same destination, which poses the problem of how to choose which source pixels set the value of the destination. This method avoids that conflict by choosing only one source pixel, always the most correct for a given mapping.

Applying this method to image rescaling, we loop over the destination pixels, determining at each location which source pixel lends its value to that destination pixel. This allows anamorphic scaling, since the horizontal and vertical mappings need not be the same. This allows both expansion of an image, where multiple destination pixels are mapped from the same source pixel, and reduction of an image, where some adjacent destination pixels are mapped from nonadjacent source pixels. These expansion and reduction methods often are referred to as *pixel replication* and *pixel sub-sampling*, respectively.

In the following pseudo-code, the scaling is conveniently defined in terms of the desired destination image size.

src_x_size:	**integer**;	*source image width*
src_y_size:	**integer**;	*source image height*
source:	**array** [0..src_x_size-1] **of array** [0..src_y_size-1] **of pixel**;	
dst_x_size:	**integer**;	*destination image width*
dst_y_size:	**integer**;	*destination image height*
destination:	**array** [0..dst_x_size-1] **of array** [0..dst_y_size-1] **of pixel**;	
sx, sy, dx, dy:	**integer**;	*source and destination coordinates*

```
begin
      dy ← 0;
      while dy < dst_y_size do
              sy ← ((dy*src_y_size)/dst_y_size);
              dx ← 0;
              while dx < dst_x_size do
                      sx ← ((dx*src_x_size)/dst_x_size);
                      destination[dx][dy] ← source[sx][sy];
                      dx ← dx + 1;
                      endloop;
              dy ← dy + 1;
              endloop;
      end;
```

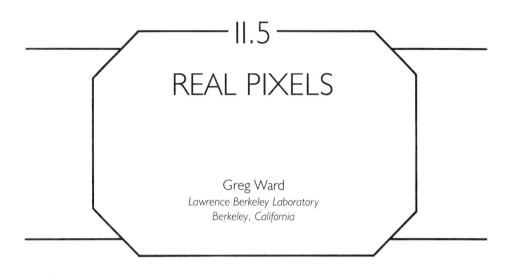

II.5

REAL PIXELS

Greg Ward

Lawrence Berkeley Laboratory
Berkeley, California

Many programs use floating point color representations internally, only to convert to 24-bit integer values when writing the results to a file. This saves disk space, but at the expense of accuracy and the ability to readjust the exposure or perform other operations that require wide dynamic range. Furthermore, if a linear mapping is used, 24 bits is inadequate for high-quality output and causes visible quantization contours in the darker regions of a print or slide.

An improved linear mapping from real color space to bytes uses random rounding as a form of predithering:

Convert a primary using random rounding:

if rval $> = 1.0$
    then ival $\leftarrow$ 255;
    else ival $\leftarrow$ 255*rval + random();

This method was suggested by Rob Cook several years ago, although it may have been floating around for some time.

It is better still to store gamma-corrected bytes rather than linear ones, since this will give the pixels greater dynamic range without sacrificing accuracy. Here is a simple table look-up routine for accomplishing this transformation:

Initialize of gamma table:
    gamtab: **array** [0..1023] **of byte**;

```
for i: integer ← 0 to 1023, i ← i + 1 do
    gamtab[i] ← 256.0*((i + .5)/1024) ^ (1.0/gamma);
```

To convert each pixel primary:
if rval > = 1.0
      then ival ← 255;
      else ival ← gamtab[floor(1024.*rval)];

It is important to use a large enough table that accuracy will not be compromised for smaller values. An alternative method is to reverse the look-up and use a 256-entry table of floating point values with a binary search routine to find the closest value, but this approach takes considerably longer and probably is not worth the small improvement in accuracy.

The ultimate solution to the problem of accurate pixel storage is to use a floating point pixel format, which is the real subject of this gem. The simplest approach is to store a short float for each of the three primaries at each pixel. On most machines, this translates to *96 unportable bits per pixel*. Many people have used this format, but nobody is bragging about it.

Fortunately, there is a better floating point format that only requires 32 bits per pixel and is completely portable between machine architectures. The idea is simple: Use an 8-bit mantissa for each primary and follow it with a single 8-bit exponent. In most floating point formats, the mantissa is normalized to lie between .5 and 1. Since this format uses the same exponent for three mantissas, only the largest value is guaranteed this normalization, and the other two may be less than .5.

For example, the color

$$[.3 \ .02 \ .1]$$

would be converted to

$$[.6 \ .04 \ .2]*2^{-1},$$

or, in 32-bit floating point format,

$$[153 \ 10 \ 51 \ 127].$$

Notice that the exponent value -1 translated to 127. It is necessary to add an offset to the unsigned value to get a signed exponent. In this case, we have chosen to add 128, giving our colors a more or less even range between values greater than 1 and less than 1. Selecting a smaller offset would favor larger values, and a larger offset would favor smaller values, but since 2^{127} is about 10^{38}, it hardly seems worth the worry.

It appears that this format favors the largest primary value at the expense of accuracy in the other two primaries. This is true, but it also is true that the largest value dominates the displayed pixel color so that the other primaries become less noticeable. The 32-bit real pixel format presented here preserves the bits that are most significant, which is the general goal of any floating point format.

Conversion to and from this format relies heavily on the math routines *frexp* and *ldexp*. *Frexp* takes a real value and returns a mantissa between .5 and 1 and an integer exponent. *Ldexp* performs the reverse operation, multiplying a real value by two to the power of an integer exponent.[1] Thus, converting from the internal floating point color representation involves picking the largest primary value, then calling *frexp*.

To convert from machine float to 32-bit real pixel:

rf, gf, bf: **real**;   *machine red, green, and blue values*
rm, gm, bm, ex: **integer**;   *red, green, and blue mantissas + exponent*

rf ← max(rf,max(gf,bf));

if v < 1e-32
    then begin
        rm ← 0;
        gm ← 0;
        bm ← 0;
        ex ← 0;
        end;
    else begin
        v ← frexp(v, e)*256./v;   *e is returned exponent*
        rm ← rf*v;
        gm ← gf*v;
        bm ← bf*v;
        ex ← e + 128;
        end;

[1]Ideally, these functions would be implemented as bit operations specific to the floating point architecture, but they are written more typically as portable C routines.

Note that there is a special case for zero. This case also is tested in the conversion back to machine floating point with *ldexp*, as follows:

To convert from 32-bit real pixel to machine float:

```
if ex = 0
    then begin
        rf ← 0.;
        gf ← 0.;
        bf ← 0.;
        end;
    else begin
        v ← ldexp(1./256., ex-128);
        rf ← (rm + .5)*v;
        gf ← (gm + .5)*v;
        bf ← (bm + .5)*v;
        end;
```

Besides the ability to perform more general image processing without losing accuracy, real pixels are great for radiosity and other lighting simulation programs, since the results can be evaluated numerically well outside the dynamic range of the display. For example, an office space with a window may have radiosities that vary over a range of 1000 : 1. It is impossible to store such values using an integer pixel format, but when the pixels are real, the image can be analyzed in many ways. The exposure can be raised and lowered dynamically, the brightnesses can be compressed, contour lines can be drawn, and values can be displayed as numbers over their positions on the screen. These capabilities can be of immense help to lighting designers and architects trying to evaluate a simulated scene for visual comfort, and they are impossible with any of the standard image storage formats.

In the end, one extra byte per pixel is not that much to pay for the benefits associated with true floating point color. Also, conventional compression techniques such as run-length encoding and Lempel–Ziv work very well with this 4-byte format—much better than machine float values, which tend to look like random bits. Thus, the image files take up only a little more space than their 24-bit counterparts.

II.6

A FAST 90-DEGREE BITMAP ROTATOR

Sue-Ken Yap
CSIRO DIT
Canberra, Australia

Introduction

This is a routine that rotates an 8×8 depth 1-bitmap clockwise by table look-up. Larger bitmaps can be rotated by division down to 8×8 tiles. Separate strides (address difference between successive rows in bitmaps) can be specified for source and destination so that the result can be written directly into the destination bitmap.

Principle

The source tile is viewed as eight rows of bytes. Each byte maps onto certain bits in the destination tile viewed as a 64-bit longword whose bits run row-wise. Eight table look-up and bit-or operations construct this longword. Finally, the longword is unpacked into 8 bytes at the destination.

The actual algorithm is modified slightly to work with nybbles and to produce two 32-bit words instead of one 64-bit longword. This reduces the size of each of the eight look-up tables from 256×64 bits to 16×32 bits.

Variations

Either transposition or rotation is possible, since the rotator allows an arbitrary *swizzle* of its input bits. For example, a different look-up table can rotate counterclockwise. Bitmap complementation can be done simultaneously by complementing the tables, changing the initial condition of the longword to all ones, and using bit-and operations in the extraction. This follows from de Morgan's theorem. This is important as the $0 = $ black, $1 = $ white conventions of digital photometry often are violated by xerographic printers, which regard $1 \Leftrightarrow$ mark $\Leftrightarrow$ black.

Acknowledgments

The idea for this gem was suggested by Alan Paeth (University of Waterloo) and implemented by the author while at the University of Rochester. The rotator was used first in a TeX DVI to raster converter described in *TUGboat* **11**(2).

See also II.7 Rotation of Run-Length Encoded Image Data, Jeff Holt, *(179) A Fast Algorithm for General Raster Rotation, Alan W. Paeth*

II.7

ROTATION OF RUN-LENGTH ENCODED IMAGE DATA

Jeff Holt
Intergraph Corporation
Huntsville, Alabama

A lot of applications require rotating raster images by 90 degrees. For example, if an image has been scanned in column major order, most software requires it to be in row major order to display—i.e., the image must be transposed. This corresponds to a 90-degree rotation, followed by inverting the order in which the lines are stored.

In general, 90-degree rotation and/or column-major-to-row major transposition is easy if the data is in expanded format—i.e., unencoded. If the image is in run-length encoded format, the image needs to be expanded completely in memory and then reconverted to run-length format. If the expanded image is larger than available memory, performance will be terrible, even on virtual memory systems, because there is no address coherency when reading out the image in rotated order.

This gem describes a simple algorithm to rotate a run-length encoded image directly. It has good performance—it has been found to be as good as or better than algorithms that expand the data before rotating, and requires much less memory. The version given rotates 16-bit data. At the end of this gem, variations to the algorithm are given for other data types, as well as some notes on performance enhancements.

The algorithm operates as follows. A structure called the *edge structure* is allocated for each line in the output (rotated) image. The edge structure is used to accumulate run-lengths for the output image. It contains:

acc_value—the pixel value being accumulated,

acc_rl—the current run-length of the value being accumulated (actually one less than the current run-length),

information to manage a linked list of buffers,

the number of run-lengths generated for the line.

The first line of the input image is used to *prime* the set of edge structures by setting the *acc_value* to the correct value for the first pixel of that line, and to initialize *acc_rl*.

Then, for each line of raster data in the input image, pixels are generated sequentially. These correspond to pixels in sequential lines of the output image. The generated pixel is compared with the *acc_value* in the edge structure for that line in the output image—the value of the run-length being accumulated for that line. If they are the same, the run-length value is incremented. If they are different, the value–run-length pair is added to the list of value–run-lengths and *acc_value* set to the current pixel, and *acc_rl* is initialized.

Variations on the Algorithm

The C code (Appendix 2) has a slight modification to the preceding algorithm. Instead of initializing the *current_run* to 1, it is initialized to zero, and always is incremented rather than being incremented only if the input and current color are the same. This will remove one branch instruction from the inner loop.

The main performance enhancements that can be made revolve around increasing cache performance. Instead of storing the current value and run being accumulated in the edge structure, they can be stored in a separate array. Then the only section of the memory usually being accessed is this array of *num_output_lines* * 4 bytes (apart from the input data, of course). The larger array of edge structures and the list of value–runs of the output image are accessed only when a value changes in a line of the output image. This means the cache is less likely to thrash.

Another performance gain from this change depends on the structure of the *cache* on some machines. When a cache hit occurs, a certain amount of data is read out—a cache line of data. For example, in the clipper chip, 16 bytes are read into a cache line buffer. A subsequent access to the data in the line gives even faster access than a cache hit. This means that while we are processing a single run-length, and hence do not need to go to memory except for the preceding array—and if this array is in cache, only one in four accesses even will require a cache read —the rest will be extremely efficient line hits.

This idea can be extended for rotating binary data, if the output image has less than 32K pixels per line.

Instead of storing value–run pairs for each output image line, store a single 16-bit integer where the bottom 15 bits represent the run-length, and the MS bit represents the color being accumulated—i.e., 0 or 1. As *cur_value*, use 0 or −1.

Then to test, do an XOR operation between *acc_run* and *cur_value*—if the result is negative, then the pixel has changed. Of course, you must mask off the top bit before storing it in the run-length list, which just consists of an array of run-lengths, with an implied toggle between runs.

This method of rotation obviously can be generalized for any size data item. For example, for 8-bit RGB data, use a longword to store the RGB values so the compare can be done by a single instruction. Larger data types may require multiple compares.

See also II.6 A Fast 90-Degree Bitmap Rotator, Sue-Ken Yap; II.8 Adaptive Run-Length Encoding, Andrew S. Glassner; (*179*) *A Fast Algorithm for General Raster Rotation, Alan W. Paeth*

II.8

ADAPTIVE RUN-LENGTH ENCODING

Andrew S. Glassner
Xerox PARC
Palo Alto, California

Many graphics programmers find that much of their disks are occupied by images. Consider that a straightforward, byte-by-byte representation of a 512-by-512 image consisting of three bytes per pixel (a *raw dump* of an image) occupies $3*2^{18}$ bytes, or about 0.75 megabytes. If many images are to be stored, it seems reasonable to try to reduce the disk space required by each image.

One approach is to use a general-purpose compaction algorithm, such as the UNIX *compress* utility. Such programs indeed may achieve high compression, but it is difficult to work with the compressed data directly. If an image is to be composited with another, or one only wishes to extract a small portion, the entire image typically must be decoded first, at considerable space and time penalty.

Some compression techniques work in two dimensions, storing regions of the picture in a data structure such as a quadtree. Again, high compression can be achieved this way for some images, but finding the best decomposition of the image can be difficult, and fast decompression of selected regions also can be hard.

A less sophisticated but simpler image storage technique is known as *run-length encoding*. Consider a gray-level image with a scanline consisting of the following 10 values:

$$(15, 15, 15, 15, 15, 15, 25, 25, 25, 25).$$

Suppose we adopt a format consisting of pairs of bytes: a *count* and a *value*. The count tells how many times to repeat the immediately following gray value. Then this line could be encoded with the four bytes

$(6, 15, 4, 25)$. This run-length form required only 4 bytes rather than 10. Since the count is only 1 byte long, we can store runs from lengths 1 to 255. We can squeeze a single extra step out of the run by realizing that we never will encode runs of length zero. So, redefine the count byte to represent one less than the actual run length; a count of 0 is a run of length 1, and 255 is a run of length 256. Thus we need only two pairs to store a 512-byte-wide scanline of constant color.

This scheme is not efficient for images where the colors change quickly. If each pixel in a scanline is different than the preceding pixel, then run-length encoding actually will double the size of the file relative to a straightforward dump, since each pixel will be preceded by a count byte with value 0 (representing a run of length 1).

To handle this situation, redefine the count byte as a signed 8-bit integer. If the value is zero or positive, then it indicates a run of length one more than its value, as described earlier; but if the count is negative, then it means that what follows is a dump: a pixel-by-pixel listing of the next few pixels, as many as the absolute value of count. This is called *adaptive run-length encoding*. For example, consider the following scanline:

$$(200, 200, 200, 200, 190, 189, 180, 180, 180, 180).$$

One way to represent this is as a 10-byte dump, requiring 11 bytes:

$$(-10, 200, 200, 200, 200, 190, 189, 180, 180, 180, 180).$$

It would be more efficient to mix runs and dumps, requiring only 7 bytes:

$$(3, 200, -2, 190, 189, 3, 180).$$

If you are working with color data, then you can consider each pixel to be a single composite color value, consisting of red, green, and blue components. Thus, rather than storing just a single byte after each count, you can store the 3 bytes encoding the red, green, and blue components. Tests for equality and runs all use the entire RGB pixel. If three pixels are to be dumped, then the dump count is still -3 (meaning three pixels), but

9 bytes of data follow. Alternatively, you may choose to encode the red, green, and blue channels separately, and compress the three channels independently.

A straightforward application of this technique usually will produce a smaller file than a raw dump, but not always. For the following discussion, C represents the length of a code, and P the length of a pixel value, both in bytes. C always is 1, but P is 1 for grayscale pictures and 3 for color images.

Consider the worst case for adaptive run-length encoding: a repeating pattern of two pixel values p_1 and p_2 in the sequence (p_1, p_2, p_2). Storing this as a raw pixel-by-pixel dump requires $3P$ bytes. An adaptive run-length encoding gives $(-1, p_1, 1, p_2)$, requiring $2(C + P)$ bytes. In general, if the pattern is repeated n times, a raw dump requires $3Pn$ bytes, and an adaptive run-length encoding requires $2n(C + P)$ bytes. If the image is grayscale, then an entire file made up of this pattern will require $4n$ bytes rather than $3n$ for a raw dump, expanding the file size by $4/3$. Happily, color pictures do not suffer, since they encode into $8n$ bytes rather than the $9n$ required by a raw dump, a savings of $8/9$. You can dream up other patterns that cost more in the encoded form than a raw dump, but unless such patterns dominate an image, you will save in the long run. Where you lose is with any picture where there are no runs at all; then you effectively end up saving a raw dump, but you pay for the extra, useless code bytes.

I recommend that you encode with a greedy algorithm: Any time you find two or more pixels of the same color in a row, encode them as a run. If the final encoded picture is larger than a raw byte-by-byte dump, then forget about it and store just the raw file. I have found this situation to be sufficiently rare that I do not bother with the test.

You can make encoded files easier to use if you encode each scanline individually, rather than trying to tie together the end of one line with the start of the next. You lose a little bit of compression this way, but you save in speed when you want direct access to some part of the image. In my implementation, I also store a header block at the top of each file, giving the offset in bytes from the start of the file to the start of each scanline. This makes it easy to quickly extract and decode small regions of the image on the fly. A 32-bit offset for each of s scanlines requires only $4s$ bytes of header, a classic space–time trade-off that buys you fast random access at the cost of a bit of extra file storage.

Acknowledgments

I first saw adaptive run-length encoding in a program written by Ephraim Cohen at the NYIT Computer Graphics Lab. Greg Abram helped me write the Ikonas microcode to encode and decode images at UNC-Chapel Hill.

See also II.7 Rotation of Run-Length Encoded Image Data, Jeff Holt; II.9 Image File Compression Made Easy, Alan W. Paeth

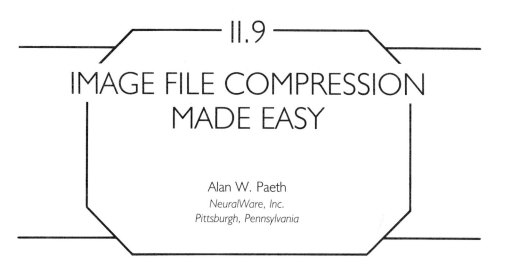

II.9

IMAGE FILE COMPRESSION MADE EASY

Alan W. Paeth
NeuralWare, Inc.
Pittsburgh, Pennsylvania

A simple predictive–corrective coding filter is derived through empirical and analytical means. Passing a 2D image through this coder in byte–serial order yields a highly redundant data stream well-suited to subsequent serial compression, as by 1D Lempel–Ziv or Huffman coders. When used to process 2D images compacted under the well-known Unix *compress* tool, treated files typically show an additional 30% reduction in size. Compared to untreated originals, cumulative compression ratios of $4:1$ are typical. The filter is demonstrably lossless and is specifically crafted for storage reduction on raster data sets of arbitrary bit precision (Paeth, 1986, 1987).

As seen in Fig. 1a, P–C coding estimates the value of the current input datum by making a prediction based on the past history of the data stream. A difference signal between the guess and the current value represents the correction to the predicted value. Given an ideal predictor, the corrector output is zero. For practical predictors, the output values are clustered about zero in symmetric fashion, leaving a data stream suitable for subsequent encoding. The efficiency of the coder may be characterized by the creation of a histogram (Fig. 2). Unlike other common schemes, such as Viterbi encoding, P–C coding is nearly its own inverse. As seen in Fig. 1b, a prediction—now based on the decoded output that has reconstructed the original—is used to provide the correction implicit with the current input value. Thus, a minor change in internal program structure allows the same code to serve as both decoder and encoder. Note that the predictor input always must be derived from previously occurring values, as the output half of the system otherwise would violate causality.

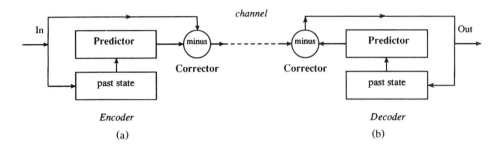

Figure 1. Prediction–correction coding.

P–C coders are a broad family. *Adaptive* (APC) coders may *learn* based on the true value of the next input; the adjustment most often is a weighted linear average. For 2D signals, the past state may be represented as a template of values that preface the current pixel (in transmission order) in both X and Y. Implementation of a simple, adaptive 2D filter for binary images is straightforward: The state of a template of N cells forms an N-bit integer, which indexes a table of predictions containing 2^N 1-bit entries. Each entry records the last output seen. Thus, any

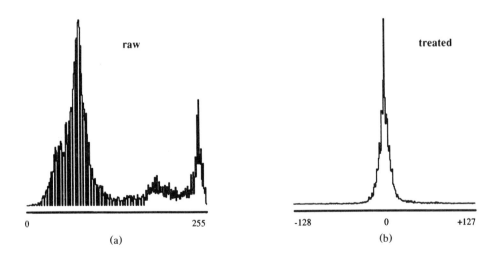

Figure 2. Data histogram: (a) raw, (b) treated.

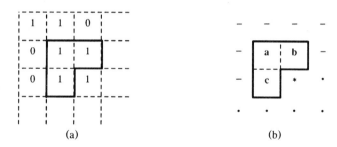

Figure 3.   2D prediction: (a) input image, (b) prediction template.

recurring template triggers a prediction that matches the unknown value discovered previously under identical local context.

A simple encoder used as a *whitening filter* does not require adapting: This is redundant to the operation of any subsequent linear compressor. Its purpose is to form a fast, nonadaptive 2D prediction based on a small set of neighboring pixels while requiring no state information on past contexts. Unfortunately, the *logical* (Binary table look-up) implementation is unsuitable: A small neighborhood of 24-bit color pixels forms too large an index. An *arithmetic* means of extension is desired; constraining the solution space simplifies the search.

A *minimum* 2D template (Fig. 3) considers neighboring values that are adjacent by edge or along the back diagonal of the current input pixel. Values previously output are indicated by ' − ', with {a, b, c} the values of particular interest. Conversely, a '.' indicates unseen raster data in which '∗' is the present input, as yet unseen by the predictor. Both logical and arithmetic models exist that estimate the value (∗). Because the predictor is to be nonadaptive, it need not save state; the multivariate function $P(a, b, c)$ models it. To reduce the solution space of any model for P, three constraints are imposed. The first is self-evident:

$$P(a, a, a) = a \qquad \text{[identity]} \quad (1).$$

The remaining two possess a compelling underlying symmetry. The second,

$$P(a, b, c) = P(a, c, b) \qquad \text{[transposition]} \quad (2),$$

guarantees an invariant predictor behavior across a transposition of the input data by row and column. Likewise:

$$P(a, b, c)' = P(a', b', c') \quad \text{[complementation]} \quad (3)$$

indicates that inversion of the raster (as with a photographic negative) yields an output that is similarly inverted.

These constraints are easily met for arithmetic prediction using Roberts's method L.R., a "poor man's Laplacian" (gradient estimator), which finds the slope along the NW/SE diagonal: $G(a, b, c) = b + c - 2a$. Adding this slope step to the variable a yields the estimate: $(*) = a + G(a, b, c)$. The predictor thus is $P(a, b, c) = b + c - a$. For images that ramp in linear fashion along any axis, the prediction is exact. Viewing the predictor output for an entire forms an image reminiscent of an *unsharp mask* convolution (Hall *et al.*, 1971).

In the case of binary prediction, empirical data was used to classify the best output as a function of eight inputs. The data was a large collection of rasters (synthetic and scanned), including digital typography, halftone, and line art. Based on the aggregate figures, the best predictions are:

a b	0 0	0 1	0 0	0 1	1 0	1 1	1 0	1 1
c $(*)$	0 (0)	0 (1)	1 (1)	1 (1)	0 (0)	0 (0)	1 (0)	1 (1) ·
300K trials	99%	66%	73%	71%	67%	90%	89%	98%

As was surmised, the empirical data satisfies all rules [1..3]. The templates are taken as the baseline case for any general predictor $P(a, b, c)$, as they satisfy both the empirical and analytical models. Note that the penultimate context and its predecessor have two of three input bits set, yet predict a zero output: These patterns are useful in detecting horizontal and vertical edges. (The binary equations that model the selection of the output data are not treated here, but are the subject of a more general paper, which also considers larger spatial templates.)

A formula modeling the template is desired in which simple pattern matching is extended arithmetically, allowing operation on rasters of arbitrary precision (Paeth, 1986, 1987). Traditional nonadaptive methods are ill-suited to binary (1 bit) data; a linear combination of integral weights often produces fractional estimates. This forms a poor prediction in the binary case, as the unseen value always is integral and on the small domain {0 1}. A fourth and final constraint already implicit in the binary template data now is adopted:

$$P(a, b, c) \text{ is an element of } \{a, b, c\} \quad [\text{membership}] \quad (4).$$

The fourth rule is satisfied easily by finding that element on the input set closest to the trial prediction, thereby forming a final prediction. Analysis shows that rules [1..3] remain invariant. Because scalar distance employs the absolute value, ambiguity in nearness is introduced should the prediction fall midway between two input values. This is resolved by introducing a tie-break order: $\{a, b, c\}$. The final prediction algorithm then is:

```
integer function predict(a, b, c: integer)
p, pa, pb, pc: integer;
    p = b + c − a;               initial estimate
    pa = abs(p − a);             distances to a, b, and c
    pb = abs(p − b);
    pc = abs(p − c);
    if (pa ≤ pb) and (pa ≤ pc) return(a);   return nearest element
    if (pb ≤ pa) and (pb ≤ pc) return(b);   in a, b, c tie-break order
    return(c);
```

This choice has the added advantage of implicitly limiting the prediction output to nonnegative values. This removes the per-datum interval test of traditional methods, used to limit predictions to the maximum range of the input. Here, the prediction output is precisely the domain of the input. For synthetic data sets of high precision, this can be of value. For instance, given an image in 24-bit precision, but having only four unique pixel colors (common to regions of bilevel color stipple or halftoning), four predictions are possible. The final estimate is the difference of two pixels; both are members of the same four-element set. Their difference set is a Cartesian product of only 16 elements. In four of 16 cases, the pixels match (a statistically common exact prediction) and a zero generated, reducing the output code set to no more than 13 combinations. In contrast, a linear method under the same conditions produces an output alphabet that is an order of magnitude larger: The final output is not sparse under byte representation.

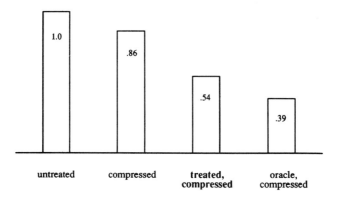

Figure 4.   Compression ratios.

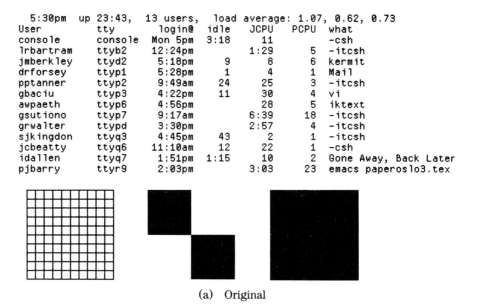

```
   5:30pm  up 23:43,  13 users,   load average: 1.07, 0.62, 0.73
User           tty          login@  idle  JCPU   PCPU  what
console        console  Mon 5pm    3:18    11         -csh
lrbartram      ttyb2     12:24pm          1:29     5  -itcsh
jmberkley      ttyd2      5:18pm      9      8      6  kermit
drforsey       ttyp1      5:28pm      1      4      1  Mail
pptanner       ttyp2      9:49am     24     25      3  -itcsh
gbaciu         ttyp3      4:22pm     11     30      4  vi
awpaeth        ttyp6      4:56pm            28      5  iktext
gsutiono       ttyp7      9:17am          6:39     18  -itcsh
grwalter       ttypd      3:30pm          2:57      4  -itcsh
sjkingdon      ttyq3      4:45pm     43      2      1  -itcsh
jcbeatty       ttyq6     11:10am     12     22      1  -csh
idallen        ttyq7      1:51pm   1:15     10      2  Gone Away, Back Later
pjbarry        ttyr9      2:03pm          3:03     23  emacs paperoslo3.tex
```

(a)   Original

Figure 5.

```
  6:30pm   up 23:43,   13 users,   load average: 1.07, 0.62, 0.73
User          tty          login@   idle   JCPU   PCPU   what
console       console      Mon 6pm  3:18    11.          -csh
lrbartram     ttyb2        12:24pm          1.:29     6   -1tcsh
jmberkley     ttyd2        6:18pm    0      8         8   kermit
drforsey      ttyp1        6:28pm    1.     4         1.  Mail
pptanner      ttyp2        9:48am    24     26        3   -1tcsh
gbaciu        ttyp3        4:22pm    11.    30        4   vi
swpaeth       ttyp6        4:56pm           28        6   1ktext
gsutiono      ttyp7        9:17am           6:38      18  -1tcsh
grwalter      ttypd        3:30pm           2:67      4   -1tcsh
sjkingdon     ttyq3        4:46pm    43     2         1.  -1tcsh
jcbeatty      ttyq6        11:10am   12     22        1.  -csh
idallen       ttyq7        1:51pm    1:16   10        2   Gone Away, Back Later
pjbarry       ttyr0        2:03pm           3:03      23  emacs paperosia3.tex
```

(b)   Prediction

(c)   Correction

Figure 5.   (*Continued*)

99

The accuracy of the hybrid predictor may be tested by pitting it against a perfect *oracle*, which peeks at the next input value $(*)$ prior to making its prediction on set $\{a, b, c\}$. (Peeking is a timeworn tradition for all successful oracles.) Also tested is a trivial 2D predictor that considers merely the input set (b); that is, the previous column element is chosen. This method satisfies rules [1, 2, 4], but not [3]. It places an added burden on the subsequent 1D coding step: Long runs of similar output value are possible, but are not necessarily clustered about zero, degrading encoding efficiency. However, adaptive 1D coders (Unix Compress) often can do well. In contrast, the two-step prediction scheme presented here supports a simplified post-coding, as by skip compression of runs of zeros. Encoding ratios are illustrated in Fig. 4; the traditional Huffman-derived entropy measure is supplanted by a file-size ratio for final sizes under Unix Compress. Figures 5a through c show the operation of the non-adaptive 2D filter at the respective stages of input, prediction, and correction.

In summary, a method for efficient, nonlinear, algebraic prediction of 2D images is demonstrated. The method is both lossless and particularly well-suited to the encoding of both synthetic and scanned raster images of arbitrary precision.

See also II.8 Adaptive Run-Length Encoding, Andrew S. Glassner

II.10

AN OPTIMAL FILTER FOR IMAGE RECONSTRUCTION

Nelson Max
Lawrence Livermore National Laboratory
Livermore, California

In a previous gem, Mark Pavicic discussed radially symmetric filter functions, optimized for several functional forms. Here, I propose another functional form, meeting somewhat different criteria.

For the purposes of image reconstruction from a sampled raster, it is important that the filter be at least C^1 smooth, so that the reconstructed image will not have Mach bands. Pavicic's filters are not C^1, resulting in creases in the sum of the filters, visible in his figures. Also, Pavicic restricted himself to radial filter functions $f(r)$, which are zero for $r \geq 1$. I do not make this restriction.

I wanted a function that was easily computed, and chose to use a nonuniform quadratic spline $g(r)$, of the form shown in Fig. 1. It consists of downward curving parabola for $0 \leq r \leq s$, and an upward curving parabola for $s \leq r \leq t$, which meet smoothly at $r = s$, and has the properties $g(0) = 1$, $g'(0) = 0$, $g(t) = 0$, and $g'(t) = 0$.

The function that satisfies these conditions is

$$g(r) = \begin{cases} 1 - \dfrac{r^2}{st} & 0 \leq r \leq s, \\[2mm] \dfrac{(t-r)^2}{t(t-s)} & s \leq r \leq t, \\[2mm] 0 & t \geq r. \end{cases}$$

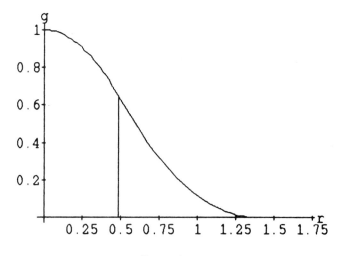

Figure 1.

The volume V under this filter is computed as a solid of revolution,

$$V = \int_0^\infty 2\pi r f(r)\, dr = 2\pi \int_0^s \left(r - \frac{r^3}{st} \right) dr + 2\pi \int_s^t \frac{r(t-r)^2}{t(t-s)}\, dr$$

$$= 2\pi \left(\frac{s^2}{2} - \frac{s^4}{4st} + \frac{t^4}{12t(t-s)} - \frac{s^2 t^2}{2t(t-s)} \right.$$

$$\left. + \frac{2s^3 t}{3t(t-s)} - \frac{s^4}{4t(t-s)} \right).$$

The filter $f(r) = \frac{1}{V} g(r)$, normalized to have unit volume, thus can be found in terms of the two parameters, s and t.

A function with constant value 1, sampled on the integer lattice $\{(i, j)\}$, will be reconstructed as

$$h(x, y) = \sum_{i=-\infty}^{\infty} \sum_{j=-\infty}^{\infty} f\left(\sqrt{(x-i)^2 + (y-j)^2} \right).$$

One condition for optimality is to minimize the difference d between the maximum value M and the minimum value m of h. This difference can become arbitrarily small as s and t approach infinity, so I limited t to be less than 2. Because of symmetry and the limited size range I allowed for t,

$$M = \max_{\substack{0 \le x \le .5 \\ 0 \le y \le .5}} \sum_{i=-1}^{2} \sum_{j=-1}^{2} f\left(\sqrt{(x-i)^2 + (y-j)^2}\right).$$

Figure 2.

For each fixed s and t, I found the critical points of $h(x, y)$ by solving the equations $\dfrac{\partial h}{\partial x} = 0$ and $\dfrac{\partial h}{\partial y} = 0$, using 2D Newton iteration, starting at all initial conditions in a 26×26 array of points inside the square of side $1/2$, and took d to be the difference between the maximum and minimum critical value.

The minimum d, equal to .885 percent, was found at $s = .4848$ and $t = 1.3778$. The RMS error between $h(x, y)$ and 1 was .261 percent, and the error volume,

$$\int_0^1 \int_0^1 abs(h(x, y) - 1)\, dx\, dy,$$

used by Pavicic was .232 percent. Figure 2 shows a raster intensity image of this $h(x, y)$ for x and y between 0 and 2, with the contrast amplified by a factor of 100. Although there is clearly visible periodic structure, the intensity varies smoothly.

The minimum RMS error of .245 percent is attained when $s = .4810$ and $t = 1.3712$, and the minimum error volume of .210 percent is attained when $s = .4792$ and $t = 1.3682$.

This work was performed under the auspices of the U.S. Department of Energy by the Lawrence Livermore National Laboratory under contract number W-7405-Eng-48.

See also (*144*) *Convenient Anti-Aliasing Filters that Minimize "Bumpy" Sampling, Mark J. Pavicic*; (*147*) *Filters for Common Resampling Tasks, Ken Turkowski*

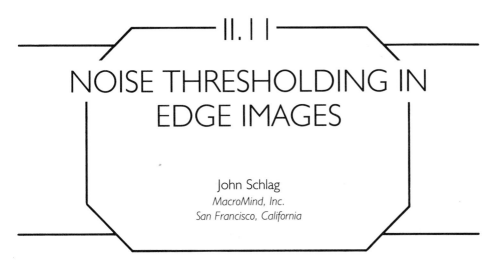

II.11

NOISE THRESHOLDING IN EDGE IMAGES

John Schlag
MacroMind, Inc.
San Francisco, California

This is actually more of a vision gem than a graphics gem, but since image processing is so often useful in computer graphics, this seems *apropos*.

First derivative filters (often called *edge detectors* in the vision literature) are often used to sharpen digitized images, or to produce a candidate set of points at which to evaluate some other operator. They also are used to obtain a surface normal perturbation from an image for bump mapping. Digitized images are typically noisy. First derivative estimators such as the *Sobel* and *Prewitt operators* (see below) accentuate this noise. Hence, it often is necessary to threshold the result of the edge operator to filter out the noise. The question then is how to pick the threshold. For those who find arbitrary (*tweak*) parameters distasteful, here is a way to at least tie the threshold to a discernible system parameter.

The two most common first derivative edge detectors are the Sobel and Prewitt operators:

$$\text{Sobel:} \quad i_x(p) \cong \begin{bmatrix} -1 & 0 & 1 \\ -2 & 0 & 2 \\ -1 & 0 & 1 \end{bmatrix} \quad i_y(p) \cong \begin{bmatrix} 1 & 2 & 1 \\ 0 & 0 & 0 \\ -1 & -2 & -1 \end{bmatrix},$$

$$\text{Prewitt:} \quad i_x(p) \cong \begin{bmatrix} -1 & 0 & 1 \\ -1 & 0 & 1 \\ -1 & 0 & 1 \end{bmatrix} \quad i_y(p) \cong \begin{bmatrix} 1 & 1 & 1 \\ 0 & 0 & 0 \\ -1 & -1 & -1 \end{bmatrix},$$

$$E(p) = \sqrt{i_x^2 + i_y^2}.$$

The 3-by-3 convolution masks are evaluated at each pixel to produce estimates of the partial derivatives of the image function. The edge function $E(p)$ produces an estimate of the magnitude of the gradient. The threshold can be based on an evaluation of the noise in the gradient

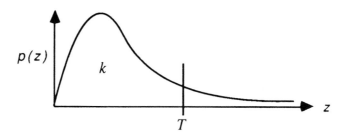

Figure 1. The Rayleigh probability density function.

domain. Assume that the noise in the input image is normal with mean zero and variance σ_n^2. Each mask forms a linear combination of the neighborhood pixels, so the noise distribution in each of the partial derivative estimates also is normal. Since the variances of independent variables add as the squares of their coefficients, the noise variance in each estimate will be $\sigma_x^2 = \sigma_y^2 = 12\sigma_n^2$ (for the Sobel masks). From probability theory (Papoulis, 1965, p. 195), the noise distribution in the edge function has a Rayleigh distribution with parameter σ_x:

$$p(z) = \frac{z}{\sigma_x^2} \exp\left(\frac{-z^2}{2\sigma_x^2}\right) \quad \text{for } z \geq 0.$$

The threshold T can be placed to eliminate a given percentage of the distribution. Integrating the density function and solving for the threshold gives $T = \sqrt{2\sigma_x^2 \ln(1/1 - k)}$, where k is the fraction of the distribution to be eliminated. If the variance σ_n^2 of the input noise is not known *a priori*, it can be measured easily from a blank image, or a flat region of an image. Alternatively, we can examine the histogram of an unthresholded edge image to find σ_x directly. Notice that we are playing fast and loose with assumptions of statistical independence, since the convolution masks are using the same pixels. Experiment confirms however, that the edge function distribution is as expected.

Similar reasoning applies in the case of *bump mapping*, where the estimates of the partials i_x and i_y are used to perturb a surface normal. In this case, $E(p)$ is never calculated, and all one need worry about is the noise distribution of the partials.

COMPUTING THE AREA, THE CIRCUMFERENCE, AND THE GENUS OF A BINARY DIGITAL IMAGE

Hanspeter Bieri, Andreas Kohler
University of Berne
Berne, Switzerland

An Example

Figure 1 shows a small *binary digital image of resolution* $8*7$ consisting of 31 black and 25 white *pixels*. Pixels are considered here to be closed unit squares, although we will assume them to be implemented as elements of a binary matrix, as is often the case. The set union of the black pixels will be called the *figure* of the image, and computing the *area*, the *circumference*, and the *genus* (or *Euler number*) of the image more precisely shall mean computing these three important properties for the figure.

Using elementary geometry, we easily verify that the area of the image in Fig. 1 is 31 and the circumference is 62. The genus of a binary digital image often is defined as the number of *connected components* of the figure minus the number of *holes*. (These are the connected components of the set complement of the figure which do not meet the border of the image.) Obviously, the image of Fig. 1 has two black connected components and three holes; therefore, its genus is -1.

The Method

In Fig. 2, the digital image of Fig. 1 is represented in a slightly different way, which makes it easy to recognize the *vertices*, *sides*, and (quadratic) *extents* of all its pixels. The main task of the method we are going to present is counting the number of vertices, sides, and extents of the black pixels in an image. Because vertices are zero-dimensional, sides one-

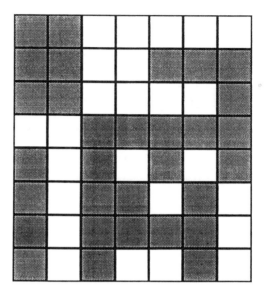

Figure 1. A binary digital image.

dimensional and extents two-dimensional, we denote these numbers by n_0, n_1, and n_2, respectively. For our example, we get $n_0 = 61$, $n_1 = 93$, $n_2 = 31$. Knowing these numbers for a given image I, it is very easy to compute the area A, the circumference C and the genus G of I by applying the following formulas:

$$A(I) = n_2,$$

$$C(I) = 2 * n_1 - 4 * n_2,$$

$$G(I) = n_0 - n_1 + n_2.$$

Now, assuming that I has resolution $m * n$ and is provided as a binary $m * n$-matrix $\mathbf{M}$, we can compute n_0, n_1, and n_2 simultaneously in one single scan of $\mathbf{M}$, e.g., row by row and from left to right. Then we only have to evaluate the three preceding formulas to determine $A(I)$, $C(I)$ and $G(I)$.

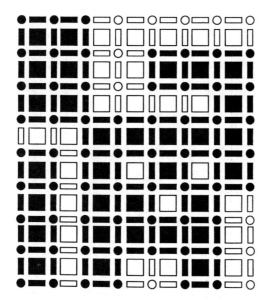

Figure 2.   The vertices, sides, and extents of all pixels in the image.

For an explanation of this method—which is based on the fact that area, circumference, and genus can be understood as additive functionals —the interested reader is referred to Bieri and Nef (1984), where the d-dimensional case is treated and where more references (several in German) are listed.

The Algorithm

To find n_0, n_1, and n_2 fast and elegantly, we add an auxiliary row and an auxiliary column of zeros to $\mathbf{M}$ and imagine the corresponding image *partitioned* in a way shown in Fig. 3. By this partitioning, every pixel vertex, pixel side, and pixel extent of I is associated with exactly one element of the (enlarged) matrix $\mathbf{M}$. For each matrix element $\mathbf{M}_{i,j}$, we call the associated vertex, horizontal side, vertical side, and pixel extent the *pixel components* at position (i, j) and denote them by $P_{i,j}$, $H_{i,j}$, $V_{i,j}$ and $E_{i,j}$, respectively (Fig. 4).

109

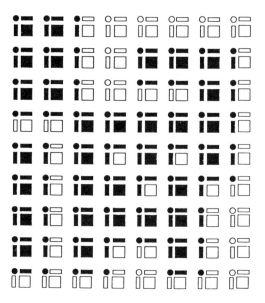

Figure 3. All pixel components belonging to the enlarged matrix.

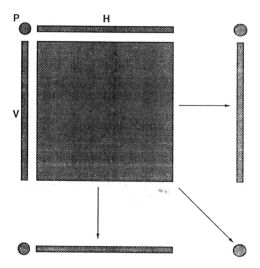

Figure 4. Five neighboring pixel components are *blackened*.

Now let us consider an element $\mathbf{M}_{i,j}$ during the scan of the matrix $\mathbf{M}$ ($0 \leq i \leq m - 1$, $0 \leq j \leq n - 1$). The following pseudo-code describes how our algorithm updates n_0, n_1 and n_2 at this position and how it *blackens* certain neighboring pixel components in case $\mathbf{M}_{i,j}$ represents a black pixel (Fig. 4). (For $i = m$ or $j = n$, only the update of n_0, n_1, and n_2 is necessary, of course.)

```
if M[i][j] = 1        black pixel
   then begin
                N[0] ← N[0] + 1;
                N[1] ← N[1] + 2;
                N[2] ← N[2] + 1;
                P[i][j + 1] ← 1;
                V[i][j + 1] ← 1;
                P[i + 1][j] ← 1;
                H[i + 1][j] ← 1;
                P[i + 1][j + 1] ← 1;
        end;
   else begin       white pixel
        if P[i][j] = 1
           then N[0] ← N[0] + 1;
        if H[i][j] = 1
           then N[1] ← N[1] + 1;
        if V[i][j] = 1
           then N[1] ← N[1] + 1;
        end;
```

Large digital images often are stored in *raster representation*, i.e., as a sequential file where row i precedes row $i + 1$. In Appendix 2, the C Implementation of our algorithm assumes the given binary digital image I to be provided in this way.

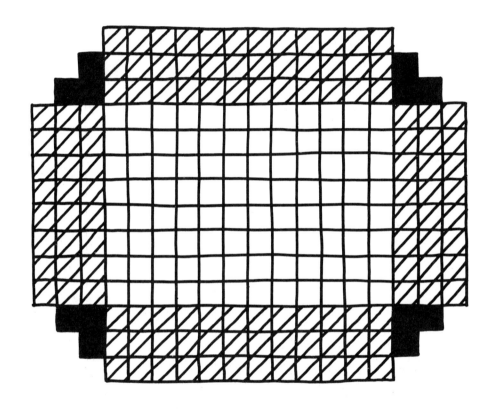

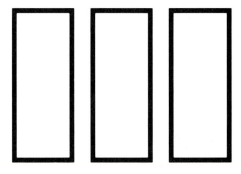

FRAME BUFFER TECHNIQUES

FRAME BUFFER TECHNIQUES

A *frame buffer* is the piece of hardware at the heart of most graphics display tasks. To the computer, this device appears essentially as a large chunk of memory, while to the user, it is the vehicle for perceiving the underlying data visually. This mapping from data to image is carried out by altering the appearance of a two-dimensional array of discrete picture elements, or *pixels*, according to the contents of corresponding memory locations. Thus, the role of modern frame buffers is to take the normally invisible contents of computer memory and present them in a visual form.

Because it is a physical piece of hardware, the frame buffer possesses certain limitations that the graphics programmer must take into account, such as resolution in pixels and the number of discrete colors each of these pixels can assume. Given the diversity and importance of these devices, it is not surprising that many techniques have been developed to make the most of their capabilities. All of the gems of this Part deal with some aspect of color as it pertains to a frame buffer.

There are many similarities between the techniques explored in this Part and those of the previous Part on image processing. These similarities stem from the fact that both frame buffer techniques and image processing are intimately linked with manipulating rectangular arrays of discrete pixels.

EFFICIENT INVERSE COLOR MAP COMPUTATION

Spencer W. Thomas
University of Michigan
Ann Arbor, Michigan

An *inverse color map* is used to translate full (RGB) colors into a limited set of colors. It might be used to drive an 8-bit color display (Apple, 1988), to perform error-propagation dithering (e.g., Floyd–Steinberg) in color (as in Gem II.3, "Color Dithering", by Spencer Thomas), or for the output phase of a color quantization algorithm (Heckbert, 1982; Gervautz and Purgathofer, 1990). Published methods for computing such color maps seem to be few and far between, and either are relatively inefficient or inexact. This gem describes a simple and efficient method for computing inverse color maps.

A *representative color* is one of the colors in the limited set. There are n representative colors. RGB colors are *quantized* to k bits by taking the top k bits of each primary as an integer in the range $0..2^k$. A *inverse color map* is a cubical array, 2^k on each side, that is indexed by quantized red, green, and blue values to obtain a color index that represents the closest (within the limits of the quantization) representative color to the given RGB color.

Two versions of the algorithm will be described. The first is simple, and illustrates the basic principle as well. It also is fairly efficient, taking approximately 24 seconds to completely fill an inverse color map ($k = 5$ and $n = 256$) on a SUN 3/60 computer. The asymptotic behavior of this algorithm is $O(n \cdot 2^{3k})$, which is achieved for relatively small values of k and n (on a SUN 3/60, the constant of proportionality is 2.8 μsec). The second version is significantly more complex, but much more efficient for large color maps, taking approximately 3.2 seconds to fill the same map. The asymptotic behavior of this algorithm is expected to be $O(\log(n) \cdot 2^{3k})$, but this limit is not reached in practice. Still, the speedup of version 2 over version 1 is significant, and improves as n and k increase.

The C Implementation for both versions is included in Appendix 2. It also is distributed freely as part of the Utah Raster Toolkit.

Incremental Distance Calculation

This algorithm is based on the following observations:

- The regions of RGB space that map to a given representative color comprise exactly those points that are closer to the given representative than to any other. This gives rise to a structure known as a *Voronoi diagram* (Preparata and Shamos, 1985) in the three-dimensional RGB space. Figure 1 (see color insert) shows one of these as a set of slices perpendicular to the red axis.

- A depth-buffered image of cones aligned with the Z axis results in a picture of a 2D Voronoi diagram. Each region consists of the points that are closest to the projection of the apex of a single cone.

- In fact, the *depth* of a point on the cone is proportional to the distance of the screen point from the projected apex of the cone. Thus, we might call the depth buffer a distance buffer instead.

- A 3D image of the RGB Voronoi diagram can be obtained by using a 3D distance buffer to render *hypercones* whose apices coincide with the representative colors.

- Since the decision to color a given voxel is based only on the relative magnitude of the distances involved, it works just as well to use the distance squared rather than the actual Euclidean distance.

- The distance squared easily can be computed incrementally using only integer addition and subtraction operations.

- Finally, for version 2, we observe that the regions are convex.

The square of the Euclidean distance from a color (r, g, b) to a representative color (r_i, g_i, b_i) is

$$d(r, g, b) = (r - r_i)^2 + (g - g_i)^2 + (b - b_i)^2.$$

The effect of incrementing one color component, say b, by a quantity x yields

$$\Delta_b(r, g, b) = d(r, g, b + x) - d(r, g, b) = x^2 - 2b_i x + 2bx.$$

The second difference,

$$\Delta_b^2(r, g, b) = \Delta_b(r, g, b + x) - \Delta_b(r, g, b) = 2x^2,$$

is a constant, assuming x is constant. Note, too, that these depend only on b, and so are independent of the values of r and g. For the pseudo-code, we assume that the input RGB values are represented with 8 bits per primary, and that $x = 2^{8-k}$. Distances are measured to the center of each quantized cell, so $x/2$ is used as the starting point instead of 0.

distbuf is a 3D array of 32-bit integers 2^k on a side. All its elements are initialized to $2^{31} - 1$.
mapbuf is a 3D array of 8-bit index values of the same size.
x ← lshift(1, 8 − k);
xsqr ← lshift(x, 8 − k);
txsqr ← xsqr*2;
The following code is executed for each color in the (forward) color map. The variable color_index is the corresponding index.
Thus, (ri, gi, bi) = color map[color_index], rdist, gdist, bdist are the computed distances for the respective nested loops
rdist ← (ri − x/2)² + (gi − x/2)² + (bi − x/2)²;
rinc, ginc, binc are the initial increments for rdist, gdist, bdist
(i.e., for r = g = b = x/2)
rinc ← 2*x*(ri − x);
ginc ← 2*x*(gi − x);
binc ← 2*x*(bi − x);
rxx, gxx, bxx are the current increment values for rdist, gdist, bdist
rxx ← rinc;
rq, gq, bq are the quantized versions of r, g, b

```
for rq ← 0 to 2^k − 1 do
    gdist ← rdist;
    gxx ← ginc;
    for gq ← 0 to 2^k − 1 do
        bdist ← gdist;
        bxx ← binc;
        for bq ← 0 to 2^k − 1 do
            if distbuf[rq][gq][bq] > bdist then
            begin
```

> *Note that in C, the subscripting is done efficiently*
> *with pointers. E.g., instead of distbuf, use a pointer*
> *distp, initialized to distbuf, and incremented*
> *each time through the blue loop.*

```
                distbuf[rq][gq][bq] ← bdist;
                mapbuf[rq][gq][bq] ← color_index;
            end;
            bdist ← bdist + bxx;
            bxx ← bxx + txsqr;
        endloop;
        gdist ← gdist + gxx;
        gxx ← gxx + txsqr;
    endloop;
    rdist ← rdist + rxx;
    rxx ← rxx + txsqr;
endloop;
```

This code visits every cell in the inverse color map for each representative color. The cost of changing a cell is not that much higher than the cost of visiting it in the first place. Therefore, the time to run will be proportional to the product of the number of representatives and the number of cells, or $n \cdot 2^{3k}$. This is borne out by experiment for values of k in the range 4–6.

Taking Advantage of Convexity

The first version of the algorithm, while quite simple, visits many inverse color map cells that it does not change because they are too far from the representative. The colors that map to a given representative lie within a convex polyhedron. We can take advantage of this fact to visit fewer cells per representative and thereby speed up the algorithm. The basic idea is simple: Start at the representative color and scan outwards until cells not in the region are encountered, then stop. In one dimension, this results in the following pseudo-code. The details of the incremental distance computation are not repeated.

```
detected_some ← false;
Note: quantize(b) = rshift(b, 8 − k)
for bq ← quantize(bi) to 2ᵏ − 1 do
    if distbuf[bq] < bdist then
    begin
            if detected_some then
                    exit;
        end;
    else begin
            detected_some ← true;
            distbuf[bq] ← bdist;
            mapbuf[bq] ← color_index;
        end;
    for bq ← quantize(bi) − 1 to 0 step − 1 do
        Pretty much the same code goes in here as in the preceding.
        Because of going down instead of up, reverse the order of incrementing:
        bxx ← bxx − txsqr;
        bdist ← bdist − bxx;
```

The multidimensional scan essentially is the same, except that for the green and red levels, the inequality test and changes to the buffer are replaced by a call on the next inner loop. The value of "detected_some" from the lower-level loop is used to determine whether a change was made, and thus whether to set "detected_some" for the higher-level loop.

Additional complexity is introduced when we realize that as green, say, scans away from the representative color, the active segment of a blue scanline might not overlap the blue value of the representative color (Fig. 2). Thus, we really should update the blue starting point so that it has a good chance of being close to the segment on the next scanline. Of course, this start-point tracking needs to be reset at the start of the next green loop (when green starts scanning down, for example, or when red has just been incremented to the next scan-plane). There are a number of variables (such as the initial distance and its increment) that are associated with the starting point; these must be updated as well.[1] The preceding code changes to look like this:

The variable names starting with 'c' are the original values of these variables at the blue center (quantize(B)). They are used to reinitialize the variables when green starts a new loop.

```
if new_green_loop then
begin
    here = quantize(B);
    binc = cbinc;
    bdist ← gdist;
    . . .
    end;
detected_some ← false;
for bq ← here to 2^k − 1 do
    if distbuf[bq] < bdist then
```
This is the same as above.
```
    else begin
        if not detected_some and bq > here then
```
First time on this scan-line, update here if necessary.
```
            here ← bq;
            binc ← bxx;
            gdist ← bdist;
            . . .
            end;
```
This is the same as above.
```
        end;
for bq ← here − 1 to 0 step − 1 do
```
essentially same code goes in here as above.

---

[1] In the green loop, two sets of some of these values (e.g., gdist) must be maintained. One set is updated from below by the blue loop, and the second set is used to update the red loop when the green starting point is changed.

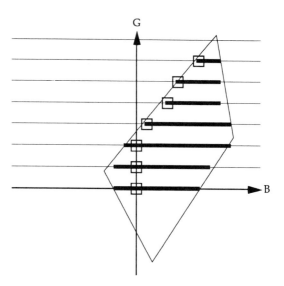

Figure 2. A sample domain in a blue–green plane, showing that the starting point of the blue scanlines may shift to the side. The solid lines indicate the changed segment (scanning up from the blue axis), and the boxes indicate the starting point of each segment.

This produces a reasonable speedup (about $7 \times$ for a map with $k = 5$), but more is possible. When the scan encounters a scanline or scan-plane on which there are no cells for the representative, it must look at all the cells on that line or plane. This causes a large number of cells to be examined uselessly. The minimum and maximum values reached during a previous scan sometimes can be used to predict the range within which any cells found on the next scan must lie. In particular, if the minimum is increasing, or the maximum decreasing, then the new scan cannot overlap the previous scan on that end (Fig. 3). This is a consequence of the convexity of the region. The min/max tracking is included in the C Implementation (Appendix 2), but will not be elaborated on here. This version showed a speedup of about $9 \times$ for a 5-bit map, and about $25 \times$ for a 6-bit map (versus $15 \times$ for the version without min/max tracking).

A final optimization splits the blue scanning loops into two halves to avoid the "if detected_some" test in the inner loop. The first loop finds the beginning of the segment and the second loop fills it.

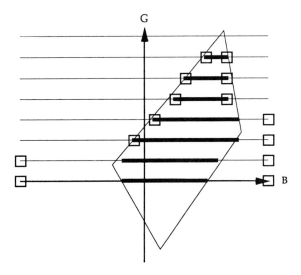

Figure 3. Adjusting the minimum and maximum for blue scanlines. The boxes show the minimum and maximum value set on each scanline, and used for the next scanline up.

What should the asymptotic behavior of this algorithm be? In the average case, with randomly distributed representative colors, the mth representative will modify approximately $1/m$ of the cells in the map. The expected number of cells modified, therefore, is

$$2^{3k} \sum_{1}^{n} \frac{1}{m} \to O(2^{3k} \log(n)).$$

The algorithm still visits an appreciable number of unmodified cells (presumably proportional to 2^{2k}), so this number forms a lower bound on the time complexity, and the observed times for $n < 256$ and $k \le 7$ do not follow this rule.

Unfortunately, version 2 of the algorithm does not produce identical results to version 1, because of an aliasing problem. If a domain is very narrow, it may be missed on some scanlines. Since the version 2 code exits as soon as a scanline (for the green loop) is empty, any cells lying past the empty scanline will be missed, and will be assigned to a different representative. However, the narrowness of the region that caused the

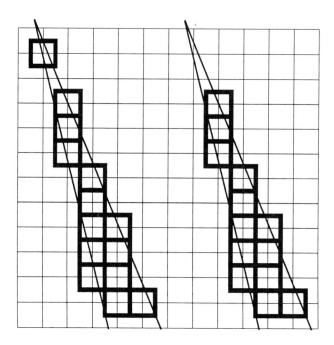

Figure 4. Aliasing of narrow domains can cause some cells to be miscolored by version 2 of the algorithm. On the left is the correct set of pixels in the domain. On the right is the set of pixels found by version 2. It stops scanning after reaching the first blank line, missing the last pixel at the top.

aliasing means that this other representative is almost as close as the original, so the effect is negligible. The aliasing problem is illustrated in Figure 4.

Color map Ordering

Version 2 of the algorithm is sensitive to the ordering of the input colors.[2] For example, if the input color map consisted solely of grays in order of increasing brightness, the loop for each representative would be expected to visit $(m - 1)/m$ cells, yielding a time complexity of $O(n \cdot 2^{3k})$. The

---

[2]This is similar to the anomalous behavior shown by the QuickSort algorithm on sorted input.

solution is simple: Randomize the input values. The *shuffle* algorithm in Morton (1990) provides exactly the effect needed here.

Results

Figure 5 (see color insert) shows a sample computer-generated image. The colors in this image were quantized to 256 representative colors. The corresponding inverse color map ($k = 6$, $n = 256$) is shown in Figure 1.

See also II.2 A Comparison of Digital Halftoning Techniques, Dale A. Schumacher; II.3 Color Dithering, Spencer W. Thomas, Rodney G. Bogart; III.2 Efficient Statistic Computations for Optimal Color Quantization, Xiaolin Wu; (*287*) *A Simple Method for Color Quantization*: *Octree Quantization*, *Michael Gervautz, Werner Purgathofer*

EFFICIENT STATISTICAL COMPUTATIONS FOR OPTIMAL COLOR QUANTIZATION

Xiaolin Wu
University of Western Ontario
London, Ontario, Canada

Introduction

Color quantization is a must when using an inexpensive 8-bit color display to display high-quality color images. Even when 24-bit full color displays become commonplace in the future, quantization still is important because it leads to significant image data compression, making extra frame buffer available for animation and reducing bandwidth requirements (a bottleneck when we go for HDTV).

Color quantization is a 3D clustering process. A color image in an RGB mode corresponds to a three-dimensional discrete density $P(\mathbf{c})$, where $\mathbf{c} = (c_r, c_g, c_b)$ in RGB space. The intensity of each primary color often is discrete and encoded by m bits; hence, $P(\mathbf{c})$ is defined on a cubic lattice S of $2^m \cdot 2^m \cdot 2^m$ points. In color image quantization, the point set S is partitioned into K subsets S_k, $1 \le k \le K$, $\Sigma_{\mathbf{c} \in S_k} P(\mathbf{c}) \ne 0$, $\bigcup_{1 \le k \le k} S_k = S$, $S_j \cap_{j \ne k} S_k = \phi$, and all colors $\mathbf{c} \in S_k$ are mapped to a representative color, $\mathbf{q}_k = (q_{kr}, q_{kg}, q_{kb})$. Given such a partition, the expected quantization error is defined as

$$E(S_1, S_2, \cdots, S_K) = \sum_{1 \le k \le K} \sum_{\mathbf{c} \in S_k} P(\mathbf{c})\Psi(\mathbf{c} - \mathbf{q}_k), \qquad (1)$$

where Ψ is a dissimilarity measure between $\mathbf{c}$ and $\mathbf{q}_k$. A suitable Ψ for human perception of colors is a research topic beyond the scope of this paper. The ubiquitous mean-square error measure is used in the following development; but test images, not just numerical errors, are used for the reader to judge the image quality.

Ideally, one would like to minimize Eq. (1) for given $P(\mathbf{c})$, Ψ, and K. The fact that there are approaching $K^{|S|}$ different partitions (Anderberg, 1973) makes optimal quantization a challenging problem for algorithm design. Many heuristic algorithms were proposed for color quantization: Heckbert's median-cut algorithm (1982), the Wu–Witten (1985) and Wan et al. (1988) variance-based algorithms, and the Gervautz–Purgathofer octree-based algorithm (1990). The median-cut algorithm partitions the color space into K boxes, each of which contains approximately the same number of pixels. This approach is better than naive uniform quantization, but far from the goal of minimizing Eq. (1). Intuitively, for the same pixel population, a large box should be allocated more representative colors than a small one; i.e., the variance should play an important role. Wu and Witten developed a divide-and-conquer strategy to minimize the marginal variance in partitioning the color space, and this work was improved by Wan et al. However, the sole reason for minimizing the marginal variance instead of true variance was that we did not have an efficient way to compute three-dimensional color statistics then. This problem will be solved in this gem, and consequently, optimizing color quantization will become computationally feasible.

Quantization Based on Variance Minimization

Color quantization is optimized through a linear search. We sweep a cutting plane across the RGB cube perpendicularly to the R, G, B axes separately, and choose the plane that minimizes the sum of variances at both sides to cut the cube into two boxes. Next, the box with the larger variance is partitioned into two smaller boxes by the same cutting criterion, and so forth, until K boxes are formed. The K means (centers of gravity) of those K boxes are selected as K representative colors.

In the preceding minimization process, for each possible cutting position in every direction, we need to evaluate the variances at both sides. Without an efficient algorithm for such statistical evaluations, the proposed optimization is impractical.

Efficient Computations of Color Statistics

In this section, we will show how the mean and the variance of any rectangular box containing n color points may be computed, respectively, in $O(1)$ time with an $O(|S|)$ time preprocessing.

Let $\mathbf{c}_i = (c_{ir}, c_{ig}, c_{ib})$ and $\mathbf{c}_j = (c_{jr}, c_{jg}, c_{jb})$ be the two points in the cubic lattice S. We say that $\mathbf{c}_j$ dominates $\mathbf{c}_i$, denoted by $\mathbf{c}_j \succ \mathbf{c}_i$, if $c_{jr} > c_{ir}$, $c_{jg} > c_{ig}$, and $c_{jb} > c_{ib}$ hold simultaneously. Any pair $\mathbf{c}_i$ and $\mathbf{c}_j$, where $\mathbf{c}_j \succ \mathbf{c}_i$, defines a three-dimensional box $\Omega(\mathbf{c}_i, \mathbf{c}_j]$ in the discrete color space, with its r, g, and b interval being $(c_{ir}, c_{jr}]$, $(c_{ig}, c_{jg}]$, and $(c_{ib}, c_{jb}]$. Notice that these intervals are open on the left but closed on the right; i.e., the lower, left, and front faces of the box are excluded, while the upper, right, and back faces are included.

If all colors $\mathbf{c} \in \Omega(\mathbf{c}_i, \mathbf{c}_j]$ are quantized to $\mathbf{q} = (q_r, q_g, q_b)$, then under the mean-square error measure, the expected quantization error for $\Omega(\mathbf{c}_i, \mathbf{c}_j]$ is defined by

$$E(\mathbf{c}_i, \mathbf{c}_j] = \sum_{\mathbf{c} \in \Omega(\mathbf{c}_i, \mathbf{c}_j]} P(\mathbf{c})(\mathbf{c} - \mathbf{q})^2, \tag{2}$$

where $(\mathbf{c} - \mathbf{q})^2 = (\mathbf{c} - \mathbf{q})(\mathbf{c} - \mathbf{q})^T$ is the squared Euclidean distance between $\mathbf{c}$ and $\mathbf{q}$. It is easy to show that Eq. (2) is minimized if the representative color $\mathbf{q}$ is set to the mean $\mu(\mathbf{c}_i, \mathbf{c}_j]$ of the box $\Omega(\mathbf{c}_i, \mathbf{c}_j]$, i.e.,

$$\mathbf{q} = \mu(\mathbf{c}_i, \mathbf{c}_j] = \frac{\displaystyle\sum_{\mathbf{c} \in \Omega(\mathbf{c}_i, \mathbf{c}_j]} \mathbf{c} P(\mathbf{c})}{\displaystyle\sum_{\mathbf{c} \in \Omega(\mathbf{c}_i, \mathbf{c}_j]} P(\mathbf{c})}. \tag{3}$$

Denote the eight vertices of the box $\Omega(\mathbf{c}_i, \mathbf{c}_j]$ by

$$\mathbf{v}_0 = (c_{ir}, c_{ig}, c_{ib}), \qquad \mathbf{v}_4 = (c_{jr}, c_{ig}, c_{ib}),$$

$$\mathbf{v}_1 = (c_{ir}, c_{ig}, c_{jb}), \qquad \mathbf{v}_5 = (c_{jr}, c_{ig}, c_{jb}),$$

$$\mathbf{v}_2 = (c_{ir}, c_{jg}, c_{ib}), \qquad \mathbf{v}_6 = (c_{jr}, c_{jg}, c_{ib}),$$

$$\mathbf{v}_3 = (c_{ir}, c_{jg}, c_{jb}), \qquad \mathbf{v}_7 = (c_{jr}, c_{jg}, c_{jb}).$$

Then by the basic rule of inclusion–exclusion of combinatorics (Liu, 1968), we have

$$\sum_{\mathbf{c}\in\Omega(\mathbf{c}_i,\mathbf{c}_j]} \mathbf{f}(\mathbf{c})P(\mathbf{c})$$

$$= \left[\sum_{\mathbf{c}\in\Omega(\mathbf{o},\mathbf{v}_7]} - \sum_{\mathbf{c}\in\Omega(\mathbf{o},\mathbf{v}_6]} - \sum_{\mathbf{c}\in\Omega(\mathbf{o},\mathbf{v}_5]} + \sum_{\mathbf{c}\in\Omega(\mathbf{o},\mathbf{v}_4]} \right.$$

$$\left. - \sum_{\mathbf{c}\in\Omega(\mathbf{o},\mathbf{v}_3]} + \sum_{c\in\Omega(\mathbf{o},\mathbf{v}_2]} + \sum_{\mathbf{c}\in\Omega(\mathbf{o},\mathbf{v}_1]} - \sum_{\mathbf{c}\in\Omega(\mathbf{o},\mathbf{v}_0]} \right] \mathbf{f}(\mathbf{c})P(\mathbf{c}). \quad (4)$$

In the preceding, vector $\mathbf{o}$ is a reference point such that

$$\sum_{\mathbf{c}\in\Omega(-\infty,\mathbf{o}]} P(\mathbf{c}) = 0. \quad (5)$$

A graphical explanation of Eq. (4) is given in Fig. 1.

Since $P(\mathbf{c})$ is defined on the finite lattice S, one can pre-compute and store the quantities,

$$\sum_{\mathbf{c}\in\Omega(\mathbf{o},\mathbf{c}_t]} \mathbf{f}(\mathbf{c})P(\mathbf{c}), \quad (6)$$

for all $\mathbf{c}_t \in S$. Then the summation $\sum_{\mathbf{c}\in\Omega(\mathbf{c}_i,\mathbf{c}_j]}\mathbf{f}(\mathbf{c})P(\mathbf{c})$ can be done in $O(1)$ time by Eq. (4), independent of the size of $\Omega(\mathbf{c}_i,\mathbf{c}_j]$. Now substitute $\mathbf{f}(\mathbf{c})$ with $\mathbf{c}^d$, $d = 0, 1, 2$, where $\mathbf{c}^0 = 1$ and $\mathbf{c}^2 = \mathbf{c}\mathbf{c}^T$, and define

$$M_d(\mathbf{c}_t) = \sum_{\mathbf{c}\in\Omega(\mathbf{o},\mathbf{c}_t]} \mathbf{c}^d P(\mathbf{c}). \quad (7)$$

Then, given a box $\Omega(\mathbf{c}_i,\mathbf{c}_j]$, its color population $w(\mathbf{c}_i,\mathbf{c}_j]$, mean $\mu(\mathbf{c}_i,\mathbf{c}_j]$,

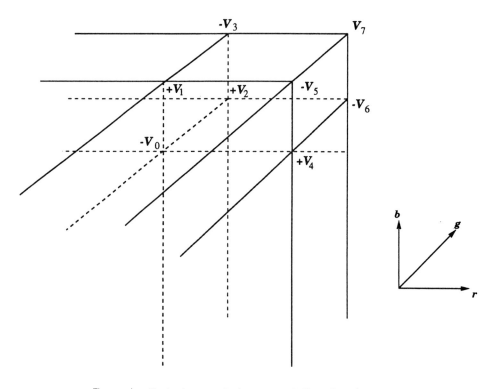

Figure 1. Inclusion–exclusion computations in color space.

and quantization error $E(\mathbf{c}_i, \mathbf{c}_j]$ (the weighted variance of the box),

$$w(\mathbf{c}_i, \mathbf{c}_j] = \sum_{\mathbf{c} \in \Omega(\mathbf{c}_i, \mathbf{c}_j]} P(\mathbf{c}) \qquad (8)$$

$$\mu(\mathbf{c}_i, \mathbf{c}_j] = \frac{\sum_{\mathbf{c} \in \Omega(\mathbf{c}_i, \mathbf{c}_j]} \mathbf{c} P(\mathbf{c})}{w(\mathbf{c}_i, \mathbf{c}_j]} \qquad (9)$$

$$E(\mathbf{c}_i, \mathbf{c}_j] = \sum_{\mathbf{c} \in \Omega(\mathbf{c}_i, \mathbf{c}_j]} \mathbf{c}^2 P(\mathbf{c}) - \frac{\left[\sum_{\mathbf{c} \in \Omega(\mathbf{c}_i, \mathbf{c}_j]} \mathbf{c} P(\mathbf{c})\right]^2}{w(\mathbf{c}_i, \mathbf{c}_j]} \qquad (10)$$

can be computed in $O(1)$ time using Eq. (4), provided that $M_d(\mathbf{c})$, $d = 0, 1, 2$, the cumulative dth moments of the discrete density $P(\mathbf{c})$ against the reference point $\mathbf{o}$, are pre-computed and stored for all $|S| = 2^{3m}$ lattice points of S. Clearly, this preprocessing requires $O(|S|)$ time and space.

If the original 24-bit pixel image was quantized directly, then $|S| = 2^{24}$, invoking excessive if not prohibitive costs. Encouragingly, it was observed by previous researchers and by the author that color image quantization on a $32 \cdot 32 \cdot 32$ rgb lattice yields visually almost the same result as on a $256 \cdot 256 \cdot 256$ lattice. Thus, the preprocessing time and space costs can be reduced to an acceptable level of $|S| = 2^{15}$ without noticeable loss of fidelity.

Algorithm Details and Analysis

Formally, optimizing the cutting of the box $\Omega(\mathbf{c}_i, \mathbf{c}_j]$ is minimizing

$$E(\mathbf{c}_i, \mathbf{c}] + E(\mathbf{c}, \mathbf{c}_j], \tag{11}$$

subject to

$$\mathbf{c} \in \left\{ c_{jr} \times c_{jg} \times (c_{ib}, c_{jb}] \right\} \cup \left\{ c_{jr} \times (c_{ig}, c_{jg}] \times c_{jb} \right\}$$

$$\cup \left\{ (c_{ir}, c_{jr}] \times c_{jg} \times c_{jb} \right\}. \tag{12}$$

With the aid of the proposed preprocessing, Eq. (11) can be evaluated in $O(1)$ time, given $\Omega(\mathbf{c}_i, \mathbf{c}_j]$ and $\mathbf{c}$. Then it can be easily shown that partitioning S into K boxes based on variance minimization needs $O(|S|^{1/3}K)$ time in the worst case and $O(|S|^{1/3}K^{2/3})$ time[1] in the average case.

---

[1] Obtained by solving the recurrence, $T(n) = 2T(n/2) + 3n^{1/3}$, for the boundary condition $T(|S|/K) = 0$.

Note, however, that the preceding analysis only gives the order of time complexity of the proposed algorithm, with no consideration of the coefficient before the O notation. Directly minimizing Eq. (11) would require as many as 76 additions, six multiplications, and two divisions for a single $\mathbf{c}$. However, since

$$E(\mathbf{c}_i, \mathbf{c}] + E(\mathbf{c}, \mathbf{c}_j] = \sum_{\mathbf{c} \in \Omega(\mathbf{c}_i, \mathbf{c}_j]} \mathbf{c}^2 P(\mathbf{c})$$

$$- \frac{\left[\sum_{\mathbf{c} \in \Omega(\mathbf{c}_i, \mathbf{c}]} \mathbf{c} P(\mathbf{c}) \right]^2}{w(\mathbf{c}_i, \mathbf{c}]} - \frac{\left[\sum_{\mathbf{c} \in \Omega(\mathbf{c}, \mathbf{c}_j]} \mathbf{c} P(\mathbf{c}) \right]^2}{w(\mathbf{c}, \mathbf{c}_j]}, \quad (13)$$

minimizing Eq. (11) is equivalent to maximizing

$$\frac{\left[\sum_{\mathbf{c} \in \Omega(\mathbf{c}_i, \mathbf{c}]} \mathbf{c} P(\mathbf{c}) \right]^2}{w(\mathbf{c}_i, \mathbf{c}]} + \frac{\left[\sum_{\mathbf{c} \in \Omega(\mathbf{c}, \mathbf{c}_j]} \mathbf{c} P(\mathbf{c}) \right]^2}{w(\mathbf{c}, \mathbf{c}_j]}$$

$$= \frac{\left[\sum_{\mathbf{c} \in \Omega(\mathbf{c}_i, \mathbf{c}]} \mathbf{c} P(\mathbf{c}) \right]^2}{w(\mathbf{c}_i, \mathbf{c}]} + \frac{\left[\sum_{\mathbf{c} \in \Omega(\mathbf{c}_i, \mathbf{c}_j]} \mathbf{c} P(\mathbf{c}) - \sum_{\mathbf{c} \in \Omega(\mathbf{c}_i, \mathbf{c}]} \mathbf{c} P(\mathbf{c}) \right]^2}{w(\mathbf{c}_i, \mathbf{c}_j] - w(\mathbf{c}_i, \mathbf{c}]}.$$

$$(14)$$

As $w(\mathbf{c}_i, \mathbf{c}_j]$ and $\sum_{\mathbf{c} \in \Omega(\mathbf{c}_i, \mathbf{c}_j]} \mathbf{c} P(\mathbf{c})$ are constants for a fixed box $\Omega(\mathbf{c}_i, \mathbf{c}_j]$, we only need to apply the inclusion–exclusion rule Eq. (4) to compute the summations $\sum_{\mathbf{c} \in \Omega(\mathbf{c}_i, \mathbf{c}]} \mathbf{c} P(\mathbf{c})$ and $w(\mathbf{c}_i, \mathbf{c}]$ for $\mathbf{c}$ of Eq. (12) in the process of maximizing Eq. (14). Furthermore, since four of eight $M_d(\mathbf{c})$ involved in Eq. (4) do not change when $\mathbf{c}$ takes on different values in one of three sets—$c_{jr} \times c_{jg} \times (c_{ib}, c_{jb}]$, $c_{jr} \times (c_{ig}, c_{jg}] \times c_{jb}$, and $(c_{ir}, c_{jr}] \times c_{jg} \times c_{jb}$—only four additions are required by $w(\mathbf{c}_i, \mathbf{c}]$ and 12 additions by $\sum_{\mathbf{c} \in \Omega(\mathbf{c}_i, \mathbf{c}]} \mathbf{c} P(\mathbf{c})$. (Note that the latter is a 3-vector). After the preceding manipulations, the new algorithm requires 25 additions, six multiplications, and two divisions per iteration.

Experimental Results

The new optimal color quantization algorithm was implemented on a SUN 3/80 workstation. It took only 10 seconds to quantize a 256×256 image. The impact of optimizing partitions is very positive. The new algorithm achieved, on average, one-third and one-ninth of mean-square errors for the median-cut and Wan et al. algorithms respectively.

Shown in Fig. 2 (see color insert) is a set of photos of a quantized ISO color test image. The picture in (a) has 256 colors and is quantized by the proposed algorithm. This image is virtually indistinguishable from the original 24-bit pixel image. In (b) is the 64-color image quantized by the proposed algorithm. Its quality is acceptable. For comparison, we also show in (c) and (d) the 64-color images quantized by the Heckbert median-cut and Wan et al. algorithms. The improvement on image quality by the new algorithm over the previous algorithms is evident.

See also II.2 A Comparison of Digital Halftoning Techniques, Dale A. Schumacher; II.3 Color Dithering, Spencer W. Thomas, Rodney G. Bogart; III.1 Efficient Inverse Color Map Computation, Spencer W. Thomas; (*287*) *A Simple Method for Quantization: Octree Quantization, Michael Gervautz, Werner Purgathofer*

III.3

A RANDOM COLOR MAP ANIMATION ALGORITHM

Ken Musgrave
Yale University
New Haven, Connecticut

Coloring deterministic fractals such as Mandelbrot and Julia sets is a time-consuming process. This process can be automated with a random color map animation algorithm that gives quite striking results as seen in the color plates I.7.1 and I.7.2. Color map animation makes iteration–fractal images *come alive* and adds considerable viewing interest; applied to more ordinary images, it can give bizarre and entertaining effects and sometimes can reveal data not readily apparent with a fixed color map.

The idea behind this algorithm is simple: Generate random sawtooth waves in red, green, and blue on the fly (Fig. 1), and push the resulting color ramps through the color look-up table. One can think of the look-up table as a window sliding along the trace of the random RGB sawtooth waves. The power of the algorithm derives from the fact that the color ramps are generated on the fly, and thus need not be stored. User input is limited to a starting seed for the underlying random number generator and parameters for the statistics of the random ramps. (These parameters can be built in, of course.) The programming work involves the creation of random-number generation routines with specific statistical character to be used in specifying the color ramps, and the interpolation of the ramps once endpoints have been specified.

For a first cut, very nice results can be had by using uniform random numbers to specify the ramp endpoints, and linear interpolation for the ramps. In fact, one simply can perform a random walk in color space (corresponding, appropriately enough, to Brownian motion) and not have to perform any interpolation at all. The choice of color space (e.g., RGB,

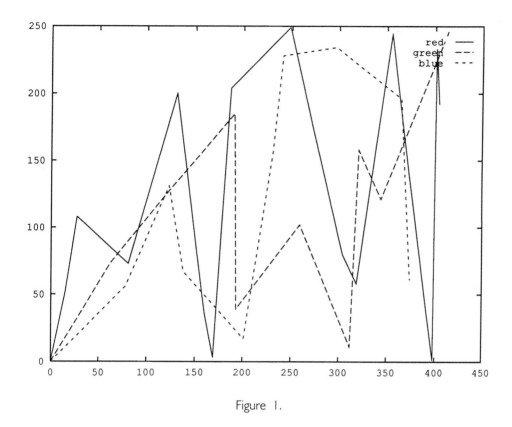

Figure 1.

HLS, etc.) is up to the programmer; we always have used the RGB color space. Linear interpolation of color ramps can be performed efficiently using a bit of standard DDA code, which you already may have lying around somewhere, or can easily lift from a basic computer graphics text.

The algorithm proceeds as follows:

0. Optionally, load a starting colormap, such as a zebra-striped grey ramp.

1. Get values from the random-number generator for ramp endpoints. Scale these values to represent intensity (i.e., 0–255) and ramp length. Maximum ramp length is a user option.

2. Assuming initial ramps start and zero intensity, shift $[0, 0, 0]$ into the low end of the color map.

3. Until the end of the next (i.e., red, green, or blue) ramp is reached, shift next interpolated color tuple into the colormap.

4. Choose endpoint for next ramp of the color ramp that has been exhausted, and go to step 3. Interpolate new ramp starting from the endpoint of the last ramp.

Note that you may wish to leave the bottom or top color map entry, which colors the interior of the M-set or J-set, fixed at some color such as black.

On modern hardware, the entire process often proceeds too rapidly, and some means, such as specification of no-ops, must be found to slow the animation down to a reasonable speed. A problem often encountered in implementation on a specific platform is side effects from writing to the color look-up table during nonvertical-retrace time; this will show up typically as a flickering noise in the display. Thus, one may have to go into low-level instructions for the frame buffer hardware to find an instruction that will assure that the writing occurs only during vertical retrace time. Personal experience indicates that when such an instruction exists, it often does not work as advertised, and that inclusion of no-ops to slow the execution usually does the trick.

Fun can be had in playing with the statistics of the random-number generator. Try Gaussian random numbers in the interval $[0, 255]$ with a mean of 127 for a pastel color map animation (more tasteful, but less spectacular). Taking Gaussian random numbers in the interval $[-256, 255]$ with mean 0 and adding 256 to negative instances gives a loud, tasteless, "postmodern" animation. Try nonlinear, e.g., cubic spline, interpolation of the color ramps. (We have found this generally less visually striking than linear interpolation.) Try reversing the direction of the animation (randomly). Try different starting maps—it takes a while to fill the color map with the random animation, but the built-in anticipation is a nice feature. A zebra-striped gray ramp, with stripes of width 2 or 3 is nice. (A width of 1 generally is very hard on the eyes.)

While the animation is, in principle, periodic, the period of the sequence is on the order of one day for a 16-bit random-number generator and about 100 years for a 32-bit generator.

Should library random-number generators be unavailable or too slow, here is one that works fine:

```
#define MULTIPLIER 25173
#define INCREMENT   13849
#define MODULUS       65535A
/*
*  pseudo-random number generator; period 65536; requires seed between
*/0 and 65535; returns random numbers between 0 and 65536.
#define RANDOM(x) (x = (MULTIPLIER * x + INCREMENT) & MODU-
LUS)
```

III.4

A FAST APPROACH TO PHIGS PLUS PSEUDO COLOR MAPPING

James Hall and Terence Lindgren
Prime CV
Bedford, Massachusetts

PHIGS PLUS allows an application to select between three color mapping models: true color mapping, pseudo color mapping and pseudo N color mapping. In all three cases, the color mapping stage receives primitives from the lighting and depth cueing stages with a color vector per vertex. Then, for interior shading method COLOR, the color mapping stage interpolates the colors across the primitive and maps the resulting colors according to the selected color mapping method. *True color mapping* sets the resulting color using either a closest fit, dithering, or directly setting the color depending on the pixel depth of the machine. If we assume that the colors are received in a normalized RGB format, then the pseudo color mapping will map the color vector onto an index that is used to select an entry from a list of colors. The major problem with this scheme is that it uses three interpolators and combines the resulting colors into an index for each pixel as we traverse the primitive. We show that it is possible by mapping the colors at the vertices first to simply interpolate the indices at each vertex.

Pseudo Color Mapping

The PHIGS PLUS specification defines *pseudo color mapping* as a method that converts colors into a single integer index that is used to select a color from a list of specified colors in a data record. The data record contains a weighting vector $[\mathbf{W1}, \mathbf{W2}, \mathbf{W3}]$ (for RGB color format) and a list of R colors. Note that an index of 1 corresponds to the first color on the list. Assuming an RGB color model for both the rendering color model and the color mapping color model, the mapping process may be defined as follows:

1. Normalize the weighting vector **W** by dividing it by the sum of its components. (This operation is independent of the interpolation process and may be done when the weighting vector is defined.)

2. Calculate $J = \text{round}((R - 1)(\mathbf{W1}*\mathbf{C1} + \mathbf{W2}*\mathbf{C2} + \mathbf{W3}*\mathbf{C3}) + 1)$ (where [**C1**, **C2**, **C3**] = [red, green, blue])

3. Use J as an index to select one of the entries in the list of colors.

4. The selected color then is displayed on the workstation as accurately as possible.

How accurately the colors are displayed on the workstation is determined by the capabilities of the underlying workstation. For true color workstations, whose pixel memory is displayed directly, mapped colors are reformatted to the correct pixel layout and output to the frame buffer. For pseudo color workstations, with a smaller frame buffer resolution whose output is mapped through a color look-up table (LUT), it is more an issue of how the LUT is managed. Since we must support both true and pseudo color mapping, at least some part of the LUT must contain a color cube to support either a closest-fit or dither scheme. If we create the largest possible color cube that the LUT size will allow, then we will get a higher-quality approximation of true color at the cost of approximating the pseudo entries. Consequently, after applying the pseudo color mapping, we must get the color from the color list and approximate it based on the current color cube. We would obtain much better performance if we directly load the color lists into the LUT so that the color indices could be written immediately into the frame buffer. Most applications tend to use only one of the color mapping methods, so a reasonable approach would be to prescan the workstation color mapping table and load the pseudo color lists into the hardware LUT, and use the remaining space to fit a color cube. In this fashion, if no pseudo color mappings are used, we would get a large color cube and a higher-quality true color approximation. As the number of pseudo color mappings increases, the quality of the true color emulation would decrease (as well as the likelihood that it would be used).

Pseudo Color Interpolation

In this section, we describe the interpolation of colors along a line and show that it is possible to map the colors at the endpoints prior to interpolation, instead of interpolating the endpoint colors and then mapping. We note that this process can be extended to fill areas (polygons) by interpolating the mapped colors along the polygon edges and performing scanline interpolation between them. We can describe the interpolation of colors along a line with endpoints $P1$ $(x1, y1, \mathbf{C1})$ and $P2(x2, y2, \mathbf{C2})$ by:

$$C = t*\mathbf{C1} + (1 - t)*\mathbf{C2}, \tag{1}$$

where

$$\mathbf{C1} = [r1, g1, b1] \text{ and } \mathbf{C2} = [r2, g2, b2].$$

The color mapping process then is defined by:

$$i = \text{round}((R - 1)(\mathbf{W1}*r + \mathbf{W2}*g + \mathbf{W3}*b) + 1).$$

We can switch to vector notation and incorporate $(R - 1)$ into $\mathbf{W}$, $\mathbf{W} = \mathbf{W}*(R - 1)$,

$$i = \text{round}((\mathbf{W}, \mathbf{C})) + 1, \tag{2}$$

combining Eqs. (1) and (2),

$$i = \text{round}((\mathbf{W}, t*\mathbf{C1} + (1 - t)*\mathbf{C2}) + 1,$$

distributing

$$i = \text{round}(t*(\mathbf{W}, \mathbf{C1}) + (1 - t)*(\mathbf{W}, \mathbf{C2})) + 1. \tag{3}$$

This shows that mapping the colors prior to interpolation is identical to interpolating the colors and then performing the pseudo color mapping; which means that we can switch accurately to a single interpolation variable for the pseudo color interpolation process.

The optimization outlined saves for each pixel four additions and three multiplications, where two of the additions are associated with updating the two extra interpolation variables and the other two are associated with the mapping operation. Moreover, we eliminate two divides associated with the two extra interpolation derivatives.

Implementation

An implementation of this scheme might prescan the workstation color mapping table and load the color lists into the hardware look-up table. This requires associating with each color mapping method entry a *lut_start* describing where in the LUT the color list was loaded. Relocating the list in this fashion allows us to drop the +1 in Eq. (3), since the first entry in the list now is at *lut_start*. Additionally instead of representing the index values as real and rounding when performing the original mapping of the vertices, we scaled the values by 4096.0 and rounded so that the indices were in an 8.12-integer format. This allows us to substitute the round in Eq. (3) with a shift right by 12, further increasing the performance. The following pseudo-code gives a general overview of an implementation:

assume we have a current color mapping state with the following format
Record color_mapping_table_entry
      begin
      w1, w2, w3: **real**;   *weighting vector with (R − 1) incorporated*

      start_lut: **integer**   *starting lut index*
      end;

shaded_line(x1, y1, x2, y2, cl, c2)   *assuming x is the major axis*
      where (x1, y1) and (x2, y2) are the endpoints of the line and c1 and c2 are the colors (red, green, blue) at those points

```
begin
          map the color at the input endpoints
  i1 ← start_lut*4096 + (w1*cl.red + w2*cl.green + w3*cl.blue)*4096;
  i2 ← start_lut*4096 + (wl*c2.red + w2*c2.green + w3*c2.blue)*4096;
  didx ← (i2 − i1) / (x2 − x1);          compute color derivative
  i ← round(i1);                         compute starting color
  for each pixel
          begin
          plot(x, y, shift_right(i, 12)); plot the current color
          i ← i + didx;                  update for next pixel
          end
end
```

III.5

MAPPING RGB TRIPLES ONTO 16 DISTINCT VALUES

Alan W. Paeth
NeuralWare, Inc.
Pittsburgh, Pennsylvania

A previous gem by the author (Paeth, 1990a) described a high-speed mapping from arbitrary RGB color descriptors onto one of 14 values, useful for creating four-bit pixel indices. This entry extends the technique in compatible fashion to 16 values by placing two mid-level gray values. The derivation once again takes advantage of descriptive solid geometry in locating the nearest (Euclidean) target point to input point. Figure 1 illustrates the partitioning of 3-space into 16 regions. Figure 2 illustrates the quantization of color triples under the algorithm.

High-speed mapping onto a small set of three-component descriptors may be achieved by the partitioning of the unit cube into subregions. This has a general application in recoding 3-vectors (color triples, surface normals) at reduced precision in symmetric fashion. Specifically, planes normal to the cube's four body diagonals (Paeth, 1990e, Fig. 6b) form 14 space partitions.

As these planes are parallel neither to the axes nor to each other, axis-separable algebraic methods (Paeth, 1990f, p. 254), which are conventionally used for quantization of larger color spaces (Gervautz and Purgathofer, 1990), must yield to non-Cartesian models, the latter easily represented geometrically. This dissection is related to the face locations of the cuboctahedron. (The latter are presented in Gem "Exact Metrics for Regular Convex Solids," later in this book (Paeth, IV.3).)

The vertices of the former solid are retained to allow upward compatibility. This preserves the primary colors of the cube's vertices at $(\pm 1, \pm 1, \pm 1)$, which are essential to many algorithms. (See also Paeth (1990f, Fig. 9).) Unfortunately, space partitioning by projection onto spherical polyhedra places no interior points: Grays in particular are absent. Worse, Steiner's theorem from 1888 (republished in 1971) indicates that four arbitrary skew planes may form no more than 15 3-space partitions: $P_3(n) = 1/6\,[n^3 + 5n + 6]$.

The addition of two gray points extends the descriptor table usefully: A uniform, linear set of four achromatic values allows the direct rendering of monochromatic images of two bits, plus their multiples (Paeth, 1990b, p. 250). The interior codes are at $(\frac{1}{3}\,\frac{1}{3}\,\frac{1}{3})$ and $(\frac{2}{3}\,\frac{2}{3}\,\frac{2}{3})$. Table I is the updated color descriptor table.

Table I.

Code	Name	Red	Green	Blue	Volume
0000	black	0	0	0	1/48
0001	olive	1/2	1/2	0	1/12
0010	purple	1/2	0	1/2	1/12
0011	red	1	0	0	1/16
0100	aqua	0	1/2	1/2	1/12
0101	green	0	1	0	1/16
0110	blue	0	0	1	1/16
0111	**lt gray**	**1/3**	**1/3**	**1/3**	**1/24**
1000	**dk gray**	**2/3**	**2/3**	**2/3**	**1/24**
1001	yellow	1	1	0	1/16
1010	magenta	1	0	1	1/16
1011	pink	1	1/2	1/2	1/12
1100	cyan	0	1	1	1/16
1101	lime	1/2	1	1/2	1/12
1110	sky	1/2	1/2	1	1/12
1111	white	1	1	1	1/48

Computation of the nearest axial gray descriptor $(\frac{c}{3}\,\frac{c}{3}\,\frac{c}{3})$ for any point in RGB space uses the equation, $c = 1/3[(R + G + B + .5)]$, valid for all space. This resembles the first half-plane equation of the previous algorithm: the test used to bisect the gray axis. To extend that algorithm, the **bit-or**ing operations that record fourfold half-space membership are permuted (with the tests not being coupled), placing the gray test in fourth position. When the three preceding boolean tests for code-bit positions 2^0 2^1 and 2^2 yield like sign, the final test with boolean result in bit 2^3 may be omitted: Code words "0000" (black) and "1111" (white) must result; codes "1000" and "0111" are inadmissible. In cases of like sign, the test point is localized to the black or white partition at the conclusion of the third test.

When these conditions arise, the fourth half-plane test may be adjusted (at execution time) by parallel displacement, recasting it in the form of a two-bit gray axis quantization test. Points lying toward the interior are placed in dark gray–light gray subregions split from the parent black–white volumes. These are represented conveniently by the previously unoccupied code words. Conditional execution of the adjustment step prior to the fourth plane test provides optional run-time back-compatibility, as seen in the following pseudo-code. (See also the C Implementation in Appendix 2.)

```
integer function remap16(R, G, B, R', G', B': real)
    rval, gval, bval,: array [0..15] of real;

    rval ← {0.,.5 ,.5 , 1.,0., 0., 0.,.333, .667, 1., 1., 1., 0.,.5 ,.5,1.}

    gval ← {0.,.5 , 0., 0.,.5, 1., 0.,.333, .667 , 1., 0.,.5 , 1., 1.,.5,1.}

    bval ← {0., 0.,.5 , 0.,.5 , 0., 1.,.333, .667 , 0., 1.,.5 , 1.,.5,1.,1.}
    dist: real ← 0.5;
    code, mask: integer ← 0;
    if   R + G − B > dist then code ← code bit-or 1
    if   R − G + B > dist then code ← code bit-or 2
    if −R + G + B > dist then code ← code bit-or 4
    dist ← 1.5; mask ← 8;
```

> The next two lines update the algorithm and may be compiled or executed conditionally to provide back-compatibility:

```
    if (code = 0) then {dist ← .5; mask ← 7;}
    else if (code = 7) then {code ← 8; dist ← 2.5; mask ← 7;}

    if R + G + B > dist then code ← code bit-or mask;
    R' = rval[code]
    G' = gval[code]
    B' = bval[code]
    return[code]
```

This yields an upward-compatible algorithm useful with old data sets. As before, *monochromatic* triples (c, c, c) yield monochromatic output. No central gray color is present: Infinitesimal test excursions away from the cubes's center at (1/2, 1/2, 1/2) yield 14 distinct colors, including two grays—only full black and full white are not represented.

A valuable geometric property of this space partitioning is that the two gray planes introduced are coincident with faces of the underlying cuboctahedron. These cut the gray body diagonal at 1/6 and 5/6 of its total length. This cube partitioning is closely related to the dissection of Euclidean 3-space into cuboctahedra and octahedra. An octahedron (whose faces are primary colors) may be split in Cartesian fashion into eight right-angled *corner* pyramids. Attaching each to the eight underlying triangular faces of a cuboctahedral core forms the color cube of the previous algorithm. In the present case, the interior, regular tetrahedra beneath the black and white corner pyramids retain intermediate gray values (Fig. 1 see color insert).

Interestingly, although many edge and face dimensions of the unit color cube have irrational measure, the dissection volumes do not: They are reciprocals of integers (Table I). Moreover, the eight primary colors, which occupy half of the descriptor table, likewise account for half of the cube's partitioned volume. Finally, the four achromatic volumes are in 1 : 2 : 2 : 1 proportion. Precisely the same ratios result when gray quantization onto two bits is performed along a one-dimensional axis, in a manner previously advocated (Paeth, 1990f, pp. 250–251). Four half-plane tests (the minimum) suffice in partitioning the (color) cube into 16 regions, though two comparisons are required to establish the displacement constant employed by the fourth test.

See also *(233) Mapping RGB Triples onto Four Bits, Alan W. Paeth*

III.6

TELEVISION COLOR ENCODING AND "HOT" BROADCAST COLORS

David Martindale
Imax Corp.
Toronto, Ontario, Canada

and

Alan W. Paeth
NeuralWare, Inc.
Pittsburgh, Pennsylvania

Introduction

Television cameras and receivers are RGB devices: They deal with color using three signals representing the intensity of red, green, and blue at each point in the image. However, television signals are not broadcast in RGB form. *RGB* is encoded into one luminance and two color-difference signals for transmission, and a color receiver decodes these signals back into *RGB* for display. The color-difference signals then may be transmitted with less bandwidth than the luminance signal, since the human visual system has poorer spatial resolution for color variation than it has for luminance variation. Also, this encoding technique provides a signal compatible with black-and-white receivers that have no color decoding circuitry.

Mathematically, the transformation from *RGB* into a luminance–color difference space is a linear change of basis, and is lossless and invertible. In the real world of television, though, the signals are represented by voltages that have maximum limits, and some *RGB* triples transform into signals that cannot be broadcast. These "unencodable" *RGB* values all are high-intensity, high-saturation colors that seldom occur in nature, but easily can be present in synthetic images. We call them *hot* colors.

We discuss the color encoding process to clarify why the problem exists. Then we discuss an algorithm for efficiently detecting hot pixels in an image, and two techniques for "cooling" them. A person selecting colors for an image may use this as a tool to avoid hot colors entirely. It also can be used to fix up already rendered images before recording them on video.

NTSC Encoding Basics

The American broadcast color television standard was developed by a group of industry experts called the National Television Systems Committee. The acronym NTSC is used now for both the committee and the standard itself.

Any color television standard must begin by specifying the chromaticities of the three primary colors that will form the color *reference frame* for the system. The actual spectral sensitivities of the sensors in the camera may not match these reference primaries, but in that case, the camera will perform a color space transform to express the color content of the scene in terms of amplitudes of the reference primaries, not the actual image sensor outputs. Similarly, if the receiver uses phosphors with chromaticities different from the reference primaries, it also will perform a color space transform to match the color that would have been produced with the reference primaries. (Well, that is the theory. Practice often differs from theory.)

For its reference primaries, the NTSC selected the chromaticities identified as *NTSC* in Table I. For the luminance (Y) signal to reflect accurately the luminance content of a scene, it must be calculated as a weighted sum of *RGB*, where the weights represent the actual contributions of each of the reference primaries towards the luminance of a reference white value. First, a reference white must be selected; the NTSC specified *CIE Standard Illuminant C* (Table II). Then we must find the linear combination of the reference primaries that gives reference white by solving the following set of equations. Here, the columns of the first matrix are the chromaticities of the reference primaries, the J's are the

Table I.   Primary Color Chromaticities.

Name	Red		Green		Blue	
	x	y	x	y	x	y
NTSC	0.67	0.33	0.21	0.71	0.14	0.08
EBU	0.64	0.33	0.29	0.60	0.15	0.06
SMPTE	0.630	0.340	0.310	0.595	0.155	0.070
HDTV ideal	0.670	0.330	0.210	0.710	0.150	0.060

Table II.   White Point Chromaticities.

Name	x	y
Illuminant C	0.3101	0.3162
Illuminant D_{65}	0.3127	0.3291

unknowns, and the right-hand matrix contains the chromaticity of reference white normalized so its y component is 1:

$$
\begin{bmatrix} x_r & x_g & x_b \\ y_r & y_g & y_b \\ z_r & z_g & z_b \end{bmatrix} * \begin{bmatrix} J_r \\ J_g \\ J_b \end{bmatrix} = \begin{bmatrix} \dfrac{x_w}{y_w} \\ 1 \\ \dfrac{z_w}{y_w} \end{bmatrix}.
$$

When this has been solved, the relative luminance contributions of the *RGB* primaries to reference white then are $J_r * y_r$, $J_g * y_g$, and $J_b * y_b$. For the NTSC primaries and Illuminant C white point, the weights are 0.299, 0.587, and 0.114 to three significant figures. The ubiquitous equation $Y = .30R + .59G + .11B$, seen so often in computer graphics, is borrowed directly from the NTSC standard. Note that these values are correct only for the NTSC primary chromaticities and white point; they are not correct for most modern RGB monitors.

In addition to the Y signal, there are two color difference values to be defined. $(B - Y)$ and $(R - Y)$ are used, since they have the nice property of going to zero on any grays in the scene, and $(G - Y)$ is less suitable because of the large amount of green in Y. The resulting values then must be scaled by some factor to keep their amplitudes within a range where they can be superimposed on the luminance signal without requiring more total voltage range. Somewhat arbitrarily, the NTSC decided to calculate the scaling factors so that any color whose *RGB* amplitudes all are less than or equal to 0.75 (after gamma correction) will be encoded into a composite signal whose peak amplitude never exceeds that of full-intensity white. The two worst-case colors are fully saturated yellow and cyan, and expressions for the encoded composite signal for these two colors yield two linear equations in two unknowns. Solving them yields the needed scaling factors, and we now can define two signals, $U = 0.493$ $(B - Y)$ and $V = 0.877 (R - Y)$. These two signals carry all of the color information, and collectively are known as *chrominance*.

The I and Q signals that are broadcast are derived from U and V via a simple linear change of basis corresponding to rotating the coordinate system $33°$: $I = V \cos(33°) - U \sin(33°)$, $Q = V \sin(33°) + U \cos(33°)$. This positions the Q axis so it carries the colors for which the eye has the poorest spatial resolution, thus minimizing the picture degradation caused by transmitting the Q signal with less bandwidth than I.

Every component of this sequence of operation (Y extraction, color difference extraction and scaling, and $33°$ change of chrominance basis vectors) is linear, so we can express the entire transformation as a single matrix. The NTSC transformation and its inverse are:

$$\begin{bmatrix} Y \\ I \\ Q \end{bmatrix} = \begin{bmatrix} 0.2989 & 0.5866 & 0.1144 \\ 0.5959 & -0.2741 & -0.3218 \\ 0.2113 & -0.5227 & 0.3113 \end{bmatrix} * \begin{bmatrix} R \\ G \\ B \end{bmatrix},$$

$$\begin{bmatrix} R \\ G \\ B \end{bmatrix} = \begin{bmatrix} 1.0 & 0.9562 & 0.6210 \\ 1.0 & -0.2717 & -0.6485 \\ 1.0 & -1.1053 & 1.7020 \end{bmatrix} * \begin{bmatrix} Y \\ I \\ Q \end{bmatrix}$$

The three signals must be combined into a single *composite* signal for broadcast or transmission over a single wire. This is done by having I and Q modulate two high-frequency signals of the same frequency but with a $90°$ phase difference between them. This can be represented by $C = I \cos(\omega t) + Q \sin(\omega t)$, where $\omega = 2\pi F_{SC}$. This sum is a single sine wave of amplitude $|C| = \text{sqrt}(I^2 + Q^2)$. When this is added to the luminance signal, the peak positive and negative excursions of the composite signal are $Y + |C|$ and $Y - |C|$.

There is one additional detail that has been ignored so far. The *RGB* signals being fed to the CRT in the receiver must be gamma-corrected to compensate for the nonlinear transfer characteristics of the CRT. The NTSC standard defines this gamma correction as being done to the *RGB* signals in the camera, before encoding to *YIQ*. As far as the NTSC encoding hardware is concerned, your frame buffer is a camera, so the signals coming from it also must include gamma correction. You may do the gamma correction with hardware or software look-up tables, have it built into your pixel quantization method, or use any other method that works. You always should use an exponent of 0.45 when doing the gamma correction, ignoring the actual gamma of your monitor. (The NTSC standard specifies gamma correction for an assumed receiver gamma of 2.2.)

The actual phosphors used in television CRTs have changed over time, and their chromaticities have not been close to the NTSC reference primaries for decades. This variation made it difficult to evaluate critically the color in television studios, and the Society of Motion Picture and Television Engineers (SMPTE) set up several committees to develop standards for these picture monitors. Eventually, recommended practices RP-37 and RP-145 (SMPTE, 1969, 1987) were published. These documents specify the phosphor chromaticities called *SMPTE* in Table I and a white reference of D_{65} (Table II). See Zavada (1988) for more information about the history of these standards.

In theory, these practices apply only to monitors used for evaluating video within television studios, while cameras, telecines[1], and home receivers continue to adhere to the original standard. However, of the broadcasters that bother to calibrate the color matrixing on their cameras and telecines, most use monitors that conform to these standards, so these picture sources are effectively being calibrated to the SMPTE standards. Thus, although the official standard has not changed, there is a new *de facto* standard for primary chromaticity.

The *RGB*-to-*YIQ* encoding still is done according to the original standard; the luminance weighting factors and chrominance scale factors have not been changed to correspond to the altered phosphors and white point. As a result, the matrix is not quite correct for the chromaticities actually used, though this causes few problems in practice.

If you have an image rendering system that can be told the chromaticities of the red, green, and blue primaries of the display for which it is rendering, you should specify chromaticities appropriate for broadcast, not the ones appropriate for your particular RGB monitor. In theory, you should use the NTSC reference primary chromaticities, but we recom-

---

[1]A telecine is a device for converting a motion picture image recorded on photographic film into a television signal.

mend that you use the SMPTE set instead. This is more likely to give color reproduction that matches that of real objects photographed in modern studios.

The Problem

Because of the particular way in which the scale factors used in the calculation of U and V were chosen, some fully saturated colors with intensities greater than 0.75 after gamma correction (0.53 before gamma correction) will have composite signal amplitudes that go above maximum white. There is some leeway for signals that go above maximum white, but not enough to handle all possible colors. The worst case occurs when either the red or blue intensity is zero and the other two components are at maximum. Such signals are unlikely to be produced by video cameras, but frame buffers will happily generate any combination of R, G, and B.

Video signal amplitudes usually are measured in IRE units, where 100 IRE is maximum white, 7.5 IRE is picture black, and 0 IRE is blanking black. At an amplitude of 120 IRE, the video transmitter becomes over-modulated, so this forms an absolute upper limit for the signal during transmission. Other video equipment, too, may clip or distort signals that exceed 120 IRE, potentially resulting in drastic color errors in the affected areas of the image. Unfortunately, full-intensity yellow and cyan encode to signals that reach 131 IRE: such colors must be reduced in intensity or saturation before they can be broadcast. To be conservative, we should limit the peak amplitude to about 110 IRE, so that even if it grows a bit through several stages of processing, it will not reach the 120 IRE hard limit. Limiting to 100 IRE is even safer, but undesirable because it further limits the colors available.

There is a second potential problem. Winkler (1990) describes how the chrominance component of an NTSC signal can be displayed on a vectorscope, and comments that colors never should be allowed to go outside the outer circle of its display. On vectorscopes available to the first author, the position of the outer circle corresponds to a chroma amplitude of 52 or 53 IRE units. To be safe, we should set the chroma amplitude limit to 50 IRE.

Although no explanation of this restriction is given by Winkler, and another source does not consider this to be a problem, it costs almost nothing to check for this condition at the same time that we check for composite signal amplitude. Thus, we provide the check; you can delete it easily if you feel it is not required.

PAL Encoding

The designers of the PAL broadcast standard used the NTSC standard as a basis, changing only what they felt needed changing for their environment. Many of the changes were in areas that do not concern us here. We will discuss only the relevant ones.

Because more total bandwidth was available, and because of the phase alternation that is used in PAL, both chrominance signals could be transmitted with the same bandwidth. Thus, there was no reason for the color space transformation from U, V to I, Q, and it was deleted. The U and V signals are used to modulate the subcarriers directly.

Instead of using the NTSC reference primaries, most PAL systems use the *EBU* reference primaries listed in Table I. Thus, you should render your images for these primary chromaticities if they are destined for PAL broadcast. PAL systems also use a D_{65} white point instead of *Illuminant C*.

Despite these changes, PAL retains exactly the same luminance weighting factors and U, V scaling factors that are used in NTSC. In matrix form, the transformation and its inverse are:

$$\begin{bmatrix} Y \\ U \\ V \end{bmatrix} = \begin{bmatrix} 0.2989 & 0.5866 & 0.1144 \\ -0.1473 & -0.2891 & 0.4364 \\ 0.6149 & -0.5145 & -0.1004 \end{bmatrix} * \begin{bmatrix} R \\ G \\ B \end{bmatrix}$$

$$\begin{bmatrix} R \\ G \\ B \end{bmatrix} = \begin{bmatrix} 1.0 & 0.0 & 1.1402 \\ 1.0 & -0.3959 & -0.5810 \\ 1.0 & 2.0294 & 0.0 \end{bmatrix} * \begin{bmatrix} Y \\ U \\ V \end{bmatrix}$$

The only difference between the NTSC and PAL matrices is the additional $33°$ rotation used to generate I and Q in NTSC.

You should do gamma correction using an exponent of 0.45 (the same as NTSC).

Component Systems

There are several systems for processing and recording video images as three separate signals that are not mixed together; these are called *component* systems. Betacam and M2 are analog component systems, while CCIR 601 is a standard digital component system. These are available for both NTSC and PAL standards. Since the luminance information is carried separately from the chrominance, there are no problems with the sum of the two being too large. In addition, the chrominance scale factors are defined so that all *RGB* colors produce chrominance signals that are within the defined range. Finally, the two chrominance signals are not added together, so the magnitude of their sum is not a concern either. See SMPTE RP-125 and 253 (1984, 1990b) for the details.

Thus, there are no color restrictions when you are recording to a component recorder—provided you will play back the recording only on a component monitor. If the signal will be encoded to composite NTSC or PAL at some point in the future, however, it may be advantageous to do hot-color processing before recording, anyway.

HDTV

The SMPTE 240M document (1988) describes an international standard for the production of HDTV images. It is a component video standard, and has all the advantages of the other component systems listed previously.

Initially, the reference phosphors are the *SMPTE* set (Table I). Eventually, the committee members hope that the colorimetry can be based on the considerably wider gamut given by the primaries labeled *HDTV ideal*. Note that the gamut of these primaries is a superset of the gamuts of the three other primary sets listed. For now, you should render for SMPTE primaries.

The white point is D_{65}. The gamma correction exponent is 0.45. The luminance weighting factors were calculated from the primaries and white point specified, and so differ from those used in NTSC and PAL. The chrominance scale factors were chosen so that there are no hot colors. The encoding and decoding matrices are:

$$\begin{bmatrix} Y \\ P_B \\ P_R \end{bmatrix} = \begin{bmatrix} 0.2122 & 0.7013 & 0.0865 \\ -0.1162 & -0.3838 & 0.5000 \\ 0.5000 & -0.4451 & -0.0549 \end{bmatrix} * \begin{bmatrix} R \\ G \\ B \end{bmatrix},$$

$$\begin{bmatrix} R \\ G \\ B \end{bmatrix} = \begin{bmatrix} 1.0 & 0.0 & 1.5755 \\ 1.0 & -0.2254 & -0.4768 \\ 1.0 & 1.8270 & 0.0 \end{bmatrix} * \begin{bmatrix} Y \\ P_B \\ P_R \end{bmatrix}.$$

The Algorithm

The hot-pixel test must be done on every pixel in an image, and thus should be fast. The "repair" section of the algorithm is likely to be used on a relatively small number of pixels, so its speed is not of such great concern.

Calculation of YIQ for each pixel potentially is quite expensive. The integer RGB values first must be decoded into a floating point number in the range [0, 1]; this may be cheap or expensive depending on the way the pixels are encoded. Then these values must be gamma-corrected, requiring three calls to a math library function. Finally, we multiply by the encoding matrix to obtain YIQ.

We can improve on this considerably by building nine look-up tables, one for each coefficient in the matrix. In each table, for each possible RGB component value, we convert the component value to float, gamma-correct it, then multiply it by the appropriate coefficient of the encoding matrix. This reduces the YIQ calculation to nine indexing operations and six additions:

$$Y = \text{tab}_{0,0}[R] + \text{tab}_{0,1}[G] + \text{tab}_{0,2}[B],$$

$$I = \text{tab}_{1,0}[R] + \text{tab}_{1,1}[G] + \text{tab}_{1,2}[B],$$

$$Q = \text{tab}_{2,0}[R] + \text{tab}_{2,1}[G] + \text{tab}_{2,2}[B].$$

Calculation of chroma amplitude involves taking a square root. Performing the test, though, only requires comparing the sizes of two expressions, so we can compare amplitude squared, and eliminate the square root:

$$\sqrt{(I^2 + Q^2)} > \text{limit}$$
$$I^2 + Q^2 > \text{limit}^2$$

The test for composite signal amplitude can be rearranged in a similar way:

$$Y + \sqrt{(I^2 + Q^2)} > \text{limit}$$
$$\sqrt{(I^2 + Q^2)} > \text{limit} - Y$$
$$I^2 + Q^2 > (\text{limit} - Y)^2$$

The simple computations just described can be done entirely in scaled integers, eliminating floating point entirely. Since the values of Y, I, and Q always are within the range $[-1, 1]$, we can choose a scale factor that gives plenty of fractional bits without risk of overflow, even on a 16-bit machine. We do have to convert to 32 bits to handle the squares, though.

There are only three integer multiplications plus seven additions, one subtraction, and two comparisons necessary in the per-pixel loop. (One squaring operation is done on a constant.) This is reasonably cheap.

Once you have found a hot pixel, you may wish to flag it in a distinctive manner so the user can see where it is. If your frame buffer does not have overlay bits, just setting the pixel to a distinctive color will do.

If you have to repair hot pixels, then the *RGB* values must be altered. This involves calculating the actual chroma amplitude, which requires taking a square root or equivalent. The C Implementation that accompanies this gem (Appendix 2) just switches to floating point for simplicity. However, if floating point is not available or is too slow, you can convert the remainder of the code to scaled integer as well. The square root also can be done with integers using an approximation technique described by the second author (Paeth, 1990b). This technique is not exact, but always errs on the side of overestimating the result. When used in this algorithm, it can result in "cooling" the color a bit too much, which is harmless.

There are two plausible ways to alter the *RGB* color to bring it within acceptable bounds. Altering the hue of the color could have extremely ugly results, so we do not consider this. That leaves saturation and intensity (luminance) open for adjustment. Changing luminance is easy. Because the color encoding transform is linear, multiplying *YIQ* by a scalar value is equivalent to multiplying *RGB* by the same scalar. Gamma correction adds a minor wrinkle: To multiply the gamma-corrected *RGB* values (and thus *YIQ* values) by a factor *K*, the linear *RGB* values must be multiplied by a factor of K^{gamma}.

Altering color saturation while leaving hue and luminance alone is only a bit more difficult. In concept, we want to scale *I* and *Q* equally by some scale factor *s*, while leaving *Y* unaltered. If **E** is the color encoding matrix and $\mathbf{E}^{-1}$ is its inverse, we wish to evaluate:

$$
\begin{bmatrix} R' \\ G' \\ B' \end{bmatrix} = \begin{bmatrix} \mathbf{E}^{-1} \end{bmatrix} * \begin{bmatrix} 1 & 0 & 0 \\ 0 & s & 0 \\ 0 & 0 & s \end{bmatrix} * \begin{bmatrix} \mathbf{E} \end{bmatrix} * \begin{bmatrix} R \\ G \\ B \end{bmatrix}
$$

If you multiply out the three 3×3 matrices, you will find that the operation performed by their product simply is:

$$
\begin{array}{ll}
R = (1-s)*Y + s*R & R = Y + s*(R-Y) \\
G = (1-s)*Y + s*G \quad \text{or} & G = Y + s*(G-Y) \\
B = (1-s)*Y + s*B & B = Y + s*(B-Y)
\end{array}
$$

In other words, perform a linear interpolation between the original pixel value and a monochrome pixel of the same luminance. In practice, this method looks awful when applied to full-intensity color bars, since their saturation must be decreased so much. However, it might be acceptable when applied to real images, and it has the advantage that it preserves the black-and-white component of the image.

Further Reading

Winkler (1990) contains an introduction to video, plus much reference material on calibrating your video equipment if you do not have a video engineer handy. Hall (1989) contains extensive discussions about color accuracy in rendering, and transforming images to a different color space. It also contains a discussion on how to handle out-of-gamut colors that goes beyond the two simple techniques discussed here. Amanatides and Mitchell (1990) provide some interesting comments about high-quality rendering for the interlaced video format.

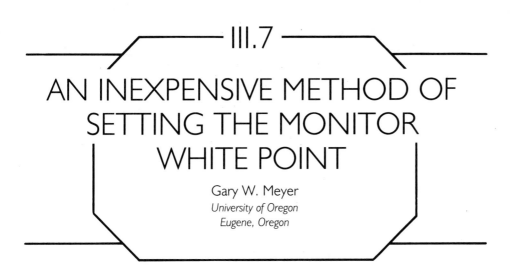

III.7

AN INEXPENSIVE METHOD OF SETTING THE MONITOR WHITE POINT

Gary W. Meyer
University of Oregon
Eugene, Oregon

Calibrating a color television monitor in terms of the CIE *XYZ* color notation system has assumed an increasingly important role in computer graphics. This adjustment has been shown to be useful in applications as diverse as two-dimensional page layout for the graphic arts and three-dimensional realistic image synthesis for commercial animation. Part of the calibration process involves setting the individual brightness and contrast controls for the three monitor guns so that a white color with known chromaticity coordinates is produced whenever $R = G = B$ (Meyer, 1990). Typically, this is thought to require an expensive color measurement device, such as a colorimeter or a color comparator (SMPTE, 1977).

In this gem, we show how a relatively inexpensive luminance meter can be used to establish this setup. We also show how the luminance meter may only need to be used once if a simple light meter with arbitrary spectral sensitivity but linear response is available. We have made use of this technique in our research for some time (Meyer, 1986). Recently, it was shown how this approach can be adapted to postpone the need for a complete monitor calibration (Lucassen and Walraven, 1990).

To employ a luminance meter in setting the monitor white point, the luminance ratio between the red, green, and blue monitor guns at equal drive must be determined. This ratio can be found by noting that the following relationship holds between the tristimulus values of the white point and the component tristimulus values produced by each of the guns,

$$\begin{bmatrix} X_R \\ Y_R \\ Z_R \end{bmatrix} + \begin{bmatrix} X_G \\ Y_G \\ Z_G \end{bmatrix} + \begin{bmatrix} X_B \\ Y_B \\ Z_B \end{bmatrix} = \begin{bmatrix} X_W \\ Y_W \\ Z_W \end{bmatrix}.$$

Using the fact that, for example,

$$X_G = Y_G \frac{x_G}{y_G},$$

where x_G and y_G are the chromaticity coordinates of the green monitor phosphor, this can be rearranged to yield

$$\begin{bmatrix} x_R/y_R & x_G/y_G & x_B/y_B \\ 1 & 1 & 1 \\ z_R/y_R & z_G/y_G & z_B/y_B \end{bmatrix} \begin{bmatrix} Y_R/Y_W \\ Y_G/Y_W \\ Y_B/Y_W \end{bmatrix} = \begin{bmatrix} x_W/y_W \\ 1 \\ z_W/y_W \end{bmatrix},$$

where x_w, y_w, and z_w are the white-point chromaticity coordinates and Y_w is the white-point luminance. From this expression, the required ratio between the gun luminances can be determined. A luminance meter can be used to set the individual brightness and contrast controls for each monitor gun so that the preceding luminance ratio is achieved.

A luminance meter may not always be available to establish these settings and, even if it is, it may not have the necessary sensitivity (due to its photopic response) to make these adjustments over the entire dynamic range of each monitor gun. It is possible, however, to make these measurements with a light sensing device of arbitrary spectral sensitivity as long as the device responds linearly to changes in intensity, the device has a response time appropriate for the monitor refresh rate, and a luminance meter is available to calibrate initially the light sensing device.

To see how this is possible, consider the spectral emission curve $KP(\lambda)$ for one of the monitor phosphors, where $P(\lambda)$ is a relative spectral

160

energy distribution curve that has the property,

$$\int P(\lambda)\, d\lambda = 1,$$

and K is a constant with units $watts\ m^{-2}\ sr^{-1}$ that scales $P(\lambda)$ to create an absolute spectral energy distribution. A luminance meter has spectral sensitivity $\bar{y}(\lambda)$ identical to the human photopic response curve and performs the following integration:

$$Y = \int KP(\lambda)\bar{y}(\lambda)\, d\lambda = K\int P(\lambda)\bar{y}(\lambda)\, d\lambda = KI_y.$$

A light sensing device with arbitrary spectral sensitivity $\bar{a}(\lambda)$ performs the following integration:

$$A = \int KP(\lambda)\bar{a}(\lambda)\, d\lambda = K\int P(\lambda)\bar{a}(\lambda)\, d\lambda = KI_a.$$

Dividing these two expressions by one another and rearranging, we see that

$$Y = \frac{I_y}{I_a} A.$$

The luminance of the phosphor, therefore, can be measured using the light sensing device with arbitrary spectral sensitivity as long as the ratio I_y/I_a has been determined. This can be done by taking the ratio of the two meter readings at several fixed phosphor intensities and averaging the result.

Given the chromaticity coordinates of the monitor phosphors, a light sensing device with linear response but arbitrary spectral sensitivity, and the short term loan of a luminance meter, it is possible to calibrate completely a color television monitor in terms of the CIE *XYZ* system. As was shown previously the light sensing device can be used to set the monitor white point and balance the monitor over its entire dynamic range. A light sensing device with flat spectral sensitivity is preferred even over a luminance meter in performing this operation because of its greater sensitivity, particularly for low blue phosphor intensities. This same light sensing device also can be used to measure the nonlinear relationship that exists between the voltage applied to the monitor guns and the amount of light that the phosphors emit (i.e., *gamma correction*) (Cowan, 1983; Brainard, 1989). In this way, a complete monitor calibration can be accomplished using one relatively inexpensive light measurement device.

III.8

SOME TIPS FOR MAKING COLOR HARDCOPY

Ken Musgrave
Yale University
New Haven, Connecticut

Obtaining high-quality color hardcopy of digital images is still more an art than a science. It is an expensive process, fraught with pitfalls and requiring much experimentation. In this gem, we seek to convey some useful knowledge and techniques. We address image quality and fidelity, and archivability and originality of computer images as artworks; we do not address problems of color gamut matching.

The essential problem of color reproduction in computer images is that of recreating one more or less arbitrary mapping from numbers to colors —the one performed by whatever reference device is deemed your *norm* —on another device or medium that has its own and, invariably, different biases. While one can endeavor to solve this problem rigorously and scientifically (Stone, et al., 1988), for some of us, just getting a reproduction that is *close* to the *original*, and in a particular preferred size and format, would be a boon—especially if it can be achieved without expensive special hardware.

The first problem we encounter in switching reproduction devices or media is dynamic range and gamma matching (Catmull, 1979; Bilson et al., 1986). We have found that a reasonable first-order approximation can be had through the following process:

Output a gray ramp, with visible tic marks on the edge at about every five gray levels. Note where the low entries of your look-up table all have gone to black, and where the high values all have gone white. (Hopefully, this will not be complicated by significantly different values for red, green, and blue.) Then remap your image to within the available contrast range, to avoid gaining contrast and potentially losing detail in highlights and/or shadows. This sort of contrast gain often occurs when mapping to photographic media, as when photographing the screen, making a C-Print or a Cibachrome print, or even when using a film recorder. Note that you may need to use a different ASA or type of film in a film recorder than that specified by the manufacturer; manufacturer's specifications sometimes are utterly apocryphal.

The next step is to reproduce the peculiar response curve of the new medium on your *standard* reference device. This means creating a *gray* ramp that resembles your *standard* gray ramp, as displayed on the new device. This new ramp may not be a gray ramp at all; it may go, for instance, from black through shades of brown to white, or show some other peculiar distortion. Reproduce this ramp on your reference device —hopefully, this simply will require a separate gamma correction to each of red, green, and blue. Now invert the mapping required to change your original gray ramp to this distorted ramp. (Inversion of exponential mappings, such as gamma corrections, just means using $1/\gamma$, where γ is the exponent used in the gamma correction.) Apply the inverse mapping to your dynamic range-adjusted image(s), which may now look rather horrible on your reference device. Print the newly distorted images. A good test is to apply the adjustments to your original gray scale and reimage it—it should be much closer to the reference ramp now.

This procedure can improve markedly the quality of first-generation output. This sometimes is not the final target, however. Sometimes, we wish to make a photographic enlargement from, for instance, a color transparency. This will require a second iteration of the procedure, to adjust for the second medium. Note that the adjustments made to your images inevitably will introduce quantization errors. We employ two techniques in our renderer to combat quantization error. First, we add white noise to the image while we have the floating point values, i.e., before quantization to 8 bits each for red, green, and blue. This has the effect of dithering the quantization lines and making them less visible and offensive. It also plays merry hell with run-length encoding. Second, we have built the inverse-distortion mapping into the renderer, as an option to be invoked when rendering images specifically for one of our favorite bogus output devices. Thus, after developing an image on our reference monitor, we can toggle the option to create images that are distorted on our reference monitor but match it closely to the hardcopy device, without introducing any extra quantization artifacts.

The final target medium may be a Duratrans, C-Print, Cibatrans, or Cibachrome photographic print, or a four-color offset print. These media are listed in order of increasing longevity. Works proffered as fine art to serious collectors must be *archival*, that is, it should be expected to last about 100 years without serious fading or degradation. No commonly available color photographic medium currently is accepted as being archival by museums and collectors.

Cibachrome and Cibatrans are positive-to-positive color printing media. C-Prints and Duratrans are negative-to-positive color printing media, and are more commonly available. C-Print and Cibachrome are opaque color prints, while Duratrans and Cibatrans are large-scale transparencies meant to be displayed back-lit in light boxes. While back-lit transparencies are a luminous medium, and thus more like a CRT display than an opaque reflection print, their life expectancy is substantially shorter, as they are directly exposed to high levels of uv-rich light from the fluorescent bulbs in the light box. Light boxes are rather expensive as well. C-Prints are rather short-lived, depending largely on exposure to light. Cibachromes are touted as being semi-archival, with good colorfastness and a life expectancy of over 50 years. Note, however, that glossy Cibachrome is purported to be longer-lived than pearl-finish Cibachrome.

Four-color offset prints made on acid-free paper with non-fugitive (i.e., colorfast) inks may be considered archival and can constitute very nice reproductions, though setup costs are high (about one to three thousand dollars) and physical dimensions may be limited. Color separations are done routinely by scanning an original image to create a digital image, from which the separations are created. With synthetic images, the intermediate *original* hardcopy may be skipped, and the separations made directly from the original digital data. (Note that medium-matching, as described previously, may need to be done here.) As artwork, the four-color offset prints now can be rightly viewed as *originals*, as no other nonvolatile visual representations exist.

High-quality color printers of various sorts are being announced with increasing frequency. While the quality can be very good, the longevity of the pigments often is rather poor. These devices remain rather expensive as well. If you cannot afford or justify the expense of such a device, look for a *service bureau*—these are commercial outfits that make a living from their stable of such devices. Whichever route you use, be prepared to pay and pay and pay—and to weep over the quality of your early results.

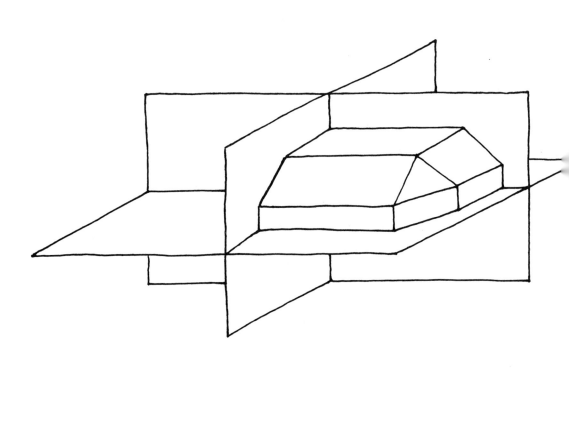

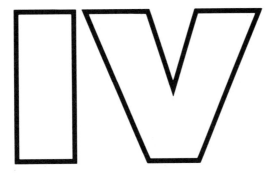

IV

3D GEOMETRY AND ALGORITHMS

3D GEOMETRY AND ALGORITHMS

One of the major uses of computer graphics is to produce visual representations of virtual three-dimensional objects. Synthetic images of hypothetical three-dimensional scenes are used in areas ranging from engineering to entertainment. Consequently, much of computer graphics is concerned with three-dimensional geometry. Within this broad subject, there are many specific, smaller problems; modeling, viewing, clipping, and shading are among them. The gems of this Part are applicable to these problems and others.

The first three gems deal with some basic properties of polyhedra and spheres, two very common types of 3D objects. More complex and general 3D geometries are addressed by the gems on *winged-edge* models and the construction of boundary representations. Three-dimensional clipping is the focus of the gem on *triangle strips*, an efficient and flexible grouping of adjacent triangles. The problem of specifying a viewing transformation for the creation of image—and the inverse problem of inferring the viewing transformation from an image—form the basis of the gems on a simple viewing geometry and view correlation, respectively. The last gem in this Part introduces the concept of *Interphong* shading, a generalization of the familiar technique of Phong shading.

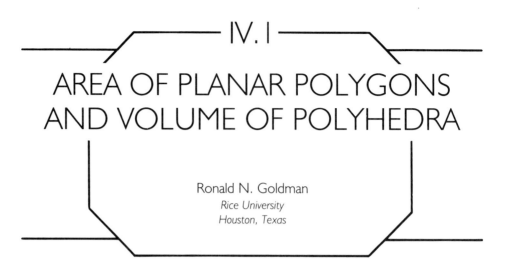

Ronald N. Goldman
Rice University
Houston, Texas

Area of a Planar Polygon

Consider a planar polygon with vertices $P_0, \ldots, P_n$. There is a simple closed formula for the area of the polygon. Let $P_{n+1} = P_0$. If the points $P_0, \ldots, P_n$ lie in the xy plane, then the following formula can be derived from Green's theorem:

$$\text{Area(Polygon)} = \frac{1}{2} \left| \sum_k P_k \times P_{k+1} \right|.$$

If the points lie on some arbitrary plane perpendicular to a unit vector $\mathbf{N}$, then from Stokes Theorem:

$$\text{Area(Polygon)} = \frac{1}{2} \left| \mathbf{N} \cdot \left\{ \sum_k P_k \times P_{k+1} \right\} \right|.$$

These two formulas are valid even for nonconvex polygons.

Volume of a Polyhedron

Consider a polyhedron with planar polygonal faces $S_0, \ldots, S_n$. There is a simple closed formula for the volume of the polyhedron. Let

$$Q_j = \text{any point on } S_j,$$

$$\mathbf{N}_j = \text{a unit outward pointing vector normal to } S_j.$$

170

Then the following formula can be derived from Gauss's theorem:

$$\text{Volume(Polyhedron)} = \frac{1}{3}\left|\sum_j (Q_j \cdot \mathbf{N}_j)\text{Area}(S_j)\right|.$$

Moreover, if $P_{0j}, \ldots, P_{mj}$ are the vertices of S_j oriented counterclockwise with respect to the outward pointing normal of S_j, then by our previous result for polygons:

$$\text{Area}(S_j) = \frac{1}{2}\left|\mathbf{N}_j \cdot \left\{\sum_k P_{kj} \times P_{k+1,j}\right\}\right|.$$

Moreover, we now can take

$$Q_j = P_{0j},$$

$$\mathbf{N}_j = \left\{(P_{1j} - P_{0j}) \times (P_{2j} - P_{0j})\right\}\big/\left|(P_{1j} - P_{0j}) \times (P_{2j} - P_{0j})\right|.$$

Putting this all together, we get the formula:

$$\text{Volume(Polyhedron)} = \frac{1}{6}\left|\left[\sum_j (P_{0j} \cdot \mathbf{N}_j)\left|\mathbf{N}_j \cdot \left\{\sum_k P_{kj} \times P_{k+1,j}\right\}\right|\right]\right|,$$

where $\mathbf{N}_j$ is defined in the preceding in terms of the vertices of the polyhedron. Notice again that these two formulas for volume are valid even for nonconvex polyhedra.

See also I.1 The Area of a Simple Polygon, Jon Rokne

IV.2

GETTING AROUND ON A SPHERE

Clifford A. Shaffer
Virginia Tech
Blacksburg, Virginia

Given a point P on a sphere, this gem describes how to compute the new coordinates that result from moving in some direction. I recently used this material when developing a browsing system for world-scale maps. When "looking down" at a position on the sphere, the user of the browsing system can shift the view to the left, right, up, or down.

The first thing to realize is that while latitude and longitude are convenient for people, most calculations for the sphere are done more easily in Cartesian coordinates. Given longitude λ, latitude ϕ, and a sphere of radius R with center at the origin of the coordinate system, the conversions are:

$$x = R \cos \lambda \cos \phi; \qquad y = R \sin \lambda \cos \phi; \qquad z = R \sin \phi;$$

$$R = \sqrt{x^2 + y^2 + z^2}; \qquad \lambda = \arctan\left(\frac{y}{x}\right); \qquad \phi = \arctan\left(\frac{z}{\sqrt{x^2 + y^2}}\right).$$

Given point P on the sphere, the plane T tangent to the sphere at P will have its normal vector going from the origin through P. Thus, the first three coefficients for the plane equation will be $T_a = P_x$, $T_b = P_y$, $T_c = P_z$. Since the plane must contain P, $T_d = -(P \cdot P)$, i.e., the negative of the dot product between the vector from the origin to P and itself.

Movement on the sphere must be in some direction. One way to specify directions is by means of a great circle G going through the current point P. In this way, we can describe movement as either along G, or in a direction at some angle at G. G will be contained in some plane J, with $J_d = 0$ (since it must go through the origin). For example, the plane for the great circle containing point P and the north pole N at $(0, 1, 0)$ will have normal $\mathbf{P} \times \mathbf{N}$, or the cross product of the vector from the origin to P with the vector from the origin to N. Taking the cross product in this order will make rotations by θ appear clockwise when looking along the direction of the normal vector from the plane.

Moving along the great circle simply will be a rotation by some angle θ. The rotation axis will be the normal vector for the plane of the great circle. Given J, the plane for some great circle, and some point P on the great circle, rotation of the point within plane J by angle θ clockwise can be done as (Faux and Pratt, 1979):

$$P'_x = \left(J_a J_a + \cos\theta(1 - J_a J_a)\right)P_x + \left(J_a J_b(1 - \cos\theta) - J_c \sin\theta\right)P_y$$

$$+ \left(J_c J_a(1 - \cos\theta) + J_b \sin\theta\right)P_z,$$

$$P'_y = \left(J_a J_b(1 - \cos\theta) + J_c \sin\theta\right)P_x + \left(J_b J_b + \cos\theta(1 - J_b J_b)\right)P_y$$

$$+ \left(J_b J_c(1 - \cos\theta) - J_a \sin\theta\right)P_z,$$

$$P'_z = \left(J_c J_a(1 - \cos\theta) - J_b \sin\theta\right)P_x + \left(J_b J_c(1 - \cos\theta) + J_a \sin\theta\right)P_y$$

$$+ \left(J_c J_c + \cos\theta(1 - J_c J_c)\right)P_z.$$

Moving in a direction perpendicular to the great circle requires computing the plane J' perpendicular to the plane J of the great circle that contains P. The normal for J' is $\mathbf{P} \times \mathbf{J_N}$, where $\mathbf{J_N}$ is the normal vector for plane J, and again, $J'_d = 0$. Note that two distinct great circle planes perpendicular to a great circle plane will not be parallel.

Finally, assume we wish to move from point P in some arbitrary direction to point P'. The direction is specified as being a clockwise angle ϕ to some great circle (with plane J) that contains P. We first must calculate the plane J' of the great circle connecting P and P'. We then can use the preceding rotation equations to calculate the actual movement. To find the new normal vector $\mathbf{J'_N}$, we simply rotate $\mathbf{J_N}$ by angle ϕ, using as the axis of rotation the vector from the origin to P. To do so, simply reverse the use of P and J, and substitute ϕ for θ, in the rotation equations.

EXACT DIHEDRAL METRICS FOR COMMON POLYHEDRA

Alan W. Paeth
NeuralWare, Inc.
Pittsburgh, Pennsylvania

Whereas decimal approximations for vertex coordinates are common, this gem gives closed-form formulae and tables for the dihedral angles of nine prototypical solids. (This is a direct extension of Paeth (1990e), which allows closed-form expressions for the vertex locations of select n-gons.) Uses include the production of coordinate tables at high precision (as seen in example), *crack prevention* in space packing lattices having no near-coincident vertices, and the generation of polyhedra using half-plane equations in the style of CAD/CAM descriptive solid modeling. The table for dihedrals for the Snub figures in analytic form is previously unpublished, and dispels the misconception requoted by Coxeter in Ball (1939) suggesting that cubic roots are needed in the analytic representation of these unusual solids.

Table I is organized by the regular (platonic) solids, quasi-regular solids (Coxeter, 1948), and their duals. All possess merely one face dihedral: the *hinge* angle δ between any two edge-adjacent polygons. These are listed as $\cos \delta$ and $\tan \delta$; $\sin \delta$ may be immediately formed as their product and does not appear. Note that supplementary angles (those that sum to $180°$ and thus form an unbroken plane) have opposite signs: $f(90° - x) = -f(90° + x)$ for f in {tan, cos}. Thus, the tetrahedron and octahedron are seen to form a common face when joined—this suggests their $2 : 1$ space packing ratio. Likewise, the cube's dihedral necessarily is zero: It forms no edge when abutted with identical copies. This condition for space packing is sufficient but not necessary: Three copies of the rhombic dodecahedron also fill space, as is suggested by a solid dihedral angle of $2\pi/3$ (Paeth, 1990g, pp. 236–239), as do two cuboctahedra and an

Table I. (Quasi) Regular Polyhedra and Duals.

Polyhedron Name	Faces	Vertices	Edges	δ	$\cos\delta$	$\tan\delta$
		Feature			Face Dihedrals	
tetrahedron	4	4	6	70.53°	$1/3$	$2\sqrt{2}$
cube	6	8	12	90°	0	∞
octahedron	8	6	12	109.47°	$-1/3$	$-2\sqrt{2}$
dodecahedron	12	20	30	116.57°	$-\sqrt{5}/5$	-2
rhombic dodecahedron	12	14	24	120°	$-1/2$	$-\sqrt{3}$
cuboctahedron	14	12	24	125.26°	$-\sqrt{3}/3$	$-\sqrt{2}$
icosahedron	20	12	30	138.19°	$-\sqrt{5}/3$	$-2\sqrt{5}/5$
icosidodecahedron	32	30	60	142.62°	$-\sqrt{(5+2\sqrt{5})}/15$	$\sqrt{5}-3$
triacontahedron	30	32	60	144°	$-(\sqrt{5}+1)/4$	$-\sqrt{(5-2\sqrt{5})}$

octahedron. (See also Fig. 1 from Gem III.5, "Mapping RGB Triples onto sixteen Distinct Values.") Other trigonometric forms may further reduce the surds. For instance, employing the halved tangent (Gem VIII.5, "A Half-Angle Identity for Digital Computation") gives the elegant series, $\{\sqrt{2}/2, 1, \sqrt{2}, \phi, \phi^2\}$, for the five platonic solids; dihedral values $\tan(\delta/2)$ are positive and go to infinity as two faces approach planarity. Under this transformation, supplementary angles have reciprocal, not complementary measures: The cube now is represented by unity. Using Table I, other identities may be derived, e.g., $\sin\delta_{i\cos a} = 2/3$.

The dodecahedron and icosahedron are strongly dependent on the golden mean. The angle formed between two adjacent (vertex) vectors of the latter may be used to derive the face dihedral of its dual dodecahedron by dotting the vectors, $(0\ 1\ \phi)\cdot(0\ 1\ -\phi)$. Closer analysis shows that the solid angle of the latter also may be derived using vectors with integral components, as with $(1\ 2\ 2)\cdot(1\ 0\ -2)$, related to the compact equation $\tan\delta_{\text{dodec}} = -2$. Similarly, the included angle of $(0\ 1\ 2)\cdot(2\ -1\ -2)$ defines the solid angle of the icosahedron.

As an example of use, the solids of fivefold symmetry most often are listed (Coxeter, 1948) *edge on* (meaning the Z axis bisects an edge). Of

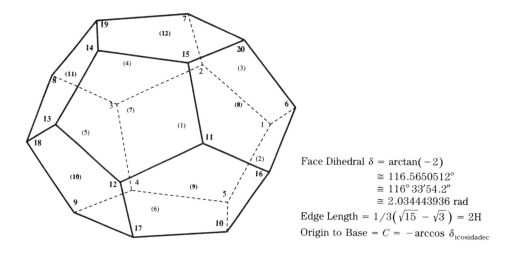

Face Dihedral $\delta = \arctan(-2)$
$\cong 116.5650512°$
$\cong 116° 33' 54.2''$
$\cong 2.034443936$ rad
Edge Length $= 1/3(\sqrt{15} - \sqrt{3}) = 2H$
Origin to Base $= C = -\arccos \delta_{\text{icosidadec}}$

	Vertices	Coordinate Values (10-digit approximations)
1 $\{B, D, -C\}$	11 $\{B, -D, C\}$	$A = 0$
2 $\{A, F, -C\}$	12 $\{A, -F, C\}$	$B = \sqrt{3}/3$ ~ .5773502692
3 $\{-B, D, -C\}$	13 $\{-B, -D, C\}$	$C = \sqrt{(5 + 2\sqrt{5})/15} = I + J$ ~ .7946544723
4 $\{-H, -I, -C\}$	14 $\{-H, I, C\}$	$D = \sqrt{(5 - 2\sqrt{5})/15} = I - J$ ~ .1875924741
5 $\{H, -I, -C\}$	15 $\{H, I, C\}$	$E = \sqrt{(10 + 2\sqrt{5})/15} = 2I$ ~ .9822469464
6 $\{G, J, -D\}$	16 $\{G, -J, D\}$	$F = \sqrt{(10 - 2\sqrt{5})/15} = 2J$ ~ .6070619982
7 $\{A, E, -D\}$	17 $\{A, -E, D\}$	$G = \sqrt{(3 + \sqrt{5})/6}$ ~ .9341723590
8 $\{-G, J, -D\}$	18 $\{-G, -J, D\}$	$H = \sqrt{(3 - \sqrt{5})/6}$ ~ .3568220898
9 $\{-B, -C, -D\}$	19 $\{-B, C, D\}$	$I = \sqrt{(5 + \sqrt{5})/30}$ ~ .4911234732
10 $\{B, -C, -D\}$	20 $\{B, C, D\}$	$J = \sqrt{(5 - \sqrt{5})/30}$ ~ .3035309991

Faces

1. $(1, 2, 3, 4, 5)$	7. $(11, 12, 13, 14, 15)$
2. $(1, 5, 10, 16, 6)$	8. $(11, 15, 20, 6, 16)$
3. $(2, 1, 6, 20, 7)$	9. $(12, 11, 16, 10, 17)$
4. $(3, 2, 7, 19, 8)$	10. $(13, 12, 17, 9, 18)$
5. $(4, 3, 8, 18, 9)$	11. $(14, 13, 18, 8, 19)$
6. $(5, 4, 9, 17, 10)$	12. $(15, 14, 19, 7, 20)$

Figure 1.   Regular Dodecahedron (face upright).

the 20 vertices in the dodecahedron, a cubic subgroup in Cartesian alignment thus is revealed. (Here $\iota = \phi^{-1} = \phi - 1$):

$$(\pm 1, \pm 1, \pm 1), (0, \pm \iota, \pm \phi), (\pm \phi, 0, \pm \iota), (\pm \iota, \pm \phi, 0).$$

Likewise, the icosahedron may be constructed from three mutually perpendicular rectangles, each having a golden aspect ratio. This also gives the edge-on representation:

$$(0, \pm \phi, \pm 1), (\pm 1, 0, \pm \phi), (\pm \phi, \pm 1, 0).$$

An aesthetic (and often more practical) dodecahedron is *face-on*: The Z axis intersects the centroid of two opposing faces. By starting with a closed-form representation for a pentagonal face (Paeth, 1990e) and then applying rotations based on the dihedral table (Table I), the desired orientation is achieved. A fully worked example is shown in Fig. 1. An inscribed cube remains evident, here at $\{\pm B, \pm C, \pm D\}$, in the list of vertices in Fig. 1. (C and D permute as the cube cannot also be face-on.)

Nearly all of the semi-regular *Archimedean* solids (whose faces are regular n-gons with more than one n in symmetric arrangement) employ these solid angles. For instance, the truncated tetrahedron adds the octahedron's dihedral for hinges between its 3-gon and 6-gon faces, suggestive of its complete truncation to the octahedron.

Unaccounted for are the *snub* figures, formed by surrounding the edges of a regular solid's faces with equilateral triangles. Snubbing the

Table II.

Face		Snub Solid	
name	vertex (θ)	name	dihedral (δ)
(none)	0°	octahedron	109.47°
triangle	60°	icosahedron	138.11°
square	**90°**	**snub cube**	**153.21° (142.98°)**
pentagon	**108°**	**snub icosahedron**	**164.17° (152.93°)**
hexagon	120°	hexagonal tiling	180°

cube and dodecahedron creates new solids; the snub octahedron is the icosahedron. This provides a good test for the snub equation relating dihedral δ to principal face to vertex angle θ:

$$4 - 3\cos\delta = \sqrt{25 + 16\sqrt{3}\,\sin\frac{\theta}{2}}$$

Likewise, snubbing a hexagonal plane tiling (which properly may be regarded as a 3-space polyhedron of infinite volume) forms the curious snub tiling of the plane. In each case, the algebraic form holds, though an obscure snub remains: The snub square anti-prism (the 85th solid in a complete enumeration of polyhedra, see (Johnson, 1966)). It has a dihedral frustratingly close to one formed given a vertex angle of $\phi = 75°$, yet yields only to other methods (Linsternik, 1963). Johnson's 84th solid, the *snub disphenoid*, is the only other snub having regular n-gon faces. It may be disregarded, as it can be decomposed into simpler solids. The Archimedean snubs are presented in Table II. A second, distinct dihedral angle is present on the two solids of interest between two equilateral triangles, and is listed in parentheses. Orthographic projections of two less-familiar solids appear below.

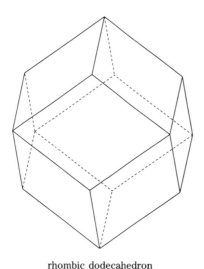

rhombic dodecahedron

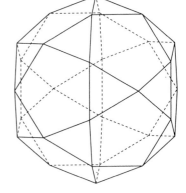

icosidadecahedron

IV

A SIMPLE VIEWING GEOMETRY

Andrew S. Glassner
Xerox PARC
Palo Alto, California

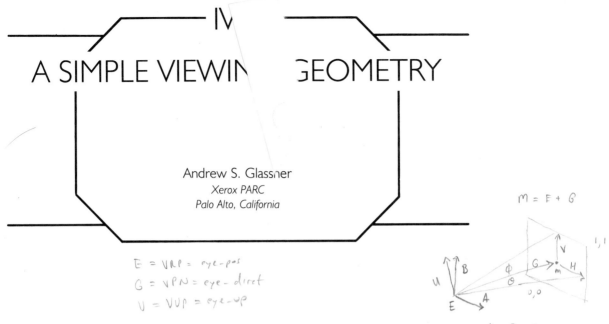

$$M = E + G$$

$$E = VRP = eye\text{-}pos$$
$$G = VPN = eye\text{-}direct$$
$$U = VUP = eye\text{-}up$$

$$A = G \times U$$

$$B = A \times G$$

$$H = A \frac{|G|}{|A|} \tan \Theta$$

$$V = B \frac{|G|}{|B|} \tan \phi$$

Sometimes, it is handy to be able to set up a simple viewing geometry. For example, packages without matrix libraries, quick preview hacks, and simple ray tracers all can benefit from a simple viewing construction. Here is one that I have found handy.

The input is a viewpoint E, a gaze direction and distance G, an up vector U, and viewing half-angles θ and φ. The output is a screen midpoint M and two vectors, H and V, which are used to sweep the screen. Figure 1 shows the setup.

First, create vector $\mathbf{A}$ by $\mathbf{A} \leftarrow \mathbf{G} \times \mathbf{U}$. (I assume right-handed cross products.) Then find $\mathbf{B}$ from $\mathbf{B} \leftarrow \mathbf{A} \times \mathbf{G}$. Vector $\mathbf{B}$ is coplanar with $\mathbf{U}$ and $\mathbf{G}$, but it is orthogonal to $\mathbf{A}$ and $\mathbf{G}$. The midpoint of the screen is found from $M \leftarrow \mathbf{E} + \mathbf{G}$. (Note that the length of $\mathbf{G}$ tells you how far away the viewscreen is located.) Vectors $\mathbf{A}$ and $\mathbf{B}$ span the viewplane, but they are the wrong size. Find the vector $\mathbf{H}$ by scaling $\mathbf{A}$ by the horizontal half-angle: $\mathbf{H} \leftarrow (\mathbf{A}|\mathbf{G}|\tan \theta)/|\mathbf{A}|$. Similarly, the vertical vector is found by $\mathbf{V} \leftarrow (\mathbf{B}|\mathbf{G}|\tan \varphi)/|\mathbf{B}|$.

Assuming your origin is in the lower left, as shown, then any point S on the screen may be specified by (sx, sy), both numbers between 0 and 1. (For example, if your frame buffer is 640 pixels wide by 480 pixels high, then $(30, 250)$ would map to $(30/639, 250/479)$). The point P on the image plane then is $P \leftarrow M + (2s_x - 1)\mathbf{H} + (2s_y - 1)\mathbf{V}$. If you prefer to have your origin in the upper left, then generate points with the equation $P \leftarrow M + (2s_x - 1)\mathbf{H} + (1 - 2s_y)\mathbf{V}$.

$$P = M + (2s_x - 1)H + (2s_y - 1)V$$

$$P = M + (2s_x - 1)H + (1 - 2s_y)V$$

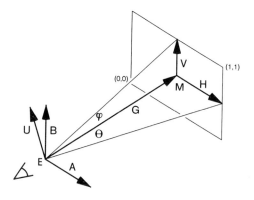

Figure 1.

If you are ray tracing, the ray equation would be $R = E + (P - E)t$. (You may wish to normalize $(P - E)$ before actually shooting the ray.)

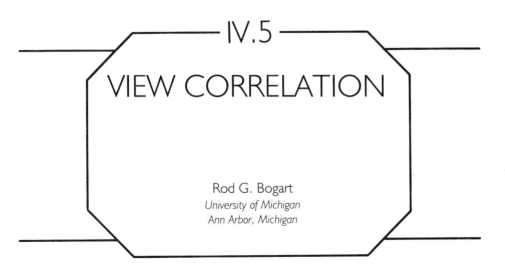

IV.5

VIEW CORRELATION

Rod G. Bogart
University of Michigan
Ann Arbor, Michigan

To combine computer-generated objects into a photographic scene, it is necessary to render the objects from the same point of view as was used to make the photo. This gem describes an iterative technique for correlating view parameters to a photograph image. The method is implemented in C (Appendix 2) as a user function with a simple driver program for testing. The following sections describe the math behind the iterative technique, some specifies about the given implementation, and an example.

This method requires that at least five points are visible in the photo image, and that the 3D coordinates of those points are known. Later, when a computer-generated object is modeled, it must be in the same 3D space as the photo objects, and must use the same units. It is not necessary for the origin to be visible in the photo image, nor does it assume a particular *up* direction.

For each of the five (or more) data points, the 2D screen point must be found. This can be done simply by examining the photo image, or by employing more advanced image processing techniques. Because this is an iterative technique, the 2D point need not be accurate to sub-pixel detail. The final set of view parameters will project the given 3D points to 2D locations that have the minimum error from the given 2D screen points.

In addition to the data points, an iterative process needs a starting value. A set of view parameters must be given that approximate the correct answer. The method is extremely forgiving; however, it does help if the starting eye position is at least in the correct octant of 3-space, and the direction of view looks towards the center of the 3D data.

Mathematical Basis

The following equations define the projection equations used, along with the partial derivatives needed for Newton iteration. The iteration process consists of finding the error with the current viewing parameters, filling the Jacobian matrix with the partial derivatives, inverting the Jacobian to find the correction values, and applying the correction values to the current viewing parameters. Right-handed coordinates and row vectors are used. The following variables are defined:

P 3D data point

E 3D eye point

T Translate by negative eye

R Viewing rotate

θ Half of horizontal view angle

r Aspect ratio for non-square pixels

x_s Half X screen width in pixels

x_c X screen centering

y_c Y screen centering

u Resulting screen X coordinate

v Resulting screen Y coordinate

The projection equations are

$$PTR = [\,a \quad b \quad c\,],$$

$$u = -\frac{x_s * a}{c * \tan \theta} + x_c,$$

$$v = -\frac{r * x_s * b}{c * \tan \theta} + y_c,$$

but it is difficult to take the partial derivatives of u and v with respect to the unknown view parameters. The partial of u with respect to a is simple, but a is dependent on the unknown eye point and rotation matrix. Therefore, the projection equations are modified so that the partial derivatives are easy to find.

Rather than subtracting the eye point from P and rotating the result (PTR), rewrite the equation by rotating each point and subtracting the results:

$$PR - ER = [\begin{array}{ccc} a & b & c \end{array}],$$

$$PR = [\begin{array}{ccc} x & y & z \end{array}],$$

$$[\begin{array}{ccc} a & b & c \end{array}] = [\begin{array}{ccc} x & y & z \end{array}] - ER,$$

$$[\begin{array}{ccc} a & b & c \end{array}] = [\begin{array}{ccc} x - er_x & y - er_y & z - er_z \end{array}].$$

The symbols er_x, etc. are just the components of the rotated eye point. The rotation matrix still is the same one as in the original projection equations. Substituting for a, b, and c gives a set of projection equations that are easy to differentiate. The expression $1/\tan\theta$ is replaced by ds, which simply is the distance to the screen divided by half the screen width:

$$u = -\frac{ds * x_s * (x - er_x)}{z - er_z} + x_c,$$

$$v = -\frac{ds * r * x_s * (y - er_y)}{z - er_z} + y_c.$$

The partial derivatives for Newton's method are found with respect to the 10 iteration parameters: er_x er_y er_z ϕ_x ϕ_y ϕ_z ds r x_c y_c. Note that x_s is constant and is known from the original photo image. The ϕ parameters are the individual rotations about the coordinate axes. Although the component rotations are not explicitly referenced in the projection equations, they are embodied in x, y, and z. Therefore, the partial $\partial u/\partial \phi_z$

can be found by the chain rule:

$$\frac{\partial u}{\partial \phi_z} = \frac{\partial u}{\partial x}\frac{\partial x}{\partial \phi_z} + \frac{\partial u}{\partial y}\frac{\partial y}{\partial \phi_z},$$

$$\frac{\partial u}{\partial x} = -\frac{ds * x_s}{z - er_z},$$

$$\frac{\partial u}{\partial y} = 0,$$

$$\frac{\partial x}{\partial \phi_z} = -y,$$

$$\frac{\partial u}{\partial \phi_z} = \frac{ds * x_s * y}{z - er_z}.$$

The partial $\partial x/\partial \phi_z$ follows from the fact that $(x, y, z) = (r \cos \phi_z, r \sin \phi_z, z)$. Therefore, $\partial x/\partial \phi_z = -r \sin \phi_z = -y$. The partial derivatives with respect to the rest of the iteration parameters are found directly, or by applications of the chain rule, and are presented in Table I.

The Jacobian matrix is simply composed of these equations evaluated for each given data point. For example, if eight data points were given, the Jacobian would have 10 rows (for the iteration parameters) and 16 columns (for the u and v partial derivative calculations for each given point).

The iteration process is simple. First, the 3D data points are projected according to the current view parameters. The projected points are compared to the measured 2D data to create a set of error terms. If the errors are below a predetermined threshold, the iteration stops. Otherwise, the Jacobian matrix is built as described previously. To produce the correction values, the Jacobian is inverted and multiplied by the error terms. Since the Jacobian probably is not a square matrix, the pseudo-inverse is calculated, $(J^{-1} = J^T(J*J^T)^{-1})$. The correction values are sub-

Table I.   Partial derivatives of u and v with respect to the 10 iteration parameters.

	u	v
er_x	$\dfrac{ds * x_s}{z - er_z}$	$0 \, .$
er_y	0	$\dfrac{ds * r * x_s}{z - er_z}$
er_z	$-\dfrac{ds * x_s * (x - er_x)}{(z - er_z)^2}$	$-\dfrac{ds * r * x_s * (y - er_y)}{(z - er_z)^2}$
ϕ_x	$\dfrac{ds * x_s * y * (x - er_x)}{(z - er_z)^2}$	$\dfrac{ds * r * x_s * z}{z - er_z} + \dfrac{ds * r * x_s * y * (y - er_y)}{(z - er_z)^2}$
ϕ_y	$-\dfrac{ds * x_s * z}{z - er_z} - \dfrac{ds * x_s * x * (x - er_x)}{(z - er_z)^2}$	$-\dfrac{ds * r * x_s * x * (y - er_y)}{(z - er_z)^2}$
ϕ_z	$\dfrac{ds * x_s * y}{z - er_z}$	$-\dfrac{ds * r * x_s * x}{z - er_z}$
ds	$-\dfrac{x_s * (x - er_x)}{z - er_z}$	$-\dfrac{r * x_s(y - er_y)}{z - er_z}$
r	0	$-\dfrac{ds * x_s(y - er_y)}{z - er_z}$
x_c	1	0
y_c	0	1

tracted from the current iteration parameters to create a new set of view parameters. Then the new view parameters are used to project the 3D points, and the process begins again.

Implementation Details

The provided C Implementation (Appendix 2) contains the view correlation routines and a simple program to test them. The test program accepts a file containing an initial view and a set of 3D points and their

2D screen locations. The program outputs the correlated view and the data points, followed by parameters suitable for a specific ray tracing program called *rayshade*.

Some renderers cannot handle arbitrary aspect ratios, so it is possible to prevent the aspect ratio from being iterated. The *include* file *view-corr.h* has a **#define** variable that can be changed to restrict the aspect ratio. The aspect ratio then should be set to 1.0 in the initial set of view parameters passed into *iterate_view_parms*.

It is important to choose appropriate 3D points for the iteration process. Although the algorithm can produce correct results with only five data points, it is advantageous to have as many points as possible. If only five points are given that all lie in a 3D plane, the process will fail. Also, if the 2D points are nearly collinear, the process will not iterate successfully. Therefore, it is best to choose points that widely span 3-space as well as spanning a large amount of screen area.

Figure 1 shows the view geometry that can result from the iterative process. The view pyramid on the left shows the line of sight as a dotted line towards the center of the screen (X_{half}, Y_{half}). However, the intended line of sight is toward another point (X_{center}, Y_{center}). The view on the right

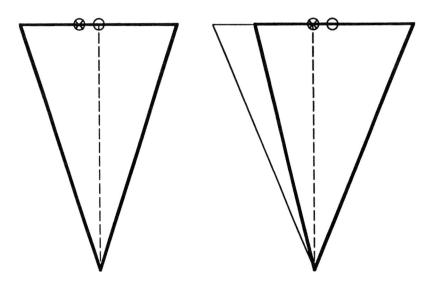

Figure 1. View pyramid geometry for rendering with iterated parameters.

shows a larger view pyramid centered at (X_{center}, Y_{center}) and completely enclosing the original screen. The correct rendering is performed by implying a large screen, then rendering a small window that is the size of the original image. During the iteration process, the *ds* value represented the field of view shown on the left. For rendering a window of a larger screen, the field of view must be scaled by the ratio of the new screen divided by the original screen.

It should be noted that the *apply_corrections* routine does not find the individual rotation parameters and subtract the correction values

Figure 2.   **Example image.**

Table II.   Initial input file for example view correlation.

200 200 200	*Eye point*
0 0 0	*Look point*
0 0 1	*Up vector*
4 1	*D/S ratio, aspect ratio*
192 192 192 192	*Half X Y screen sizes, Xcenter Ycenter*
7	*Number of data points*
50 0 6 57 113	*X Y Z ScreenX ScreenY*
0 50 6 326 156	
25 25 48 198 265	
5 0 21 151 251	
50 50 6 230 39	
0 25 48 249 315	
20 35 18 239 167	

from them. This would work only for very small changes to the rotation parameters. Instead, the correction values are built into a single matrix, and appended to the current view matrix.

Example

The structure shown in Fig. 2 was built from bricks with known dimensions. Therefore, it was simple to choose a set of 3D points and the corresponding 2D screen locations of those points. The exact input for the *viewfind* program is shown in Table II. The comments to the right are not part of the input file.

Table III.   Parameters for use with *rayshade* for the example image.

```
screen 608 582
window 224 198 607 581
eyep 248.932765 149.991910 239.688754
lookp 248.350545 149.572529 238.992235
up −0.592104 −0.368372 0.716740
fov 25.338186 24.858782
```

Figure 3. Example image with computer-generated objects.

With this input file, the iteration stops after 36 steps, with a root-mean-squared error of 0.446954. The final *rayshade* parameters are shown in Table III. If the initial guess for the up vector is changed to $(0, 1, 0)$, the iteration takes 116 steps to reach the same values. When the up vector is changed to $(0, 1, 0)$, the eye point is set to $(100, 1000, -500)$, and the look point is set to $(300, 300, 300)$, the iteration takes 272 steps. On current CPUs, 272 iterations occur in a few seconds.

Figure 3 shows some additional bricks added by rendering an image of the two towers with the new *rayshade* parameters. The raytraced image then was composited over the original photo image.

Although this gem is intended for use with photographic data, it can be tested by producing an image of known data with known parameters. Then the iterated parameters can be compared to the original data.

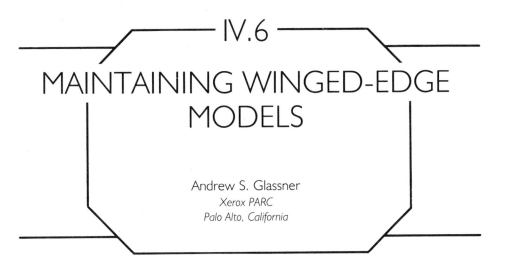

IV.6
MAINTAINING WINGED-EDGE MODELS

Andrew S. Glassner
Xerox PARC
Palo Alto, California

The *winged-edge* data structure is a powerful mechanism for manipulating polyhedral models. The basic idea rests on the idea of an edge and its adjacent polygons. The name is derived by imagining the two polygons as a butterfly's wings, and the edge as the butterfly's body separating them. This simple concept provides a basis for implementing a variety of powerful tools for performing high-level operations on models. The references (Baumgart, 1974), (Baumgart, 1975), and (Hanrahan, 1982) provide details on such high-level operations as object–object intersection, union, difference, and collision detection.

There are several fundamental operations that a winged-edge library must support. Each operation requires carefully moving and adjusting a variety of pointers. To illustrate the type of problem that must be solved, consider the task of inserting a new node N into a simple doubly linked list between nodes A and B. Each node has two pointers, *prev* and *next*, pointing to the previous and next node, respectively. At the time of insertion, $A.next = B$ and $B.prev = A$. If you insert node N by setting $A.next \leftarrow N$, and then set $N.next \leftarrow A.next$, you are in big trouble, since after assignment, $N.next$ will point to N, not B. If you make those assignments in the opposite order, all is well. This sort of problem is greatly multiplied when moving pointers in a winged-edge library—you have to make sure you do things in just the right order, or disaster will ensue.

The purpose of this note is to describe how I solved some of what I found to be the trickiest pointer-stitching problems in implementing a winged-edge library. A complete description of such a library would be long and only repeat the information in the references. Rather, I will suggest a general architecture and data structures, and give recipes for performing those basic mechanisms that require some care to implement correctly.

I like the architecture suggested by Pat Hanrahan. The general structure is that faces, edges, and vertices each are stored in a ring (a doubly linked list). A *WShape* contains three rings, one each for faces, edges, and vertices. Each edge ring entry points to a data structure called *WEdgeData*, which contains the information for that edge. Each face contains an edge ring describing the edges around that face. Each vertex contains an edge ring of all edges around that vertex. All duplicate instantiations of an edge point to a single *WEdgeData* structure. (This contains a pointer back to its *owner* in the master edge ring in the *WShape*.) Notice that there is a lot of redundancy in this architecture—that helps speed up searches and complex operations, which typically start from a face, edge, or vertex ad work from there. Figure 1 is a pictorial description of a *WShape*.

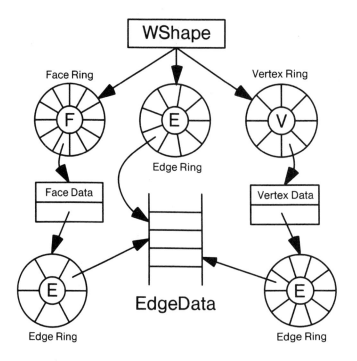

Figure 1.

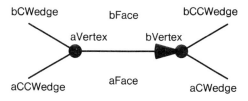

Figure 2.

The fundamental building block in the system is the *edge*, represented by an instance of the *WEdgeData* data structure. An edge is a directed connection between two vertices (from *aVertex* to *bVertex*). Each edge separates two faces. (Viewing the edge as in Figure 2, *aFace* is below and *bFace* is above; when following an edge *aFace* is on the right looking down onto the outside of the surface, and *bFace* is on the left.) An edge has four *wings*; these are the first edges around the vertex encountered in the specified direction. Referring to Fig. 2, on *aFace* we travel clockwise from the edge to reach *aCWedge*, and counterclockwise to reach *aCCWedge*; we travel similarly for *bFace* and its wings, *bCWedge* and *bCCWedge*. Note that other edges may share *aVertex* and lie between *aCCWedge* and *bCWedge*, but we only store these two *outermost* edges in the *WEdgeData* data structure.

The basic data structures to implement this library are the *WShape*, *WFace*, *WEdge*, *WVertex*, and *WEdgeData*. The basic components of these structures are given as follows. I have augmented the basic data with an *index* field and a *clientData* field; the former is for bookkeeping and debugging, and the latter is a place for users of the library to store a pointer to any information they wish to associate with an individual element.

ClockDirection: **type**{*cw, ccw*};

WShape: **type record**[

vertexRing:	WVertex ← **nil**,
edgeRing:	WEdge ← **nil**,
faceRing:	WFace ← **nil**,
next, previous:	WShape ← **nil**,
index:	**int** ← 0,
clientData:	**ref any** ← **nil**

];

```
WFace: type record[
        edgeRing:               WEdge ← nil,
        next, previous:         WFace ← nil,
        index:                  nil ← 0,
        clientData:             ref any ← nil
        ];

WEdgeData: type record[
        aCWedge, bCWedge:       WEdge ← nil,
        aCCWedge, bCCWedge: WEdge ← nil,
        aVertex, bVertex:       WVertex ← nil,
        aFace, bFace:           WFace ← nil,
        index:                  int ← 0,
        owner:                  WEdge ← nil,
        clientData:             ref any ← nil
        ];

WEdge: type record[
        edgeData:               WEdgeData ← nil,
        next, previous:         WEdge ← nil,
        clientData:             ref any ← nil
        ];

WVertex: type record[
        basicVertex:            point,
        edgeRing:               WEdge ← nil,
        next, previous:         WVertex ← nil,
        index:                  int ← 0,
        clientData:             ref any ← nil
        ];
```

With these data structures in hand, we can consider some of the functions a winged-edge library needs to support. One common operation when constructing a model is embodied in the procedure *SetWings*. This takes a pair of edges with a common vertex, and determines their wing information. There are eight ways the edges might be related when they come into the procedure; Fig. 3 indicates how to set the pointers. (This is adapted from page 22 of Baumgart (1974).) In the figure, *aF* and *bF* stand for *aFace* and *bFace*, and *aCW*, *bCW*, *aCCW*, and *bCCW* stand for the edges with those prefixes.

e1.aV = e2.aV	e1.aV = e2.bV	e1.bV = e2.aV	e1.bV = e2.bV
e1 e2	e1 e2	e1 e2	e1 e2
e1.bF = a2.aF	e1.bF = a2.bF	e1.aF = e2.aF	e1.aF = e2.bF
e1.bCW ← e2	e1.bCW ← e2	e1.aCW ← e2	e1.aCW ← e2
e2.aCCW ← e1	e2.bCCW←e1	e2.aCCW ← e1	e2.bCCW ← e1
e2 e1	e2 e1	e2 e1	e2 e1
e1.aF = e2.bF	e1.aF = e2.aF	e1.bF = e2.bF	e1.bF = e2.aF
e1.aCCW ← e2	e1.aCCW ← e2	e1.bCCW ← e2	e1.bCCW ← e2
e2.bCW ← e1	e2.aCW ← e1	e2.bCW ← e1	e2.aCW ← e1

Figure 3.

The input to *SetWings* is two edges, *e1* and *e2*. The four columns distinguish the four cases that identify the vertex shared by the edges. Each column has two illustrated cases, depending on how the edges are shared. The cases are identified using the equality just under each picture. When a diagram is identified as describing this pair of edges, the assignments below the test are applied to the input edges. For example, suppose your input is two edges, *e1* and *e2*. If *e1.aVertex = e2.bVertex*, then you are in the second column. Then if *e1.aFace = e2.aFace*, you are in the bottom half of the second column, and you would set *e1.aCCWedge ← e2* and *e2.aCWedge ← e1*.

Consider next a useful routine called *NextFaceAroundVertex*. This takes a vertex, a face, and a direction, and returns the next face around that vertex in the given direction. Begin by finding any edge that is on the input face and contains that vertex. (Call this edge *e*.) As with the previous procedure, there are eight possible geometric configurations; identifying the one at hand allows you to determine the next face around the vertex. We assume a procedure called *FaceAcrossEdge*, which ac-

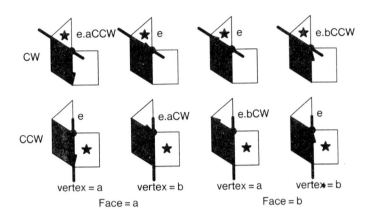

Figure 4.

cepts an edge and face, and returns the other face sharing that edge. (Such a procedure is easy; if the input face is *edge.aFace*, return *edge.bFace*, and vice versa.)

Figure 4 illustrates the logic behind *NextFaceAroundVertex*. In the diagram, the input vertex is common to all three shapes; it is marked with a circle. The input face is shaded in gray. Edge *e*, the edge you find on the face and vertex, is indicated with an arrow. In each portion of the figure, the desired face is marked with a star; the triangle is the next face clockwise, and the rectangle is the next face counterclockwise. In each case, we return the face across an edge with respect to the input face; the correct edge to use is shown in bold. In four cases, that edge is just *e*; the other four cases each use one of the wings of *e*. The legends refer to the position of the passed-in vertex and face with respect to *e*. Each case is marked with the name of the edged used to find the next face, opposite the input face; this edge is marked in bold.

For example, suppose you are given *inputFace* and *inputVertex* and the direction *clockwise*. Since clockwise was specified, you know you care about the upper row of the chart. You search the vertex or face for an edge *e* on that vertex and face. Now, find on which side of *e* lies *inputFace*; suppose *inputFace* = *e.bFace*, which is the situation for the two rightmost columns. To distinguish now between the two rightmost entries on the top row, find which vertex of *e* is *inputVertex*; suppose *e.bVertex* = *inputVertex*. Then you are in the rightmost column of the

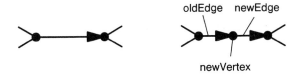

oldEdge   newEdge

newVertex

Figure 5.

top row, or the upper right corner, and you would call *FaceAcrossEdge* (*e.bCCWedge*, *inputFace*) to find and return the new face.

Consider next the basic operations when modifying a winged-edge model: These typically are known as *Euler operators*, since they preserve the Euler characteristic number of the model. One of the basic Euler operators is *SplitEdge*, which simply inserts a new vertex into a single edge, splitting it in two, as shown in Fig. 5.

I say *simply* advisedly, since finding the proper sequence in which to move the pointers can be a little tricky to get right. Part of the problem is that the data structure I described before has a lot of redundancy, so there are many pointers to move. As with the linked-list example, you have to make sure you move your pointers in the right order or you will end up with disaster. Figure 6 shows the order of interconnect of the links. The diagram follows Fig. 5; the bold edge and vertex on the right side are the new elements. A * indicates that a copy of the indicated edge

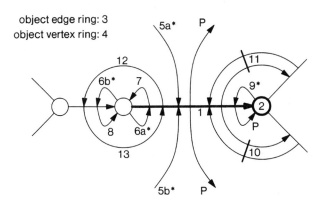

Figure 6.

is created (but not the data to which it points). The links marked with a P are inherited from the input (or parent) edge.

Step 1: Create the new edge and its data structures.

Step 2: Create the new vertex and its data structures.

Step 3: Hook the edge into the object edge ring.

Step 4: Hook the vertex into the object vertex ring.

Step 5: Hook the new edge into the edge rings for both faces.

Step 6: Point the new vertex at the two edges.

Step 7: Set up the starting vertex of the new edge.

Step 8: Direct the old edge to the new vertex.

Step 9: Hook back the old *bVertex* into the new edge.

Step 10: Connect the *aCW* wings.

Step 11: Connect the *bCCW* wings.

Step 12: Connect the back wings of the new edge to the old edge.

Step 13: Connect the front wings of the old edge to the new edge.

Another common operation is *RemoveEdge*. This routine accepts an edge as input, and removes that edge, merging the two faces that share it, Figure 7 shows the order for setting the links.

Step 1: Delete the pointer from vertex a to the edge.

Step 2: Delete the pointer from vertex b to the edge.

Step 3: Repoint all edges pointing to face b to point to face a.

Step 4: Build the new edge ring for face a.

Step 5: Link the old wings on *aVertex*.

Step 6: Link the old wings on *bVertex*.

Step 7: Delete *bFace* from object.

Step 8: Delete edge from object.

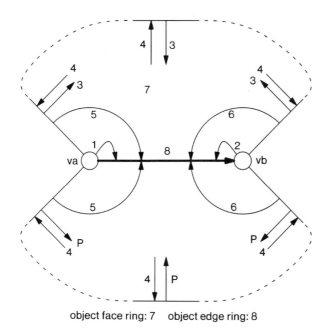

object face ring: 7   object edge ring: 8

Figure 7.

The opposite operation is *InsertBridge*, which takes two vertices as inputs and builds a new edge between them. In Fig. 8, the edge is directed from v1 to v2. A * indicates that a copy of the indicated edge is created (but not the data to which it points). The new edge is shown in bold. Links labeled with P are inherited from the input (or parent) configuration.

Step 1: Create the new edge.

Step 2: Add the new edge to the object's edge ring.

Step 3: Create the new face.

Step 4: Add the new face to the object's face ring.

Step 5: Assign the first vertex to the new edge's tail.

Step 6: Assign the second vertex to the new edge's head.

Step 7: Insert the new edge into the edge list at the head vertex.

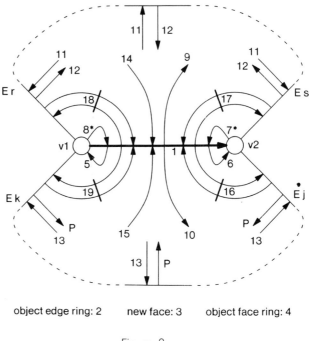

object edge ring: 2   new face: 3   object face ring: 4

Figure 8.

Step 8: Insert the new edge into the edge list at the tail vertex.

Step 9: Link the new edge to the new face.

Step 10: Link the new edge to the old face.

Step 11: Build the edge ring for the new face.

Step 12: Set the edges around the new face to point to the new face.

Step 13: Build the edge ring for the old face, and point the edges at the new face.

Step 14: Link the new face to the new edge.

Step 15: Link the old face to the new edge.

Step 16: Set the new edge's aCW wings.

Step 17: Set the new edge's $bCCW$ wings.

Step 18: Set the new edge's *bCW* wings.

Step 19: Set the new edge's *aCCW* wings.

Cleanup: Reclaim old face edge ring, and replace old face edge ring with new.

The information given in this gem certainly is not enough to implement an entire library; I have provided only some signposts around what I found to be the most twisting parts of the road. For more information on winged-edge data structures and their use, please consult the references.

QUADTREE / OCTREE-TO-BOUNDARY CONVERSION

Claudio Montani and Roberto Scopigno
Consiglio Nazionale delle Ricerche
Pisa, Italy

Introduction

Numerous and widely differentiated are the coding schemes proposed for the representation and manipulation of two-dimensional and three-dimensional spatial information: from analytical to vectorial, from raster to cellular or hierarchical, from parametric to algebraic. Each of these representation schemes presents peculiar characteristics with reference to the storage costs, the efficiency of the algorithms, the simplicity of the data manipulation, and so on. For these reasons, it is common to use multiple data representation schemes to fulfil the required space–time efficiency. The quest for efficient scheme conversion algorithms always has been a central theme in the problem of the representation of spatial data.

An algorithm for the conversion from hierarchical representation (quadtree or octree) (Samet *et al.*, 1988, 1990) to boundary is presented in this gem. The algorithm returns the boundary of the represented objects in terms of a list of polygon borders (2D case) or a list of faces (3D case). The proposed approach can be applied easily to raster or voxel representation, too.

The algorithm computes the boundary of the represented regions (or faces), taking into account possible holes, and requires only one complete visit of the hierarchical structure. The hierarchical structure is visited with a simple depth-first criterion, and more complex neighbor-finding techniques (Samet, 1982) are not requested (Dyer, 1980); this characteristic made it possible to apply this conversion algorithm on both pointer and pointerless QT/OT (Gargantini, 1982a, 1982b), with the same efficiency. The algorithm makes use of a two-step approach: It first converts

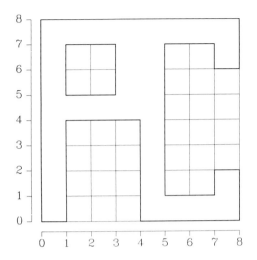

Figure 1.   A simple example of 2D drawing.

the hierarchical structure in a raster-based temporary data structure, the Parallel Connected Stripes (PCS) (Montani, 1984); then the boundary of the represented regions is reconstructed by working on the PCS representation. This representation made it possible to reconstruct efficiently the maximal connected polygonal borders/regions that constitute a boundary representation of the original hierarchical data. The polygonal borders are returned in the common 4-directions Freeman's chains (Freeman, 1974); the algorithm returns clockwise boundaries of the represented regions or objects and counterclockwise boundaries of the holes.

The PCS Representation Scheme

Figure 2 shows the PCS representation (Montani, 1984) for the regions of the binary map of Fig. 1. The original 2D space is subdivided into horizontal *stripes* of thickness equal to the step size of the reference grid (for simplicity's sake, the step size being 1 in our examples); the intersection of each stripe with the regions of the map generates a set of rectangular *substripes* corresponding to the part of the regions internal to the stripe.

Each stripe can be described by storing its ordinate (the ordinate of the lower side), the number of substripes, and the list of the abscissas of the

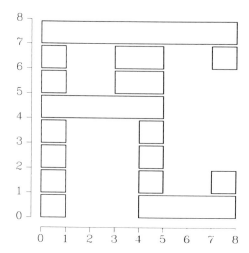

Figure 2.   The PCS representation of the example in Fig. 1.

Table I.   Numerical representation of the PCS data structure for the example in Fig. 2.

Stripe ordinate	# substripes	substripe 1		substripe 2		substripe 3	
		west	east	west	east	west	east
7	1	0	8				
6	3	0	1	3	5	7	8
5	2	0	1	3	5		
4	1	0	5				
3	2	0	1	4	5		
2	2	0	1	4	5		
1	3	0	1	4	5	7	8
0	2	0	1	4	8		

west and east sides of each substripe. Table I shows this information for the example of Fig. 2.

PCS-to-Boundary Conversion

The conversion from PCS representation to boundary is very simple. (Actually, the algorithm returns 4-directions Freeman's chains (Freeman, 1974).) It is possible to *walk* from one substripe of y ordinate to one of

$y + 1$ or $y - 1$ ordinate only if these are *connected* (i.e., have one horizontal side or part of it in common); it is possible to *walk* from one substripe of y ordinate to another of the same ordinate only if there is a substripe of $y + 1$ or $y - 1$ ordinate connecting them.

The algorithm consists of two steps: a first step in which a starting point for the chain is searched for (*PCS_To_Chain* procedure) and a second step in which the chain is constructed *walking* through the stripes (*Bottom_Up* and *Top_Down* procedures). The first step is repeated until all of the outer boundaries (or holes) of the data structure have been detected. To avoid endless reconstruction, each substripe side already considered in the conversion process is marked.

The *PCS_To_Chain* procedure (Fig. 3) searches for a substripe with at least one unmarked side. If the unmarked side is the west side of the S_y^i substripe (i.e., the ith substripe in the stripe of ordinate y), the point $(Absc(S_y^i, W), y)$ is chosen as the beginning point of the output chain, and the algorithm starts to reconstruct clockwise the boundary of a region, activating the *Bottom_Up* procedure (Fig. 4) on the substripe S_y^i.

```
PCS_to_Chain( )
    begin
        for y: integer ← YMIN, y ← y + 1 WHILE y < YMAX do
            for i: integer ← 0, i ← i + 1 WHILE i < Ss_Num(y) do
                begin
                    if Check_Mark(Sᵢy, W) = FALSE then
                        begin
                            Init_Chain(Absc(Sᵢy, W), y);
                            Bottom_Up(Sᵢy);
                            Display_Chain( );
                        end;
                    else if Check_Mark(Sᵢy, E) = FALSE then
                        begin
                            Init_Chain(Absc(Sᵢy, E), y + 1);
                            Top_Down(Sᵢy);
                            Display_Chain( );
                        end;
                endloop;
    end PCS_to_Chain;
```

Figure 3. *PCS_to_Chain* procedure.

```
Bottom_Up(S^i_y)
    begin
        if Check_Mark(S^i_y, W) = FALSE then
            begin
Fig. 6a         Add_Link(1,'1');
                Mark(S^i_y, W);
                for k: integer ← 0, k ← k + 1 while k < Ss_Num(y + 1) do
                    if (Absc(S^i_y, W) < Absc(s^k_{y+1}, E)) and
                            (Absc(S^i_y, E) > Absc(S^k_{y+1}, W)) do
                        begin
                            p ← Absc(S^k_{y+1}, W);
                            if Absc(S^i_y, W) ≤ p then
                                begin
Fig. 6b/c                       Add_Link(p-Absc(S^i_y, W),'0');
                                    Bottom_Up(S^k_{y+1});
                                    return;
                                end;
                            else if (i = 0) or (Absc(S^{i-1}_y, E) ≤ p) then
                                begin
Fig. 6g                         Add_Link(Absc(S^i_y, W) − p,'2');
                                    Bottom_Up(S^k_{y+1});
                                    return;
                                end;
                            else
                                begin
Fig. 6f                         Add_Link(Absc(S^i_y, W) − Absc(S^{i-1}_y, E),'2');
                                    Top_Down(S^{i-1}_y);
                                    return;
                                end;
                        end;
Fig. 6e         Add_Link(Absc(S^i_y, E) − Absc(S^i_y, W),'0');
                Top_Down(S^i_y);
            end;
    end Bottom_Up;
```

Figure 4. *Bottom_Up* procedure.

Alternatively, if the west side of the substripe is marked and the east side is not, we indicate with $(Absc(S_y^i, E), y + 1)$ the beginning point of the output chain and go on to reconstruct counterclockwise the boundary of a hole activating the *Top_Down* procedure (Fig. 5) on S_y^i. With $Absc(S_y^i, P)$, we indicate the abscissa of the P side (west or east) of the S_y^i substripe.

The certainty in considering that the first case deals only with the outer frontier of a region, and the second only with holes, holds because:

(a) the starting point is searched from the bottom upwards and from left to right, and

(b) by definition of the PCS, the non-empty space is on the right of each west side (i.e., the *inside* of a region), while the empty space is on the right of the east sides.

The different directions (clockwise and counterclockwise) of the chains describing the outer boundaries or the holes of the regions are not obtained by adopting different procedures or inverting the chains returned, but, conversely, using the same algorithm that follows the sides and the bases of the substripes, which always leaves the *inside* of the regions to the right and the *outside* to the left.

The recursive procedure *Bottom_Up* is invoked on a substripe S_y^i; it adds an upward vertical link to the current chain and then searches in the stripe of ordinate $y + 1$ (scanning from left to right) for a substripe top-connected to S_y^i.

If such a substripe (S_{y+1}^k) exists and

$$Absc\left(S_y^i, W\right) \le Absc\left(S_{y+1}^k, W\right),$$

the procedure (Figs. 6B and 6C) produces the leftward horizontal links associated to the upper side of S_y^i not adjacent to S_{y+1}^k; then, *Bottom_Up* invokes itself on the S_{y+1}^k substripe.

If, otherwise, the top-connected substripe S_{y+1}^k is in the opposite relation with S_y^i (Fig. 6D),

$$Absc\left(S_y^i, W\right) > Absc\left(S_{y+1}^k, W\right),$$

the procedure analyzes the position of the $(i - 1)$th substripe of the ordinate y. In the case of Fig. 6F, *Bottom_Up* returns a set of leftward horizontal links and then it activates *Top_Down* on the substripe S_y^{i-1}.

Top_Down(S_y^i)
   begin
      if Check_Mark(S_y^i, E) = FALSE **then**
         begin

Fig. 7a
           Add_Link(1,'3');
           Mark(S_y^i, E);
           for k: **integer** $\leftarrow$ Ss_Num(y − 1) − 1, k $\leftarrow$ k − 1 **while** k $\geq$ 0 **do**
             if (Absc(S_y^i, W) < Absc(S_{y-1}^k, E)) **and**
                    (Absc(S_y^i, E) > Absc(S_{y-1}^k, W)) **do**
               begin
                  p $\leftarrow$ Absc(S_{y-1}^k,E);
                  if Absc(S_y^i, E) $\geq$ p **then**
                    begin

Fig. 7b/c
                      Add_Link(Absc(S_y^i, E) − p,'2');
                      Top_Down(S_{y-1}^k);
                      return;
                  end;
                else if (i = Ss_Num(y) − 1) **or**
                      (Absc(S_y^{i+1}, W) $\geq$ p) **then**
                  begin

Fig. 7g
                      Add_Link(p-Absc(S_y^i, E),'0');
                      Top_down(S_{y-1}^k);
                      return;
                  end;
                else
                  begin

Fig. 7f
                      Add_Link(Absc(S_y^{i+1}, W) − Absc(S_y^i, E),'0');
                      Bottom_Up(s_y^{i+1});
                      return;
                  end;
              end;

Fig. 7e
           Add_Link(Absc(S_y^i, E) − Absc(S_y^i, W),'2');
           Bottom_Up(S_y^i);
        end;
     end Top_Down;

Figure 5. *Top_Down* procedure.

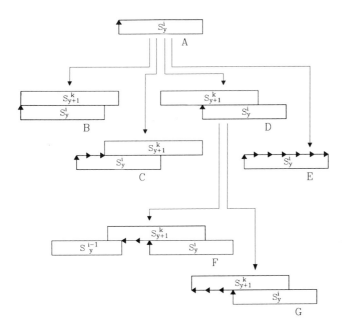

Figure 6. *Bottom_Up* procedure: possible situations during the bottom-up boundary reconstruction.

Conversely, as in Fig. 6G, *Bottom_Up* invokes itself on the S_{y+1}^k substripe.

Finally, if a top-connected substripe S_{y+1}^k does not exist (Fig. 6E), the procedure adds to the output chain $Absc(S_y^i, W) - Absc(S_y^i, E)$ rightward horizontal links and invokes *Top_Down* on the same substripe.

Similarly, changing appropriately the terms and directions of movement, the *Top_Down* procedure (Fig. 7) can be described. Table II shows the Freeman chains produced by the application of the algorithm to the example of Fig. 2. It also shows which procedure has produced the links in the chains to give a clearer idea of the conversion process.

The pseudo-code procedures of Figs. 3, 4, and 5 make use of the following simple functions:

Ss_Num(y): returns the number of substripes belonging to the stripe of ordinate y;

Absc(S_y^i, P): returns the abscissa of the P side (West or East) of the ith substripe of the stripe of ordinate y;

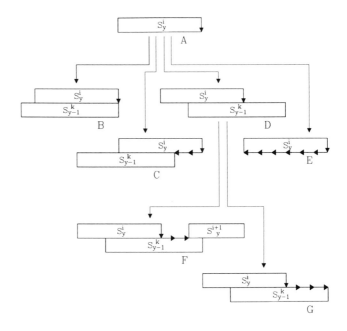

Figure 7. *Top_Down* procedure: possible situations during the top-down boundary reconstruction.

Mark(S_y^i, P): marks the P side (west or east) of the substripe S_y^i;

Check_Mark(S_y^i, P): returns *false* if the P side of the substripe S_y^i is marked, *true* otherwise;

Init_Chain(x, y): initializes a new Freeman chain with starting point (x, y);

Add_Link(n, t): adds to the current chain n links (possibly none) of type t (being t in the range $\{0, 1, 2, 3\}$);

Return_Chain$()$: returns the constructed Freeman chain; the effective action is implementation-dependent: the returned chain actually can be displayed or stored.

It is worthwhile to note that the algorithm returns clockwise boundaries of the regions and counterclockwise boundaries of the holes. This characteristic is found to be very important for the correct management and subsequent processing of returned information.

Table 2. Applying the PCS-to-chains conversion algorithm to the example of Fig. 2.

Starting Point	Boundary Type	Procedure	Links
(0, 0)	Outer	Bottom_Up	1 1 1 1 1 1 1 1 0 0 0 0 0 0 0 0
		Top_Down	3 3 2
		Bottom_Up	1 2 2
		Top_Down	3 3 3 3 3 3 0 0
		Bottom_Up	1 0
		Top_Down	3 3 2 2 2 2
		Bottom_Up	1 1 1 1 2 2
		Top_Down	3 3 3 3 2
		Bottom_Up	**stop**
(1, 6)	Hole	Top_Down	3 0 0
		Bottom_Up	1 1 2 2
		Top_Down	3 **stop**

Because the horizontal links of the output chains are produced as connections between two vertical links, the computational complexity of the *PCS_To_Chain* algorithm is proportional to the number of substripes of the PCS data structure rather than to the perimeter of the regions. In real cases, the search for a top-connected or bottom-connected substripe is proportional to the number of distinct regions and holes of the map.

Quadtree-to-Boundary Conversion

The *Quadtree-to-Boundary* conversion is realized by first applying a *Quadtree-to-PCS* conversion and then reconstructing the boundary of the represented regions by using the former *PCS-to-Chain* procedure.

The recursive procedure *Quadtree-to-PCS* (Fig. 8) here is defined for the binary pointer-based quadtree, and can be extended easily to the more general case of n-level pointer or pointerless quadtree. The parameters of the *Quadtree-to-PCS* procedure are the pointer Q to the quadtree, the *width* of the space $2^n * 2^n$ of definition of the quadtree ($width = 2^n$), and the coordinate x, y of the lower left corner of the

```
Quadtree_to_PCS (Q, width, x, y)
    begin
        if Node_Type(Q) = BLACK then
            for i: integer ← 0, i ← i + 1, while i < width do
                begin
                    Side_Insert (x, y + i);
                    Side_Insert (x + width, y + i);
                end;
        else if Node_Type (Q) = GRAY then
            begin
                hw = width / 2;
                Quadtree_to_PCS (Son(Q, NW), hw, x, y + hw);
                Quadtree_to_PCS (Son(Q, NE), hw, x + hw, y + hw);
                Quadtree_to_PCS (Son(Q, SW), hw, x, y);
                Quadtree_to_PCS (Son(Q, SE), hw, x + hw, y);
            end;
    end Quadtree_to_PCS;
```

Figure 8.   *Quadtree_to_PCS* procedure.

definition space with respect to a global coordinate space. The procedure visits the quadtree and, for each *black* node, inserts in the PCS data structure the set of substripes corresponding to the node. For each node at level i in the quadtree, 2^{n-i} substripes of length 2^{n-i} will be inserted in the PCS.

The following simple functions are used in the pseudo-code description of *Quadtree-to-PCS* procedure:

Node_Type (Q): returns the type (Black, White, or Gray) of the node Q;

Side_Insert (x, y): inserts in the stripe y of the PCS data structure a substripe side with abscissa x; the sides are inserted into stripe y in ascending order with respect to the abscissa value. If a side with the same x value is contained already in the PCS, then the new side is not inserted and the old one is deleted; in this way, two substripes with a side in common are unified in a single one;

Son(Q, P): returns the pointer to the P son (with P in {NW, NE, SW, SE}) of the Q node.

The procedure *Quadtree-to-PCS* returns a PCS data structure in which a list of sides is associated to each stripe, ordered by increasing abscissa value. By definition, the odd sides in the list are west sides of substripes, while the even are east sides; moreover, by definition of the procedure *Side_Insert*, each couple of successive odd and even sides in each stripe individuates one of the maximal length substripes obtained by intersecting the area described by the quadtree with that stripe. Figure 9

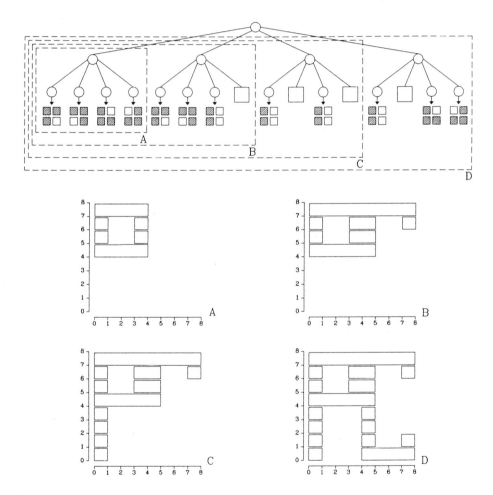

Figure 9. The making of the PCS data structure during the depth-first visit of the quadtree.

shows the conversion steps required to convert the quadtree representing the regions of the example in Fig. 1.

The complexity of the *Quadtree-to-PCS* algorithm simply is proportional to the number of black nodes in the quadtree.

Octree-to-Boundary Conversion

To introduce the three dimensional extension of the preceding algorithms, the *Octree-to-Boundary* conversion algorithm, let us describe how to convert a simple octree composed of one black node only (Fig. 10); let the width of the node be 2^n. We define six different PCSs, the first couple representing the planes $X = 0$ and $X = 2^n$ parallel to the plane YZ; the second couple, $Z = 0$ and $Z = 2^n$ parallel to the plane XY; and the third couple, $Y = 0$ and $Y = 2^n$ parallel to the plane ZX. We then can convert the octree by defining the six PCSs representing the six faces of the root black node. Once the six PCSs are constructed, it is possible to apply the *PCS-to-Chain* procedure to each of them and, therefore, obtain

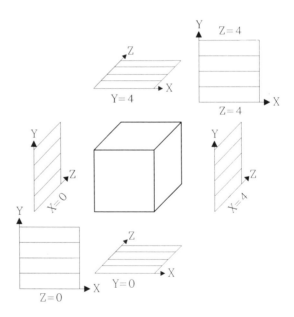

Figure 10.   Converting a Black node of an octree into six PCS data structures.

```
Octree_to_PCS(Q, width, x, y, z)
    begin
        if Node_Type(Q) = BLACK then
            for i: integer ← 0, i ← i + 1, while i < width do
                begin
                    Side_Insert_XY(z, x, y + i);
                    Side_Insert_XY(z, x + width, y + i);
                    Side_Insert_XY(z + width, x, y + i);
                    Side_Insert_XY(z + width, x + width, y + i);
                    Side_Insert_ZY(x, z, y + i);
                    Side_Insert_ZY(x, z + width, y + i);
                    Side_Insert_ZY(z + width, z, y + i);
                    Side_Insert_ZY(x + width, z + width, y + i);
                    Side_Insert_XZ(y, x, z + i);
                    Side_Insert_XZ(y, x + width, z + i);
                    Side_Insert_XZ(y + width, x, z + i);
                    Side_Insert_XZ(y + width, x + width, z + i);
                end;
        else if Node_Type(Q) = GRAY then
            begin
                hw = width / 2;
                Octree_to_PCS(Son(Q, FNW), hw, x, y + hw, z);
                Octree_to_PCS(Son(Q, FNE), hw, x + hw, y + hw, z);
                Octree_to_PCS(Son(Q, FSW), hw, x, y, z);
                Octree_to_PCS(Son(Q, FSE), hw, x + hw, y, z);
                Octree_to_PCS(Son(Q, BNW), hw, x, y + hw, z + hw);
                Octree_to_PCS(Son(Q, BNE), hw, x + hw, y + hw, z + hw);
                Octree_to_PCS(Son(Q, BSW), hw, x, y, z + hw);
                Octree_to_PCS(Son(Q, BSE), hw, x + hw, y, z + hw);
            end;
    end Quadtree_to_PCS;
```

Figure 11. *Octree_to_PCS* procedure.

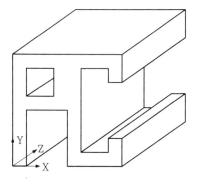

Figure 12. A 3D example.

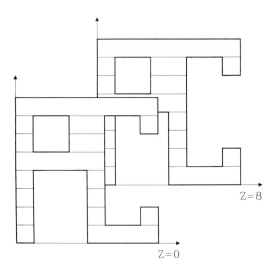

Figure 13. The PCS data structures for the *XY* faces of the example.

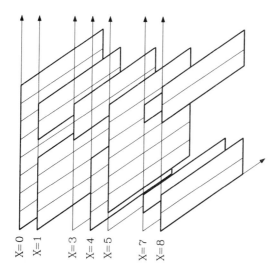

X=0 X=1 X=3 X=4 X=5 X=7 X=8

Figure 14.   The PCS data structures for the *YZ* faces of the example.

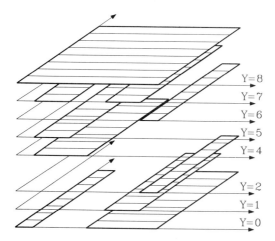

Y=8
Y=7
Y=6
Y=5
Y=4
Y=2
Y=1
Y=0

Figure 15.   The PCS data structures for the *XZ* faces of the example.

the Freeman encoded description of the polygonal faces that bound the polyhedrical volume represented by the octree.

The former approach is generalized in the *Octree-to-PCS* procedure in Fig. 11. For each black node of the octree, the six faces are converted in substripes and inserted into six PCSs, each of them associated to the plane on which the faces of the node lie. The procedure makes use of the following simple functions:

Side_Insert_XY (z, x, y): inserts a substripe side of y ordinate and x abscissa in the PCS that represents the plane $Z = z$;

Side_Insert_ZY (x, z, y): inserts a substripe side having ordinate y and abscissa z in the PCS that represents the plane $X = x$;

Side_Insert_XZ (y, x, z): inserts a substripe side having ordinate z and abscissa x in the PCS that represents the plane $Y = y$.

Analogously to the *Side_Insert* procedure described for the *Quadtree-to-Boundary* conversion algorithm, in each of the preceding routines, couples of sides with identical coordinates are deleted from the PCS data structure. The conversion of the obtained set of PCSs into Freeman chains is the same as the 2D case.

In Figs. 13–15 are the three sets of faces returned by the algorithm when applied to the example of Fig. 12.

IV.8

THREE-DIMENSIONAL HOMOGENEOUS CLIPPING OF TRIANGLE STRIPS

Patrick-Gilles Maillot
Sun Microsystems, Inc.
Mountain View, California

Introduction

Triangle strips are among the *complex* primitives handled by most 3D graphics software packages. One of the most expensive operations in graphics is to perform clipping. This gem presents a solution that takes into account the specific organization of the list of points provided with a triangle strip to achieve up to 50,000 + triangle clippings per second in software.

Some of the principles discussed here can be applied to other, simpler graphic structures, such as multi-bounded polygons, to improve the efficiency of standard clipping methods. The same principles also have been applied to quadrilateral mesh clipping.

One easy way of optimizing a graphics pipeline operation is to keep the primitive (and its logic) all along the graphics pipeline. Unfortunately, some operations of the pipeline can modify, or break, the logical structure of the initial primitive. This typically is the case of clipping, where a triangle can be changed (clipped) into a nine-sided polygon after the clipping operation against six planes.

This gem proposes a method to clip triangle strips in 3D homogeneous coordinates, in the general case of a non-normalized clipping volume, accepting a triangle strip structure at the input of the clipping process, and giving a triangle strip structure at the output.

Data Study

While described by *a list of points*, triangle strips also have a logical organization that should be considered during the clipping step. A trian-

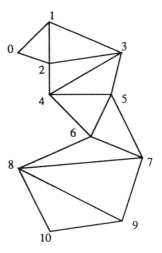

Figure 1. A triangle strip.

gle strip consists of an ordered list of n vertices $[v_0, v_1, \ldots, v_{n-1}]$ that define a sequence of $n - 2$ triangles. The triangles in the strip share common edges. Thus, the $k\,th$ triangle is formed of vertices $k, k + 1,$ $k + 2$. Figure 1 is a pictorial example of a triangle strip.

Algorithm Study

We propose clipping the primitives using a method derived from the Sutherland–Hodgman algorithm (1974). This means that the clipping calculations will be limited to determining intersections with one clipping plane at a time, separating the primitive into two regions: the *inside* and the *outside*. These calculations will be repeated as many times as needed to scan all the enabled clipping planes.

   This method involves a lot of computations as well as memory operations. However, since we operate in a three-dimensional space, and the vertices can have both normal and color information, it seems to be the most efficient. Each intersection (computed only when needed) is based on the parametric equation of the edge from one vertex to another:

$$P \leftarrow \lambda P_2 + (1 - \lambda)P_1,$$
$$\lambda \in [0.0, 1.0].$$

The value of λ is used to compute the intersection vertex coordinates (P), and also can be used to interpolate linearly the color and normal data generally associated with the intersection vertex.

The intersection, in the case of a line segment, has to be evaluated only when the endpoints of that line lie in opposite regions. If a bit is assigned to each point, with a 1 meaning *lies outside* and a 0 meaning *lies inside*, then the intersection will be computed only when (bit[P_i] $\otimes$ bit[P_{i+1}]) is set, meaning that one point lies outside and the other one lies inside the clipping region. If both bits are set, that means the entire line segment is outside the clipping region. The entire line segment is inside the clipping region when both bits are equal to 0. This approach, presented in Maillot's thesis (1986), offers the advantage of using fast operations to check for trivial cases, and provides a way to keep intermediate results available for the next point. In the case of a triangle, we can take advantage of three points at a time.

A triangle strip is (obviously) composed of triangles. Each triangle can be considered separately for the intersection calculations. However, the implementation of the clipping algorithm should provide a way to avoid multiple equivalent calculations by taking advantage of the logical organization of the vertices. As a triangle is composed of three points, and the clipping process is organized in n steps, n being the number of enabled clip planes, each point of the triangle can be *in* or *out* of the interior half space determined by the current clipping plane. This produces eight different situations to examine when computing the clipped result of a triangle with a given clipping plane. The drawings of Fig. 2 show the different cases and the resulting output that has to be generated by the clipper to maintain the logical organization of the triangle strip. The triangle strip clipping algorithm can generate some triangles with an area of zero. By doing this, the triangle strip structure can be maintained even when a triangle degenerates into a quad after clipping with a clip-plane.

There are special cases when clipping a triangle with clipping codes equal to 011, or 110. The code 011 indicates that the current triangle has its two first points outside, and the third point of the triangle is inside the clipping boundary. In this particular case, a new triangle strip should be issued. Even in the case of a single triangle strip input, it is possible to have more than one triangle strip after the clipping operation. Figure 3 explains such a situation.

There is a way, however, to avoid the multiple triangle strips at the clipper output, and this helps to simplify the triangle strip rendering. The

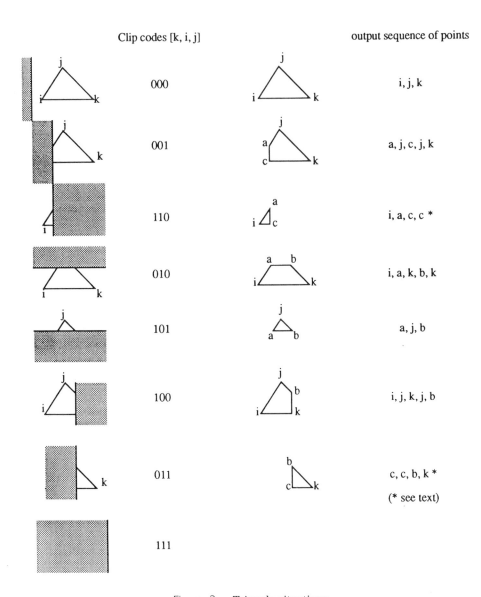

Figure 2. Triangle situations.

222

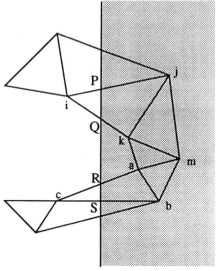

...

i, j, k: clipping code 110, generates i, P, Q
j, k, m: clipping code 111, culled
k, m, a: clipping code 111, culled
m, a, b: clipping code 111, culled
a, b, c: clipping code 011, generates R, S, c

...

A new triangle should be issued when clipping a, b, c

Figure 3. Multiple triangle strips created by the clipping operation. A new triangle should be issued when clipping a, b, c.

solution, proposed in the case presented in Fig. 3, is to duplicate the points Q and R so that three degenerate triangles are issued to keep the logic of the original triangle strip. The implementation proposed in this gem takes advantage of this method. It should be noted that this can be applied only when the rendering stage, further *down* in the graphics pipeline, knows how to deal with degenerate triangles.

Memory Considerations

The standard clipping algorithm proposed by Sutherland–Hodgman implies a lot of memory operations. A detailed introduction to the principle of the algorithm is presented in Foley *et al.* (1990), showing the different steps used to clip a polygon in 2D or 3D. Although it is mentioned that the reentrant characteristic of the original algorithm avoids the need for intermediate storage, the cost implied in stack operations and recursive calls probably is not well-suited in the case of a software implementation with large data structures.

While keeping the same general intersection principles, this gem proposes a different approach, necessitating intermediate storage, but limiting the number of calls to the inner portions of the clipping algorithm to the number of active clipping planes. The algorithm only propagates pointers to points, and not the points themselves, from one stage of the clipper to the next stage, thus avoiding expensive memory copy operations.

Homogeneous Clipping Against a Non-Normalized Clipping Volume

Most of the algorithms presented in the literature and proposing a clipping in homogeneous coordinates only deal with a normalized clipping volume. In fact, it may be more interesting for a software implementation of a graphics pipeline to perform all the transformations using a single matrix, and then perform the clipping against a clip-volume in homogeneous device coordinates. The graphics pipeline is simplified in terms of number steps to perform, but the clipping operation needs more attention.

Clipping against a normalized clip volume means that the clip volume is $[-1, 1] \times [-1, 1] \times [0, 1]$. In this gem, the clipping operation uses a general, non-normalized, clipping volume $[x\min, x\max] \times [y\min, y\max] \times [z\min, z\max]$. In a homogeneous coordinates system, the basic clipping equation is:

$$-w \leq c \leq w,$$

with $w > 0$, and c the value of the x, y, or z coordinate.

In the case of a non-normalized clipping volume, the basic clipping equation becomes:

$$w * x\min \leq x \leq w * x\max,$$

$$w * y\min \leq y \leq w * y\max,$$

$$w * z\min \leq z \leq w * z\max,$$

with $w > 0$.

Detailed explanations about clipping against a nonuniform clipping volume, as well as a general description of the clipping problems, can be found in Maillot's thesis (1986).

Implementation

The algorithm proposed here supports the case where the w components of the vertices of the triangle strip are positive. Clipping for negative w's requires changing the clipping equation (an exercise left to the reader), and supporting lines with end vertices having both positive and negative w's requires two passes by the clipping algorithm to render both positive and negative sections, one for each clipping equation. Figure 4 shows the result of clipping a single triangle with coordinates $(1, 0, 0, 1)$, $(0, 1, 0, 1)$, and $(0, 0, 1, 1)$, compared to a triangle with coordinates $(1, 0, 0, 1)$, $(0, 1, 0, -1)$, and $(0, 0, 1, -1)$.

To implement the clipping algorithm for triangle strips, we define the following data structures:

```
H_point: record [
        coords: array[0..3] of real;
];
```

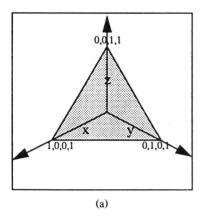
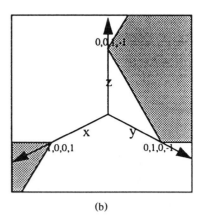

(a)   (b)

Figure 4. Effect of positive and negative w components: (a) all w components are positive; (b) w components are positive and negative.

This structure holds a single homogeneous point with coordinates x, y, z, and w.

```
H_list: record [
    num_hpoints: integer;
    hpoint: array[] of H_point;
];
```

This structure holds a list of homogeneous points with coordinates x, y, z, and w.

```
Clip_ctx: record [

    cl_plane: array[0..5] of real;

    cl_tbdone: char;

    pointers_bucket_0: array[] of array[] of H_point;

    integer pointers_bucket_0_max;

    pointers_bucket_1: array[] of array[] of H_point;

    pointers_bucket_1_max: integer;

    hpoints_bucket: array[] of H_point;

    hpoints_bucket_max: integer;

    hpoints_bucket_index: integer;

];
```

This structure holds the current state of the clipper. Storage is made for pointers to points, and intermediate values of different clipping parameters. *cl_plane*[] represents the six values of $x$min, $x$max, $y$min, $y$max, $z$min, $z$max of the clipping volume. *cl_tbdone* is composed of 6 bits; bit 0 is set if clipping has to be done on $x$min, bit 1 is assigned to $x$max, and so on, up to bit 5, assigned to the clip condition on $z$max.

The following is the pseudo-code for the clipping of a triangle strip. To simplify the presentation of the code, some portions appear in "⟨ ⟩" in the pseudo-code. These are related to memory management, making sure enough memory has been allocated, or ensuring the copy of data. Please refer to the actual C Implementation proposed in Appendix 2 for a complete description of the tasks to be performed.

The pseudo-code also makes reference to macros. These are used in the computation of intersections, or when moving pointers to points from one stage of the clipper to the other one. The C Implementation gives a complete description of these macros.

> *3D triangle strip clipper. A triangle strip is made of vertices logically organized in triangles (. . .). The first triangle is composed of the vertices 0, 1, and 2. The second triangle is represented by the vertices 1, 2, and 3, and so on until the last vertex.*
>
> *The triangle strip clipper clips the triangle strip against one to six boundaries organized in a [xmin, xmax, ymin, ymax, zmin, zmax] order. Each clip plane can be enabled / disabled by controlling the clip_ctx^ cl_tbdone [0..5] flags. Each flag affects the respective clip plane of clip_ctx^ cl_plane[0..5].*
>
> *As presented in the algorithm, a triangle strip outputs only one triangle strip. This is possible if degenerate triangles are acceptable.*
>
> *Notes:*
> *This basically is a Sutherland – Hodgman algorithm, but a nonre- ursive version. Some "shortcuts" have been employed in the in- tersection calculations in homogeneous coordinates.*

h3d_strip_clip(clip_ctx, in, out)
{

At init, set the previous stage pointers to the input points values.

    n_cur_s ← in^ num_hpoints;
    if clip_ctx^ pointers_bucket_0_max < (n_cur_s + 64) **then begin**
        ⟨Ensure memory for pointers_bucket_0⟩
    end;
    if clip_ctx^ pointers_bucket_1_max < (n_cur_s + 64) **then begin**
        ⟨Ensure memory for pointers_bucket_1⟩
    end;

```
cur_stage ← clip_ctx^ pointers_bucket_0;
for i: integer ← 0, i < n_cur_s, i ← i + 1 do
    cur_stage[i] ← &(in^ hpoints[i]);
endloop;
C ← clip_ctx^ hpoints_bucket;
clip_ctx^ hpoints_bucket_index ← 0;
```

For each of the clipping planes, clip (if necessary).
```
        for i: integer ← 0, i < 6 and n_cur_s > 2, i ← i + 1 do
        if (clip_ctx^ cl_tbdone ≫ i) & 1 then begin
        c ← i ≫ 1;
        ⟨Switch memory between current and previous⟩
        n_cur_s ← 0;
```

Start clipping of the previous stage, for the ith clip plane.
Output points go in the current_stage memory.
Process the first point of the triangle strip.

```
        clip_code ← 0;
        n ← 0;
        COMPUTE_INTER_3D(Q, Q_plan, 1)
```

Now, process the second point of the triangle strip.

```
        n ← 1;
        COMPUT_INTER_3D(R, R_plan, 2)
```

(Q, R) represents the first line segment of the first triangle of
the triangle strip. Need to clip it as a line to ensure the first two points.
```
        n ← clip_code ≫ 1;
        select n from
            0: begin      Q and R inside
               POINT_COPY(Q)
               POINT_COPY(R)
               end;
            1: begin      Q outside, R inside
               POINT_INTER_3D(Q, Q_plan, R, R_plan)
               POINT_COPY(R)
               end;
```

```
        2: begin      Q inside, R outside
           POINT_COPY(Q)
           POINT_INTER_3D(Q, Q plan, R, R plan)
           end;
        3:            Q and R outside
     endcase;
```

Process each subsequent point of the triangle strip.
P, Q, R form the (n − 2)ith triangle of the strip.

```
        for n: integer ← 2, n < n_pre_s, n ← n + 1 do
           clip_code ← clip_code ≫ 1;
           P ← Q;
           Q ← R;
           P_plan ← Q_plan;
           Q_plan ← R_plan;
           COMPUT_INTER_3D(R, R_plan, 2)
           if n_cur_max < (n_cur_s + 3) then begin
              ⟨Ensure that enough memory is available⟩
           end;
```

clip_code now has 3 bits that represent the "position" of the triangle in
respect to the clip boundary. 8 different cases can occur.

```
        select clip_code from
           0: begin          all inside
              POINT_COPY(R)
              end;
           1: begin          P outside, Q and R inside
              POINT_INTER_3D(R, R_plan, P, P_plan)
              POINT_COPY(Q)
              POINT_COPY(R)
              end;
           2: begin          P inside, Q outside and R inside
              POINT_COPY(R)
              POINT_INTER_3D(Q, Q_plan, R, R_plan)
              POINT_COPY(R)
              end;
           3: begin          P and Q outside, R inside
              POINT_INTER_3D(R, R_plan, P, P_plan)
              ⟨Duplicate the point just computed⟩
```

```
                    POINT_INTER_3D(Q, Q_plan, R, R_plan)
                    POINT_COPY(R)
                    end;
                4: begin            P and Q inside, R outside
                    POINT_INTER_3D(R, R_plan, P, P_plan)
                    POINT_COPY(Q)
                    POINT_INTER_3D(Q, Q_plan, R, R_plan)
                    end;
                5: begin            P outside, Q inside, R outside
                    POINT_INTER_3D(Q, Q_plan, R, R_plan)
                    end;
                6: begin P inside, Q and R outside
                    POINT_INTER_3D(R, R_plan, P, P_plan)
                    ⟨Duplicate the point just computed⟩
                    end;
                7:                  P, Q and R outside
            endcase;
            endloop;
            end;
        endloop;
```

The triangle strip has been clipped against all (enabled) clipping planes. "Copy" the result to the output.

```
                if n_cur_s > 2 then
                    begin
                        for i: integer ← 0, i < n_cur_s, i ← i + 1 do
                            out^ hpoints[i] ← *(cur_stage[i]);
                        endloop;
                        out^ num_hpoints ← n_cur_s;
                    end;
                else
                    out^ num_hpoints ← 0;
                return;
            };
```

Conclusion

This gem has presented a different approach to 3D homogeneous clipping of complex primitives. Most of the particularities presented here—reorganization of the Sutherland–Hodgman algorithm, intersection computations, nonuniform clipping volume, etc.—can be used in any 3D polygon clipping. The performance of the proposed algorithm for all clip planes enabled is better than 23,000 triangles (trivial acceptance or trivial reject) per second on a Sun-Sparc Station 330, with the C Implementation given in Appendix 2, and for triangle strips of 10 or more triangles. The efficiency of the clipping algorithm varies with the number of triangles per triangle strip. The worst case of the algorithm—one triangle per triangle strip—still clips at an honorable speed of 10,000 + triangles per second.

The specific case of single triangles should be optimized separately. An implementation limited to clipping against uniform volumes also gives better performances.

The method presented here also has been applied in the case of quadrilateral meshes. The clipping operation is performed one quad-mesh row at a time, and potentially can generate several quad-mesh rows at the output of the clipping algorithm. Because quads are composed of four points, the algorithm takes two points at a time, and the core of the clipping process necessitates 16 different cases.

IV.9

INTERPHONG SHADING

Nadia Magnenat Thalmann
University of Geneva
Geneva, Switzerland,

Daniel Thalmann
Swiss Federal Institute of Technology
Lausanne, Switzerland

and

Hong Tong Minh
University of Waterloo
Waterloo, Ontario, Canada

Overview

InterPhong shading is a modified version of the popular Phong shading. When applied to a facet-based object, it is able to give a rough or smooth appearance depending on the variation between the normals of the facets. For example, we may apply it to a sphere, a cube, or a cylinder. This varying shading also may be considered as a continuous model between faceted shading and Phong shading. This property is very important for shading objects obtained by shape interpolation between two different objects, such as a sphere and a cube. The InterPhong shading also has been used for rendering synthetic actors. In particular, it has been used for rendering Marilyn Monroe and Humphrey Bogart in the film, *Rendezvous à Montréal*.

Introduction

Since 1970, various illumination and shading models have been proposed, as described by several authors (Rogers, 1985; Lorif, 1986; Magnenat Thalmann and Thalmann, 1987a). Hall (1986) proposes a classification into three groups:

1. Incremental shading techniques and empirical illumination models.

2. Ray tracing and translational illumination models.

3. Analytical models and radiosity techniques.

232

In this Gem, we are concerned with the first kind of shading models. These models traditionally are implemented with scanline rendering systems and will be reviewed in the next section. It is evident that the better the results that an algorithm provides, the more expensive it is in terms of CPU time. However, the choice of shading techniques also is dependent on the shape of objects. For example, Phong shading is well adapted to spheres, and faceted shading is suitable for cubes. Now consider the transformation of a sphere into a cube using an in-between algorithm. What kind of shading model should be used to shade any in-between object? This gem tries to answer this question by introducing a new kind of shading dependent on the shape of objects. The new shading model, called the *InterPhong model*, also may be considered as a continuous model between faceted shading and Phong shading. One application of this algorithm is to shade faceted-based objects obtained from a general shape interpolation (Hong *et al.*, 1988). As objects change, their shading is changed automatically.

Review of Incremental and Empirical Shading Techniques

The first illumination model that took into account the three components of ambient, diffuse, and specular light was devised by Bui-Tuong Phong (1975). Intensity I in this model is given by:

$$I = I_{\mathbf{a}} + I_{\mathbf{d}} + I_{\mathbf{s}}, \tag{1}$$

where I_{a} is reflection due to ambient light, $I_{\mathbf{d}}$ is diffuse reflection, and $I_{\mathbf{s}}$ is specular reflection.

Diffuse reflection is defined as in Lambert's law, which means for m_{s} light sources:

$$I_{\mathrm{d}} = k_{\mathrm{d}} C_{\mathbf{s}} \sum_{j}^{m_{\mathrm{s}}} I_{lj} (N \cdot \mathbf{L_j}), \tag{2}$$

where k_{d} is the diffuse reflection coefficient, N is the unit surface normal, I_{lj} is the intensity of the jth source, C_{s} is the surface color, $\mathbf{L_j}$ is the vector in the direction of the jth light source, and m_s is the number of light sources.

Specular reflection is defined as:

$$I_s = k_s C_r \sum_j^{m_s} I_{l\,j} (N \cdot \mathbf{H_j})^n,\tag{3}$$

where k_s is the specular reflection coefficient and C_r is the reflective color surface. The exponent n depends on the surface and determines how glossy this surface is; $\mathbf{H_j}$ is the vector in the direction halfway between the observer and the jth light source.

Surface shading may be defined as the distribution of light over an illuminated surface. For each type of object model (set of polygons, algebraic surface, patches), shading can be calculated using the preceding reflection model. However, reflection models do not directly provide ways of calculating the complete shading of an object, but only the intensity of light as specific points. The shading techniques used depend on the type of object. For polygon meshes, three basic ways of shading objects have been developed—faceted shading, Gouraud shading, and Phong shading.

Faceted shading was first introduced by Bouknight (1970). It involves calculating a single intensity for each polygon. This implies the following assumptions:

1. The light source is at infinity.

2. The observer is at infinity.

3. The polygons are not an approximation of a curved surface.

The first two assumptions are required so that the dot products $N \cdot \mathbf{L_j}$ and $N \cdot \mathbf{H_j}$ are constant in the calculations of intensity. The third assumption is made because each polygonal facet of an object will have a slightly different intensity from its neighbors. This produces good results for a cube, but very poor ones for a sphere.

Gouraud (1971) introduced an intensity interpolation shading method that eliminates the discontinuities of constant shading. The principle of *Gouraud shading* is as follows:

1. For each vertex common to several polygons, the normal to each polygon is computed as a vector perpendicular to the plane of that polygon.

2. For each vertex, a unique normal is calculated by averaging the surface normals obtained previously.

3. Vertex intensities are calculated by using the vertex normals and a light model.

4. As each polygon has a different shading at each vertex, the shading at any point inside the polygon is found by linear interpolation of vertex intensities along each edge and then between edges along each scanline.

Bui-Tuong Phong (1972) has proposed a normal–vector interpolation shading method. This means that instead of interpolating intensities as in Gouraud shading, Phong interpolates the surface normal vector. With this approach, the shading of a point is computed from the orientation of the approximated normal. With Phong shading, a better approximation of the curvature of the surface is obtained, and highlights due to the simulation of specular reflection are rendered much better. However, the method requires more computation, since three normal components must be computed, rather than one shading value, and the vector at each point must be normalized before evaluating the shading function. The linear interpolation scheme used in the Phong algorithm to approximate the orientation of the normal does not guarantee a continuous first derivative of the shading function across an edge of a polygonal model. In particular, where there is an abrupt change in the orientation of two adjacent polygons along a common edge, the *Mach band effect* is possible. This means that a subjective brightness may be visible along this edge. The effect usually is much less visible in the Phong model than in the Gouraud model. However, Duff (1979) shows that Phong shading can produce worse Mach bands than Gouraud shading, notably for spheres and cylinders. Moreover, both techniques render concave polygons incorrectly. Duff has discovered another great problem in the computer animation of shaded objects with the Gouraud and Phong algorithms. If an object and its light source are rotated together in the image plane, the shading of the object can change contrary to expectations. This is due to the fact that the interpolation of intensities (or normals) is carried out using values on a scanline, and when objects and lights are rotated, the scanlines do not cut the edges at the same points. Duff proposes alleviating this problem by interpolating intensities (or normals) in a rotation-independent manner; he avoids the use of values by the use of an appropriate interpolator depending only on the vertices of the polygon.

InterPhong Shading

Faceted shading is the quickest and easiest of the shading techniques. It is more appropriate for rendering cubes than spheres. However, it is not realistic for perspective views and/or point light sources. One way of improving realism in this case is to recalculate the intensity at each pixel, because only the normal is constant at any point of a given facet, not the viewer direction and light direction. This process is almost as expensive as the Phong shading, although no interpolation across facets is performed. We call this type of shading *modified faceted shading*. This

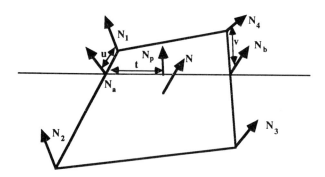

Figure 1. Normal interpolation.

shading is realistic for a cube, while Phong shading is a good way (in a facet-based environment) of rendering a sphere. Now consider the transformation of a sphere to a cube using an in-between algorithm. What kind of shading model should be used to shade any in-between object? Though we may decide that an object that is 50% sphere and 50% cube may be rendered using Phong shading, this is not true for a 99.9% cube and 0.1% sphere. We have to introduce a varying shading model between the faceted (or modified faceted) model and the Phong model. We call this the InterPhong model. To explain this model, consider, as shown in Fig. 1, a point P belonging to a facet with normal N. The interpolated normal N_p according to the Phong method is:

$$N_p = N_a + t(N_b - N_a),\tag{4}$$

$$N_a = N_1 + u(N_2 - N_1),$$

$$N_b = N_4 + v(N_3 - N_4),$$

with $\{t, u, v\} \in [0, 1]$.

We now replace N_p by a new value calculated as:

$$N_{p\text{new}} = N_p + f(N - N_p),\tag{5}$$

with

$$f = \left(|N - N_p| + \beta_1(2 - |N - N_p|)\right)\frac{\beta_2}{2}.\tag{6}$$

Several cases may be considered to explain the role of β_1 and β_2:

1. $\beta_1 = 0$. In this case, we have $f = \dfrac{|N - N_p|\beta_2}{2}$. The algorithm will decide to give a rough or smooth appearance depending on the variation

between the normals of the facets. (The polygon facet edges are left sharp or smoothed.) β_2 is a real positive number; when the tension β_2 is decreased, the characteristics of the Phong model are emphasized. Otherwise, when the tension β_2 is greater than 1, the characteristics of the faceted model are emphasized. β_2 is called the *shading tension*.

2. $\beta_1 = 1$. In this case, we have $f = \beta_2$. The user may select a value between 0 and 1 for the tension parameter β_2 to obtain an interpolated shading between faceted shading and Phong shading. For example, if $\beta_2 = 0.75$, we have 75% of faceted shading and 25% of Phong shading. For $\beta_2 = 1$, we have the faceted shading, and for $\beta_2 = 0$, standard Phong shading.

3. $0 < \beta_1 < 1$. This is a combination of the two previous cases. For example, if $\beta_2 = 0.25$, we obtain a shading with 25% of effects from the interpolation (between Phong shading and faceted shading) and 75% from the edge emphasizing process. (See first case.)

As β_1 is a measure of the dependence on the variation between the normals of the facets; we call it the *nonlocality tension*.

Analysis of the New Formula

The use of a new $N_{p\,new}$ calculated by Eq. (5) solves two problems:

1. The dependence of the *texture* of the display of a graphical object on the scanlines.

2. The undesirable smoothing of certain regions.

For example, consider the cube of Fig. 2; we observe that N_{p1} depends on N_1, N_2, and N_4, and N_{p2} depends on N_2, N_3, and N_4. This implies a kind of texture that varies depending on the scanned areas. Moreover, at the vertex S, the cube will be *rounded* and the common edges will be difficult to distinguish. The problems are solved by moving the normal N_p to the facet normal N, which is the *only true information*.

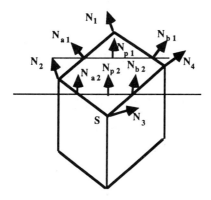

Figure 2.   Vertex dependence.

To simplify the explanations, consider the case with $\beta_1 = 0$ and $\beta_2 = 1$. We have:

$$\frac{N_{p\,\text{new}} - N_p = |N - N_p|(N - N_p)}{2}.\tag{7}$$

If the normal variations between the adjacent facets are small (smooth surfaces), as shown in Fig. 3, the normals N_p and/or N_p' should not be very different from N and/or N'.

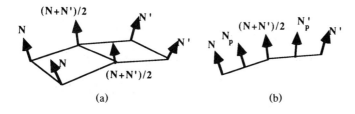

(a)   (b)

Figure 3.   Normals for adjacent facets: a) in 3D; b) in 2D.

This implies that

$$\frac{|N_{p\,new} - N_p| = |N - N_p|^2}{2} \rightarrow 0 \tag{8}$$

and

$$\frac{|N'_{p\,new} - N'_p| = |N' - N'_p|^2}{2} \rightarrow 0,$$

as $N \cong N_p$ (and $N' \cong N'_p$), $N_{p\,new} \rightarrow N_p$ (and $N'_{p\,new} \rightarrow N'_p$); the new shading model preserves the Phong characteristics.

For a cube, $|N - N_p|$ is not negligible and

$$N_{p\,new} = \frac{N_p + |N - N_p|(N - N_p)}{2}$$

is very near the original normal N. This means that the various adjacent facets will have different new normals, which emphasize the edges.

If we assume that all normals are normalized, the constant "2" in Eq. (6) comes from $|N - N_p| < |N| + |N_p| < 1 + 1 = 2$. This is the maximum correction allowed and corresponds to $N - N_p$.

From a performance point of view, as all norms in R^n are topologically equivalent, we may use $|N| = |N_x| + |N_y| + |N_z|$, which implies

- 3 absolute values and 2 additions for the norms,
- 3 subtractions for $N - N_p$,
- 1 multiplication and 1 division for $|N - N_p|(N - N_p)/2$
- 3 additions for $N_{p\,new} = N_p + |N - N_p|(N - N_p)/2$

This is an extra cost of 10 arithmetic operations and three absolute values.

Applications of InterPhong Shading

One possible application of InterPhong shading is the rendering of human faces. As it was noted in the film, *Rendez-vous à Montréal* (Magnenat Thalmann and Thalmann, 1987b), Phong shading is convenient for the face of a synthetic actress, but the result is too smooth for a synthetic actor. Fig. 4 (see color insert) shows various shadings for the face of a synthetic actor.

The InterPhong shading model may be considered as a continuous model between faceted shading and Phong shading. This property is very much important for shading objects obtained by shape interpolation between two different objects, such as a sphere and a cube.

Figure 5 (see back cover) shows an example of transformation of a sphere into a dodecahedron with a continuous shading interpolation from Phong shading to faceted shading (InterPhong shading).

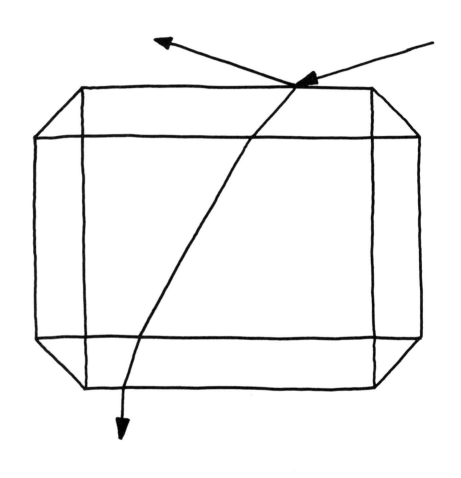

V

RAY TRACING

RAY TRACING

Ray tracing is one of the most popular techniques for high-fidelity image synthesis because of its wide variety of optical effects and its conceptual simplicity. First introduced to the realm of computer graphics by Appel [68], it was later extended into its now-familiar recursive form by Whitted, 1980. Since then, ray tracing has been widely used to generate images of striking realism, and continues to be a topic of vigorous research. Much of the appeal of ray tracing stems from its faithful simulation of basic geometrical optics. By tracing individual rays of light into a hypothetical 3D scene and obeying laws for refraction and reflection, the overall characteristics of transparent and reflective surfaces can be simulated. These characteristics remain the unmistakable hallmarks of ray-traced imagery.

In the context of more recent global illumination algorithms, ray tracing is taking on a new life as a powerful tool for solving subproblems. (Examples of this can be found in the following Part on the radiosity method). It is clear that ray tracing will have an important role to play for a long time, whether used directly for image synthesis or as the foundation for other algorithms. Its generality makes it an ideal research vehicle, lending itself to a panoply of essential graphics operations and optical effects.

The gems of this Part address methods for computing ray intersections with polyhedra, triangles, and tori, as well as large collections of such objects by use of object hierarchies and spatial subdivision. The last three gems discuss techniques for use in shadow calculations and in the simulation of translucent objects, two important effects in ray tracing's wide repertoire.

V. I

FAST RAY – CONVEX POLYHEDRON INTERSECTION

Eric Haines

3D / Eye, Inc.
Ithaca, New York

The standard solution to ray–polyhedron intersection is to test the ray against each polygon and find the closest intersection, if any. If the polyhedron is convex, the ray–polyhedron test can be accelerated by considering the *polyhedron* to be the space inside a set of planes. This definition also drastically reduces the memory requirements for such polyhedra, as none of the vertices and their connectivities need to be stored; only the plane equations for the faces are needed. Finally, the ray–polyhedron test outlined here avoids the problems that can occur when the shared edge of two polygons is intersected by a ray, since there no longer are any edges. There is no chance of a ray "slipping through the cracks" by having its intersection point on an edge not considered being inside either polygon.

The algorithm is based on the ideas of Roth (1981) and Kay and Kajiya (1986). The basic idea is that each plane of the polyhedron defines a half-space: All points to one side of this space are considered inside the plane (also considering points on the plane as inside). The logical intersection of the half-spaces of all the convex polyhedron's planes is the volume defined by the polyhedron. Introducing a ray into this definition changes the problem from three dimensions to one. The intersection of each plane by the ray creates a line segment (unbounded at one end) made of a set of points inside the plane's half-space. By taking the logical intersection of all ray–plane line segments, we find the line segment (if any) in which the ray passes through the polyhedron.

The ray is defined by:

$$R_{\text{origin}} = R_o = [x_o y_o z_o],$$

$$\mathbf{R}_{\text{direction}} = \mathbf{R_d} = [x_d y_d z_d],$$

where $x_d^2 + y_d^2 + z_d^2 = 1$ (i.e., normalized).

The set of points on the ray is represented by the function:

$$R(t) = R_0 + \mathbf{R_d^*} t,$$

where $t > 0$.

In addition, in ray tracing, it is useful to keep track of t_{max}, the maximum valid distance along the ray. In shadow testing, t_{max} is set to the distance of the light from the ray's origin. For rays in which the closest object hit is desired, t_{max} is initialized to *infinity* (i.e., some arbitrarily large distance), then updated to the distance of the object currently the closest as testing progresses. An object intersected beyond t_{max} does not need to be tested further—for example, for shadow testing, such an object is beyond the light.

We initialize the distances t_{near} to *negative infinity* and t_{far} to t_{max}. These will be used to keep track of the logical intersection of the half-spaces with the ray. If t_{near} ever becomes greater than t_{far}, the ray misses the polyhedron and testing is done.

Each plane is defined in terms of $[a, b, c, d]$, which defines the plane as:

$$a*x + b*y + c*z + d = 0.$$

$\mathbf{P_n}$ is the plane's normal, $[a, b, c]$.

The distance from the ray's origin to the intersection with the plane P is simply:

$$t = -\nu_n / \nu_d,$$

where:

$$\nu_n = \mathbf{P_n} \cdot R_o + d,$$

$$\nu_d = \mathbf{P_n} \cdot \mathbf{R_d}.$$

If ν_d is 0, then the ray is parallel to the plane and no intersection takes place. In such a case, we check if the ray origin is inside the plane's half-space. If ν_n is positive, then the ray origin is outside the plane's half-space. In this case, the ray must miss the polyhedron, so testing is done.

Otherwise, the plane is categorized as front-facing or back-facing. If ν_d is positive, the plane faces away from the ray, so this plane is a back-face of the polyhedron; else, the plane is a front-face. If a back-face, the plane can affect t_{far}. If the computed t is less than 0, then the polyhedron is

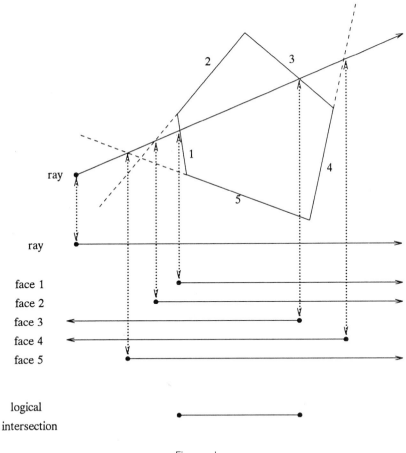

Figure 1.

behind the ray and so is missed. If t is less than t_{far}, t_{far} is updated to t. Similarly, if the plane is a front-face, t_{near} is set to t if t is greater than t_{near}. If t_{near} ever is greater than t_{far}, the ray must miss the polyhedron. Else, the ray hits, with t_{near} being the entry distance (possibly negative) and t_{far} being the distance where the ray exits the convex polyhedron. If t_{near} is negative, the ray originates inside the polyhedron; in this case, check if t_{far} is less than t_{max}; if it is, then t_{far} is the first valid intersection.

An example of this process is shown in Fig. 1. A two-dimensional view of a ray and a set of five planes forming a polyhedron is shown. Below this is the set of segments formed by the ray and the five faces. The ray intersects the plane formed by face 1 and so defines a set of points along the ray inside the half-space to the right of this intersection. The ray intersects the plane of face 2 (shown as a dashed line) at a closer distance, even though the face itself is missed. Face 3 is a back-face and creates a half-space open to the left. Face 4 also is missed, but its plane still defines a half-space. Finally, plane 5 forms a front-face half-space.

The segment in which the line defined by the ray passes through the polyhedron is the logical intersection of the five face segments; that is, where all of these segments overlap. Comparing this segment with the ray's own segment gives which (if either) of the intersection points is the closest along the ray. If there is no logical intersection, the ray misses.

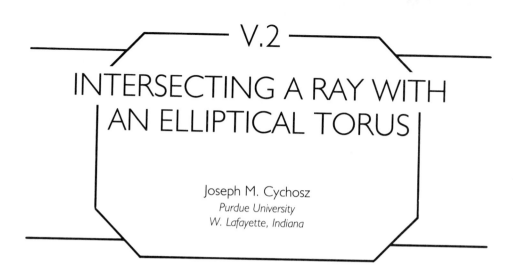

V.2

INTERSECTING A RAY WITH AN ELLIPTICAL TORUS

Joseph M. Cychosz
Purdue University
W. Lafayette, Indiana

Introduction

This gem presents the mathematics and computations required for determining the points of intersection between a ray and a torus. Also presented is an efficient bounding method for tori.

The Equation of an Elliptical Torus

An elliptical torus can be generated by sweeping an ellipse about a given axis. Figure 1 illustrates the resulting cross section of an elliptical torus that has been swept about the y axis. The cross section consists of two ellipses of radii a and b, centered at $x = \pm r$, $y = 0$. By sweeping the ellipses circularly about the y axis, a torus of radius r and centered at the origin is formed.

In an approach analogous to that taken by Glassner *et al.* (1989), the equation of the two elliptical cross sections is given by

$$\left(\frac{(x-r)^2}{a^2} + \frac{y^2}{b^2} - 1 \right)\left(\frac{(x+r)^2}{a^2} + \frac{y^2}{b^2} - 1 \right) = 0, \qquad (1)$$

which can be expressed as

$$\left(b^2(x-r)^2 + a^2y^2 - a^2b^2 \right)\left(b^2(x+r)^2 + a^2y^2 - a^2b^2 \right) = 0. \quad (2)$$

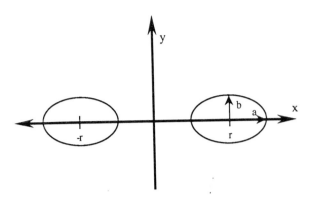

Figure 1. Cross section of an elliptical torus.

Equation (2) can be rearranged to yield the following equation,

$$\left((x+r)^2 + \frac{a^2}{b^2}y^2 + (r^2 - a^2)\right)^2 - 4r^2x^2 = 0. \tag{3}$$

By substituting p for a^2/b^2, A_0 for $4r^2$, and B_0 for $(r^2 - a^2)$, Eq. (3) is rewritten as

$$\left(x^2 + py^2 + B_0\right)^2 - A_0x^2 = 0. \tag{4}$$

By setting $y = 0$ in the preceding equation, we find that $x^2 = r^2$. The torus now can be formed by substituting the sweeping function, $r^2 = x^2 + z^2$, for x^2 in the cross-sectional function presented in Eq. (4). The equation for the elliptical torus thus becomes

$$\left(x^2 + z^2 + py^2 + B_0\right)^2 - A_0(x^2 + z^2) = 0, \tag{5}$$

where p, A_0, and B_0 are constants defined previously that control the shape of the torus.

Intersection of a Ray with a Torus

The intersection of a ray with a torus can be found by substituting the ray equations shown in Eqs. (6a)–(6c) into Eq. (5), the torus equation, the intersection of a ray with a torus is defined in Eq. (7) as follows:

$$x = x_0 + \alpha_x t, \tag{6a}$$

$$y = y_0 + \alpha_y t, \tag{6b}$$

$$z = z_0 + \alpha_z t, \tag{6c}$$

$$\left(t^2\left(\alpha_x^2 + p\alpha_y^2 + \alpha_z^2\right) + 2t(x_0\alpha_x + py_0\alpha_y + z_0\alpha_z)\right.$$

$$\left. + \left(x_0^2 + py_0^2 + z_0^2\right) + B_0\right)^2$$

$$- A_0\left(t^2\left(\alpha_x^2 + \alpha_z^2\right) + 2t(x_0\alpha_x + z_0\alpha_z) + \left(x_0^2 + z_0^2\right)\right) = 0. \tag{7}$$

The real roots of the quartic equation presented in Eq. (7) define the distances along the ray where the ray intersects the torus. Eq. (7) can be rearranged into the following form:

$$c_4 t^4 + c_3 t^3 + c_2 t^2 + c_1 t + c_0 = 0,$$

where

$$c_4 = \left(\alpha_x^2 + p\alpha_y^2 + \alpha_z^2\right)^2,$$

$$c_3 = 4(x_0\alpha_x + py_0\alpha_y + z_0\alpha_z)\left(\alpha_x^2 + p\alpha_y^2 + \alpha_z^2\right),$$

$$c_2 = 4(x_0\alpha_x + py_0\alpha_y + z_0\alpha_z)^2$$

$$+ 2\left(x_0^2 + py_0^2 + z_0^2 + B_0\right)\left(\alpha_x^2 + p\alpha_y^2 + \alpha_z^2\right) - A_0\left(\alpha_x^2 + \alpha_z^2\right),$$

$$c_1 = 4(x_0\alpha_x + py_0\alpha_y + z_0\alpha_z)\left(x_0^2 + py_0^2 + z_0^2 + B_0\right)$$

$$- 2A_0(x_0\alpha_x + z_0\alpha_z),$$

$$c_0 = \left(x_0^2 + py_0^2 + z_0^2 + B_0\right)^2 - A_0\left(x_0^2 + z_0^2\right).$$

253

Using the substitutions developed by Cashwell and Everett (1969), the quartic in normalized form is as follows:

$$c_4 = 1,$$

$$c_3 = 2m,$$

$$c_2 = m^2 + 2u - qf,$$

$$c_1 = 2mu - ql,$$

$$c_0 = u^2 - qt,$$

where

$$f = 1 - \alpha_y^2, \quad g = f + p\alpha_y^2, \quad l = 2(x_0\alpha_x + z_0\alpha_z), \quad t = x_0^2 + z_0^2,$$

$$q = \frac{A_0}{g^2}, \quad m = \frac{(l + 2py_0\alpha_y)}{g}, \quad u = \frac{(t + py_0^2 + B_0)}{g}.$$

To intersect a ray with a torus that has been arbitrarily positioned and oriented, the ray base and direction cosines must be transformed into the coordinate system of a torus positioned at the origin and oriented in the x-z plane. This can be done by use of a coordinate transformation matrix established from the orthonormal basis created from the axis of rotation and the local x axis. The transformation matrix is defined as follows:

$$\mathbf{T} = \begin{bmatrix} & \mathbf{U} & & 0 \\ & \mathbf{N} & & 0 \\ \mathbf{U} & \times & \mathbf{N} & 0 \\ -\mathbf{C}_x & -\mathbf{C}_y & -\mathbf{C}_z & 1 \end{bmatrix},$$

where $\mathbf{U}$ defines the local x axis of the torus, $\mathbf{N}$ defines the local y axis (i.e., the axis of rotation) of the torus, and $\mathbf{C}$ is location of the center of the torus.

Efficient Bounding of Tori

A common bounding method is to enclose an object within a sphere. When the ray does not intersect the bounding sphere, there is no need to calculate the intersection points of the ray with the enclosed object, thus

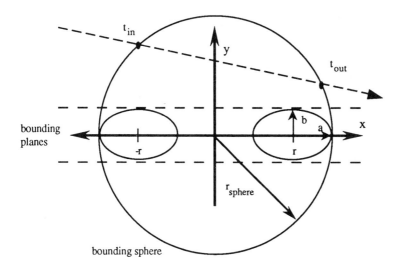

Figure 2. Efficient toroidal bounding.

eliminating unnecessary computation. A torus can be enclosed easily within a sphere positioned at the center of the torus and with a radius as follows:

$$r_{\text{sphere}} = r + \max(a, b).$$

However, this bounding approach results in a significantly large void volume as depicted in Fig. 2. To reduce the resulting void volume, the torus is sandwiched between two planes located $\pm b$ off of the x–z plane. The vertical distances of the intersection points of the sphere then are tested to determine if the ray passes either completely above or below the torus. Since the torus lies in the x–z plane, only the y component of the intersection locations on the sphere are of interest. The ray misses the torus if the following relationship is true:

$$y_{\text{in}} = y_0' + a_y' t_{\text{in}},$$

$$y_{\text{out}} = y_0' + a_y' t_{\text{out}},$$

$$(y_{\text{in}} > b \quad and \quad y_{\text{out}} > b) \ or \ (y_{\text{in}} < -b \quad and \quad y_{\text{out}} < -b),$$

where t_{in} and t_{out} are the intersection distances to the bounding sphere.

Determining the Surface Normal of a Torus

The normal at any given point on the surface of the torus can be computed by evaluating the gradient (i.e., the partial derivatives of the surface function with respect to each of the variables, x, y, and z) of the surface at the point. Given the hit point P, the surface normal $\mathbf{N}$ is defined as follows:

$$P' = P \times \mathbf{T}$$

$$d = \sqrt{P'^2_x + P'^2_z},$$

$$f = \frac{2(d - r)}{(da^2)},$$

$$\mathbf{N}'_x = P'_x f,$$

$$\mathbf{N}'_y = \frac{2P'_y}{b^2},$$

$$\mathbf{N}'_z = P'_z f,$$

$$\mathbf{N} = \mathbf{N}' \times \mathbf{T}^T_{33}.$$

The normal in world coordinate space is found by transforming the normal from the local coordinate space by using the inverse of the coordinate transformation matrix $\mathbf{T}$. Since the upper 3×3 matrix in $\mathbf{T}$ is an orthonormal basis, the inverse simply is the transpose of the upper 3×3.

RAY – TRIANGLE INTERSECTION USING BINARY RECURSIVE SUBDIVISION

Douglas Voorhies
Apollo Systems Division
Hewlett-Packard Co.
Chelmsford, Massachusetts

and

David Kirk
California Institute of Technology
Pasadena, California

The Problem

Determine if a line segment and a triangle intersect. If so, calculate the XYZ coordinates of that intersection, and the corresponding U, V triangle location.

Initial Information

The line segment is defined by XYZ endpoint coordinates. (See Fig. 1.) The triangle is defined by XYZ vertex coordinates, with the coefficients of its $AX + BY + CZ + D = 0$ plane equation available as well.

Constraints

To make the solution effective in both hardware and software, the number of calculations (especially multiplications) must be minimized, with more difficult operations such as divides, roots, and transcendentals avoided entirely. Integer arithmetic is preferable to floating point, again to permit efficient hardware implementation.

The Method

The 3D intersection problem is decomposed into a series of 1D intersection problems: along the ray, along the triangle sides, and along an axis.

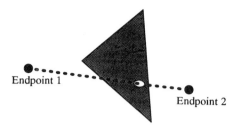

Figure 1.

The U, V parameters are determined partially as a side effect of the intersection calculation. There are three steps in total:

1. Finding the intersection of the ray with the plane of the triangle.

2. Determining if that point lies inside or outside of the triangle itself.

3. Completing the computation of the intersection point's triangle U, V parameters.

Step 1: Ray – Plane Intersection

The plane of the triangle is stored as coefficients (A, B, C, D) of the plane equation: $AX + BY + CZ + D = 0$. This equation may be thought of as representing the 1-norm (Manhattan) distance from the plane: $AX + BY + CZ + D = Manhattan$ $distance$, where the scaling factors for the three axes may not be equal.

By evaluating this function for endpoint 1 and endpoint 2, we get the signed distance above or below the plane for these two points. (This calculation requires six multiplications and six additions.) If these two distances are not zero and agree in sign, then both are on the same side of the plane, and the line interval does not intersect the plane. If one distance is zero, then that endpoint is the intersection point, and we can skip to the next step. If both are zero, the line segment and the triangle are coplanar to within the precision of the addresses, and are presumed to not intersect.

If the endpoint distances are nonzero and differ in sign, then the plane passes through or between these endpoints. The intersection of the plane with the line segment between the endpoints may be found by recursive subdivision of the interval. The interval is shortened by half each iteration by taking the interval's current endpoints and averaging them, thus computing the interval midpoint. The Manhattan distances also are averaged, producing the Manhattan distance for that midpoint. Each division of the interval produces a choice of two sub-intervals; the one whose end Manhattan distances differ in sign is pursued. (Each iteration requires four additions, four shifts, and a zero detect.) Thus:

Initially: End 1 & End 2 define the line segment
(XYZ and distance from plane)
until $(Distnew = 0)$ **do**
Compute Midpoint:
$\qquad$ Xnew $\leftarrow$ $(X1 + X2)/2$;
$\qquad$ Ynew $\leftarrow$ $(Y1 + Y2)/2$;
$\qquad$ Znew $\leftarrow$ $(Z1 + Z2)/2$;
$\qquad$ Distnew $\leftarrow$ $(Dist1 + Dist2)/2$;
Choose new interval:
$\qquad$ **if** $(SIGN(Dist1) = SIGN(Distnew))$ **then** End1 $\leftarrow$ New;
$\qquad\qquad\qquad\qquad\qquad\qquad\qquad\qquad$ **else** End2 $\leftarrow$ New;
$\qquad$ **endloop;**
Whereupon (XYZ)new is the intersection point

Step 2: Point – Triangle Intersection

The second part of the algorithm determines if the intersection point lies inside the triangle. This implicitly is a 2D problem, since the plane intersection point and the triangle are coplanar. The coordinate whose axis is most orthogonal to the plane simply is dropped, thus projecting the intersection point and the triangle on to the plane of the remaining axes. Its determination involves two 1D procedures, with the first procedure carrying an extra coordinate along for use in the second.

After dropping the coordinate for one axis, we project the intersection point and triangle vertices on to one of the remaining two axes (by simply selecting that axis's coordinate); this is shown in Fig. 2. Either axis could be used, but the one along which the triangle's extent is greatest preserves more precision. The intersection point's projection on to this axis will lie within the extent of either zero or two triangle edges. If no triangle edge overlaps the intersection point's projection, then the line segment and the triangle do not intersect.

For those two edges whose extents overlap the intersection point in the chosen axis's dimension, we must find the actual triangle edge locations that project on to the same axis location as the intersection point. We use recursive subdivision separately on both triangle edges to converge upon these points. Each subdivision begins with the vertices for its edge and subdivides the edge recursively. On each iteration, the axis projection of the new midpoint is compared with that of the intersection point, and the sub-interval whose projection contains the intersection point's projection is pursued. Eventually, both edges converge on 2D locations having the axis coordinate equal to the intersection point. (This calculation requires two additions, one subtraction, and two shifts per edge iteration, for a total of four additions, two subtractions, and four shifts per iteration.) In Step 3, we will want the pattern of subdivision decisions that converge on these edge points; to save them requires two shift registers.

In the following algorithm definition, we use the notation L, M, and S to represent the axes (among X, Y, and Z) in which the particular triangle's extents are largest, medium, and smallest, respectively:

Initially: End 1 and End 2 are the (L, M) triangle edge vertices
   Orientation $=$ " $+$ " if $L2 > L1$ else Orientation $=$ " $-$ "
until $(Ldist = 0)$ **do**
Compute Midpoint:
   $Lnew \leftarrow (L1 + L2)/2;$
   $Mnew \leftarrow (M1 + M2)/2;$
   $Ldist \leftarrow Lnew - Lintersection;$
Choose new interval:
   if $(SIGN(Ldist) = Orientation)$ **then** $End2 \leftarrow New;$
                              else $End1 \leftarrow New;$
   endloop;
Whereupon $(L, M)new$ is edge point with $Lnew = Lintersection$

We now look at the span between these two edge points and do 1D comparisons in the M dimension. If the intersection point lies on the span between these two edge locations, then the intersection point is inside the triangle, and the intersection test succeeds; otherwise, it is

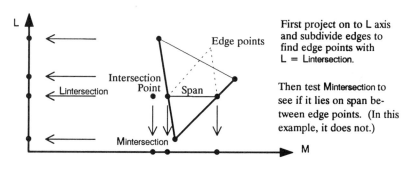

First project on to L axis and subdivide edges to find edge points with L = Lintersection.

Then test Mintersection to see if it lies on span between edge points. (In this example, it does not.)

Figure 2.

outside, and the intersection test fails. (This requires only two comparisons of Mintersection against the two MnewS). Figure 2 illustrates the projection on to the M axis as well.

Step 3: U, V Computation

If intersected triangles are assumed to have a canonical U, V mapping of $0, 0, 0, 1$, and $1, 0$ at the three vertices, as shown in Fig. 3, then the U, V values at the two edge points are available directly.

The pattern of subdivision decisions (or the pattern subtracted from 1) encodes the U or V value for the resulting edge point. For example, if one edge point is two-thirds of the way from the $0, 0$ vertex to the $1, 0$ vertex, then the subdivision decisions proceed: far interval, near interval, far interval, near interval..., etc. Expressing this pattern as a binary

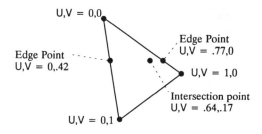

Figure 3.

fraction (.1010101010101010) gives the U parameter of this example point.

Edge Vertices	Parameter Values at Edge Point	
	U	V
$0,0 \rightarrow 0,1$	0	subdivision fraction
$0,0 \rightarrow 1,0$	subdivision fraction	0
$0,1 \rightarrow 1,0$	subdivision fraction	1-subdivision fraction

Given the U, V values for the two edge points, the U, V value for the intersection point that lies on the span between them can be computed by yet another recursive subdivision of this span. The edge point M coordinates and U, V parameters are averaged to determine midpoint values for each iteration. Mmidpoint is compared with Mintersection to determine which sub-interval to pursue. When these M coordinates are equal, the U, V values are correct for the intersection point. (This requires three additions, one subtraction, and three shifts.)

Initially: End 1 and End 2 are the two (M, U, V) triangle edge points
Orientation = "+" if M2 > M1 else Orientation = "−"
until (Mintersection = Mnew) **do**
Compute Midpoint:
  Mnew ← (M1 + M2)/2
  Unew ← (U1 + U2)/2
  Vnew ← (V1 + V2)/2
  Mdist ← Mnew − Mintersection
Choose new interval:
  if (SIGN(Mdist) = Orientation) **then** End2 ← New
                        else End1 ← New
  endloop;
Whereupon (U, V)new is parametric triangle location
for the intersection point

Conclusion

This method substitutes binary recursive subdivision for division in finding intersection points along line segments. By using only simple arithmetic operations, it is suitable for use on computers with weak floating-point capability, or even directly in hardware. An advantage is that part of the computation needed to determine the U, V triangle location of the intersection point simply is a side effect of deciding whether there is any intersection. A disadvantage is the need for the triangle's plane equation coefficients in addition to the vertexes.

This intersection technique solves the 3D ray–triangle intersection problem by reducing it to a sequence of 1D and 2D problems. This aspect of the algorithm is useful regardless of whether binary recursive subdivision or division is used.

See also (*390*) An Efficient Ray–Polygon Intersection, Didier Badouel; (*394*) Fast Ray–Polygon Intersection, Andrew Woo

IMPROVED RAY TAGGING FOR VOXEL-BASED RAY TRACING

David Kirk
California Institute of Technology
Pasadena, California
and
James Arvo
Apollo Systems Division of Hewlett-Packard
Chelmsford, Massachusetts

Introduction

A common difficulty that arises in ray tracing spatially subdivided scenes is caused by objects that penetrate more than one voxel. The problem is a degradation in performance due to repeated ray–object intersection tests between the same ray and object. These redundant tests occur when a ray steps through several voxels occupied by the same object before finding an intersection. One strategy that avoids this problem is to employ a *mailbox* as described by Arnaldi *et al*. (1987). A mailbox, in this context, is a means of storing intersection results with objects to avoid redundant calculations. Each object is assigned a mailbox and each distinct ray is tagged with a unique number. When an object is tested for intersection, the results of the test and the ray tag are stored in the object's mailbox. Before testing each object, the tag stored in its mailbox is compared against that of the current ray. If they match, the ray has been tested previously against this object and the results can be retrieved without being recalculated.

Unfortunately, this scheme can break down when the world object hierarchy contains multiple instances of spatial subdivision *aggregate objects*; that is, collections of objects bundled with a ray intersection technique based on an octree, a uniform grid, or some other spatial data structure. In such a scene, several intersections may occur between a ray and instances of an aggregate object, each instance being geometrically distinct in the world coordinate system. Therefore, to use the tagging scheme correctly, we must be careful to distinguish between child objects within different instances. One way to do this is to update a ray's tag

264

```
Octree_Intersect(Ray, Octree, Hit_data)
     Ray : struct;                    Ray origin, direction, etc.
     Octree : struct;                 Local data for octree.
     Hit_data : struct;               Details of intersection.
begin
     Incremental local intersection invocation counter.
     Octree.tag ← Octree.tag + 1;
     Walk through voxels, looking for first intersection.
     repeat
          get next Voxel of Octree pierced by Ray;
          Test all objects in current voxel
          for each Child associated with Voxel begin
               if Octree.tag = Child.tag Then
                    This_test ← Child.mailbox;
               else begin
                    Intersect_Object(Ray, Child.Object, This_test);
                    Child.mailbox ← This_test;
                    Child.tag ← Octree.tag;
                    end;
               if This_test is a closer hit than Hit_data then
                    Hit_data ← This_test;
               endfor;
          until intersection found or no more voxels;
     end
```

Figure 1.   A procedure for using local ray–object intersection tags.

whenever it encounters an instance of an aggregate object, thereby invalidating the previous contents of the mailboxes. However, this can be awkward because knowledge about ray tags must percolate throughout every part of the ray tracer, even modules completely divorced from spatial subdivision. In particular, the ray tag would need to be updated every time a new ray is generated or transformed.

An Improved Technique

A better approach stems from the observation that the items that need to be tagged are not rays at all, but intersection queries between rays and aggregate objects. Therefore, the ray tag can be replaced by invocation counters residing only within aggregate objects based on spatial subdivision. The tag then is part of the private data of an aggregate and is incremented each time its ray-intersection technique is invoked on behalf of any instance. The mailboxes are still associated with child objects within the aggregate, and the tag is compared with the contents of these mailboxes, as before (Figure 1).

The benefits of this approach are two-fold. First, the ray tag and mailbox concepts are localized to where they are used. Therefore, the bulk of the ray tracer can remain unaffected by them; tags need not be copied or updated when rays are created or transformed. The second benefit is that redundant intersection tests are avoided completely, even in the presence of instanced aggregate objects.

As object-oriented programming techniques are adopted more widely in ray tracing implementations, it will become common to encapsulate basic ray tracing operations such as ray–aggregate intersection queries, CSG operations, and shaders within *objects* that behave much as simple primitives (Kirk and Arvo, 1988). Observations about the locality of information allow us to hide data structures within the objects, removing them from the main body of the ray tracer, as we have done here with ray tags.

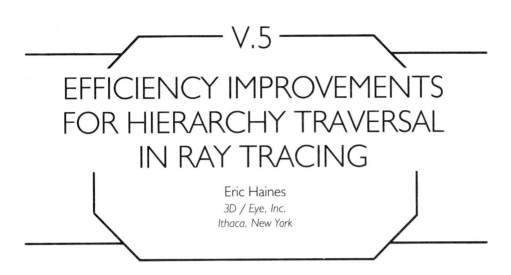

V.5

EFFICIENCY IMPROVEMENTS FOR HIERARCHY TRAVERSAL IN RAY TRACING

Eric Haines
3D / Eye, Inc.
Ithaca, New York

One common scheme for accelerating ray tracing is using a hierarchical set of bounding volumes. In this scheme, a tree structure is formed in which the root is a bounding volume enclosing all objects in the scene, and each child is an object or a bounding volume containing more objects or volumes (Rubin and Whitted, 1980; Weghorst *et al.*, 1984). Such a hierarchy can be formed manually or by various algorithms (Kay and Kajiya, 1986; Goldsmith and Salmon, 1987). The hierarchy is accessed by testing a ray against the root volume. If it hits, the volume is *opened up* and the objects or volumes within are tested for intersection. This process continues until the entire tree is traversed, at which time the closest intersection is returned. What follows are improved tree traversal techniques, many of which have not been published before or have been overlooked.

One simple improvement is to use the current closest intersection distance as an upper bound on how far the ray travels. For example, if the ray hits a sphere at some distance, there is no good reason to examine the contents of any bounding volumes beyond this distance. For that matter, if a polygon is intersected at a distance beyond this upper bound, the polygon must be missed (and so the inside–outside test for the polygon can be avoided).

Kay and Kajiya improved upon the traversal process by keeping track of intersected bounding volumes and their intersection distances. The closest volume on this list is retrieved via heap sort, then is opened and examined. If at any time the retrieved volume is beyond the upper bound distance, then the rest of the volumes must be missed and so the process is complete. Jeff Goldsmith and I have noted that this sorting process should not be done for shadow rays, since any intersection found will block the light.

Caching is a technique that can improve efficiency in traversal. *Shadow object caching* is a good example of the method (Haines and Greenberg, 1986). At each intersection node in the ray tree, store a set of object pointers, one per light source. Set each pointer initially to null. Whenever a shadow test is done at this node and for a given light, store the object hit by the ray in the pointer location (or store null if no object is hit). At the beginning of each shadow test, check if there is an object for this light at the node. If so, test this object first. If the ray hits the object, no more testing is needed. Otherwise, continue shadow testing as before.

The principle is simple enough: An object that blocked the last shadow ray for a node and light probably is going to block the next ray. Using Arnaldi's *mailboxes* technique of marking objects (Arnaldi, *et al.*, 1987) avoids testing the object twice (once in the cache and once during regular traversal). The mailbox algorithm is to give each ray a unique ID, and store this ID in the object when it is tested against the ray. At the beginning of any intersection test, if the object's ID matches the ray's ID, then the object already has been tested against the ray.

Another technique is to save transparent objects for later intersection while performing shadow testing (or, memory permitting, to have a separate hierarchy for them altogether). Only if no opaque object is hit do the transparent objects need to be tested. The idea here is to avoid doing work on transparent objects when, in fact, the light does not reach the object.

Caching also can be applied to tracing *shading* rays; that is, eye, reflection, or refraction rays. Keep track of the closest object (if any) last intersected at the node and test this object first. If the object is hit, there now is a good upper bound on the ray's length. Bounding volumes beyond this distance are discarded, which can cut down considerably on the amount of the hierarchy traversed. In fact, this minor addition can give much of the benefit of Kay and Kajiya's heap sort scheme with much less implementation and overhead. It also can aid Kay and Kajiya's method by helping to prune the tree immediately.

There are a variety of techniques that improve the traversal process itself. One *top-down* preprocess method is to open bounding volumes that contain an endpoint of the ray. For example, a large number of rays originate from the eye location. So, before tracing any of them, test the

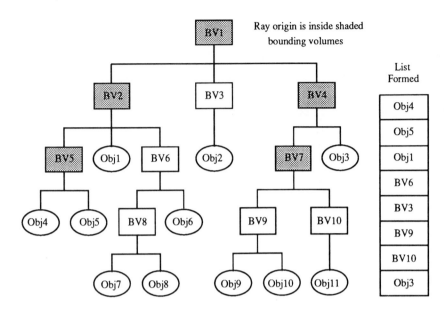

Figure 1. Top-down list formation.

eye's location against the root bounding volume. If it is inside, this box always must be hit; recursively test the eye location on down the tree. Put the bounding volumes not enclosing the eye location, and all objects found inside opened bounding volumes, on a list. Use this list of objects for testing all rays from the eye. In this way, unneeded intersection tests are eliminated at the start. The same process can be done for each point light source.

This list formation process is shown in Fig. 1. In this example, the ray origin is found to be inside bounding volume 1; so, this bounding volume is opened and the ray origin is tested against the three children. The origin is found to be in bounding volume 2, so its children are tested. Bounding volume 5 also encloses the origin, so its children are examined. These children both are objects, so they are put on the test list. Checking the other children of BV2, object 1 is put on the list, and BV6 is tested against the origin. This time, the ray's origin is not inside the bounding volume, so BV6 is put on the list. This traversal process continues until the entire tree has been classified.

A *bottom-up* method can be done on the fly for rays originating on an object. All ancestors of the originating object must be hit by these rays. Beginning at the parent bounding volume of the originating object, test each son against the ray. Move to the parent of this bounding volume, and test all sons except this one. Continue moving up the tree through each ancestor until done. This traversal has two advantages. The obvious one is that the object's ancestor bounding volumes never have to be tested against the rays. The other advantage is that objects relatively close to the object are tested first for intersection, thus providing a possible upper bound early in the process. This approach was used successfully in the early Cornell ray tracer.

This process is similar to caching in that the lists formed can be reused for rays originating from the same object. Instead of traversing and intersecting, simply move up the hierarchy from the originating object and store the direct sons of these ancestors (except for the originating sons). This list stays the same throughout the rendering, so it can be used whenever a ray begins on that object. If keeping all lists around for the duration of the process costs too much memory, an alternative is to keep the lists in a similar fashion to shadow cache objects: Store the object's list at the intersection node. If the originating object is the same for the next ray starting from this node, then this list can be reused; otherwise, it is freed and a new list formed. Note that the list at a node can be used for a large number of rays: the reflection ray, the refraction ray, and all shadow rays from this object. Amortizing the cost of forming this list once over the number of rays per node and the number of times the node has the same object usually gives a minimal cost per ray for list management.

An example of how this process works is shown in Fig. 2. A ray originates on object 7; so, object 7 itself is stored for later testing in the list. This object is shown in parentheses, since one could avoid storing it if it is guaranteed that the ray cannot intersect this originating object (e.g., a ray originating on a polygon cannot re-intersect this polygon). The parent bounding volume 8 is opened and its other son, object 8, is put on the list. The parent of BV8 is BV6, which then is opened, and its other son, object 6, is placed on the list. This process continues until the root node, BV1, is opened.

A further traversal enhancement is combining the top-down and bottom-up approaches. Say there is a list for a given object at a given node. If the next ray originates on a different object, we normally would rebuild

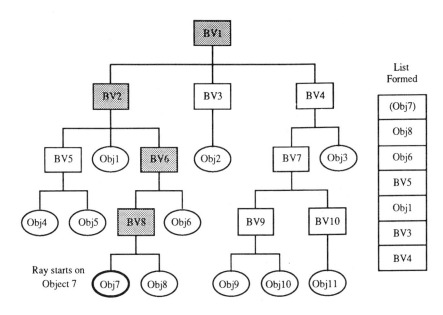

Figure 2.   Bottom-up traversal.

the list. However, what if the ray's origin is inside the bounding volume of the list's originating object? If so, the ray must hit all the bounding volumes eliminated when the list was made, and so the list can be reused for this ray.

It is interesting to note that rays that originate slightly outside the bounding volume still can use the list—in fact, *any* ray can use the list. However, the further the ray is from the bounding volume that formed the list, the worse the traversal time. Some bounding volumes will be open on the list that the ray would not have opened, and some bounding volumes that could have been culled by removing the ancestors will have to be tested against the ray instead.

As shown before, there is much benefit in obtaining a close intersection early on in traversal. This suggests another simple scheme, which is to reorder the hierarchical tree so that objects are before bounding volumes in the list of sons of a bounding volume. All things being equal, it is better to find an intersection with an object quickly, and possibly prune bounding volumes early on. Sorting the list of sons in this way suggests other schemes, such as putting larger objects first in the list, on the theory that larger objects are more likely to be hit. Another scheme is to put objects that are quick to test first. For example, if a sphere and a spline patch are equally likely to be hit by a ray, it is better to test the sphere first, as this may obtain an upper bound that quickly prunes the spline from any testing at all. Sorting by the ratio of hits to tests (found empirically from testing) is another possibility. A combination of all of these factors may be the best sorting scheme.

Likewise, bounding volumes could be sorted by various characteristics. Size and simplicity of intersection both apply as sort keys. Another factor is the number of descendants in the tree. In general, less descendants means that fewer bounding volumes will have to be traversed before reaching objects. Our goal is to test objects as soon as possible, so bounding volumes with fewer descendants generally are preferable.

For specialized applications, i.e., for a scene rendered with only eye rays, the sons could be sorted by the distance along the main direction of rays. Objects close by then would be tested before those further behind. This idea simply is performing a Kay and Kajiya sort as a preprocess. Little work has been done on sorting the hierarchy to date, so this whole area deserves exploration.

As has been shown, there are many methods for speeding hierarchy access for ray tracing. Some, such as shadow caching and eye-ray list building, almost always are worth doing. Others, such as object list building, are more dependent upon weighing the savings of the new algorithm versus the additional setup and access costs. Most of the techniques described in this gem are simple to implement and test, and each can yield some bit of savings.

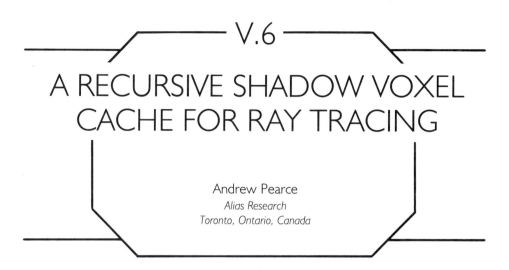

V.6

A RECURSIVE SHADOW VOXEL CACHE FOR RAY TRACING

Andrew Pearce
Alias Research
Toronto, Ontario, Canada

This gem describes a simple technique for speeding up shadow ray computation if you are ray tracing scenes that exploit any type of spatial subdivision.

When ray tracing shadow rays, it is a good idea to store a pointer to the last object that caused a shadow with each light source in a *shadow cache* (Haines and Greenberg, 1986). The next shadow ray towards any light source first is intersected with the object in the shadow cache, and if an intersection occurs, the point we are shading can be declared to be in shadow with respect to that light source. This works because it is not necessary to know *which* object shadows a light source; it is sufficient to know simply that an object does shadow a light source. The shadow cache technique exploits object coherence in shadowing.

However, if you are ray tracing surface tessellations, the amount of object coherence in the shadow is minimal, since the tessellated triangles produced usually are quite small. It is a simple matter to extend the shadow cache idea to include the caching of the *voxel* in which the last object to shadow the light was intersected, in a *voxel cache* with each light source. If the shadow-cached object does not shadow the light source, then one of the objects in the vicinity (as enclosed by the voxel) likely will, so all of the objects in the voxel are tested for intersection to see if they might shadow the light.

David Jevans added the comment that if the last shadow ray towards a given light source was spawned from a primary ray, and the current shadow ray was spawned from a reflection ray, then the information in the shadow and voxel cache is useless, and probably will waste computation by intersecting objects that could not possibly shadow the light source. What he suggests is that a tree of shadow voxel caches be stored with each light source. To access the shadow voxel cache tree, the history of each ray is kept at all times; a ray's history describes uniquely its position in the shading tree for the current primary (eye) ray. To keep track of the current ray's history, a simple bit table can be employed (called *path* in the code).

The shadow voxel cache will waste computation when the spawning point for the shadow rays moves drastically. Therefore, the shadow voxel cache trees should be cleared at the end of each scanline unless scanlines are traced in alternating directions (i.e., even scanlines sweep left to right across the screen, odd scanlines sweep right to left). There is no way to avoid wasting computation when the spawning point is changed drastically due to highly curved objects or transitioning between objects; one must hope that the benefits of the shadow voxel cache tree outweigh this little bit of wasted computation, and, in practice, I have found this technique to be very effective.

V.7

AVOIDING INCORRECT SHADOW INTERSECTIONS FOR RAY TRACING

Andrew Pearce
Alias Research
Toronto, Ontario, Canada

This gem is a quick way to avoid intersecting the object that generated the shadow ray when ray tracing, and is appropriate for planar objects.

Due to floating-point precision problems, many ray tracers add a small epsilon to the starting position of the shadow ray (along the direction of its travel) to avoid intersecting the object that has just been intersected. If the epsilon is not added, then it is possible that the shadow ray will find an intersection with the object it is supposed to be shading (right at the origin of the shadow ray), resulting in an incorrect shadow.

When ray tracing objects that are contained in most types of spatial subdivision structures, it is possible to intersect an object that spans multiple voxels more than once. A simple technique—which is mentioned by Arnaldi *et al.* (1987), Pearce (1987), and Amanatides and Woo (1987) —is to assign a unique identification number to each ray so that objects will be tested for intersection with any given ray only once. Once an object is tested for intersection, the ray's number is stored in a *last-ray* field in that object. Before intersecting an object, the ray's number and the last-ray field in the object are compared; if the numbers match, then the object already has been encountered and tested in a previous voxel and has been eliminated from the set of possible intersections, so no further processing is done on that object.

An advantage of saving ray numbers with each object is that the shadow test easily can ignore the spawning object simply by setting the object's last-ray field to the shadow ray's number before starting the shadow test. However, if the objects are nonplanar and can curve around to self-shadow, then the traditional epsilon method (or something similar) must be used.

A BODY COLOR MODEL: ABSORPTION OF LIGHT THROUGH TRANSLUCENT MEDIA

Mark E. Lee
Amoco Production Company
Tulsa Research Center
Tulsa, Oklahoma

and

Samuel P. Uselton
Computer Sciences Corporation
NASA Ames Research Center
Moffett Field, California

Introduction

Body color is the result of the selective absorption of certain wavelengths of light as the light travels through a medium. The ability to use body color is important both in realistic image synthesis and in scientific visualization. The attenuation and color shift of light traveling through an almost transparent medium provide important visual cues to the thickness, density, and shape of the object being traversed. Traditional graphics shading models have concentrated on shading at surfaces, which is sufficient for many objects. However, including the ability to model the body color of those objects that act as filters enhances the realism and, in some cases, improves the interpretability of the images produced.

Theoretical Basis

The theory of physical optics is used to derive formulas for calculating the attenuation of the intensity of light as it passes through translucent materials. Absorption occurs when light waves lose energy as they travel through a medium. The amount of energy absorbed increases with the thickness of the medium. If the medium absorbs more energy in one wavelength than others, then the overall color of the light changes as it travels through the absorbing medium. This is the principle behind colored filters. An absorbing medium exhibits body color as distinguished from surface color, since the color comes from light that has traveled a distance through the medium. Surface color comes by the reflection of light at the surface. Paints give their color primarily by absorption. Metals give their color predominantly by reflection (Jenkins and White, 1937).

All of the formulas in this gem are stated for a single wavelength. If the color space being used is based on a continuous range of wavelengths, then all of the terms in the formulas are functions over the continuous range of wavelengths. If the color space is discrete in wavelength, such as an RGB color space, then all of the terms are vectors with one element for each discrete wavelength.

Absorption by Homogeneous Media

The basic absorption formula is derived from the amount of absorption in the medium through layers of unit thickness (Jenkins and White, 1937). Suppose that the light wave enters a medium layered in unit thicknesses. The intensity of the wave entering the medium is I_0. The intensity of the wave as it enters the second layer will be a fraction q of the initial intensity I_0, such that

$$I_1 = qI_0.$$

As the wave exits the second layer, then the new intensity I_2 is

$$I_2 = qI_1 = q^2I_0.$$

The same effect takes place as the wave moves from layer to layer. After n layers,

$$I_n = q^nI_0.$$

Therefore, as the layers become infinitely thin,

$$I_x = q^xI_0$$

for some distance x. The factor q is called the *transmission coefficient* (Jenkins and White, 1937) and represents the fraction of the intensity of light remaining after traveling a unit distance through the volume. This version of the absorption model is the model proposed by Kay and Greenberg (1979) and Hall (Hall and Greenberg, 1983).

The same general formula can be derived in a different manner (Jenkins and White, 1937). For an infinitely small thickness, dx, the fraction of the intensity absorbed is proportional to dx by the following equation:

$$\frac{dI}{I} = -A dx,$$

where dI/I is the fraction of the intensity absorbed in the thickness, dx. The factor A is the fraction of incident intensity absorbed per unit thickness for small thicknesses. By integrating both sides of the equation, the final intensity can be derived for any distance travelled. Using the fact that when $x = 0$, $I = I_0$, the equation

$$\int_{I_0}^{I_x} \frac{dI}{I} = -\int_0^x A dx,$$

yields

$$I_x = I_0 e^{-(Ax)}.$$

This result is Lambert's law of absorption. A is called the *absorption coefficient* of the medium (Jenkins and White, 1937). Values for this parameter for specific real materials sometimes can be found in various references (Gubareff *et al.*, 1960; Purdue University, 1970a, 1970b, 1970c).

Another measure of absorption sometimes is more readily available. It is called the *extinction coefficient*, k_0, and is related to the absorption coefficient in the following manner:

$$A = \frac{4\pi k_0}{\lambda_0},$$

where λ_0 is the wavelength measured in a vacuum (Jenkins and White, 1937). If the wavelength in a vacuum, λ_0, is replaced by the wavelength in the material, λ, then k_0 can be replaced by k by using the relationship, $k_0 = nk$, where n is the index of refraction for the medium, which implies that

$$A = \frac{4\pi k}{\lambda}.$$

The term k is called the *absorption index*. Both the extinction coefficient and the absorption index can be found sometimes in the literature (Gubareff *et al.*, 1960; Purdue University, 1970a, 1970b, 1970c). Sometimes, the term k is used for the extinction coefficient instead of the absorption index and care must be exercised when using the literature to determine whether the extinction coefficient or the absorption index is being specified.

By substituting these two relationships for A, the absorption formulas now can be stated as

$$I_x = q^x I_0,$$

$$= I_0 e^{-(Ax)},$$

$$= I_0 e^{\frac{-(4\pi k_0 x)}{\lambda_0}},$$

$$= I_0 e^{\frac{-(4\pi k x)}{\lambda}},$$

where x is the distance traveled (Born and Wolf, 1975; Jenkins and White, 1937). Any of the preceding formulations may be used depending on the availability of the necessary parameters.

Absorption through Inhomogeneous Media

Suppose that the absorptive medium is not constant throughout the volume, but is defined as a function of position. Now the extinction coefficient becomes the function $A(x)$, where x represents distance and

$$\frac{dI}{I} = -A(x)dx.$$

When integrating over the thickness through the volume, then

$$\int_{I_0}^{I_x} \frac{dI}{I} = -\int_0^x A(x)\,dx \quad \text{results in} \quad I_x = I_0 e^{-\int_0^x A(x)\,dx}.$$

Since

$$A(x) = \frac{4\pi k_0(x)}{\lambda_0} \quad \text{and} \quad k_0(x) = nk(x),$$

then

$$I_x = I_0 e^{-\int_0^x A(x)\,dx},$$

$$= I_0 e^{-\int_0^x \frac{4\pi k_0(x)}{\lambda_0}\,dx},$$

$$= I_0 e^{-\int_0^x \frac{4\pi k(x)}{\lambda}\,dx}.$$

Now an integral still remains for evaluation. For some applications, the media being traversed is piecewise homogeneous or varies smoothly in some known fashion and the integral can be evaluated directly. For other applications and various graphical display methods, the integrals cannot be evaluated directly. For some applications, numerical integration algorithms such as Gaussian quadrature can be applied, while for other applications, statistical techniques such as Monte Carlo methods must be applied. The best evaluation methods are highly application- and display method-dependent and must be chosen wisely.

Once again, remember that the absorption formulas contain a wavelength factor. The absorption factors are wavelength-dependent and must be specified for every wavelength that is to be sampled, allowing certain wavelengths to be absorbed at higher rates than others. Filters operate on this principle. Some wavelengths are absorbed completely, while others are allowed to pass untouched, causing an overall shift in the color of the light to be perceived.

Reflection of Light

As a side note, the reflection of light from a conducting medium (medium with free electrons) also is affected by the extinction coefficient. The Fresnel formulas determine the fraction of the intensity of the light wave that will be reflected. For more on this subject, please see the appendix for the next gem in this book.

Conclusions

We have derived several equivalent absorption formulations, each of which can be used depending on the application and the availability of data. For stable numerical computation, we prefer transforming the data into the form using the absorption coefficient. Unstable conditions for the exponential function, such as underflow and overflow, are detected easily and avoided.

See also V.9 More Shadow Attenuation for Ray Tracing Transparent or Translucent Objects, Mark E. Lee, Samuel P. Uselton; (*397*) *Shadow Attenuation for Ray Tracing Transparent Objects, Andrew Pearce*

V.9
MORE SHADOW ATTENUATION FOR RAY TRACING TRANSPARENT OR TRANSLUCENT OBJECTS

Mark E. Lee
Amoco Production Company
Tulsa Research Company
Tulsa, Oklahoma

and

Samuel P. Uselton
Computer Sciences Corporation
NASA Ames Research Center
Moffett Field, California

Approximations for Shadow Generation

This gem contains the derivation of an approximation for the calculation of a shadow attenuation term for shadow generation.

Why is an approximation necessary? An accurate, general, computable algorithm for calculating the amount of light that passes through transparent surfaces to reach the point being illuminated is difficult to construct. Objects such as glass lenses tend to focus light onto the point being illuminated. To demonstrate the difficulty in constructing an accurate model, consider the light being focused through a simple lens. The solution for light being focused through a lens onto a single point on the surface is a continuous area of the lens. Determination of the focusing areas for arbitrary multiple transparent surfaces is extremely difficult. However, if focusing effects are ignored, the shadow model becomes much simpler.

Pearce (1990) presented one such approximation. We would like to present another approximation that has been used by the ray-tracing project at the University of Tulsa (Lee *et al.*, 1986).

The Naive Scheme

Let S be the shadow attenuation factor for the amount of light that reaches the point to be illuminated. A naive scheme for calculating the S term sends a ray back in the light source direction and determines if any objects lie between the point of interest and the light source. If any objects obstruct the path of the ray between the point of interest and the light source, then the point is assumed to be in shadow and $S = 0$;

otherwise, the point is not shadowed and $S = 1$. This scheme works efficiently; however, for transparent surfaces, the amount of shadow is incorrect. A certain amount of light still travels through the transparent surface to reach the intersection point and the shadow is not completely dark ($0 \leq S \leq 1$). A better approximation is necessary.

An Improved Scheme

For many shading models, such as the Hall model (Hall and Greenberg, 1983; Hall, 1983; Glassner, 1989), the amount of light that passes through the interface between two media (generally a surface) is $I_0 k_t T$, where I_0 is the amount of light incident to the interface, k_t is the transmission coefficient from the shading equation (in our application, the same as k_s, the specular reflection coefficient), and $T = 1 - F$, where T is the Fresnel transmission curve and F is the Fresnel reflectance curve. (See the appendix for this gem for the calculation of the Fresnel reflectance curve.) The new approximation procedure now will construct the shadow attenuation term S from the same transmission factor, $k_t T$, used for the refraction of a ray through a surface interface. A ray is sent from the point of interest to the light source and all points of ray–surface intersection are calculated. Unlike the refraction of a ray at the interface between two media, the direction of the light ray is not altered at such points. By not bending the light ray at each interface, the problem of determining the path of light from the light source through transparent objects onto other surfaces has been eliminated. The ray proceeds from intersection point to intersection point, calculating new transmission

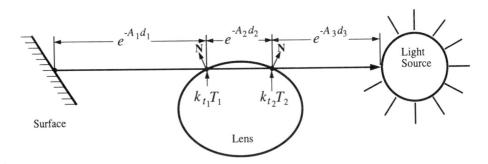

Figure 1.　Calculation of shadow through lens.

factors and weighting the current shadow attenuation term S by these transmission factors to generate the new shadow attenuation term. Also, as light passes through absorbing media, the amount of absorption should be factored into the shadow attenuation term. (See preceding gem, on body color.)

The attenuation term S is calculated as follows:

Procedure Shadow_ray()
  $S = 1$
  send a ray to the light source and generate intersection list
  for j = 1 to number_of_intersections **or** until reach light source
      get jth intersection **point**
      compute distance, d, through previous medium with absorption factor, A
      $S = Se^{(-Ad)}$ *attenuation of light by absorption*
      compute Fresnel transmission curve, T, for the surface interface
      $S = Sk_tT$ *attenuation of light by surface transmission factor*
  repeat
end.

When the light source is reached, S contains the shadow attenuation term for scaling the amount of light that reached the point being illuminated.

Figure 1 demonstrates the shadow algorithm. As the ray leaves the intersection point and reaches the lens, the absorption factor for medium 1 and the transmission factor for the interface between medium 1 and medium 2 are factored into the S term. The process continues until the ray reaches the light source, where the final term is:

$$S = e^{(-A_1d_1)}k_{t_1}T_1e^{(-A_2d_2)}k_{t_2}T_2e^{(-A_3d_3)}.$$

Notice that, since the absorption and transmission factors are present in the equation, the equation is now wavelength-dependent. (See preceding gem, on body color.) The wavelength dependency allows certain wavelengths to be absorbed at higher rates than others, causing an overall shift in the color of the light to be perceived and permitting the shadows to be colored by the filtering of light by various media. The images in the stratified sampling paper by Lee, Redner, and Uselton (1985) contain examples of colored shadows generated by using this technique. Note also the dark edges and light center of the shadow cast by the solid glass wineglass stem.

This approximation can be extended further by taking diffuse transmission of light into account. Let T_s be the specular transmission curve as before (previously called T). Let T_d be the diffuse transmission curve, k_{st} be the specular transmission coefficient (previously called k_t), and k_{dt} be the diffuse transmission coefficient (Glassner, 1989). In our project at the University of Tulsa, $k_{st} = k_s$, the specular reflectance coefficient, and $k_{dt} = k_d$, the diffuse reflectance coefficient. Now, $T_s = 1 - F_s$ as before, and using conservation of energy principles, $T_d = 1 - F_d$, where F_d is the diffuse reflectance curve. The new shadow attenuation through the interface between two media can be modeled as $k_{st}T_s + k_{dt}T_d$. This might make for a more accurate approximation for shadows generated by frosted glass. However, most diffusely reflecting objects are opaque and Haines's idea of testing for opaque objects first when calculating shadows definitely should be used before applying this shadowing approximation.

Appendix

Wavelength-Dependent Reflection and Refraction

The reflection of light from a *conducting medium* (medium with free electrons) is affected by both the extinction coefficient and the index of refraction. The Fresnel formulas determine the fraction of the intensity of the light wave that will be reflected (Born and Wolf, 1975; Cook, 1982; Cook and Torrance, 1982; Jenkins and White, 1937; Sparrow and Cess, 1970; Wiebelt, 1966). Brighter reflections, such as reflections from metallic surfaces, are due to increased motion by free electrons under the force of a light wave. The motion is greatest at the most resonant frequencies, which occur where the values of the extinction coefficient are greatest. The effective reflectance is a weighted average of the reflectance in the direction parallel to the electric field and the reflectance in the direction perpendicular to the electric field. If the incident light is unpolarized, then the weights of the parallel and perpendicular terms are equal (Born and Wolf, 1975; Ditchburn, 1976; Jenkins and White, 1937; Wiebelt, 1966).

Special care must be taken that the complex index of refraction, $n_c + ik_0$, for the Fresnel formulas not be confused with the geometric index of refraction, n, used by ray tracing for determining the direction of refraction. When $k_0 = 0$, as is the case for dielectric materials such as glass and plastic, then the geometric index of refraction, n, is the same as the real portion of the complex index of refraction, n_c (i.e., the complex index of refraction now is real, as for dielectric media); otherwise, n_c and n are different.

Approximations for Applying the Fresnel Formulas

Unfortunately, the Fresnel formulas for a conducting medium (metals) are not readily available or applicable except for the interface between metals and air ($n_c = 1$, $k_0 = 0$). However, as Cook points out (Cook, 1982; Cook and Torrance, 1982), the Fresnel formulas are only weakly dependent on k_0 and, therefore, the appearance of a metallic surface is not degraded too severely using the Fresnel formulas for the interface between dielectric surfaces ($k_0 = 0$), which are well-defined. The Fresnel formulas for dielectric materials (Born and Wolf, 1975; Ditchburn, 1976; Sparrow and Cess, 1970; Wiebelt, 1966) are:

$$r_\parallel = \frac{n_t \cos \theta_i - n_i \cos \theta_t}{n_t \cos \theta_i + n_i \cos \theta_t},$$

$$r_\perp = \frac{n_i \cos \theta_i - n_t \cos \theta_t}{n_i \cos \theta_i + n_t \cos \theta_t},$$

$$F_\parallel = r_\parallel^2,$$

$$F_\perp = r_\perp^2, \quad \text{and}$$

$$F = \tfrac{1}{2}(F_\parallel + F_\perp),$$

where

n_i is the index of refraction for the medium of incidence,

n_t is the index of refraction for the medium of transmittance,

θ_i is the angle of incidence,

θ_t is the angle of refraction,

$r_{\parallel}$ is the ratio of the amplitude of the incident wave and the reflected wave for the direction parallel to the electric field,

$r_{\perp}$ is the ratio of the amplitude of the incident wave and the reflected wave for the direction perpendicular to the electric field,

$F_{\parallel}$ is the reflectivity value for the direction parallel to the electric field,

$F_{\perp}$ is the reflectivity value for the direction perpendicular to the electric field,

F is the total reflectivity value when the incident light wave energy is unpolarized.

The formula $F = 1/2(F_{\parallel} + F_{\perp})$ holds only under the assumption that the energy incident to the dielectric interface is completely unpolarized. The energy leaving the surface is polarized or partially polarized for all angles except 0 and 90 degrees. However, since no polarization information is being maintained by the majority of all existing shading models, the assumption must be made that the incident energy is completely unpolarized.

The cosine terms are calculated as follows:

$$\cos \theta_i = \begin{cases} \mathbf{V} \cdot \mathbf{H} & \text{for shading model applications,} \\ \mathbf{V} \cdot \mathbf{N} & \text{for reflected ray weight calculations,} \\ \mathbf{L} \cdot \mathbf{N} & \text{for shadow ray attenuation calculations,} \end{cases}$$

$$\cos \theta_t = \sqrt{1 - \left((n_i^2/n_t^2)(1 - \cos^2 \theta_i) \right)},$$

where

$\mathbf{L}$ is the ray from the point to be illuminated to the light source,

$\mathbf{N}$ is the surface normal,

$\mathbf{V}$ is the incident or viewing ray, and

$\mathbf{H} = (\mathbf{V} + \mathbf{L})/|\mathbf{V} + \mathbf{L}|$.

The term T is the Fresnel transmission term that determines the amount of light to be transmitted for a particular wavelength. Assuming a conservation of energy, the sum of the intensity of light reflected and the intensity of light transmitted must equal the intensity of light incident on the surface interface, which implies that $T = 1 - F$.

Since the Fresnel formulas are well-defined only for dielectric media, the values of $n_c + ik_0$ for conducting media must be converted to the geometric index of refraction, n. Generating the refracted ray at a surface intersection also requires the geometric index of refraction. An approximation can be used to derive the geometric index of refraction, n, from the complex index of refraction, $n_c + ik_0$. At normal incidence, the reflectance equation becomes:

$$F = \frac{(n_c - 1)^2 + k_0^2}{(n_c + 1)^2 + k_0^2},$$

where F is the effective reflectance. Using the geometric index of refraction in place of the complex index of refraction, the reflectance equation becomes:

$$F = \frac{(n - 1)^2}{(n + 1)^2}.$$

Solving for n yields:

$$n = \frac{1 + \sqrt{F}}{1 - \sqrt{F}}.$$

By using the effective reflectance calculated using the complex index of refraction with this last equation, an approximation to the geometric index of refraction, n, has been derived (Cook, 1982; Cook and Torrance, 1982).

See also V.8 A Body Color Model: Absorption of Light through Translucent Media, Mark E. Lee, Samuel P. Uselton

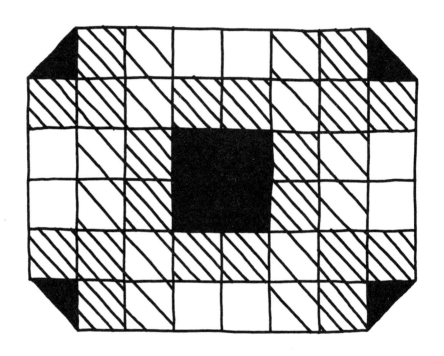

VI

RADIOSITY

RADIOSITY

The *radiosity* approach to image synthesis was introduced by Goral *et al.* (1984) and is now well-established as one of the preeminent algorithms for creating high-quality images. Based on ideas from an engineering discipline known as radiative heat transfer, the radiosity approach has as its central tenet a fundamental physical principle that is ignored almost entirely by techniques such as ray tracing—the principle of energy conservation. Although the standard ray-tracing effects of specular reflection and refraction are much more difficult to incorporate into this approach, radiosity excels at computing global lighting in which energy is balanced among diffuse surfaces that radiate and re-radiate light *ad infinitum*.

Initially, radiosity appeared to be a radical departure from ray tracing, with the sharp difference easily discernible in the images generated by each method. Ray tracing boasted curved shiny objects with brilliant reflections, while radiosity images revealed soft shadows and color bleeding among flat diffuse surfaces—subtle effects that add realism to images of more commonplace settings, such as room interiors. Although the two algorithms seemed worlds apart, current research is bridging the gap to yield techniques that enjoy the strengths of both. The view-dependent nature of ray tracing makes it indispensable for precise reflections, while the physically based nature of radiosity makes it an ideal paradigm for physically accurate simulations. The gems in this Part focus on different aspects of the radiosity approach. The first gem describes how a radiosity

293

renderer can be implemented based on familiar rendering software. The next two gems describe small improvements to relatively well-known radiosity approaches. The last two gems focus on the use of ray tracing within the context of radiosity.

VI.1
IMPLEMENTING PROGRESSIVE RADIOSITY WITH USER-PROVIDED POLYGON DISPLAY ROUTINES

Shenchang Eric Chen
Apple Computer, Inc.
Cupertino, California

Introduction

Radiosity has emerged in recent years as a popular rendering technique. The main advantage of radiosity is its capability of simulating diffuse interreflection or so-called color bleeding effects. This advantage has enabled radiosity images to be highly realistic, since most surfaces in the real world are diffuse. Another characteristic of typical diffuse radiosity is that the rendering is view-independent: Intensities are computed in world space on some discrete surface points. This allows fast viewing of radiosity results from different positions.

While a naive ray tracer can be implemented fairly easily and compactly (as in the case of Paul Heckbert, who has a ray tracer printed on his business card), implementing a radiosity program generally is regarded as an enormous task. This is evident in that there still is no public domain radiosity code available, to the author's knowledge; yet if we assume some tools are available, a naive radiosity renderer actually is quite simple to implement.

The main computation in radiosity is the computation of *form factors*, which are geometrical relationships between surfaces (Goral *et al.*, 1984). Form factors can be computed using a hemi-cube technique (Cohen and Greenberg, 1985), which mainly involves hidden surface removal. Therefore, if we assume some polygon display tools such as z buffer or ray casting are available, then implementing a radiosity program is very simple. The availability of such kinds of tools generally is not a problem. A number of polygon scan converters and ray tracers are published in previous gems. Most graphics workstations now have z buffer methods implemented in hardware and may be used to speed up the hemi-cube computation.

In the following sections, an implementation of progressive radiosity (Cohen *et al.*, 1988) is presented and its C Implementation also is given in Appendix 2. The implementation assumes all the surfaces are ideal diffuse and have been tessellated into patches (shooters of radiosity) and elements (receivers of radiosity). It does not perform any adaptive subdivision and ignores the aliasing problems caused by the hemi-cube method as noted by Baum *et al.* (1989) and Wallace *et al.* (1989). The program is easily transportable to different platforms because it assumes some user-provided polygon drawing routines are available. An additional advantage of this approach is that it allows users to experiment with different hidden surface algorithms to accelerate the hemi-cube computation, which may account for 90% of the total computation.

Progressive Radiosity

Progressive radiosity uses an iterative solution to compute the results. Each iteration basically consists of the following steps:

Find Shooting Patch: Find the next shooting patch that has the greatest unshot energy (i.e., the energy to be distributed). If the unshot energy is less than a fraction of the sum of the initially emitted energy, then stop the solution.

Compute Form Factors: Place a hemi-cube on the center of the shooting patch and orient it to the patch's normal direction. Project every element to all five faces of the hemi-cube. Sum the delta form factors associated with each hemi-cube pixel to compute form factors from the shooting patch to every element.

Distribute Radiosity: Distribute the unshot radiosity of the shooting patch to every element.

Display Results: Display all the elements with colors determined from the element's radiosity.

Figure 1 illustrates the process.

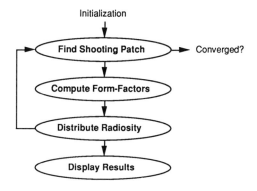

Figure 1. Progressive radiosity.

Implementation

The program *rad.c* takes an array of *patches* and *elements* as input and performs rendering on them. The patch and element are two different levels of subdivision of a surface. The patches actually are surface sample points that contain locations, normals, areas, surface attributes, etc. The shape of a patch is not needed in our implementation. The patch subdivision can be very coarse and usually is a function of the surface's radiosity, size, and position. Varying patch subdivision is equivalent to approximating an area light with different numbers of point lights and has a similar speed and quality trade-off. Each patch is subdivided further into elements, which contain additional information such as shapes and patches to which they belong. Since elements are used to display the results, varying element subdivision is analogous to varying image resolutions in ray tracing.

This program makes use of three user-provided routines to perform hemi-cube computation and display of results:

BeginDraw: This function should clear the frame buffer with a background color and prepare it for drawing. It also sets up a view transformation that will be used by all the subsequent drawings of polygons.

DrawPolygon: This function should transform, clip, and scan–convert a polygon into a frame buffer, and should perform hidden surface removal. Each polygon is drawn with a constant color.

EndDraw: The function should guarantee all the polygons are drawn to the frame buffer and the content of the buffer is ready to be accessed by the caller.

Notice that the preceding routines also can be implemented with a ray tracer, which stores polygons in a list when *DrawPolygon* is called and starts tracing rays when *EndDraw* is called.

Since the drawing routines are assumed to perform only flat shading, each polygon in the image is shaded with a constant color computed from the element radiosity. To generate smoothly shaded images, bilinear interpolation of the element radiosities can be used to obtain colors of the element vertices. Then Gouraud shading (1971) can be used to display the image.

A test program *room.c* is included as a demonstration. (See C Implementation in Appendix II.)

A CUBIC TETRAHEDRAL | ADAPTATION OF THE | HEMI-CUBE ALGORITHM

Jeffrey C. Beran-Koehn and Mark J. Pavicic
North Dakota State University
Fargo, North Dakota

The *hemi-cube algorithm* has become the most popular method of calculating radiosity solutions for complex environments containing hidden surfaces and shadows (Cohen and Greenberg, 1985). A cubic tetrahedral adaptation of this algorithm increases performance by reducing the number of projection planes from five to three, while maintaining the simplicity of the required clipping and projection operations.

The hemi-cube algorithm calculates the amount of light landing on a patch from every other patch by transforming the environment so that the receiving patch's center is at the origin and its normal coincides with the positive z axis. An imaginary cube is constructed around the center of the receiving patch. The upper half of this cube provides four half-faces and one full face onto which the environment is projected. Each of these faces is divided into square pixels at a given resolution. The hemi-cube is illustrated in Fig. 1.

Every patch in the environment that is above, or intersects, the $z = 0$ plane is clipped so that it lies within only one of the five view volumes defined by the planes: $z = 0$, $z = x$, $z = -x$, $z = y$, $z = -y$, $x = y$, and $x = -y$. These patches then are projected onto the appropriate face of the cube by a perspective projection and hidden-surface removal is done with a depth-buffering algorithm.

A cubic tetrahedron may be constructed by slicing a cube with a plane that passes through three of the cube's vertices. Using a cube that is identical to the one described before, select the following vertices to define the slicing plane: $V_1 = (-r, r, r)$, $V_2 = (r, -r, r)$, $V_3 = (r, r, -r)$. The apex of the cubic tetrahedron is at the point $A = (r, r, r)$, and the center of the cubic tetrahedron's base is located at the point $C =$

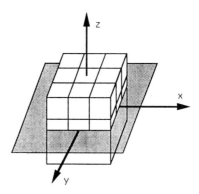

Figure 1. The hemi-cube.

$(r/3, r/3, r/3)$. To locate the center of the cubic tetrahedron's base at the origin, the cube is translated $-r/3$ units along the $x, y,$ and z axes (i.e., $V_i' = V_i - C$, $A' = A - C$, and $C' = 0$). Figure 2 illustrates this cubic tetrahedron. The plane equation of the base of the cubic tetrahedron now is $x + y = -z$. The equation of the plane containing C', A', and V_1' is $z = y$. The plane containing C', A', and V_2' is described by the equation $z = x$, while C', A', and V_3' define a plane whose equation is $x = y$.

To use this cubic tetrahedral approach, the environment is transformed so the center of the receiving patch is at the origin and the patch's normal

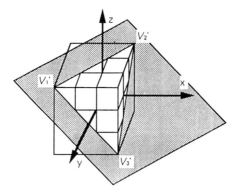

Figure 2. The cubic tetrahedron.

coincides with the vector $(1, 1, 1)$. An imaginary cubic tetrahedron is constructed from a cube and the plane containing the receiving patch as described previously. This defines three faces onto which the environment is to be projected. Every patch in the environment that is above, or intersects, the $x + y = -z$ plane is clipped so that it lies within only one of the three view volumes defined by the planes: $x + y = -z$, $z = y$, $z = x$, and $x = y$. Thus, the cubic tetrahedron retains the property that only simple comparisons are required to determine on which side of a clipping plane any point lies. Each patch, located above the $x + y = -z$ plane, is projected onto the appropriate face of the cubic tetrahedron by a perspective projection. The projections for the cubic tetrahedron and the hemi-cube differ only in the distance between the center of projection and the projection plane. As is the case with the hemi-cube algorithm, hidden-surface removal is done with a depth-buffering algorithm.

The first advantage of the cubic tetrahedral adaptation is the fact that each of the faces is identical. The hemi-cube uses four half-faces and one full face of a cube, thus requiring the top face to be treated differently than the four side faces.

The cubic tetrahedral adaptation also increases the performance of the hemi-cube algorithm. The cubic tetrahedron partitions the environment into three view volumes instead of five. This coarser partitioning results in fewer patches that must be clipped. This is an important result because for each patch that is clipped, not only must the intersection of the patch with an edge of a view volume be calculated, but another patch is created. This new patch creates additional work in the projection and hidden-surface portions of the algorithm. The reduction in the clipping, and, therefore, in the number of projection and hidden-surface calculations, is achieved while maintaining the ease with which these operations are performed.

The cubic tetrahedral adaptation samples the environment with half as many pixels as would be used by the hemi-cube algorithm at a given resolution. The four half-faces and one full face of the hemi-cube sample the environment with three times the number of pixels located on one full face of the cube. The three faces of the cubic tetrahedron sample the environment with only one and one-half times the number of pixels located on one full face of the cube. Therefore, to sample the environment with the same number of pixels as the hemi-cube, the number of pixels on the cubic tetrahedron must be doubled. This does not affect performance, since the number of pixels used for hidden-surface removal and form-factor calculations now is identical for both geometries. The doubling, however, does slightly increase the storage requirements of the delta form-factor look-up table (Cohen and Greenberg, 1985). Let n be the number of pixels on one full face of the cube. Then the hemi-cube's look-up table contains $n/8 + n/4$, or $3n/8$ values. Doubling the number of pixels on the cubic tetrahedron results in a look-up table containing $n/2$ values.

The cubic tetrahedron provides an attractive adaptation of the hemi-cube algorithm. It replaces the five faces of the hemi-cube with three symmetrical faces. These faces are constructed in such a manner as to maintain the efficiency of the clipping and projection operations. The number of patches that are clipped is reduced, resulting in a reduction of the number of projection and hidden-surface calculations performed. This performance increase is accompanied by only a slight increase in the amount of storage required for the delta form-factor look-up table.

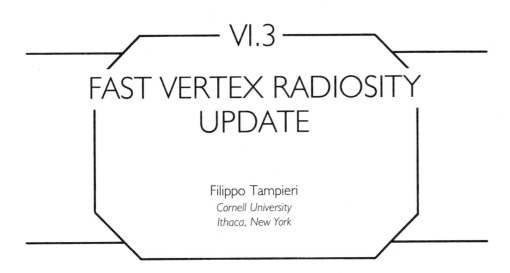

VI.3

FAST VERTEX RADIOSITY UPDATE

Filippo Tampieri
Cornell University
Ithaca, New York

Here is a simple method for fast progressive refinement radiosity using ray-traced form factors that, at each iteration of the algorithm, reduces the number of surfaces whose radiosity needs to be updated.

At each iteration of progressive refinement radiosity, a shooting patch is selected and the radiosity of all the mesh vertices in the environment must be updated with its contribution. A simple approach consists of traversing sequentially a list of these vertices and updating each one in turn. The update involves tracing one or more shadow rays to determine occlusions for the computation of the vertex-to-shooting patch form factor and can be pretty expensive. If the vertex is behind the shooting patch, though, the entire computation can be avoided, since, in this case, there can be no energy reaching the vertex. Let the vertex location be denoted by P and the plane on which the shooting patch lies be denoted by N and d, where $N = [a, b, c]$ and $ax + by + cz + d = 0$ is the equation of the plane, then:

> **if** $N \cdot P + d \leq 0$ **then**
> > *vertex P is behind the shooting patch*
>
> **else**
> > *vertex P is in front of the shooting patch*

Thus, a simple dot product is sufficient to cull a vertex out of consideration. The culling operation, though, can be much more effective at speeding up the update pass if applied to a group of mesh vertices all at once.

If the environment is viewed as consisting of a set of surfaces, mesh vertices can be grouped according to which surface they lie on. If the surfaces all are polygons, then each surface can be culled easily by testing its corners; if its corners all are behind the shooting patch, then none of its mesh vertices can receive any energy and no further work is necessary. However, if at least one corner is in front of the shooting patch, then all of its mesh vertices must be processed, since some of them might receive energy.

Bounding boxes can be used to develop a faster and more general method of determining whether a surface is behind a shooting patch. If the surface is enclosed in a bounding box, then it can be culled out of consideration if its bounding box is behind the shooting patch.

Here is an algorithm that determines whether or not an axis-aligned box is completely behind a given plane, using only a few comparisons and a single dot product. The idea is as follows: Choose the corner of the box that is in front of the plane and the furthest away from it, or that which is the closest to the plane if no corner lies in front of the plane. (Ties are broken arbitrarily.) If the chosen corner is behind the plane, then all the other corners must be behind the plane as well, which implies that the bounding box itself and its contents are completely behind the plane and thus can be culled safely out of consideration. In Fig. 1, the chosen corner is circled for the three most representative cases.

The choice is made simply by selecting that corner whose x, y, and z components are the largest when the corresponding component of the plane normal is positive, and the smallest when the corresponding component of the plane normal is negative. (If the component of the plane normal is zero, any choice will do.)

Let the axis-aligned box be denoted by its minimum and maximum corners, $C^{\min}$ and $C^{\max}$, and the plane be denoted by N and d as before;

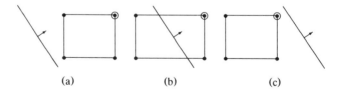

(a)   (b)   (c)

Figure 1.

304

then:

1. **for** i **in** x y z **do**
      if $N_i \geq 0.$ **then**
            $P_i := C_i^{\max}$
      else
            $P_i := C_i^{\min}$;
2. **if** $N \cdot P + \mathrm{d} \leq 0.$ **then**
      the box is completely behind the plane
   else
      the box is at least partially in front of the plane

Step 1 chooses the appropriate corner of the bounding box and step 2 checks whether the corner is behind the plane of the shooting patch. On large surfaces and fine meshes, this method may cull hundreds or even thousands of mesh vertices in a single operation.

The idea of using bounding boxes can be carried even further. If the surfaces in the environment are organized in a hierarchy of bounding boxes, then entire groups of surfaces are eliminated from consideration when the bounding box associated to an interior node of the hierarchy is found to lie completely behind the plane of the shooting patch. The whole environment now is updated by traversing the hierarchy recursively, starting from the root, testing at each node whether its bounding box is completely behind the shooting patch, and examining its children only if that is not the case.

See also VI.I Implementing Progressive Radiosity with User-Provided Polygon Display Routines, Shenchang Eric Chen

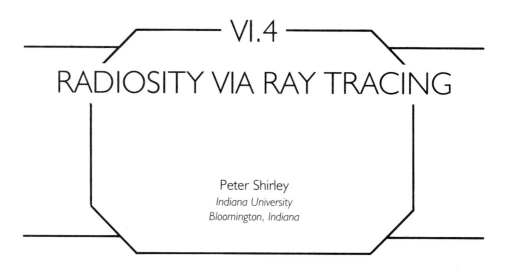

VI.4

RADIOSITY VIA RAY TRACING

Peter Shirley

Indiana University
Bloomington, Indiana

In a radiosity program, the indirect lighting that contributes to surface color is calculated explicitly. This is used in place of the less accurate *ambient* term usually used in computer graphics. Radiosity solutions are applicable to scenes that are made up of *diffuse* reflectors (i.e., matte objects). Recently, *progressive refinement* radiosity has become popular. In progressive refinement solutions, power is transported within the environment until we have an estimate for the power reflected from each surface. If ray tracing is used to transport the power, a radiosity program is not hard to write.

Progressive Refinement Radiosity

The simplest way to implement (and understand) a radiosity program is as a brute force physical simulation. Assume that the entire environment is divided into N surface zones z_i.

For each zone, we should find the average reflectivity, R_i. The unknowns we would like to solve for are the radiances L_i of all z_i. Radiance can be thought of as surface brightness, and sometimes is called intensity in the computer graphics literature. For our purposes, we can use *radiance* and *brightness* interchangeably.

In a physical simulation, it is easier to deal with power than radiance. Power simply is the energy per unit time. For example, a light bulb that emits 60 joules per second is a 60-watt bulb. Given the power Φ_i leaving z_i, we can find the radiance L_i:

$$L_i = \frac{\Phi_i}{\pi A_i},$$

where A_i is the surface area of z_i.

Assume the power emitted from z_i is known to be Φ_i^{emit}. This quantity will be zero for zones that are not *luminaires* (light sources). In a progressive refinement solution, we send the power from the luminaires to all other zones. We then have these zones send the power they reflect. This process is repeated until most of the power is absorbed. To accomplish this, we need to define Φ_i^{unsent}, the accumulated power of z_i that has not yet been propagated to other zones. We now can outline a simple program to estimate L_i for every surface:

> **for** $i = 1$ to N
> $\Phi_i^{unsent} = \Phi_i = \Phi_i^{emit}$
> **for** b $= 1$ to B
>   **for** $i = 1$ to N
>   Send Φ_i^{unsent} to other surfaces
> $\Phi_i^{unsent} = 0$
>   **for** $i = 1$ to N
> $L_i = \Phi_i/(\pi A_i)$

This algorithm loops through all the zones B times. B can be thought of as the approximate number of interreflections we model (we actually model approximately $1.5B$ interreflections), and values somewhere between 4 and 20 should produce good results. Each zone sends its unsent power once to the other zones in each iteration of the loop. The difficult part of the algorithm is the line *Send Φ_i^{unsent} to other surfaces*. Here, power is sent to many z_j, raising the values for Φ_j and Φ_j^{unsent}. This can be accomplished using projection techniques or ray tracing. In the next section, the easiest ray tracing method is described.

Sending the Power with Rays

When the zone z_i sends its accumulated power out into the environment, the quantity sent in a particular direction is proportional to $\cos \theta$, where θ is the angle between the direction and the surface normal of z_i. We could calculate explicitly the power transferred from z_i to every z_j based on the geometrical relationship of z_i and z_j. The fraction of power leaving z_i that directly gets to z_j is called the form factor F_{ij}. Instead, we implicitly can estimate F_{ij} by using a Monte Carlo simulation.

Because we know z_i reflects/emits power in a cosine distribution, we could divide Φ_i^{unsent} into r packets, and send each packet in a random direction. These directions should have a cosine density, rather than being uniformly random. The power carried in each packet would be transferred fully to whatever zone, z_j, is hit by the packet (seen in the direction the packet is sent). In pseudo-code, this idea becomes:

$$\phi = \Phi_i^{unsent}/r$$
for $k = 1$ to r
    Choose a random direction (θ, φ)
    Choose a random point p on z_j
    Find zone z_k hit by ray from p in direction (θ, φ)
    $\Phi_k = \Phi_k + R_k \phi$
    $\Phi_k^{unsent} = \Phi_k^{unsent} + R_k \phi$

One way to think of this is as a simulation where r *photons* are sent from z_i. There are two details that need to be fleshed out. The first is how many rays r we should send. We certainly should not use the same r for each surface, because we would rather send many rays from a bright zone, and no rays from a zone with no unsent power. A good method is to make r directly proportional to Φ_i^{unsent}, so a zone with twice as much power as another zone will send twice as many rays.

We also need a way to choose random (θ, φ) with the right distribution: The probability of a particular direction is proportional to $\cos \theta$. For a particular ray, we choose a random pair (ξ_1, ξ_2) uniformly from the unit square $(0 \le \xi_j < 1)$. We get the direction (θ, φ) by applying the transformations $\theta = \arccos(\sqrt{1 - \xi_1})$, and $\varphi = 2\pi\xi_2$. Be sure to remember that (θ, φ) are the coordinates relative to the surface normal, and not the global Cartesian axes.

Extensions

There are a few things we need to add to our solution for it to be useful. Most importantly, we need to *smooth* our solution. If we simply flat-shaded every z_i using L_i, then we would end up with obvious zone boundaries, giving a *quilting* effect. The standard solution is to interpolate zone colors to the zone vertices, and then Gouraud shade each zone. Because we want color to vary continuously across an object (e.g., the wall in a room), vertices shared by adjacent zones should have exactly one color. The simplest way to find vertex colors that meet this constraint is to set each vertex color to the average of L_i for all z_i that have that vertex on their boundaries.

Another basic thing we need to add is color. This is done by representing the power, reflectance, and radiance variables as sets of values. If an RGB color model is used, each variable would have a red, a green, and a blue component. If we want to use a more sophisticated color model, we can represent each variable at a set of specified wavelengths.

Non-diffuse luminaires can be added by distributing the rays first sent from luminaires according to some density other than the cosine density. For example, we could make the density proportional to $\cos^n \theta$, where n is a user-defined *phong* exponent. For this, we use the transformations $\theta = \arccos((1 - \xi_1)^{1/(n+1)})$, $\varphi = 2\pi\xi_2$.

If we want to make images of complex scenes, we will want to use texture mapping. We can think of this as allowing each zone to have a reflectivity that varies across its surface; so each z_i will have a reflectivity function $R(p)$ defined for all points p on the zone. The average reflectance, R_i, can be found by integrating $R(p)$ over the surface of z_i and dividing by A_i. If we use Monte Carlo integration, this amounts to averaging $R(p_j)$ for several points p_j randomly taken from the surface of z_i. We can proceed with the standard radiosity solution. When we normally would display a point p on a zone z_i as color $L(p)$ (found from Gouraud shading), instead use $R(p)L(p)/R_i$. In effect, this transforms the radiosity solution to one of incoming light rather than reflected light, which we then can multiply by reflectance.

Mirrors can be added to our solution by letting the power carrying rays reflect from them with appropriate loss in power (attenuation by the reflectivity of the mirror). These mirrors will not have any stored color (as their color varies directionally), but they can be rendered with a standard ray tracing program.

Further Reading

The first radiosity paper, which gives insight into the original thinking behind radiosity methods, is by Goral *et al.* (1984). The hemi-cube, an alternative to ray tracing, and the interpolation to zone vertices is discussed by Cohen and Greenberg (1985). The progressive refinement approach is described by Cohen *et al.* (1988). Ray tracing for radiosity is discussed by Malley (1988), Sillion and Puech (1989), Wallace *et al.* (1989), and Airey *et al.* (1990). More information on Gouraud shading and modeling techniques for polygons with shared vertices can be found in Foley *et al.* (1990). Radiosity techniques for heat transfer, as well as much of the underlying physics, can be found in the book by Siegel and Howell (1981).

See also VI.I Implementing Progressive Radiosity with User-Provided Polygon Display Routines, Shenchang Eric Chen

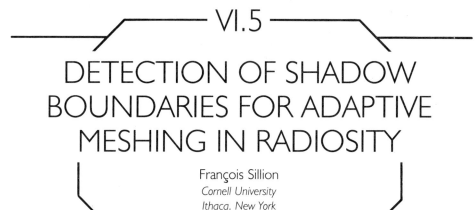

VI.5

DETECTION OF SHADOW BOUNDARIES FOR ADAPTIVE MESHING IN RADIOSITY

François Sillion
Cornell University
Ithaca, New York

Background

Radiosity algorithms attempt to compute the global interreflection of light in an environment composed of diffuse surfaces. Most implementations of the radiosity approach break the surfaces in a scene into *patches* in a meshing stage, and these patches are used as secondary illuminators in the course of the solution. Radiosity textures also have been used to encode the illumination information without complicating the geometrical description (Heckbert, 1990).

The radiosity (diffused intensity) across a patch typically is interpolated bilinearly from radiosities at the vertices, which means that the accuracy of the illumination on a surface is influenced directly by the size of the mesh elements (or the texture resolution). Typically, we would like to concentrate smaller elements in the regions of sharp intensity variations, such as shadow boundaries, while limiting the subdivision of surfaces with gentle illumination variations.

We place ourselves in the context of *progressive radiosity*, where successive steps of the solution can be described as *shooting* light from a selected patch. Since we would like our mesh (or texture) to depend on illumination, we have to base our subdivision criterion on the results of the simulation. This means that after each shooting step, we want to decide which areas to subdivide, based on the results of the current shot.

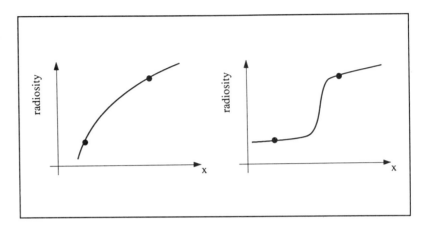

Figure 1. Two cases with the same difference in vertex intensities. Only the one with a shadow boundary should require subdivision, since it cannot be rendered by bilinear interpolation.

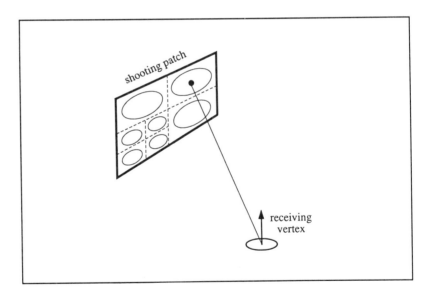

Figure 2. Ray-traced form factors.

Unfortunately, it is difficult to base a decision on intensity comparisons alone (Fig. 1). What we really want to detect are cases where bilinear interpolation will not capture the real intensity variations.

The idea presented here is equally applicable to meshed and textured environments. We show that, using ray casting to compute area-to-differential-area form factors as explained by Wallace *et al.* (1989), it is easy, in fact, to detect true shadow boundaries, by keeping track of the visibility of the shooting patch at each receiving vertex. This information then can be used in the subdivision criterion.

Obtaining a "Visibility Index"

When using ray casting to compute form factors, a shooting patch is selected, and each vertex in the environment mesh is visited in turn. At each vertex, the shooting patch is sampled at one or several locations (as a variety of sampling algorithms can be implemented), and for each sample point, a ray is cast to determine potential occlusion. Each sample point has an area associated with it, and a *delta form factor* is computed by approximating the region around the sample point with a disk of the same area (Fig. 2). An *area-to-differential-area* form factor (Wallace *et al.*, 1989) then is computed as an area-weighted average of the delta form factors.

Suppose now that we associate a *visibility* value to each ray; that is, 0.0 if the sample point is obstructed from the vertex, 1.0 otherwise. We then can compute the same area-weighted average of this visibility variable, and obtain a *patch visibility index* that can be stored with the vertex. Depending on the amount of storage that one is willing to allocate, this can be as simple as a 1 bit value, or a more precise quantity.

Subdivision Criteria

After a complete radiosity shot—that is, when all vertices have been visited—is the time to examine the current mesh or texture, and to decide whether to subdivide further. Each edge of the mesh is considered in turn, and the chosen subdivision criterion is applied to decide of that edge needs to be split. If yes, the edge and the neighboring mesh elements are split, and radiosity is shot from the shooting patch to all newly created vertices. The same criterion then can be applied recursively to the newly created edges.

As was shown in Fig. 1, the difference in intensities at the endpoints of an edge is not relevant as a criterion: It would require a low threshold to detect faint (but important for the picture) shadow boundaries, which would result in unnecessary subdivision in open areas.

We advocate the use of different thresholds for edges that cross or do not cross a shadow boundary: Using the visibility variable that was just described, shadow boundaries are identified trivially, and the lower threshold can be used. When no shadow boundary is crossed, a different criterion can be used; for example, based on the actual 3D intensity gradient. It is possible then to trigger adaptive subdivision on faint shadow boundaries, without subdividing all the *open areas* on the surfaces.

The algorithm can be summarized as:

Select shooting patch
   For each vertex
      -**for** each sample point on the patch
         use your favorite sampling method
       compute delta form factor
       compute visibility   *1 or 0*
      -average (area weighted) form factor
      -average (area weighted) visibility
   End For

   For each edge
      If visibility of endpoints are different
      Then
       apply shadow boundary criterion.
      Else
       apply normal criterion.
      Subdivide or not according to criterion
   End For

See also VI.1 Implementing Progressive Radiosity with User-Provided Polygon Display Routines, Shenchang Eric Chen; VI.4 Radiosity via Ray Tracing, Peter Shirley

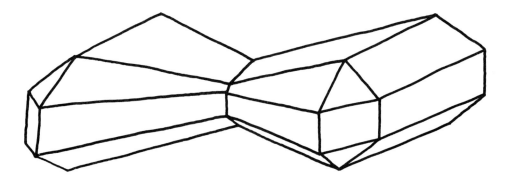

VII

MATRIX TECHNIQUES

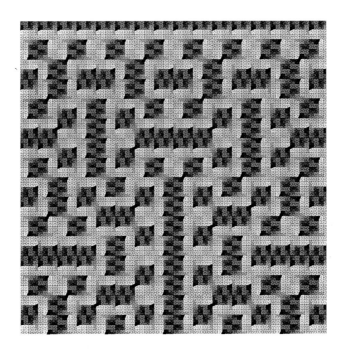

I.7 Figures I and 2.   These plates show the Peano curve in two dimensions with 8 subdivisions, or "bits of precision," at 512 by 512 resolution. Thus alternating pixels are covered by the curve. The two images represent the same curve, as seen at different points in a colormap animation performed by ran_ramp. Note the changing patterns created by the colormap animation.

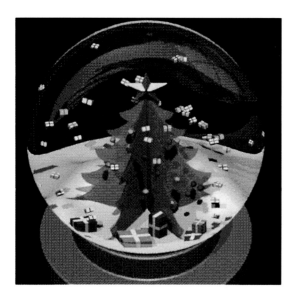

II.3 Figure I. A multilevel image dithered with ordered dither.

II.3 Figure 3. A sample image dithered to the ordered dither colormap, using multilevel error-propagation dither.

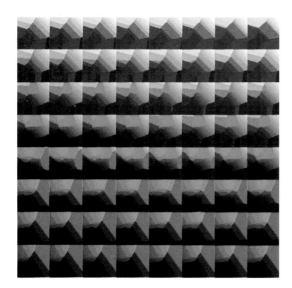

III.I Figure I. A color Voronoi diagram. The colors were derived by quantizing the Christmas tree image in Fig. 5.

III.I Figure 5. A test image. (See Fig. 1.)

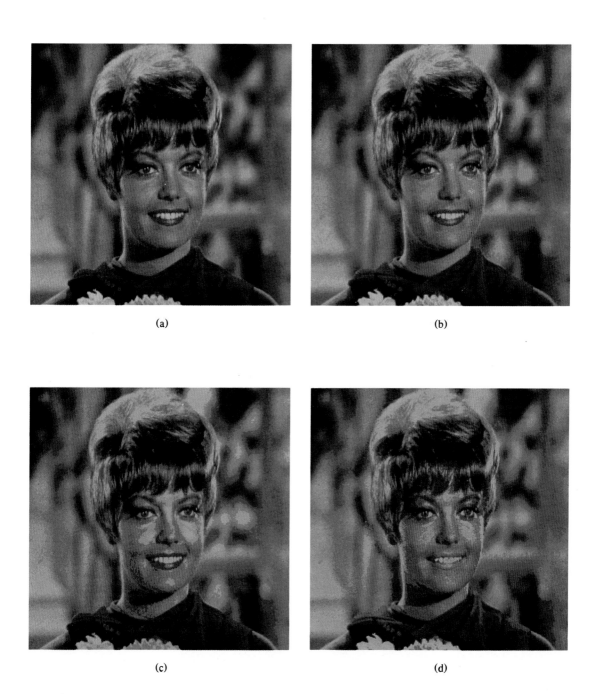

III.2 Figure 2. (a) 256-color image quantized by Wu's algorithm; (b) 64-color image quantized by Wu's algorithm; (c) 64-color image quantized by Heckbert's algorithm; (d) 64-color image quantized by the Wan *et al.* algorithm.

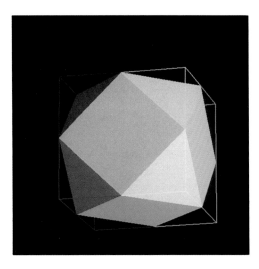

III.5 Figure 1. Partitioning of 3-space into 16 regions.

III.5 Figure 2. Quantization of color triples under the algorithm.

(a)   (b)   (c)   (d)

IV.9 Figure 4. A synthetic actor: a) faceted shading; b) Phong shading; c) InterPhong shading with $\beta_1 = 0$ and $\beta_2 = 1$; d) InterPhong shading with $\beta_1 = 0$ and $\beta_2 = 5$.

MATRIX TECHNIQUES

The mathematical foundation and predominant language of computer graphics come from linear algebra, and perhaps the most fundamental element of this vocabulary is the matrix. Virtually every graphics application rests at some level upon linear transformations in *screen* coordinates, *world* coordinates, or *homogeneous* coordinates, expressed as 2×2, 3×3, and 4×4 matrices. Operations involving these matrices are sprinkled liberally throughout every manner of graphics program, from image processing to ray tracing. Their utility is made clear by the preponderance of hardware graphics devices designed to accelerate matrix transformations, as well as by mathematical expositions in which they provide concise notation. The gems of this Part are devoted to constructing, decomposing, representing, and operating on matrices.

VII.1

DECOMPOSING A MATRIX INTO SIMPLE TRANSFORMATIONS

Spencer W. Thomas
University of Michigan
Ann Arbor, Michigan

Sometimes, it is useful to be able to extract a sequence of simple transformations (scale, rotate, etc.) that will reproduce a given transformation matrix. This gem provides a way to do that. In particular, given (almost[1]) any 4×4 transformation matrix $\mathbf{M}$, it will compute the arguments to the following sequence of transformations, such that concatenating the transformations will reproduce the original matrix (to within a homogeneous scale factor):

$$\text{Scale}(s_x, s_y, s_z)\text{Shear}_{xy}^2 \text{ Shear}_{xz} \text{ Shear}_{yz} \text{ Rotate}_x \text{ Rotate}_y$$

$$\text{Rotate}_z \text{Translate}(t_x, t_y, t_z)$$

$$\text{Perspective}(p_x, p_y, p_z, p_w).$$

This routine has been used for tasks such as removing the shears from a rotation matrix, for feeding an arbitrary transformation to a graphics system that only *understands* a particular sequence of transformations (which is particularly useful when dealing with rotations), or for any other application in which you want just part of the transformation sequence.

---

[1]The only constraint is that the product of the $[4, 4]$ element with the determinant of the upper left 3×3 component of the matrix be nonzero.

[2]Shear_{xy} shears the x coordinate as the y coordinate changes. The matrix corresponding to this transformation is

$$\begin{bmatrix} 1 & 0 & 0 \\ s_{xy} & 1 & 0 \\ 0 & 0 & 1 \end{bmatrix}.$$

320

The Algorithm

The algorithm works by *undoing* the transformation sequence in reverse order. It first determines perspective elements that, when *removed* from the matrix, will leave the last column (the *perspective partition*) as $(0, 0, 0, 1)^T$. Then it extracts the translations. This leaves a 3×3 matrix comprising the scales, shears, and rotations. It is decomposed from the left, extracting first the scaling factors and then the shearing components, leaving a pure rotation matrix. This is broken down into three consecutive rotations.

Extracting the perspective components is the messiest part. Essentially, we need to solve the matrix equation:

$$
\begin{bmatrix}
\mathbf{M}_{1,1} & \mathbf{M}_{1,2} & \mathbf{M}_{1,3} & \mathbf{M}_{1,4} \\
\mathbf{M}_{2,1} & \mathbf{M}_{2,2} & \mathbf{M}_{2,3} & \mathbf{M}_{2,4} \\
\mathbf{M}_{3,1} & \mathbf{M}_{3,2} & \mathbf{M}_{3,3} & \mathbf{M}_{3,4} \\
\mathbf{M}_{4,1} & \mathbf{M}_{4,2} & \mathbf{M}_{4,3} & \mathbf{M}_{4,4}
\end{bmatrix}
$$

$$
=
\begin{bmatrix}
\mathbf{M}_{1,1} & \mathbf{M}_{1,2} & \mathbf{M}_{1,3} & 0 \\
\mathbf{M}_{2,1} & \mathbf{M}_{2,2} & \mathbf{M}_{2,3} & 0 \\
\mathbf{M}_{3,1} & \mathbf{M}_{3,2} & \mathbf{M}_{3,3} & 0 \\
\mathbf{M}_{4,1} & \mathbf{M}_{4,2} & \mathbf{M}_{4,3} & 1
\end{bmatrix}
\begin{bmatrix}
1 & 0 & 0 & p_x \\
0 & 1 & 0 & p_y \\
0 & 0 & 1 & p_z \\
0 & 0 & 0 & p_w
\end{bmatrix},
$$

which reduces to:

$$
\begin{bmatrix}
\mathbf{M}_{1,4} \\
\mathbf{M}_{2,4} \\
\mathbf{M}_{3,4} \\
\mathbf{M}_{4,4}
\end{bmatrix}
=
\begin{bmatrix}
\mathbf{M}_{1,1} & \mathbf{M}_{1,2} & \mathbf{M}_{1,3} & 0 \\
\mathbf{M}_{2,1} & \mathbf{M}_{2,2} & \mathbf{M}_{2,3} & 0 \\
\mathbf{M}_{3,1} & \mathbf{M}_{3,2} & \mathbf{M}_{3,3} & 0 \\
\mathbf{M}_{4,1} & \mathbf{M}_{4,2} & \mathbf{M}_{4,3} & 1
\end{bmatrix}
\begin{bmatrix}
p_x \\
p_y \\
p_z \\
p_w
\end{bmatrix}.
$$

Assuming that the upper left 3×3 partition of $\mathbf{M}$ is not singular, this can be solved easily for p_x, p_y, p_z, and p_w. Since some of the later steps will not work if this partition is singular, this is not a serious defect.

The next step is to extract the translations. This is trivial; we find $t_x = \mathbf{M}_{4,1}$, $t_y = \mathbf{M}_{4,2}$, and $t_z = \mathbf{M}_{4,3}$. At this point, we are left with a 3×3 matrix, $\mathbf{M}' = \mathbf{M}_{1..3,1..3}$.

The process of finding the scaling factors and shear parameters is interleaved. First, find $s_x = |\mathbf{M}_1'|$. Then, compute an initial value for the xy shear factor, $s_{xy} = \mathbf{M}_1' \cdot \mathbf{M}_2'$. (This is too large by the y scaling factor.) The second row of the matrix is made orthogonal to the first by setting $\mathbf{M}_2' \leftarrow \mathbf{M}_2' - s_{xy}\mathbf{M}_1'$. Then the y scaling factor, s_y, is the length of the modified second row. The second row is normalized, and s_{xy} is divided by s_y to get its final value. The xz and yz shear factors are computed as in the preceding, the third row is made orthogonal to the first two rows, the z scaling factor is computed, the third row is normalized, and the xz and yz shear factors are rescaled.

The resulting matrix now is a pure rotation matrix, except that it might still include a scale factor of -1. If the determinant of the matrix is -1, negate the matrix and all three scaling factors. Call the resulting matrix $\mathbf{R}$.

Finally, we need to decompose the rotation matrix into a sequence of rotations about the x, y, and z axes. If the rotation angle about x is α, that about y is β, and that about z is γ, then the composite rotation is:

$$
\mathbf{R} = \begin{bmatrix}
\cos\{\beta\}\cos\{\gamma\} & \cos\{\beta\}\sin\{\gamma\} & -\sin\{\beta\} \\
\begin{matrix}\sin\{\alpha\}\sin\{\beta\}\cos\{\gamma\} \\ -\cos\{\alpha\}\sin\{\gamma\}\end{matrix} & \begin{matrix}\sin\{\alpha\}\sin\{\beta\}\sin\{\gamma\} \\ +\cos\{\alpha\}\cos\{\gamma\}\end{matrix} & \sin\{\alpha\}\cos\{\beta\} \\
\begin{matrix}\cos\{\alpha\}\sin\{\beta\}\cos\{\gamma\} \\ +\sin\{\alpha\}\sin\{\gamma\}\end{matrix} & \begin{matrix}\cos\{\alpha\}\sin\{\beta\}\sin\{\gamma\} \\ -\sin\{\alpha\}\cos\{\gamma\}\end{matrix} & \cos\{\alpha\}\cos\{\beta\}
\end{bmatrix}.
$$

Thus, $\beta = \arcsin(-\mathbf{R}_{1,3})$. If $\cos(\beta) \neq 0$, α is derived easily from $\mathbf{R}_{2,3}$ and $\mathbf{R}_{3,3}$, and γ from $\mathbf{R}_{1,2}$ and $\mathbf{R}_{1,1}$. If $\cos(\beta) = 0$, then $\mathbf{R}$ reduces to:

$$
\begin{bmatrix}
0 & 0 & \pm 1 \\
\sin\{\alpha \pm \gamma\} & \cos\{\alpha \pm \gamma\} & 0 \\
\cos\{\alpha \pm \gamma\} & -\sin\{\alpha \pm \gamma\} & 0
\end{bmatrix}.
$$

In this case, we arbitrarily set γ to 0 and derive α from $\mathbf{R}_{2,1}$ and $\mathbf{R}_{2,2}$. This finishes the decomposition.

See also VII.2 Recovering the Data from the Transformation Matrix, Ronald N. Goldman

VII.2

RECOVERING THE DATA FROM THE TRANSFORMATION MATRIX

Ronald N. Goldman
Rice University
Houston, Texas

In *Graphics Gems* ("Matrices and Transformations"), we showed how to construct the 4×4 matrices for affine and projective transformations—rigid motion, scaling, and projections—which were defined relative to some arbitrary positions and orientations described by scalars, points, and vectors. In this volume, we added the 4×4 matrices for shear and pseudo-perspective. Now we shall show how to retrieve the defining data—scalars, points, and vectors—from the 4×4 matrix when we know the type of transformation represented by the matrix. This is useful, for example, when we concatenate matrices for rotations around different axes and then want to know the axis and angle of the resulting rotation.

Most of the affine and projective transformations we discuss have fixed points and fixed directions—that is, values that are left invariant by the transformation. These fixed values show up as eigenvectors of the transformation matrix. (In keeping with standard usage, we shall use the term eigenvector even when the fixed value actually is a point rather than a vector). The data we seek to extract often are simply eigenvectors of the transformation matrix.

Briefly, an eigenvector v of a transformation T is any nonzero vector such that

$$\mathrm{T}(v) = \beta \mathrm{I}(v) = \beta v,$$

where I is the identity transformation. The scalar β is called an eigenvalue of T, and v is said to be an eigenvector of T corresponding to the eigenvalue β. The eigenvalues of T are the roots of the equation:

$$\text{Det}(\mathbf{T} - \beta\mathbf{I}) = 0$$

where $\mathbf{I}$ is the identity matrix of the same size as the matrix $\mathbf{T}$. There are well-known algorithms for computing eigenvalues and eigenvectors; readers not familiar with these concepts should consult a standard linear algebra text.

We shall adopt the following notation:

$$\mathbf{M} = 4 \times 4 \text{ matrix,}$$

$$\mathbf{M_{33}} = \text{upper left } 3 \times 3 \text{ submatrix of } \mathbf{M},$$

$$\mathbf{M_{34}} = \text{upper } 3 \times 4 \text{ submatrix of } \mathbf{M},$$

$$\mathbf{M_{43}} = \text{left } 4 \times 3 \text{ submatrix of } \mathbf{M},$$

$$\mathbf{M}^{\mathrm{T}} = \text{transpose of } \mathbf{M},$$

$$\text{Trace } (\mathbf{M_{33}}) = \sum_k \mathbf{M_{33}}(k, k) = \mathbf{M}(1, 1) + \mathbf{M}(2, 2) + \mathbf{M}(3, 3).$$

Armed with these concepts and this notation, we are ready now to extract the data from the transformation matrices. Note that in many cases, the data is not unique. For example, if we define a plane by a point and a unit vector, the point is not unique. Usually, this point is an eigenvector of the transformation matrix relative to some fixed eigenvalue. If we do not specify further, then any such eigenvector will suffice. Often, too, we will require a unit eigenvector corresponding to some eigenvalue β. Such an eigenvector is found readily by computing any eigenvector v corresponding to the eigenvalue β and then normalizing its length to one, since, by linearity, if v is an eigenvector corresponding to the eigenvalue β, then cv also is an eigenvector corresponding to the eigenvalue β.

Translation

Let

$$w = \text{Translation vector}$$

Given

$$\mathbf{T}(w) = \text{Translation matrix}$$

Compute

$$w = \text{Fourth row of } \mathbf{T}(w) = (0, 0, 0, 1) * \mathbf{T}(w)$$

Rotation

Let

$$L = \text{Axis line}$$

$$w = \text{Unit vector parallel to } L$$

$$Q = \text{Point on } L$$

$$\phi = \text{Angle of rotation}$$

Given

$$\mathbf{R} = \mathbf{R}(w, \phi, Q) = \text{Rotation matrix}$$

Compute

$$\cos \phi = \frac{(\text{Trace}(\mathbf{R}_{33}) - 1)}{2}$$

$$w = \text{Unit eigenvector of } \mathbf{R}_{33} \text{ corresponding to the eigenvalue 1}$$

$$Q = \text{Any eigenvector of } \mathbf{R} \text{ corresponding to the eigenvalue 1}$$

$$\sin \phi = \frac{\{\mathbf{R}(1, 2) + (\cos \phi - 1)w_1 w_2\}}{w_3}$$

Notice that the sign of $\sin \phi$ depends on the choice of w, since both w and $-w$ are eigenvectors of $\mathbf{R}_{33}$ corresponding to the eigenvalue 1. Therefore, we cannot find ϕ without first deciding on the choice of w.

Mirror Image

Let

$$S = \text{Mirror plane}$$

$$n = \text{Unit vector perpendicular to } S$$

$$Q = \text{Point on } S$$

Given

$$\mathbf{M} = \mathbf{M}(n, Q) = \text{Mirror matrix}$$

Compute

$$n = \text{Unit eigenvector of } \mathbf{M}_{33} \text{ corresponding to the eigenvalue } -1$$

$$Q = \text{Any eigenvector of } \mathbf{M} \text{ corresponding to the eigenvalue } +1$$

Scaling

Let

$$Q = \text{Scaling origin}$$

$$c = \text{Scaling factor}$$

$$w = \text{Scaling direction}$$

a. Uniform scaling
   Given

$$\mathbf{S} = \mathbf{S}(Q, c) = \text{Scaling matrix}$$

Compute

$$c = \frac{\text{Trace}(\mathbf{S}_{33})}{3}$$

Q = Any eigenvector of S corresponding to the eigenvalue 1

b. Nonuniform scaling
   Given

$$\mathbf{S} = \mathbf{S}(Q, c, w) = \text{Scaling matrix}$$

Compute

$$c = \text{Trace}(\mathbf{S}_{33}) - 2$$

w = Unit eigenvector of $\mathbf{S}_{33}$ corresponding to the eigenvalue c

Q = Any eigenvector of $\mathbf{S}$ corresponding to the eigenvalue 1

Shear

Let

$$S = \text{Shearing plane}$$

$$v = \text{Unit vector perpendicular to } S$$

$$Q = \text{Point on } S$$

$$w = \text{Unit shearing direction vector}$$

$$\phi = \text{Shearing angle}$$

Given

$$\mathbf{S} = \text{Shear}(Q, v, w, \phi) = \text{Shearing matrix}$$

Compute

w_1, w_2 = independent eigenvectors of $\mathbf{S_{33}}$ corresponding to the eigenvalue 1

$$v = \frac{w_1 \times w_2}{|w_1 \times w_2|}$$

$$\tan \phi = |v * (\mathbf{S} - \mathbf{I})_{\mathbf{33}}|$$

$$w = \frac{v * (\mathbf{S} - \mathbf{I})_{\mathbf{33}}}{\tan \phi}$$

Q = any eigenvector of $\mathbf{S}$ corresponding to the eigenvalue 1

Projection

Let

S = Image plane

n = Unit vector perpendicular to S

Q = Point on S

w = Unit vector parallel to projection direction

R = Perspective point

a. Orthogonal projection
   Given

$$\mathbf{O} = \mathbf{O}\,\text{proj}(n, Q) = \text{Projection matrix}$$

Compute

n = Unit eigenvector of $\mathbf{O}_{33}$ corresponding to the eigenvalue 0

Q = Any eigenvector of $\mathbf{O}$ corresponding to the eigenvalue 1

b. Parallel projection
Given

$$\mathbf{P} = \mathbf{P}\,\mathrm{proj}(n, Q, w) = \text{Projection matrix}$$

Compute

Q = Any eigenvector of $\mathbf{P}$ corresponding to the eigenvalue 1

w = Unit eigenvector of $\mathbf{P}_{33}$ corresponding to the eigenvalue 0

n = Unit eigenvector of $\mathbf{P}_{33}^{\mathrm{T}}$ corresponding to the eigenvalue 0

$$= \frac{w * \left\{(\mathbf{I} - \mathbf{P})_{33}^{\mathrm{T}}\right\}}{\left| w * \left\{(\mathbf{I} - \mathbf{P})_{33}^{\mathrm{T}}\right\}\right|}$$

c. Pseudo-perspective
Given

$$\mathbf{P} = \mathrm{Pseudo}(n, Q, R) = \text{Pseudo-perspective matrix}$$

Compute

Q = Any eigenvector of $\mathbf{P}$ not corresponding to the eigenvalue 0

n^{T} = First three entries of the fourth column of $\mathbf{P} = \mathbf{P}_{34} * (0, 0, 0, 1)^{\mathrm{T}}$

$$R = -\frac{\left\{(0, 0, 0, 1) * \mathbf{P}_{43} + (Q \cdot n)n\right\}}{(Q \cdot n)}$$

d. Perspective
Given

$$\mathbf{P} = \mathrm{Persp}(n, Q, R) = \text{Perspective matrix}$$

Compute

Q = Any eigenvector of $\mathbf{P}$ not corresponding to the eigenvalue 0

n^{T} = − First three entries of the fourth column of $\mathbf{P}$ = $-\mathbf{P_{34}} * (0, 0, 0, 1)^{\mathrm{T}}$

R = eigenvector of $\mathbf{P}$ corresponding to the eigenvalue 0

$$= \frac{(0, 0, 0, 1) * \mathbf{P_{43}}}{(Q \cdot n)}$$

See also VII.1 Decomposing a Matrix into Simple Transformations, Spencer W. Thomas

VII.3

TRANSFORMATIONS AS EXPONENTIALS

Ronald N. Goldman
Rice University
Houston, Texas

Introduction

Consider two rotations around the same axis. Concatenating these two transformations is equivalent to adding the rotation angles; that is, the product of two such rotation matrices is equivalent to a single rotation matrix where the angles are added. Thus, multiplication of rotations is like the adding of angles. There is another well-known function in mathematics where multiplication can be performed through addition: the *exponential*. Multiplying two exponentials is equivalent to adding their exponents. Of course, this observation is the basis of standard logarithms. We shall show here that this connection between rotation and exponentials is more than simply a coincidence; indeed, rotations—and many of the other nonsingular transformations that we often encounter in computer graphics—are exponential matrices.

The Exponential Matrix

Let $\mathbf{M}$ be a square matrix. We define the matrix $e^{\mathbf{M}}$ by the usual infinite series for the exponential. Let $\mathbf{I}$ denote the identity matrix. Then

$$e^{\mathbf{M}} = \mathbf{I} + \mathbf{M} + \frac{\mathbf{M}^2}{2!} + \frac{\mathbf{M}^3}{3!} + \cdots = \sum_k \frac{\mathbf{M}^k}{k!}.$$

For any constant $c > 0$, we define $c^{\mathbf{M}}$ by

$$c^{\mathbf{M}} = e^{\ln(c)\mathbf{M}}.$$

The matrix exponential function behaves in many ways like the ordinary scalar exponential function. We list some of its main properties below:

- $e^{\mathbf{M}} * e^{-\mathbf{M}} = \mathbf{I}$

- $e^{\mathbf{M}} * e^{\mathbf{N}} = e^{\mathbf{M}+\mathbf{N}}$ whenever $\mathbf{MN} = \mathbf{NM}$

- $\mathbf{R}e^{\mathbf{M}}\mathbf{R}^{-1} = e^{\mathbf{RMR}^{-1}}$

- $\mathrm{Det}(e^{\mathbf{M}}) = e^{\mathrm{Trace}(\mathbf{M})}$

In the last equation, Det is the usual determinant function and Trace is the sum of the diagonal terms of $\mathbf{M}$; that is,

$$\mathrm{Trace}(\mathbf{M}) = \sum_{k} \mathbf{M}_{\mathbf{kk}}.$$

Notice that by the first property $e^{\mathbf{M}}$ always is invertible, so only nonsingular matrices can be exponentials.

Tensor Product and Cross Product

Before we can proceed further, we need to recall some notation that was used in *Graphics Gems* ("Matrices and Transformations") and in this book ("More Matrices and Transformations") to construct the matrices for the transformations rotation, mirror image, scaling, and shear. Since we are interested primarily in transformations of 3-space, we confine ourselves to 3×3 matrices.

a. **Identity**

$$I = \begin{vmatrix} 1 & 0 & 0 \\ 0 & 1 & 0 \\ 0 & 0 & 1 \end{vmatrix}$$

b. **Tensor Product**

$$v \otimes w = \begin{vmatrix} v_1 w_1 & v_1 w_2 & v_1 w_3 \\ v_2 w_1 & v_2 w_2 & v_2 w_3 \\ v_3 w_1 & v_3 w_2 & v_3 w_3 \end{vmatrix} = \begin{vmatrix} v_1 \\ v_2 \\ v_3 \end{vmatrix} * \begin{vmatrix} w_1 & w_2 & w_3 \end{vmatrix}$$

c. **Cross Product**

$$w\mathbf{x}_- = \begin{vmatrix} 0 & w_3 & -w_2 \\ -w_3 & 0 & w_1 \\ w_2 & -w_1 & 0 \end{vmatrix}$$

d. **Observations**

$$u * (v \otimes w) = (u \cdot v)w$$

$$u * (w\mathbf{x}_-) = w \times u$$

$$(v \otimes w)^k = (v \cdot w)^{k-1}(v \otimes w) \qquad k \geq 1$$

$$v \cdot w = 0 \quad \text{implies} \quad e^{d(v \otimes w)} = I + d(v \otimes w)$$

$$w \cdot w = 1 \quad \text{implies} \quad e^{d(w \otimes w)} = I + (e^d - 1)(w \otimes w)$$

$$(w\mathbf{x}_-)^2 = w \otimes w - I \quad \text{and} \quad (w\mathbf{x}_-)^3 = -w\mathbf{x}_-$$

$$(w\mathbf{x}_-)^{2k} = (-1)^k (I - w \otimes w) \quad \text{and} \quad (w\mathbf{x}_-)^{2k+1} = (-1)^k w\mathbf{x}_-$$

Linear Transformations

We shall focus our attention on the following five linear transformations, which are standard in computer graphics. Notice that we do not include any projections, since projections are singular and, therefore, cannot be exponentials. By convention, all the vectors below are unit vectors.

$\text{rot}(w, \phi)$ = rotation around the axis vector w through the angle ϕ,

$\text{mir}(n)$ = mirror image in the plane perpendicular to the vector n,

$\text{scale}(c)$ = scaling in all directions by a constant $c > 0$,

$\text{scale}(c, w)$ = scaling only in the direction parallel to the vector w by a constant $c > 0$,

$\text{shear}(v, w, \phi)$ = shearing orthogonal to the plane perpendicular to the vector v by the angle ϕ in the direction parallel to the vector w, which is perpendicular to the vector v.

Here, we consider only the 3×3 matrices defined by these transformations, not the 4×4 matrices discussed in previous articles. We can think of this in two ways. The fourth row of the transformation matrix stores a translation. If our transformations are defined by lines or planes that pass through the origin, then this fourth row does not contribute anything and is not required. Alternatively, we can think of applying our transformations only to vectors, not to points. In this case, the fourth row again contributes nothing, since vectors remain invariant under translation. In any event, we are dealing here with linear, rather than affine, transformations.

Now, in previous articles ("Matrices and Transformations," in *Graphics Gems*, and "More Matrices and Transformations," in this book), we

335

have shown that:

$$\text{rot}(w, \phi) = (\cos \phi)\text{I} + (1 - \cos \phi)w \otimes w + (\sin \phi)w\text{x}_-,$$

$$\text{mir}(n) = \text{I} - 2n \otimes n,$$

$$\text{scale}(c) = c\text{I},$$

$$\text{scale}(c, w) = \text{I} + (c - 1)w \otimes w,$$

$$\text{shear}(v, w, \phi) = \text{I} + (\tan \phi)v \otimes w.$$

Each of these transformation matrices is nonsingular and, it turns out, each can be represented as an exponential. Indeed, using the definitions and the properties of the exponential map, the tensor product, and the cross product, it is not difficult to show that:

$$\text{rot}(w, \phi) = e^{\phi(w\text{x}_-)},$$

$$\text{mir}(n) = e^{i\pi(n \otimes n)}, \qquad (i = \sqrt{-1})$$

$$\text{scale}(c) = c^{\text{I}},$$

$$\text{scale}(c, w) = c^{w \otimes w},$$

$$\text{shear}(,v\, w, \phi) = e^{(\tan \phi)v \otimes w}.$$

One immediate application of these exponentials is that they make it particularly easy to compute determinants. Recall that:

$$\text{Det}(e^{\mathbf{M}}) = e^{\text{Trace}(\mathbf{M})}.$$

Moreover, it is easy to verify that:

$$\text{Trace}(\text{I}) = 3$$

$$\text{Trace}(v \otimes w) = v \cdot w$$

$$\text{Trace}(w\text{x}_-) = 0.$$

Therefore,

$$\text{Det}\{\text{rot}(w, \phi)\} = e^0 = 1,$$

$$\text{Det}\{\text{mir}(n)\} = e^{i\pi} = -1,$$

$$\text{Det}\{\text{scale}(c)\} = e^{3\ln(c)} = c^3,$$

$$\text{Det}\{\text{scale}(c, w)\} = e^{\ln(c)} = c,$$

$$\text{Det}\{\text{shear}(v, w, \phi)\} = e^0 = 1.$$

The most interesting of these exponentials by far is the one for rotation. As we said at the start, rotation mimics the exponential function, since multiplication of rotations around the same axis is akin to adding angles. This observation is immediate from the properties of the exponential map, since:

$$\text{rot}(w, \phi_1) * \text{rot}(w, \phi_2) = e^{\phi_1(w\mathbf{x}_-)} * e^{\phi_2(w\mathbf{x}_-)},$$

$$= e^{(\phi_1 + \phi_2)(w\mathbf{x}_-)},$$

$$= \text{rot}(w, \phi_1 + \phi_2).$$

Since exponentials are particularly simple to manipulate, the exponential map also may be useful for discovering other identities relating the standard linear transformations of computer graphics.

VII.4

MORE MATRICES AND TRANSFORMATIONS: SHEAR AND PSEUDO-PERSPECTIVE

Ronald N. Goldman
Rice University
Houston, Texas

In *Graphics Gems* ("Matrices and Transformations"), we showed how to construct the matrices for affine and projective transformations—rotation, mirror image, scaling, and projections—which were not defined relative to the origin and coordinate axes, but rather relative to some arbitrary positions and orientations. Two fundamental transformations we omitted from that discussion were shear and pseudo-perspective. Here, we construct the matrices for these two important transformations. We begin by recalling some notation.

Notation

    a.   Identity

$$I = \begin{vmatrix} 1 & 0 & 0 \\ 0 & 1 & 0 \\ 0 & 0 & 1 \end{vmatrix}$$

    b.   Tensor Product

$$v \otimes w = \begin{vmatrix} v_1 w_1 & v_1 w_2 & v_1 w_3 \\ v_2 w_1 & v_2 w_2 & v_2 w_3 \\ v_3 w_1 & v_3 w_2 & v_3 w_3 \end{vmatrix} = \begin{vmatrix} v_1 \\ v_2 \\ v_3 \end{vmatrix} * \begin{vmatrix} w_1 & w_2 & w_3 \end{vmatrix}$$

338

Observations

$$u * \mathrm{I} = u$$

$$u * (v \otimes w) = (u \cdot v)w$$

Shear

A shear is defined in terms of a shearing plane S, a unit vector w in S, and an angle ϕ. Given any point P, project P orthogonally onto a point P' in the shearing plane S. Now, slide P parallel to w to a point P'', so that $\angle P''P'P = \phi$. The point P'' is the result of applying the shearing transformation to the point P. (See Fig. 1.)

To construct the 4×4 matrix which represents shear, let

S = Shearing plane

v = Unit vector perpendicular to S

Q = Point on S

w = Unit vector in S (i.e., unit vector perpendicular to v)

ϕ = Shear angle

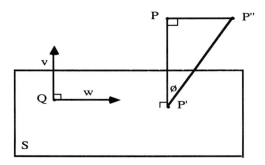

Figure 1.   The geometry of a shear.

Then the shear transformation is given by the 4×4 matrix:

$$\text{Shear}(Q, v, w, \phi) = \begin{vmatrix} I + \tan\phi\,(v \otimes w) & 0 \\ -(Q \cdot v)w & 1 \end{vmatrix}$$

It is easy to verify by direct computation that

$$\text{Det}\{\text{Shear}(Q, v, w, \phi)\} = 1.$$

Therefore, shearing preserves volumes.

Pseudo-Perspective

If we perform perspective projection before clipping, we lose the ability to clip in depth. To avoid this problem, we must put depth back into the perspective transformation; that is, we want a transformation that gives us both perspective and depth. Usually, this is done by factoring perspective projection through orthogonal projection. Thus, we want a pseudo-perspective transformation that preserves relative depth such that:

$$\text{Perspective} = (\text{Pseudo-Perspective}) * (\text{Orthogonal Projection}).$$

To construct the 4×4 matrix that represents pseudo-perspective, let

$$S = \text{Perspective plane}$$

$$Q = \text{Point on } S$$

$$\mathbf{N} = \text{Unit vector perpendicular to } S$$

$$R = \text{Perspective point}$$

Then the pseudo-perspective transformation is given by the 4×4 matrix:

$$\text{Pseudo}(\mathbf{N}, Q, R) = \begin{vmatrix} \{(Q - R) \cdot \mathbf{N}\}I + \mathbf{N} \otimes R + \mathbf{N} \otimes \mathbf{N} & {}^{T}\mathbf{N} \\ -(Q \cdot N)(R + \mathbf{N}) & -R \cdot N \end{vmatrix}$$

where ${}^{T}\mathbf{N}$ denotes the transpose of the row vector $\mathbf{N}$.

See also (472) *Matrices and Transformations, Ronald Goldman*

VII.5
FAST MATRIX INVERSION

Kevin Wu
Sun Microsystems, Inc.
Mountain View, California

Problem Statement

Performing matrix operations quickly is especially important when a graphics program changes the state of the transformation pipeline frequently. Matrix inversion can be relatively slow compared with other matrix operations because inversion requires careful checking and handling to avoid numerical instabilities resulting from roundoff error and to determine when a matrix is singular. However, a general-purpose matrix inversion procedure is not necessary for special types of matrices. Indeed, when speed is more important than code size, a graphics programmer can benefit greatly by identifying groups of matrices that have simple inverses and providing a special matrix inversion procedure for each type. This gem describes inversion of 4×4 matrices for types that commonly arise in 3D computer graphics. Note that previous gems (Carling, 1990; Turkowski, 1990) have given examples where a matrix inverse is needed, including texture mapping and normal vector transformation.

Building Blocks

Graphics books—for example, Foley and van Dam (1982) and Newman and Sproull (1979)—describe how to construct general geometric transformations by concatenating matrix representations of the basic operations: translation, scaling, and rotation. We denote the 3D transformations with 4×4 matrices:

- $\mathbf{T}(t_x, t_y, t_z)$ is a translation matrix.
- $\mathbf{S}(s_x, s_y, s_z)$ is a scale matrix.
- $\mathbf{R}$ is a rotation matrix in (x, y, z) coordinate space.

We adopt the convention of treating points in homogeneous space as row vectors of the form $[wx \ wy \ wz \ w]$, $w \neq 0$. These matrices are suitable for developing the ideas in the following sections, but some graphics programmers may find it convenient to consider other building blocks, such as shear.

Basic Group Theory

A *group* is an algebraic object useful for characterizing symmetries and permutations. For example, all crystalline lattices can be classified by applying group theory. Gilbert (1976) gives a good introduction to the subject. Our interest in groups comes from the desire to define the scope of special matrix types.

Definition I   A *group* $(G, \cdot)$ is a set G together with a binary operation $\cdot$ satisfying the following axioms.

1. *Closure*: $a \cdot b \in G$ for all $a, b \in G$.

2. *Associativity*: $(a \cdot b) \cdot c = a \cdot (b \cdot c)$ for all $a, b, c \in G$.

3. *Identity*: There exists an *identity* element $e \in G$, such that $e \cdot a = a \cdot e = a$ for all $a \in G$.

4. *Inverse*: Each element $a \in G$ has an *inverse* element $a^{-1} \in G$, such that $a^{-1} \cdot a = a \cdot a^{-1} = e$.

For our purposes, the set G is a particular type of matrix with a certain form and set of properties. The operation $\cdot$ is matrix multiplication. When the operation of a group is clearly understood, we can denote the group by only its underlying set. Hereafter, we denote the matrix group $(G, \cdot)$

by simply G with the matrix multiplication operation implicit. Note that the fourth axiom limits our attention to nonsingular matrices. A singular matrix has no inverse, so in practice, a matrix inversion procedure must check for this condition.

Matrix Groups in Graphics

The following matrix groups can occur frequently in graphics applications, so they deserve special attention.

Basic Matrix Groups

Each of the elementary matrix types together with matrix multiplication is a group. These are useful groups:

- *Identity Matrix Group*: $\mathscr{I} = \{\mathbf{I}\}$.
- *Translation Matrix Group*: $\mathscr{T} = \{\mathbf{T}(t_x, t_y, t_z)\}$.
- *Isotropic Scale Matrix Group*: $\mathscr{S}_i = \{\mathbf{S}(s, s, s)|s \neq 0\}$.
- *Anisotropic Scale Matrix Group*: $\mathscr{S}_a = \{\mathbf{S}(s_x, s_y, s_z)|s_x, s_y, s_z \neq 0\}$.
- *Rotation Matrix Group*: $\mathscr{R} = \{\mathbf{R}\}$.

The Window-to-Viewport Matrix Group $\mathscr{W}$

$$\left\{ \mathbf{T}(t_x, t_y, t_z), \mathbf{S}(s_x, s_y, s_z)|s_x, s_y, s_z \neq 0 \right\} \subset \mathscr{W}$$

Transformation of a window to a viewport is the last stage of a typical graphics transformation pipeline. It involves scaling and translation, but not rotation. A matrix of this form also may appear in other parts of a transformation pipeline.

The Length-Preserving Matrix Group $\mathscr{P}_l$

$$\left\{ \mathbf{T}(t_x, t_y, t_z), \mathbf{R} \right\} \subset \mathscr{P}_l$$

A graphics program sometimes can benefit from knowing when a matrix always preserves the distances between points and the lengths of direction vectors. For example, when a unit light direction vector or unit surface normal vector passes through such a matrix, the program does not need to normalize the vector after transformation, saving three multiplications and divisions and a square root per vector.

The Angle-Preserving Matrix Group $\mathscr{P}_a$

$$\left\{\mathbf{T}(t_x, t_y, t_z), \mathbf{R}, \mathbf{S}(s, s, s) \middle| s \neq 0\right\} \subset \mathscr{P}_a$$

A matrix that preserves angles allows lighting calculations to take place in model coordinates. Instead of transforming surface normals to world coordinates and performing lighting there, we can transform the lights back to model coordinates to calculate the reflected light. This is beneficial when there are fewer lights than surface normals in a particular model space. Since angles are preserved, so are dot products (after renormalizing direction vectors). Some local light sources may have attenuation properties that cause the intensity of light reaching the surface to diminish with its distance from the light source. In such a situation, the uniform scaling factor must be applied to distances in model coordinates.

The Affine Matrix Group $\mathscr{A}$

$$\left\{\mathbf{T}(t_x, t_y, t_z), \mathbf{R}, \mathbf{S}(s_x, s_y, s_z) \middle| s_x, s_y, s_z \neq 0\right\} \subset \mathscr{A}$$

An *affine* matrix preserves the straightness of lines and the parallelism of parallel lines, but possibly alters distances between points or the angles between lines. Thus, an affine matrix can perform anisotropic scaling. Perspective projection is an example of a transformation that is not affine. However, parallel projection is affine. In addition, the model transformation that maps points from model coordinates to world coordinates almost always is affine.

The Nonsingular Matrix Group $\mathscr{N}$

All the preceding groups are subgroups of the *nonsingular* matrix group. Perspective matrices are included in this group as well. We denote it by $\mathscr{N}$.

Table 1.   Elementary Matrices and Matrix Groups.

Elementary Matrix	Matrix Group								
	$\mathscr{I}$	$\mathscr{T}$	$\mathscr{S}_i$	$\mathscr{S}_a$	$\mathscr{R}$	$\mathscr{W}$	$\mathscr{P}_l$	$\mathscr{P}_a$	$\mathscr{A}$
I	•	•	•	•	•	•	•	•	•
$\mathbf{T}(t_x, t_y, t_z)$	•					•	•	•	•
$\mathbf{S}(s, s, s)$			•	•		•		•	•
$\mathbf{S}(s_x, s_y, s_z)$			•			•			•
R					•	•	•		•

Membership and Privileges

The preceding section introduced the matrix groups by listing the elementary matrices that belong to each group; these are the columns in Table I. Now, we examine each elementary matrix and tabulate its memberships to the matrix groups; these are the rows of Table I.

A graphics program can take advantage of this information in the following way. We assign each group to a bit in a flag word and associate this flag word or *membership record* with each matrix in a graphics program. The program has utilities for constructing each of the elementary matrices. For example, a utility takes a translation vector and returns a translation matrix. In addition, it sets the membership record associated with this matrix according to the second row of Table I.

The graphics program takes advantage of the definition of a group when it multiplies two matrices. Since a group is closed under its operation, the product of two matrices is a member of the groups to which both operands belong: The program simply intersects the operands' membership records using logical AND to obtain the record of the product. When the program needs to calculate the inverse of a matrix, its membership record establishes its privilege to use a fast matrix inversion procedure.

As an aside, we note that a graphics program also can use the membership records to optimize matrix multiplication. Each matrix group has a characteristic form, often with many zeros and ones. As a previous gem (Thompson, 1990) has observed, a programmer can eliminate extraneous multiplications and additions and unroll the loops according to the memberships of the two matrices. Perhaps more importantly, a programmer can optimize multiplication of points by a matrix because thousands of points may require the geometric mapping of the matrix.

Matrix Inversion

The membership record associated with a matrix determines how much effort a graphics program requires to invert the matrix. The program determines the group that has the fastest inversion procedure among the matrix's eligible groups and calls that procedure. The fourth axiom in a group's definition states that the inverse belongs to the same groups as the original matrix. By implication, the inverse has the same form as the original, so some of the zeros and ones occupy the same positions.

Inverses of the Elementary Matrices

The inverses of the elementary matrices are straightforward:

- *Identity*: $\mathbf{I}^{-1} = \mathbf{I}$.
- *Translation*: $\mathbf{T}^{-1}(t_x, t_y, t_z) = \mathbf{T}(-t_x, -t_y, -t_z)$.
- *Scale*: $\mathbf{S}^{-1}(s_x, s_y, s_z) = \mathbf{S}(s_x^{-1}, s_y^{-1}, s_z^{-1})$, $s_x, s_y, s_z \neq 0$.
- *Rotation*: $\mathbf{R}^{-1} = \mathbf{R}^{\mathrm{T}}$

Evaluation Strategy

A graphics program can evaluate inverses on the fly (automatic evaluation) or on demand (lazy evaluation).

Given the inverses of the preceding elementary matrices, the program automatically can evaluate the inverse when it multiplies two matrices according to the rule, $(\mathbf{AB})^{-1} = \mathbf{B}^{-1}\mathbf{A}^{-1}$, provided $\mathbf{A}$ and $\mathbf{B}$ are invertible. This approach requires that the inverse always is available. Therefore, matrix multiplication runs at half its normal speed because the multiplication utility must find the product of two matrices and the two inverses.

Lazy evaluation allows matrix multiplication to run at full speed because the graphics program never evaluates the product of inverses. An inversion utility explicitly evaluates an inverse as required. In practice, a typical graphics program usually performs many more matrix multiplications than inversions so lazy evaluation gives better overall system performance. The following two sections describe additional special-case inversion techniques for use with lazy evaluation that complement the ones in the preceding section.

Inverse of a Window-to-Viewport Matrix

The inverse of a window-to-viewport matrix is useful in picking when the pick device gives locations in the device coordinates of the viewport and the pick aperture conceptually resides in the virtual device coordinates of the window:

$$
\begin{bmatrix}
s_x & 0 & 0 & 0 \\
0 & s_y & 0 & 0 \\
0 & 0 & s_z & 0 \\
t_x & t_y & t_z & 1
\end{bmatrix}^{-1}
=
\begin{bmatrix}
\dfrac{1}{s_x} & 0 & 0 & 0 \\
0 & \dfrac{1}{s_y} & 0 & 0 \\
0 & 0 & \dfrac{1}{s_z} & 0 \\
\dfrac{-t_x}{s_x} & \dfrac{-t_y}{s_y} & \dfrac{-t_z}{s_z} & 1
\end{bmatrix}, \ s_x, s_y, s_z \neq 0.
$$

Inverse of an Affine Matrix

The product of any combination of the elementary matrices always is affine. A typical 3D graphics program probably needs to find the inverse of matrices in the affine group $\mathcal{A}$ and the nonsingular group $\mathcal{N}$ more often than any other groups. A general-purpose matrix inversion procedure is necessary for $\mathcal{N}$. However, a faster procedure is possible for $\mathcal{A}$ because the last column always is $[0\ 0\ 0\ 1]^{T}$. A fact applicable to the inverse of block matrices (for example, Kailath, 1980) serves as the starting point:

$$
\mathbf{M}^{-1} = \begin{bmatrix} \mathbf{A} & \mathbf{0} \\ \mathbf{C} & \mathbf{B} \end{bmatrix}^{-1} = \begin{bmatrix} \mathbf{A}^{-1} & \mathbf{0} \\ -\mathbf{B}^{-1}\mathbf{C}\mathbf{A}^{-1} & \mathbf{B}^{-1} \end{bmatrix}.
$$

This holds for any square submatrices **A** and **B** as long as their inverses exist. For our affine matrices, we let **A** be the upper-left 3×3 submatrix of **M** and **B** be 1. Then this result simplifies to

$$\mathbf{M}^{-1} = \begin{bmatrix} \mathbf{A} & \mathbf{0} \\ \mathbf{C} & 1 \end{bmatrix}^{-1} = \begin{bmatrix} \mathbf{A}^{-1} & \mathbf{0} \\ -\mathbf{CA}^{-1} & 1 \end{bmatrix}.$$

The effort required to calculate the inverse of the 3×3 matrix **A** is much less than that for a general 4×4 matrix.

One method for finding the inverse of a general matrix involves determinants as described in a previous gem (Carling, 1990): $\mathbf{A}^{-1} = \mathbf{A}^*/\det(\mathbf{A})$, where $\mathbf{A}^*$ is the adjoint matrix of **A** and $\det(\mathbf{A})$ is the determinant of **A**. If the dimension of **A** is n, the number of multiplications for this method is $\mathcal{O}((n + 1)!)$ for large n.

Another inversion technique is Gauss–Jordan elimination. In practice, a related technique—LU decomposition with partial pivoting and backsubstitution—is more efficient and robust. *Numerical Recipes in C* (Press et al., 1988) describes this in some detail and gives a C Implementation. The operations count is $\mathcal{O}(n^3)$, and the book claims there is no better way to find the inverse. LU decomposition has much overhead and bookkeeping, including many tests and loops. In addition, partial pivoting requires exchanging rows. These extra steps can count for more than the floating-point arithmetic, depending on the hardware.

Some test runs for calculating the inverse of affine matrices on a SUN SPARCstation 330 demonstrated that the adjoint approach is twice as fast as LU decomposition after unrolling the loops, substituting constants for the variable indices, and eliminating extraneous tests; both these implementations treat affine matrices as block matrices. This adjoint technique is three times faster than a procedure capable of inverting any nonsingular 4×4 matrix using LU decomposition and no block matrices. However, numerical analysts agree that Gaussian elimination techniques like LU decomposition with pivoting are more stable in the presence of roundoff error than determinant methods. The graphics programmer needs to decide whether the risk is worth the improved performance.

A C Implementation for calculating the inverse of a 3D affine matrix is included in Appendix 2. It finds $\mathbf{A}^{-1}$ from the adjoint matrix and $\mathbf{M}^{-1}$ from the equation for inverting block matrices.

Inverse of a Nonsingular Matrix

A 4×4 matrix belonging to the nonsingular matrix group $\mathcal{N}$ requires a general matrix inversion procedure. Some test runs (again, on a SPARC-station 330) have shown that LU decomposition is faster than the adjoint method, but the ratio is less than a factor of two. The results may differ on a host machine with different floating-point performance relative to nonarithmetic performance, but LU decomposition with partial pivoting is more stable numerically.

Summary

A graphics programmer can take the following steps to improve the performance of 3D matrix inversion for special types of matrices commonly found in computer graphics:

1. Provide a set of utilities for constructing a basic set of elementary matrices.

2. Associate a membership record with each matrix that describes the matrix groups to which the matrix belongs. The utilities in the previous step initialize the matrix's membership record.

3. The matrix multiplication utility determines the membership record of a product by intersecting the records of the two operand matrices.

4. The matrix inversion utility inverts a matrix by calling the fastest of the procedures associated with the groups in the matrix's membership record.

VII.6

QUATERNIONS AND 4 × 4 MATRICES

Ken Shoemake
Otter Enterprises
Palo Alto, California

Quaternions are steadily replacing Euler angles as the internal representation of orientations, presumably because of such advantages as are detailed in Shoemake (1985, 1989). What is not so obvious from that paper, however, is that they mesh remarkably well with 4 × 4 homogeneous matrices.

Matrix multiplication can be used quite nicely for quaternion multiplication, since quaternions are, in fact, four-component homogeneous coordinates for orientations, and since they multiply linearly. Consider a quaternion q as a 4-vector, written (x_q, y_q, z_q, w_q), or as just (x, y, z, w) when context makes it clear. The quaternion product $p \blacklozenge q$ is a linear function of either p or q, so two different matrix forms are possible. (Transpose these when using row vectors.) They are:

$$p \blacklozenge q = \mathbf{L}(p)q = \begin{bmatrix} w_p & -z_p & y_p & x_p \\ z_p & w_p & -x_p & y_p \\ -y_p & x_p & w_p & z_p \\ -x_p & -y_p & -z_p & w_p \end{bmatrix} \begin{bmatrix} x_q \\ y_q \\ z_q \\ w_q \end{bmatrix}$$

and

$$p \blacklozenge q = \mathbf{R}(q)p = \begin{bmatrix} w_q & z_q & -y_q & x_q \\ -z_q & w_q & x_q & y_q \\ y_q & -x_q & w_q & z_q \\ -x_q & -y_q & -z_q & w_q \end{bmatrix} \begin{bmatrix} x_p \\ y_p \\ z_p \\ w_p \end{bmatrix}$$

Using these **L** and **R** matrices, we can readily convert a quaternion to a homogeneous rotation matrix. Recall that a quaternion q rotates a vector v using the product $q \blacklozenge v \blacklozenge q^{-1}$, where $q^{-1} = q^*/N(q)$. In the common case of a unit quaternion, $q^{-1} = q^*$. This permits the rotation matrix to be computed from the components of q—since q^* is merely $(-x, -y, -z, w)$—as

$$\mathbf{Rot}(q) = \mathbf{L}(q)\mathbf{R}(q^*),$$

so that a hardware matrix multiplier can do all the conversion work. Isn't that nice?

More specifically, suppose you are using hardware matrix multiplication to compose a series of matrices that will be applied to row vectors in right-handed coordinates, as in $v\mathbf{SNQTP}$, where **Q** is to be derived from a quaternion, $q = (x, y, z, w)$. Then instead of **Q**, compose with **L**(q) and **R**(q^*), so that the sequence is $v\mathbf{SNRLTP}$. For row vectors, we want the transpose form of **L** and **R**, so we have

$$\mathbf{Q}_{\text{row}} = \mathbf{R}_{\text{row}}(q^*)\mathbf{L}_{\text{row}}(q) = \begin{bmatrix} w & z & -y & -x \\ -z & w & x & -y \\ y & -x & w & -z \\ x & y & z & w \end{bmatrix}$$

$$\times \begin{bmatrix} w & z & -y & x \\ -z & w & x & y \\ y & -x & w & z \\ -x & -y & -z & w \end{bmatrix}.$$

Because the desired result is a *homogeneous* rotation matrix, an overall scale factor can be ignored; thus, q^* can be used instead of q^{-1} even if $N(q) = q \blacklozenge q^* = x^2 + y^2 + z^2 + w^2$ is not equal to one. Be aware, however, that some systems do not implement matrix manipulations carefully, and will misbehave if the bottom right entry of the matrix is not 1. Even when normalization is desired, it is not necessary to compute a square root; only addition, subtraction, multiplication, and division are used.

Notice that only the last row and column of the two matrices differ, and then only by transposition or sign change. (This may seem obvious, but one programmer's "obvious" is another's "obscure", and perhaps pointing it out will save someone time.) Although these two matrices may look peculiar to the average computer graphicist, multiplying them confirms that the result is a matrix with the expected zeros in the last row and column, with 1 in the corner for a unit quaternion.

$$
\mathbf{Q}_{\text{row}} =
\begin{bmatrix}
w^2 + x^2 - y^2 - z^2 & 2xy - 2wz & 2xz + 2wy & 0 \\
2xy + 2wz & w^2 - x^2 + y^2 - z^2 & 2yz - 2wx & 0 \\
2xz - 2wy & 2yz + 2wx & w^2 - x^2 - y^2 + z^2 & 0 \\
0 & 0 & 0 & w^2 + x^2 + y^2 + z^2
\end{bmatrix}.
$$

Fans of 4D should note that any rotation of a 4-vector v can be written as $p \blacklozenge q \blacklozenge v \blacklozenge q^{-1} \blacklozenge p$, which is translated easily into matrices using this same approach. The q quaternion controls rotation in the planes excluding w—namely x-y, x-z, and y-z—while the p quaternion controls rotation in the planes including w—namely w-x, w-y, and w-z.

Converting a homogeneous matrix back to a quaternion also is relatively easy, as the $\mathbf{Q}_{\text{row}}$ matrix has a great deal of structure that can be exploited. To preserve numerical precision, one must adapt to the specific matrix given, but the structure also makes that elegant. Observe that the difference, $\mathbf{Q}_{\text{row}}$ minus its transpose, has a simple form:

$$
\mathbf{Q}_{\text{row}} - \mathbf{Q}_{\text{row}}^{\text{T}} =
\begin{bmatrix}
0 & -4wz & 4wy & 0 \\
4wz & 0 & -4wx & 0 \\
-4wy & 4wx & 0 & 0 \\
0 & 0 & 0 & 0
\end{bmatrix}.
$$

Clearly, it is easy to find x, y, and z when w is known, so long as w is not zero—or, for better precision, so long as w is not nearly zero. On the other hand, the sum of $\mathbf{Q}_{\text{row}}$ plus its transpose also is simple, if we ignore the diagonal:

$$
\mathbf{Q}_{\text{row}} + \mathbf{Q}_{\text{row}}^{\text{T}} - \text{diagonal} =
\begin{bmatrix}
0 & 4xy & 4xz & 0 \\
4xy & 0 & 4yz & 0 \\
4xz & 4yz & 0 & 0 \\
0 & 0 & 0 & 0
\end{bmatrix}.
$$

So, knowing any one of x, y, or z also makes it easy to find the others, and to find w (using the difference matrix). In particular, if (i, j, k) is a

cyclic permutation of $(0, 1, 2)$, then

$$w = \frac{\mathbf{Q}[k, j] - \mathbf{Q}[j, k]}{q[i]}, \qquad q[j] = \frac{\mathbf{Q}[i, j] + \mathbf{Q}[j, i]}{q[i]},$$

$$q[k] = \frac{\mathbf{Q}[i, k] + \mathbf{Q}[k, i]}{q[i]}.$$

Now observe that the trace of the homogeneous matrix (the sum of the diagonal elements) always will be $4w^2$. Denoting the diagonal elements by X, Y, Z, and W, one finds all possibilities:

$$4x^2 = X - Y - Z + W,$$

$$4y^2 = -X + Y - Z + W,$$

$$4z^2 = -X - Y + Z + W,$$

$$4w^2 = X + Y + Z + W.$$

Except for w, the computation is $q[i] = \text{Sqrt}(\mathbf{Q}[i, i] - \mathbf{Q}[j, j] - \mathbf{Q}[k, k] + \mathbf{Q}[3, 3])/2$. Since a divide almost certainly is cheaper than a square root, it is better to compute just one of these, preferably the largest, since that will give the best precision for the divides; but look at the diagonal elements again, and let $S = w^2 - x^2 - y^2 - z^2$. Then $X = S + 2x^2$, $Y = S + 2y^2$, $Z = S + 2z^2$, and $T = X + Y + Z = S + 2w^2$. Clearly, which of X, Y, Z, or T is largest indicates which of x, y, z, or w is largest. (T is the trace of the upper-left 3×3 corner of the homogeneous matrix.)

See also (*498*) Using Quaternions for Coding 3D Transformations, Patrick-Gilles Maillot

VII.7

RANDOM ROTATION MATRICES

James Arvo

Apollo Systems Division of Hewlett-Packard
Chelmsford, Massachusetts

It is sometimes convenient to generate arbitrary 3×3 rotation matrices for use in creating randomized models, random animation sequences, or for use in stochastic simulations. The following routine (Fig. 1) maps three random variables in the range $[0, 1]$ onto the set of orthogonal 3×3 matrices with positive determinant; that is, the set of all rotations in 3-space. This mapping is one-to-one on the domain $(0, 1) \times (0, 1) \times (0, 1)$. The algorithm works by first constructing a unit quaternion from the three random variables, then converting the quaternion into an orthogonal matrix. If the random variables are independent and uniformly distributed in $[0, 1]$, the resulting rotations will also be uniformly distributed.

Random _ Rotation _ Matrix(x_1, x_2, x_2, M)

    x_1, x_2, x_3: **real**;

    M: **matrix3**;

begin

    Use the random variables x_1 and x_2 to determine the axis of rotation in cylindrical coordinates.

    z: **real** $\leftarrow x_1$;

    θ: **real** $\leftarrow 2\pi x_2$;

    r: **real** $\leftarrow \sqrt{1 - z^2}$;

Figure 1.

Use the random variable x_3 to determine the half-angle rotation, ω, about this axis.

ω: **real** $\leftarrow \pi x_3$;

Map (z, θ, r, ω) to a unit quaternion (a, b, c, d).

a: **real** $\leftarrow \cos(\omega)$;
b: **real** $\leftarrow \sin(\omega)\cos(\theta)\, r$;
c: **real** $\leftarrow \sin(\omega)\sin(\theta)\, r$;
d: **real** $\leftarrow \sin(\omega)\, z$;

Construct an orthogonal matrix corresponding to (a, b, c, d). This matrix has positive determinant, so it is a rotation.

$$M \leftarrow \begin{bmatrix} 1 - 2(c^2 + d^2) & 2(bc + ad) & 2(bd - ac) \\ 2(bc - ad) & 1 - 2(b^2 + d^2) & 2(cd + ab) \\ 2(bd + ac) & 2(cd - ab) & 1 - 2(b^2 + c^2) \end{bmatrix}$$

end

Figure 1. *(Continued)*

See also VII.6 Quaternions and 4 × 4 Matrices, Ken Shoemake; (*498*) *Using Quaternions for Coding 3D Transformations, Patrick-Gilles Maillot*

VII.8

CLASSIFYING SMALL SPARSE MATRICES

James Arvo
Apollo Systems Division of Hewlett-Packard
Chelmsford, Massachusetts

Zero Structures

Small matrices, such as 3×3 or 4×4, are ubiquitous in computer graphics. They are used to transform everything from rays and normal vectors in ray tracing to vectors and polygons in traditional display list processing. Because these matrices are often formed by concatenating several simpler matrices, such as rotations, translations, changes of scale, and reflections, they frequently contain a number of zero elements: i.e., they are frequently *sparse*. If a given sparse matrix is used for many transformations, its *zero structure* can be exploited to minimize the total number of floating-point operations. To do this, we propose tagging each matrix with an integer *form index* indicating its zero structure and subsequently using this index to branch to optimized handlers for each zero structure; that is, code in which the zero additions and multiplications have been removed.

Because a 3×3 matrix has 2^9, or 512, possible zero structures, nearly half of which are guaranteed to be singular (247 of them, to be exact), it would seem unreasonable to supply special-purpose code for every case. A compromise is to pick a small number of common zero structures and optimize only these. The frequency with which these sparse matrices arise in a given application will determine whether using the form index will be beneficial. However, because the added cost of a branch is typically very small (depending upon the compiler and machine architecture), there is little to lose and potentially much to gain in using this approach.

Form indices also make it possible to optimize space by storing only nonzero elements. However, it is often more convenient to store the full matrix because this allows non-time-critical code and preexisting libraries to operate on these matrices in the normal fashion, oblivious to zero structures.

Classifying a Matrix

Figure 1 enumerates a set of 16 common zero structures for 3×3 matrices. Included are six *permutations*, three *rotations*, and the seven distinct forms resulting from permuting the rows and columns of the simple rotations. Note that the labels *permutation* and *rotation* pertain only to the structure and do not imply that the matrix is a true permutation or rotation. This can be determined only by considering the values of the nonzero elements, which is unnecessary for our purposes.

Though we could deduce a zero structure for a matrix from the zero structures of its component matrices and the order of concatenation, it is

Even Permutations

$$P_1 = \begin{bmatrix} * & 0 & 0 \\ 0 & * & 0 \\ 0 & 0 & * \end{bmatrix} \quad P_2 = \begin{bmatrix} 0 & * & 0 \\ 0 & 0 & * \\ * & 0 & 0 \end{bmatrix} \quad P_3 = \begin{bmatrix} 0 & 0 & * \\ * & 0 & 0 \\ 0 & * & 0 \end{bmatrix}$$

Odd Permutations

$$P_4 = \begin{bmatrix} 0 & * & 0 \\ * & 0 & 0 \\ 0 & 0 & * \end{bmatrix} \quad P_5 = \begin{bmatrix} * & 0 & 0 \\ 0 & 0 & * \\ 0 & * & 0 \end{bmatrix} \quad P_6 = \begin{bmatrix} 0 & 0 & * \\ 0 & * & 0 \\ * & 0 & 0 \end{bmatrix}$$

Simple Rotations

$$R_x = \begin{bmatrix} * & 0 & 0 \\ 0 & * & * \\ 0 & * & * \end{bmatrix} \quad R_y = \begin{bmatrix} * & 0 & * \\ 0 & * & 0 \\ * & 0 & * \end{bmatrix} \quad R_z = \begin{bmatrix} * & * & 0 \\ * & * & 0 \\ 0 & 0 & * \end{bmatrix}$$

Combinations

$$C_1 = \begin{bmatrix} * & 0 & * \\ 0 & * & 0 \\ * & 0 & * \end{bmatrix} \quad C_2 = \begin{bmatrix} 0 & 0 & * \\ * & * & 0 \\ * & * & 0 \end{bmatrix} \quad C_3 = \begin{bmatrix} 0 & * & * \\ 0 & * & * \\ * & 0 & 0 \end{bmatrix}$$

$$C_4 = \begin{bmatrix} 0 & * & 0 \\ * & 0 & * \\ * & 0 & * \end{bmatrix} \quad C_5 = \begin{bmatrix} * & * & 0 \\ 0 & 0 & * \\ * & * & 0 \end{bmatrix} \quad C_6 = \begin{bmatrix} * & 0 & * \\ * & 0 & * \\ 0 & * & 0 \end{bmatrix} \quad C_7 = \begin{bmatrix} 0 & * & * \\ * & 0 & 0 \\ 0 & * & * \end{bmatrix}$$

Figure 1. Sixteen common zero structures for a 3×3 matrix.

far easier to do this after the matrix has been computed. This makes it unnecessary for the modeling operations to have any knowledge of zero structures, and it also takes advantage of fortuitous cancellations that introduce additional zeros.

The algorithm in Fig. 2 is a fast and convenient way to determine which of the zero structures of Fig. 1 apply to a given 3×3 matrix. Rather than using deeply nested if-then-elses, which can be cumbersome, this proce-

Classify _ Matrix(M):**integer**

    M:Matrix3;

Begin

    Initialize "form" by oring all possibilities together.

    form:**integer** $\leftarrow P_1 \cup \ldots P_6 \cup R_* \cup C_1 \cup \ldots C_6$;

    Eliminate possibilities due to non-zeros on the diagonal.

    if $M[0][0] \neq 0$ **then** form $\leftarrow$ form $\cap (P_1 \cup P_5 \cup R_* \cup C_1 \cup C_5 \cup C_6)$;

    if $M[1][1] \neq 0$ **then** form $\leftarrow$ form $\cap (P_1 \cup P_6 \cup R_* \cup C_1 \cup C_2 \cup C_3)$;

    if $M[2][2] \neq 0$ **then** form $\leftarrow$ form $\cap (P_1 \cup P_4 \cup R_* \cup C_1 \cup C_4 \cup C_7)$;

    Eliminate possibilities due to non-zeros in the upper triangle.

    if $M[0][1] \neq 0$ **then** form $\leftarrow$ form $\cap (P_2 \cup P_4 \cup R_z \cup C_3 \cup C_4 \cup C_5 \cup C_7)$;

    if $M[0][2] \neq 0$ **then** form $\leftarrow$ form $\cap (P_3 \cup P_6 \cup R_y \cup C_1 \cup C_2 \cup C_3 \cup C_6 \cup C_7)$;

    if $M[1][2] \neq 0$ **then** form $\leftarrow$ form $\cap (P_2 \cup P_5 \cup R_x \cup C_3 \cup C_4 \cup C_5 \cup C_6)$;

    Eliminate possibilities due to non-zeros in the lower triangle.

    if $M[1][0] \neq 0$ **then** form $\leftarrow$ form $\cap (P_3 \cup P_4 \cup R_z \cup C_2 \cup C_4 \cup C_6 \cup C_7)$;

    if $M[2][0] \neq 0$ **then** form $\leftarrow$ form $\cap (P_2 \cup P_6 \cup R_y \cup C_1 \cup C_2 \cup C_3 \cup C_4 \cup C_5)$;

    if $M[2][1] \neq 0$ **then** form $\leftarrow$ form $\cap (P_3 \cup P_5 \cup R_x \cup C_2 \cup C_5 \cup C_6 \cup C_7)$;

    return[form]

    end

Figure 2. A function for identifying the zero structure of 3×3 matrices. Here, $\cap$ means *bitwise-and*, $\cup$ means *bitwise-or*, and R_* is an abbreviation for $(R_x \cup R_y \cup R_z)$.

dure maintains a bit-vector of possible classifications, which is narrowed down by examining each matrix element in sequence. Only nonzero elements constrain the possible classifications because starred elements may be anything, including zero. Thus, for each nonzero element, we reset the bits corresponding to forms in which that element is zero. Any reasonable compiler will replace the *or* expressions in Fig. 2 with the equivalent constants at compile time.

```
Sparse_Mat_Vect_Mult(M, form, a, b)
    M:Matrix3;
    form:integer;
    a:vector3;
    b:vector3;
begin
    select form from
        P₁:begin
            b.x ← M[0][0] * a.x;
            b.y ← M[1][1] * a.y;
            b.z ← M[2][2] * a.z;

            end

        P₂:begin
            b.x ← M[2][0] * a.x;
            b.y ← M[0][1] * a.y;
            b.z ← M[1][2] * a.z;

            end
            ⋮
        DENSE:   Resort to traditional matrix multiply

        endcase

    end
```

Figure 3.   A procedure for multiplying a sparse matrix by a vector.

Figure 3 shows how one might use the form index to speed up matrix–vector products. Operations such as matrix inversion and matrix–matrix multiplications can also enjoy the extra information supplied by the form index; but be warned that in the case of inversion, most *but not all* matrices have the same zero structure as their inverses. For example, the inverse of a P_2 matrix has the form of P_3, and vice versa.

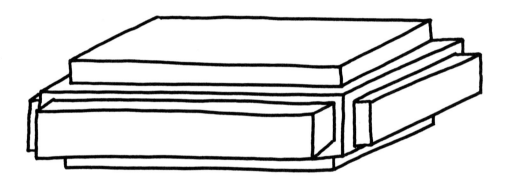

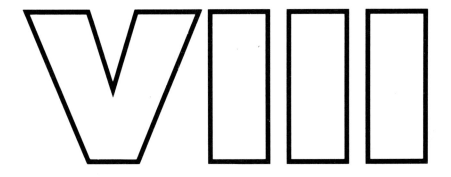

VIII

NUMERICAL AND
PROGRAMMING
TECHNIQUES

NUMERICAL AND PROGRAMMING TECHNIQUES

Computer graphics is replete with programming tricks and careful numerical techniques, both of which deal with the myriad mathematical problems that every graphics programmer encounters. Solutions often come from clever mathematical identities, special numerical algorithms, and shrewd programming. The gems of this Part present methods for counting bits,useful trigonometric identities, and methods for fast approximations and evaluation of familiar functions such as square root and arctangent, as well as the more exotic *noise* function.

VIII. I

BIT PICKING

Ken Shoemake
Otter Enterprises
Palo Alto, California

One bit raster graphics is not dead yet, and the use of bit vectors probably will never die—which is merely an excuse to propagate one of the prettiest little hacks on a binary computer. Some computer architectures, such as the Motorola 68020, include an instruction for finding the highest 1-bit set in a word, presumably to assist in software normalization of floating-point operation results. This high 1 finding can be quite handy for other bit vector operations as well. Finding the lowest 1-bit set in a word is a different matter. However, using the properties of 2's-complement arithmetic, it can be done easily. Simply take the bit-wise AND of the word and its negative; the result will be a word containing just the lowest 1-bit. If n is exactly a power of 2, then $n == (n \& -n)$ is TRUE, otherwise not. One example of the use of this technique is in stepping through 1 bit in a word, which is used to record pixel coverage for anti-aliasing. Why does it work? Here is a picture (Table I):

Table I.

n	0	0	0	1	1	1	0	0	1	0	1	0	0	0	0	0
$!n$	1	1	1	0	0	0	1	1	0	1	0	1	1	1	1	1
$+1$	0	0	0	0	0	0	0	0	0	0	0	0	0	0	0	1
$-n$	1	1	1	0	0	0	1	1	0	1	1	0	0	0	0	0
n	0	0	0	1	1	1	0	0	1	0	1	0	0	0	0	0
$n \& -n$	0	0	0	0	0	0	0	0	0	0	1	0	0	0	0	0

Remember that $-n$ in 2's-complement arithmetic is $!n + 1$; carry propagation is effectively doing the search.

See also VIII.3 Fast In-Line Manipulations: Of Integers, Fields, and Bit Counting, Alan W. Paeth, David Schilling

VIII.2

FASTER FOURIER TRANSFORM

Ken Shoemake
Otter Enterprises
Palo Alto, California

Fast Fourier Transform algorithms have been explored pretty thoroughly, and vary from quite terse to highly optimized. It is not hard to find source code, as in Press *et al.* (1988) or Burrus and Parks (1985). However, there is one task common to every in-place algorithm that can be made faster, namely, the *flipped bit count* shuffling of data that occurs before or after the transform proper.

Historically, folks have tried to come up with clever ways either to flip the bits of an ordinary counter or to make a flipped counter; but there is another possibly pointed out by Evans (1987). Notice in Table 1 that, first, all rearrangements involve simply swapping pairs; and second, that some indices do not change (the *palindromes* 000, 010, 101, and 111). Both these properties hold in larger cases as well, and suggest trying to generate only the pairs that must be swapped. For a length 1024 FFT, this means enumerating 496 indices—less than half the total.

When the bits are flipped, $abcxyz$ turns into $zyxcba$—as, for example, 101011 becomes 110101—and vice versa. A way to avoid duplications and palindromes can be found by splitting the bits in half, as in 101 011. When zyx is strictly greater than abc, $zyxcba$ is strictly greater than

Table I.

		Decimal	0	1	2	3	4	5	6	7
Index	in	Binary	000	001	010	011	100	101	110	111
Index	out	Binary	000	100	010	110	001	101	011	111
		Decimal	0	4	2	6	1	5	3	7

368

abcxyz, and cannot be a palindrome. A simple enumeration strategy for a length $n = 2^{2k}$ FFT thus is possible:

```
shift = k >> 1; half = 1 << shift;
h = k − shift;
for (low = 1; low + +; low < half) {
        limit = flip (low, h); top = limit << shift;
        for (high = 0; high + +; high < limit) {
                SWAP (data[(high << shift) + low],
                    data[top + flip (high, h)]);
            }
    }
```

More subtly, the same code works when $n = 2^{2k+1}$, because of the way in which h is computed. One further speedup, now possible because only small values of h will occur, is to implement *flip* using a table look-up. For a 1024-point FFT, the table need hold only 32 entries.

Why does the code work for odd numbers of bits? First, the flipping, shifting, and adding leave the middle bit unchanged. Second, the inner-

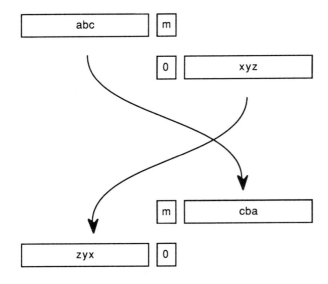

Figure 1.

most loop generates both 0 and 1 for the middle bit, so both cases are considered. Finally, $zyx0$ strictly greater than $abcm$ implies zyx is strictly greater than abc, which still guarantees no duplicates or palindromes. Figure 1 shows the odd-bits case; the even-bits case omits the m bit in the middle.

VIII.3

OF INTEGERS, FIELDS, AND BIT COUNTING

Alan W. Paeth
NeuralWare Inc.
Pittsburgh, Pennsylvania

David Schilling
Software Consultant
Bellevue, Washington

Inner loops common to graphics code may benefit from short, register-based in-line code. These may exploit mixed arithmetic–logical operation on integers to achieve high performance at small cost. Two techniques useful for bit manipulation within a single register are described. The first increments (disjoint) fields within machine words; the second tallies the number of bits set. Both are helpful particularly in manipulating RGB pixels within a single machine word without resort to the (re)packing of each component, a valuable property exploited elsewhere (Paeth, 1990a).

Basics

Consider hardware that represents integers in the nearly universal 2's-complement binary form. Bitwise logical negation "not()" is an arithmetic 1's-complement operation, differing by one unit from arithmetic negation "−" on such machines. They may be equated: $\text{not}(A) = -(A + 1)$. Negating both sides yields an incremental form; a decrement may be derived in like manner:

$$A \leftarrow -\text{not}(A) \quad \Leftrightarrow \quad A \leftarrow A + 1,$$

$$A \leftarrow \text{not}(-A) \quad \Leftrightarrow \quad A \leftarrow A - 1.$$

The latter places the logical operation outermost, allowing it to be absorbed further. For instance, the expression, "X **bit-and** $(Y - 1)$" and equivalent "X **and-not** $(-Y)$," become "X **bit-clear** $(-Y)$" on architectures having only a **bit-clear** (e.g., a Vax).

Counting through Bits under Mask

A binary integer of 2^N non-adjacent bits may be *counted* (incremented through its 2^N unique states) in simple fashion by using a mask of active bits. This situation commonly occurs when a machine word represents a color pixel of three adjacent integers, most often bytes representing RGB values. As an example, hexadecimal mask "808080" has 3 bits set. These define the most significant bits for each primary in a 24-bit pixel descriptor. Counting up through this *scattered* integer generates the eight bounding corners of the color cube at 50% intensity. Conversely, the 6-bit mask of "030303" may define low-order unused *dither* bits when representing data having only 6 bits per color channel on a 24-bit display; counting under the second mask enumerates all possible intermediate dither values.

A minimal implementation requires two registers: a mask of those bits that are *live* in the partitioned integer, plus the current count value, initially zero. Successive values may be generated using the brief fragment:

$$\text{count} = \text{count} - \text{mask},$$

$$\text{count} = \text{count } \textbf{bit-and} \text{ mask}.$$

This form combines logical and arithmetic operations to achieve the desired effect. The operation is minimal in that no more than the two original registers are employed. Also, both machine instructions are of the compact two-op form, $\langle \text{reg} A \text{ op} = \text{reg} B \rangle$.

To understand why this works, recall that subtraction of mask in the first statement may be expressed as the addition of the 2's-complement of mask. This form may be represented in turn by the 1's-complement of mask plus 1: $-\text{mask} = \text{not}(\text{mask}) + 1$. The rewrite gives:

$$\text{count} = \text{count} + \text{not}(\text{mask}) + 1,$$

$$\text{count} = \text{count} \ \textbf{bit-and} \ \text{mask},$$

where the unit constant serves to increment the count. The inclusion of *not(mask)* provides a carry path across those bits in mask that are unoccupied, allowing low-bit carry-outs to advance to the carry-in of the next active bit. The second statement zeros out carry-chain scaffolding, thereby vacating bit positions unused in register *count*. The cycle then is ready to repeat.

Tallying the **on** bits in an Integer

Bit-tallying is a common tool in a programmer's kit. In graphics scenarios, it is used most often when the target word represents a portion of a raster. For instance, consider a binary output device in which **on** bits represent marks (e.g., a laser printer). Tallying 1's in the input data stream provides an estimate of the local or global density of the print. Similarly, counting the **on** bits within a 4×4 spatial mask can convert a binary raster of size $4N \times 4M$ into a grayscale raster of size $N \times M$. In both examples, a significant portion of the input may be off/unmarked: a counting method with cost proportional to the number of **on** bits may be beneficial.

A straightforward approach employs byte-indexed tables. Based on machine architecture and implementation specifics, this may be the fastest technique.

Here, a 256-entry table indexed by byte—whose *N*th entry is the number of bits present in its byte index *N*—solves the problem for 8-bit words. For 32-bit *long* words, the word first is broken into 4 bytes. Each is tallied using the table method. The four values then are summed. The summing may be done implicitly by forming the remainder modulo 255, as explained at the conclusion of this gem. The table method has constant cost, but still may lose to the following bit-based methods on machines for which byte alignment and indexing are expensive, or when rasters are very sparse or full, but not both.

A less intuitive scheme with running time proportional to the number of set bits likewise may take advantage of *mixed* arithmetic–logical operations. For sufficiently sparse rasters, this method often provides asymptotically better running time:

```
integer function tally(bits)
count: integer ← 0;
while (bits < > 0)
      begin
      bits = bits bit-and (bits − 1)
or use "bits = bits bit-clear (-bits)"
      count = count + 1
      end
```

This algorithm is strongly suggestive of the first item in this gem. Bit **and**ing any integer with its predecessor zeros the rightmost bit set (up to and including the word's rightmost/least significant bit); for instance, the operation, ABCD0300 **bit-and** ABCD02FF = ABCD0200. Bits then may be tallied and discerded until the word is zero.

For *dense* rasters whose words have many bits set, the method likewise is fast: Given as 32-bit word W, the complemented word W' may be counted and the value $32 − C(W')$ returned. A hybrid *bipolar* algorithm performing both tests in line-by-line parallel has been suggested (Booth, 1989) for fast symmetric performance. Here, each inner loop has twice the cost, but the code terminates at most in half the number of steps, as no more than half the bits can be both 1 and 0. This gives identical worst-case performances and a chance to end early for words that are either empty or full.

Analysis reveals a subtlety: The algorithm generally is not useful. Even with no penalty for overhead in parallel execution, this hybrid scheme is slower on average by 1.73 times. This is a consequence of the binomial theorem on the distribution of bits. For a 32-bit integer of random bit settings, the number of patterns having between 15 and 17 bits set (and as many off) is 40.33%; most often, any algorithm will terminate near the

16th cycle. Comparing hybrid to simple, the former does twice the work for each step. Put another way, the twin halting conditions and associated work buy little improvement; they tend to occur at roughly the same moment.

Finally, counting may be done by viewing a long word as 32 1-bit tallies. These are regrouped (by addition) as 16 2-bit tallies, continuing for $\log_2$ (word-length) steps, at which point a 32-bit tally is left. This method has many variations; three are provided in the C Implementation. Once partial tallying has created four adjacent byte counts (the same format as the first tally algorithm), a remainder step may be employed to complete the task (Beeler *et al.*, 1972). The modulus allows the casting out of $N - 1$'s in any base $N > 2$; the digital root test (digit sums) for divisibility by 9 in base 10 is a well-known example. In the case at hand:

$$N = (d_3 d_2 d_1 d_0) = \sum_{i=0}^{3} d_i 2^{8i},$$

$$N \bmod 255 = \left[\sum_{i=0}^{3} d_i (2^{8i} \bmod 255) \right] \bmod 255,$$

$$= (d_3 + d_2 + d_1 + d_0) \bmod 255,$$

$$= d_3 + d_2 + d_1 + d_0.$$

The last step discards the modulus, as the value of the sum at most is 32. Performing the modulus on eight hex digits would employ "mod 15" and introduces ambiguity; an interesting, compact algorithm employing the modulus 31 with minor correction for ambiguity appears as the final C code algorithm.

A pseudo-code example follows:

integer function tally32(a)
a: unsigned long **integer**;   a: 32 × 1-bit
tallies

> **begin**
> mask = 1431655765;   hex 55555555
> a = (a **bit-and** mask) + (a **rshift** 1) **bit-and** mask;   a: 16 × 2-bit tallies
>
> mask = 858993459;   hex 33333333
> a = (a **bit-and** mask) + (a **rshift** 2) **bit-and** mask;   a: 8 × 4-bit tallies
>
> mask = 117901063;   hex 07070707
> a = (a **bit-and** mask) + (a **rshift** 4) **bit-and** mask;   a: 4 × 8-bit tallies
>
> **return**(a mod 255)   *sum the bytes by*
> **end**   *casting out 255's.*

on machines for which modulus is expensive, the **return** *may be replaced with this coda:*

> mask = 2031647;   hex 001f001f
> a = (a **bit-and** mask) + (a **rshift** 8) **bit-and** mask;   a: 2 × 8-bit tallies
> mask = 63;   hex 0000003f
> a = (a **bit-and** mask) + (a **rshift** 16) **bit-and** mask; a: 1 × 32-bit tally
> **return**(a)   done.
> **end**

See also VIII.1 Bit Picking, Ken Shoemake

VIII.4

USING GEOMETRIC CONSTRUCTIONS TO INTERPOLATE ORIENTATION WITH QUATERNIONS

John Schlag
MacroMind, Inc.
San Francisco, California

Quaternions have been established as a useful representation for interpolating 3D orientation in computer animation. In keeping with traditional computer animation practices, we would like both interpolating and approximating splines. These can be derived easily by applying the geometric constructions known for linear splines.

Shoemake (1985) provided a scheme for deriving Bézier control points from a sequence of quaternions. This provides an interpolating spline for quaternions, but the construction is somewhat more complicated than necessary. The most common interpolating spline in use probably is the *Catmull–Rom spline*. In 1988, Barry and Goldman (1988) obligingly provided a geometric construction for Catmull–Rom splines. This produces an interpolating spline directly from the control points, without the construction of auxiliary Bézier points. For an approximating spline, a geometric construction for *B*-splines is well-known (de Boor, 1972).

Barry and Goldman represent geometric constructions as a triangle with the four control points at the bottom, the result point at the top, and weighting functions for the intermediate results on each arc; for example, the nonuniform B-spline construction:

$$P_0^3(t)$$

$$\frac{t_{q+1} - t}{t_{q+1} - t_q} \qquad \frac{t - t_q}{t_{q+1} - t_q}$$

$$P_{-1}^2(t) \qquad\qquad\qquad P_0^2(t)$$

$$\frac{t_{q+1} - t}{t_{q+1} - t_{q-1}} \qquad \frac{t - t_{q-1}}{t_{q+1} - t_{q-1}} \qquad \frac{t_{q+2} - t}{t_{q+2} - t_q} \qquad \frac{t - t_q}{t_{q+2} - t_q}$$

$$P_{-2}^1(t) \qquad\qquad\qquad P_{-1}^1(t) \qquad\qquad\qquad P_0^1(t)$$

$$\frac{t_{q+1} - t}{t_{q+1} - t_{q-2}} \quad \frac{t - t_{q-2}}{t_{q+1} - t_{q-2}} \quad \frac{t_{q+2} - t}{t_{q+2} - t_{q-1}} \quad \frac{t - t_{q-1}}{t_{q+2} - t_{q-1}} \quad \frac{t_{q+3} - t}{t_{q+3} - t_q} \quad \frac{t - t_q}{t_{q+3} - t_q}$$

$$P_{-3} \qquad\qquad\qquad P_{-2} \qquad\qquad\qquad P_{-1} \qquad\qquad\qquad P_0$$

This notation can be compressed considerably, since each pair of points is blended with coefficients that sum to one (i.e., the points are linearly interpolated, or *lerped*). By collapsing such coefficients and deleting the points, we get the six-entry triangle:

$$\frac{t - t_q}{t_{q+1} - t_q}$$

$$\frac{t - t_{q-1}}{t_{q+1} - t_{q-1}} \qquad\qquad \frac{t - t_q}{t_{q+2} - t_q}$$

$$\frac{t - t_{q-2}}{t_{q+1} - t_{q-2}} \qquad \frac{t - t_{q-1}}{t_{q+2} - t_{q-1}} \qquad \frac{t - t_q}{t_{q+3} - t_q}$$

In the uniform case (with knot values $t_i = i$), this reduces to:

$$t$$

$$\frac{t + 1}{2} \qquad\qquad \frac{t}{2}$$

$$\frac{t + 2}{3} \qquad\qquad \frac{t + 1}{3} \qquad\qquad \frac{t}{3}$$

Similarly, the Catmull–Rom construction is

$$
\begin{array}{ccccc}
& & t & & \\
& \dfrac{t+1}{2} & & \dfrac{t}{2} & \\
t+1 & & t & & t-1
\end{array}
$$

and the Bezier construction is simply

$$
\begin{array}{ccccc}
& & t & & \\
& t & & t & \\
t & & t & & t
\end{array}
$$

For our purposes, the most useful consequence of expressing the constructions as lerping pairs of points together is that they can be readily applied to any domain where an analog to *lerp* exists. For quaternions, the analog to lerp is *slerp*, for spherical linear interpolation (Shoemake, 1985):

$$
\text{slerp}(q_1, q_2, u) = \frac{\sin(1-u)\theta}{\sin\theta} q_1 + \frac{\sin u\theta}{\sin\theta} q_2, \text{ where } \cos\theta = q_1 \cdot q_2.
$$

For example:

```
function qCatmullRom(
        q00, q01, q02, q03: quaternion; t: real
): quaternion;
        q10, q11, q12, q20, q21: quaternion;
begin
        q10 ← slerp(q00, q01, t + 1);
        q11 ← slerp(q01, q02, t);
        q12 ← slerp(q02, q03, t − 1);
        q20 ← slerp(q10, q11, (t + 1)/2);
        q21 ← slerp(q11, q12, t/2);
        return [slerp(q20, q21, t)];
endproc qCatmullRom
```

The implementation of the other constructions differs only in the third arguments to slerp().

See also VII.6 Quaternions and 4×4 Matrices, Ken Shoemake; (498) *Using Quaternions for Coding 3D Transformations, Patrick-Gilles Maillot*

A HALF-ANGLE IDENTITY FOR DIGITAL COMPUTATION: THE JOYS OF THE HALVED TANGENT

Alan W. Paeth
NeuralWare Inc.
Pittsburgh, Pennsylvania

Trigonometric transformations are common to distant corners of graphics, ranging from cartography to ray tracing. However, the formulae that underpin their related algorithms often make heavy use of the basic trigonometric functions $\tan \theta$, $\sin \theta$, or $\cos \theta$, their reciprocals, and often their half-angle forms. The values typically occur in pairs; $[\cos \theta, \sin \theta]$ is a common example. Algorithms employing parallel trigonometric expressions may benefit from a transformation that expresses all trigonometric forms in terms of one: $\tan(\theta/2)$. This gem derives the half-angle identity and reveals a wide variety of uses.

Trigonometric formulae are derived conventionally through geometric means on a right triangle of unit hypotenuse. We substitute an isosceles triangle symmetric about the x axis on the Cartesian plane and proceed by way of analytic geometry. Its three vertices are located at the origin and at a pair of conjugate points (Fig. 1).

Here, the base is of length $2y$, the congruent sides are $\sqrt{x^2 + y^2}$. By regarding these common sides as vectors, the cosine of their included angle is equated to their dot (inner) product, normalized by the product of their lengths (Fig. 2a). Because the cosine represents the quotient of two sides (adjacent over hypotenuse) in a conventional right triangle, application of Pythagoras's theorem finds the third side of this *rectified* triangle (Fig. 2b). It likewise has base angle α. Thus, $\sin \alpha = 2xy/x^2 + y^2$, $\tan \alpha = 2xy/x^2 - y^2$. Note that the side equations in Fig. 2b contain no roots: They are integral for integrals x and y. Figure 2b thus rederives the familiar generator of all Pythagorean triangles (Paeth, 1990c). All right triangles of integer sides (solving the familiar $i^2 + j^2 = k^2$) may be

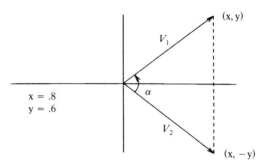

Figure 1.

defined by at least one integer pair (x, y). For instance, the pair $(2, 1)$ yields the $[3, 4, 5]$ Egyptian triangle of antiquity.

Bisecting the angle α in Fig. 1 shows that $\tan(\alpha/2) = y/x$. Setting $x = 1$ in the equations for both tangent and half-tangent provide the basis of formulae interrelating functions of the angle and half-angle. Although half-angle identities of full angles are common (Glassner, 1990a), their inverses are infrequently tabulated. Reexpressing the trigonometric identities for the right triangle in Fig. 2b in terms of $x = 1$, $T = y = \tan \alpha/2$ yields:

$$\cos \alpha = \frac{1 - T^2}{1 + T^2}, \quad \sin \alpha = \frac{2T}{1 + T^2}, \quad \tan \alpha = \frac{2T}{1 - T^2},$$

$$\cos\frac{\alpha}{2} = \sqrt{\frac{1}{1 + T^2}}, \quad \sin\frac{\alpha}{2} = \sqrt{\frac{T^2}{1 + T^2}}, \quad \tan\frac{\alpha}{2} = T(\alpha).$$

By substituting the trigonometric value $T = \tan \alpha/2$ for the angular value

$$\cos \alpha = \frac{V_1 \cdot V_2}{|V_1||V_2|} = \frac{x^2 - y^2}{x^2 + y^2}$$

(a)   (b)

Figure 2.

382

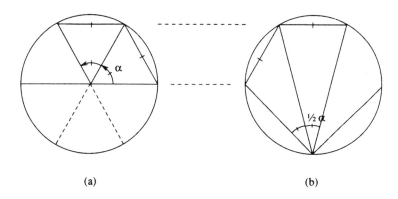

(a)   (b)

Figure 3.   a) Circle with radials; b) circle with fan.

α, equations involving the sine, cosine, and tangent of α may proceed without resorting further to radicals or trig libraries; four-function hardware floating-point often suffices. The savings can be substantial, as when large (hemispherical) cartographic [lat, lon] data sets are precomputed off-line under the transformation T. In this case, further savings exist when the half-tangent form appears explicitly, as with Mercator's conformal projection (Paeth, 1990c), or with the stereographic conformal projection, which follows.

The form $[\cos\theta, \sin\theta]$ is bound intimately to the unit circle by the foundational identity $e^{i\theta} = \cos\theta + i\sin\theta$. By this expression, the complex Nth roots of unity form the vertices of a regular N-gon. Because $T(\theta)$ substitutes so freely for $[\cos, \sin]$, intuition suggests a geometric model involving the half-angle and a circle, analogous to the conventional model. Both appear in Fig. 3.

A constant rotation θ in Fig. 3a yields linear circumferential motion. Remarkably, the same is true in Fig. 3b, where a viewer at the edge need turn at only half the rate and through a half-circumference, while viewing the same instantaneous horizon as a central observer in Fig. 3a. In short, a chord's angular subtense to a point anywhere on the circle's perimeter is half the angular subtense at the center. A geometric proof (omitted) constructs congruent isosceles triangles that have the circle's base and center in common, but which have different points along the perimeter. Euclid derives a general case; a lucid account appears in Polya (1962).

The identities given allow the familiar reexpression of parametric circular plotting through rational polynomials. Here, the LHS is the familiar unit vector of rotation with $\alpha = 2\arctan(T)$ substituted. The RHS may be derived from the tables previously given, yielding:

$$\left[\cos(2\arctan(T)), \sin(2\arctan(T))\right] = \left[\frac{1 - T^2}{1 + T^2}, \frac{2T}{1 + T^2}\right],$$

as appearing in Newman and Sproull (1979) and elsewhere. When T is a half-tangent function of angle α, the circumferential motion is uniform. When T is taken as the (linear) independent parameter, the angular rate is no longer constant, but does not deviate considerably; The half-tangent is strongly linear through much of its domain, as seen by the Taylor expansion of both the function and its inverse about $x = 0$:

$$2T(x) = 2\tan\left(\frac{x}{2}\right) = x + \frac{1}{12}x^3 + \frac{1}{120}x^5 + O(x)^7,$$

$$2\arctan\left(\frac{x}{2}\right) = x - \frac{1}{12}x^3 + \frac{1}{80}x^5 + O(x)^7.$$

This reveals the alternate forms $2\tan(x/2)$ and $2\arctan(x/2)$, which may be employed preferentially to inherit the valuable property $x \cong 0 \to F(x) \cong x$, shared by $\sin(x)$ and $\tan(x)$. This form is familiar to the geometry of viewport specification and, more generally, to problems of geometric optics: $2\tan(\theta/2)$ relates an angular field of view to a linear field viewed at a unit distance. This occurs often enough to merit an example.

A 35 mm format camera (with $1.5:1$ aspect ratio giving a 42 mm film diagonal) equipped with a 210 mm telephoto lens has a field–distance ratio of $42:210 = 1/5$. Substitution into the second Taylor expansion gives the angular field: $2\tan^{-1}(1/10) \sim 2/10$ radians $\sim 11.4°$ (half-field if the leading 2 is omitted). Here, merely the approximation's first term is retained, as the field is narrow.

Interestingly, a nonrectilinear *fish-eye* lens enforces this approximation at wide angles; angular field distance then gives linear displacement at the film plane, allowing the imaging of a hemispherical extent (or more) in cases where an ideal *pinhole* lens would require an infinite film plane.

The close relation between the half-tangent and the conventional rotation form $[\cos\theta, \sin\theta]$ also may be implicit. For instance, raster rotation using shearing (Paeth, 1990a) employs three 2×2 identity matrices, each with one off-diagonal, nonzero element. This element is $-\tan(\theta/2)$ for the central matrix, bracketed by matrices having $\sin\theta$ on the off-diagonal. Not surprisingly, the algorithm admits particularly accurate special cases when the off-diagonals are small rationals. These are related directly to Pythagorean forms (Paeth, 1990c). In particular, the generator pair $(1, 1)$ yields a *flat* right triangle with sides $(0, 1, 1)$, allowing for 90-degree rotation of all integer coefficients as a well-known special case (Guibas and Stolfi, 1982).

This model reveals other domains in which the half-tangent appears. The drawing in Fig. 3b is suggestive of the Lambertian radiosity model, which characterizes ideal diffuse reflective surfaces. This specific model also may be extended to 3-space by rotation about an axis containing the base point and center of the opposite chord. The latter becomes a circle (all points of common subtense) on the sphere, while its projection remains circular. This illustrates the basis of the stereographic polar projection (Paeth, 1990d). A plot (Paeth, 1990d, Fig. 5) illustrates the remarkable property unique to this conformal mapping: Circles are preserved under transformation between chart and globe. The equation that relates azimuthal chart distance to spherical subtense is $2\tan(\chi/2)$, where χ is co-latitude (zero at the pole).

Elsewhere, the function is useful in problems of general trigonometry. A concise identity (Glassner, 1990a) relates the half-tangents of two base angles in a plane triangle to the ratio of their respective legs (Fig. 4a). Extension to oblique spherical triangles necessarily adds a trigonometric form: The legs of spherical triangles are measured in terms of angular subtense. Another introduction of the half-tangent suffices (Fig. 4b).

$$\frac{T(A-B)}{T(A+B)} = \frac{a-b}{a+b} \qquad \frac{T(A-B)}{T(A+B)} = \frac{T(a-b)}{T(a+b)}$$

(a) (b)

Figure 4. a) Planar; b) spherical.

From a computational point of view, the function $T(x) = \tan(x/2)$ is desirable because it is odd-valued: $T(-x) = -T(x)$. In contrast, even functions such as $\cos(x)$ and $\sqrt{x}$ discard x's sign. Similarly, transformations involving the square root introduce a sign ambiguity, recovered through cumbersome forms such as $\text{sign}(x)\sqrt{F(x)}$. Under substitution, $T(x)$ remains superior to other odd trigonometric functions, such as $S = \sin(x)$, whose expression of the cosine, $\cos(x) = \sqrt{(1 - S^2)}$, is unstable for $S \sim 1$. However, there are other means to form $[\cos, \sin]$ in parallel with high accuracy, e.g., Cordic techniques (Turkowski, 1990).

$T(\theta)$ moves the tangent's bothersome singularity at $\pm\pi/2$ outward to $\pm\pi$: the function is defined on the entire circumferential domain $(-\pi \ldots +\pi)$, where its range is $[-\infty \ldots \infty]$. Note that the point-at-infinity is a pole having no sign; this is suggested by the stereographic projection's antipodal point, which lies in no unique direction away from the chart origin. In many cases, a half-circle or hemispherical domain suffices for T and the range then is the convenient $[-1 \ldots 1]$, as was seen in the rational–parametric circle drawer. The π likewise may be removed from the domain by reexpressing $T(x)$ in circumferential units (Shoemake, 1990).

It is ironic that trigonometric identities based on a single form are not more common today. In times past, problems of navigation and astronomy—which provided mathematics many of its riches—preferentially employed half-angle forms, such as the haversine $(\text{hav}(x) = 1/2 \, \text{vers}(x) = 1/2[1 - \cos x] = \sin^2 x/2 = T^2/1 + T^2)$. By these, the reckoner of a ship's company could (among his other duties) navigate during adverse circumstances with reference merely to sums and to a single table. Today, a misplaced sign has less dire consequences (usually!) for the reckoner. Still, the opportunity to optimize code under a unified model while implicitly accounting for the bothersome ambiguities of four-quadrant trigonometry is not ignored easily.

VIII.6

AN INTEGER SQUARE ROOT ALGORITHM

Christopher J. Musial
New Horizons Software
St. Louis, Missouri

Some algorithms that perform a square root operation may require only the integer portion of the result, rather than the entire floating-point number. An example may be arranging a list of items into a *nearly square* table: The table will have the same number of rows and columns, with the last row/column possibly being empty or incomplete. The overhead of a full floating-point calculation is not necessary in this case. The algorithm presented here calculates the largest integer, which is less than or equal to the square root of a given integer n, i.e., $\lfloor \sqrt{n} \rfloor$.

Given n as the number for which the square root is required and s as the integer square root we are seeking, iteratively perform the operation,

$$s_{i+1} \leftarrow \frac{s_i + \dfrac{x}{s_i}}{2},$$

until s_{i+1} becomes greater than or equal to s_i, at which point s_i is the integer square root we are seeking. Prior to starting the iteration, s_i is assigned the value $n/2$. Note that the divisions are carried out in integer arithmetic. The pseudo-code for this procedure is:

```
procedure isqr (n: unsigned long int);
begin
  nextTrial: unsigned int ← n/2;
  currentAnswer;
```

```
if n ≤ 1 then return [n];
do
  begin
    currentAnswer ← nextTrial;
    nextTrial ← (nextTrial + n / nextTrial) / 2;
    end;
  until nextTrial ≥ currentAnswer;
  return [currentAnswer];
end;
```

See also (424) *A High Speed, Low Precision Square Root, Paul Lalonde, Robert Dawson*

VIII.7

FAST APPROXIMATION TO THE ARCTANGENT

Ron Capelli
IBM Corp.
Poughkeepsie, New York

Given the components of a vector (dx, dy), the inverse trigonometric arctangent function is used to determine precisely the angle that the vector makes with respect to the x axis. The function arctan2(dy, dx) is provided in many program libraries so that the function can be defined for all values of dx and dy (except the single case where both dx and dy are zero).

A useful measure of vector angle can be constructed by a piecewise continuous function, using only three comparisons, one division, and one or two add/subtract operations. This represents significantly fewer operations than a standard implementation of arctan2.

The segments of the piecewise continuous function are determined by the octant in which the vector lies. The octant can be determined by three comparisons of dx with respect to 0, dy with respect to 0, and dx with respect to dy. For octants where abs$(dx) >$ abs(dy), dy/dx is evaluated. For octants where abs$(dx) <$ abs(dy), dx/dy is evaluated. Finally, so that the segments join with both C^0 and C^1 continuity, the absolute value of the quotient is subtracted from 1 for the odd octants, and the octant number is added to the result. This algorithm is summarized in Fig. 1, with the comparisons satisfied for each octant shown inside the circle, and the piecewise function evaluation for each octant shown outside the circle.

Figure 2 is a graph of the function for all angles. The function is monotonically increasing, so it is ideal for use as a key for sorting vectors by angle. Such a sort, for example, is used in determining the convex hull of a set of points using Graham's scan algorithm (Graham, 1972; Lee and Preparata, 1984).

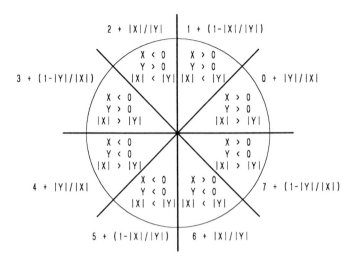

Figure 1. Octants and piecewise function evaluation.

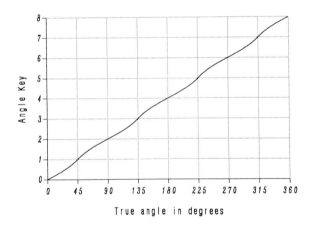

Figure 2. Graph of piecewise continuous function.

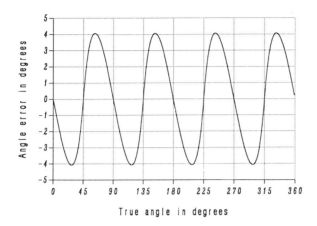

Figure 3.   Graph of arctangent approximation error.

As presented, this function returns a value greater than or equal to zero, and less than 8. This range often is useful as is, or it can be remapped easily to radians (or degrees) to provide an approximation to the arctangent. Figure 3 is a graph of the error of the approximation. The maximum error is less than 4.1 degrees, just over 1% of a full circle. Thus, the approximation is safe for point-in-polygon testing using algebraic sums of angles when the number of polygon vertices is small.

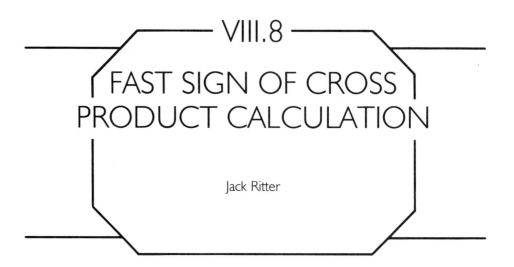

FAST SIGN OF CROSS PRODUCT CALCULATION

Jack Ritter

This gem provides a quick method of determining the sign of a 2D cross product. (If the plane defined by the two vectors is a general 3D plane, a transformation that aligns the plane to one of the three coordinate planes should be pre-applied to all points, to convert the problem into 2D.) In computer graphics, there are many cases where the cross product is computed, but only the *sign* is really needed. Four such cases are:

1. Back face culling (in screen space).

2. Determining the winding, or handedness, of two consecutive edges in a polygon, or looking at all consecutive pairs to determine whether the polygon is convex (e.g., if all signs agree). Handedness also is referred to as *into/out of the page*.

3. Determining the two outer corners of a pair of 2D wide lines joined at the ends, so as to fill in the hole with a bevel joint, mitered joint, etc.

4. Determining if a point is inside a triangle.

Typically, the full cross product is computed, and compared to zero. The calculation of a floating-point 2D cross product is of the form:

$$a*b - c*d,$$

where two fp multiplications, one fp subtraction, and one fp compare (to 0) are needed. This can be simplified by converting the problem into fixed point, and looking at the signs of a, b, c, and d, *before* doing the multiplication. Half the time, no multiplications are necessary, and the other half of the time, two *fixed-point*, 16-bit multiplications are required. To convert a fp number to a fixed point, scaling often is necessary. The algorithm uses signed short integers, so the fp numbers should scale to the order of: $-32K \rightarrow 32K$. This guarantees that only 16×16 fixed-point multiplications will be compiled, and not calls to complex math routines (like _lmul). The C Implementation (Appendix 2) uses a scaling of 16384; e.g., the original fp numbers are assumed to be in the range of $-1.0 \rightarrow 1.0$. The scale factor always should be a power of 2, so the compiler generates a fp shift, and *not* a fp multiplication.

Sometimes, the quantities a, b, c, and d are known only as relative differences (e.g., $a2 - a1$ instead of a). In these cases, it might be worth it to pass all eight floating-point numbers to the routine, convert all eight to fixed point, and then do the four subtractions in fixed point.

VIII.9

INTERVAL SAMPLING

Ken Shoemake
Otter Enterprises
Palo Alto, California

To sample an interval evenly with a predetermined number of points is easy. Sampling evenly when the number of points needed is not known in advance is less obvious. What is needed is a sequence of points that breaks the interval up as evenly as possible with each new point. Ramshaw (1978) showed one special way to do this is optimal according to several different criteria. For simplicity, assume your interval is the unit interval. (A simple linear map $t \to (b - a)t + a$ will convert from $[0 \ldots 1]$ to $[a \ldots b]$.) Then the sequence of sample points x_k is given by $x_k = (\log_2(2k + 1)) \bmod 1.0$, where modulo 1.0 means to take the fractional part. Here in the accompanying table are the first few samples:

k	x_k
1	0.584963
2	0.321928
3	0.807355
4	0.169925
5	0.459432
6	0.700440
7	0.906891
8	0.087463

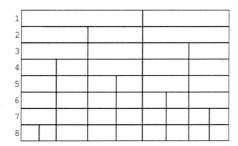

Figure 1.

Figure 1 is a graphical depiction of the partitioning obtained. For k sample points, the fragments obtained are all roughly of length $1/(k + 1)$.

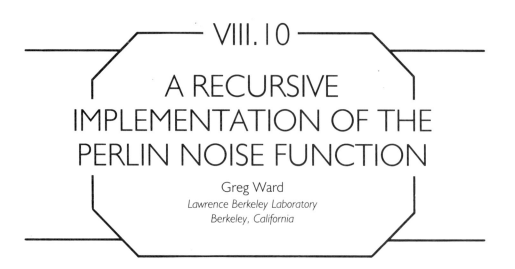

VIII.10

A RECURSIVE IMPLEMENTATION OF THE PERLIN NOISE FUNCTION

Greg Ward
Lawrence Berkeley Laboratory
Berkeley, California

Since its introduction at SIGGRAPH '85, Ken Perlin's three-dimensional noise function has found its way into a great many renderers (Perlin, 1985). The idea is to create a basis function that varies randomly between -1 and 1 throughout 3-space with an autocorrelation distance of about 1 in every direction. Such a function can serve as the building block for a wide variety of procedural textures. An additional proviso of the Perlin noise function is that it should not have pronounced harmonics; i.e., it should look like a sine function with a wiggling amplitude and no origin (Fig. 1). This enables the programmer to build up almost any desired random function by summing harmonics of the basic function, similar to a Fourier reconstruction.

There is no one correct way to write a random noise function, but some approaches are simpler or more efficient than others. One popular approach, suggested by Perlin in his 1985 paper, is to use random values and gradients assigned to a rectilinear grid throughout 3-space, then interpolate between them using Hermite splines. Although this does not produce a function that is completely free of rotational biases, it is good enough for most rendering applications. The C Implementation (Appendix II) is based on this simple approach.

The initial requirement of the implementation is a mapping from integer 3-space to random gradients and values, for which there are two basic approaches. The first approach is to use a hashing function to map integer triplets to a (possibly small) table of random numbers. The second approach is to use some uniformly distributed random function of three integers. The first method tends to be faster and more reliable, although

396

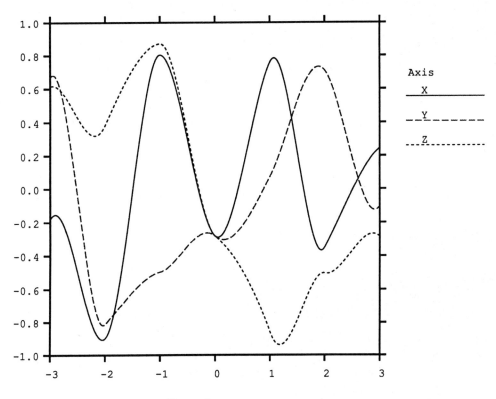

Figure 1. Perlin noise function.

the second method has the potential to produce more random results (but be careful—it is much easier to write a bad random function than one might think!). Once an algorithm has been chosen for assigning random vectors with components between −1 and 1 to integer lattice points, Hermite interpolation can be used to compute the function value at any point in 3-space.

The following pseudo-code function returns a random real value between −1 and 1 based on a single integer argument. Since its value from one integer to the next essentially is uncorrelated, random functions of more arguments can be constructed by using a sum of prime multiples as shown for the marcros *rand3a*, *rand3b*, *rand3c*, and *rand3d* that follow.

Frand: return a pseudo-random real between −1 and 1 from an integer seed

The following assumes a 32-bit two's-complement integer architecture

MAXINT: **integer** ← 1shift(1,32)-1; *All ones except sign bit*

function frand(s: **integer**): **real**;
begin

First, hash s as a preventive measure
s ← 1shift(s,13) **bit-xor** s;

Next, use a third order odd polynomial, better than linear
s ← (s*(s*s*15731 + 789221) + 1376312589) **bit-and** MAXINT;

Convert result to −1 to 1 range
rval ← 1.0 − s*2.0/MAXINT;

return rval;

end; *End of frand*

Define macros for different random functions of 3 integers:

macro rand3a(x, y, z)   frand(67*(x) + 59*(y) + 71*(z))
macro rand3b(x, y, z)   frand(73*(x) + 79*(y) + 83*(z))
macro rand3c(x, y, z)   frand(89*(x) + 97*(y) + 101*(z))
macro rand3d(x, y, z)   frand(103*(x) + 107*(y) + 109*(z))

In our implementation of three-dimensional Hermite interpolation, recursion is used to reduce the apparent complexity. A single function—whose job is to interpolate points and tangents in N dimensions—is written. If N is greater than 0, then it calls itself on each half of the next lower-order function ($N − 1$) and interpolates the results with a Hermite cubic function. If N is 0, then the function simply returns the point and tangent vector at the specified corner from the random lattice mapping.

Figure 2 shows eight lattice points surrounding a point in 3-space. The random values at these points are used to compute four points interpolated in x, which in turn are interpolated in y, then in z to compute the final value.

The following pseudo-code implements this algorithm. A macro defines the Hermite polynomial, and a home base routine assigns global variables and calls the recursive function that performs the actual interpolation.

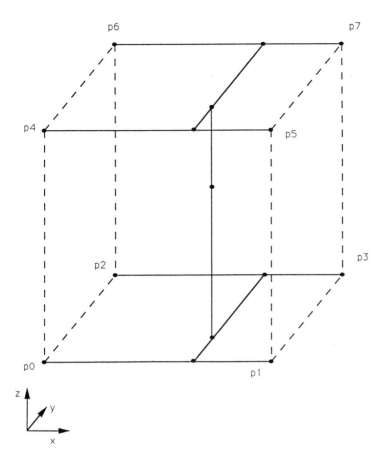

Figure 2.

One-dimensional Hermite polynomial:

$2tt - 3tt + 1$

macro   hermite(p0,p1,r0,r1,t)(p0*((2.*t − 3.)*t*t + 1.) +
                    p1*(−2.*t + 3.)*t*t + $-2ttt + 3tt$
                    r0*((t − 2.)*t + 1.)*t + $(tt - 2t + 1)t \rightarrow ttt - 2tt + t$
                    r1*(t − 1.)*t*t) $ttt - tt$

Global variable for the cube containing the point: $tt, ttt, +5 = ttt - tt,$

xlim: **array** [0..2] **of array** [0..1] **of integer**; $vo 32 = 3tt - 2ttt$

399

Global variable for the fractional parts for each coordinate:

xarg: **array** [0..2] **of real**;

Define type for gradient plus value in 4D array
GradV: **array** [0..3] **of real**;

function noise3(x: **point**): GradV;
nval: GradV;
begin

    Assign global variables for cube and fractional part
    xlim[0][0] ← floor(x[0]);
    xlim[0][1] ← xlim[0][0] + 1;
    xlim[1][0] ← floor(x[1]);
    xlim[1][1] ← xlim[1][0] + 1;
    xlim[2][0] ← floor(x[2]);
    xlim[2][1] ← xlim[2][0] + 1;
    xarg[0] ← x[0] − xlim[0][0];
    xarg[1] ← x[1] − xlim[1][0];
    xarg[2] ← x[2] − xlim[2][0];

    Call recursive interpolation function
    interpolate(f, 0, 3);

    return nval;

    end; *End of noise3*

Interpolate n-dimensional noise function

interpolate(**var** f: GradV; i, n: **integer**)
f0, f1: GradV; *results for first and second halves*
begin
    if n = 0
        then begin *at zero, just return lattice value*
        f[0] ← rand3a(xlim[0][i **bit-and** 1],
                xlim[1][rshift(i,1) **bit-and** 1],
                xlim[2][rshift(i,2)]);
        f[1] ← rand3b(xlim[0][i **bit-and** 1],
                xlim[1][rshift(i,1) **bit-and** 1],
                xlim[2][rshift(i,2)]);

```
            f[2] ← rand3c(xlim[0][i bit-and 1],
                        xlim[1][rshift(i,1) bit-and 1],
                        xlim[2][4shift(i,2)]);
            f[3] ← rand3d(xlim[0][i bit-and 1],
                        xlim[1][rshift(i,1) bit-and 1],
                        xlim[2][rshift(i,2)]);
        return,
        end;
    n ← n − 1;                      decrease order
    interpolate(f0, i, n);              compute first half
    interpolate(f1, i|1 ≪ n, n);        compute second half
                use linear interpolation for slopes
    f[0] ← lerp(xarg[n], f0[0], f1[0]);
    f[1] ← lerp(xarg[n], f0[1], f1[1]);
    f[2] ← lerp(xarg[n], f0[2], f1[2]);
                use hermite interpolation for value
    f[3] ← hermite(f0[3], f1[3], f0[n], f1[n], xarg[n]);
    end; End of interpolate
```

Thanks to this algorithm's recursive nature, it is easy to extend it to noise functions of higher dimensions. One only would need to add extra gradient components to the random number lattice mapping and increase the number of linear interpolations a like amount.

The author's experience with this implementation has proven it to be both fast and reliable, producing pleasing patterns without discernible repetition or statistical bias.

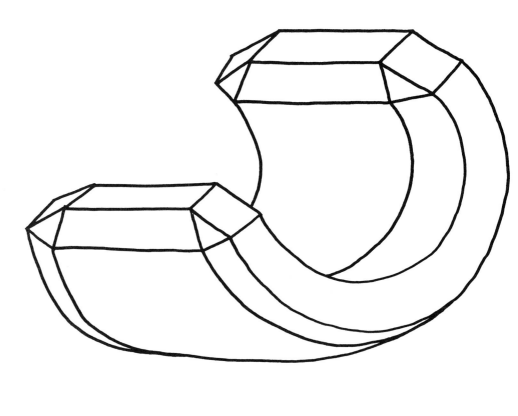

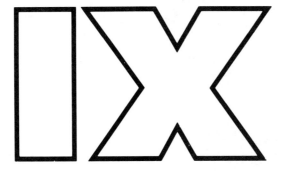

IX

CURVES AND
SURFACES

CURVES AND
SURFACES

The gems of this Part explore several theoretical and practical aspects of curves and surfaces. The first four gems provide new techniques for efficient evaluation and manipulation of polynomial representations, such as those based on Bézier curves. These are computationally convenient and provide a fairly compact means of representing complex surfaces.

The last three gems focus on curves related to the circle. It may be surprising that interesting and challenging problems remain even in this simple and familiar shape, but within the realm of computer graphics, there always will be a need to draw circles and arcs with increasing speed and fidelity. Toward this end, the final gems address approximation of circular arcs, plotting great circles, and anti-aliasing of circles.

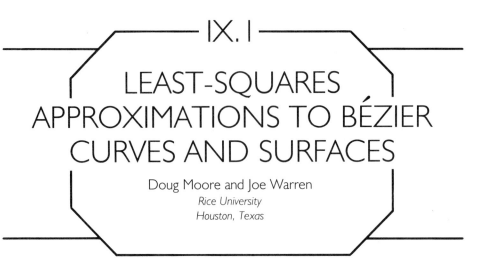

IX.1

LEAST-SQUARES APPROXIMATIONS TO BÉZIER CURVES AND SURFACES

Doug Moore and Joe Warren
Rice University
Houston, Texas

Problem

In computer graphics, the need to approximate a high-degree curve or surface by a lower-degree curve or surface often arises. One popular method used to select approximations is the least-squares technique. This gem discusses the use of least-squares to produce optimal approximations of lower degree to Bézier curves and surfaces.

Univariate Approximation

Let $p(t)$ be a polynomial of degree n written in Bernstein basis form:

$$p(t) = \sum_{j=0}^{n} p_j B_j^n(t).$$

Here, the Bernstein basis functions $B_j^n(t)$ are of the form:

$$B_j^n(t) = \frac{n!}{j!(n-j)!} t^j (1-t)^{n-j}.$$

We wish to compute a polynomial $q(t)$ of degree m,

$$q(t) = \sum_{j=0}^{m} q_j B_j^m(t),$$

that best approximates $p(t)$ under some mathematically precise measure of approximation error.

The least-squares method (Lawson and Hanson, 1974) provides one such measure. To use it, we define the residual as the average squared difference between $p(t)$ and $q(t)$ over the unit interval,

$$R = \int_0^1 \left(\sum_{j=0}^m q_j B_j^m(t) - \sum_{j=0}^n p_j B_j^n(t) \right)^2 dt,$$

and seek coefficients q_j that minimize the residual. For fixed $p(t)$, the residual is a quadratic expression in the coefficients q_j. It is minimized where all of its derivatives $\partial/\partial q_i$ vanish. From elementary calculus, the vanishing of the derivatives means that

$$\int_0^1 \sum_{j=0}^m q_j B_i^m(t) B_j^m(t)\, dt = \int_0^1 \sum_{j=0}^n p_j B_i^m(t) B_j^n(t)\, dt$$

for all $0 \leq i \leq m$.

Such an equation can be simplified by applying the rules for products and integrals of Bernstein polynomials (Farin, 1988). The result is a matrix equation of the form,

$$\mathbf{Aq} = \mathbf{Bp}, \tag{1}$$

where $\mathbf{A}$ is in $\mathscr{R}^{(m+1)\times(m+1)}$ and $\mathbf{B}$ is in $\mathscr{R}^{(m+1)\times(n+1)}$. The entries of $\mathbf{A}$ and $\mathbf{B}$ can be written as:

$$(2m+1)a_{ij} = \frac{\binom{m}{j}}{\binom{2m}{i+j}}, \quad (m+n+1)b_{ij} = \frac{\binom{n}{j}}{\binom{m+n}{i+j}}.$$

In practice, the degrees of $p(t)$ and $q(t)$ usually are fixed. In such cases, it is possible to precompute the matrix $\mathbf{A}^{-1}\mathbf{B}$ and avoid repeatedly solving Eq. (1). If $m = 1$, this matrix, $\mathbf{C} = \mathbf{A}^{-1}\mathbf{B}$, has a particularly simple form:

$$c_{0j} = \frac{2}{(n+1)(n+2)}(1 + 2n - 3j),$$

$$c_{1j} = \frac{2}{(n+1)(n+2)}(1 - n + 3j).$$

For example, the best-fitting linear function $q(t)$ to a given cubic polynomial $p(t)$ has coefficients:

$$q_0 = \frac{1}{10}(7p_0 + 4p_1 + p_2 - 2p_3),$$

$$q_1 = \frac{1}{10}(-2p_0 + p_1 + 4p_2 + 7p_3).$$

To approximate a parametric Bézier curve, we apply the method to each of the component polynomials $x(t)$ and $y(t)$ separately. An example of the application of this technique appears in Fig. 1, in which a degree 12 parametric curve is reduced to a degree 3 curve. If the line segment $L(t)$ connects the points $p(t)$ and $q(t)$ on the two curves, then the least-squares fitting cubic curve minimizes the average value of the squared length of $L(t)$.

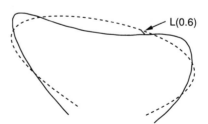

Figure 1.   Cubic curve approximating degree 12 curve.

Multivariate Approximation

A more general problem is the fitting of a Bézier surface, or its higher-dimensional analog, with a lower-degree surface. The multivariate Bernstein polynomials behave very much like their univariate counterparts, so with appropriate notation, an explanation of the general multivariate result is no more difficult to understand than the univariate result.

A multivariate Bernstein polynomial (de Boor, 1987) of dimension d is defined over a d-simplex, where a 2-simplex is a triangle and a 3-simplex is a tetrahedron. For concreteness, consider in particular the simplex S with vertices at the origin and at $\mathbf{e}_1, \ldots, \mathbf{e}_d$, where $\mathbf{e}_i$ is a point on the x_i axis one unit from the origin. For convenience, define x_0 as $1 - \sum_{i=1}^{d} x_i$.

The index set for the degree n Bernstein polynomials of dimension d is denoted as Δ_d^n; it consists of all the $(d + 1)$-tuples of nonnegative integers that sum to n. For an element $\mathbf{i} \in \Delta_d^n$, $\mathbf{i}_k$ is the kth index, $\mathbf{i}!$ denotes the product of the factorials of the indices, and $\mathbf{x}^i$ denotes the product of the terms $x_0^{i_0} \ldots x_d^{i_d}$. In this notation, a Bernstein basis function can be expressed as:

$$B_{\mathbf{i}}(\mathbf{x}) = \frac{n!}{\mathbf{i}!} \mathbf{x}^i,$$

and a polynomial in Bernstein basis form as:

$$p(\mathbf{t}) = \sum_{\mathbf{i} \in \Delta_d^n} p_{\mathbf{i}} B_{\mathbf{i}}(\mathbf{t}).$$

Using this notation, the derivation in the multivariate case closely matches the derivation in the univariate case. Given $p(\mathbf{t})$, we wish to find a $q(\mathbf{t})$ that minimizes the residual,

$$R = \int_S \left(\sum_{\mathbf{j} \in \Delta_d^m} q_{\mathbf{j}} B_{\mathbf{j}}(\mathbf{t}) - \sum_{\mathbf{j} \in \Delta_d^n} p_{\mathbf{j}} B_{\mathbf{j}}(\mathbf{t}) \right)^2 d\mathbf{t}.$$

This expression is minimized where the partial derivatives $\partial/\partial q_{\mathbf{i}}$ vanish, so that

$$\int_S \sum_{\mathbf{j} \in \Delta_d^m} q_{\mathbf{j}} B_{\mathbf{i}}(\mathbf{t}) B_{\mathbf{j}}(\mathbf{t}) \, d\mathbf{t} = \int_S \sum_{\mathbf{j} \in \Delta_d^n} p_{\mathbf{j}} B_{\mathbf{i}}(\mathbf{t}) B_{\mathbf{j}}(\mathbf{t}) \, d\mathbf{t}$$

for each $\mathbf{i} \in \Delta_d^m$. Again, the product and integration rules for multivariate Bernstein polynomials (de Boor, 1987) permit simplifications of this expression to the matrix equation,

$$\mathbf{Aq} = \mathbf{Bp},$$

where the matrix $\mathbf{A}$ is in $\mathscr{R}^{|\Delta_d^m| \times |\Delta_d^m|}$ and the matrix B is in $\mathscr{R}^{|\Delta_d^m| \times |\Delta_d^n|}$, where

$$|\Delta_d^k| = \binom{k + d}{k}.$$

The entries of A and B are given by the expressions,

$$a_{\mathbf{ij}} = \frac{m! d! (\mathbf{i} + \mathbf{j})!}{(2m + d)! \mathbf{j}!}, \, b_{\mathbf{ij}} = \frac{n! d! (\mathbf{i} + \mathbf{j})!}{(m + n + d)! \mathbf{j}!}.$$

In the linear case, $m = 1$, this expression can be simplified further. The elements of $\mathbf{A}^{-1}$ are given by:

$$a_{\mathbf{ii}}^{-1} = (d + 1)^2,$$

$$a_{\mathbf{ij}}^{-1} = -(d + 1) \ (\mathbf{i} \neq \mathbf{j}).$$

Since $m = 1$, the indices of the coefficients $q_{\mathbf{i}}$ are in Δ_d^1, and each index $\mathbf{i}$ is of the form $\mathbf{e}_k$ for $0 \leq k \leq d$. The $q_{\mathbf{e}_k}$ can be expressed in terms of the $p_{\mathbf{j}}$ as:

$$q_{\mathbf{e}_k} = \frac{n! (d + 1)!}{(n + d + 1)!} \sum_{\mathbf{j} \in \Delta_d^n} (1 - n + (d + 2) \mathbf{j}_k) p_j,$$

where $\mathbf{j}_k$ denotes the kth entry of $\mathbf{j}$.

For example, if $n = d = 2$, then

$$q_{100} = \frac{1}{10}(7p_{200} + 3p_{110} + 3p_{101} - p_{020} - p_{011} - p_{002}),$$

$$q_{010} = \frac{1}{10}(7p_{020} + 3p_{110} + 3p_{011} - p_{200} - p_{101} - p_{002}),$$

$$q_{001} = \frac{1}{10}(7p_{002} + 3p_{101} + 3p_{011} - p_{200} - p_{110} - p_{020}).$$

See also IX.2 Beyond Bézier Curves, Ken Shoemake; IX.6 Geometrically Continuous Cubic Bézier Curves, Hans-Peter Seidel

IX.2

BEYOND BÉZIER CURVES

Ken Shoemake
Otter Enterprises
Palo Alto, California

Bézier curves are deservedly popular, because the control points have a geometrical relationship to the curve, unlike polynomial coefficients. By associating a homogeneous weight with each control point, it is possible to describe rational curves—and hence, conics—as well. Surfaces can be described with tensor products of curves, giving four-sided Bézier patches; and solids as well as higher-dimensional volumes can be described by an extension of the same technique. This is not the only way to proceed, however. Instead, one can construct Bézier triangles, tetrahedra and so on (de Boor, 1987). These *Bézier simplices* have been exploited recently by Loop and De Rose (1989, 1990) as a way to construct patches with any number of sides, and from these, surfaces of arbitrary topology.

Evaluation to find points on Bézier simplices can be accomplished by a generalization of the recursive geometric de Casteljau algorithm for curves. One tricky part in doing this is simply managing the bookkeeping, since the algorithms and data structures are most naturally expressed in terms of what are called *multi-indices*. For a curve, these may seem like an unnecessary complication; for higher dimensions, they are a great help. Here in Fig. 1 are examples of a cubic curve and a cubic triangle, with control points labeled by their multi-indices. The sum of the indices is the parametric degree; here, it is 3.

Evaluation of the curve or surface recursively reduces the degree to zero, which gives a point. A convenient way to describe the process is to give the parameter values for the point as affine coordinates with respect to a simplex. For a point $2/3$ of the way along the curve, the coordinates are $(1/3, 2/3)$. Each edge of the control polygon for a curve has two endpoints, which are summed in these proportions to give a point of the

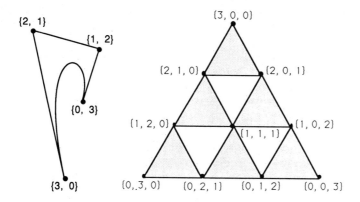

Figure 1.   a) Cubic curve; b) cubic triangle.

next lower-degree control polygon. The affine coordinates always sum to 1, or else this would not make sense; also, this constraint removes one degree of freedom, leaving only a single effective parameter for a curve, as expected. Be careful not to confuse the index for a control point—which is only a label—with its coordinates. In implementation terms, the multi-index gives a location in an array, while the coordinates are the contents of that location. Thus, the point with multi-index $\{1, 2\}$ could have coordinates $(1.3, -2.4, 2)$ and control a space curve, not just a planar curve. For a degree 2 curve, the indices will be $\{2, 0\}$, $\{1, 1\}$, and $\{0, 2\}$; for degree 1 (a line), they will be $\{1, 0\}$ and $\{0, 1\}$; and finally, for degree 0 (a point), the index is $\{0, 0\}$ (Table I).

Table I.

Degree 3	Degree 2		Degree 1		Degree 0	
index	from	index	from	index	from	index
$\{3, 0\}$	$\{3, 0\}, \{2, 1\}$	$\{2, 0\}$	$\{2, 0\}, \{1, 1\}$	$\{1, 0\}$	$\{1, 0\}, \{0, 1\}$	$\{0, 0\}$
$\{2, 1\}$	$\{2, 1\}, \{1, 2\}$	$\{1, 1\}$	$\{1, 1\}, \{0, 2\}$	$\{0, 1\}$		
$\{1, 2\}$	$\{1, 2\}, \{0, 3\}$	$\{0, 2\}$				
$\{0, 3\}$						

Table II.

| Degree 2 | Degree 1 | | Degree 0 | |
index	from	index	from	index
$\{2,0,0\}$	$\{2,0,0\}, \{1,1,0\}, \{1,0,1\}$	$\{1,0,0\}$	$\{1,0,0\}, \{0,1,0\}, \{0,0,1\}$	$\{0,0,0\}$
$\{1,1,0\}$	$\{1,1,0\}, \{0,2,0\}, \{0,1,1\}$	$\{0,1,0\}$		
$\{1,0,1\}$	$\{1,0,1\}, \{0,1,1\}, \{0,0,2\}$	$\{0,0,1\}$		
$\{0,2,0\}$				
$\{0,1,1\}$				
$\{0,0,2\}$				

The dependency follows a very simple pattern: $p[\hat{\imath}] = \Sigma t[k]p[\hat{\imath} + \hat{e}_k]$, where $\hat{\imath} + \hat{e}_k$ adds 1 to each component of the multi-index $\hat{\imath}$ in turn. For triangles, the pattern holds, but there now are three control points to sum, and the affine coordinates are three-tuples, $t = (t_0, t_1, t_2)$, with $\Sigma t_k = 1$. (See Fig. 1 and Table II. To save space, the table shows only the evaluation of a quadratic triangle.) While it is possible to store the points in a multi-dimensional array, it also is wasteful. The triangular cubic patch would store only 10 points in a $4^3 = 64$ entry array, while the points for one of Loop and De Rose's S-patches of depth 6 and five sides

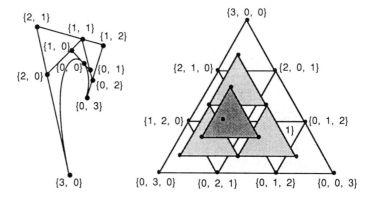

Figure 2.

Table III.

Degree 3	Degree 2		Degree 1		Degree 0	
at	from	at	from	at	from	at
0	0 1 2	0	0 1 2	0	0 1 2	0
1	1 3 4	1	1 3 4	1		
2	2 4 5	2	2 4 5	2		
3	3 6 7	3				
4	4 7 8	4				
5	5 8 9	5				
6						
7						
8						
9						

would use only 210 out of $7^5 = 16,807$ entries! Fortunately, one can systematically enumerate the control points to allow systematic indexing, and so use entries in a one-dimensional array without any waste.

To enumerate through all multi-indices for degree d and $n + 1$ slots, decrement the first index i_0 from d down to 0, and for each value of i_0, recurse to enumerate the multi-indices for degree $d - i_0$ and one less slot. For degree 0 or for only one slot (a special case), there is only one control point. For higher degrees or more slots, #Points$(d, n) =$ #Points$(d - 1, n) +$ #Points$(d, n - 1)$. The closed form #Points(d, n) $= (d + n)!/d!n!$ clearly is symmetric in its arguments. With this order, evaluation is very regular, as can be seen in the case of a cubic triangle (Table III).

Study of this and similar examples reveals that for a given number of slots, there really is only one dependency list, with lower degrees using smaller portions of it. Also, a point always depends on the higher degree point at the same array index (and never on points with lower indices); so, for a modest investment in precalculated tables, all the multi-index bookkeeping goes away.

To build the dependency tables, it helps to know how to compute an offset from a multi-index. This turns out to be another recursive process. The idea behind the offset calculation is that before we get to the offset for the leading index i_0, we first must have enumerated all larger indices.

When the degree is zero, the offset is zero; this is where the recursion bottoms out. Otherwise, the offset is the sum of $\#\text{Points}(d - i_0 - 1, n)$ and the offset for the shorter multi-index, $\{i_1, \ldots, i_n\}$. (For the case when $i_0 = d$, it is necessary to extend the definition of $\#\text{Points}$ to return 0 when d is negative.) Remember that the degree is the sum of the indices, so the shorter multi-index has degree $d - i_0$, and the recursion will terminate after all the nonzero indices have been picked off.

A SIMPLE FORMULATION FOR CURVE INTERPOLATION WITH VARIABLE CONTROL POINT APPROXIMATION

John Schlag
MacroMind, Inc.
San Francisco, California

Curve interpolation for computer animation often requires some sort of shape control beyond the values of the control points. This gem presents a hybrid scheme—based on techniques presented by Kochanek and Bartels (1984) and Duff (1984)—that provides control over tension, bias, continuity, and approximation. (The terms *approximation* and *interpolation* are used interchangeably, although they are complementary, similar to the terms *transparency* and *opacity* in rendering.)

Kochanek and Bartels (1984) provide an elegant formulation for tension, continuity, and bias control based on the blending of tangents:

$$P'_{i-1}(1) = \frac{(1 - t)(1 - c)(1 + b)}{2}(P_i - P_{i-1})$$

$$+ \frac{(1 - t)(1 + c)(1 - b)}{2}(P_{i+1} - P_i),$$

$$P'_i(0) = \frac{(1 - t)(1 + c)(1 + b)}{2}(P_i - P_{i-1})$$

$$+ \frac{(1 - t)(1 - c)(1 - b)}{2}(P_{i+1} - P_i).$$

where $P'_{i-1}(1)$ is the incoming tangent at P_i (i.e., the tangent of arc $i - 1$ evaluated at $t = 1$) and $P'_i(0)$ is the outgoing tangent at P_i, and t, c, and b are tension, continuity, and bias. Two control points, P_i and P_{i+1}, and the tangents computed at these control points, $P'_i(0)$ and $P'_i(1)$ are then used for Hermite interpolation.

Duff (1984), on the other hand, provides a five-parameter family of splines with control over bias, tension, and approximation:

$$P(0) = \text{lerp}\left(P_i, \text{lerp}(P_{i-1}, P_{i+1}, \sigma), \iota\right),$$

$$P(1) = \text{lerp}(P_{i+1}, \text{lerp}\left(P_i, P_{i+2}, \sigma\right), \iota),$$

$$P'(0) = (1 - \gamma)\tau \, \text{lerp}\left(P_i - P_{i-1}, P_{i+1} - P_i, \delta\right),$$

$$P'(1) = \gamma\tau \, \text{lerp}\left(P_{i+1} + P_i, P_{i+2} - P_{i+1}, \delta\right),$$

where σ, ι, γ, τ, and δ are interpreted as *slew, interpolation, geometricity, tension,* and *direction*, respectively. Note that, unfortunately, the term *tension* is used both for interpolating splines, in which the tension controls the velocity at the control points, and for approximating splines, in which the tension controls the degree to which the curve approaches the control points.

The Kochanek–Bartels formulation provides superior control over tangents by breaking the tangent at a point into incoming and outgoing tangents, thus providing control over continuity. Duff's formulation provides the additional parameter necessary for control over approximation. These methods can be easily combined by using Duff's formulation with σ = .5 to calculate the endpoints $P(0)$ and $P(1)$, and the Kochanek–Bartels formulation to calculate the tangents $P'(0)$ and $P'(1)$:

$$P(0) = \text{lerp}\left(P_i, \frac{P_{i-1} + P_{i+1}}{2}, \iota\right),$$

$$P(1) = \text{lerp}\left(P_{i+1}, \frac{P_i + P_{i+2}}{2}, \iota\right),$$

$$P'(0) = \frac{(1 - t)(1 + c)(1 + b)}{2}(P_i - P_{i-1})$$

$$+ \frac{(1 - t)(1 - c)(1 - b)}{2}(P_{i+1} - P_i),$$

$$P'(1) = \frac{(1 - t)(1 - c)(1 + b)}{2}(P_{i+1} - P_i)$$

$$+ \frac{(1 - t)(1 + c)(1 - b)}{2}(P_{i+2} - P_{i+1}).$$

With $t = c = b = 0$, the value $\iota = 1/3$ generates B-splines, and $\iota = 0$ generates Catmull–Rom splines.

Note that the Kochanek–Bartels formulation includes corrections to the tangents for knot spacing (omitted until now for clarity):

$$\text{adjusted } P'(0) = P'(0)\frac{2N_{i-1}}{N_{i-1} + N_i},$$

$$\text{adjusted } P'(1) = P'(1)\frac{2N_{i+1}}{N_i + N_{i+1}}.$$

Now for some observations regarding the user interface to these parameters: The most obvious approach is to provide sliders or some other controls for t, b, c, and ι. Another approach is to let the user edit the tangents directly. This works especially well for 2D position (Adobe, 1988). This technique can be extended to 3D in a number of ways. First, the technique can be limited to 1D—as in a function editor—and then applied to each scalar. This is often the only alternative, especially when the motion parameter being interpolated has no intuitive geometric meaning. Alternatively, we can observe that, according to the rules of good traditional animation (Lasseter, 1987), animation is often staged from the side. This suggests that mapping 2D interaction onto a plane parallel to the image plane of a 3D view window would be acceptable. Finally, of course, three orthogonal views can be used, if necessary, to provide complete control.

IX.4

SYMMETRIC EVALUATION OF POLYNOMIALS

Terence Lindgren
Prime Computervision
Bedford, Massachusetts

Parametric curves and surfaces are widely used primitives in computer graphics. PHIGS PLUS, in fact, makes NURBS curves and surfaces fundamental primitives. It is very common to renderers to find polyline representations for curves and facet representations for surfaces. Typically, these representations come from evaluating the curve or surface at a set of points and connecting them in the natural way. The efficient evaluation of these primitives is important to any renderer interested in speed. The mathematical form of the primitive is important to both the application and the renderer. Often, CAD/CAM applications represent geometry in the *B*-Spline basis or the Berstein basis because these bases have significant geometric interpretations; other applications might use a power series with the more familiar power basis, $\{1, t, t*t, \ldots\}$. Unfortunately, many of these different bases are difficult to render quickly within the constraints of most graphics subsystems. However, the power basis is not one of the difficult ones, and renderers commonly change to the power basis prior to evaluation (Boehm, 1984).

Before the advent of fast floating-point multipliers, these polynomials might have been evaluated with forward differencing; but with multiplier speeds comparable to adder speeds, a polynomial can be evaluated realistically by Horner's rule; that is,

$$F[t] = \sum_{i=0}^{N} \alpha i \cdot t^i$$

can be evaluated at t by the loop:·

F ← a$_n$;

  for i = N − 1 to 0
   begin

F ← F*t + a$_i$;

   end

We will examine this technique and subsequent calculations in terms of the number of multiplications and the number of additions the operation takes. If the degree of the polynomial is N, then Horner's rule requires N multiplications and N additions to evaluate a point t in the domain. A multivariate polynomial, like those that would be used to represent the coordinate functions of a parametric surface,

$$F[t, s] = \sum_{i=0}^{N} \sum_{j=0}^{M} \alpha_{ij} \cdot s^{j} * t^{i},$$

would use $(N + 1)(M + 1) − 1$ multiplications and $(N + 1)(M + 1) − 1$ additions to evaluate a point (s, t) in the domain by Horner's rule.

The polynomials we encounter in computer graphics, especially those arising originally as NURBS, are defined neither over an infinite domain nor over an interval that is symmetric about the origin. Both the interval of definition $[a, b]$ and the point at which the power series is centered are unrestricted. For power series centered at some point c, we can evaluate points in the domain by applying Horner's rule to the quantity $(t − c)$, reducing the problem of evaluating a power series to ones centered at 0. Of particular interest to us are power series centered at the midpoint m of the domain $[a, b]$; that is,

$$F[t] = \sum_{i=0}^{N} \beta_{i} \cdot (t − m)^{i}.$$

Henceforth, we will consider only power series centered at 0.

Certain polynomials have some very simple properties. Some are even or odd functions. A function H is even if

$$H[−t] = H[t],$$

and is odd if

$$H[-t] = -H[t].$$

Moreover, any polynomial is the sum of an even and an odd function. The even function is determined by those terms with even powers, and the odd function is determined by those terms with odd powers,

$$F[t] = E[t] + O[t].$$

Since $O[t]$ is all terms with odd powers from F, we immediately see that we may rewrite $O[t]$ as

$$O[t] = t*E'[t],$$

where E' is an even function. So we may write F as

$$F[t] = E[t] + t*E'[t], \tag{1}$$

and we now are free to recognize

$$F[-t] = E[t] - t*E'[t].$$

With this observation, we are in a position to state the simple work saving evaluation technique, which we will call *symmetric evaluation*. Note that we do assume that the power series is centered at the midpoint of the segment or patch.

> **for** t ≥ 0, generate F[t] and F[−t].
> *Construct a power series (centered at the midpoint of the segment).*
> Calculate E and E' as in Eq. (1)
> Calculate t*t.
> *Use Horner's Rule to evaluate both E and E' as polynomials in t*t.*
> Multiply E' by t.
> Create the sum, F[t], and difference, F[−t], of E[t] and t*E'[t].

The price we pay for calculating two symmetric points of a polynomial of degree N is a multiplication to set up $t*t$, N multiplications and $N - 1$ additions to calculate E and E', and two additions to calculate the sum and the difference; So, for a single polynomial, the total work is

$N + 1$ multiplications and $N + 1$ additions. Evaluation of polynomials in two variables presents an opportunity for even greater savings. We center a power series at the midpoint of a patch just as we did for the midpoint of a segment and proceed in a similar way as before.

If we evaluate the multivariate polynomial as if it were $N + 2$ univariate polynomials, as

$$F[t, s] = \sum_{i=0}^{N} \left(\sum_{j=0}^{M} \alpha_{ij} \cdot s^j \right) * t^i$$

would indicate, our savings are more impressive. We may evaluate symmetrically four points with a cost of $(N + 1)M + 2N + 2$ multiplications and $(N + 1)(M + 3)$ additions. Compare this to the $4((N + 1)(M + 1) - 1)$ multiplications and $4((N + 1)(M + 1) - 1)$ additions needed for traditional evaluation.

Actually, the savings are greater for a parametric surface; not only are there at least three coordinate polynomials to be evaluated, but the surface's partial derivatives also will need to be evaluated. After all, we will want to shade the surface, so we will need the partials to calculate the surface normal at the evaluation points. The cost for this work traditionally is $4*$(number of coordinate functions)$*(3NM + 2(N + M) - 2)$ multiplications and additions; while the cost for symmetric evaluation is (number of coordinate functions)$*(3NM + 5N + 3M - 2)$ multiplications and (number of coordinate functions)$*(3NM + 6N + 4M + 3)$ additions.

Finally, as an illustration, let us look at the actual savings obtained evaluating symmetric points and their partials on an integral bicubic patch. Traditional evaluation costs 444 multiplications and 444 additions, whereas symmetric evaluation costs only 149 multiplications and 180 additions.

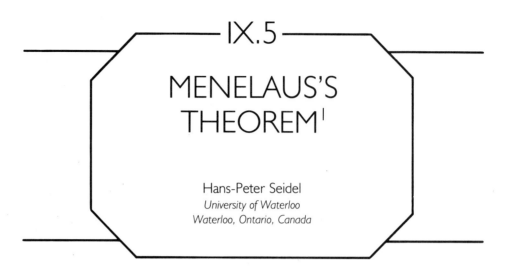

IX.5

MENELAUS'S THEOREM[1]

Hans-Peter Seidel
University of Waterloo
Waterloo, Ontario, Canada

Introduction

Menelaus's theorem has been known since the ancient Greeks, but is surprisingly unfamiliar today. It often is a handy tool in curve and surface design, since it relates the ratios between different control points in a simple intuitive way. In particular, Menelaus's theorem can be used for knot insertion in B-splines, β-splines, and NURBS.

Menelaus's Theorem

Menelaus's theorem can be stated as follows: Consider the triangle $\triangle(ABC)$ together with the points $D \in BC$, $E \in CA$, and $F \in AB$ as shown in Fig. 1. Menelaus's theorem says that the points

$$D, E, F \text{ are collinear iff } \frac{\overline{BD}}{\overline{DC}} \cdot \frac{\overline{CE}}{\overline{EA}} \cdot \frac{\overline{AF}}{\overline{FB}} = -1.$$

(The negative sign is due to the fact that the ratio $\overline{BD} / \overline{DC}$ for a point D outside of $\overline{BC}$ is negative).

[1]This work has been supported partly by the Natural Sciences and Engineering Research Council of Canada through Strategic Operating Grant STR0040527.

424

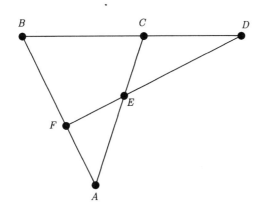

Figure 1.   Menelaus's theorem.

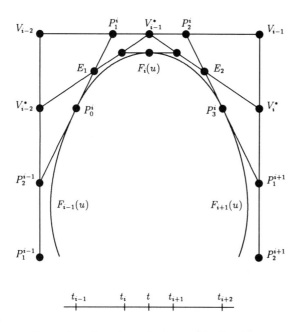

Figure 2.   Knot insertion for cubic B-splines.

Application

An application of Menelaus's theorem is shown in Fig. 2. The figure illustrates how Menelaus's theorem can be used for knot insertion into B-splines: Shown in the ith segment of a cubic B-spline curve F over the knot vector,

$$T = (\ldots, t_{i-1}, t_i, t_{i+1}, t_{i+2}, \ldots),$$

together with the B-spline control points $\ldots, V_{i-2}, V_{i-1}, \ldots$ and the Bézier points $\ldots, P_1^{i-1}, \ldots, P_2^{i+1}, \ldots$ of the adjacent segments. Also depicted are the new control points $V_{i-2}^*, \ldots, V_i^*$ after inserting the new knot t between t_i and t_{i+1}.

Note that Fig. 2 contains two of Menelaus's figures: One figure comes from the triangle, $\triangle(A_1, B_1, C_1) = \triangle(P_2^{i-1}, V_{i-2}, P_1^i)$, together with the points, $D_1 = V_{i-1}^*$, E_1, and $F_1 = V_{i-2}^*$, while the other figure comes from the triangle, $\triangle(A_2, B_2, C_2) = \triangle(P_1^{i+1}, V_{i-1}, P_2^i)$, together with the points, $D_2 = V_{i-1}^*$, E_2, and $F_2 = V_i^*$.

Since the points,

$$E_1 = \frac{t - t_i}{t_{i+1} - t_i} P_1^i + \frac{t_{i+1} - t}{t_{i+1} - t_i} P_0^i,$$

$$V_{i-1}^* = \frac{t - t_i}{t_{i+1} - t_i} P_2^i + \frac{t_{i+1} - t}{t_{i+1} - t_i} P_1^i,$$

$$E_2 = \frac{t - t_i}{t_{i+1} - t_i} P_3^i + \frac{t_{i+1} - t}{t_{i+1} - t_i} P_2^i,$$

are given by the de Casteljau algorithm, a simple calculation using Menelaus's theorem shows

$$V_{i-2}^* = \frac{t - t_i}{t_{i+1} - t_i} V_{i-2} + \frac{t_{i+1} - t}{t_{i+1} - t_i} P_2^{i-1},$$

and

$$V_i^* = \frac{t - t_i}{t_{i+1} - t_i} P_1^{i+1} + \frac{t_{i+1} - t}{t_{i+1} - t_i} V^{i-1},$$

and using the relationship between the Bézier points and the *B*-spline control points, we see that the new control points V_j^* are given as:

$$V_j^* = \frac{t - t_i}{t_{i+1} - t_i} V_j + \frac{t_{i+1} - t}{t_{i+1} - t_i} V_{j-1}, \qquad j = i - 2, \ldots, i.$$

Thus, we have derived the well-known insertion algorithm for *B*-splines from a simple theorem on 2D geometry. In a similar fashion, Menelaus's theorem can be used for knot insertion in nonuniform β-splines and NURBS.

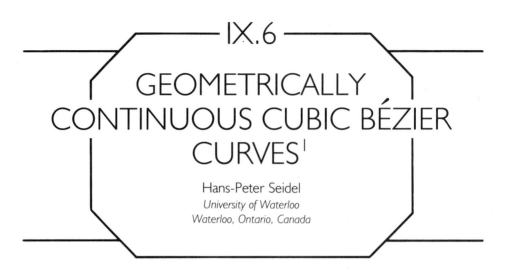

IX.6

GEOMETRICALLY CONTINUOUS CUBIC BÉZIER CURVES[1]

Hans-Peter Seidel
University of Waterloo
Waterloo, Ontario, Canada

Introduction

Traditionally, curves and surfaces in computer graphics and computer-aided design have been required to be parametrically C^k-continuous. However, for many applications, this notion of continuity is far too restrictive: Figure 1 shows two cubic Bézier curves,

$$F(u) = \sum_{i=0}^{3} B_i^n(u) P_i,$$

and

$$H(u) = \sum_{i=0}^{3} B_i^3(u) R_i,$$

in the plane. Here,

$$B_i^3(u) = \binom{3}{i} u^i (1-u)^{3-i}, \qquad i = 0, \ldots, 3$$

are the Bernstein polynomials, and the points $P_0, \ldots, P_3$, and $R_0, \ldots, R_3$, respectively, are the Bézier points. The problem is to fill the gap between

[1]This work has been supported partly by the Natural Sciences and Engineering Research Council of Canada through Strategic Operating Grant STR0040527.

428

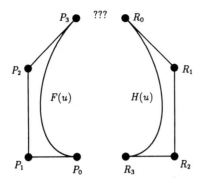

Figure I. Gap between P_3 and R_0.

P_3 and R_0 by another cubic Bézier curve,

$$G(u) = \sum_{i=0}^{3} B_i^3(u)Q_i,$$

in such a way that the resulting composite curve is as *smooth* as possible.

Suppose we wish to fill the gap between the given curves F and H in such a way that the resulting composite curve is parametrically C^1-continuous. Using the well-known derivative formulas for Bézier curves,

$$G'(0) = 3(Q_1 - Q_0), G''(0) = 6(Q_2 - 2Q_1 + Q_0),$$

and

$$G'(1) = 3(Q_3 - Q_2), G''(1) = 6(Q_3 - 2Q_2 + Q_1),$$

we see that a C^1-joint at $F(1) = G(0)$ implies:

$$Q_0 = P_3 \text{ and } Q_1 = 2P_3 - P_2,$$

while a C^1-joint at $G(1) = H(0)$ gives:

$$Q_3 = R_0 \text{ and } Q_2 = 2R_0 - R_1.$$

429

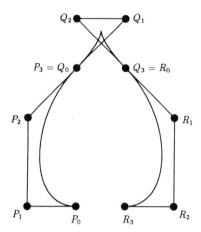

Figure 2. C^1-solution with a cusp.

In particular, our requirement for an overall C^1-curve completely determines the Bézier curve G that bridges the gap between F and H. So far, it seems that the preceding two equations provide an easy solution to an easy problem.

Second thoughts arise when we actually take a look at the curve G that we have just computed (Fig. 2). Disaster has happened: By insisting on parametric C^1-continuity at the joints $G(0)$ and $G(1)$, we actually have introduced a cusp. Our solution G is totally unacceptable!

Parametric versus Geometric Continuity

The problem with our solution G in the previous section stems from the fact that we have insisted on *parametric* continuity instead of *geometric* continuity: Instead of looking at the continuity of a specific parametrization, we have to look at the continuity of the shape of the curve, which is independent under possible reparametrization. Thus, we say that two curves join with *geometric continuity* if the curves are parametrically continuous under reparametrization. In other words, two curves F and G are G^k-continuous at a parameter s if there exists a reparametrization ϕ (which preserves the given orientation of the curve) such that $F(\phi(u))$ and $G(u)$ are C^k-continuous at s. Using the chain rule of differentiation, it easily is seen that G^k-continuity is equivalent to the well-known β-constraints:

$$G'(s) = \beta_1 F'(s),$$

$$G''(s) = \beta_1^2 F''(s) + \beta_2 F'(s),$$

$$G'''(s) = \beta_1^3 F'''(s) + 3\beta_1\beta_2 F''(s) + \beta_3 F'(s).$$

$$\vdots$$

$$G^{(k)}(s) = \sum_{j=0}^{k} \sum_{\substack{i_1+i_2+\ldots+i_k=j, \\ i_1+2i_2+\ldots+ki_k=k,}} \frac{k!}{i_1!(1!)^{i_1} \cdots i_k!(k!)^{i_k}} \beta_1^{i_1} \cdots \beta_k^{i_k} F^{(j)}(s),$$

where $\beta_k = \phi^{(k)}(s)$, and $\beta_1 > 0$, since ϕ preserves the given orientation. The parameters β_i also are called *shape parameters*. We pause to remark that G^1-continuity is equivalent to a continuous unit tangent, while G^2-continuity is equivalent to a continuous curvature vector.

Geometrically Continuous Bézier Curves

How can we exploit the preceding conditions to join two cubic Bézier curves with a given order of geometric continuity? Consider two cubic Bézier curves,

$$F(\tilde{u}) = \sum_{i=0}^{3} B_i^3(\tilde{u})P_i \quad \text{and} \quad G(\tilde{v}) = \sum_{i=0}^{3} B_i^3(\tilde{v})Q_i,$$

over the intervals $[r, s]$ and $[s, t]$, respectively, so that the local parameters $\tilde{u}$ and $\tilde{v}$ are given as:

$$\tilde{u} = \frac{u - r}{s - r} \quad (u \in [r, s]) \quad \text{and} \quad \tilde{v} = \frac{v - s}{t - s} \quad (v \in [s, t]).$$

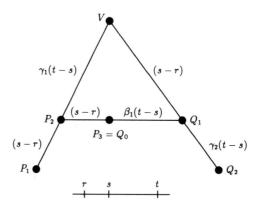

Figure 3. C^1-joint between two cubic Bézier curves.

To join F and G with G^1-continuity, it is necessary and sufficient that the Bézier points

$$P_2, P_3 = Q_0, Q_1 \text{ are collinear,}$$

and satisfy the ratios,

$$\overline{P_2 P_3} : \overline{Q_0 Q_1} = (s - r) : \beta_1 (t - s).$$

This follows immediately from the β-constraints and the well-known derivative formula for Bézier curves, and is depicted in Fig. 3.

Things become slightly more complicated for G^2-continuity. (See Fig. 4.)

It can be shown that F and G are G^2-continuous at s precisely if the Bézier points,

$$P_1, P_2, P_3 = Q_0, Q_1, Q_2, \text{ are coplanar,}$$

Figure 4. G^2-joint between two cubic Bézier curves.

and satisfy the ratios,

$$\overline{P_1 P_2} : \overline{P_2 V} = (s - r) : \gamma_1 (t - s) \quad \text{and} \quad \overline{VQ_1} : \overline{Q_1 Q_2} = (s - r) : \gamma_2 (t - s),$$

for parameters γ_1, γ_2, with

$$\gamma_1 \gamma_2 = \beta_1^2.$$

Thus, instead of directly using the shape parameters β_1 and β_2, it sometimes is advantageous to use the shape parameters β_1 and γ_1 instead. For those who are curious, the (ugly) relationship between the γ's and the β's is given as:

$$\gamma_1 = \frac{2\beta_1^2 (\beta_1 (t - s) + (s - r))}{\beta_2 (t - s)(s - r) + 2\beta_1 (\beta_1 (t - s) + (s - r))}$$

and

$$\gamma_2 = \frac{\beta_2 (t - s)(s - r) + 2\beta_1 (\beta_1 (t - s) + (s - r))}{2(\beta_1 (t - s) + (s - r))}.$$

Using geometric continuity instead of parametric continuity, it now is easy to come up with a simple satisfactory solution to our original problem of filling the gap between two given cubic Bézier curves F and H by another cubic Bézier curve,

$$G(u) = \sum_{i=0}^{3} B_i^n(u) Q_i,$$

in such a way that the resulting composite curve is as smooth as possible.

All we have to do is move the Bézier points Q_1 and Q_2 somewhere on the lines $P_2 P_3$ and $R_0 R_1$ a little bit closer to the endpoints P_3 and R_0. This will avoid the cusp in the C^1-solution, and, according to Fig. 3, will produce a G^1-curve overall; but we can do even better than that. Note that the exact positioning of the vertices Q_1 and Q_2 on the lines $P_2 P_3$ and $R_0 R_1$ still leaves us with one degree of freedom for each point. Using the symmetry of the given problem, we can exploit this freedom to

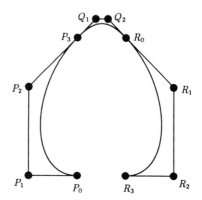

Figure 5. G^2-solution: The resulting composite curve has a continuous unit tangent, and, in addition, is curvature-continuous everywhere.

arrange the Bézier points Q_1 and Q_2 of G in such a way that the ratios of Fig. 4 are satisfied. Thus, the resulting curve not only will be C^1, but, in addition, will have continuous curvature throughout. This solution is shown in Fig. 5.

See also IX.1 Least-Squares Approximations to Bézier Curves and Surfaces, Doug Moore, Joe Warren; IX.2 Beyond Bézier Curves, Ken Shoemake

IX.7

A GOOD STRAIGHT-LINE APPROXIMATION OF A CIRCULAR ARC

Christopher J. Musial
New Horizons Software
St. Louis, Missouri

Many geometric algorithms and spatial modeling systems work with straight lines and straight-line polygons. Because the world does not always consist of straight lines, the need often arises for approximating a circular arc with line segments. The simplest approximation is to select points along the curve at a spacing that gives sufficient accuracy and then join these points together into a polyline. One of the major deficiencies with this approach is that the length of the resulting polyline is less than the arc length of the original curve. If perimeter calculation is a requirement, this type of approximation is unacceptable.

In addition to maintaining the original length, the polyline also must start and stop at the same endpoints as the arc. Because we are imposing two constraints on the curve, there are two variables we must calculate.

The first is the angle formed between the tangent vector at the start of the arc with the first segment in the approximating polyline (α). (By symmetry, this also is the angle between the last segment and the tangent line at the end of the curve.)

The second variable is the incremental angle between two adjacent polyline segments (ϕ). Figure 1 shows these two angles. (In Fig. 1 and throughout this discussion, clockwise arcs are assumed. Counterclockwise arcs will be explained later.)

Before we can begin the calculation, we first must determine the number of segments to use in the polyline based on the maximum allowable distance between the polyline and the arc. If the polyline circumscribes the arc, it will be longer than the arc; likewise, if the polyline is inscribed within the arc, it will be shorter than the arc. Therefore, a polyline with the same length as the arc will be somewhere

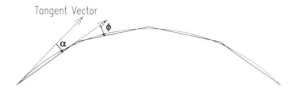

Figure 1.

between being inscribed and circumscribed. By choosing the number of segments based on the curve-to-chord distance of error for an inscribed polyline, we will be sure to be within the tolerance for the polyline at which we are aiming. Figure 2 shows the curve-to-chord distance for an inscribed polyline.

The distance d between a circular arc with an internal angle θ and a radius R, and the chord joining its two endpoints, is

$$d = R\left(1 - \cos\frac{\theta}{2}\right). \tag{1}$$

If this distance is too large, split the curve by dividing θ and the arc length in half. Repeating the preceding procedure until we get a curve-to-chord distance within the acceptable tolerance, the length of each segment in the polyline is that of the last arc length, and the number of segments is $2^{\text{number of splits}}$.

The preceding step satisfied the first criterion we were after: The sum of each segment in the polyline will equal the arc length of the curve. The second criterion—having the same start and end points as the arc—will

Figure 2.

be met by forcing the horizontal span of the polyline to equal the chord length of the curve.

The horizontal span is the sum of the projection of each segment onto the x axis, which simply is the segment length times the cosine of the segment's direction vector. This problem becomes one of calculating the segment directions, and thus the two angles, α and ϕ.

If $\mathbf{T}$ is the tangent vector at the start of the arc, the direction vector of the first polyline segment is $\mathbf{T} - \alpha$, the direction vector of the next segment is $\mathbf{T} - \alpha - \phi$, $\mathbf{T} - \alpha - 2\phi$, and so on. Thus, forcing the total span to be equal to the chord length of the arc, we get the equation:

$$\text{segLen} \sum_{i=0}^{n-1} \cos(\mathbf{T} - \alpha - i\phi) = \text{chordLen}, \tag{2}$$

where n is the number of segments in the polyline, segLen is the length of each segment in the polyline, and chordLen is the length of the chord of the arc.

Figure 3 shows the values we need. Only four segments are used in the approximation for ease of viewing.

We know that the total deflection of the circular arc is the same as its internal angle, θ. We also know that the total deflection of the polyline

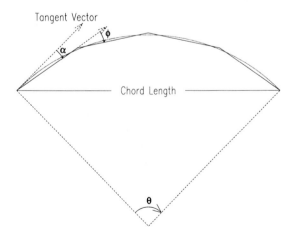

Figure 3.

plus the two α's at either end equals the deflection of the curve, so

$$2\alpha + (n - 1)\phi = \theta, \quad \text{or} \tag{3a}$$

$$\alpha = \frac{\theta - (n - 1)\phi}{2}. \tag{3b}$$

Substituting for α in Eq. (2) and rearranging, we get

$$\text{segLen} \sum_{i=0}^{n-1} \cos\left(\mathbf{T} - \frac{\theta - (n - 1)\phi}{2} - i\phi\right) - \text{chordLen} = 0. \tag{4}$$

From here, you may use your favorite convergence algorithm to calculate ϕ. Both α and ϕ are positive, so using Eq. (3a), we can calculate the range of values for α and ϕ as:

$$0 < \alpha < \frac{\theta}{2}, \tag{5a}$$

$$0 < \phi < \frac{\theta}{n - 1}. \tag{5b}$$

Equation (4) is a well-behaved function as shown in Fig. 4. This is a graph of Eq. (4) for an arc with $\theta = 90°$, radius $= 100$, $\mathbf{T} = 45°$, and $n = 32$. The chord length is calculated as 141.4214 and the segment length as 4.9087. Along the x axis are values of ϕ. The y axis is the left side of Eq. (4). The value of ϕ we need is where the plot crosses $y = 0$.

The result of the left side of Eq. (4) for the different trial values of ϕ is the error to be minimized, which is the difference between the span of the polyline and the chord length of the arc. Once Eq. (4) gives an answer within the acceptable tolerance, use Eq. (3b) to calculate α.

For counterclockwise curves, use the same procedure as before, and then negate the values of α and ϕ.

In this discussion, we oriented the curve such that the chord is parallel with the x axis. When this is not the case (and it usually is not), calculate α and ϕ as if it were, but use the true tangent vector of the arc when

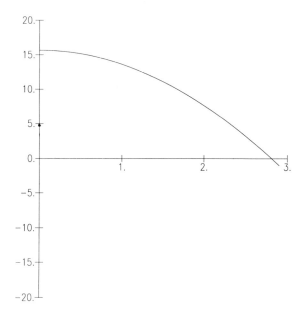

Figure 4.

calculating the direction vectors of the polyline segments as described in the following.

Knowing the starting point and direction of the first segment $(\mathbf{T} - \alpha)$, and the direction vector for each succeeding segment $(\mathbf{T} - \alpha - (i - 1)\phi)$, the polyline now may be constructed.

The C Implementation (Appendix II) uses linear interpolation as the convergence method, and also shows how to calculate the polyline vertices once α and ϕ are available.

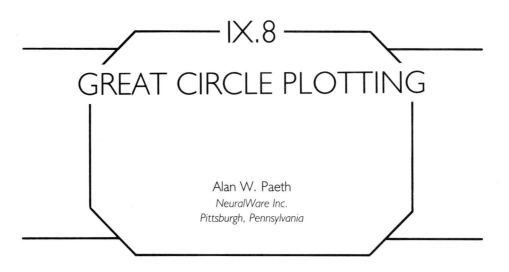

IX.8

GREAT CIRCLE PLOTTING

Alan W. Paeth
NeuralWare Inc.
Pittsburgh, Pennsylvania

A great circle comprises those points common to a sphere and a plane, the latter passing through the former's center. Great circles partition a sphere into equal hemispheres and form *geodesics*: lines of minimal length spanning two points on the sphere's surface. These properties make them ubiquitous to charts and other applications involving spherical coordinates. Examples include the instantaneous ground track of a satellite (with orbital planes containing the center of the body), the Earth's present day/night terminator (the sun illuminating one hemisphere), and the way followed by a long-haul airline route or a radio wave (the shortest path having the least expended energy). By deriving the equations for a great circle in analytic form, the equations of projection—or algorithms for plotting—can be created easily. A simple [lat/lon] chart (Fig. 1) illustrates the great circles forming the day/night terminators on consecutive months during fall in the Northern Hemisphere.

Plotting great circles is especially difficult when the track passes near a pole: Pronounced shifts in instantaneous heading arise. In particular, cylindrical projections for paths of high inclination are decidedly curved. Great circles cannot be approximated suitably by generating points along the linear path spanning (lat1, lon2) and (lat2, lon2). Common charts cannot easily account for this curve's shape, save for two azimuthal projections: the stereographic and gnomonic (Paeth, 1990g). Neither of these can depict an entire globe on a chart of finite extent.

A simple analytic expression for the great circle interrelates the circle's latitude and longitude by way of parametric longitude and inclination. The final formula then may be easily reexpressed in other projections such as

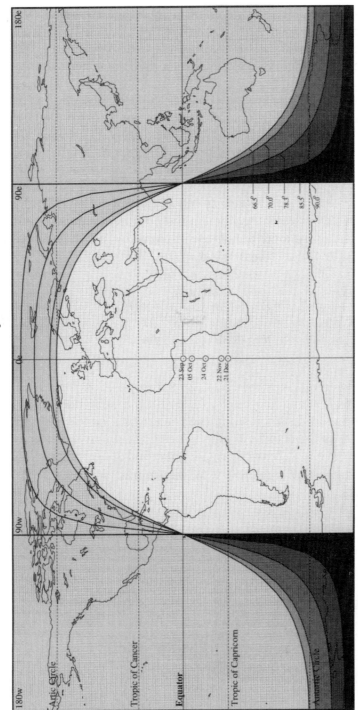

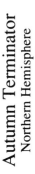

Figure 1. Autumn terminator (Northern Hemisphere).

441

Mercator's. Although problems of navigation traditionally were both difficult and of central importance to Renaissance mathematics (Dörre, 1965), the analytic vector geometry of the last century simplifies the derivation considerably; explicit reference to spherical trigonometry is not needed.

Without loss of generality, consider the central section of a sphere by a plane. If the plane fully contains the equator (a great circle with defining plane XY), the problem is solved immediately. Otherwise, the equator is intersected at two nodes. Without loss of generality, these may be placed at the locations $\pm 90°$, i.e., rotated onto the Y axis with subsequent offsetting of all values of longitude. Any great circle now may be modeled as a parametric equatorial circle (no Z component) and local longitude L: [$\cos L, \sin L, 0$], which may be expressed in rectangular coordinates. This circle then is rotated about the Y axis by an inclination ρ. This is expressed by the matrix product in the RHS:

$$
\begin{bmatrix} X \\ Y \\ Z \end{bmatrix} = \begin{bmatrix} \cos\rho & \cos L \\ & \sin L \\ -\sin\rho & \cos L \end{bmatrix} = \begin{bmatrix} \cos\rho & 0 & \sin\rho \\ 0 & 1 & 0 \\ -\sin\rho & 0 & \cos\rho \end{bmatrix} \begin{bmatrix} \cos L \\ \sin L \\ 0 \end{bmatrix}.
$$

The **LHS** vector gives the (X, Y, Z) space position for a uniform angular motion by L along the circle. (L is both a subtended angle and linear circumferential distance along the track.) As a check, note that $X^2 + Y^2 + Z^2 = 1$, as expected: All points formed lie upon the surface of the unit sphere. Conversion between rectangular and spherical coordinates (Paeth, 1990b) states that $\tan \text{lon} = Y/X$, and $\tan \text{lat} = z/\sqrt{X^2 + Y^2}$. Substitution yields:

$$
\tan \text{lon} = \frac{\sin L}{\cos\rho \cos L} = \sec\rho \tan L,
$$

implying that

$$
\tan L = \cos\rho \tan \text{lon}. \tag{1}
$$

Similarly,

$$\tan \text{lat} = \frac{-\sin \rho \cos L}{\sqrt{\cos^2 \rho \cos^2 L + \sin^2 L}} .\tag{2}$$

A simplification of Eq. (2) is sought to rework it in nonparametric form, thereby yielding an expression for latitude in terms of longitude and inclination. This is possible by substituting Eq. (1) in Eq. (2), with other trigonometric functions of L reexpressed in terms of the tangent, as needed:

	Identity used
$\tan \text{lat} = \dfrac{-\sin \rho \sqrt{\dfrac{1}{1 + \cos^2 \rho \tan^2 \text{lon}}}}{\sqrt{\dfrac{\cos^2 \rho}{1 + \cos^2 \rho \tan^2 \text{lon}} + \dfrac{\cos^2 \rho \tan^2 \text{lon}}{1 + \cos^2 \rho \tan^2 \text{lon}}}}$	$\cos^2 L = \dfrac{1}{1 + \tan^2 L}$ $\sin^2 L = \dfrac{\tan^2 L}{1 + \tan^2 L}$
$= -\sin \rho \sqrt{\dfrac{1}{\cos^2 \rho + \cos^2 \rho \tan^2 \text{lon}}}$	$1 + \tan^2 \text{lon}$
$= \dfrac{-\sin \rho}{\cos \rho} \sqrt{\dfrac{1}{1 + \tan^2 \text{lon}}}$	$= \sec^2 \text{lon} \rightarrow$ $\dfrac{1}{1 + \tan^2 \text{lon}}$ $= \cos^2 \text{lon}$

$$\tan \text{lat} = \pm \tan \rho \cos \text{lon},\tag{3a}$$

or (with proper choice of sign)

$$\text{lat} = \arctan(\tan \rho \cos \text{lon}).\tag{3b}$$

As a double-check of the equation, note that:

lon = 0   → lat = ρ (inclination being the maximum latitude at center),

lon = ± 90 → lot = 0   (nodes crossed at $\pm 90°$ for any inclination).

For illustration, four annotated values of inclination are plotted under a global Plate Carre's cylindrical equidistant chart (Paeth, 1990g; Maling, 1973). The maximum inclination occurs at the equinox, when day equals night everywhere on the globe. Here, the sun's declination (celestial latitude) is zero; it lies over the equator. Thus, the colatitude (angle to the North Pole) is 90 degrees and the tan ρ in Eq. (3b) goes to infinity. Minimum inclination (colatitude) corresponds to the sun's maximum declination (latitude) at $-23.5°$. The sun achieves this maximum on December 21 and momentarily is stationary in celestial declination; hence the term *winter solstice*. The globe's subsolar points on the solstice likewise are at $-23.5°$ and define the Tropic of Capricorn, appearing as a dotted line on the chart. (Capricorn, Latin for *goat*, is the name of the constellation in which the sun resided on the solstice at the time of the naming of the constellations; owing to the precession of the equinoxes, Sagittarius, Latin for *archer*, would now be the proper choice).

To use the technique to plot a great circle between two points on the surface of a sphere, vector geometry aids the derivation of inclination angle. Points (lat0, lon0) and (lat1, lon1) are treated as unit vectors in spherical coordinates $(R = 1)$ and then transformed into rectangular coordinates (Paeth, 1990g). The cross-product $[x_0, y_0, z_0] \times [x_1, y_1, z_1]$ $= [y_0 z_1 - y_1 z_0, x_0 z_1 - x_1 z_0, x_0 y_1 - x_1 y_0]$ is the unit normal vector to that plane common to both vectors and to the origin. The cross-axis then may be returned to spherical coordinates, yielding a longitude and latitude value.

The latitude is converted to colatitude: colat = $90°$ − lat to form an inclination value. For instance, eastward travel along the equator (lat = 0) yields a normal vector through the North Pole (lat = $90°$, colat = $0°$); travel thus is in a plane having zero inclination. The longitude of this normal vector likewise provides the offset angle in longitude for proper placement of the nodes.

For use in forming analytic, closed-form formulae, the *tan lat* term of the RHS of Eq. (3a) may be substituted directly for projection formulae expressed in terms of this function. For instance, Mercator's projection, $y = \ln \tan(\mathrm{lon}/2 + \pi/4)$, may be rewritten using the little-known substitution, $\tan(x/2 \pm \pi/4) = \pm \tan x \pm \sqrt{1 + \tan^2 x}$ (derived by the author and used to great advantage in Paeth (1990a)), which then may be expressed as $y = \sinh^{-1}(-\tan \rho \cos \mathrm{lon})$, yielding a simple analytic expression for great circles plotted on cylindrical, conformal maps of globular scale.

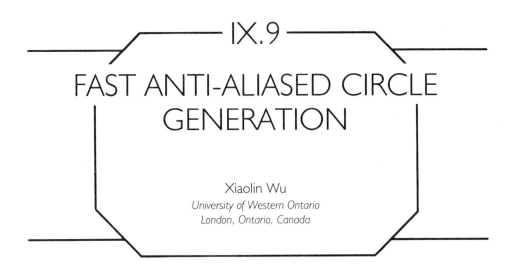

IX.9

FAST ANTI-ALIASED CIRCLE GENERATION

Xiaolin Wu
University of Western Ontario
London, Ontario, Canada

This gem proposes an elegant technique to render anti-aliased circles with even fewer number of operations than Bresenham's incremental circle algorithm (1977). The success is credited to a simple two-point anti-aliasing scheme and the use of a table of size $\sqrt{2}/4R_{max}$, where R_{max} is the maximum circle radius allowed by the new algorithm.

Simple Two-Point Anti-Aliasing Scheme

Due to the eight-way symmetry of the circle, it suffices to consider the circle $x^2 + y^2 = r^2$ in the first octant. To suppress the image jaggies caused by insufficient spatial sampling on a grayscale display, we may plot all pixels immediately to the right and left of the true circular arc (Fig. 1) with their intensities inversely proportional to their distances to the arc. To keep even intensity on the digital circle, we let the total intensity I of two horizontally adjacent pixels be a constant. Let $I(i, j)$ be the pixel value at the raster point (i, j); then the linear intensity interpolation between the two adjacent pixels is given by:

$$I\left(\left\lfloor\sqrt{r^2 - j^2}\right\rfloor, j\right) = I\left(\left\lceil\sqrt{r^2 - j^2}\right\rceil - \sqrt{r^2 - j^2}\right),$$

$$I\left(\left\lceil\sqrt{r^2 - j^2}\right\rceil, j\right) = I - I\left(\left\lfloor\sqrt{r^2 - j^2}\right\rfloor, j\right), \qquad 1 \leq j \leq \frac{r}{\sqrt{2}}. \quad (1)$$

Now we derive the algorithm to compute Eq. (1) as j marches in the y axis from 0 to $r/\sqrt{2}$ in scan-converting the first octant circular arc. The

446

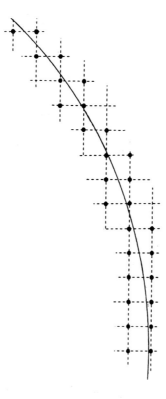

Figure I.   Anti-aliasing pixel band.

first issue is to determine when the integer-valued function $\left\lceil \sqrt{r^2 - j^2} \right\rceil$ decreases by 1 as j increases. We need the critical values t such that $\left\lceil \sqrt{r^2 - (t-1)^2} \right\rceil - \left\lceil \sqrt{r^2 - t^2} \right\rceil = 1$ to move the pixel band being plotted to the left by one step. This computation can be simplified by the following lemma.

LEMMA I   *The relation*

$$\left\lceil \sqrt{r^2 - (t-1)^2} \right\rceil - \left\lceil \sqrt{r^2 - t^2} \right\rceil = 1$$

holds if and only if

$$\left\lceil \sqrt{r^2 - (t-1)^2} \right\rceil - \sqrt{r^2 - (t-1)^2} > \left\lceil \sqrt{r^2 - t^2} \right\rceil - \sqrt{r^2 - t^2} .$$

447

Proof. Since $\sqrt{r^2 - j^2}$ is decreasing monotonically in j,

$$\left\lceil \sqrt{r^2 - (t-1)^2} \right\rceil - \sqrt{r^2 - (t-1)^2} > \left\lceil \sqrt{r^2 - t^2} \right\rceil - \sqrt{r^2 - t^2}$$

implies

$$\left\lceil \sqrt{r^2 - (t-1)^2} \right\rceil - \left\lceil \sqrt{r^2 - t^2} \right\rceil > 0;$$

but in the first octant, we have

$$\sqrt{r^2 - (t-1)^2} - \sqrt{r^2 - t^2} \leq 1,$$

prohibiting

$$\left\lceil \sqrt{r^2 - (t-1)^2} \right\rceil - \left\lceil \sqrt{r^2 - t^2} \right\rceil > 1;$$

hence,

$$\left\lceil \sqrt{r^2 - (t-1)^2} \right\rceil - \left\lceil \sqrt{r^2 - t^2} \right\rceil = 1.$$

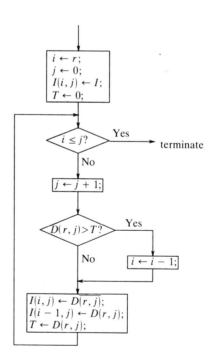

Figure 2. Wu's anti-aliased circle algorithm for first octant.

448

The only–if part can be proven by contradiction. Assume that

$$\left\lceil \sqrt{r^2 - (t-1)^2} \right\rceil - \left\lceil \sqrt{r^2 - t^2} \right\rceil = 1,$$

but

$$\left\lceil \sqrt{r^2 - (t-1)^2} \right\rceil - \sqrt{r^2 - (t-1)^2} \le \left\lceil \sqrt{r^2 - t^2} \right\rceil - \sqrt{r^2 - t^2}.$$

This requires $\sqrt{r^2 - (t-1)^2} - \sqrt{r^2 - t^2} > 1$, an impossibility in the first octant. $\qquad\square$

For given r, the values $\left\lceil \sqrt{r^2 - j^2} \right\rceil - \sqrt{r^2 - j^2}$, $1 \le j \le r/\sqrt{2}$, serve dual purposes: determining the pixel positions as suggested by the preceding lemma and determining the pixel intensities as in Eq. (1). Let the intensity range for the display be from 0 to $2^m - 1$, and define the integer variable:

$$D(r, j) = \left\lfloor (2^m - 1)\left(\left\lceil \sqrt{r^2 - j^2} \right\rceil - \sqrt{r^2 - j^2} \right) + 0.5 \right\rfloor. \qquad (2)$$

Figure 3. Bresenham's circles (left) and Wu's anti-aliased circles (right).

449

Then it follows from Eq. (1) that

$$I\left(\left\lfloor\sqrt{r^2 - j^2}\right\rfloor, j\right) = D(r, j),$$

$$I\left(\left\lfloor\sqrt{r^2 - j^2}\right\rfloor, j\right) = \overline{D(r, j)}, \ 1 \le j \le \frac{r}{\sqrt{2}}, \tag{3}$$

where $\overline{D(r, j)}$ is the integer value obtained through bitwise-inverse operation on $D(r, j)$, since $I\left(\left\lfloor\sqrt{r^2 - j^2}\right\rfloor, j\right) + I\left(\left\lfloor\sqrt{r^2 - j^2}\right\rfloor, j\right) = I = 2^m - 1$, and since the intensity values are integers. By Eq. (2), every decrement of the function, $\left\lfloor\sqrt{r^2 - j^2}\right\rfloor - \sqrt{r^2 - j^2}$ as j increases, is reflected by a decrement of $D(r, j)$; thus, $D(r, j)$ can be used to control the scan conversion of the circle. The new anti-aliased circle algorithm based on precomputed $D(r, j)$ is extremely simple and fast. The algorithm for the first octant is described by the flowchart in Fig. 2.

The inner loop of the anti-aliased circle algorithm requires even fewer operations than Bresenham's circle algorithm. Of course, the gains in image quality and scan-conversion speed are obtained by using the $D(r, j)$ table. If R_{max} is the maximum radius handled by the circle generator, then the table size will be $\sqrt{2}/4 R_{max}$. It is my opinion that the rapidly decreasing memory cost makes the preceding simple idea a viable solution to real-time anti-aliased circle generation. For instance, for a 64K-bytes ROM, the preceding algorithm can display anti-aliased circular arcs of radius up to 430. Without the precomputed table $D(r, j)$, the anti-aliased circle algorithm can be implemented by computing the function $D(r, j)$.

The performance of the new anti-aliased circle algorithm is demonstrated by Fig. 3.

See also (105) *Rendering Anti-Aliased Lines, Kelvin Thompson*

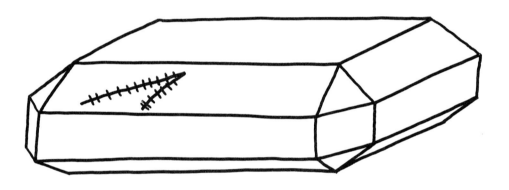

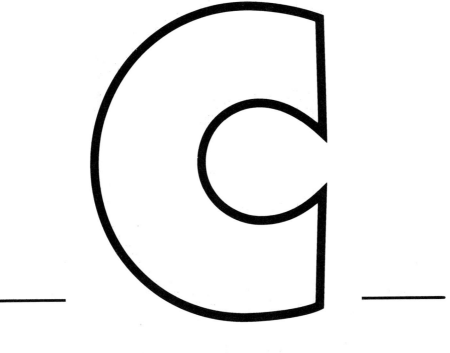

APPENDIX I
C UTILITIES

GRAPHICS GEMS C HEADER FILE

Andrew Glassner

```c
#ifndef GG_H
#define GG_H 1

/*********************/
/* 2d geometry types */
/*********************/

typedef struct Point2Struct {      /* 2d point */
    double x, y;
    } Point2;
typedef Point2 Vector2;

typedef struct IntPoint2Struct {   /* 2d integer point */
    int x, y;
    } IntPoint2;

typedef struct Matrix3Struct {     /* 3-by-3 matrix */
    double element[3][3];
    } Matrix3;

typedef struct Box2dStruct {       /* 2d box */
    Point2 min, max;
    } Box2;

/*********************/
/* 3d geometry types */
/*********************/

typedef struct Point3Struct {      /* 3d point */
    double x, y, z;
    } Point3;
typedef Point3 Vector3;

typedef struct IntPoint3Struct {   /* 3d integer point */
    int x, y, z;
    } IntPoint3;
```

```c
typedef struct Matrix4Struct {        /* 4-by-4 matrix */
    double element[4][4];
    } Matrix4;

typedef struct Box3dStruct {          /* 3d box */
    Point3 min, max;
    } Box3;
```

```c
/***********************/
/* one-argument macros */
/***********************/

/* absolute value of a */
#define ABS(a)          (((a)<0) ? -(a) : (a))

/* round a to nearest integer towards 0 */
#define FLOOR(a)        ((a)>0 ? (int)(a) : -(int)(-a))

/* round a to nearest integer away from 0 */
#define CEILING(a) \
((a)==(int)(a) ? (a) : (a)>0 ? 1+(int)(a) : -(1+(int)(-a)))

/* round a to nearest int */
#define ROUND(a)        ((a)>0 ? (int)(a+0.5) : -(int)(0.5-a))

/* take sign of a, either -1, 0, or 1 */
#define ZSGN(a)         (((a)<0) ? -1 : (a)>0 ? 1 : 0)

/* take binary sign of a, either -1, or 1 if >= 0 */
#define SGN(a)          (((a)<0) ? -1 : 0)

/* shout if something that should be true isn't */
#define ASSERT(x) \
if (!(x)) fprintf(stderr,' Assert failed: x\n');

/* square a */
#define SQR(a)          ((a)*(a))

/***********************/
/* two-argument macros */
/***********************/

/* find minimum of a and b */
#define MIN(a,b)      (((a)<(b))?(a):(b))

/* find maximum of a and b */
#define MAX(a,b)      (((a)>(b))?(a):(b))

/* swap a and b (see Gem by Wyvill) */
#define SWAP(a,b)     { a^=b; b^=a; a^=b; }

/* linear interpolation from l (when a=0) to h (when a=1)*/
/* (equal to (a*h)+((1-a)*l) */
#define LERP(a,l,h)  ((l)+(((h)-(l))*(a)))
```

```
/* clamp the input to the specified range */
#define CLAMP(v,l,h)     ((v)<(l) ? (l) : (v) > (h) ? (h) : v)

/*****************************/
/* memory allocation macros */
/*****************************/

/* create a new instance of a structure (see Gem by Hultquist) */
#define NEWSTRUCT(x)     (struct x *)(malloc((unsigned)sizeof(struct x)))

/* create a new instance of a type */
#define NEWTYPE(x)   (x *)(malloc((unsigned)sizeof(x)))

/********************/
/* useful constants */
/********************/

#define PI          3.141592    /* the venerable pi */
#define PITIMES2    6.283185    /* 2 * pi */
#define PIOVER2     1.570796    /* pi / 2 */
#define E           2.718282    /* the venerable e */
#define SQRT2       1.414214    /* sqrt(2) */
#define SQRT3       1.732051    /* sqrt(3) */
#define GOLDEN      1.618034    /* the golden ratio */
#define DTOR        0.017453    /* convert degrees to radians */
#define RTOD        57.29578    /* convert radians to degrees */

/************/
/* booleans */
/************/

#define TRUE    1
#define FALSE   0
#define ON      1
#define OFF     0
typedef int boolean;        /* boolean data type */
typedef boolean flag;       /* flag data type */

extern double V2SquaredLength(), V2Length();
extern double V2Dot(), V2DistanceBetween2Points();
extern Vector2 *V2Negate(), *V2Normalize(), *V2Scale(), *V2Add(), *V2Sub();
extern Vector2 *V2Lerp(), *V2Combine(), *V2Mul(), *V2MakePerpendicular();
extern Vector2 *V2New(), *V2Duplicate();
extern Point2 *V2MulPointByProjMatrix();
extern Matrix3 *V2MatMul(), *TransposeMatrix3();
extern double V3SquaredLength(), V3Length();
extern double V3Dot(), V3DistanceBetween2Points();
extern Vector3 *V3Normalize(), *V3Scale(), *V3Add(), *V3Sub();
extern Vector3 *V3Lerp(), *V3Combine(), *V3Mul(), *V3Cross();
extern Vector3 *V3New(), *V3Duplicate();
extern Point3 *V3MulPointByMatrix(), *V3MulPointByProjMatrix();
extern Matrix4 *V3MatMul();
extern double RegulaFalsi(), NewtonRaphson(), findroot();
#endif
```

2D & 3D VECTOR LIBRARY

Andrew Glassner

(corrected and extended by Rod G. Bogart)

```c
#include <math.h>
#include "GraphicsGems.h"

/******************/
/*   2d Library   */
/******************/

/* returns squared length of input vector */
double V2SquaredLength(a)
Vector2 *a;
{   return((a->x * a->x)+(a->y * a->y));
    };

/* returns length of input vector */
double V2Length(a)
Vector2 *a;
{
    return(sqrt(V2SquaredLength(a)));
    };

/* negates the input vector and returns it */
Vector2 *V2Negate(v)
Vector2 *v;
{
    v->x = -v->x;   v->y = -v->y;
    return(v);
    };

/* normalizes the input vector and returns it */
Vector2 *V2Normalize(v)
Vector2 *v;
{
double len = V2Length(v);
    if (len != 0.0) { v->x /= len;   v->y /= len; };
    return(v);
    };
```

```c
/* scales the input vector to the new length and returns it */
Vector2 *V2Scale(v, newlen)
Vector2 *v;
double newlen;
{
double len = V2Length(v);
    if (len != 0.0) { v->x *= newlen/len;   v->y *= newlen/len; };
    return(v);
    };

/* return vector sum c = a+b */
Vector2 *V2Add(a, b, c)
Vector2 *a, *b, *c;
{
    c->x = a->x+b->x;   c->y = a->y+b->y;
    return(c);
    };

/* return vector difference c = a-b */
Vector2 *V2Sub(a, b, c)
Vector2 *a, *b, *c;
{
    c->x = a->x-b->x;   c->y = a->y-b->y;
    return(c);
    };

/* return the dot product of vectors a and b */
double V2Dot(a, b)
Vector2 *a, *b;
{
    return((a->x*b->x)+(a->y*b->y));
    };

/* linearly interpolate between vectors by an amount alpha */
/* and return the resulting vector. */
/* When alpha=0, result=lo.  When alpha=1, result=hi. */
Vector2 *V2Lerp(lo, hi, alpha, result)
Vector2 *lo, *hi, *result;
double alpha;
{
    result->x = LERP(alpha, lo->x, hi->x);
    result->y = LERP(alpha, lo->y, hi->y);
    return(result);
    };


/* make a linear combination of two vectors and return the result. */
/* result = (a * ascl) + (b * bscl) */
Vector2 *V2Combine (a, b, result, ascl, bscl)
Vector2 *a, *b, *result;
double ascl, bscl;
{
    result->x = (ascl * a->x) + (bscl * b->x);
    result->y = (ascl * a->y) + (bscl * b->y);
    return(result);
    };
```

```
/* multiply two vectors together component-wise */
Vector2 *V2Mul (a, b, result)
Vector2 *a, *b, *result;
{
    result->x = a->x * b->x;
    result->y = a->y * b->y;
    return(result);
    };

/* return the distance between two points */
double V2DistanceBetween2Points(a, b)
Point2 *a, *b;
{
double dx = a->x - b->x;
double dy = a->y - b->y;
    return(sqrt((dx*dx)+(dy*dy)));
    };

/* return the vector perpendicular to the input vector a */
Vector2 *V2MakePerpendicular(a, ap)
Vector2 *a, *ap;
{
    ap->x = -a->y;
    ap->y = a->x;
    return(ap);
    };

/* create, initialize, and return a new vector */
Vector2 *V2New(x, y)
double x, y;
{
Vector2 *v = NEWTYPE(Vector2);
    v->x = x;   v->y = y;
    return(v);
    };


/* create, initialize, and return a duplicate vector */
Vector2 *V2Duplicate(a)
Vector2 *a;
{
Vector2 *v = NEWTYPE(Vector2);
    v->x = a->x;   v->y = a->y;
    return(v);
    };

/* multiply a point by a projective matrix and return the transformed point */
Point2 *V2MulPointByProjMatrix(pin, m, pout)
Point2 *pin, *pout;
Matrix3 *m;
{
double w;
    pout->x = (pin->x * m->element[0][0]) +
              (pin->y * m->element[1][0]) + m->element[2][0];
    pout->y = (pin->x * m->element[0][1]) +
              (pin->y * m->element[1][1]) + m->element[2][1];
    w =       (pin->x * m->element[0][2]) +
              (pin->y * m->element[1][2]) + m->element[2][2];
    if (w != 0.0) { pout->x /= w;  pout->y /= w; }
    return(pout);
```

460

```
    };

/* multiply together matrices c = ab */
/* note that c must not point to either of the input matrices */
Matrix3 *V2MatMul(a, b, c)
Matrix3 *a, *b, *c;
{
int i, j, k;
    for (i=0; i<3; i++) {
        for (j=0; j<3; j++) {
            c->element[i][j] = 0;
            for (k=0; k<3; k++) c->element[i][j] +=
                    a->element[i][k] * b->element[k][j];
            };
        };
    return(c);
    };

/* transpose matrix a, return b */
Matrix3 *TransposeMatrix3(a, b)
Matrix3 *a, *b;
{
int i, j;
    for (i=0; i<3; i++) {
        for (j=0; j<3; j++)
            b->element[i][j] = a->element[j][i];
        };
    return(b);
    };




/******************/
/*   3d Library   */
/******************/

/* returns squared length of input vector */
double V3SquaredLength(a)
Vector3 *a;
{
    return((a->x * a->x)+(a->y * a->y)+(a->z * a->z));
    };

/* returns length of input vector */
double V3Length(a)
Vector3 *a;
{
    return(sqrt(V3SquaredLength(a)));
    };

/* negates the input vector and returns it */
Vector3 *V3Negate(v)
Vector3 *v;
{
    v->x = -v->x;   v->y = -v->y;   v->z = -v->z;
    return(v);
    };
```

```
/* normalizes the input vector and returns it */
Vector3 *V3Normalize(v)
Vector3 *v;
{
double len = V3Length(v);
    if (len != 0.0) { v->x /= len;  v->y /= len;  v->z /= len; };
    return(v);
    };


/* scales the input vector to the new length and returns it */
Vector3 *V3Scale(v, newlen)
Vector3 *v;          ,
double newlen;
{
double len = V3Length(v);
    if (len != 0.0) {
    v->x *= newlen/len;  v->y *= newlen/len;  v->z *= newlen/len;
    };
    return(v);
    };


/* return vector sum c = a+b */
Vector3 *V3Add(a, b, c)
Vector3 *a, *b, *c;
{
    c->x = a->x+b->x;  c->y = a->y+b->y;  c->z = a->z+b->z;
    return(c);
    };

/* return vector difference c = a-b */
Vector3 *V3Sub(a, b, c)
Vector3 *a, *b, *c;
{
    c->x = a->x-b->x;  c->y = a->y-b->y;  c->z = a->z-b->z;
    return(c);
    };

/* return the dot product of vectors a and b */
double V3Dot(a, b)
Vector3 *a, *b;
{
    return((a->x*b->x)+(a->y*b->y)+(a->z*b->z));
    };

/* linearly interpolate between vectors by an amount alpha */
/* and return the resulting vector. */
/* When alpha=0, result=lo.  When alpha=1, result=hi. */
Vector3 *V3Lerp(lo, hi, alpha, result)
Vector3 *lo, *hi, *result;
double alpha;
{
    result->x = LERP(alpha, lo->x, hi->x);
    result->y = LERP(alpha, lo->y, hi->y);
    result->z = LERP(alpha, lo->z, hi->z);
    return(result);
    };
```

```
/* make a linear combination of two vectors and return the result. */
/* result = (a * ascl) + (b * bscl) */
Vector3 *V3Combine (a, b, result, ascl, bscl)
Vector3 *a, *b, *result;
double ascl, bscl;
{
    result->x = (ascl * a->x) + (bscl * b->x);
    result->y = (ascl * a->y) + (bscl * b->y);
    result->y = (ascl * a->z) + (bscl * b->z);
    return(result);
    };


/* multiply two vectors together component-wise and return the result */
Vector3 *V3Mul (a, b, result)
Vector3 *a, *b, *result;
{
    result->x = a->x * b->x;
    result->y = a->y * b->y;
    result->z = a->z * b->z;
    return(result);
    };

/* return the distance between two points */
double V3DistanceBetween2Points(a, b)
Point3 *a, *b;
{
double dx = a->x - b->x;
double dy = a->y - b->y;
double dz = a->z - b->z;
    return(sqrt((dx*dx)+(dy*dy)+(dz*dz)));
    };

/* return the cross product c = a cross b */
Vector3 *V3Cross(a, b, c)
Vector3 *a, *b, *c;
{
    c->x = (a->y*b->z) - (a->z*b->y);
    c->y = (a->z*b->x) - (a->x*b->z);
    c->z = (a->x*b->y) - (a->y*b->x);
    return(c);
    };

/* create, initialize, and return a new vector */
Vector3 *V3New(x, y, z)
double x, y, z;
{
Vector3 *v = NEWTYPE(Vector3);
    v->x = x;   v->y = y;   v->z = z;
    return(v);
    };

/* create, initialize, and return a duplicate vector */
Vector3 *V3Duplicate(a)
Vector3 *a;
{
Vector3 *v = NEWTYPE(Vector3);
    v->x = a->x;   v->y = a->y;   v->z = a->z;
    return(v);
    };
```

```
/* multiply a point by a matrix and return the transformed point */
Point3 *V3MulPointByMatrix(pin, m, pout)
Point3 *pin, *pout;
Matrix3 *m;
{
    pout->x = (pin->x * m->element[0][0]) + (pin->y * m->element[1][0]) +
              (pin->z * m->element[2][0]);
    pout->y = (pin->x * m->element[0][1]) + (pin->y * m->element[1][1]) +
              (pin->z * m->element[2][1]);
    pout->z = (pin->x * m->element[0][2]) + (pin->y * m->element[1][2]) +
              (pin->z * m->element[2][2]);
    return(pout);
    };


/* multiply a point by a projective matrix and return the transformed point */
Point3 *V3MulPointByProjMatrix(pin, m, pout)
Point3 *pin, *pout;
Matrix4 *m;
{
double w;
    pout->x = (pin->x * m->element[0][0]) +(pin->y * m->element[1][0]) +
              (pin->z * m->element[2][0]) + m->element[3][0];
    pout->y = (pin->x * m->element[0][1]) +(pin->y * m->element[1][1]) +
              (pin->z * m->element[2][1]) + m->element[3][1];
    pout->z = (pin->x * m->element[0][2]) +(pin->y * m->element[1][2]) +
              (pin->z * m->element[2][2]) + m->element[3][2];
    w =       (pin->x * m->element[0][3]) +(pin->y * m->element[1][3]) +
              (pin->z * m->element[2][3]) + m->element[3][3];
    if (w != 0.0) { pout->x /= w;  pout->y /= w;  pout->z /= w; }
    return(pout);
    };


/* multiply together matrices c = ab */
/* note that c must not point to either of the input matrices */
Matrix4 *V3MatMul(a, b, c)
Matrix4 *a, *b, *c;
{
int i, j, k;
    for (i=0; i<4; i++) {
        for (j=0; j<4; j++) {
            c->element[i][j] = 0;
            for (k=0; k<4; k++) c->element[i][j] +=
                a->element[i][k] * b->element[k][j];
            };
        };
    return(c);
    };


/* binary greatest common divisor by Silver and Terzian.  See Knuth */
/* both inputs must be >= 0 */
gcd(u, v)
int u, v;
{
int k, t, f;
    if ((u<0) || (v<0)) return(1); /* error if u<0 or v<0 */
    k = 0;  f = 1;
    while ((0 == (u%2)) && (0 == (v%2))) {
        k++;  u>>=1;  v>>=1,  f*=2;
        };
```

```
        if (u&01) { t = -v;  goto B4; } else { t = u; }
        B3: if (t > 0) { t >>= 1; } else { t = -((-t) >> 1); }; 
        B4: if (0 == (t%2)) goto B3;

        if (t > 0) u = t; else v = -t;
        if (0 != (t = u - v)) goto B3;
        return(u*f);
        };
```

```
/***********************/
/*   Useful Routines   */
/***********************/

/* return roots of ax^2+bx+c */
/* stable algebra derived from Numerical Recipes by Press et al.*/
int quadraticRoots(a, b, c, roots)
double a, b, c, *roots;
{
double d, q;
int count = 0;
        d = (b*b)-(4*a*c);
        if (d < 0.0) { *roots = *(roots+1) = 0.0;  return(0); };
        q =  -0.5 * (b + (SGN(b)*sqrt(d)));
        if (a != 0.0)  { *roots++ = q/a; count++; }
        if (q != 0.0) { *roots++ = c/q; count++; }
        return(count);
        };


/* generic 1d regula-falsi step.  f is function to evaluate */
/* interval known to contain root is given in left, right */
/* returns new estimate */
double RegulaFalsi(f, left, right)
double (*f)(), left, right;
{
double d = (*f)(right) - (*f)(left);
        if (d != 0.0) return (right - (*f)(right)*(right-left)/d);
        return((left+right)/2.0);
        };

/* generic 1d Newton-Raphson step. f is function, df is derivative */
/* x is current best guess for root location. Returns new estimate */
double NewtonRaphson(f, df, x)
double (*f)(), (*df)(), x;
{
double d = (*df)(x);
        if (d != 0.0) return (x-((*f)(x)/d));
        return(x-1.0);
        };


/* hybrid 1d Newton-Raphson/Regula Falsi root finder. */
/* input function f and its derivative df, an interval */
/* left, right known to contain the root, and an error tolerance */
/* Based on Blinn */
double findroot(left, right, tolerance, f, df)
double left, right, tolerance;
double (*f)(), (*df)();
{
double newx = left;
```

```
    while (ABS((*f)(newx)) > tolerance) {
        newx = NewtonRaphson(f, df, newx);
        if (newx < left || newx > right)
            newx = RegulaFalsi(f, left, right);
        if ((*f)(newx) * (*f)(left) <= 0.0) right = newx;
            else left = newx;
    };
return(newx);
};
```

USEFUL C MACROS FOR VECTOR OPERATIONS

Steve Hollasch

```
/****************************************************************
 *   The following macros handle most vector operations, the exceptions
 *   usually being complex equations with four or more vectors.
 *
 *   An alternate form for the multiple-statement macros is the
 *   "if (1) macro_body else" form.  This allows for temporary variable
 *   declaration and control-flow constructs, but cannot be used
 *   everywhere a function call could, as with the form used here.
 *
 *   Note that since the vector arguments are not enclosed in parentheses
 *   in the macro body, you can scale the vector arguments in the macro
 *   calls, e.g. Vec2Op(vec1,=,scalar*vec2).
 *
 *   Here are some example uses of the following macros:
 *
 *       printf ("vector = <%lf %lf %lf>\n", VecList(vector));
 *       vector_dot = VecDot (vec1,vec2);
 *       norm = VecNorm (vector);
 *       VecScalar (vector, /=, norm);
 *       VecScalar (vector, *=,.scale);
 *       Vec3Scalar (Xaxis, =, 1.0, 0.0, 0.0);
 *       Vec3Scalar (vector, *=, Xshear, Yshear, Zshear);
 *       Vec2Op (vector, =, Xaxis);
 *       Vec2Op (vector, +=, norm * Xaxis);
 *       Vec3Op (vec1, =, vec2, =, Xaxis);
 *       Vec3Op (vec1, =, vec2, -, vec3);
 *       Vec3Op (vec1, +=, scale2 * vec2, -, scale3 * vec3);
 *       VecCross (vec1, -=, vec2, X, vec3);
 *       VecCrossSafe (vec1, =, vec1, X, Xaxis);
 ****************************************************************/

#include <math.h>              /* Needed for the sqrt() definition. */
```

```
    /* Vector type definition.  If you define colors in the same manner,
    ** you can also use these macros for color vector operations.  */

typedef long float  Vector[3];


    /* VecList enumerates the vector fields for function calls. */

#define VecList(V)         V[0],V[1],V[2]

    /* This macro computes the dot product of two vectors. */

#define VecDot(A,B)        ((A[0]*B[0]) + (A[1]*B[1]) + (A[2]*B[2]))

    /* This macro computes the norm of the vector. */

#define VecNorm(V)         sqrt(VecDot(V,V))

    /* VecScalar provides for scalar operations on a vector. */

#define VecScalar(V,assign_op,k) \
(  V[0] assign_op k, \
   V[1] assign_op k, \
   V[2] assign_op k  \
)

    /* Vec3Scalar provides for scalar-vector operations that have three
    ** distinct scalar factors. */

#define Vec3Scalar(V,assign_op,a,b,c) \
(  V[0] assign_op a, \
   V[1] assign_op b, \
   V[2] assign_op c  \
)

    /* Vec2Op provides for operations with two vectors. */

#define Vec2Op(A,assign_op,B) \
(  A[0] assign_op B[0], \
   A[1] assign_op B[1], \
   A[2] assign_op B[2]  \
)

    /* Vec3Op handles vector operations with three vectors. */

#define Vec3Op(A,assign_op,B,op,C) \
(  A[0] assign_op B[0] op C[0], \
   A[1] assign_op B[1] op C[1], \
   A[2] assign_op B[2] op C[2]  \
)
```

```
/* The cross product macros come in two flavors.  VecCross() requires
** that all three vectors must be distinct.  With the VecCrossSafe()
** macro, it's OK to do A <- A X B, but this requires the temporary
** vector for storage, which in turn requires the "if (1) ... else"
** form.  As an alternative, a global temporary vector could be used.
*/

#define VecCross(A,assign_op,B,dummy_op,C) \
(   A[0] assign_op (B[1]*C[2]) - (B[2]*C[1]), \
    A[1] assign_op (B[2]*C[0]) - (B[0]*C[2]), \
    A[2] assign_op (B[0]*C[1]) - (B[1]*C[0])  \
)

#define VecCrossSafe(A,assign_op,B,dummy_op,C) \
if (1) { auto Vector Temp; \
    Temp[0] = (B[1]*C[2]) - (B[2]*C[1]); \
    Temp[1] = (B[2]*C[0]) - (B[0]*C[2]); \
    Temp[2] = (B[0]*C[1]) - (B[1]*C[0]); \
    A[0] assign_op Temp[0]; \
    A[1] assign_op Temp[1]; \
    A[2] assign_op Temp[2]; \
} else
```

main{

}

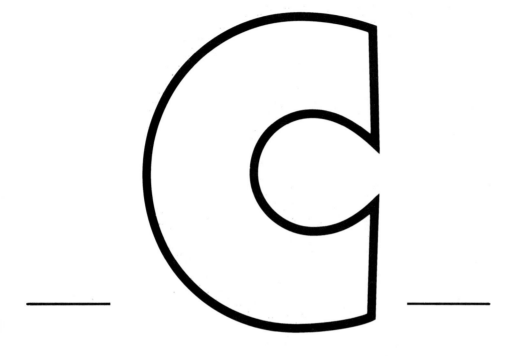

APPENDIX II
C IMPLEMENTATIONS

INTERSECTION OF LINE SEGMENTS

(page 7)

Mukesh Prasad

```
/* lines_intersect:
 *    This function computes whether two line segments,
 *    respectively joining the input points (x1,y1) -- (x2,y2)
 *    and the input points (x3,y3) -- (x4,y4) intersect.
 *    If the lines intersect, the output variables x, y are
 *    set to coordinates of the point of intersection.
 *
 *    All values are in integers.  The returned value is rounded
 *    to the nearest integer point.
 *
 *    If non-integral grid points are relevant, the function
 *    can easily be transformed by substituting floating point
 *    calculations instead of integer calculations.
 *
 *    Entry
 *        x1, y1,  x2, y2   Coordinates of endpoints of one segment.
 *        x3, y3,  x4, y4   Coordinates of endpoints of other segment.
 *
 *    Exit
 *        x, y              Coordinates of intersection point.
 *
 *    The value returned by the function is one of:
 *
 *        DONT_INTERSECT    0
 *        DO_INTERSECT      1
 *        COLLINEAR         2
 *
 * Error condititions:
 *
 *    Depending upon the possible ranges, and particularly on 16-bit
 *    computers, care should be taken to protect from overflow.
 *
 *    In the following code, 'long' values have been used for this
 *    purpose, instead of 'int'.
 *
 */
```

```
#define DONT_INTERSECT    0
#define DO_INTERSECT      1
#define COLLINEAR         2

/****************************************************************
 *                                                              *
 *     NOTE:  The following macro to determine if two numbers   *
 *     have the same sign, is for 2's complement number         *
 *     representation.  It will need to be modified for other   *
 *     number systems.                                          *
 *                                                              *
 ****************************************************************/

#define SAME_SIGNS( a, b )  \
        (((long) ((unsigned long) a ^ (unsigned long) b)) >= 0 )

int lines_intersect( x1, y1,    /* First line segment */
            x2, y2,

            x3, y3,    /* Second line segment */
            x4, y4,

            x,
            y          /* Output value:
                        * point of intersection */
               )
long
    x1, y1, x2, y2, x3, y3, x4, y4,
    *x, *y;
{
    long a1, a2, b1, b2, c1, c2; /* Coefficients of line eqns. */
    long r1, r2, r3, r4;         /* 'Sign' values */
    long denom, offset, num;     /* Intermediate values */

    /* Compute a1, b1, c1, where line joining points 1 and 2
     * is "a1 x  +  b1 y  +  c1  =  0".
     */

    a1 = y2 - y1;
    b1 = x1 - x2;
    c1 = x2 * y1 - x1 * y2;

    /* Compute r3 and r4.
     */


    r3 = a1 * x3 + b1 * y3 + c1;
    r4 = a1 * x4 + b1 * y4 + c1;

    /* Check signs of r3 and r4.  If both point 3 and point 4 lie on
     * same side of line 1, the line segments do not intersect.
     */

    if ( r3 != 0 &&
         r4 != 0 &&
         SAME_SIGNS( r3, r4 ))
        return ( DONT_INTERSECT );
```

```c
/* Compute a2, b2, c2 */

a2 = y4 - y3;
b2 = x3 - x4;
c2 = x4 * y3 - x3 * y4;

/* Compute r1 and r2 */

r1 = a2 * x1 + b2 * y1 + c2;
r2 = a2 * x2 + b2 * y2 + c2;

/* Check signs of r1 and r2.  If both point 1 and point 2 lie
 * on same side of second line segment, the line segments do
 * not intersect.
 */

if ( r1 != 0 &&
     r2 != 0 &&
     SAME_SIGNS( r1, r2 ))
    return ( DONT_INTERSECT );

/* Line segments intersect: compute intersection point.
 */

denom = a1 * b2 - a2 * b1;
if ( denom == 0 )
    return ( COLLINEAR );
offset = denom < 0 ? - denom / 2 : denom / 2;

/* The denom/2 is to get rounding instead of truncating.  It
 * is added or subtracted to the numerator, depending upon the
 * sign of the numerator.
 */

num = b1 * c2 - b2 * c1;
*x = ( num < 0 ? num - offset : num + offset ) / denom;

num = a2 * c1 - a1 * c2;
*y = ( num < 0 ? num - offset : num + offset ) / denom;

return ( DO_INTERSECT );
} /* lines_intersect */

/* A main program to test the function.
 */

main()
{
    long x1, x2, x3, x4, y1, y2, y3, y4;
    long x, y;

    for (;;) {
        printf( "X1, Y1: " );
scanf( "%ld %ld", &x1, &y1 );
        printf( "X2, Y2: " );
scanf( "%ld %ld", &x2, &y2 );
        printf( "X3, Y3: " );
scanf( "%ld %ld", &x3, &y3 );
        printf( "X4, Y4: " );
scanf( "%ld %ld", &x4, &y4 );
```

```
    switch ( lines_intersect( x1, y1, x2, y2, x3, y3, x4, y4, &x, &y )) {
        case DONT_INTERSECT:
         printf( "Lines don't intersect\n" );
         break;
        case COLLINEAR:
                    printf( "Lines are collinear\n" );
                    break;
        case DO_INTERSECT:
         printf( "Lines intersect at %ld,%ld\n", x, y );
                    break;
        }
    }
} /* main */
```

A PEANO CURVE GENERATION ALGORITHM

(page 25)

Ken Musgrave

```c
/* main.c */
/* generates a peano curve in n dimensions to m bits precision */

/* Ken Musgrave */
/* June 1986 */


#include <stdio.h>
#include <math.h>
#include "types.h"

vector      coord, last_coord;


main(argc, argv)

int         argc;
char        *argv[];

{
    int             i, pos=0;

            /* get command-line args */
    if ( argc != 3 )
            {
            fprintf( stderr, "usage: %s dim prec\n", argv[0] );
            exit(0);
            }

    dimensions = atoi( argv[1] );
    if ( dimensions<1 || dimensions>MAX_DIMENSIONS )
            {
            fprintf( stderr, "%s: can't work in %d dimensions!\n", argv[0], dimensions );
            exit(-1);
            }
```

```
        precision = atoi( argv[2] );
        if ( precision<0 || precision>MAX_PRECISION-1 )
                {
                fprintf( stderr, "%s: can't work with %d bits of precision!\n", argv[0], precision );
                exit(-1);
                }

        printf("%s: filling %d dimensions to %d bits of precision\n", argv[0], dimensions, precision );

        /* intialize */
        for ( i=0; i<dimensions; i++ )
                {
                bitmask[i] = 1 << ( dimensions - i - 1 );
                bytemask |= 1 << i;
                last_coord[i] = 0;
                }

        recurse( coord, last_coord, (int)pow(2.0,(double)precision), dimensions );

}   /* main() */



                /* recursive routine to call "peano()" */
recurse( coord, last_coord, iterations, level )

vector          coord, last_coord;
int             iterations, level;

{

        int                     i;
        static int              n=0;

        if ( level > 0 )
                for ( i=0; i<iterations; i++ )
                        recurse( coord, last_coord, iterations, level-1 );
        else            {
                        /* get x,y coord of position n on peano curve */
                peano( coord, n++ );
                for ( i=0; i<dimensions; i++ )
                        printf("%d ", coord[i] );
                printf("\n");

                        /* "last_coord" tracks where we came from, if needed */
                for ( i=0; i<precision; i++ )
                        last_coord[i] = coord[i];
                }

}   /* recurse() */

/* peano.c */
/* space-filling peano curve algorithm. */
/* fills n-space with a 1d peano curve. */

/* Ken Musgrave */
/* June 1986 */
```

```
#include "types.h"


peano( coord, point )
/* determine the n-space coordinate of "point" on the peano curve */

vector        coord;
int           point;

{
        int                 i;

        zero( sigma );                          /* initialize necessary arrays */
        zero( tilde_sigma );
        zero( tilde_tau );

        build_rho( point );
        for( i=0; i<precision; i++ )
                J[i] = principal_pos( rho[i] );
        build_sigma();
        build_tau();
        build_tilde_sigma();
        build_tilde_tau();
        build_omega();
        build_alpha();

        v_convert( alpha, coord );

}  /* peano() */



build_rho( point )
/* build "rho" array */

int           point;

{
        int                 i, mask=bytemask;

        for( i=0; i<precision; i++ )
                {
                rho[precision-i-1] = ( point & mask ) >> ( i * dimensions );
                mask <<= dimensions;
                }

}  /* build_rho() */
```

```
principal_pos( a_byte )
/* find principal position of "a_byte" */

byte        a_byte;

{
    int     nth_bit, i=1;

    nth_bit = a_byte & 0x01;
    for( i=1; i<dimensions; i++ )
            {
            if ( ( ( a_byte & bitmask[dimensions−i−1] ) >> i ) != nth_bit )
                return( dimensions − i );
                }

    return( dimensions );                   /* all bits are the same */

} /* principal_pos() */



build_sigma()
/* build "sigma" array */
{
    int     i, bit;

    for( i=0; i<precision; i++ )
            {
            sigma[i] |= rho[i] & bitmask[0];
            for ( bit=1; bit<dimensions; bit++ )
                    {
                    sigma[i] |= ( rho[i] & bitmask[bit] )
                                    ^ ( ( rho[i] & bitmask[bit−1] ) >> 1 );
                    }
            }

} /* build_sigma() */
```

480

```
build_tau()
/* build "tau" array */
{
        int             parity, bit, i, j;
        byte            temp_byte;

        for( i=0; i<precision; i++ )
                {
                parity = 0;
                                                        /* complement nth bit */
                if ( sigma[i] & bitmask[dimensions-1] )
                        tau[i] = sigma[i] - 1;          /* nth bit was 1 */
                else
                        tau[i] = sigma[i] + 1;          /* nth bit was 0 */

                for ( j=0; j<dimensions; j++ )          /* find parity */
                        if ( tau[i] & bitmask[j] )
                                parity++;

                if ( ODD( parity ) )                    /* complement principal bit */
                        {
                        bit = J[i] - 1;                 /* get index of principal bit */

                                                        /* get bit in question */
                        temp_byte = tau[i] & bitmask[bit];
                        tau[i] |= bitmask[bit];         /* set the bit to 1 */
                        tau[i] &= ~temp_byte;           /* assign complement */
                        }
                } /* for */

} /* build_tau() */



build_tilde_sigma()
/* build "tilde_sigma" array */
{
        int     i, shift=0;

        tilde_sigma[0] = sigma[0];
        for( i=1; i<precision; i++ )
                {
                shift += J[i-1] - 1;
                shift %= dimensions;
                tilde_sigma[i] = RT_CSHFT( sigma[i], shift, dimensions, bytemask );
                }

} /* build_tilde_sigma() */
```

481

```
build_tilde_tau()
/* build "tilde_tau" array */
{
     int    i, shift=0;

     tilde_tau[0]  =  tau[0];
     for( i=1; i<precision; i++ )
             {
             shift += J[i-1] - 1;
             shift %= dimensions;
             tilde_tau[i] = RT_CSHFT( tau[i], shift, dimensions, bytemask );
             }

}  /* build_tilde_tau() */




build_omega()
/* build "omega" array */
{
     int    i;

     omega[0]  =  0;
     for( i=1; i<precision; i++ )
             omega[i] = omega[i-1] ^ tilde_tau[i-1];

}  /* build_omega() */




build_alpha()
/* build "alpha" array */
{
     int    i;

     for( i=0; i<precision; i++ )
             alpha[i] = omega[i] ^ tilde_sigma[i];

}  /* build_alpha() */
```

```
zero( array )
/* initialize "array" to zeros */

r_array      array;

{
     int    i;

     for ( i=0; i<precision; i++ )
          array[i] = 0;

}  /* zero() */



v_convert( alpha, coord )
/* convert "alpha" array into n_space coordinate vector */

r_array      alpha;
vector       coord;

{
     int              i, j, bit, a_bitmask=1;

     for ( i=0; i<dimensions; i++ )
          {
          coord[i] = 0;
          bit = precision;
          for ( j=0; j<precision; j++ )                /* extract each bit of coord i */
               coord[i] |= ( ( alpha[j] & a_bitmask ) << —bit ) >> i;
          a_bitmask <<= 1;
          }

}  /* v_convert() */

/* types.h */
/* types and #define's for peano curve algorithm */

/* Ken Musgrave */
/* June 1986 */
```

```
#define FB_SIZE            1024                    /* frame buffer size */

#define MAX_DIMENSIONS     5                       /* dimensionality of space */
#define MAX_PRECISION      11                      /* number of bits /dimension −1 */

#define ODD(x)             ( ( (x) & 0x1 )  ?  1 : 0 )

                                                   /* right circular shift */
#define RT_CSHFT( byte, shift, dimensions, bytemask ) \
        (((((byte) >> (shift)) | ((byte) << dimensions − (shift))) & bytemask)


typedef char        byte;                   /* size must be >= MAX_PRECISION */

typedef int         vector[MAX_DIMENSIONS];     /* n−space vector */

typedef byte        r_array[MAX_PRECISION];     /* vector of type "r" in algo */


/* global variable section */

int         J[MAX_PRECISION];                   /* storage for principal positions */

                                                /* global arrays */
r_array     rho, sigma, tau, tilde_sigma, tilde_tau, omega, alpha;

byte        bitmask[MAX_DIMENSIONS];            /* to be filled with bit masks */

int         dimensions;                         /* number of dimensions being filled */
int         precision;                          /* number of bits of precision used */
byte        bytemask;                           /* masks "dimensions" bits */
```

SPACE-FILLING CURVES AND
A MEASURE OF COHERENCE

(page 26)

Douglas Voorhies

```
/*****************************************************************
peano recursively draws a Peano curve
orient -- is either +1 or -1
angle -- is 0, 90, 180, or 270
level -- is initially the desired recursion depth

step moves to the next pixel in direction angle and marks it
*****************************************************************/

peano (orient,angle,level)
long orient, *angle, level;
{
    if (level-- <= 0) return;          /* Stop recursion?    */
    peano(orient,angle,level);         /* Recurse            */
    step(*angle);                      /* Step to next pixel */
    peano(-orient,angle,level);        /* Recurse            */
    step(*angle);                      /* Step to next pixel */
    peano(orient,angle,level);         /* Recurse            */
    *angle -= orient * 90;             /* Turn               */
    step(*angle);                      /* Step to next pixel */
    *angle -= orient * 90;             /* Turn               */
    peano(-orient,angle,level);        /* Recurse            */
    step(*angle);                      /* Step to next pixel */
    peano(orient,angle,level);         /* Recurse            */
    step(*angle);                      /* Step to next pixel */
    peano(-orient,angle,level);        /* Recurse            */
    *angle += orient * 90;             /* Turn               */
    step(*angle);                      /* Step to next pixel */
    *angle += orient * 90;             /* Turn               */
    peano(orient,angle,level);         /* Recurse            */
    step(*angle);                      /* Step to next pixel */
    peano(-orient,angle,level);        /* Recurse            */
    step(*angle);                      /* Step to next pixel */
    peano(orient,angle,level);         /* Recurse            */
}
```

```
/******************************************************************
hilbert recursively draws a Hilbert curve
orient -- is either +1 or -1
angle -- is 0, 90, 180, or 270
level -- is initially the desired recursion depth

step moves to the next pixel in direction angle and marks it
******************************************************************/

hilbert (orient,angle,level)
long orient, *angle, level;
{
    if (level-- <= 0) return;              /* Stop recursion?   */
    *angle += orient * 90;                 /* Turn              */
    hilbert(-orient,angle,level);          /* Recurse           */
    step(*angle);                          /* Step to next pixel */
    *angle -= orient * 90;                 /* Turn              */
    hilbert(orient,angle,level);           /* Recurse           */
    step(*angle);                          /* Step to next pixel */
    hilbert(orient,angle,level);           /* Recurse           */
    *angle -= orient * 90;                 /* Turn              */
    step(*angle);                          /* Step to next pixel */
    hilbert(-orient,angle,level);          /* Recurse           */
    *angle += orient * 90;                 /* Turn              */
}
```

SCANLINE COHERENT
SHAPE ALGEBRA

(page 31)

Jonathan E. Steinhart

```c
struct  segment {
    struct  segment *next;        /* next segment element */
    int             x;            /* x coordinate of this element */
};

struct  span    {
    struct  span    *next;        /* next span element */
    struct  segment *x;           /* start of segment list for this span */
    int             y;            /* y coordinate of this span */
};

struct  segment *
segment_copy(x)
struct  segment *x;                        /* the segment to copy */
{
    extern  char        *malloc();         /* memory allocator */

    struct  segment     **sp;              /* segment list insertion point*/
    struct  segment     *segment;          /* head of result segment list */

    /*
     *  Copy the segment until we hit the end.
     */

    for (sp = &segment; x != (struct segment *)0; x = x->next) {
        *sp = (struct segment *)malloc(sizeof (struct segment));
        (*sp)->x = x->x;
        sp = &(*sp)->next;
    }

    *sp = (struct segment *)0;

    return (segment);
}

struct  span    *
shape_copy(shape)
struct  span    *shape;                    /* the shape to copy */
{
    extern  char        *malloc();         /* memory allocator */
```

```
    struct   segment    **sp;            /* segment list insertion point*/
    struct   segment    *segment;        /* head of result segment list */
    struct   segment    *x;              /* operand segment pointer */
    struct   span       **rp;            /* result list insertion point */
    struct   span       *result;         /* head of result span list */

    /*
     *  Run down the spans until we hit the end.
     */

    for (rp = &result; shape != (struct span *)0; shape = shape->next) {
        *rp = (struct span *)malloc(sizeof (struct span));
        (*rp)->y = shape->y;

        /*
         *  Run down the segment until we hit the end.
         */

        sp = &segment;

        for (x = shape->x; x != (struct segment *)0; x = x->next) {
            *sp = (struct segment *)malloc(sizeof (struct segment));
            (*sp)->x = x->x;
            sp = &(*sp)->next;
        }

        /*
         *  Terminate the segment, attach it to the span, move on.
         */

        *sp = (struct segment *)0;
        (*rp)->x = segment;
        rp = &(*rp)->next;
    }

    *rp = (struct span *)0;

    return (result);
}

struct   span     *
span_copy(span)
struct   span     *span;                    /* the span to copy */
{
    extern   char        *malloc();          /* memory allocator */
    extern   struct   segment *segment_copy(); /* copy a segment desc */

    struct   span          *result;          /* result span list head */

    /*
     *  Copy a single span.
     */

    result = (struct span *)malloc(sizeof (struct span));
    result->y = span->y;
    result->x = segment_copy(span->x);
```

488

```
        result->next = (struct span *)0;

        return (result);
}

struct  span     *
shape_intersect(shape1, shape2)
struct  span     *shape1;          /* first shape operand */
struct  span     *shape2;          /* second shape operand */
{
        extern  char     *malloc();        /* memory allocator */

        int              flag;             /* segment state flag */
        int              old;              /* old segment state flag */
        int              test;             /* comparison test value */
        int              x;                /* current x value */
        int              y;                /* current y value */
        struct  segment **sp;              /* segment list insertion point */
        struct  segment *segment;          /* head of result segment list */
        struct  segment *p1;               /* first operand segment pointer */
        struct  segment *p2;               /* second operand segment pointer */
        struct  segment *x1;               /* first operand segment */
        struct  segment *x2;               /* second operand segment */
        struct  span     **rp;             /* result list insertion point */
        struct  span     *result;          /* head of result span list */

        /*
         * The result is empty if either shape operand is empty.
         */

        if (shape1 == (struct span *)0 || shape2 == (struct span *)0)
            return ((struct span *)0);

        /*
         * Initialize the result list and list insertion pointer.
         */

        result = (struct span *)0;
        rp = &result;

        /*
         * Initialize the segment pointers.  This ensures that we always
         * have valid operands to process even if one shape begins before
         * the other.
         */

        x1 = x2 = (struct segment *)0;

        /*
         * Process the spans until either shape ends.  We know that we're
         * done when either shape terminates for intersections.
         */
```

```
while (shape1 != (struct span *)0 && shape2 != (struct span *)0) {

    /*
     * Compute the test value.  The value is negative if the first
     * shape is behind the second shape, positive if the first shape
     * is ahead of the second one, and zero if they're at the same
     * coordinate.
     *
     * Advance whichever shape is behind; both if they're even.
     * Extract the y value from the span so that we have it
     * after the list is advanced.  Also extract the segment.
     */

    if ((test = shape1->y - shape2->y) <= 0) {
        y = shape1->y;
        x1 = shape1->x;
        shape1 = shape1->next;
    }

    if (test >= 0) {
        y = shape2->y;
        x2 = shape2->x;
        shape2 = shape2->next;
    }

    /*
     * Initialize the state flags, and new segment pointers.
     */

    flag = old = 0;
    segment = (struct segment *)0;
    sp = &segment;

    /*
     * Process the segments until either one terminates.
     */

    p1 = x1;
    p2 = x2;

    while (p1 != (struct segment *)0 && p2 != (struct segment *)0) {

        /*
         * Compute the test value.  The value is negative if the
         * first shape behind the second shape, positive if the
         * first shape is ahead of the  second one, and zero if
         * they're at the same coordinate.
         *
         * Advance whichever shape is behind; both if they're even.
         * Extract the x value from the segment so that we have it
         * after the list is advanced.  Update the state flag.
         */

        if ((test = p1->x - p2->x) <= 0) {
            x = p1->x;
            flag ^= 1;
            p1 = p1->next;
        }
```

490

```
        if (test >= 0) {
            x = p2->x;
            flag ^= 2;
            p2 = p2->next;
        }

        /*
         * A transition in/out of state 3 indicates an intersection.
         * Add a new segment element to record the coordinate.
         * Save the state value for transition out checking.
         */

        if (flag == 3 || old == 3) {
            *sp = (struct segment *)malloc(sizeof (struct segment));
            (*sp)->x = x;
            sp = &(*sp)->next;
        }

        old = flag;
    }

    /*
     * Add a new span to the result if there's anything in the
     * segment.  Also add a span if there's already something in
     * the result list because we need to mark the vertical gap.
     */

    if (segment != (struct segment *)0 || result != (struct span *)0) {
        *sp = (struct segment *)0;
        *rp = (struct span *)malloc(sizeof (struct span));
        (*rp)->x = segment;
        (*rp)->y = y;
        rp = &(*rp)->next;
    }
}

/*
 * Terminate the result list and return it.
 */

*rp = (struct span *)0;

return (result);
}

struct  span    *
shape_union(shape1, shape2)
struct  span    *shape1;                    /* first shape operand */
struct  span    *shape2;                    /* second shape operand */
{
    extern  char        *malloc();          /* memory allocator */
    extern  struct  segment *segment_copy();/* copy segment description*/
    extern  struct  span    *shape_copy();  /* copy shape description */

    int         flag;           /* segment state flag */
    int         old;            /* old segment state flag */
```

```
int            test;            /* comparison test value */
int            x;               /* current x value */
int            y;               /* current y value */
struct   segment **sp;          /* segment list insertion point */
struct   segment *segment;      /* head of result segment list */
struct   segment *p1;           /* first operand segment pointer */
struct   segment *p2;           /* second operand segment pointer */
struct   segment *x1;           /* first operand segment */
struct   segment *x2;           /* second operand segment */
struct   span    **rp;          /* result list insertion point */
struct   span    *result;       /* head of result span list */

/*
 *  The result is the second shape if the first shape is empty, the
 *  first shape if the second shape is empty.  This yields an empty
 *  shape result if both operands are empty.
 */

if (shape1 == (struct span *)0)
    return (shape_copy(shape2));

else if (shape2 == (struct span *)0)
    return (shape_copy(shape1));

/*
 *  Initialize the result list and list insertion pointer.
 */

result = (struct span *)0;
rp = &result;

/*
 *  Initialize the segment pointers.  This ensures that we always
 *  have valid operands to process even if one shape begins before
 *  the other.
 */

x1 = x2 = (struct segment *)0;

/*
 *  Copy all spans from either the first shape or the second shape
 *  that come before the first span of the second shape or first
 *  shape to the result.  This is faster than using the generic
 *  outer loop.
 */

if (shape1->y < shape2->y) {
    while (shape1 != (struct span *)0 && shape1->y < shape2->y) {
        *rp = span_copy(shape1);
        x1 = shape1->x;
        rp = &(*rp)->next;
        shape1 = shape1->next;
    }
}
```

```
    else if (shape2->y < shape1->y) {
        while (shape2 != (struct span *)0 && shape2->y < shape1->y) {
            *rp = span_copy(shape2);
            x2 = shape2->x;
            rp = &(*rp)->next;
            shape2 = shape2->next;
        }
    }
}

/*
 *  Process the area in which the shapes overlap vertically.
 */

while (shape1 != (struct span *)0 && shape2 != (struct span *)0) {

    /*
     *  Compute the test value.  The value is negative if the first
     *  shape is behind the second shape, positive if the first shape
     *  is ahead of the second one, and zero if they're at the same
     *  coordinate.
     *
     *  Advance whichever shape is behind; both if they're even.
     *  Extract the y value from the span so that we have it
     *  after the list is advanced.  Also extract the segment.
     */

    if ((test = shape1->y - shape2->y) <= 0) {
        y = shape1->y;
        x1 = shape1->x;
        shape1 = shape1->next;
    }

    if (test >= 0) {
        y = shape2->y;
        x2 = shape2->x;
        shape2 = shape2->next;
    }

    /*
     *  The result segment is empty if both operand segments are
     *  empty.  The result segment is the second operand segment
     *  if the first operand segment is empty and vice versa.
     */

    if (x1 == (struct segment *)0 && x2 == (struct segment *)0)
        segment = (struct segment *)0;

    else if (x1 == (struct segment *)0)
        segment = segment_copy(x2);

    else if (x2 == (struct segment *)0)
        segment = segment_copy(x1);

    /*
     *  Both operands have non-empty segments.
     */
```

```
else {
    /*
     * Initialize the state flags and new segment pointers.
     */

    flag = old = 0;
    segment = (struct segment *)0;
    sp = &segment;

    /*
     * Process the segments until either one terminates.
     */

    p1 = x1;
    p2 = x2;

    while (p1!=(struct segment *)0 && p2!=(struct segment *)0) {

        /*
         * Compute the test value.  The value is negative if the
         * first shape behind the second shape, positive if the
         * first shape is ahead of the second one, and zero if
         * they're at the same coordinate.
         *
         * Advance whichever shape is behind; both if they're
         * even.  Extract the x value from the segment so that
         * we have it after the list is advanced.  Update the
         * state flag.
         */

        if ((test = p1->x - p2->x) <= 0) {
            x = p1->x;
            flag ^= 1;
            p1 = p1->next;
        }

        if (test >= 0) {
            x = p2->x;
            flag ^= 2;
            p2 = p2->next;
        }

        /*
         * A transition in or out of state 0 indicates a union.
         * Add a new segment element to record the coordinate.
         * Save the state value for transition out checking.
         */

        if (flag == 0 || old == 0) {
            *sp = (struct segment *)malloc(sizeof (struct segment));
            (*sp)->x = x;
            sp = &(*sp)->next;
        }

        old = flag;
    }
```

```c
        /*
         *  Copy anything left over in whatever segment
         *  wasn't finshed to the result.
         */

        while (p1 != (struct segment *)0) {
            *sp = (struct segment *)malloc(sizeof (struct segment));
            (*sp)->x = p1->x;
            sp = &(*sp)->next;
            p1 = p1->next;
        }

        while (p2 != (struct segment *)0) {
            *sp = (struct segment *)malloc(sizeof (struct segment));
            (*sp)->x = p2->x;
            sp = &(*sp)->next;
            p2 = p2->next;
        }

        *sp = (struct segment *)0;
    }

    /*
     *  Add a new span to the result if there's anything in the
     *  segment.  Also add a span if there's already something in
     *  the result list because we need to mark the vertical gap.
     */

    if (segment != (struct segment *)0 || result != (struct span *)0) {
        *rp = (struct span *)malloc(sizeof (struct span));
        (*rp)->x = segment;
        (*rp)->y = y;
        rp = &(*rp)->next;
    }
}

/*
 *  Copy the spans from whichever shape continues past the other one
 *  to the result.
 */

if (shape1 != (struct span *)0) {
    while (shape1 != (struct span *)0) {
        *rp = span_copy(shape1);
        rp = &(*rp)->next;
        shape1 = shape1->next;
    }
}
else {
    while (shape2 != (struct span *)0) {
        *rp = span_copy(shape2);
        rp = &(*rp)->next;
        shape2 = shape2->next;
    }
}
```

```
        /*
         *  Terminate the result list and return it.
         */

        *rp = (struct span *)0;

        return (result);
}

struct    span    *
shape_difference(shape1, shape2)
struct    span    *shape1;                    /* first shape operand */
struct    span    *shape2;                    /* second shape operand */
{
        extern    char         *malloc();        /* memory allocator */
        extern    struct    segment *segment_copy();/* copy segment description*/
        extern    struct    span    *shape_copy();  /* copy shape description */

        int             flag;            /* segment state flag */
        int             old;             /* old segment state flag */
        int             test;            /* comparison test value */
        int             x;               /* current x value */
        int             y;               /* current y value */
        struct    segment **sp;          /* segment list insertion point */
        struct    segment *segment;      /* head of result segment list */
        struct    segment *p1;           /* first operand segment pointer */
        struct    segment *p2;           /* second operand segment pointer */
        struct    segment *x1;           /* first operand segment */
        struct    segment *x2;           /* second operand segment */
        struct    span    **rp;          /* result list insertion point */
        struct    span    *result;       /* head of result span list */

        /*
         *  The result is empty if the first shape is empty, the first shape
         *  if the second shape is empty.
         */

        if (shape1 == (struct span *)0)
            return ((struct span *)0);

        else if (shape2 == (struct span *)0)
            return (shape_copy(shape1));

        /*
         *  Initialize the result and the result list insertion pointer.
         */

        result = (struct span *)0;
        rp = &result;

        /*
         *  Initialize the segment pointers.  This ensures that we always
         *  have valid operands to process even if one shape begins before
         *  the other.
         */

        x1 = x2 = (struct segment *)0;
```

496

```
/*
 * Copy all spans from the first shape that come before the first
 * span of the second shape to the result.  Skip any spans in the
 * second shape that come before the first span in the first shape.
 * This is faster than using the generic outer loop.
 */

if (shape1->y < shape2->y) {
    while (shape1 != (struct span *)0 && shape1->y < shape2->y) {
        *rp = span_copy(shape1);
        x1 = shape1->x;
        rp = &(*rp)->next;
        shape1 = shape1->next;
    }
}
else if (shape2->y < shape1->y) {
    while (shape2->y < shape1->y) {
        x2 = shape2->x;
        shape2 = shape2->next;
    }
}

/*
 * Process the area in which the shapes overlap vertically.
 */

while (shape1 != (struct span *)0 && shape2 != (struct span *)0) {

    /*
     * Compute the test value.  The value is negative if the first
     * shape is behind the second shape, positive if the first shape
     * is ahead of the second one, and zero if they're at the same
     * coordinate.
     *
     * Advance whichever shape is behind; both if they're even.
     * Extract the y value from the span so that we have it
     * after the list is advanced.  Also extract the segment.
     */

    if ((test = shape1->y - shape2->y) <= 0) {
        y = shape1->y;
        x1 = shape1->x;
        shape1 = shape1->next;
    }

    if (test >= 0) {
        y = shape2->y;
        x2 = shape2->x;
        shape2 = shape2->next;
    }

    /*
     * The result segment is empty if the second operand segment is
     * empty.  The result segment is the first operand segment if
     * the second operand segment is empty.
     */
```

```
else if (x1 == (struct segment *)0)
    segment = (struct segment *)0;

else if (x2 == (struct segment *)0)
    segment = segment_copy(x1);

/*
 *  Both operands have non-empty segments.
 */

else {
    /*
     * Initialize the state flags and new segment pointers.
     */

    flag = old = 0;
    segment = (struct segment *)0;
    sp = &segment;

    /*
     *  Process the segments until either one terminates.
     */

    p1 = x1;
    p2 = x2;

    while (p1!=(struct segment *)0 && p2!=(struct segment *)0) {

        /*
         *  Compute the test value.  The value is negative if the
         *  first shape behind the second shape, positive if the
         *  first shape is ahead of the second one, and zero if
         *  they're at the same coordinate.
         *
         *  Advance whichever shape is behind; both if they're
         *  even.  Extract the x value from the segment so that
         *  we have it after the list is advanced.  Update the
         *  state flag.
         */

        if ((test = p1->x - p2->x) <= 0) {
            x = p1->x;
            flag ^= 1;
            p1 = p1->next;
        }

        if (test >= 0) {
            x = p2->x;
            flag ^= 2;
            p2 = p2->next;
        }

        /*
         *  A transition in/out of state 1 indicates difference.
         *  Add a new segment element to record the coordinate.
         *  Save the state value for transition out checking.
         */
```

498

```
            if (flag == 1 || old == 1) {
                *sp = (struct segment *)malloc(sizeof (struct segment));
                (*sp)->x = x;
                sp = &(*sp)->next;
            }

            old = flag;
        }

        /*
         *  Copy anything left over in the first segment
         *  to the result.
         */

        while (p1 != (struct segment *)0) {
            *sp = (struct segment *)malloc(sizeof (struct segment));
            (*sp)->x = p1->x;
            sp = &(*sp)->next;
            p1 = p1->next;
        }

        *sp = (struct segment *)0;
    }

    /*
     *  Add a new span to the result if there's anything in the
     *  segment.  Also add a span if there's already something in
     *  the result list because we need to mark the vertical gap.
     */

    if (segment != (struct segment *)0 || result != (struct span *)0) {
        *rp = (struct span *)malloc(sizeof (struct span));
        (*rp)->x = segment;
        (*rp)->y = y;
        rp = &(*rp)->next;
    }
}

/*
 *  Copy any leftover spans from the first shape to the result.
 */

while (shape1 != (struct span *)0) {
    *rp = span_copy(shape1);
    rp = &(*rp)->next;
    shape1 = shape1->next;
}

/*
 *  Terminate the result list and return it.
 */

*rp = (struct span *)0;

return (result);
}
```

```
struct  span    *
shape_translate(shape, x, y)
struct  span    *shape;              /* shape to translate */
int             x;                   /* x translation */
int             y;                   /* y translation */
{
    struct  segment *segment;        /* segment list pointer */
    struct  span    *span;           /* span list pointer */

    /*
     *  Add the y offset to each span.
     */

    for (span = shape; span != (struct span *)0; span = span->next) {
        span->y += y;

        /*
         *  Add the x offset to each segment.
         */

        for (segment = span->x;
          segment != (struct segment *)0; segment = segment->next)
            segment->x += x;
    }

    return (shape);
}

struct  span    *
shape_box(x, y, width, height)
int             x;                   /* x coordinate of rectangle */
int             y;                   /* y coordinate of rectangle */
int             width;               /* width of rectangle */
int             height;              /* height of rectangle */
{
    extern  char        *malloc();   /* memory allocator */

    struct  span        *result;     /* head of result span list */

    /*
     *  Make a shape from the box description.
     */

    result = (struct span *)malloc(sizeof (struct span));
    result->y = y;

    result->next = (struct span *)malloc(sizeof (struct span));
    result->next->y = y + height;
    result->next->next = (struct span *)0;

    result->x = (struct segment *)malloc(sizeof (struct segment));
    result->x->x = x;

    result->x->next = (struct segment *)malloc(sizeof (struct segment));
    result->x->next->x = x + width;
    result->x->next->next = (struct segment *)0;

    return (result);
}
```

```c
struct  span     *
shape_tmp_box(x, y, width, height)
int       x;                          /* x coordinate of rectangle */
int       y;                          /* y coordinate of rectangle */
int       width;                      /* width of rectangle */
int       height;                     /* height of rectangle */
{
    static  struct  segment x2 = {  0,    0 };
    static  struct  segment x1 = {  &x2,  0 };

    static  struct  span    y2 = {    0,    0,    0 };
    static  struct  span    y1 = {  &y2,  &x1,    0 };

    /*
     * Make a shape from the box description in static storage.
     */

    y1.y = y;
    y2.y = y + height;
    x1.x = x;
    x2.x = x + width;

    return (&y1);
}

void
shape_free(shape)
struct  span    *shape;               /* the shape to free */
{
    extern  int         free();       /* free allocated memory */

    struct  segment     *fx;          /* segment free pointer */
    struct  segment     *x;           /* operand segment pointer */
    struct  span        *fy;          /* span free pointer */

    /*
     * Free all of the spans and segments.
     */

    while (shape != (struct span *)0) {
        for (x = shape->x; x != (struct segment *)0; ) {
            fx = x;
            x = x->next;
            (void)free((char *)fx);
        }

        fy = shape;
        shape = shape->next;
        (void)free((char *)fy);
    }

    return;
}
```

A COMPARISON OF DIGITAL HALFTONING TECHNIQUES

(page 57)

Dale A. Schumacher

```
/************************************************************************

         Digital Halftoning with Threshold and Diffusion Dithers

 ************************************************************************/
#include <stdio.h>
#include <string.h>
#include <malloc.h>

typedef unsigned char    Pixel;

typedef struct {
        int     xsize;          /* horizontal size of the image in Pixels */
        int     ysize;          /* vertical size of the image in Pixels */
        Pixel * data;           /* pointer to first scanline of image */
        int     span;           /* byte offset between two scanlines */
} Image;

#define WHITE_PIXEL     (255)
#define BLACK_PIXEL     (0)

#define MUL(x,y)        (((long)(x))*((long)(y)))
#define DIV(x,y)        (((long)(x))/((long)(y)))

static char *
next_token(f)
FILE *f;
{
        static char delim[] = " \t\r\n";
        static char *t = NULL;
        static char lnbuf[256];
        char *p;

        while(t == NULL) {                      /* nothing in the buffer */
                if(fgets(lnbuf, sizeof(lnbuf), f)) {    /* read a line */
                        if(p = strchr(lnbuf, '#')) {    /* clip any comment */
                                *p = '\0';
                        }
                        t = strtok(lnbuf, delim);       /* get first token */
                } else {
                        return(NULL);
                }
```

```
        }
        p = t;
        t = strtok(NULL, delim);                        /* get next token */
        return(p);
}

Image *
new_image(xsize, ysize) /* create a blank image */
int xsize;
int ysize;
{
        Image *image;

        if((image = (Image *)malloc(sizeof(Image)))
        && (image->data = (Pixel *)calloc(ysize, xsize))) {
                image->xsize = xsize;
                image->ysize = ysize;
                image->span = xsize;
        }
        return(image);
}

Image *
load_image(f)            /* read image from file */
FILE *f;
{
        char *p;
        int width, height;
        Image *image;

        if(((p = next_token(f)) && (strcmp(p, "Bm") == 0))
        && ((p = next_token(f)) && ((width = atoi(p)) > 0))
        && ((p = next_token(f)) && ((height = atoi(p)) > 0))
        && ((p = next_token(f)) && (strcmp(p, "8") == 0))
        && (image = new_image(width, height))
        && (fread(image->data, width, height, f) == height)) {
                return(image);              /* load successful */
        } else {
                return(NULL);               /* load failed */
        }
}

int
save_image(f, image)     /* write image to file */
FILE *f;
Image *image;
{
        char *p;
        int width, height;

        fprintf(f, "Bm # PXM 8-bit greyscale image\n");
        fprintf(f, "%d %d 8 # width height depth\n",
                image->xsize, image->ysize);
        if(fwrite(image->data, image->xsize, image->ysize, f) == image->ysize) {
                return(0);                  /* save successful */
        } else {
                return(-1);                 /* save failed */
        }
}
```

```
Pixel
get_pixel(image, x, y)
Image *image;
int x;
int y;
{
        static Image *im = NULL;
        static int yy = -1;
        static Pixel *p = NULL;

        if((x < 0) || (x >= image->xsize) || (y < 0) || (y >= image->ysize)) {
                return(0);
        }
        if((im != image) || (yy != y)) {
                im = image;
                yy = y;
                p = image->data + (y * image->span);
        }
        return(p[x]);
}

Pixel
put_pixel(image, x, y, data)
Image *image;
int x;
int y;
Pixel data;
{
        static Image *im = NULL;
        static int yy = -1;
        static Pixel *p = NULL;

        if((x < 0) || (x >= image->xsize) || (y < 0) || (y >= image->ysize)) {
                return(0);
        }
        if((im != image) || (yy != y)) {
                im = image;
                yy = y;
                p = image->data + (y * image->span);
        }
        return(p[x] = data);
}


/*******************************************************************

                Threshold Dithering

*******************************************************************/

struct thesh_params {
        int n;                  /* number of output levels */
        Image *tp;              /* threshold "image" */
};
```

```
Image *
threshold_dither(ip, parm)
Image *ip;                      /* input image */
struct thresh_params *parm;     /* threshold parameters */
{
        int n, x, y, xsize, ysize, mx, my, mxsize, mysize, range, base;
        Pixel v, t;
        Image *tp, *op;

        n = parm->tp;
        tp = parm->tp;
        xsize = ip->xsize;
        ysize = ip->ysize;
        mxsize = tp->xsize;
        mysize = tp->ysize;
        if((op = new_image(xsize, ysize)) == NULL) {
                return(NULL);
        }
        --n;                            /* convert to number of ranges */
        range = DIV(WHITE_PIXEL, n);    /* compute quantization step size */
        for(y = 0; y < ip->ysize; ++y) {
                my = (y % mysize);
                for(x = 0; x < ip->xsize; ++x) {
                        mx = (x % mxsize);
                        v = get_pixel(ip, x, y);
                        t = get_pixel(tp, mx, my);
                        t = DIV(MUL(t, range), WHITE_PIXEL);
                        base = (v / range) * range;
                        if((v - base) > t) {
                                put_pixel(op, x, y, base + range);
                        } else {
                                put_pixel(op, x, y, base);
                        }
                }
        }
        return(op);
}


/*******************************************************************

                Diffusion Dithering

*******************************************************************/

int     W_fs[3][3] = {                  /* Floyd and Steinberg */
                {       0,      0,      0       },
                {       0,      0,      7       },
                {       3,      5,      1       }
};

int     W_jjn[5][5] = {                 /* Jarvis, Judice and Ninke */
                {       0,      0,      0,      0,      0       },
                {       0,      0,      0,      0,      0       },
                {       0,      0,      0,      7,      5       },
                {       3,      5,      7,      5,      3       },
                {       1,      3,      5,      3,      1       }
};
```

```
int     W_s[5][5] = {                           /* Stucki */
        {       0,      0,      0,      0,      0       },
        {       0,      0,      0,      0,      0       },
        {       0,      0,      0,      8,      4       },
        {       2,      4,      8,      4,      2       },
        {       1,      2,      4,      2,      1       }
};

#define mp_fs    &W_fs[0][1][1]
#define mp_jjn   &W_jjn[2][2]
#define mp_s     &W_s[2][2]

#define mw_fs    1
#define mw_jjn   2
#define mw_s     2

#define CLAMP(n,l,h)    ((n) < (l) ? (l) : ((n) > (h) ? (h) : (n)))
#define WEIGHT(i,j)     (*(mp + (i) + (j * ((2 * mw) + 1))))

struct diff_params {
        int n;                          /* number of output levels */
        int *mp;                        /* matrix pointer */
        int mw;                         /* matrix width (from -mw to +mw) */
};

Image *
diffusion_dither(ip, dp)
Image *ip;                  /* input image */
struct diff_params *parm;
{
        int *mp, mw, n;
        int x, y, xsize, ysize, mx, my;
        int sum, range, base, error, esum;
        int u, v, t, r0, r1;
        Image *op;

        n = parm->n;
        mp = parm->mp;
        mw = parm->mw;
        xsize = ip->xsize;
        ysize = ip->ysize;
        if((op = new_image(xsize, ysize)) == NULL) {
                return(NULL);
        }
        --n;                            /* convert to number of ranges */
        range = DIV(WHITE_PIXEL, n);    /* compute quantization step size */
        sum = 0;
        for(my = -mw; my <= mw; ++my) { /* compute filter weighting sum */
                for(mx = -mw; mx <= mw; ++mx) {
                        sum += WEIGHT(mx, my);
                }
        }
        for(y = 0; y < ip->ysize; ++y) {/* process image with normal raster */
                for(x = 0; x < ip->xsize; ++x) {
                        u = get_pixel(ip, x, y);
                        if(u <= BLACK_PIXEL) {
                                v = BLACK_PIXEL;
                        } else if(u >= WHITE_PIXEL) {
                                v = WHITE_PIXEL;
                        } else {
```

```
                                      base = (u / range) * range;
                                      t = (range / 2);
                                      if((u - base) > t) {
                                              v = base + range;
                                      } else {
                                              v = base;
                                      }
                              }
                              put_pixel(op, x, y, v);
                              error = u - v;              /* distribute error */
                              esum = error;
                              for(my = 0/*-mw*/; my <= mw; ++my) {
                                      for(mx = -mw; mx <= mw; ++mx) {
                                              if((u = WEIGHT(mx, my)) == 0) {
                                                      continue;
                                              }
                                              v = get_pixel(ip, x + mx, y + my);
                                              u = (error * u) / sum;
                                              if((mx == mw) && (my == mw)) {
                                                      u = esum;
                                              }
                                              esum -= u;
                                              v += u;
                                              v = CLAMP(v, BLACK_PIXEL, WHITE_PIXEL);
                                              put_pixel(ip, x + mx, y + my, v);
                                      }
                              }
                      }
              }
              return(op);
}


/**********************************************************************

    This routine is a nice framework for testing graphics algorithms

**********************************************************************/
#define setbinary(f)        /*((f)->_flag |= _IOBIN)*/

int
pixel_process(infname, outfname, fn, aux)
char *infname;                /* name of the input file, or NULL for stdin */
char *outfname;               /* name of the output file, or NULL for stdout */
Pixel *(*fn)();               /* pointer to pixel processing routine */
char *aux;                    /* pointer to auxiliary data need by the routine */
{
        FILE *infile;
        FILE *outfile;
        Image *inimage;
        Image *outimage;

        if((infname == NULL)
        || (infname[0] == '\0')
        || ((infname[0] == '-') && (infname[1] == '\0'))) {
                infile = stdin;
                setbinary(infile);
                infname = "<stdin>";
        } else {
                if((infile = fopen(infname, "rb")) == NULL) {
```

507

```c
                            fprintf(stderr, "error opening input file %s\n",
                                     infname);
                            return(-1);
                    }
            }
            if((inimage = load_image(infile)) == NULL) {
                    fprintf(stderr, "error loading image from %s\n", infname);
                    return(-1);
            }
            if((outfname == NULL)
            || (outfname[0] == '\0')
            || ((outfname[0] == '-') && (outfname[1] == '\0'))) {
                    outfile = stdout;
                    setbinary(outfile);
                    outfname = "<stdout>";
            } else {
                    if((outfile = fopen(outfname, "wb")) == NULL) {
                            fprintf(stderr, "error opening output file %s\n",
                                     outfname);
                            return(-1);
                    }
            }
            if((outimage = (*fn)(inimage, aux)) == NULL) {
                    fprintf(stderr, "error processing image\n");
                    return(-1);
            }
            if(save_image(outfile, outimage) != 0) {
                    fprintf(stderr, "error saving image to %s\n", outfname);
                    return(-1);
            }
            return(0);
}

/*=============================================================================*/
```

508

COLOR DITHERING

(page 72)

Spencer W. Thomas and Rod G. Bogart

```
/*
 * dither.c - Functions for RGB color dithering.
 *
 * Author:    Spencer W. Thomas
 *            Computer Science Dept.
 *            University of Utah
 * Date:      Mon Feb  2 1987
 */

#include <math.h>

void   make_square();

static int magic4x4[4][4] =  {
        0, 14,   3, 13,
       11,  5,   8,  6,
       12,  2,  15,  1,
        7,  9,   4, 10
};

/* basic dithering macro */
#define DMAP(v,x,y)        (modN[v]>magic[x][y] ? divN[v] + 1 : divN[v])

/***************************************************************
 * dithermap
 *
 * Create a color dithering map with a given number of intensity levels.
 * Inputs:
 *    levels:              Intensity levels per primary.
 *    gamma:        Display gamma value.
 * Outputs:
 *    rgbmap:             Generated color map.
 *    divN:         "div" function for dithering.
 *    modN:         "mod" function for dithering.
 * Assumptions:
 *    rgbmap will hold levels^3 entries.
 * Algorithm:
 *    Compute gamma compensation map.
 *    N = 255.0 / (levels - 1) is number of pixel values per level.
```

```
 *      Compute rgbmap with red ramping fastest, green slower, and blue
 *      slowest (treat it as if it were rgbmap[levels][levels][levels][3]).
 *      Call make_square to get divN, modN, and magic
 *
 * Note:
 *      Call dithergb( x, y, r, g, b, levels, divN, modN, magic ) for index
 *      into rgbmap for a given color/location pair, or use
 *          rw = y % 16; cl = x % 16;
 *          DMAP(v,col,row) =def (divN[v] + (modN[v]>magic[col][row] ? 1:0))
 *          DMAP(r,cl,rw) + DMAP(g,cl,rw)*levels + DMAP(b,cl,rw)*levels^2
 *      if you don't want function call overhead.
 */
void
dithermap( levels, gamma, rgbmap, divN, modN, magic )
double gamma;
int rgbmap[][3];
int divN[256];
int modN[256];
int magic[16][16];
{
    double N;
    register int i;
    int levelsq, levelsc;
    int gammamap[256];

    for ( i = 0; i < 256; i++ )
        gammamap[i] = (int)(0.5 + 255 * pow( i / 255.0, 1.0/gamma ));

    levelsq = levels*levels;    /* squared */
    levelsc = levels*levelsq;   /* and cubed */

    N = 255.0 / (levels - 1);       /* Get size of each step */

    /*
     * Set up the color map entries.
     */
    for (i = 0; i < levelsc; i++) {
        rgbmap[i][0] = gammamap[(int)(0.5 + (i%levels) * N)];
        rgbmap[i][1] = gammamap[(int)(0.5 + ((i/levels)%levels) * N)];
        rgbmap[i][2] = gammamap[(int)(0.5 + ((i/levelsq)%levels) * N)];
    }

    make_square( N, divN, modN, magic );
}


/********************************************************************
 * TAG( bwdithermap )
 *
 * Create a b&w dithering map with a given number of intensity levels.
 * Inputs:
 *      levels:         Intensity levels.
 *      gamma:          Display gamma value.
 * Outputs:
 *      bwmap:          Generated black & white map.
 *      divN:           "div" function for dithering.
 *      modN:           "mod" function for dithering.
```

510

```
 * Assumptions:
 *      bwmap will hold levels entries.
 * Algorithm:
 *      As above.
 * Note:
 *      Call ditherbw( x, y, val, divN, modN, magic ) to get index into
 *      bwmap for a given color/location pair, or use
 *          row = y % 16; col = x % 16;
 *          divN[val] + (modN[val]>magic[col][row] ? 1 : 0)
 *      if you don't want function call overhead.
 *      On a 1-bit display, use
 *          divN[val] > magic[col][row] ? 1 : 0
 */
void
bwdithermap( levels, gamma, bwmap, divN, modN, magic )
double gamma;
int bwmap[];
int divN[256];
int modN[256];
int magic[16][16];
{
    double N;
    register int i;
    int gammamap[256];

    for ( i = 0; i < 256; i++ )
       gammamap[i] = (int)(0.5 + 255 * pow( i / 255.0, 1.0/gamma ));

    N = 255.0 / (levels - 1);    /* Get size of each step */

    /*
     * Set up the color map entries.
     */
    for(i = 0; i < levels; i++)
       bwmap[i] = gammamap[(int)(0.5 + i * N)];

    make_square( N, divN, modN, magic );
}


/***************************************************************
 * TAG( make_square )
 *
 * Build the magic square for a given number of levels.
 * Inputs:
 *      N:              Pixel values per level (255.0 / levels).
 * Outputs:
 *      divN:           Integer value of pixval / N
 *      modN:           Integer remainder between pixval and divN[pixval]*N
 *      magic:          Magic square for dithering to N sublevels.
 * Assumptions:
 *
 * Algorithm:
 *      divN[pixval] = (int)(pixval / N) maps pixval to its level.
 *      modN[pixval] = pixval - (int)(N * divN[pixval]) maps pixval to
 *      its sublevel, and is used in the dithering computation.
 *      The magic square is computed as the (modified) outer product of
```

```
 *      a 4x4 magic square with itself.
 *      magic[4*k + i][4*l + j] = (magic4x4[i][j] + magic4x4[k][l]/16.0)
 *      multiplied by an appropriate factor to get the correct dithering
 *      range.
 */
void
make_square( N, divN, modN, magic )
double N;
int divN[256];
int modN[256];
int magic[16][16] ;
{
    register int i, j, k, l;
    double magicfact;

    for ( i = 0; i < 256; i++ )
    {
      divN[i] = (int)(i / N);
      modN[i] = i - (int)(N * divN[i]);
    }
    modN[255] = 0;          /* always */

    /*
     * Expand 4x4 dither pattern to 16x16.  4x4 leaves obvious patterning,
     * and doesn't give us full intensity range (only 17 sublevels).
     *
     * magicfact is (N - 1)/16 so we get numbers in the matrix from 0 to
     * N - 1: mod N gives numbers in 0 to N - 1, don't ever want all
     * pixels incremented to the next level (this is reserved for the
     * pixel value with mod N == 0 at the next level).
     */
    magicfact = (N - 1) / 16.;
    for ( i = 0; i < 4; i++ )
      for ( j = 0; j < 4; j++ )
          for ( k = 0; k < 4; k++ )
             for ( l = 0; l < 4; l++ )
                 magic[4*k+i][4*l+j] =
                    (int)(0.5 + magic4x4[i][j] * magicfact +
                          (magic4x4[k][l] / 16.) * magicfact);
}


/******************************************************************
 * TAG( dithergb )
 *
 * Return dithered RGB value.
 * Inputs:
 *      x:          X location on screen of this pixel.
 *      y:          Y location on screen of this pixel.
 *      r, g, b:    Color at this pixel (0 - 255 range).
 *      levels:         Number of levels in this map.
 *      divN, modN: From dithermap.
 *      magic:      Magic square from dithermap.
 * Outputs:
 *      Returns color map index for dithered pixelv value.
 * Assumptions:
 *      divN, modN, magic were set up properly.
```

```
 * Algorithm:
 *      see "Note:" in dithermap comment.
 */
dithergb( x, y, r, g, b, levels, divN, modN, magic )
int divN[256];
int modN[256];
int magic[16][16];
{
    int col = x % 16, row = y % 16;

    return DMAP(r, col, row) +
        DMAP(g, col, row) * levels +
            DMAP(b, col, row) * levels*levels;
}


/******************************************************************
 * TAG( ditherbw )
 *
 * Return dithered black & white value.
 * Inputs:
 *      x:              X location on screen of this pixel.
 *      y:              Y location on screen of this pixel.
 *      val:            Intensity at this pixel (0 - 255 range).
 *      divN, modN:     From dithermap.
 *      magic:          Magic square from dithermap.
 * Outputs:
 *      Returns color map index for dithered pixel value.
 * Assumptions:
 *      divN, modN, magic were set up properly.
 * Algorithm:
 *      see "Note:" in bwdithermap comment.
 */
ditherbw( x, y, val, divN, modN, magic )
int divN[256];
int modN[256];
int magic[16][16];
{
    int col = x % 16, row = y % 16;

    return DMAP(val, col, row);
}
```

A FAST 90-DEGREE BITMAP ROTATOR

(page 84)

Sue-Ken Yap

```
/*
**      Rotate an 8x8 tile clockwise by table lookup
**      and write to destination directly.
**      Large bitmaps can be rotated an 8x8 tile at a time.
**      The extraction is done a nybble at a time to reduce the
**      size of the tables.
**
**      Input parameters:
**      src             starting address of source 8x8 tile
**      srcstep         difference in byte address between
**                      adjacent rows in source bitmap
**      dst             starting address of destination 8x8 tile
**      dststep         difference in byte address between
**                      adjacent rows in destination bitmap
*/

typedef long    bit32;

#define table(name,n)\
        static bit32 name[16] =\
        {\
                0x00000000<<n, 0x00000001<<n, 0x00000100<<n, 0x00000101<<n,\
                0x00010000<<n, 0x00010001<<n, 0x00010100<<n, 0x00010101<<n,\
                0x01000000<<n, 0x01000001<<n, 0x01000100<<n, 0x01000101<<n,\
                0x01010000<<n, 0x01010001<<n, 0x01010100<<n, 0x01010101<<n,\
        };

table(ltab0,7)
table(ltab1,6)
table(ltab2,5)
table(ltab3,4)
table(ltab4,3)
table(ltab5,2)
table(ltab6,1)
table(ltab7,0)
```

```
void rotate8x8(src, srcstep, dst, dststep)
        unsigned char    *src, *dst;
        int              srcstep, dststep;
{

        register unsigned char  *p;
        register int    pstep, lownyb, hinyb;
        register bit32  low, hi;

        low = hi = 0;

#define extract(d,t)\
        lownyb = *d & 0xf; hinyb = *d >> 4;\
        low |= t[lownyb]; hi |= t[hinyb]; d += pstep;

        p = src; pstep = srcstep;
        extract(p,ltab0) extract(p,ltab1) extract(p,ltab2) extract(p,ltab3)
        extract(p,ltab4) extract(p,ltab5) extract(p,ltab6) extract(p,ltab7)


#define unpack(d,w)\
        *d = w & 0xff;            d += pstep;\
        *d = (w >> 8) & 0xff;    d += pstep;\
        *d = (w >> 16) & 0xff;   d += pstep;\
        *d = (w >> 24) & 0xff;

        p = dst; pstep = dststep;
        unpack(p,low) p += pstep; unpack(p,hi)
}
```

ROTATION OF RUN-LENGTH ENCODED IMAGE DATA

(page 86)

Jeff Holt

```
/**********************************************************************
 *
 *       This file contains routines to perform 90 degree rotation/
 *       row/column major transposition of runlength encoded data
 *       directly, without expanding the data.
 *       For input data the code expects a buffer consisting of
 *       unsigned shorts as follows :
 *
 *       wtf      - (short) words of data for first raster line
 *       color1
 *       run1
 *       color2
 *       run2
 *       .
 *       .
 *       runn
 *       colorn           where wtf = n * 2
 *       wtf
 *       color1
 *       run1
 *       etc
 *
 *       The code depends on the integrity of the data, and does not
 *       check for consistency. The sum of the runs should add to exactly
 *       the number of pixels per scan line, or internal memory may be
 *       corrupted. Checking for data integrity could easily be added,
 *       however this will affect performance.
 *
 **********************************************************************/

extern unsigned char *malloc(), *realloc(), *calloc();

typedef unsigned short   ushort;


#define MALLOCF          -1       /* return error code */
```

```c
struct _ROT_s                    /* rotate data structure */
{
        int     pix_pl;
        int     no_lines;

        int     *init_arrays;    /* addr of initial set of rl arrays */

struct  lstruct_s *ls_start;     /* array of edge structures */
struct  lstruct_s *ls_end;       /* points to last edge structure */
}
        rd;

struct  lstruct_s        /* "edge" structure to hold output line info */
{
        ushort  acc_rl;          /* accumulating runlength */
        ushort  acc_value;       /* value being accumulated */

        ushort  *rlptr;          /* ->next runlength position */
        ushort  *rlend;          /* last addr for current array */
        int     *array;          /* first output runlength array */
        int     *csa;            /* current output runlength array */
        int     wtf;             /* accumulating # words of runlengths */
};

#define RLWORDS 100     /* shorts in runlength array NOTE : MUST BE EVEN */

/***********************************************************************
 *
 *      int     _ROT_10(iptr,pix_pl,no_lines,optr,trans)
 *      ushort  *iptr;          ptr to input buffer
 *      ushort  **optr;         returned pointer to output buffer
 *      int     pix_pl;         pixels per line in input image
 *      int     no_lines;       number of lines in input image
 *      int     rot;            true => transpose, else rotate 90
 *
 *      This function takes runlength encoded 16 bit data in the above
 *      format, and returns either rotated or transposed data (depending
 *      on the flag "trans"). A buffer is malloced for the output data
 *      and the address of this buffer is returned in "obuff".
 *
 ***********************************************************************/

int     _ROT_10(iptr,pix_pl,no_lines,optr,trans)
ushort  *iptr;
ushort  **optr;
int     pix_pl;
int     no_lines;
int     trans;
{
        int     status,i;
        int     wtf;
        int     line;

        int     tot_words;       /* total words of rotated data */
        int     shorts;          /* shorts in line of rotated data */
```

```
            int     obytes;            /* size of output buffer */
            unsigned short  *obuff;
            unsigned short  *wtfptr;

    /*
       initialize line routines
    */
            printf("Starting rotation....\n");

            status = _ROT_10_init(&rd,pix_pl,no_lines);
            if(status)
                    return(status);

            wtf = *iptr++;
            status = _ROT_10_prime(&rd,iptr);
            if(status)
                    return(status);

            iptr += wtf;

            for ( i=1 ; i < no_lines ; i++ )
            {
                    wtf = *iptr++;
                    if ( (i & 0xFFC0) == i )
                    {
                            printf("\rprocessing line %d",i+1);
                    }
                    status = _ROT_10_line(&rd,iptr);
                    if(status)
                            return(status);

                    iptr += wtf;
            }
            printf("\rProcessed %d lines         \n",i);

            status = _ROT_10_rotate(&rd,&tot_words);
            if(status)
                    return(status);

            printf("Finished rotation, move data...\n");

    /*
      allocate buffer - NOTE: may want to deallocate input buffer here
    */
            obytes = (tot_words + pix_pl) * 2;
            obuff = (unsigned short *)malloc(obytes);
            if ( ! obuff )
                    return(MALLOCF);

            *optr = obuff;
```

518

```
/*
  move the data
*/
        for ( i = 0 ; i < pix_pl ; i++ )
        {
                wtfptr = obuff++;

                if ( trans )
                        line = i;
                else
                        line = pix_pl - i - 1;

                shorts = _ROT_10_get_line(&rd,obuff,line);
                if(status)
                        return(status);

                *wtfptr = shorts;

                obuff = &obuff[shorts];
        }
        printf("Finished rotation\n");

        return(0);
}
/***********************************************************************
*
*       int     _ROT_10_init(me,pix_pl,no_lines)
*       struct _ROT_s   *me;
*       int     pix_pl,no_lines;
*
*       This routine initializes the rotation data structures.
*       It initializes the rotate data structure specified, allocates
*       an array of edge structures, and initial buffers to store
*       output runlengths.
*
***********************************************************************/
int     _ROT_10_init(me,pix_pl,no_lines)
struct _ROT_s   *me;
{
        struct lstruct_s
                *ls_start,              /* ptr to start of array of structs */
                *ls_end,                /* ptr to end of array of structs */
                *lsptr;                 /* moves through above array */

        int     size;
        int     *lptr;
        int     *mptr,*next;

        me->pix_pl = pix_pl;
        me->no_lines = no_lines;
```

```
/*
    allocate data structures :
        o lstruct array : accumulating runlengths and control
        o initial acc runlength arrays
*/

        lptr = (int *)malloc(pix_pl*sizeof(struct lstruct_s));
        if ( ! lptr )
                return(MALLOCF);                 /* couldnt get it */
        me->ls_start = (struct lstruct_s *)lptr;

        lptr = (int *)malloc( (RLWORDS*2 + 4) * pix_pl );
        if ( ! lptr )
                return(MALLOCF);
        me->init_arrays = lptr;

/*
    initialize data structs :
        init edge structure array
        (rl arrays are dont care)
*/
        ls_start = me->ls_start;
        ls_end = &ls_start[pix_pl];
        me->ls_end = ls_end;

        lptr = me->init_arrays;
        for ( lsptr = ls_start ; lsptr < ls_end ; lsptr++ )
        {
                *lptr = 0;                          /* zero linkage pointer */
                lsptr->array = lptr;                /* initial array */
                lsptr->csa = lptr;                  /* current sub-array */

                lptr++;                             /* skip linkage */
                lsptr->rlptr = (ushort *)lptr;      /* first rl slot */

                lptr = &lptr[RLWORDS/2];                   /* skip to next sub */
                lsptr->rlend = (ushort *)lptr;      /* = end +1 of prev */

                lsptr->wtf = 0;

        }
        return(0);
}

/*****************************************************************************
 *
 *      int        _ROT_10_prime(me,data)
 *      struct  _ROT_s *me;
 *      unsigned int *data;
 *
 *      This routine proceses the first line of raster data,
 *      initializing acc_rl and acc_value in the edge structures
 *
 *****************************************************************************/
```

```c
int       _ROT_10_prime(me,rlptr)
struct _ROT_s *me;
ushort  *rlptr;
{
        struct lstruct_s  *lsptr;        /* scan edge array */
        struct lstruct_s  *lsend;        /* end of scan */

        int       pixel;
        int       run;

        lsptr = me->ls_start;
        lsend = me->ls_end;

        while ( lsptr < lsend )
        {
                pixel = *rlptr++;
                run = *rlptr++;
                while ( run-- > 0 )
                {
                        lsptr->acc_value = pixel;        /* value to accum */
                        lsptr->acc_rl = 0;               /* 1 less than run */
                        lsptr++;
                }
        }
        return(0);
}
/**********************************************************************
 *
 *        int       _ROT_10_line(me,data)
 *        struct _ROT_s *me;
 *        unsigned int *data;
 *
 *        This routine proceses one line of raster data, unwinding runlengths
 *        and rewinding in the other direction.
 *
 **********************************************************************/

int       _ROT_10_line(me,rlptr)
struct _ROT_s *me;
ushort  *rlptr;
{
        struct lstruct_s  *lsptr;        /* scan edge array */
        struct lstruct_s  *lsend;        /* end of scan */
        int       *mptr;                 /* malloc data ptr */

        int       pixel;
        int       run;

        lsptr = me->ls_start;
        lsend = me->ls_end;
```

```
                while ( lsptr < lsend )
                {
                        pixel = *rlptr++;
                        run = *rlptr++;
                        while ( run-- > 0 )
                        {
                                lsptr->acc_rl++;
                                if ( pixel != lsptr->acc_value )        /* if diff */
                                {
                                        if ( lsptr->rlptr == lsptr->rlend )
                                        {
                                                mptr = (int *)malloc(RLWORDS*2 + 4);
                                                if ( ! mptr )
                                                        return(MALLOCF);

                                                lsptr->wtf += RLWORDS;
                                                *lsptr->csa = (int)mptr; /* link */
                                                lsptr->csa = mptr;
                                                *mptr = 0;

                                                lsptr->rlptr = (ushort *)++mptr;
                                                lsptr->rlend = (ushort *)&mptr[RLWORDS/2];
                                        }
                                        *lsptr->rlptr++ = lsptr->acc_value;
                                        *lsptr->rlptr++ = lsptr->acc_rl;

                                        lsptr->acc_value = pixel;
                                        lsptr->acc_rl = 0;
                                }
                                lsptr++;
                        }
                }
                return(0);
}

/********************************************************************
*
*       int     _ROT_10_rotate(me,size)
*       struct _ROT_s *me;
*       int     *size;
*
*       This routine cleans up and gets ready to return the data to the
*       caller :
*          o writes the last runlength into the buffer array
*          o passes back total image size as number of short words
*          o initialize return edge pointer.
*
********************************************************************/
int     _ROT_10_rotate(me,isize)
struct _ROT_s   *me;
        int     *isize;
{
        struct lstruct_s  *lsptr,*lsend;        /* scan edge array */
        int     *mptr;
        ushort  *sptr;                  /* temp pointer */

        int     tot_wtf;
```

522

```
        tot_wtf = 0;

        lsptr = me->ls_start;
        lsend = me->ls_end;
        while ( lsptr < lsend )
        {
                if ( lsptr->rlptr == lsptr->rlend )
                {
                        mptr = (int *)malloc(12);
                        if ( ! mptr )
                                return(MALLOCF);

                        *lsptr->csa = (int)mptr;          /* link */
                        lsptr->csa = mptr;
                        *mptr = 0;
                        lsptr->rlptr = (ushort *)++mptr;
                        lsptr->rlend = (ushort *)&mptr[2];
                        lsptr->wtf += RLWORDS;
                }
                *lsptr->rlptr++ = lsptr->acc_value;
                *lsptr->rlptr++ = lsptr->acc_rl + 1;

                sptr = (ushort *)(lsptr->csa + 1);

                lsptr->wtf += lsptr->rlptr - sptr;
                tot_wtf += lsptr->wtf;
                lsptr++;
        }
        *isize = tot_wtf;
        return(0);
}
/***********************************************************************
 *
 *      int     _ROT_10_get_line(me,buff,lno)
 *      struct _ROT_s *me;
 *      ushort  *buff;
 *      int     lno;
 *
 *      This routine copies one line of data into the passed buffer, and
 *      returns the number of short words written to the output buffer.
 *      lno is the line number of data to be returned - [0,pix_pl - 1]
 *
 ***********************************************************************/

int     _ROT_10_get_line(me,sbuff,lno)
struct _ROT_s *me;
ushort *sbuff;
int     lno;
{
        int     wtf,j;
        struct lstruct_s *lsptr;
        int     *mptr;
        ushort *rlptr;
        ushort *start;
```

```
        lsptr = &me->ls_start[lno];                    /* return pointer */

        start = sbuff;
        wtf = lsptr->wtf;                              /* words of data */

        for ( mptr = lsptr->array ; mptr ; mptr = (int *)*mptr )
        {
                rlptr = (ushort *)&mptr[1];
                if ( *mptr )        /* full array */
                {
                        for ( j = 0 ; j < RLWORDS ; j++ )
                                *sbuff++ = *rlptr++;

                        wtf -= RLWORDS;
                }
                else
                {
                        for ( j = 0 ; j < wtf ; j++ )
                                *sbuff++ = *rlptr++;
                }
        }
        return(sbuff - start);
}
```

COMPUTING THE AREA, THE CIRCUMFERENCE, AND THE GENUS OF A BINARY DIGITAL IMAGE

(page 107)

Hanspeter Bieri and Andreas Kohler

```
/*****************************************************
Compute the area, the circumference and the genus
(Euler number) of a digital image.
All input is supposed to come from a file which has
to be specified as a commandline parameter.
*****************************************************/

#include <stdio.h>
#include <stdlib.h>
#include <malloc.h>

typedef short bool;
#define TRUE  1
#define FALSE 0


int main(int argc, char *argv[])
{
  long  N[3],          /* Number of vertices, sides, extents  */
        area,          /* Area of the digital image           */
        circumf,       /* Circumference of the digital image  */
        genus;         /* Genus of the digital image          */
  void  comp_ver_sid_ext(long *, char *);

  /* Exit, if there is no filename given on the command line */
  if (argc < 2) { /* no arguments given */
    fprintf(stderr, "ERROR: No filename specified\n\n");
    exit(1);
    };

  /* Initialization of variables */
  N[0] = N[1] = N[2] = area = circumf = genus = 0;

  /* Compute number of vertices, sides and extents */
  comp_ver_sid_ext(N, argv[1]);

  /* Compute area, circumference and genus */
  area = N[2];
  circumf = 2*N[1] - 4*N[2];
  genus = N[0] - N[1] + N[2];
```

```
/* Output of the results on stdout */
printf("\n\nThe results for the tested image are:\n");
printf("   Area          :  %10ld\n", area);
printf("   Circumference :  %10ld\n", circumf);
printf("   Genus         :  %10ld\n", genus);

} /* main() */



/****************************************************************
   Function for reading in the imagefile and computing the
   values N[0], N[1] and N[2]. The file which contains the
   digital image must have the following structure:
   #rows #columns          (=header)
   row[0]                  (length = #columns)
   row[1]
      .
      .
      .
   row[#rows]
****************************************************************/
void comp_ver_sid_ext(long *N_array, char *filename)
{
  long cols, rows;          /* Number of columns and rows             */
  bool *one_row=NULL,       /* One row of the digital image           */
       *P_actual=NULL,      /* vertex components of actual row        */
       *P_next=NULL,        /* vertex components of next row          */
       *V_actual=NULL,      /* vertical components of actual row      */
       *V_next=NULL,        /*    "        "      of next    "        */
       *H_actual=NULL,      /* horizontal components of actual row    */
       *H_next=NULL;        /*    "        "      of next    "        */
  bool *temp=NULL;          /* auxiliary pointer for swapping arrays  */
  long I, J;                /* Variables for indexing arrays          */
  FILE *datafile;

  /* Read number of rows and number of columns from sdtin */
  datafile = fopen(filename, "r");
  fscanf(datafile, "%ld %ld", &rows, &cols);

  /* Allocate space for the arrays */
  one_row  = (bool *) malloc((cols+1) * sizeof(bool));
  P_actual = (bool *) malloc((cols+1) * sizeof(bool));
  P_next   = (bool *) malloc((cols+1) * sizeof(bool));
  V_actual = (bool *) malloc((cols+1) * sizeof(bool));
  V_next   = (bool *) malloc((cols+1) * sizeof(bool));
  H_actual = (bool *) malloc((cols+1) * sizeof(bool));
  H_next   = (bool *) malloc((cols+1) * sizeof(bool));

  /* Initialize above arrays as all FALSE. Not necessary but save! */
  for (I=0; I <= cols; I++) {
    one_row[I]  = FALSE;
    P_actual[I] = FALSE;
    P_next[I]   = FALSE;
    V_actual[I] = FALSE;
    V_next[I]   = FALSE;
    H_actual[I] = FALSE;
    H_next[I]   = FALSE;
  };
```

```
/* Do all the computation */
for (I = 0; I <= rows; I++) {
  /* Read row I into one_row. For last row all items are FALSE */
  if (I < rows)
    for (J = 0; J < cols; fscanf(datafile, "%hd", &one_row[J++]));
  else
    for (J = 0; J < cols; one_row[J++] = FALSE);


  /* Scan over row I of the digital image */
  for (J = 0; J <= cols; J++) {
    if (one_row[J]) {  /* the pixel is black */
      N_array[0] += 1;
      N_array[1] += 2;
      N_array[2] += 1;
      P_actual[J+1] = TRUE;
      V_actual[J+1] = TRUE;
      P_next[J]  = TRUE;
      H_next[J]  = TRUE;
      P_next[J+1] = TRUE;
      }
    else {    /* the pixel is white */
      if (P_actual[J]) N_array[0] += 1;
      if (H_actual[J]) N_array[1] += 1;
      if (V_actual[J]) N_array[1] += 1;
      }
    };

  /* Copy next-arrays to actual-arrays */
  if (I < rows) {  /* not for last pass */
    temp = P_actual;
    P_actual = P_next;
    P_next = temp;
    temp = V_actual;
    V_actual = V_next;
    V_next = temp;
    temp = H_actual;
    H_actual = H_next;
    H_next = temp;

    /* Reinitialize all next-arrays to FALSE */
    for (J = 0; J <= cols; J++)
      P_next[J] = V_next[J] = H_next[J] = FALSE;
    }
  }
}
```

EFFICIENT INVERSE COLOR MAP COMPUTATION

(page 116)

Spencer W. Thomas

```
/*
 * inv_cmap.c - Compute an inverse colormap.
 *
 * Author:  Spencer W. Thomas
 *          EECS Dept.
 *          University of Michigan
 */

#include <math.h>
#include <stdio.h>

/******************************************************************
 * inv_cmap_1 - Compute an inverse colormap efficiently (version 1).
 *
 * Inputs:
 *   colors:    Number of colors in the forward colormap.
 *   colormap:  The forward colormap.
 *   bits:      Number of quantization bits.  The inverse
 *              colormap will have (2^bits)^3 entries.
 *   dist_buf:  An array of (2^bits)^3 long integers to be
 *              used as scratch space.
 * Outputs:
 *   rgbmap:    The output inverse colormap.  The entry
 *              rgbmap[(r<<(2*bits)) + (g<<bits) + b]
 *              is the colormap entry that is closest to the
 *              (quantized) color (r,g,b).
 * Assumptions:
 *      Quantization is performed by right shift (low order bits are
 *      truncated).  Thus, the distance to a quantized color is
 *      actually measured to the color at the center of the cell
 *      (i.e., to r+.5, g+.5, b+.5, if (r,g,b) is a quantized color).
 * Algorithm:
 *      Uses a "distance buffer" algorithm.  See the Gem
 *      "Efficient Inverse Colormap Computation."
 */
void inv_cmap_1( colors, colormap, bits, dist_buf, rgbmap )
int colors, bits;
unsigned char *colormap[3], *rgbmap;
unsigned long *dist_buf;
```

528

```
{
    register unsigned long *dp;
    register unsigned char *rgbp;
    register long bdist, bxx;
    register int b, i;
    int nbits = 8 - bits;
    register int colormax = 1 << bits;
    register long xsqr = 1 << (2 * nbits);
    int x = 1 << nbits;
    int rinc, ginc, binc, r, g;
    long rdist, gdist, rxx, gxx;

    for ( i = 0; i < colors; i++ ) {
        rdist = colormap[0][i] - x/2;
        gdist = colormap[1][i] - x/2;
        bdist = colormap[2][i] - x/2;
        rdist = rdist*rdist + gdist*gdist + bdist*bdist;

        rinc = 2 * (xsqr - (colormap[0][i] << nbits));
        ginc = 2 * (xsqr - (colormap[1][i] << nbits));
        binc = 2 * (xsqr - (colormap[2][i] << nbits));
        dp = dist_buf;
        rgbp = rgbmap;
        for ( r = 0, rxx = rinc;
              r < colormax;
              rdist += rxx, r++, rxx += xsqr + xsqr )
            for ( g = 0, gdist = rdist, gxx = ginc;
                  g < colormax;
                  gdist += gxx, g++, gxx += xsqr + xsqr )
            for ( b = 0, bdist = gdist, bxx = binc;
                  b < colormax;
                  bdist += bxx, b++, dp++, rgbp++, bxx += xsqr + xsqr ) {
                if ( i == 0 || *dp > bdist ) {
                    *dp = bdist;
                    *rgbp = i;
                }
            }
    }
}

/* Variables used to communicate between the "loop" subroutines below.
 * If I had a good macro facility, I'd do it all in-line and wouldn't
 * need these.  It would probably be more efficient, too.
 */
static int bcenter, gcenter, rcenter;      /* Quantized color. */
static long gdist, rdist, cdist;           /* Current distances. */
static long cbinc, cginc, crinc;           /* Increment at starting point. */
static unsigned long *gdp, *rdp, *cdp;     /* Pointers into distbuf. */
static unsigned char *grgbp, *rrgbp, *crgbp;   /* Ptr into rgbmap. */
static int gstride, rstride;               /* Step one in green, red. */
static long x, xsqr, colormax;             /* Index of this color. */
static int cindex;
```

```
/**********************************************************************
 * inv_cmap_2 - Compute an inverse colormap more efficiently (version 2).
 *
 * Inputs:
 *      As above.
 * Outputs:
 *      As above.
 * Assumptions:
 *      As above.
 * Algorithm:
 *      Uses a "distance buffer" algorithm.
 *      Distances are computed "outward" from each color.
 *      See the gem "Efficient Inverse Colormap Computation."
 */
void inv_cmap_2( colors, colormap, bits, dist_buf, rgbmap )
int colors, bits;
unsigned char *colormap[3], *rgbmap;
unsigned long *dist_buf;
{
    int nbits = 8 - bits;

    colormax = 1 << bits;
    x = 1 << nbits;
    xsqr = 1 << (2 * nbits);

    /* Compute "strides" for accessing the arrays. */
    gstride = colormax;
    rstride = colormax * colormax;

    maxfill( dist_buf, colormax );

    for ( cindex = 0; cindex < colors; cindex++ ) {
        /* The initial position is the cell containing the colormap
         * entry.  We get this by quantizing the colormap values.
         */
        rcenter = colormap[0][cindex] >> nbits;
        gcenter = colormap[1][cindex] >> nbits;
        bcenter = colormap[2][cindex] >> nbits;

        rdist = colormap[0][cindex] - (rcenter * x + x/2);
        gdist = colormap[1][cindex] - (gcenter * x + x/2);
        cdist = colormap[2][cindex] - (bcenter * x + x/2);
        cdist = rdist*rdist + gdist*gdist + cdist*cdist;

        crinc = 2 * ((rcenter + 1) * xsqr - (colormap[0][cindex] * x));
        cginc = 2 * ((gcenter + 1) * xsqr - (colormap[1][cindex] * x));
        cbinc = 2 * ((bcenter + 1) * xsqr - (colormap[2][cindex] * x));

        /* Array starting points. */
        cdp = dist_buf + rcenter * rstride + gcenter * gstride + bcenter;
        crgbp = rgbmap + rcenter * rstride + gcenter * gstride + bcenter;

        (void)redloop();
    }
}
```

```
/* redloop -- loop up and down from red center. */
int redloop()
{
    int detect, r, first;
    long txsqr = xsqr + xsqr;
    static int here, min, max;
    static long rxx;

    detect = 0;

    /* Basic loop up. */
    for ( r = rcenter, rdist = cdist, rxx = crinc,
            rdp = cdp, rrgbp = crgbp, first = 1;
          r < colormax;
          r++, rdp += rstride, rrgbp += rstride,
            rdist += rxx, rxx += txsqr, first = 0 ) {
        if ( greenloop( first ) )
            detect = 1;
        else if ( detect )
            break;
    }

    /* Basic loop down. */
    for ( r = rcenter - 1, rxx = crinc - txsqr, rdist = cdist - rxx,
            rdp = cdp - rstride, rrgbp = crgbp - rstride, first = 1;
          r >= 0;
          r--, rdp -= rstride, rrgbp -= rstride,
            rxx -= txsqr, rdist -= rxx, first = 0 ) {
        if ( greenloop( first ) )
            detect = 1;
        else if ( detect )
            break;
    }

    return detect;
}

/* greenloop -- loop up and down from green center. */
int
greenloop( restart )
{
    int detect, g, first;
    long txsqr = xsqr + xsqr;
    static int here, min, max;
    static int prevmax, prevmin;        /* For tracking min and max. */
    int thismax, thismin;
    static long ginc, gxx, gcdist;      /* "gc" variables maintain correct */
    static unsigned long *gcdp;         /* values for bcenter position, */
    static unsigned char *gcrgbp;       /* despite changes by blueloop */
                                        /* to gdist, gdp, grgbp. */

    /* Red loop restarted, reset variables to "center" position. */
    if ( restart ) {
        here = gcenter;
        min = 0;
        max = colormax - 1;
```

```
            ginc = cginc;
            prevmax = 0;
            prevmin = colormax;
        }

        /* Finding actual min and max on this line. */
        thismin = min;
        thismax = max;
        detect = 0;

        /* Basic loop up. */
        for ( g = here, gcdist = gdist = rdist, gxx = ginc,
                gcdp = gdp = rdp, gcrgbp = grgbp = rrgbp, first = 1;
              g <= max;
              g++, gdp += gstride, gcdp += gstride,
               grgbp += gstride, gcrgbp += gstride,
               gdist += gxx, gcdist += gxx, gxx += txsqr, first = 0 ) {
            if ( blueloop( first ) ) {
                if ( !detect ) {
                    /* Remember here and associated data! */
                    if ( g > here ) {
                        here = g;
                        rdp = gcdp;
                        rrgbp = gcrgbp;
                        rdist = gcdist;
                        ginc = gxx;
                        thismin = here;
                    }
                    detect = 1;
                }
            }
            else if ( detect ) {
                thismax = g - 1;
                break;
            }
        }

        /* Basic loop down. */
        for ( g = here - 1, gxx = ginc - txsqr, gcdist = gdist = rdist - gxx,
                gcdp = gdp = rdp - gstride, gcrgbp = grgbp = rrgbp - gstride,
                first = 1;
              g >= min;
              g--, gdp -= gstride, gcdp -= gstride,
               grgbp -= gstride, gcrgbp -= gstride,
               gxx -= txsqr, gdist -= gxx, gcdist -= gxx, first = 0 ) {
            if ( blueloop( first ) ) {
                if ( !detect ) {
                    /* Remember here! */
                    here = g;
                    rdp = gcdp;
                    rrgbp = gcrgbp;
                    rdist = gcdist;
                    ginc = gxx;
                    thismax = here;
                    detect = 1;
                }
            }
```

```
        }
        else if ( detect ) {
            thismin = g + 1;
            break;
        }
    }

    /* If we saw something, update the edge trackers.  Only
     * tracks edges that are "shrinking" (min increasing, max
     * decreasing.
     */
    if ( detect ) {
        if ( thismax < prevmax )
            max = thismax;
        prevmax = thismax;

        if ( thismin > prevmin )
            min = thismin;
        prevmin = thismin;
    }

    return detect;
}

/* blueloop -- loop up and down from blue center. */
int blueloop( restart )
{
    int detect;
    /* These are all registers on a Sun 3.  Your mileage may differ. */
    register unsigned long *dp;
    register unsigned char *rgbp;
    register long bdist, bxx;
    register int b, i = cindex;
    register long txsqr = xsqr + xsqr;
    register int lim;          /* For min & max, avoid extra registers. */
    static int here, min, max;
    static int prevmin, prevmax;    /* For tracking min and max. */
    int thismin, thismax;
    static long binc;

    if ( restart ) {
        here = bcenter;
        min = 0;
        max = colormax - 1;
        binc = cbinc;
        prevmin = colormax;
        prevmax = 0;
    }

    detect = 0;
    thismin = min;
    thismax = max;

    /* Basic loop up. */
```

```
/* First loop just finds first applicable cell. */
for ( b = here, bdist = gdist, bxx = binc, dp = gdp, rgbp = grgbp,
        lim = max;
      b <= lim;
      b++, dp++, rgbp++, bdist += bxx, bxx += txsqr ) {
    if ( *dp > bdist ) {
        /* Remember new 'here' and associated data! */
        if ( b > here ) {
            here = b;
            gdp = dp;
            grgbp = rgbp;
            gdist = bdist;
            binc = bxx;
            thismin = here;
        }
        detect = 1;
        break;
    }
}
/* Second loop fills in a run of closer cells. */
for ( ;
      b <= lim;
      b++, dp++, rgbp++, bdist += bxx, bxx += txsqr ) {
    if ( *dp > bdist ) {
        *dp = bdist;
        *rgbp = i;
    } else {
        thismax = b - 1;
        break;
    }
}


/* Basic loop down. */
/* Do initializations here, since the 'find' loop might not get
 * executed.
 */
lim = min;
b = here - 1;
bxx = binc - txsqr;
bdist = gdist - bxx;
dp = gdp - 1;
rgbp = grgbp - 1;
/* The 'find' loop is executed only if we didn't already find
 * something.
 */
if ( !detect )
    for ( ;
          b >= lim;
          b--, dp--, rgbp--, bxx -= txsqr, bdist -= bxx ) {
        if ( *dp > bdist ) {
            /* Remember here! */
            /* No test for b against here necessary because b <
             * here by definition.
             */
            here = b;
            gdp = dp;
```

```
                grgbp = rgbp;
                gdist = bdist;
                binc = bxx;
                thismax = here;
                detect = 1;
                break;
            }
        }
    /* The 'update' loop. */
    for ( ;
            b >= lim;
            b--, dp--, rgbp--, bxx -= txsqr, bdist -= bxx ) {
        if ( *dp > bdist ) {
            *dp = bdist;
            *rgbp = i;
        } else {
            thismin = b + 1;
            break;
        }
    }
    }

    /* If we saw something, update the edge trackers. */
    if ( detect ) {
        /* Only tracks edges that are "shrinking" (min increasing, max
         * decreasing).
         */
        if ( thismax < prevmax )
            max = thismax;
        if ( thismin > prevmin )
            min = thismin;

        /* Remember the min and max values. */
        prevmax = thismax;
        prevmin = thismin;
    }

    return detect;
}

/* Fill a buffer with the largest unsigned long. */
maxfill( buffer, side )
unsigned long *buffer;
long side;
{
    register unsigned long maxv = ~0L;
    register long i;
    register unsigned long *bp;

    for ( i = colormax * colormax * colormax, bp = buffer;
            i > 0;
            i--, bp++ )
        *bp = maxv;
}
```

A RANDOM COLOR MAP
ANIMATION ALGORITHM

(page 134)

Ken Musgrave

```
/* copyright Ken Musgrave */
/* March 1985 */

/* ran.ramp.c */

/**********************************************************************
*
*     Usage: ran.ramp [ -g ] [ -z ]
*
*     Performs random continuous changes to the color map of the AED512.
*
*     The idea is to use three DDA's with endpoint input from a random
* number generator.  The three DDA's generate random sawtooth waves
* of values for red, green, and blue.  These waves of values are pushed
* through the lookup table from entry 254 down to entry 0.
*
*     NOTE:   Entry 255 remains black.
*
********************************************************************** /

#include <stdio.h>
#include <ctype.h>
#include <signal.h>

#define TRUE    1
#define FALSE   0

#define MAXENTRY            256
#define MAXINDEX            255
#define DELAY              8

#define MULTIPLIER 25173
#define INCREMENT  13849
#define MODULUS        65535
```

```c
/*
 *  pseudo-random number generator; period 65536; requires seed between
 *  0 and 65535; returns random numbers between 0 and 65536.
 */
#define RANDOM(x)   (MULTIPLIER * x + INCREMENT) & MODULUS

                                    /* signal variables */
int         quit = FALSE;
int         stop = FALSE;

                                    /* variables for color DDAs */
float       ry1, ry2, gy1, gy2, by1, by2, rinc, ginc, binc,
            r_xsteps, g_xsteps, b_xsteps;
int                 r_xcount, g_xcount, b_xcount;

                                    /* user input variables */
int                 seed, maxsteps;

                                    /* arrays for color lookup table values */
unsigned char r[MAXENTRY], g[MAXENTRY], b[MAXENTRY];

main ( argc, argv )

int         argc;
char        *argv[];

{

    register int                i;

    int                         reply, delay;

                                    /* signal functions, see below */
    int                 inter();
    int                 suspend();
printf("Please enter seed:   (0-100)\n");
scanf("%d", &seed );
                                    /* scale "seed" to range 0 - 65535 */
seed = (int) seed * 655.35;

printf("Please enter maximum length of color ramp:   (10-100)\n");
scanf("%d", &maxsteps );

r_xcount = r_xsteps = g_xcount = g_xsteps = b_xcount = b_xsteps = 0;
ry2 = gy2 = by2 = 0;

fb_init();

                                    /* if specified, set initial map option */
if ( argc == 2 )
    {

                                    /* check for -g option for gray scale */
```

537

```
if ( argv[1][0] == '-' && argv[1][1] == 'g' )
        {
        for ( i=0; i<MAXINDEX; i++ )
             r[i] = g[i] = b[i] = i;
        r[MAXINDEX] = g[MAXINDEX] = b[MAXINDEX] = 0;
        }
                                    /* check for -z option for zebra scale */
else if ( argv[1][0] == '-' && argv[1][1] == 'z' )
        {
        for ( i=0; i<MAXINDEX; i+=4 )
             {
             r[i] = r[i+1] = g[i] = g[i+1] = b[i] = b[i+1] = i*4 /5;
             r[i+2] = r[i+3] = g[i+2] = g[i+3] = b[i+2] = b[i+3] = i*4 /5 +51;
             }
        r[MAXINDEX] = g[MAXINDEX] = b[MAXINDEX] = 0;
        }
    }
else
                                    /* initialize the color map to black */
    for ( i=0; i<MAXINDEX; i++ )
        r[i] = g[i] = b[i] = 0;

fb_setmap(0, MAXINDEX, r, g, b);

while (!quit)
    {
                                    /* suspend program execution on control-Z */
    if (stop)
        {
        fb_done();
        printf("\nSave lookup table? (y/n) ");
        while ( isspace( reply = getchar() ) );
        if ( reply == 'y' )
             save_lut();
        kill(getpid(), SIGSTOP);
        stop = FALSE;
        fb_init();
        }
                                    /* move each entry in color
                                       map arrays down one place */
    for ( i=0; i<(MAXINDEX -1); i++)
        {
        r[i] = r[i+1];
        g[i] = g[i+1];
        b[i] = b[i+1];
        }
                                    /* get new high color map entries */
    r[MAXINDEX -1] = dda_red();
    g[MAXINDEX -1] = dda_green();
    b[MAXINDEX -1] = dda_blue();

                                    /* send new color maps to the AED */
    for (delay = 0; delay < DELAY ; delay++)
             fb_setmap(0, MAXINDEX, r, g, b);
```

```
            }
        fb_done();
}
```

```
inter()                                    /* function for halting program with
{                                             control–C  */
    quit = TRUE;
}
```

```
suspend()                                  /* function for suspending program with
{                                             control–Z  */
    stop = TRUE;
}
```

```
/*

 * produces random ramps in intensity for the red portion of the color

 * lookup table

 */

dda_red()
{
    register int   temp;

    if ( r_xcount >= (int) r_xsteps )      /* if at end of ramp... */
    {
                                           /* make the end of last ramp the
                                              beginning of next ramp */
        ry1 = ry2;
                                           /* define end of next ramp */
        seed = RANDOM(seed);
                                           /* assign a new (scaled) end point */
        ry2 = MAXINDEX * ( seed / 65535.0 );
        seed = RANDOM(seed);
                                           /* get a new ramp length */
        r_xsteps = ( maxsteps * ( seed / 65535.0 ) );
                                           /* find the intensity increment per step */
        if ( r_xsteps != 0 )
            rinc = ( ry2 – ry1 ) / r_xsteps;
        else
            rinc = 0;
        r_xcount = 0;
    }
```

```c
        temp  =  (int)  ry1;
        ry1  +=  rinc;
        r_xcount++;
        return  temp;
}

    /*

    * produces random ramps in intensity for the green portion of the color

    * lookup table

    * /

dda_green()
{

        register int    temp;

        if ( g_xcount >= (int) g_xsteps )
        {
                                        /* make the end of last ramp the
                                           beginning of next ramp * /
            gy1  =  gy2;
                                        /* define end of next ramp * /
            seed  =  RANDOM(seed);
            gy2  =    MAXINDEX  *  ( seed  / 65535.0 );
            seed  =  RANDOM(seed);
            g_xsteps  = ( maxsteps  *  ( seed  / 65535.0 ) );
                                        /* find the intensity increment per step * /
            if ( g_xsteps != 0 )
                    ginc  = ( gy2 – gy1 )  / g_xsteps;
            else
                    ginc  =  0;
            g_xcount  =  0;
        }
        temp  =  (int) gy1;
        gy1  +=  ginc;
        g_xcount++;
        return  temp;
}

    /*

    * produces random ramps in intensity for the blue portion of the color

    * lookup table

    * /

dda_blue()
{
```

```c
        register int    temp;

        if ( b_xcount >= (int) b_xsteps )
        {
                                            /* make the end of last ramp the
                                                beginning of next ramp */
                by1 = by2;
                                            /* define end of next ramp */
                seed = RANDOM(seed);
                by2 =   MAXINDEX * ( seed  / 65535.0 );
                seed = RANDOM(seed);
                b_xsteps = ( maxsteps * ( seed  / 65535.0 ) );
                                            /* find the intensity increment per step */
                if ( b_xsteps != 0 )
                     binc = ( by2 - by1 ) / b_xsteps;
                else
                     binc = 0;
                b_xcount = 0;
        }
        temp = (int) by1;
        by1 += binc;
        b_xcount++;
        return temp;
}


                                            /* save the lookup table to a file */
save_lut()
    {

    FILE            *fp, *fopen();
    char            filename[40];
    int             i;

    getchar();                              /* read leading newline char */
    printf("Enter filename for lookup table:   ");
    gets( filename );
    fp = fopen( filename, "w" );

    for ( i=0; i<MAXINDEX; i++ )
            fprintf( fp, "%3d %3d %3d\n", r[i], g[i], b[i] );

    fclose( fp );

    } /* end save_lut */
```

TELEVISION COLOR ENCODING AND "HOT" BROADCAST COLORS

(page 147)

David Martindale and Alan W. Paeth

```
/*
 * hot.c - Scan an image for pixels with RGB values that will give
 *   "unsafe" values of chrominance signal or composite signal
 *   amplitude when encoded into an NTSC or PAL colour signal.
 *   (This happens for certain high-intensity high-saturation colours
 *   that are rare in real scenes, but can easily be present
 *   in synthetic images.)
 *
 *   Such pixels can be flagged so the user may then choose other
 *   colours.  Or, the offending pixels can be made "safe"
 *   in a manner that preserves hue.
 *
 *   There are two reasonable ways to make a pixel "safe":
 *   We can reduce its intensity (luminance) while leaving
 *   hue and saturation the same.  Or, we can reduce saturation
 *   while leaving hue and luminance the same.  A #define selects
 *   which strategy to use.
 *
 * Note to the user: You must add your own read_pixel() and write_pixel()
 *   routines.  You may have to modify pix_decode() and pix_encode().
 *   MAXPIX, WID, and HGT are likely to need modification.
 */

/*
 * Originally written as "ikNTSC.c" by Alan Wm Paeth,
 *   University of Waterloo, August, 1985
 * Updated by Dave Martindale, Imax Systems Corp., December 1990
 */

/*
 * Compile-time options.
 *
 * Define either NTSC or PAL as 1 to select the colour system.
 * Define the other one as zero, or leave it undefined.
 *
 * Define FLAG_HOT as 1 if you want "hot" pixels set to black
 *   to identify them.  Otherwise they will be made safe.
 *
```

```
 * Define REDUCE_SAT as 1 if you want hot pixels to be repaired by
 * reducing their saturation.  By default, luminance is reduced.
 *
 * CHROMA_LIM is the limit (in IRE units) of the overall
 * chrominance amplitude; it should be 50 or perhaps
 * very slightly higher.
 *
 * COMPOS_LIM is the maximum amplitude (in IRE units) allowed for
 * the composite signal.  A value of 100 is the maximum
 * monochrome white, and is always safe.   120 is the absolute
 * limit for NTSC broadcasting, since the transmitter's carrier
 * goes to zero with 120 IRE input signal.  Generally, 110
 * is a good compromise - it allows somewhat brighter colours
 * than 100, while staying safely away from the hard limit.
 */

#define NTSC        1
#define PAL         0
#define FLAG_HOT    0
#define REDUCE_SAT  0


#define CHROMA_LIM      50.0        /* chroma amplitude limit */
#define COMPOS_LIM      110.0       /* max IRE amplitude */

#if NTSC
/*
 * RGB to YIQ encoding matrix.
 */
double code_matrix[3][3] = {
     0.2989,      0.5866,      0.1144,
     0.5959,     -0.2741,     -0.3218,
     0.2113,     -0.5227,      0.3113,
};

#define PEDESTAL    7.5     /* 7.5 IRE black pedestal */
#define GAMMA       2.2
#endif NTSC

#if PAL
/*
 * RGB to YUV encoding matrix.
 */
double code_matrix[3][3] = {
     0.2989,      0.5866,      0.1144,
    -0.1473,     -0.2891,      0.4364,
     0.6149,     -0.5145,     -0.1004,
};

#define PEDESTAL    0.0     /* no pedestal in PAL */
#define GAMMA       2.8
#endif PAL


#define SCALE   8192                /* scale factor: do floats with int math */
#define MAXPIX  255                 /* white value */
#define WID 1024                /* FB dimensions */
#define HGT 768
```

```
typedef struct {
    unsigned char    r, g, b;
} Pixel;

int tab[3][3][MAXPIX+1];      /* multiply lookup table */
double  chroma_lim;                 /* chroma limit */
double  compos_lim;                 /* composite amplitude limit */
long    ichroma_lim2;               /* chroma limit squared (scaled integer) */
int icompos_lim;               /* composite amplitude limit (scaled integer) */

double  pix_decode(), gc(), inv_gc();
int pix_encode(), hot();

main()
{
    Pixel    p;
    int row, col;

    build_tab();

    for (col=0; col<WID; col++) {
        for(row=0; row<HGT; row++) {
            read_pixel(row, col, &p);
            if (hot(&p)) {
                write_pixel(row, col, &p);
            }
        }
    }
}

/*
 * build_tab: Build multiply lookup table.
 *
 * For each possible pixel value, decode value into floating-point
 * intensity.  Then do gamma correction required by the video
 * standard.  Scale the result by our fixed-point scale factor.
 * Then calculate 9 lookup table entries for this pixel value.
 *
 * We also calculate floating-point and scaled integer versions
 * of our limits here.  This prevents evaluating expressions every pixel
 * when the compiler is too stupid to evaluate constant-valued
 * floating-point expressions at compile time.
 *
 * For convenience, the limits are #defined using IRE units.
 * We must convert them here into the units in which YIQ
 * are measured.  The conversion from IRE to internal units
 * depends on the pedestal level in use, since as Y goes from
 * 0 to 1, the signal goes from the pedestal level to 100 IRE.
 * Chroma is always scaled to remain consistent with Y.
 */

build_tab()
{
    register double f;
    register int     pv;
```

```
    for (pv = 0; pv <= MAXPIX; pv++) {
        f = SCALE * gc(pix_decode(pv));
        tab[0][0][pv] = (int)(f * code_matrix[0][0] + 0.5);
        tab[0][1][pv] = (int)(f * code_matrix[0][1] + 0.5);
        tab[0][2][pv] = (int)(f * code_matrix[0][2] + 0.5);
        tab[1][0][pv] = (int)(f * code_matrix[1][0] + 0.5);
        tab[1][1][pv] = (int)(f * code_matrix[1][1] + 0.5);
        tab[1][2][pv] = (int)(f * code_matrix[1][2] + 0.5);
        tab[2][0][pv] = (int)(f * code_matrix[2][0] + 0.5);
        tab[2][1][pv] = (int)(f * code_matrix[2][1] + 0.5);
        tab[2][2][pv] = (int)(f * code_matrix[2][2] + 0.5);
    }

    chroma_lim = (double)CHROMA_LIM / (100.0 - PEDESTAL);
    compos_lim = ((double)COMPOS_LIM - PEDESTAL) / (100.0 - PEDESTAL);

    ichroma_lim2 = (int)(chroma_lim * SCALE + 0.5);
    ichroma_lim2 *= ichroma_lim2;
    icompos_lim = (int)(compos_lim * SCALE + 0.5);
}

int
hot(p)
Pixel    *p;
{
    register int     r, g, b;
    register int     y, i, q;
    register long    y2, c2;
    double           pr, pg, pb;
#if REDUCE_SAT
    double           py;
#endif
    register double  fy, fc, t, scale;
#if !FLAG_HOT
    static int       prev_r = 0, prev_g = 0, prev_b = 0;
    static int       new_r, new_g, new_b;
#endif
    extern double    pow(), hypot();

    r = p->r;
    g = p->g;
    b = p->b;

    /*
     * Pixel decoding, gamma correction, and matrix multiplication
     * all done by lookup table.
     *
     * "i" and "q" are the two chrominance components;
     * they are I and Q for NTSC.
     * For PAL, "i" is U (scaled B-Y) and "q" is V (scaled R-Y).
     * Since we only care about the length of the chroma vector,
     * not its angle, we don't care which is which.
     */
    y = tab[0][0][r] + tab[0][1][g] + tab[0][2][b];
    i = tab[1][0][r] + tab[1][1][g] + tab[1][2][b];
    q = tab[2][0][r] + tab[2][1][g] + tab[2][2][b];
```

```
    /*
     * Check to see if the chrominance vector is too long or the
     * composite waveform amplitude is too large.
     *
     * Chrominance is too large if
     *
     *   sqrt(i^2, q^2)  >  chroma_lim.
     *
     * The composite signal amplitude is too large if
     *
     *   y + sqrt(i^2, q^2)  >  compos_lim.
     *
     * We avoid doing the sqrt by checking
     *
     *   i^2 + q^2  >  chroma_lim^2
     * and
     *   y + sqrt(i^2 + q^2)  >  compos_lim
     *   sqrt(i^2 + q^2)  >  compos_lim - y
     *   i^2 + q^2  >  (compos_lim - y)^2
     *
     */

    c2 = (long)i * i + (long)q * q;
    y2 = (long)icompos_lim - y;
    y2 *= y2;
    if (c2 <= ichroma_lim2 && c2 <= y2) /* no problems */
        return 0;

    /*
     * Pixel is hot, choose desired (compilation time controlled) strategy
     */
#if FLAG_HOT
    /*
     * Set the hot pixel to black to identify it.
     */
    p->r = p->g = p->b = 0;
#else FLAG_HOT
    /*
     * Optimization: cache the last-computed hot pixel.
     */
    if (r == prev_r && g == prev_g && b == prev_b) {
        p->r = new_r;
        p->g = new_g;
        p->b = new_b;
        return 1;
    }
    prev_r = r;
    prev_g = g;
    prev_b = b;

    /*
     * Get Y and chroma amplitudes in floating point.
     *
     * If your C library doesn't have hypot(), just use
     * hypot(a,b) = sqrt(a*a, b*b);
     *
     * Then extract linear (un-gamma-corrected) floating-point
     * pixel RGB values.
     */
    fy = (double)y / SCALE;
```

```
        fc = hypot((double)i / SCALE, (double)q / SCALE);

        pr = pix_decode(r);
        pg = pix_decode(g);
        pb = pix_decode(b);

        /*
         * Reducing overall pixel intensity by scaling
         * R, G, and B reduces Y, I, and Q by the same factor.
         * This changes luminance but not saturation, since saturation
         * is determined by the chroma/luminance ratio.
         *
         * On the other hand, by linearly interpolating between the
         * original pixel value and a grey pixel with the same
         * luminance (R=G=B=Y), we change saturation without
         * affecting luminance.
         */

#if !REDUCE_SAT
        /*
         * Calculate a scale factor that will bring the pixel
         * within both chroma and composite limits, if we scale
         * luminance and chroma simultaneously.
         *
         * The calculated chrominance reduction applies to the
         * gamma-corrected RGB values that are the input to
         * the RGB-to-YIQ operation.  Multiplying the
         * original un-gamma-corrected pixel values by
         * the scaling factor raised to the "gamma" power
         * is equivalent, and avoids calling gc() and inv_gc()
         * three times each.
         */
        scale = chroma_lim / fc;
        t = compos_lim / (fy + fc);
        if (t < scale)
            scale = t;
        scale = pow(scale, GAMMA);

        r = pix_encode(scale * pr);
        g = pix_encode(scale * pg);
        b = pix_encode(scale * pb);
#else REDUCE_SAT
        /*
         * Calculate a scale factor that will bring the pixel
         * within both chroma and composite limits, if we scale
         * chroma while leaving luminance unchanged.
         *
         * We have to interpolate gamma-corrected RGB values,
         * so we must convert from linear to gamma-corrected
         * before interpolation and then back to linear afterwards.
         */
        scale = chroma_lim / fc;
        t = (compos_lim - fy) / fc;
        if (t < scale)
            scale = t;
```

```
            pr = gc(pr);
            pg = gc(pg);
            pb = gc(pb);
            py = pr * code_matrix[0][0] + pg * code_matrix[0][1]
                + pb * code_matrix[0][2];
            r = pix_encode(inv_gc(py + scale * (pr - py)));
            g = pix_encode(inv_gc(py + scale * (pg - py)));
            b = pix_encode(inv_gc(py + scale * (pb - py)));
#endif REDUCE_SAT

        p->r = new_r = r;
        p->g = new_g = g;
        p->b = new_b = b;
#endif FLAG_HOT
        return 1;
}

/*
 * gc: apply the gamma correction specified for this video standard.
 * inv_gc: inverse function of gc.
 *
 * These are generally just a call to pow(), but be careful!
 * Future standards may use more complex functions.
 * (e.g. SMPTE 240M's "electro-optic transfer characteristic").
 */

double
gc(x)
double  x;
{
        extern double   pow();

        return pow(x, 1.0 / GAMMA);
}

double
inv_gc(x)
double  x;
{
        extern double   pow();

        return pow(x, GAMMA);
}

/*
 * pix_decode: decode an integer pixel value into a floating-point
 *  intensity in the range [0, 1].
 *
 * pix_encode: encode a floating-point intensity into an integer
 *  pixel value.
 *
 * The code given here assumes simple linear encoding; you must change
 * these routines if you use a different pixel encoding technique.
 */
```

548

```
double
pix_decode(v)
int v;
{
    return (double)v / MAXPIX;
}

int
pix_encode(v)
double  v;
{
    return (int)(v * MAXPIX + 0.5);
}
```

VIEW CORRELATION
(page 181)

Rod G. Bogart

```c
/*
 * viewfind.c - Simple program to read view and screen data, then run view
 * correlation on it, and dump the results suitable for a raytracing program.
 *
 * Author:     Rod G. Bogart
 * Date:       Oct 15 1990
 * Copyright (c) 1990, University of Michigan
 *
 */
#include <stdio.h>
#include <math.h>
#include "GraphicsGems.h"
#include "matrix.h"
#include "viewcorr.h"

main(argc, argv)
char **argv;
{
    ViewData datapts;
    ViewParms view_parms;
    int i, num_iterations = 0;

    if (argc >= 2)
        num_iterations = atoi(argv[1]);
    read_points_and_view(stdin, &datapts, &view_parms );
    iterate_view_parms( &datapts, &view_parms, num_iterations );
    dump_points_and_view(stdout, &datapts, &view_parms );
    dump_rayshade_parms(stdout, &view_parms);
}

read_points_and_view( infile, datapts, view_parms )
FILE * infile;
ViewData *datapts;
ViewParms *view_parms;
{
    int i;
    Matrix3 *vm;
    Point3 lookp, up;
    Point3 xvec, yvec, zvec;
```

```
    /* read viewparms first, then data points */

    fscanf(infile,"%lf %lf %lf",&(view_parms->eye.x),&(view_parms->eye.y),
            &(view_parms->eye.z));
    fscanf(infile,"%lf %lf %lf",&(lookp.x),&(lookp.y),&(lookp.z));
    fscanf(infile,"%lf %lf %lf",&(up.x),&(up.y),&(up.z));

    /* make coordinate frame unit vectors from eye, lookp, and up */
    V3Sub(&view_parms->eye, &lookp, &zvec);
    V3Normalize( &zvec );
    V3Normalize( &up );
    V3Cross(&up, &zvec, &xvec);
    V3Cross(&zvec, &xvec, &yvec);
    V3Normalize( &xvec );
    V3Normalize( &yvec );

    /* Store the coordinate frame unit vectors as columns to create
     * a rotation matrix
     */
    vm = &(view_parms->view);
    vm->element[0][0] = xvec.x;
    vm->element[0][1] = yvec.x;
    vm->element[0][2] = zvec.x;
    vm->element[1][0] = xvec.y;
    vm->element[1][1] = yvec.y;
    vm->element[1][2] = zvec.y;
    vm->element[2][0] = xvec.z;
    vm->element[2][1] = yvec.z;
    vm->element[2][2] = zvec.z;

    propagate_rotate_change( view_parms );

    fscanf(infile,"%lf %lf",&(view_parms->d_over_s),&(view_parms->aspect));
    fscanf(infile,"%lf %lf %lf %lf",&(view_parms->halfx),&(view_parms->halfy),
            &(view_parms->xcenter),&(view_parms->ycenter));

    fscanf(infile,"%d",&datapts->numpts);
    datapts->pts = (Point3 *) malloc(datapts->numpts * sizeof(Point3));
    datapts->scrpts = (Point2 *) malloc(datapts->numpts * sizeof(Point2));
    for(i=0; i < datapts->numpts; i++)
    {
        fscanf(infile,"%lf %lf %lf",&datapts->pts[i].x,&datapts->pts[i].y,
                &datapts->pts[i].z);
        fscanf(infile,"%lf %lf",&datapts->scrpts[i].x,&datapts->scrpts[i].y);
    }
}

dump_points_and_view( dumpfile, datapts, view_parms )
FILE * dumpfile;
ViewData *datapts;
ViewParms *view_parms;
{
    int i;
    Matrix3 *vm;
    Point3 dov, tmp, up;
```

```
        tmp.x = 0.0;
        tmp.y = 0.0;
        tmp.z = -1.0;
        V3MulPointByMatrix(&tmp, &view_parms->viewinv, &dov);
        tmp.x = 0.0;
        tmp.y = 1.0;
        tmp.z = 0.0;
        V3MulPointByMatrix(&tmp, &view_parms->viewinv, &up);

        fprintf(dumpfile,"%lf %lf %lf\n",view_parms->eye.x,view_parms->eye.y,
                view_parms->eye.z);

        fprintf(dumpfile,"%lf %lf %lf\n",
                view_parms->eye.x + dov.x,
                view_parms->eye.y + dov.y,
                view_parms->eye.z + dov.z);
        fprintf(dumpfile,"%lf %lf %lf\n", up.x, up.y, up.z);

        fprintf(dumpfile,"%lf %lf\n",view_parms->d_over_s,view_parms->aspect);
        fprintf(dumpfile,"%lf %lf %lf %lf\n",view_parms->halfx, view_parms->halfy,
                view_parms->xcenter, view_parms->ycenter);

        fprintf(dumpfile,"%d\n",datapts->numpts);
        for(i=0; i < datapts->numpts; i++)
        {
            fprintf(dumpfile,"%lf %lf %lf ",datapts->pts[i].x,datapts->pts[i].y,
                    datapts->pts[i].z);
            fprintf(dumpfile,"%lf %lf\n",datapts->scrpts[i].x,
                    datapts->scrpts[i].y);
        }
}

dump_rayshade_parms( dumpfile, view_parms )
FILE * dumpfile;
ViewParms *view_parms;
{
    double ds;
    int halfx, halfy;
    Point3 dov, tmp, up;

    tmp.x = 0.0;
    tmp.y = 0.0;
    tmp.z = -1.0;
    V3MulPointByMatrix(&tmp, &view_parms->viewinv, &dov);
    tmp.x = 0.0;
    tmp.y = 1.0;
    tmp.z = 0.0;
    V3MulPointByMatrix(&tmp, &view_parms->viewinv, &up);

    if (view_parms->halfx > view_parms->xcenter) {
        halfx = (int) (2.0*view_parms->halfx - view_parms->xcenter);
    }
    else
        halfx = view_parms->xcenter;
    if (view_parms->halfy > view_parms->ycenter) {
        halfy = (int) (2.0*view_parms->halfy - view_parms->ycenter);
    }
    else
        halfy = view_parms->ycenter;
```

552

```c
        ds = view_parms->d_over_s;
        if (ds < 0.0) {
            V3Negate(&up);
            ds = -ds;
        }
        fprintf(dumpfile,"screen %d %d\n", halfx * 2, halfy * 2);
        fprintf(dumpfile,"window %d %d %d %d\n",
                (int) (halfx - view_parms->xcenter),
                (int) (halfy - view_parms->ycenter),
                (int) (halfx - view_parms->xcenter) +
                (int) (view_parms->halfx*2 - 1),
                (int) (halfy - view_parms->ycenter) +
                (int) (view_parms->halfy*2 - 1));
        fprintf(dumpfile,"eyep %lf %lf %lf\n", view_parms->eye.x,
                view_parms->eye.y, view_parms->eye.z);
        fprintf(dumpfile,"lookp %lf %lf %lf\n",
                view_parms->eye.x + dov.x,
                view_parms->eye.y + dov.y,
                view_parms->eye.z + dov.z);
        fprintf(dumpfile,"up %lf %lf %lf\n", up.x, up.y, up.z);
        fprintf(dumpfile,"fov %lf %lf\n",
                atan(((double) halfx / view_parms->halfx) *
                        (1.0/ds)) * RTOD * 2.0,
                atan(((double) halfy / view_parms->halfx) *
                        (1.0/(ds * view_parms->aspect))) * RTOD * 2.0);
}

/* viewcorr.h
 *      The global types for view correlation routines.
 */


typedef struct ViewParmsStruct {
    Point3 eye;                     /* projection point */
    Matrix3 view;                   /* 3x3 rotation matrix */
    Matrix3 viewinv;                /* 3x3 inverse rotation matrix */
    double d_over_s;                /* distance to screen / half screen width */
    double aspect;                  /* aspect ratio (for non-square pixels) */
    double halfx, halfy;            /* half of screen resolutions */
    double xcenter, ycenter;        /* center of image */
} ViewParms;

typedef struct ViewDataStruct {
    int numpts;                     /* number of data points */
    Point3 *pts;                    /* array of three D data points */
    Point2 *scrpts;                 /* array of screen data points */
} ViewData;

/* If you cannot handle arbitrary aspect ratios, change the following define
 * to an undef.  The iteration will happen with the aspect ratio given in
 * the initial set of ViewParms.
 */
#define ITERATE_ASPECT_RATIO

#ifdef ITERATE_ASPECT_RATIO
#define NUM_VIEW_PARMS 10
#else
#define NUM_VIEW_PARMS 9
#endif
```

```c
/*
 * viewcorr.c - Iterate the view parameters.
 *
 *
 * Author:      Rod G. Bogart
 * Date:        Oct 15 1990
 * Copyright (c) 1990, University of Michigan
 *
 */
#include <stdio.h>
#include <math.h>
#include "GraphicsGems.h"
#include "matrix.h"
#include "viewcorr.h"

iterate_view_parms( datapts, view_parms, num_iterations )
ViewData *datapts;
ViewParms *view_parms;
int num_iterations;
{
    Matrix errors, jacobian, corrections;
    int i,j;
    double rootmeansqr, last_rootmeansqr;

    /* allocate Matrix stuff */
    errors = NewMatrix(datapts->numpts*2, 1);
    jacobian = NewMatrix(datapts->numpts*2, NUM_VIEW_PARMS);
    corrections = NewMatrix(NUM_VIEW_PARMS, 1);

    if (num_iterations <= 0) {
        num_iterations = 10000;
    }
    last_rootmeansqr = 0.0;
    for (i = 0; i < num_iterations; i++)
    {
        measure_errors( datapts, view_parms, errors, &rootmeansqr );
        if (ABS(rootmeansqr - last_rootmeansqr) < 1E-8) {
            /* quit when rootmeansqr stays the same */
            break;
        }
        last_rootmeansqr = rootmeansqr;
        if (rootmeansqr > (0.1 * view_parms->halfx))
            /* When the error terms are large, the corrections become too
             * extreme, and knock the whole thing into outer space.  Sooo,
             * shrink the error terms, to cause the corrections to happen
             * a small amount at a time.  Note: dividing by the rootmeansqr
             * may be a little extreme, but it does slow down the erratic
             * behaviour.
             */
            for (j = 0; j < datapts->numpts; j++)
            {
                errors[0][j*2] /= rootmeansqr;
                errors[0][j*2+1] /= rootmeansqr;
            }
        build_jacobian( datapts, view_parms, jacobian );
        find_corrections( datapts, jacobian, errors, corrections );
        apply_corrections( corrections, view_parms );
    }
```

```
        FreeMatrix(errors, 1);
        FreeMatrix(jacobian, NUM_VIEW_PARMS);
        FreeMatrix(corrections, 1);
    }


measure_errors( datapts, view_parms, errors, rootmeansqr )
ViewData *datapts;
Matrix errors;
ViewParms *view_parms;
double *rootmeansqr;
{
    int i;
    double sqrs=0.0;
    Point2 screenpt;

    for (i = 0; i < datapts->numpts; i++)
    {
        screen_project( &datapts->pts[i], view_parms, &screenpt );
        errors[0][i*2 + 0] = screenpt.x - datapts->scrpts[i].x;
        errors[0][i*2 + 1] = screenpt.y - datapts->scrpts[i].y;
        sqrs += SQR(errors[0][i*2 + 0]) + SQR(errors[0][i*2 + 1]);
    }
    *rootmeansqr = sqrt( sqrs / (datapts->numpts*2.0) );
}


build_jacobian( datapts, view_parms, jacobian )
ViewData *datapts;
Matrix jacobian;
ViewParms *view_parms;
{
    int i;
    Point3 xyz, eR;

    /* The jacobian matrix has at least 10 columns (u and v for 5 pts)
     * and 10 rows (10 iteration parameters).  The iteration parameters will
     * be ordered: eRx eRy eRz phi_x phi_y phi_z ds xcenter ycenter aspect
     * from the top down.
     */

    V3MulPointByMatrix(&view_parms->eye, &view_parms->view, &eR);
    for (i = 0; i < datapts->numpts; i++)
    {
        V3MulPointByMatrix(&datapts->pts[i], &view_parms->view, &xyz);

        store_u_partials( &xyz, &eR, view_parms, i, jacobian );
        store_v_partials( &xyz, &eR, view_parms, i, jacobian );
    }
}


store_u_partials( xyz, eR, view_parms, ptnum, jacobian )
Point3 *xyz, *eR;
Matrix jacobian;
ViewParms *view_parms;
int ptnum;
{
    double x_min_eR, z_min_eR;
    int i2;
```

555

```
    i2 = ptnum*2;
    x_min_eR = xyz->x - eR->x;
    z_min_eR = xyz->z - eR->z;

    jacobian[0][i2] = view_parms->d_over_s * view_parms->halfx / z_min_eR;
    jacobian[1][i2] = 0.0;
    jacobian[2][i2] = - view_parms->d_over_s * view_parms->halfx * x_min_eR
        / SQR( z_min_eR );

    jacobian[3][i2] = view_parms->d_over_s * view_parms->halfx * xyz->y
        * x_min_eR / SQR( z_min_eR );
    jacobian[4][i2] = - (view_parms->d_over_s * view_parms->halfx * xyz->z
                        / z_min_eR)
        - (view_parms->d_over_s * view_parms->halfx * xyz->x * x_min_eR
            / SQR( z_min_eR ));
    jacobian[5][i2] = view_parms->d_over_s * view_parms->halfx * xyz->y
        / z_min_eR;

    jacobian[6][i2] = - view_parms->halfx * x_min_eR / z_min_eR;
    jacobian[7][i2] = 1.0;
    jacobian[8][i2] = 0.0;
#ifdef ITERATE_ASPECT_RATIO
    jacobian[9][i2] = 0.0;
#endif
}

store_v_partials( xyz, eR, view_parms, ptnum, jacobian )
Point3 *xyz, *eR;
Matrix jacobian;
ViewParms *view_parms;
int ptnum;
{
    double y_min_eR, z_min_eR, d_over_s;
    int i2;

    i2 = ptnum*2 + 1;
    y_min_eR = xyz->y - eR->y;
    z_min_eR = xyz->z - eR->z;
    d_over_s = view_parms->d_over_s * view_parms->aspect;

    jacobian[0][i2] = 0.0;
    jacobian[1][i2] = d_over_s * view_parms->halfx / z_min_eR;
    jacobian[2][i2] = - d_over_s * view_parms->halfx * y_min_eR
        / SQR( z_min_eR );

    jacobian[3][i2] = (d_over_s * view_parms->halfx * xyz->z
                        / z_min_eR)
        + (d_over_s * view_parms->halfx * xyz->y * y_min_eR
            / SQR( z_min_eR ));
    jacobian[4][i2] = - d_over_s * view_parms->halfx * xyz->x
        * y_min_eR / SQR( z_min_eR );
    jacobian[5][i2] = - d_over_s * view_parms->halfx * xyz->x
        / z_min_eR;
```

```
        jacobian[6][i2] = - view_parms->aspect * view_parms->halfx * y_min_eR
            / z_min_eR;
        jacobian[7][i2] = 0.0;
        jacobian[8][i2] = 1.0;
#ifdef ITERATE_ASPECT_RATIO
        jacobian[9][i2] = - view_parms->d_over_s * view_parms->halfx * y_min_eR
            / z_min_eR;
#endif
}

find_corrections( datapts, jacobian, errors, corrections )
ViewData *datapts;
Matrix jacobian, errors, corrections;
{
    Matrix jacobian_transpose, combo_inverse, error_J_transpose;
    int i;

    /* The corrections matrix is the error matrix times the inverse
     * of the Jacobian.  Since the Jacobian may not be square, the
     * pseudo-inverse is used:
     *            -1        T        T -1
     *   C = E  J    =   E  J   (J  J )
     */
    for (i = 0; i < NUM_VIEW_PARMS; i++)
        corrections[0][i] = 0.0;

    jacobian_transpose = NewMatrix(NUM_VIEW_PARMS, datapts->numpts*2);
    combo_inverse = NewMatrix(NUM_VIEW_PARMS, NUM_VIEW_PARMS);

    TransposeMatrix( jacobian, jacobian_transpose,
                    NUM_VIEW_PARMS, datapts->numpts*2 );
    MultMatrix( jacobian, jacobian_transpose, combo_inverse,
                NUM_VIEW_PARMS, datapts->numpts*2, NUM_VIEW_PARMS );
    if (InvertMatrix( combo_inverse, NUM_VIEW_PARMS ) == 0.0)
    {
        fprintf(stderr,"Could not invert matrix in iteration!!!\n");
        FreeMatrix(jacobian_transpose, datapts->numpts*2);
        FreeMatrix(combo_inverse, NUM_VIEW_PARMS);
        return;
    }

    error_J_transpose = NewMatrix(NUM_VIEW_PARMS, 1);
    MultMatrix( errors, jacobian_transpose, error_J_transpose, 1,
                datapts->numpts*2, NUM_VIEW_PARMS );
    MultMatrix( error_J_transpose, combo_inverse, corrections, 1,
                NUM_VIEW_PARMS, NUM_VIEW_PARMS );
    FreeMatrix(jacobian_transpose, datapts->numpts*2);
    FreeMatrix(combo_inverse, NUM_VIEW_PARMS);
    FreeMatrix(error_J_transpose, 1);
}

apply_corrections( corrections, view_parms )
Matrix corrections;
ViewParms *view_parms;
{
    ViewParms current_parms;
    Point3 eR;
    Matrix3 inc_rotate;
```

```
    current_parms = *view_parms;

    build_rotate(&inc_rotate,
                -corrections[0][3], -corrections[0][4], -corrections[0][5]);
    V2MatMul(&current_parms.view, &inc_rotate, &view_parms->view);
    propagate_rotate_change( view_parms );

    V3MulPointByMatrix(&current_parms.eye, &current_parms.view, &eR);
    eR.x -= corrections[0][0];
    eR.y -= corrections[0][1];
    eR.z -= corrections[0][2];
    V3MulPointByMatrix(&eR, &view_parms->viewinv, &view_parms->eye);
    view_parms->d_over_s -= corrections[0][6];
    view_parms->xcenter -= corrections[0][7];
    view_parms->ycenter -= corrections[0][8];
#ifdef ITERATE_ASPECT_RATIO
    view_parms->aspect -= corrections[0][9];
#endif
    return;
}


propagate_rotate_change( view_parms )
ViewParms *view_parms;
{
    /* inverse is just the transpose of a rotate matrix */
    TransposeMatrix3(&view_parms->view, &view_parms->viewinv);
}


rotate_mat(m, rot_angle, pos_sin_index, neg_sin_index)
Matrix3 *m;
double rot_angle;
int pos_sin_index, neg_sin_index;
{
    double cos_theta, sin_theta;
    int i,j;

    cos_theta = cos( rot_angle );    sin_theta = sin( rot_angle );
    for (i = 0; i < 3; i++)
        for (j = 0; j < 3; j++)
            m->element[i][j] = (i==j) ? 1.0 : 0.0;
    m->element[pos_sin_index][pos_sin_index] = cos_theta;
    m->element[neg_sin_index][neg_sin_index] = cos_theta;
    m->element[pos_sin_index][neg_sin_index] = sin_theta;
    m->element[neg_sin_index][pos_sin_index] = -sin_theta;
}


build_rotate( m, rot_x, rot_y, rot_z )
Matrix3 *m;
double rot_x, rot_y, rot_z;
{
    Matrix3 tmpmat, rotate;

    /* m = Xrotate
     * tmpmat = [m] [Yrotate]
     * m = [tmpmat] [Zrotate]
     */
```

```c
    rotate_mat(m, rot_x, 1, 2);
    rotate_mat(&rotate, rot_y, 2, 0);
    V2MatMul(m, &rotate, &tmpmat);
    rotate_mat(&rotate, rot_z, 0, 1);
    V2MatMul(&tmpmat, &rotate, m);
}

screen_project(datapt, view_parms, screenpt)
Point3 *datapt;
ViewParms *view_parms;
Point2 *screenpt;
{
    Point3 xyz, data_minus_eye;
    int i;

    V3Sub(datapt, &view_parms->eye, &data_minus_eye);
    V3MulPointByMatrix(&data_minus_eye, &view_parms->view, &xyz);
    screenpt->x = - (view_parms->d_over_s * view_parms->halfx * xyz.x
                    / xyz.z) + view_parms->xcenter;
    screenpt->y = - (view_parms->aspect * view_parms->d_over_s
                    * view_parms->halfx * xyz.y
                    / xyz.z) + view_parms->ycenter;
}

/* matrix.h
 *      The type and externs for matrix routines.
 */

typedef double ** Matrix;

extern double InvertMatrix();
extern Matrix NewMatrix();

/*
 * matrix.c - Simple routines for general sized matrices.
 *
 */

#include <stdio.h>
#include <math.h>
#include "matrix.h"


double
InvertMatrix(mat,actual_size)
Matrix mat;                     /* Holds the original and inverse */
int actual_size;                /* Actual size of matrix in use, (high_subscript+1)*/
{
    int i,j,k;
                                        /* Locations of pivot elements */
    int *pvt_i, *pvt_j;
    double pvt_val;                     /* Value of current pivot element */
    double hold;                        /* Temporary storage */
    double determ;                      /* Determinant */
```

```
determ = 1.0;

pvt_i = (int *) malloc(actual_size * sizeof(int));
pvt_j = (int *) malloc(actual_size * sizeof(int));

for (k = 0; k < actual_size; k++)
{
    /* Locate k'th pivot element */
    pvt_val = mat[k][k];                    /* Initialize for search */
    pvt_i[k] = k;
    pvt_j[k] = k;
    for (i = k; i < actual_size; i++)
      for (j = k; j < actual_size; j++)
        if (fabs(mat[i][j]) > fabs(pvt_val))
        {
            pvt_i[k] = i;
            pvt_j[k] = j;
            pvt_val = mat[i][j];
        }
    /* Product of pivots, gives determinant when finished */
    determ *= pvt_val;
    if (determ == 0.0) {
     /* Matrix is singular (zero determinant). */
        free(pvt_i);
        free(pvt_j);
        return (0.0);
    }

    /* "Interchange" rows (with sign change stuff) */
    i = pvt_i[k];
    if (i != k)                             /* If rows are different */
      for (j = 0; j < actual_size; j++)
      {
        hold = -mat[k][j];
        mat[k][j] = mat[i][j];
        mat[i][j] = hold;
      }

    /* "Interchange" columns */
    j = pvt_j[k];
    if (j != k)                             /* If columns are different */
      for (i = 0; i < actual_size; i++)
      {
        hold = -mat[i][k];
        mat[i][k] = mat[i][j];
        mat[i][j] = hold;
      }
    /* Divide column by minus pivot value */
    for (i = 0; i < actual_size; i++)
      if (i != k)                           /* Don't touch the pivot entry */
        mat[i][k] /= ( -pvt_val) ;  /* (Tricky C syntax for division) */

    /* Reduce the matrix */
    for (i = 0; i < actual_size; i++)
    {
        hold = mat[i][k];
        for (j = 0; j < actual_size; j++)
          if ( i != k && j != k )   /* Don't touch pivot. */
            mat[i][j] += hold * mat[k][j];
    }
```

```
          /* Divide row by pivot */
          for (j = 0; j < actual_size; j++)
            if (j != k)                         /* Don't touch the pivot! */
              mat[k][j] /= pvt_val;

          /* Replace pivot by reciprocal (at last we can touch it). */
          mat[k][k] = 1.0/pvt_val;
      }

      /* That was most of the work, one final pass of row/column interchange */
      /* to finish */
      for (k = actual_size-2; k >= 0; k--)  /* Don't need to work with 1 by 1 */
                                            /* corner */
      {
          i = pvt_j[k];               /* Rows to swap correspond to pivot COLUMN */
          if (i != k)                         /* If rows are different */
            for(j = 0; j < actual_size; j++)
            {
              hold = mat[k][j];
              mat[k][j] = -mat[i][j];
              mat[i][j] = hold;
            }

          j = pvt_i[k];               /* Columns to swap correspond to pivot ROW */
          if (j != k)                         /* If columns are different */
            for (i = 0; i < actual_size; i++)
            {
              hold = mat[i][k];
              mat[i][k] = -mat[i][j];
              mat[i][j] = hold;
            }
      }

      free(pvt_i);
      free(pvt_j);
      return(determ);
}

Matrix
NewMatrix(cols, rows)
int cols,rows;
{
    int i;
    Matrix newM;
    newM = (double **) malloc(rows * sizeof(double *));
    for(i = 0; i < rows; i++)
        newM[i] = (double *) malloc(cols * sizeof(double));
    return newM;
}

FreeMatrix(mat, rows)
Matrix mat;
int rows;
{
    int i;
    for(i = 0; i < rows; i++)
        free(mat[i]);
    free(mat);
}
```

```
TransposeMatrix(inM, outM, cols, rows)
Matrix inM, outM;
int cols,rows;
{
    int tempI, tempJ;
    for(tempI=0; tempI < rows; tempI++)
        for(tempJ=0; tempJ < cols; tempJ++)
            outM[tempI][tempJ] = inM[tempJ][tempI];
}


MultMatrix(firstM, secondM, outM, firstrows, cols, secondcols)
Matrix firstM, secondM, outM;
int firstrows, cols, secondcols;
{
    int i,j,k;
    double sum;

    for(i=0; i < secondcols; i++)
        for(j=0; j < firstrows; j++)
        {
            sum = 0.0;
            for(k=0; k < cols; k++)
                sum += firstM[j][k] * secondM[k][i];
            outM[j][i] = sum;
        }
}
```

THREE-DIMENSIONAL
HOMOGENEOUS CLIPPING
OF TRIANGLE STRIPS

(page 219)

Patrick-Gilles Maillot

```
/*
 * 3D point structure
 */
typedef struct {
  float           coords[4];
} H_point;

typedef struct {
  int             num_hpoints;
  H_point         *hpoints;
} H_list;

typedef struct {
float           cl_plane[6];
  unsigned char cl_tbdone;
  H_point       **pointers_bucket_0;
  int           pointers_bucket_0_max;
  H_point       **pointers_bucket_1;
  int           pointers_bucket_1_max;
  H_point       *hpoints_bucket;
  int           hpoints_bucket_max;
  int           hpoints_bucket_index;
} Clip_ctx;

/*
 *
 *   Space coding information:
```

```
*
* This 3D clipping function is based on the intersection of
* lines using a line segment parametric equation:
*
*   Let P a point on the line segment, then if A and B are the
*   extremes points of the line segment, we can write:
*   P = l * B + (1 - l) * A, with l = [0..1]
*
*
* Furthermore, The space is coded as following: we use a six-bit word
* in which each bit represents the interior of a half space separated by
* the infinite clip plane. Each clip plane is defined by one coordinate
* only and thus is parallel to the system's axes.
* A 0 bit means "interior", while
* a 1 bit means "exterior".
*
*/


/*
 * Intersection macros
 */

#define COMPUTE_INTER_3D(P, P_plan, S) \
  P = pre_stage[n]; \
  P_plan = P->coords[i >> 1] - clip_ctx->cl_plane[i] * P->coords[3]; \
  if (i & 1) clip_code |= ((P_plan > 0.) << S); \
  else clip_code |= ((P_plan < 0.) << S);


#define POINT_INTER_3D(P, P_plan, Q, Q_plan) \
  if (clip_ctx->hpoints_bucket_index >= clip_ctx->hpoints_bucket_max) { \
      if (clip_ctx->hpoints_bucket) { \
         C = (H_point *)realloc(clip_ctx->hpoints_bucket, \
         (clip_ctx->hpoints_bucket_max + 128) * sizeof(H_point)); \
      } else { \
         C = (H_point *)malloc((clip_ctx->hpoints_bucket_max + 128) \
            * sizeof(H_point)); \
      } \
      if (C) { \
         clip_ctx->hpoints_bucket_max += 128; \
         clip_ctx->hpoints_bucket = C; \
      } else { \
         out->num_hpoints = 0; \
         return; \
      } \
   } \
```

564

```
    lambda = P_plan / (P_plan - Q_plan); \
    C->coords[0] = P->coords[0] + lambda * (Q->coords[0] - P->coords[0]); \
    C->coords[1] = P->coords[1] + lambda * (Q->coords[1] - P->coords[1]); \
    C->coords[2] = P->coords[2] + lambda * (Q->coords[2] - P->coords[2]); \
    C->coords[3] = P->coords[3] + lambda * (Q->coords[3] - P->coords[3]); \
    cur_stage[n_cur_s] = C; \
    n_cur_s += 1; \
    clip_ctx->hpoints_bucket_index += 1; \
    C += 1;

#define POINT_COPY(P) \
    cur_stage[n_cur_s] = P; \
    n_cur_s += 1;


/*
 *    h3d_strip_clip:
 *        3D triangle strip clipper. A triangle strip is made of
 *        vertices logocally organized in triangles (...). The first
 *        triangle is composed of the vertices 0, 1, and 2. The second
 *        triangle is represented by the vertices 1, 2, and 3, and so
 *        on until the last vertex.
 *
 *        The triangle strip clipper clips the triangle strip against
 *        one to six boundaries organized in a [xmin, xmax, ymin, ymax,
 *        zmin, zmax] order.Each clip plane can be enabled/disabled by
 *        controlling the clip_ctx->cl_tbdone[0..5] flags. Each flag
 *        affects the respective clip plane of clip_ctx->cl_plane[0..5].
 *
 *        As presented in the algorithm, a triangle strip outputs only
 *        one triangle strip. This is possible if degenerate triangles
 *        are acceptable.
 *
 * Notes:
 *    This is basically a Sutherland-Hodgman algorithm. But a non-recursive
 *    version. Some "shortcuts" have been employed in the intersection cal-
 *    culations in homogeneous coordinates.
 *
 */

h3d_strip_clip(clip_ctx, in, out)
register Clip_ctx   *clip_ctx;
register H_list     *in;
register H_list     *out;
{
```

```
register H_point          **pre_stage, **cur_stage, **tmp_stage;
register H_point          *P, *Q, *R, *C;
register int              n_pre_s, n_cur_s, n_cur_max;
register int              i, n, c;
register unsigned char clip_code;
double                    lambda;
float                     P_plan, Q_plan, R_plan;

/*
 * At init, set the previous stage point to the input points values.
 */

n_cur_s = in->num_hpoints;
if (clip_ctx->pointers_bucket_0_max < (n_cur_s + 64)) {
  if (pre_stage = (H_point **)malloc((n_cur_s + 64) * sizeof(H_point *))) {
    if (clip_ctx->pointers_bucket_0)
      free(clip_ctx->pointers_bucket_0);
    clip_ctx->pointers_bucket_0 = pre_stage;
    clip_ctx->pointers_bucket_0_max = n_cur_s + 64;
  } else {
    out->num_hpoints = 0;
    return;
  }
}
if (clip_ctx->pointers_bucket_1_max < (n_cur_s + 64)) {
  if (pre_stage = (H_point **)malloc((n_cur_s + 64) * sizeof(H_point *))) {
    if (clip_ctx->pointers_bucket_1)
      free(clip_ctx->pointers_bucket_1);
    clip_ctx->pointers_bucket_1 = pre_stage;
    clip_ctx->pointers_bucket_1_max = n_cur_s + 64;
  } else {
    out->num_hpoints = 0;
    return;
  }
}
cur_stage = clip_ctx->pointers_bucket_0;
for (i = 0; i < n_cur_s; i++)
  cur_stage[i] = &(in->hpoints[i]);

C = clip_ctx->hpoints_bucket;
clip_ctx->hpoints_bucket_index = 0;
/*
 * For each of the clipping plane, clip (if necessary).
```

```
 */
for (i = 0; (i < 6 && n_cur_s > 2); i++) {
  if ((clip_ctx->cl_tbdone >> i) & 1) {
     c = i >> 1;
/*
 * switch memory between current and previous.
 */
     pre_stage = cur_stage;
     n_pre_s = n_cur_s;
     if (cur_stage == clip_ctx->pointers_bucket_0) {
        cur_stage = clip_ctx->pointers_bucket_1;
        n_cur_max = clip_ctx->pointers_bucket_1_max;
     } else {
        cur_stage = clip_ctx->pointers_bucket_0;
        n_cur_max = clip_ctx->pointers_bucket_0_max;
     }
     n_cur_s = 0;
/*
 * Start clipping of the previous stage, for the ith clip plane.
 * Output points go in the current_stage memory.
 */
/*
 * Start clipping of the triangle strip from the "previous" stage
 * into the "current" stage, for the ith clip plane.
 *
 * Process the first point of the triangle strip.
 *
 * NOTE: Facet indices only have to be processed after first two points in
 * triangle strip have been taken care of.
 */
     clip_code = 0;
     n = 0;
     COMPUTE_INTER_3D(Q, Q_plan, 1)

/*
 * Now, process the second point of the triangle strip.
 */
     n = 1;
     COMPUTE_INTER_3D(R, R_plan, 2)
/*
 * (Q, R) represents the first line segment of the first triangle of
 * the triangle strip (still following?). We need to clip it as a line
 * to ensure the first two points.
 */
```

```
        n = clip_code >> 1;
        switch (n) {
            case 0:          /* Q and R inside */
                POINT_COPY(Q)
                POINT_COPY(R)
                break;
            case 1:          /* Q outside, R inside */
                POINT_INTER_3D(Q, Q_plan, R, R_plan)
                POINT_COPY(R)
                break;
            case 2:          /* Q inside, R outside */
                POINT_COPY(Q)
                POINT_INTER_3D(Q, Q_plan, R, R_plan)
                break;
            case 3:          /* Q and R outside */
            default:
                break;
        }

/*
 * Process each subsequent point of the triangle strip.
 * P, Q, R form the (n-2)ith triangle of the srtip.
 */
    for (n = 2; n < n_pre_s; n++) {

        clip_code >>= 1;
        P = Q;
        Q = R;
        P_plan = Q_plan;
        Q_plan = R_plan;

        COMPUTE_INTER_3D(R, R_plan, 2)
/*
 * We need to ensure that enough memory is available.
 */
        if (n_cur_max < n_cur_s + 3) {
            tmp_stage = (H_point **)realloc(cur_stage, (n_cur_max + 64)
                    * sizeof (H_point *));
            if (tmp_stage) {
                if (cur_stage == clip_ctx->pointers_bucket_0) {
                    clip_ctx->pointers_bucket_0_max += 64;
                } else {
                    clip_ctx->pointers_bucket_1_max += 64;
                }
```

568

```
          } else {
             out->num_hpoints = 0;
             return;
          }
          cur_stage = tmp_stage;
          n_cur_max += 64;
       }
/*
 * clip_code has now 3 bits that represent the "position" of the triangle in
 * respect to the clip boundary. 8 different cases can occur.
 */
       switch (clip_code) {
           case 0:          /* all inside */
              POINT_COPY(R)
              break;
           case 1:          /* P outside, Q and R inside */
              POINT_INTER_3D(R, R_plan, P, P_plan)
              POINT_COPY(Q)
              POINT_COPY(R)
              break;
           case 2:          /* P inside, Q outside and R inside */
              POINT_COPY(R)
              POINT_INTER_3D(Q, Q_plan, R, R_plan)
              POINT_COPY(R)
              break;
           case 3:          /* P and Q outside, R inside */
              POINT_INTER_3D(R, R_plan, P, P_plan)
              memcpy((char *)(cur_stage + n_cur_s),
                     (char *)(cur_stage + n_cur_s - 1),
                     sizeof(H_point));
              n_cur_s += 1;
              POINT_INTER_3D(Q, Q_plan, R, R_plan)
              POINT_COPY(R)
              break;
           case 4:          /* P and Q inside, R outside */
              POINT_INTER_3D(R, R_plan, P, P_plan)
              POINT_COPY(Q)
              POINT_INTER_3D(Q, Q_plan, R, R_plan)
              break;
           case 5:          /* P outside, Q inside, R outside */
              POINT_INTER_3D(Q, Q_plan, R, R_plan)
              break;
```

```
            case 6:           /* P inside, Q and R outside */
                POINT_INTER_3D(R, R_plan, P, P_plan)
                memcpy((char *)(cur_stage + n_cur_s),
                        (char *)(cur_stage + n_cur_s - 1),
                        sizeof(H_point));
                n_cur_s += 1;
                break;
            case 7:           /* P, Q and R outside */
            default:
                break;
        }
    }
}
/*
 * The triangle strip has been clipped against all (enabled) clipping
 * planes.
 * "Copy" the result to the output.
 */
if (n_cur_s > 2) {
    for (i = 0; i < n_cur_s; i++)
        out->hpoints[i] = *(cur_stage[i]);
    out->num_hpoints = n_cur_s;
} else {
    out->num_hpoints = 0;
}
return;
}
```

INTERPHONG SHADING

(page 232)

Nadia Magnenat Thalmann, Daniel Thalmann, and Hong Tong Minh

```
/**************************************************************************
                InterPhong shading for Scan-line rendering algorithms

InterPhong shading has been used for rendering the synthetic actors Marilyn
Monroe and Humphrey Bogart in the film "Rendez-vous à Montréal" directed by Nadia
Magnenat Thalmann and Daniel Thalmann, 1987

**************************************************************************/

#include <math.h>
#include "gems.h"

#define RESANTI          3839
#define NBMAXSOURCES     10
#define SQRT3_2          3.464101615
#define NIL              0

typedef struct {
        double r, g, b;
} Colors;

typedef struct {
        Colors coul;
        double w, n;
} RecCoul;

/*      Declaration of types used for the datastructures that represent the
        information of a figure for the treatment by scanline ( software
rendering )
 */

typedef struct blocedge {
        struct blocedge *edsuiv;        /* next edge in the list */
        struct blocpoly *ptpoly1, *ptpoly2;  /* polygons sharing this edge */
        double x, dx;           /* Xmin and Xdelta */
        double z, dz;           /* Zmin and Zdelta */
        double ymax; /* maximum Y of edge */
        double nx, dnx, ny, dny, nz, dnz;
        double px, dpx, py, dpy, pz, dpz;
} BlockEdge;
```

```c
typedef struct blocpoly {
        struct blocpoly *polsuiv;        /* next polygon in the list */
        struct T_ptedge *ptlisttrie;
        RecCoul refl;    /* polygon characteristics color, spec.
                          coeff., ... */
        Colors coulpoly;        /* polygon shading */
        Vector3 normalctri;
        double bias, tension;
} BlockPoly;

typedef struct T_ptedge {
        BlockEdge *ptedtrie;
        struct T_ptedge *ptedsuiv;
} PtEdge;

/*
 * Declaration of types concerning the calculated image for the
 * current scanline ( Z-buffer )
 */

typedef struct scanbuf_el {
        Colors c,                               /* final color of this pixel */
                polycolor;                      /* initial color of visible polygon
*/
} ScanBufType [RESANTI + 1];

typedef struct epthbuf_el {
        double depth;                           /* depth of opaque pixel */
} DepthBufType [RESANTI + 1];

typedef struct           {
        int     xmin, xmax;
} PosBufType;

/*
 * Declaration of data structure types to store light source information
 */

static PosBufType        posbuffer;

ScanBufType _scanbuffer;                         /* Z-buffer */
DepthBufType _depthbuffer;

static
void intphong(nestime, noriginal, bias, tension)
Vector3 *nestime, *noriginal;
double bias, tension;

/*

    Purpose: interphong interpolation
    Arguments
        nestime        : estimated normal
        noriginal      : original normal
        bias, tension  : bias and tension
*/
```

572

```
{
        double  fact;
        Vector3 vtemp;

        V3Sub (noriginal, nestime, &vtemp);
        fact = fabs(vtemp.x) + fabs(vtemp.y) + fabs(vtemp.z);
        fact = (fact + bias * (SQRT3_2 - fact)) * tension;
        V3Scale (vtemp,fact*V3Length (vtemp));
        V3Add (nestime, &vtemp,nestime);
        V3Normalize (nestime);
}

/*===========================================================*/

static
void shadepoly(ptpoly)
BlockPoly        *ptpoly;

/*

    Purpose: shades a polygon on the current scanline
    Arguments
        ptpoly          : polygon to render
        noscline        : current scanline
*/

{
        BlockEdge       *edge1, *edge2;
        PtEdge  *tripedtrie;
        int             xx;
        double          dxx;
        double          zz, dzz;
        double          diffx;
        double          dnnx, dnny, dnnz;
        Vector3 normal, unitn;
        double          dppx, dppy, dppz;
        Vector3 point;
        Colors  cc;
        RecCoul ptrefl;
        register struct scanbuf_el      *scanel ;
        register struct depthbuf_el     *depthel ;

        tripedtrie = ptpoly->ptlisttrie;
        ptrefl = ptpoly->refl;
        while (tripedtrie != (PtEdge *)NIL)
        {
                edge1 = tripedtrie->ptedtrie;
                if (tripedtrie->ptedsuiv != (PtEdge *)NIL)
                {
                        tripedtrie = tripedtrie->ptedsuiv;
                        edge2 = tripedtrie->ptedtrie;
                }
                else
                        abort(" Odd number of edges on scanline");

                dxx = edge2->x - edge1->x;          /* distance between edges
                                                      on current scanline */
```

```
        if (dxx < 1.0)                         /* crossing edges ? */
                dxx = 1.0;
        dxx = 1.0 / dxx;                        /* increment per pixel */
        xx = Trunc(edge1->x) + 1;              /* first pixel to be
                                                  colored */

        diffx = xx - edge1->x;

        dzz = (edge2->z - edge1->z) * dxx;
        zz = edge1->z + dzz * diffx;

        if (xx < posbuffer.xmin)
                posbuffer.xmin = xx;
        if (edge2->x > posbuffer.xmax)
                posbuffer.xmax = Trunc(edge2->x);

        dnnx = (edge2->nx - edge1->nx) * dxx;
        dnny = (edge2->ny - edge1->ny) * dxx;
        dnnz = (edge2->nz - edge1->nz) * dxx;
        normal.x = (edge1->nx + dnnx * diffx) + dnnx;
        normal.y = (edge1->ny + dnny * diffx) + dnny;
        normal.z = (edge1->nz + dnnz * diffx) + dnnz;
        dppx = (edge2->px - edge1->px) * dxx;
        dppy = (edge2->py - edge1->py) * dxx;
        dppz = (edge2->pz - edge1->pz) * dxx;
        point.x = (edge1->px + dppx * diffx) + dppx;
        point.y = (edge1->py + dppy * diffx) + dppy;
        point.z = (edge1->pz + dppz * diffx) + dppz;

        while (xx <= edge2->x)
        {
                scanel = &_scanbuffer[xx];
                depthel = &_depthbuffer[xx];

                if (zz < depthel->depth)
                {
                        unity(normal, &unitn);
                        intphong(&unitn, &ptpoly->normalctri,
                                ptpoly->bias, ptpoly->tension);
                        cc = ptpoly->coulpoly;
                        depthel->depth = zz;
                        scanel->polycolor = ptrefl.coul;
                        scanel->c = cc;
                }
                xx = xx + 1;
                zz = zz + dzz;
                normal.x = normal.x + dnnx;
                normal.y = normal.y + dnny;
                normal.z = normal.z + dnnz;
                point.x = point.x + dppx;
                point.y = point.y + dppy;
                point.z = point.z + dppz;
        }
        break ;
        tripedtrie = tripedtrie->ptedsuiv;
    }
  }
```

574

FAST RAY – CONVEX POLYHEDRON INTERSECTION
(page 247)

Eric Haines

```
/* Ray-Convex Polyhedron Intersection Test by Eric Haines
 *
 * This test checks the ray against each face of a polyhedron, checking whether
 * the set of intersection points found for each ray-plane intersection
 * overlaps the previous intersection results.  If there is no overlap (i.e.
 * no line segment along the ray that is inside the polyhedron), then the
 * ray misses and returns 0; else 1 is returned if the ray is entering the
 * polyhedron, -1 if the ray originates inside the polyhedron.  If there is
 * an intersection, the distance and the normal of the face hit is returned.
 */

#include <math.h>
#include "GraphicsGems.h"

#ifndef HUGE_VAL
#define HUGE_VAL 1.7976931348623157e+308
#endif

typedef struct Point4Struct {          /* 4d point */
        double x, y, z, w;
        } Point4;

/* fast macro version of V3Dot, usable with Point4 */
#define DOT3( a, b ) ( (a)->x*(b)->x + (a)->y*(b)->y + (a)->z*(b)->z )

/* return codes */
#define MISSED     0
#define FRONTFACE  1
#define BACKFACE  -1

int RayCvxPolyhedronInt( org, dir, tmax, phdrn, ph_num, tresult, norm )
Point3 *org, *dir ;          /* origin and direction of ray */
double tmax ;                /* maximum useful distance along ray */
Point4 *phdrn ;              /* list of planes in convex polyhedron */
int ph_num ;                 /* number of planes in convex polyhedron */
double *tresult ;            /* returned: distance of intersection along ray */
Point3 *norm ;               /* returned: normal of face hit */
{
Point4 *pln ;       /* plane equation */
double tnear, tfar, t, vn, vd ;
int fnorm_num, bnorm_num ;   /* front/back face # hit */
```

```
tnear = -HUGE_VAL ;
tfar = tmax ;

/* Test each plane in polyhedron */
for ( pln = &phdrn[ph_num-1] ; ph_num-- ; pln-- ) {
    /* Compute intersection point T and sidedness */
    vd = DOT3( dir, pln ) ;
    vn = DOT3( org, pln ) + pln->w ;
    if ( vd == 0.0 ) {
        /* ray is parallel to plane - check if ray origin is inside plane's
           half-space */
        if ( vn > 0.0 )
            /* ray origin is outside half-space */
            return ( MISSED ) ;
    } else {
        /* ray not parallel - get distance to plane */
        t = -vn / vd ;
        if ( vd < 0.0 ) {
            /* front face - T is a near point */
            if ( t > tfar ) return ( MISSED ) ;
            if ( t > tnear ) {
                /* hit near face, update normal */
                fnorm_num = ph_num ;
                tnear = t ;
            }
        } else {
            /* back face - T is a far point */
            if ( t < 0.0 ) return ( MISSED ) ;
            if ( t < tfar ) {
                /* hit near face, update normal */
                bnorm_num = ph_num ;
                tfar = t ;
            }
        }
    }
}

/* survived all tests */
/* Note: if ray originates on polyhedron, may want to change 0.0 to some
 * epsilon to avoid intersecting the originating face.
 */
if ( tnear >= 0.0 ) {
    /* outside, hitting front face */
    *norm = *(Point3 *)&phdrn[fnorm_num] ;
    *tresult = tnear ;
    return ( FRONTFACE ) ;
} else {
    if ( tfar < tmax ) {
        /* inside, hitting back face */
        *norm = *(Point3 *)&phdrn[bnorm_num] ;
        *tresult = tfar ;
        return ( BACKFACE ) ;
    } else {
        /* inside, but back face beyond tmax */
        return ( MISSED ) ;
    }
}
}
```

INTERSECTING A RAY WITH AN ELLIPTICAL TORUS

(page 251)

Joseph M. Cychosz

```
#include          <math.h>
#include          "GraphicsGems.h"


/* ---- inttor.c - Intersect a ray with a torus. ------------------------ */
/*                                                                         */
/*                                                                         */
/*      Description:                                                       */
/*           Inttor determines the intersection of a ray with a torus.     */
/*                                                                         */
/*      On entry:                                                          */
/*           raybase = The coordinate defining the base of the            */
/*                        intersecting ray.                                */
/*           raycos  = The direction cosines of the above ray.            */
/*           center  = The center location of the torus.                  */
/*           radius  = The major radius of the torus.                     */
/*           rplane  = The minor radius in the plane of the torus.        */
/*           rnorm   = The minor radius normal to the plane of the torus. */
/*           tran    = A 4x4 transformation matrix that will position     */
/*                        the torus at the origin and orient it such that  */
/*                        the plane of the torus lyes in the x-z plane.    */
/*                                                                         */
/*      On return:                                                         */
/*           nhits   = The number of intersections the ray makes with     */
/*                        the torus.                                       */
/*           rhits   = The entering/leaving distances of the              */
/*                        intersections.                                   */
/*                                                                         */
/*      Returns:  True if the ray intersects the torus.                   */
/*                                                                         */
/* ----------------------------------------------------------------------- */
```

```
int        inttor    (raybase, raycos, center, radius, rplane, rnorm, tran, nhits, rhits)

           Point3    raybase;                 /* Base of the intersection ray */
           Vector3   raycos;                  /* Direction cosines of the ray */
           Point3    center;                  /* Center of the torus          */
           double    radius;                  /* Major radius of the torus    */
           double    rplane;                  /* Minor planer radius          */
           double    rnorm;                   /* Minor normal radius          */
           Matrix4   tran;                     /* Transformation matrix        */
           int *     nhits;                   /* Number of intersections      */
           double    rhits[4];                /* Intersection distances       */

{
           int       hit;                     /* True if ray intersects torus */
           double    rsphere;                 /* Bounding sphere radius        */
           Vector3   Base, Dcos;              /* Transformed intersection ray  */
           double    rmin, rmax;              /* Root bounds                   */
           double    yin, yout;
           double    rho, a0, b0;             /* Related constants             */
           double    f, l, t, g, q, m, u;     /* Ray dependent terms           */
           double    C[5];                    /* Quartic coefficents           */

extern     int       intsph ();              /* Intersect ray with sphere     */
extern     int       SolveQuartic ();        /* Solve quartic equation        */


           *nhits  = 0;

/*         Compute the intersection of the ray with a bounding sphere.         */

           rsphere = radius + MAX (rplane, rnorm);
           hit     = intsph (raybase, raycos, center, rsphere, &rmin, &rmax);

           if  (!hit) return (hit);          /* If ray misses bounding sphere*/

/*         Transform the intersection ray                                      */

           Base = raybase;
           Dcos = raycos;
           V3MulPointByMatrix  (&Base, &tran);
           V3MulVectorByMatrix (&Dcos, &tran);

/*         Bound the torus by two parallel planes rnorm from the x-z plane.    */

           yin  = Base.y + rmin * Dcos.y;
           yout = Base.y + rmax * Dcos.y;
           hit  = !( (yin >  rnorm && yout >  rnorm) ||
                     (yin < -rnorm && yout < -rnorm) );

           if  (!hit) return (hit);          /* If ray is above/below torus. */
```

```
/*      Compute constants related to the torus.                         */

        rho = rplane*rplane / (rnorm*rnorm);
        a0  = 4. * radius*radius;
        b0  = radius*radius - rplane*rplane;

/*      Compute ray dependent terms.                                    */

        f = 1. - Dcos.y*Dcos.y;
        l = 2. * (Base.x*Dcos.x + Base.z*Dcos.z);
        t = Base.x*Base.x + Base.z*Base.z;
        g = f + rho * Dcos.y*Dcos.y;
        q = a0 / (g*g);
        m = (l + 2.*rho*Dcos.y*Base.y) / g;
        u = (t +    rho*Base.y*Base.y + b0) / g;

/*      Compute the coefficients of the quartic.                        */

        C[4] = 1.0;
        C[3] = 2. * m;
        C[2] = m*m + 2.*u - q*f;
        C[1] = 2.*m*u - q*l;
        C[0] = u*u - q*t;

/*      Use quartic root solver found in "Graphics Gems" by Jochen      */
/*      Schwarze.                                                       */

        *nhits = SolveQuartic (C,rhits);
        return (*nhits != 0);
}



/* ---- intsph.c - Intersect a ray with a sphere. ---------------------- */
/*                                                                       */
/*                                                                       */
/*      Description:                                                     */
/*          Intsph determines the intersection of a ray with a sphere.   */
/*                                                                       */
/*      On entry:                                                        */
/*          raybase = The coordinate defining the base of the           */
/*                    intersecting ray.                                 */
/*          raycos  = The direction cosines of the above ray.           */
/*          center  = The center location of the sphere.                */
/*          radius  = The radius of the sphere.                         */
/*                                                                       */
/*      On return:                                                       */
/*          rin     = The entering distance of the intersection.        */
/*          rout    = The leaving  distance of the intersection.        */
/*                                                                       */
/*      Returns:  True if the ray intersects the sphere.                */
/*                                                                       */
/* --------------------------------------------------------------------- */
```

```
int      intsph   (raybase,raycos,center,radius,rin,rout)

         Point3    raybase;                   /* Base of the intersection ray */
         Vector3   raycos;                    /* Direction cosines of the ray */
         Point3    center;                    /* Center of the sphere         */
         double    radius;                    /* Radius of the sphere         */
         double    *rin;                       /* Entering distance            */
         double    *rout;                      /* Leaving distance             */

{
         int       hit;                       /* True if ray intersects sphere */
         double    dx, dy, dz; /* Ray base to sphere center               */
         double    bsq, u, disc;
         double    root;


         dx   = raybase.x - center.x;
         dy   = raybase.y - center.y;
         dz   = raybase.z - center.z;
         bsq  = dx*raycos.x + dy*raycos.y + dz*raycos.z;
         u    = dx*dx + dy*dy + dz*dz - radius*radius;
         disc = bsq*bsq - u;

         hit  = (disc >= 0.0);

         if  (hit) {                           /* If ray hits sphere           */
             root  = sqrt (disc);
             *rin  = -bsq - root;              /*    entering distance         */
             *rout = -bsq + root;              /*    leaving distanc           */
         }

         return (hit);
}
```

A RECURSIVE SHADOW VOXEL CACHE FOR RAY TRACING

(page 273)

Andrew Pearce

When Spawning a Refraction Ray:

```
Mask = 0x01 << Spawning_ray_level;
path = path | Mask;                /* Turn on correct bit. */
trace( /* refraction ray */ );
path = path & ~Mask;
```

When Spawning Reflection Ray:

```
Mask = 0x01 << Spawning_ray_level;
path = path & ~Mask;              /* Turn off correct bit. */
trace( /* reflection ray */ );
```

```
typedef struct _stree {
    Object_Rec      *last_object;
    Voxel_Rec       *last_voxel;
    struct _stree  *refraction_ray;
    struct _stree  *reflection_ray;
} Shadow_Tree;

float check_shadowing(ray, light, path, Spawning_ray_level)
Ray_Rec   *ray;   /* ray from shading point to light source */
Light_Rec *light; /* the light source we are interested in */
int       path;   /* bit table: current position in vision ray tree */
int       Spawning_ray_level; /* level of ray spawning this shadow ray */
{
```

```
    unsigned int   Mask;
    Shadow_Tree  *cache;

    cache = light->cache_tree;
    Mask = 0x01;
    /* If the spawning ray's level is 0 (primary ray), then we */
    /* use the head of the cache_tree. */
    for (i = 0; i < Spawning_ray_level; ++i) {
        if (Mask & path) cache = cache->refraction_ray;
        else             cache = cache->reflection_ray;
        Mask = Mask << 1; /* Shift mask left 1 bit */
    }


if (cache->last_object != NULL) {
    /* intersect_object() marks object as having been */
    /* intersected by this ray. */
    hit = intersect_object( ray, cache->last_object, &object);

    if (hit) {
        /* You may want to check that the hit was actually in the */
        /* last_voxel at this point and null the last_voxel if not. */
        return(1.0); /* full shadowing */
    }
    cache->last_object = NULL; /* object was not hit */

    if (cache->last_voxel != NULL) { /* implied !hit */

        /* intersect_object_in_voxel_for_shadows() returns TRUE */
        /* on first affirmed intersection with an opaque object. */
        /* It ignores transparent objects altogether. */
        hit = intersect_objects_in_voxel_for_shadows( ray,
                                    cache->last_voxel, &object);
        if (hit) {
            cache->last_object = object;
            /* You may want to check if the hit was actually in the */
            /* last_voxel at this point & NULL last_voxel if not. */
            return(1.0);
        }
        cache->last_voxel = NULL; /* voxel did not supply a hit */
    }
}


/* traverse_voxels_for_shadows() DOES intersect transparent objects */
/* and sorts the intersections for proper attenuation of the light  */
/* intensity. If multiple objects are hit, then one of the          */
/* intersections must be transparent, and the object returned is the*/
```

IMPLEMENTING PROGRESSIVE RADIOSITY WITH USER-PROVIDED POLYGON DISPLAY ROUTINES

(page 295)

Shenchang Eric Chen

```
/*****************************************************************************
 *    rad.h
 *
 *    This is the headerfile which defines the data structures used in rad.c
 *****************************************************************************/

#define kNumberOfRadSamples 3

typedef struct { float x, y, z; } TPoint3f;
typedef TPoint3f TVector3f;
typedef struct { unsigned char a, r, g, b;} TColor32b;

typedef struct {
    double samples[kNumberOfRadSamples];
} TSpectra;

typedef struct {
    TSpectra* reflectance; /* diffuse reflectance of the patch */
    TSpectra* emission; /* emission of the patch */
    TPoint3f center;/* center of the patch where hemi-cubes will be placed */
    TVector3f normal;   /* normal of the patch; for orienting the hemi-cube */
    TSpectra unshotRad; /* unshot radiosity of the patch */
    double area;/* area of the patch */
} TPatch;

typedef struct {
    unsigned short nVerts;   /* number of vertices of the element */
    unsigned long* verts;    /* vertices */
    TVector3f normal;    /* normal of the element; for backface removal */
    TSpectra rad;    /* total radiosity of the element */
    double area;/* area of the patch */
    TPatch* patch;   /* pointer to the parent patch */
} TElement;

typedef struct {
    TPoint3f camera;/* camera location */
    TPoint3f lookat;/* point of interest */
    TVector3f up;    /* view up vector */
    float fovx, fovy;    /* field of view in x, y (in degree) */
    float near, far;/* distance from the camera to the near and far planes */
    unsigned short xRes, yRes;   /* resolution of the buffer */
```

```
    unsigned long* buffer;   /* pointer to the buffer */
} TView;

/* radiosity input parameters */
typedef struct {
    double threshold; /* convergence threshold (fraction of the total emitted
                        energy) */
    unsigned long nPatches; /* number of patches */
    TPatch *patches; /* patches */
    unsigned long nElements; /* number of elements */
    TElement *elements; /* elements */
    unsigned long nPoints;   /* nubmer of element vertices */
    TPoint3f *points;   /* element vertices */
    TView displayView;   /* view to display the results */
    unsigned short hemicubeRes; /* hemi-cube resolution */
    float worldSize; /* approximate diameter of the bounding sphere of the world.
            used for placing near and far planes in the hemi-cube computation*/
    float intensityScale;   /* used to scale intensity for display */
} TRadParams;

/* initialization */
void InitRad(TRadParams *p);
/* main iterative loop */
void DoRad();
/* final clean up */
void CleanUpRad();

/* The following routines should be provided by the user */

/* Clear buffer. Set up view transformation */
void BeginDraw(
TView *view,     /* the viewing parameters and frame buffer to draw to*/
unsigned long color /* color used to clear the buffer */
);

/* Draw a 3-d polygon with a constant color */
void DrawPolygon(
int nPts, /* number of points in the polygon */
TPoint3f *pts, /* points of the polygon */
TVector3f* normal, /* normal of the polygon */
unsigned long color /* color to be drawn with */
);

/* Finish the drawing of polygons to the frame buffer */
void EndDraw();
```

584

```
/****************************************************************************
*   rad.c
*
*   This program contains three functions that should be called in sequence to
*   perform radiosity rendering:
*   InitRad(): Initialize radiosity.
*   DoRad(): Perform the main radiosity iteration loop.
*   CleanUpRad(): Clean up.
*
*   The following routines are assumed to be provided by the user:
*   BeginDraw()
*   DrawPolygon()
*   EndDraw()
*   Refer to rad.h for details
****************************************************************************/

#include "Rad.h"
#include <math.h>
#include <stdlib.h>

#define kMaxPolyPoints   255
#define PI   3.1415926
#define AddVector(c,a,b)  (c).x=(a).x+(b).x,  (c).y=(a).y+(b).y,  (c).z=(a).z+(b).z
#define SubVector(c,a,b)  (c).x=(a).x-(b).x,  (c).y=(a).y-(b).y,  (c).z=(a).z-(b).z
#define CrossVector(c,a,b)    (c).x = (a).y*(b).z - (a).z*(b).y, \
                              (c).y = (a).z*(b).x - (a).x*(b).z, \
                              (c).z = (a).x*(b).y - (a).y*(b).x
#define DotVector(a,b)  (a).x*(b).x + (a).y*(b).y + (a).z*(b).z
#define ScaleVector(c,s)  (c).x*=(s),  (c).y*=(s),  (c).z*=(s)
#define NormalizeVector(n,a)      ((n)=sqrt(DotVector(a,a)), \
                                  (n)?((a).x/=n, (a).y/=n, (a).z/=n):0)


typedef struct {
    TView    view;          /* we only need to store one face of the hemi-cube */
    double* topFactors;  /* delta form-factors(weight for each pixel) of the top
                     face */
    double* sideFactors; /* delta form-factors of the side faces */
} THemicube;

static TRadParams *params;   /* input parameters */
static THemicube hemicube;   /* one hemi-cube */
static double *formfactors; /* a form-factor array which has the same length as
```

```
                                 the number of elements */
static double totalEnergy;      /* total emitted energy; used for convergence
                                 checking */

static const TSpectra black = { 0, 0, 0 };   /* for initialization */
static int FindShootPatch(unsigned long *shootPatch);
static void SumFactors(double* formfactors, int xRes, int yRes,
    unsigned long* buf, double* deltaFactors);
static void MakeTopFactors(int hres, double* deltaFactors);
static void MakeSideFactors(int hres, double* deltaFactors);
static void ComputeFormfactors(unsigned long shootPatch);
static void DistributeRad(unsigned long shootPatch);
static void DisplayResults(TView* view);
static void DrawElement(TElement* ep, unsigned long color);
static TColor32b SpectraToRGB(TSpectra* spectra);


/* Initialize radiosity based on the input parameters p */
void InitRad(TRadParams *p)
{
    int n;
    int hRes;
    unsigned long i;
    int j;
    TPatch* pp;
    TElement* ep;

    params = p;

    /* initialize hemi-cube */
    hemicube.view.fovx = 90;
    hemicube.view.fovy = 90;
    /* make sure hemicube resolution is an even number */
    hRes = ((int)(params->hemicubeRes/2.0+0.5))*2;
    hemicube.view.xRes = hemicube.view.yRes = hRes;
    n = hRes*hRes;
    hemicube.view.buffer = calloc(n, sizeof(unsigned long));
    hemicube.view.near = params->worldSize*0.001;
    hemicube.view.far = params->worldSize;

    /* take advantage of the symmetry in the delta form-factors */
    hemicube.topFactors= calloc(n/4, sizeof(double));
    hemicube.sideFactors= calloc(n/4, sizeof(double));
    MakeTopFactors(hRes/2, hemicube.topFactors);
    MakeSideFactors(hRes/2, hemicube.sideFactors);

    formfactors = calloc(params->nElements, sizeof(double));

    /* initialize radiosity */
    pp = params->patches;
    for (i=params->nPatches; i--; pp++)
        pp->unshotRad = *(pp->emission);
    ep = params->elements;
    for (i=params->nElements; i--; ep++)
        ep->rad = *(ep->patch->emission);

    /* compute total energy */
    totalEnergy = 0;
    pp = params->patches;
```

```
        for (i=params->nPatches; i--; pp++)
            for (j=0; j<kNumberOfRadSamples; j++)
                totalEnergy += pp->emission->samples[j] * pp->area;

    DisplayResults(&params->displayView);

}

/* Main iterative loop */
void DoRad()
{
    unsigned long shootPatch;

    while (FindShootPatch(&shootPatch))
    {
        ComputeFormfactors(shootPatch);
        DistributeRad(shootPatch);
        DisplayResults(&params->displayView);
    }

}

/* Clean up */
void CleanUpRad()
{
    free(hemicube.topFactors);
    free(hemicube.sideFactors);
    free(hemicube.view.buffer);
    free(formfactors);

}

/* Find the next shooting patch based on the unshot energy of each patch */
/* Return 0 if convergence is reached; otherwise, return 1 */
static int FindShootPatch(unsigned long *shootPatch)
{
    int i, j;
    double energySum, error, maxEnergySum=0;
    TPatch* ep;

    ep = params->patches;
    for (i=0; i< params->nPatches; i++, ep++)
    {
        energySum =0;
        for (j=0; j<kNumberOfRadSamples; j++)
            energySum += ep->unshotRad.samples[j] * ep->area;

        if (energySum > maxEnergySum)
        {
            *shootPatch = i;
            maxEnergySum = energySum;
        }
    }

    error = maxEnergySum / totalEnergy;

    /* check convergence */
    if (error < params->threshold)
        return (0);       /* converged */
    else
```

```
        return (1);


}


/* Find out the index to the delta form-factors arrary */
#define Index(i) ((i)<hres? i: (hres-1- ((i)%hres)))

/* Use the largest 32bit unsigned long for background */
#define kBackgroundItem 0xffffffff

/* Convert a hemi-cube face to form-factors */
static void SumFactors(
double* formfactors, /* output */
int xRes, int yRes, /* resolution of the hemi-cube face */
unsigned long* buf, /* we only need the storage of the top hemi-cube face */
double* deltaFactors /* delta form-factors for each hemi-cube pixel */
)
{
    int i, j;
    int ii, jj;
    unsigned long *ip=buf;
    int hres = xRes/2;
    for (i=0; i<yRes; i++)
    {
        ii= Index(i)*hres;
        for (j=0; j<xRes; j++, ip++)
            if ((*ip) != kBackgroundItem)
            {
                jj = Index(j);
                formfactors[*ip] += deltaFactors[ii+jj];
            }
    }
}

/* Create the delta form-factors for the top face of hemi-cube */
/* Only need to compute 1/4 of the form-factors because of the 4-way symmetry */
static void MakeTopFactors(
int hres, /* half resolution of the face */
double* deltaFactors /* output */
)
{
    int j,k;
    double xSq , ySq, xylSq;
    double n= hres;
    double* wp;
    double dj, dk;

    wp = deltaFactors;
    for (j=0; j<hres; j++)
    {
        dj = (double)j;
        ySq = (n - (j+0.5)) / n;
        ySq *= ySq;
        for ( k=0 ; k<hres ; k++ )
        {
            dk = (double)k;
            xSq = ( n - (k + 0.5) ) / n;
            xSq *= xSq;
```

588

```
                    xy1Sq =  xSq + ySq + 1.0 ;
                    xy1Sq *= xy1Sq;
                    *wp++ = 1.0 / (xy1Sq * PI * n * n);
            }
        }
}


/* Create the delta form-factors for the side face of hemi-cube */
/* Only need to compute 1/4 of the form-factors because of the 4-way symmetry */
static void MakeSideFactors(
int hres, /* half resolution of the face */
double* deltaFactors /* output */
)
{
    int j,k;
    double x, xSq , y, ySq, xy1, xy1Sq;
    double n= hres;
    double* wp;
    double dj, dk;

    wp = deltaFactors;
    for (j=0; j<hres; j++)
    {
        dj = (double)j;
        y = (n - (dj+0.5)) / n;
        ySq = y*y;
        for ( k=0 ; k<hres ; k++ )
        {
            dk = (double)k;
            x = ( n - (dk + 0.5) ) / n;
            xSq = x*x;
            xy1 =   xSq + ySq + 1.0 ;
            xy1Sq = xy1*xy1;
            *wp++ = y / (xy1Sq * PI * n * n);
        }
    }
}


/* Use drand48 instead if it is supported */
#define RandomFloat ((float)(rand())/(float)RAND_MAX)

/* Compute form-factors from the shooting patch to every elements */
static void ComputeFormfactors(unsigned long shootPatch)
{
    unsigned long i;
    TVector3f    up[5];
    TPoint3f     lookat[5];
    TPoint3f     center;
    TVector3f    normal, tangentU, tangentV, vec;
    int face;
    double       norm;
    TPatch*      sp;
    double*      fp;
    TElement*    ep;

    /* get the center of shootPatch */
    sp = &(params->patches[shootPatch]);
    center = sp->center;
    normal = sp->normal;
```

```
/* rotate the hemi-cube along the normal axis of the patch randomly */
/* this will reduce the hemi-cube aliasing artifacts */
do {
    vec.x = RandomFloat;
    vec.y = RandomFloat;
    vec.z = RandomFloat;
    /* get a tangent vector */
    CrossVector(tangentU, normal, vec);
    NormalizeVector(norm, tangentU);
} while (norm==0);   /* bad choice of the radom vector */

/* compute tangentV */
CrossVector(tangentV, normal, tangentU);

/* assign the lookats and ups for each hemicube face */
AddVector(lookat[0], center, normal);
up[0] = tangentU;
AddVector(lookat[1], center, tangentU);
up[1] = normal;
AddVector(lookat[2], center, tangentV);
up[2] = normal;
SubVector(lookat[3], center, tangentU);
up[3] = normal;
SubVector(lookat[4], center, tangentV);
up[4] = normal;

/* position the hemicube at the center of the shooting patch */
hemicube.view.camera = center;

/* clear the formfactors */
fp = formfactors;
for (i=params->nElements; i--; fp++)
    *fp = 0.0;

for (face=0; face < 5; face++)
{
    hemicube.view.lookat = lookat[face];
    hemicube.view.up = up[face];

    /* draw elements */
    BeginDraw(&(hemicube.view), kBackgroundItem);
    for (i=0; i< params->nElements; i++)
        DrawElement(&params->elements[i], i);
        /* color element i with its index */
    EndDraw();

    /* get formfactors */
    if (face==0)
        SumFactors(formfactors, hemicube.view.xRes, hemicube.view.yRes,
            hemicube.view.buffer, hemicube.topFactors);
    else
        SumFactors(formfactors, hemicube.view.xRes, hemicube.view.yRes/2,
            hemicube.view.buffer, hemicube.sideFactors);
}

/* compute reciprocal form-factors */
ep = params->elements;
fp   formfactors;
for (i=params->nElements; i--; ep++, fp++)
```

```
        {
            *fp *= sp->area / ep->area;

            /* This is a potential source of hemi-cube aliasing */
            /* To do this right, we need to subdivide the shooting patch
               and reshoot. For now we just clip it to unity */
            if ((*fp) > 1.0)      *fp ==1.0;
        }
    }
}

/* Distribute radiosity form shootPatch to every element */
/* Reset the shooter's unshot radiosity to 0 */
static void DistributeRad(unsigned long shootPatch)
{
    unsigned long i;
    int j;
    TPatch* sp;
    TElement* ep;
    double* fp;
    TSpectra deltaRad;
    double w;

    sp = &(params->patches[shootPatch]);

    /* distribute unshotRad to every element */
    ep = params->elements;
    fp = formfactors;
    for (i=params->nElements; i--; ep++, fp++)
    {
        if ((*fp) != 0.0)
        {
            for (j=0; j<kNumberOfRadSamples; j++)
                deltaRad.samples[j] =   sp->unshotRad.samples[j] * (*fp) *
                                       ep->patch->reflectance->samples[j];

            /* incremental element's radiosity and patch's unshot radiosity */
            w = ep->area/ep->patch->area;
            for (j=0; j<kNumberOfRadSamples; j++)
            {
                ep->rad.samples[j] += deltaRad.samples[j];
                ep->patch->unshotRad.samples[j] += deltaRad.samples[j] * w;
            }
        }
    }

    /* reset shooting patch's unshot radiosity */
    sp->unshotRad = black;
}

/* Convert a TSpectra (radiosity) to a TColor32b (rgb color) */
/* Assume the first three samples of the spectra are the r, g, b colors */
/* More elaborated color space transformation could be performed here */
static TColor32b
SpectraToRGB(TSpectra* spectra)
{
    TColor32b   c;
    TSpectra    r;
    double   max=1.0;
```

```
    int k;

    for (k=kNumberOfRadSamples; k--;) {
        if (spectra->samples[k] > max)
            max = spectra->samples[k];
    }
    /* Clip the intensity*/
    r = *spectra;
    if (max>1.0) {
        for (k=kNumberOfRadSamples; k--; )
            r.samples[k] /= max;
    }

    /* Convert to a 32-bit color; Assume the first 3 samples in TSpectra
    are the r, g, b colors we want. Otherwise, do color conversion here */
    c.a= 0;
    c.r= (unsigned char) (r.samples[0] * 255.0 + 0.5);
    c.g= (unsigned char) (r.samples[1] * 255.0 + 0.5);
    c.b= (unsigned char) (r.samples[2] * 255.0 + 0.5);

    return c;
}


static void
DisplayResults(TView* view)
{
    unsigned long i;
    register TElement* ep;

    BeginDraw(view, 0);
    ep = params->elements;
    for (i=0; i< params->nElements; i++, ep++) {
        TColor32b    c;
        TSpectra  s;
        int k;
        for (k=kNumberOfRadSamples; k--; )
            s.samples[k] = ep->rad.samples[k]*params->intensityScale;

        /* quantize color */
        c = SpectraToRGB(&s);
        DrawElement(ep, *(unsigned long*)&c);
    }

    EndDraw();

}

static void
DrawElement(TElement* ep, unsigned long color)
{
    static TPoint3f pts[kMaxPolyPoints];
    int nPts = ep->nVerts;
    int j;
    for (j=0; j<nPts; j++)
        pts[j] = params->points[ep->verts[j]];

    DrawPolygon(nPts, pts, &ep->normal, color);

}
```

```
/****************************************************************
*    room.c
*
*    This is a test program which constrcuts the Cornell radiosity room with
*    a ceiling light and two boxes inside. The side faces of the boxes are not
*    directly illuminated by the light. Therefore, they are a good example of
*    the color bleeding effects.
*    This program calls IniRad(), DoRad() and CleanUpRad() in rad.c to perform
*    the radiosity rendering.
****************************************************************/

#include "rad.h"

/* a quadrilateral */
typedef struct {
    short verts[4]; /* vertices of the quadrilateral */
    short patchLevel; /* patch subdivision level (how fine to subdivide the
                    quadrilateral?) */
    short elementLevel; /* element subdivision level (how fine to subdivide a
                    patch?) */
    float area; /* area of the quadrilateral */
    TVector3f normal; /* normal of the quadrilateral */
    TSpectra* reflectance; /* diffuse reflectance of the quadrilateral */
    TSpectra* emission; /* emission of the quadrilateral */
} TQuad;

/* Input parameters */
TRadParams  params = {
    0.001,              /* convergence threshold */
    0, 0, 0, 0, 0, 0,   /* patches, elements and points; initialize these in
                        InitParams */
    {{ 108, 120, 400 }, /* camera location */
    { 108, 100, 100 },  /* look at point */
    { 0, 1, 0 },        /* up vector */
    60, 60,             /* field of view in x, y*/
    1, 550,             /* near, far */
    200, 200,           /* resolution x, y */
    0 },                /* buffer */
    100,                /* hemi-cube resolution */
    250,                /* approximate diameter of the room */
    50,                 /* intensity scale */
}
```

```
TPoint3f roomPoints[] = {
    0, 0, 0,
    216, 0, 0,
    216, 0, 215,
    0, 0, 215,
    0, 221, 0,
    216, 221, 0,
    216, 221, 215,
    0, 221, 215,
    85.5, 220, 90,
    130.5, 220, 90,
    130.5, 220, 130,
    85.5, 220, 130,
    53.104, 0, 64.104,
    109.36, 0, 96.604,
    76.896, 0, 152.896,
    20.604, 0, 120.396,
    53.104, 65, 64.104,
    109.36, 65, 96.604,
    76.896, 65, 152.896,
    20.604, 65, 120.396,
    134.104, 0, 67.104,
    190.396, 0, 99.604,
    157.896, 0, 155.896,
    101.604, 0, 123.396,
    134.104, 130, 67.104,
    190.396, 130, 99.604,
    157.896, 130, 155.896,
    101.604, 130, 123.396
};

const TSpectra red = { 0.80, 0.10, 0.075 };
const TSpectra yellow = { 0.9, 0.8, 0.1 };
const TSpectra blue = { 0.075, 0.10, 0.35 };
const TSpectra white = { 1.0, 1.0, 1.0 };
const TSpectra lightGrey = { 0.9, 0.9, 0.9 };
const TSpectra black = { 0.0, 0.0, 0.0 };

/* Assume a right-handed coordinate system */
/* Polygon vertices follow counter-clockwise order when viewing from front */
#define numberOfPolys   18
TQuad roomPolys[numberOfPolys] = {
    {4, 5, 6, 7, 2, 8, 216*215, 0, -1, 0, &lightGrey, &black}, /* ceiling */
    {0, 3, 2, 1, 3, 8, 216*215, 0, 1, 0, &lightGrey, &black}, /* floor */
    {0, 4, 7, 3, 2, 8, 221*215, 1, 0, 0, &red, &black}, /* wall */
    {0, 1, 5, 4, 2, 8, 221*216, 0, 0, 1, &lightGrey, &black}, /* wall */
    {2, 6, 5, 1, 2, 8, 221*215, -1, 0, 0, &blue, &black}, /* wall */
    {8, 9, 10, 11, 2, 1, 40*45, 0, -1, 0, &black, &white}, /* light */
    {16, 19, 18, 17, 1, 5, 65*65, 0, 1, 0, &yellow, &black}, /* box 1 */
    {12, 13, 14, 15, 1, 1, 65*65, 0, -1, 0, &yellow, &black},
    {12, 15, 19, 16, 1, 5, 65*65, -0.866, 0, -0.5, &yellow, &black},
    {12, 16, 17, 13, 1, 5, 65*65, 0.5, 0, -0.866, &yellow, &black},
    {14, 13, 17, 18, 1, 5, 65*65, 0.866, 0, 0.5, &yellow, &black},
    {14, 18, 19, 15, 1, 5, 65*65, -0.5, 0, 0.866, &yellow, &black},
    {24, 27, 26, 25, 1, 5, 65*65, 0, 1, 0, &lightGrey, &black}, /* box 2 */
    {20, 21, 22, 23, 1, 1, 65*65, 0, -1, 0, &lightGrey, &black},
    {20, 23, 27, 24, 1, 6, 65*130, -0.866, 0, -0.5, &lightGrey, &black},
    {20, 24, 25, 21, 1, 6, 65*130, 0.5, 0, -0.866, &lightGrey, &black},
```

```
    {22, 21, 25, 26, 1, 6, 65*130, 0.866, 0, 0.5, &lightGrey, &black},
    {22, 26, 27, 23, 1, 6, 65*130, -0.5, 0, 0.866, &lightGrey, &black},
};


/* Compute the xyz coordinates of a point on a quadrilateral given its u, v
coordinates using bi-linear mapping */
void UVToXYZ(const TPoint3f quad[4], float u, float v, TPoint3f* xyz)
{
    xyz->x = quad[0].x * (1-u)*(1-v) + quad[1].x * (1-u)*v + quad[2].x * u*v +
            quad[3].x * u*(1-v);
    xyz->y = quad[0].y * (1-u)*(1-v) + quad[1].y * (1-u)*v + quad[2].y * u*v +
            quad[3].y * u*(1-v);
    xyz->z = quad[0].z * (1-u)*(1-v) + quad[1].z * (1-u)*v + quad[2].z * u*v +
            quad[3].z * u*(1-v);
}

#define Index(i, j)  ((i)*(nv+1)+(j))

int iOffset;        /* index offset to the point array */
TPatch* pPatch;
TElement* pElement;
TPoint3f* pPoint;

/* Mesh a quarilateral into patches and elements */
/* Output goes to pPatch, pElement, pPoint */
void MeshQuad(TQuad* quad)
{
    TPoint3f pts[4];
    int nu, nv;
    double  du, dv;
    int i, j;
    double u, v;
    int nPts=0;
    float fi, fj;
    int pi, pj;

    /* Calculate element vertices */
    for (i=0; i<4; i++)
        pts[i] = roomPoints[quad->verts[i]];
    nu = nv = quad->patchLevel * quad->elementLevel+1;
    du = 1.0 / (nu-1); dv = 1.0 / (nv-1);
    for (i = 0, u = 0; i < nu; i++, u += du)
        for (j = 0, v = 0; j < nv; j++, v += dv, nPts++)
            UVToXYZ(pts, u, v, pPoint++);

    /* Calculate elements */
    nu = nv = quad->patchLevel*quad->elementLevel;
    du = 1.0 / nu; dv = 1.0 / nv;
    for (i = 0, u = du/2.0; i < nu; i++, u += du)
        for (j = 0, v = dv/2.0; j < nv; j++, v += dv, pElement++) {
            pElement->normal = quad->normal;
            pElement->nVerts = 4;
            pElement->verts = (unsigned long*)calloc(4, sizeof(unsigned long));
            pElement->verts[0] = Index(i, j)+iOffset;
            pElement->verts[1] = Index(i+1, j)+iOffset;
            pElement->verts[2] = Index(i+1, j+1)+iOffset;
            pElement->verts[3] = Index(i, j+1)+iOffset;
            pElement->area = quad->area / (nu*nv);
            /* find out the parent patch */
```

```
                fi = (float)i/(float)nu;
                fj = (float)j/(float)nv;
                pi = (int)(fi*(float)(quad->patchLevel));
                pj = (int)(fj*(float)(quad->patchLevel));
                pElement->patch = pPatch+pi*quad->patchLevel+pj;
        }

        /* Calculate patches */
        nu = quad->patchLevel; nv=quad->patchLevel;
        du = 1.0 / nu; dv = 1.0 / nv;
        for (i = 0, u = du/2.0; i < nu; i++, u += du)
            for (j = 0, v = dv/2.0; j < nv; j++, v += dv, pPatch++) {
                UVToXYZ(pts, u, v, &pPatch->center);
                pPatch->normal = quad->normal;
                pPatch->reflectance = quad->reflectance;
                pPatch->emission = quad->emission;
                pPatch->area = quad->area / (nu*nv);
            }

        iOffset += nPts;
}


/* Initialize input parameters */
void InitParams()
{
    int i, n=0;

    /* compute the total number of patches */
    params.nPatches=0;
    for (i=numberOfPolys; i--; )
        params.nPatches += roomPolys[i].patchLevel*roomPolys[i].patchLevel;
    params.patches = (TPatch*)calloc(params.nPatches, sizeof(TPatch));

    /* compute the total number of elements */
    params.nElements=0;
    for (i=numberOfPolys; i--; )
        params.nElements += roomPolys[i].elementLevel*roomPolys[i].patchLevel*
                        roomPolys[i].elementLevel*roomPolys[i].patchLevel;
    params.elements = (TElement*)calloc(params.nElements, sizeof(TElement));

    /* compute the total number of element vertices */
    params.nPoints=0;
    for (i=numberOfPolys; i--; )
        params.nPoints += (roomPolys[i].elementLevel*roomPolys[i].patchLevel+1)*
                        (roomPolys[i].elementLevel*roomPolys[i].patchLevel+1);
    params.points = (TPoint3f*)calloc(params.nPoints, sizeof(TPoint3f));

    /* mesh the room to patches and elements */
    iOffset = 0;
    pPatch= params.patches;
    pElement= params.elements;
    pPoint= params.points;
    for (i=0; i<numberOfPolys; i++)
        MeshQuad(&roomPolys[i]);

    params.displayView.buffer= (unsigned long*)calloc(
        params.displayView.xRes*params.displayView.yRes, sizeof(unsigned long));

}
```

```
void main()
{
    InitParams();
    InitRad(&params);
    DoRad();
    CleanUpRad();
}
```

FAST VERTEX RADIOSITY UPDATE

(page 303)

Filippo Tampieri

```
#define FALSE 0
#define TRUE 1
#define DOT(A,B) (A[0] * B[0] + A[1] * B[1] + A[2] * B[2])

/*
        vertexIsBehindPlane returns TRUE if point P is behind the
        plane of normal N and coefficient d, FALSE otherwise.
*/
vertexIsBehindPlane(P, N, d)
float P[3], N[3], d;
{
        return(DOT(N, P) + d <= 0. ? TRUE : FALSE);
}


/*
        boxIsBehindPlane returns TRUE if the axis-aligned box of
        minimum corner Cmin and maximum corner Cmax is behind the
        plane of normal N and coefficient d, FALSE otherwise.
*/
boxIsBehindPlane(Cmin, Cmax, N, d)
float Cmin[3], Cmax[3], N[3], d;
{
        register int i;
        float P[3];

        /*
                assign to P the corner further away
                along the direction of normal N
        */
        for(i = 0; i < 3 ; i++)
                P[i] = N[i] >= 0. ? Cmax[i] : Cmin[i];

        /* test P against the input plane */
        return(vertexIsBehindPlane(P, N, d));
}
```

DECOMPOSING
A MATRIX INTO SIMPLE
TRANSFORMATIONS
(page 320)

Spencer W. Thomas

```
/*
 * unmatrix.h - Definitions for using unmatrix
 *
 * Author:   Spencer W. Thomas
 *           University of Michigan
 */

/* The unmatrix subroutine fills in a vector of floating point
 * values.  These symbols make it easier to get the data back out.
 */

enum unmatrix_indices {
        U_SCALEX,
        U_SCALEY,
        U_SCALEZ,
        U_SHEARXY,
        U_SHEARXZ,
        U_SHEARYZ,
        U_ROTATEX,
        U_ROTATEY,
        U_ROTATEZ,
        U_TRANSX,
        U_TRANSY,
        U_TRANSZ,
        U_PERSPX,
        U_PERSPY,
        U_PERSPZ,
        U_PERSPW
};
```

```
/* unmatrix.c - given a 4x4 matrix, decompose it into standard operations.
 *
 * Author:    Spencer W. Thomas
 *            University of Michigan
 */

/* unmatrix - Decompose a non-degenerate 4x4 transformation matrix into
 *     the sequence of transformations that produced it.
 * [Sx][Sy][Sz][Shearx/y][Sx/z][Sz/y][Rx][Ry][Rz][Tx][Ty][Tz][P(x,y,z,w)]
 *
 * The coefficient of each transformation is returned in the corresponding
 * element of the vector tran.
 *
 * Returns 1 upon success, 0 if the matrix is singular.
 */
unmatrix( mat, tran )
Matrix4 *mat;
double tran[16];
{
        register int i, j;
        Matrix4 locmat;
        Matrix4 pmat, invpmat;
        /* Vector4 type and functions need to be added to the common set. */
        Vector4 prhs, psol;
        Point3 row[3];

        locmat = *mat;
        /* Normalize the matrix. */
        if ( pmat.element[3][3] != 0 )
              for ( i=0; i<4;i++ )
                    for ( j=0; j<4; j++ )
                            locmat.element[i][j] /= locmat.element[3][3];
        /* pmat is used to solve for perspective, but it also provides
         * an easy way to test for singularity of the upper 3x3 component.
         */
        pmat = locmat;
        for ( i=0; i<3; i++ )
              pmat.element[i][3] = 0;
        pmat.element[4][3] = 1;

        if ( det4x4(pmat) == 0.0 )
                return 0;

        /* First, isolate perspective.  This is the messiest. */
        if ( locmat.element[0][3] != 0 || locmat.element[1][3] != 0 ||
              locmat.element[2][3] != 0 ) {
              /* prhs is the right hand side of the equation. */
              prhs.x = locmat.element[0][3];
              prhs.y = locmat.element[1][3];
              prhs.z = locmat.element[2][3];
              prhs.w = locmat.element[3][3];

              /* Solve the equation by inverting pmat and multiplying
               * prhs by the inverse.  (This is the easiest way, not
               * necessarily the best.)
               * inverse function (and det4x4, above) from the Matrix
```

```
         * Inversion gem in the first volume.
         */
        inverse( &pmat, &invpmat );
        psol = *V4MulPointByMatrix(&prhs, &invpmat);

        /* Stuff the answer away. */
        tran[U_PERSPX] = psol.x;
        tran[U_PERSPY] = psol.y;
        tran[U_PERSPZ] = psol.z;
        tran[U_PERSPW] = psol.w;
        /* Clear the perspective partition. */
        locmat.element[0][3] = locmat.element[1][3] =
                locmat.element[2][3] = 0;
        locmat.element[3][3] = 1;
} else          /* No perspective. */
        tran[U_PERSPX] = tran[U_PERSPY] = tran[U_PERSPZ] =
                tran[U_PERSPW] = 0;

/* Next take care of translation (easy). */
for ( i=0; i<3; i++ ) {
        tran[U_TRANSX + i] = locmat.element[3][i];
        locmat.element[3][i] = 0;
}

/* Now get scale and shear. */
for ( i=0; i<3; i++ ) {
        row[i].x = locmat.element[i][0];
        row[i].y = locmat.element[i][1];
        row[i].z = locmat.element[i][2];
}

/* Compute X scale factor and normalize first row. */
tran[U_SCALEX] = V3Length(&row[0]);
(void)V3Normalize(&row[0]);

/* Compute XY shear factor and make 2nd row orthogonal to 1st. */
tran[U_SHEARXY] = V3Dot(&row[0], &row[1]);
(void)V3Combine(&row[1], &row[0], &row[1], 1.0, -tran[U_SHEARXY]);

/* Now, compute Y scale and normalize 2nd row. */
tran[U_SCALEY] = V3Length(&row[1]);
(void)V3Normalize(&row[1]);
tran[U_SHEARXY] /= tran[U_SCALEY];

/* Compute XZ and YZ shears, orthogonalize 3rd row. */
tran[U_SHEARXZ] = V3Dot(&row[0], &row[2]);
(void)V3Combine(&row[2], &row[0], &row[2], 1.0, -tran[U_SHEARXZ]);
tran[U_SHEARYZ] = V3Dot(&row[1], &row[2]);
(void)V3Combine(&row[2], &row[1], &row[2], 1.0, -tran[U_SHEARYZ]);

/* Next, get Z scale and normalize 3rd row. */
tran[U_SCALEZ] = V3Length(&row[2]);
(void)V3Normalize(&row[2]);
tran[U_SHEARXZ] /= tran[U_SCALEZ];
tran[U_SHEARYZ] /= tran[U_SCALEZ];
```

```
      /* At this point, the matrix (in rows[]) is orthonormal.
       * Check for a coordinate system flip.  If the determinant
       * is -1, then negate the matrix and the scaling factors.
       */
      if ( V3Dot( &row[0], V3Cross( &row[1], &row[2]) ) < 0 )
            for ( i = 0; i < 3; i++ ) {
                  tran[U_SCALEX+i] *= -1;
                  row[i].x *= -1;
                  row[i].y *= -1;
                  row[i].z *= -1;
            }

      /* Now, get the rotations out, as described in the gem. */
      tran[U_ROTATEY] = asin(-row[0].z);
      if ( cos(tran[U_ROTATEY]) != 0 ) {
            tran[U_ROTATEX] = atan2(row[1].z, row[2].z);
            tran[U_ROTATEZ] = atan2(row[0].y, row[0].x);
      } else {
            tran[U_ROTATEX] = atan2(row[1].x, row[1].y);
            tran[U_ROTATEZ] = 0;
      }
      /* All done! */
      return 1;
}
```

FAST MATRIX INVERSION

(page 342)

Kevin Wu

```
#include "GraphicsGems.h"
#include <stdio.h>

/****
 *
 * affine_matrix4_inverse
 *
 * Computes the inverse of a 3D affine matrix; i.e. a matrix with a dimen-
 * sionality of 4 where the right column has the entries (0, 0, 0, 1).
 *
 * This procedure treats the 4 by 4 matrix as a block matrix and
 * calculates the inverse of one submatrix for a significant perform-
 * ance improvement over a general procedure that can invert any non-
 * singular matrix:
 *
 *           --        --  -1      --            --
 *           |          |          |             |
 *           | A      0 |          |    A        0 |
 *    -1     |          |          |   -1         |
 *   M    =  |          |     =    |             |
 *           |          |          |       -1    |
 *           | C      1 |          | -C  A      1 |
 *           |          |          |             |
 *           --        --          --           --
 *
 *   where      M is a 4 by 4 matrix,
 *              A is the 3 by 3 upper left submatrix of M,
 *              C is the 1 by 3 lower left submatrix of M.
 *
 * Input:
 *   in   - 3D affine matrix
 *
 * Output:
 *   out  - inverse of 3D affine matrix
 *
 * Returned value:
 *   TRUE   if input matrix is nonsingular
 *   FALSE  otherwise
 *
 ***/
```

```
boolean
affine_matrix4_inverse (in, out)
    register  Matrix4  *in;
    register  Matrix4  *out;
{
    register  double     det_1;
              double     pos, neg, temp;

#define ACCUMULATE       \
    if (temp >= 0.0)     \
        pos += temp;     \
    else                 \
        neg += temp;

#define PRECISION_LIMIT (1.0e-15)

    /*
     * Calculate the determinant of submatrix A and determine if the
     * the matrix is singular as limited by the double precision
     * floating-point data representation.
     */
    pos = neg = 0.0;
    temp =  in->element[0][0] * in->element[1][1] * in->element[2][2];
    ACCUMULATE
    temp =  in->element[0][1] * in->element[1][2] * in->element[2][0];
    ACCUMULATE
    temp =  in->element[0][2] * in->element[1][0] * in->element[2][1];
    ACCUMULATE
    temp = -in->element[0][2] * in->element[1][1] * in->element[2][0];
    ACCUMULATE
    temp = -in->element[0][1] * in->element[1][0] * in->element[2][2];
    ACCUMULATE
    temp = -in->element[0][0] * in->element[1][2] * in->element[2][1];
    ACCUMULATE
    det_1 = pos + neg;

    /* Is the submatrix A singular? */
    temp = det_1 / (pos - neg);

    if (ABS(temp) < PRECISION_LIMIT) {

        /* Matrix M has no inverse */
        fprintf (stderr, "affine_matrix4_inverse: singular matrix\n");
        return FALSE;
    }

    else {

        /* Calculate inverse(A) = adj(A) / det(A) */
        det_1 = 1.0 / det_1;
        out->element[0][0] =   ( in->element[1][1] * in->element[2][2] -
                                 in->element[1][2] * in->element[2][1] )
                             * det_1;
        out->element[1][0] = - ( in->element[1][0] * in->element[2][2] -
                                 in->element[1][2] * in->element[2][0] )
                             * det_1;
```

```
out->element[2][0] =     ( in->element[1][0] * in->element[2][1] -
                           in->element[1][1] * in->element[2][0] )
                      * det_1;
out->element[0][1] = -   ( in->element[0][1] * in->element[2][2] -
                           in->element[0][2] * in->element[2][1] )
                      * det_1;
out->element[1][1] =     ( in->element[0][0] * in->element[2][2] -
                           in->element[0][2] * in->element[2][0] )
                      * det_1;
out->element[2][1] = -   ( in->element[0][0] * in->element[2][1] -
                           in->element[0][1] * in->element[2][0] )
                      * det_1;
out->element[0][2] =     ( in->element[0][1] * in->element[1][2] -
                           in->element[0][2] * in->element[1][1] )
                      * det_1;
out->element[1][2] = -   ( in->element[0][0] * in->element[1][2] -
                           in->element[0][2] * in->element[1][0] )
                      * det_1;
out->element[2][2] =     ( in->element[0][0] * in->element[1][1] -
                           in->element[0][1] * in->element[1][0] )
                      * det_1;

/* Calculate -C * inverse(A) */
out->element[3][0] = - ( in->element[3][0] * out->element[0][0] +
                         in->element[3][1] * out->element[1][0] +
                         in->element[3][2] * out->element[2][0] );
out->element[3][1] = - ( in->element[3][0] * out->element[0][1] +
                         in->element[3][1] * out->element[1][1] +
                         in->element[3][2] * out->element[2][1] );
out->element[3][2] = - ( in->element[3][0] * out->element[0][2] +
                         in->element[3][1] * out->element[1][2] +
                         in->element[3][2] * out->element[2][2] );

/* Fill in last column */
out->element[0][3] = out->element[1][3] = out->element[2][3] = 0.0;
out->element[3][3] = 1.0;

return TRUE;
}

}
```

RANDOM ROTATION MATRICES

(page 355)

James Arvo

```
#include "GraphicsGems.h"

/*============================================================================*
 *                                                                            *
 *    This routine maps three values (x[0], x[1], x[2]) to a 3x3 rotation     *
 *    matrix, M.  If x0, x1, and x2 are uniformly distributed random numbers  *
 *    in [0,1], then M will be a random rotation matrix.                      *
 *                                                                            *
 *============================================================================*/
void Rand_rotation( x, M )
float x[];
Matrix3 *M;
    {
    float    a, b, c, d, s;
    float    z, r, theta, omega;
    float    bb, cc, dd;
    float    ab, ac, ad;
    float    bc, bd, cd;

    /* Use the random variables x[0] and x[1] to determine the axis of  */
    /* rotation in cylindrical coordinates and the random variable x[2] */
    /* to determine the amount of rotation, omega, about this axis.     */

    z = x[0];
    r = sqrt( 1 - z * z );
    theta = 2.0 * PI * x[1];
    omega = PI * x[2];

    /* Compute the unit quaternion (a,b,c,d) where a is the cosine of   */
    /* half the rotation angle and the axis vector (b,c,d) is determined */
    /* by "r", "theta" and "z" computed above.                         */

    s = sin( omega );
    a = cos( omega );
    b = s * cos( theta ) * r;
    c = s * sin( theta ) * r;
    d = s * z;
```

```c
/* Compute all the pairwise products of a, b, c, and d, except a * a. */

bb = b * b;    cc = c * c;    dd = d * d;
ab = a * b;    ac = a * c;    ad = a * d;
bc = b * c;    bd = b * d;    cd = c * d;

/* Construct an orthogonal matrix corresponding to  */
/* the unit quaternion (a,b,c,d).                   */

M->element[0][0] = 1.0 - 2.0 * ( cc + dd );
M->element[0][1] =       2.0 * ( bc + ad );
M->element[0][2] =       2.0 * ( bd - ac );

M->element[1][0] =       2.0 * ( bc - ad );
M->element[1][1] = 1.0 - 2.0 * ( bb + dd );
M->element[1][2] =       2.0 * ( cd + ab );

M->element[2][0] =       2.0 * ( bd + ac );
M->element[2][1] =       2.0 * ( cd - ab );
M->element[2][2] = 1.0 - 2.0 * ( bb + cc );

} /* Rand_rotation */
```

CLASSIFYING SMALL SPARSE MATRICES

(page 357)

James Arvo

```
#include "GraphicsGems.h"

/*=========================================================================*
 *                                                                         *
 * This function classifies a 3x3 matrix according to its zero structure.  *
 * It returns an unsigned integer in which each bit signifies a zero       *
 * structure that describes the given matrix.  If all bits are zero it     *
 * means the matrix is dense or does not fit any of these 16 forms.        *
 *                                                                         *
 *                                                                         *
 *   Permutations:                                                         *
 *                                                                         *
 *    * 0 0      0 * 0      0 0 *      0 * 0      * 0 0      0 0 *          *
 *    0 * 0      0 0 *      * 0 0      * 0 0      0 0 *      0 * 0          *
 *    0 0 *      * 0 0      0 * 0      0 0 *      0 * 0      * 0 0          *
 *                                                                         *
 *    P1         P2         P3         P4         P5         P6            *
 *                                                                         *
 *                                                                         *
 *   Simple Rotations:                                                     *
 *                                                                         *
 *    * 0 0      * 0 *      * * 0                                          *
 *    0 * *      0 * 0      * * 0                                          *
 *    0 * *      * 0 *      0 0 *                                          *
 *                                                                         *
 *    RX         RY         RZ                                            *
 *                                                                         *
 *                                                                         *
 *   Permutations of the simple rotations:                                 *
 *                                                                         *
 *    * 0 *      0 0 *      0 * *      0 * 0      * * 0      * 0 *      0 * *  *
 *    0 * 0      * * 0      0 * *      * 0 *      0 0 *      * 0 *      * 0 0  *
 *    * 0 *      * * 0      * 0 0      * 0 *      * * 0      0 * 0      0 * *  *
 *                                                                         *
 *    C1         C2         C3         C4         C5         C6         C7    *
 *                                                                         *
 *=========================================================================*/
```

608

```
#define P1 (1<< 0)
#define P2 (1<< 1)
#define P3 (1<< 2)
#define P4 (1<< 3)
#define P5 (1<< 4)
#define P6 (1<< 5)
#define RX (1<< 6)
#define RY (1<< 7)
#define RZ (1<< 8)
#define C1 (1<< 9)
#define C2 (1<<10)
#define C3 (1<<11)
#define C4 (1<<12)
#define C5 (1<<13)
#define C6 (1<<14)
#define C7 (1<<15)

unsigned int classify_matrix( M )
Matrix3  M;
    {
    unsigned int form = 0xFFFF;

    /* Classify based on the diagonal elements. */

    if( M.element[0][0] != 0 ) form &= P1 | P5 | RX | RY | RZ | C1 | C5 | C6;
    if( M.element[1][1] != 0 ) form &= P1 | P6 | RX | RY | RZ | C1 | C2 | C3;
    if( M.element[2][2] != 0 ) form &= P1 | P4 | RX | RY | RZ | C1 | C4 | C7;

    /* Classify based on the upper triangular elements. */

    if( M.element[0][1] != 0 ) form &= P2 | P4 | RZ | C3 | C4 | C5 | C7;
    if( M.element[0][2] != 0 ) form &= P3 | P6 | RY | C1 | C2 | C3 | C6 | C7;
    if( M.element[1][2] != 0 ) form &= P2 | P5 | RX | C3 | C4 | C5 | C6;

    /* Classify based on the lower triangular elements. */

    if( M.element[1][0] != 0 ) form &= P3 | P4 | RZ | C2 | C4 | C6 | C7;
    if( M.element[2][0] != 0 ) form &= P2 | P6 | RY | C1 | C2 | C3 | C4 | C5;
    if( M.element[2][1] != 0 ) form &= P3 | P5 | RX | C2 | C5 | C6 | C7;

    return( form );
    }
```

OF INTEGERS, FIELDS,
AND BIT COUNTING

(page 371)

Alan W. Paeth and David Schilling

```
/*
 * bit32on - count the 1 bits in a 32-bit long integer. Three varients are
 *           provided (the second accepts further code revision); one will
 *           be ''best'' based on the nature of the data and the hardware.
 *           Use of "register" directives may also yield further speed-up.
 *           The user is urged to perform comparative analysis for a given
 *           architecture and to study the assembler output, or to hand code.
 *           This code has been thoroughly tested by the second author.
 *
 * Alan W. Paeth
 * David Schilling
 */

int bit32on1(a)
  unsigned long a;
  {
  int c;
  c = 0;
  while( a != 0 )         /* until no bits remain, */
    {
    c++;                  /* "tally" ho, then */
    a = a &~ -a;          /* clear lowest bit */
    }
  return(c);
  }

int bit32on2(a)
  unsigned long a;                                   /* a: 32  1-bit tallies */
  {
  a = (a&0x55555555) + ((a>>1) &(0x55555555));  /* a: 16  2-bit tallies */
  a = (a&0x33333333) + ((a>>2) &(0x33333333));  /* a:  8  4-bit tallies */
  a = (a&0x07070707) + ((a>>4) &(0x07070707));  /* a:  4  8-bit tallies */
/* a &= 255; return(a); may replace what follows */
  a = (a&0x000F000F) + ((a>>8) &(0x000F000F));  /* a:  2 16-bit tallies */
  a = (a&0x0000001F) + ((a>>16)&(0x0000001F));  /* a:  1 32-bit tally */
  return(a);
  }
```

610

```
int bit32on3(a)
    unsigned long a;
    {
    unsigned long mask, sum;
    if (a == 0)                    /* a common case */
        return(0);
    else if (a == 0xffffffff)      /* ditto, but the early return is essential: */
        return(32);                /* it leaves mod 31 (not 33) final states */
    mask = 0x42108421L;
    sum = a & mask;                /* 5x: accumulate through a 1-in-5 sieve */
    sum += (a>>=1) & mask;
    sum += (a>>=1) & mask;
    sum += (a>>=1) & mask;
    sum += (a>>=1) & mask;
    sum %= (mask = 31);            /* casting out mod 31 (save that constant) */
    return(sum ? sum : mask);      /* return bits (zero indicated 31 bits on) */
    }
```

AN INTEGER SQUARE ROOT ALGORITHM

(page 387)

Christopher J. Musial

```
/************************************************************************

This routine returns the largest integer which is less than or equal to the
square root of the passed number.

Entry:
   n - the number for which the integer square root is required.

Return value:  The largest integer less than or equal to the square
               root of lnum.

************************************************************************/

unsigned int isqr (n)
    unsigned long int n;
{
    unsigned long int nextTrial=n>>1, currentAnswer;

    if (n <= 1)  return((unsigned int)n);

    do
    {
        currentAnswer = nextTrial;
        nextTrial = (nextTrial + n/nextTrial) >> 1;
    } while (nextTrial < currentAnswer);

    return ((unsigned int)currentAnswer);
}
```

FAST SIGN OF CROSS PRODUCT CALCULATION

(page 392)

Jack Ritter

```
#define SCALE 16384
int find_sign(a,b,c,d) /* return sign: -1,0, or 1 */
double a,b,c,d;
{
register short sign_mask = 0x8000;  /* sign bit of a short*/
register short as,bs,cs,ds,left_sign,right_sign,t;
long left_prod,right_prod;
/* the compiler should generate fp SHIFTS */
as = (short)SCALE*a;  bs = (short)SCALE*b;
cs = (short)SCALE*c;  ds = (short)SCALE*d;
/* compute signs of as*bs, and cs*ds */
if ( (as==0) || (bs==0) )
   left_sign = 0;
else
   left_sign  = (as & sign_mask) ^ (bs & sign_mask);
if ( (cs==0) || (ds==0) )
   right_sign = 0;
else
   right_sign = (cs & sign_mask) ^ (ds & sign_mask);
if (left_sign && !right_sign)
   return (-1); /* as*bs is < 0 and cs*ds > 0 */
if (!left_sign && right_sign)
   return (1); /* as*bs is > 0 and cs*ds < 0 */
/* At this point, half of all cases have been resolved. */
/* The left/right signs are now either both positive, */
/* or both negative.  If both negative, we SWAP as & cs, */
/* and bs & ds, because negation reverses inequality */
if (left_sign)   { /* both neg. */
   t = ABS(as); as = ABS(cs); cs = t;
   t = ABS(bs); bs = ABS(ds); ds = t; }
left_prod  = as*bs; /* 16x16 bit -> 32 bit */
right_prod = cs*ds;
if (left_prod < right_prod)
   return (-1);
```

```
if (left_prod > right_prod)
    return (1);
/* At this point, the answer will be ZERO. */
/* Since only 16 bits of accuracy are being used, */
/* the caller may want to do the full floating point */
/* calculation when a ZERO is returned, */
/* since his original FP numbers had more accuracy. */
/* Parellelism is in the eye of the beholder. */
return (0);
}
```

$(2t - 3)tt + 1 \longrightarrow 2ttt - 3tt + 1$

$(-2t + 3)tt \longrightarrow 3tt - 2ttt$

$(t - 2)t + 1)t \longrightarrow (tt - 2t + 1)t \longrightarrow ttt - 2tt + t$

$(t-1)tt \longrightarrow ttt - tt$

$\overset{t+t}{\text{calculate}} : \overset{t+t}{tt} \longrightarrow \overset{(2tt)}{tt + tt} \longrightarrow \overset{(3tt)}{+ tt}$

$+t \longrightarrow ttt \longrightarrow \overset{(2ttt)}{ttt + ttt}$

$5t = ttt - tt \qquad 32ver = (2ttt - 3tt)$

Pass in to hermite: ttt, $2ttt$, tt, $2tt$, $3tt$. (optional)

$\underbrace{\text{FP reg}}$

$\rightarrow h(p0, p1, r0, r1, t, 5t, 32vr, tt)$

$= \quad p0 * (1 - 32ver +) +$

$p1 * (32vr) +$

$r0 * (5t - tt + t) +$

$r1 * (5t)$

614

A RECURSIVE IMPLEMENTATION OF THE PERLIN NOISE FUNCTION

(page 396)

Greg Ward

```
#define   hermite(p0,p1,r0,r1,t)   (          p0 *((2. *t−3.) *t *t+1.)  +
                                               p1 *(−2. *t+3.) *t *t  +
                                               r0 *((t−2.) *t+1.) *t  +
                                               r1 *(t−1.) *t *t  )

#define   rand3a(x,y,z)        frand(67 *(x)+59 *(y)+71 *(z))
#define   rand3b(x,y,z)        frand(73 *(x)+79 *(y)+83 *(z))
#define   rand3c(x,y,z)        frand(89 *(x)+97 *(y)+101 *(z))
#define   rand3d(x,y,z)        frand(103 *(x)+107 *(y)+109 *(z))

long    xlim[3][2];                 /* integer bounds for point */
double  xarg[3];                    /* fractional part */

double
frand(s)                            /* get random number from seed */
register  long   s;
{
        s = s<<13 ^ s;
        return(  1.0 − ((s *(s *s *15731+789221)+1376312589)&0x7fffffff)
                     / 1073741824.0 );

}

interpolate(f, i, n)                     /* interpolate noise function */
double   f[4];                       /* returned tangent and value */
register int    i, n;                /* location and order */
{
        double   f0[4], f1[4];           /* results for first and second halves */

        if (n == 0) {                    /* at zero, just return lattice value */
                f[0] = rand3a(xlim[0][i&1],xlim[1][i>>1&1],xlim[2][i>>2]);
                f[1] = rand3b(xlim[0][i&1],xlim[1][i>>1&1],xlim[2][i>>2]);
                f[2] = rand3c(xlim[0][i&1],xlim[1][i>>1&1],xlim[2][i>>2]);
                f[3] = rand3d(xlim[0][i&1],xlim[1][i>>1&1],xlim[2][i>>2]);
                return;
```

```
        }
        n—;                                      /* decrease order */
        interpolate(f0, i, n);                             /* compute first half */
        interpolate(f1, i | 1<<n, n);                      /* compute second half */
                                        /* use linear interpolation for slopes */
        f[0] = (1.0−xarg[n])*f0[0] + xarg[n]*f1[0];
        f[1] = (1.0−xarg[n])*f0[1] + xarg[n]*f1[1];
        f[2] = (1.0−xarg[n])*f0[2] + xarg[n]*f1[2];
                                        /* use hermite interpolation for value */
        f[3] = hermite(f0[3], f1[3], f0[n], f1[n], xarg[n]);
}

double *
noise3(x)                                /* compute the noise function */
double   x[3];
{
        extern double  floor();
        static double  f[4];

        xlim[0][0] = floor(x[0]); xlim[0][1] = xlim[0][0] + 1;
        xlim[1][0] = floor(x[1]); xlim[1][1] = xlim[1][0] + 1;
        xlim[2][0] = floor(x[2]); xlim[2][1] = xlim[2][0] + 1;
        xarg[0] = x[0] − xlim[0][0];
        xarg[1] = x[1] − xlim[1][0];
        xarg[2] = x[2] − xlim[2][0];
        interpolate(f, 0, 3);
        return(f);
}
```

616

A GOOD STRAIGHT-LINE APPROXIMATION OF A CIRCULAR ARC

(page 435)

Christopher J. Musial

```
/**********************************************************************

Compute parameters for a polyline which approximates a circular arc,
maintaining the arc length and start and end positions.

Entry:
  radius - radius of the arc
  angle - central angle of the arc, in radians.  The arc is clockwise if
          angle>0; counterclockwise of angle<0
  curveTolerance - Maximum allowable distance between the curve and any
                   part of the polyline
  polylineTolerance - Maximum allowable difference between the span of
                      the polyline and the chord length of the arc,
                      measured along the axis of the chord

Exit:
  segmentLength - the length of each segment in the polyline
  initialAngle - Angle between the tangent vector of the arc at its
                 initial point and the first segment of the polyline.
                 Subtract this value from the arc's tangent vector to
                 get the direction vector of the initial polyline
                 segment.
  incrementalAngle - Difference in the direction vectors of 2 adjacent
                     polyline segments.  Subtract this value from the
                     direction vector of 1 segment to get the direction
                     vector of the following segment.

Return value:  The number of segments in the polyline.

**********************************************************************/

#include <math.h>

#define PI 3.141592653589793
#define degToRad(deg) ((deg)*PI/180.)   /* convert degrees to radians */
```

```
int arcApprox (radius, angle, curveTolerance, polylineTolerance,
               segmentLength, initialAngle, incrementalAngle)
    double radius;
    double angle;
    double curveTolerance;
    double polylineTolerance;
    double *segmentLength;
    double *initialAngle;
    double *incrementalAngle;
{
    int direction, i, numSegments, numTries=0;
    double curveToChord, arcLength, chordLength, spanLength,
           startTangent, trialAngles[2], trialErrors[2],
           tempAngle=angle/2.;

/* We'll only work with clockwise curves for now.  If this is
   counterclockwise, we'll adjust the returned angles later. */

    direction = (angle > 0) ? 1 : -1;
    if (angle < 0.)   angle = -angle;

/* Calculate the number of segments needed for the polyline */

    curveToChord = radius * (1. - cos(tempAngle/2.));
    for (numSegments = 2; curveToChord > curveTolerance; )
    {
        numSegments *= 2;
        tempAngle /= 2.;
        curveToChord = radius * (1. - cos(tempAngle/2.));
    }

/* Calculate the various curve parameters */

    arcLength = radius * angle;
    chordLength = 2. * radius * sin(angle/2.);
    startTangent = angle / 2.;

    *segmentLength = arcLength / numSegments;
    do
    {
     /* Come up with the next trial value for the incremental angle */

        switch (numTries)
        {
            case 0:

             /* First time - use the low end of the range */

                *incrementalAngle = 0.;
                break;

            case 1:

             /* Second time - use the high end of the range.  Save the
                trial values from the previous calculation for later
                use.  */
```

618

```
                trialAngles[0] = *incrementalAngle;
                trialErrors[0] = spanLength - chordLength;
                *incrementalAngle = angle / (numSegments - 1);
                break;

            default:

                /* Calculate the next trial value by linear interpolation
                   of the previous 2 trials.  */

                trialAngles[1] = *incrementalAngle;
                trialErrors[1] = spanLength - chordLength;
                *incrementalAngle =
                    (trialAngles[1]-trialAngles[0]) * -trialErrors[1] /
                    (trialErrors[1] -trialErrors[0]) + trialAngles[1];

                trialAngles[0] = trialAngles[1];
                trialErrors[0]  = trialErrors[1];
        }

    /* Calculate the polyline span for new incremental angle */

        for (spanLength = 0, i = 0; i < numSegments; i++)
        {
            *initialAngle = (angle - (numSegments-1)* *incrementalAngle)/2;
            spanLength += cos (startTangent - *initialAngle -
                            i * *incrementalAngle);
        }
        spanLength *= *segmentLength;
        numTries++;
    } while (fabs(spanLength-chordLength) > polylineTolerance);

    if (direction < 0)
    {
      *initialAngle = - *initialAngle;
      *incrementalAngle = -*incrementalAngle;
    }

    return(numSegments);
}

main()
{
    double x[100], y[100];
    double centralAngle, iniAng, incAng, radius, segLen, startTangent;
    int nsegs, nvertices;

    radius = 100.;
    centralAngle = degToRad (90);

    nsegs = arcApprox (radius, centralAngle, 1., .00001,
                    &segLen, &iniAng, &incAng);

    x[0] = 1000.;     /* Coordinates of the start of the arc  */
    y[0] = 1000.;
    startTangent = degToRad (30);
```

```
/* Calculate the coordinates of each vertex in the polyline.  When
   finished, x[] and y[] will contain the coordinates of each vertex,
   and nvertices will be the number of vertices */

for (nvertices=0; nvertices < nsegs; nvertices++)
{
    double direction;

    direction = startTangent - iniAng - nvertices*incAng;
    x[nvertices+1] = x[nvertices] + segLen * cos(direction);
    y[nvertices+1] = y[nvertices] + segLen * sin(direction);
}
    .
    .
    .
}
```

REFERENCES

Adobe Systems, Inc. (1988). *User's Guide to Adobe Illustrator 88.* (IX.3 A Simple Formulation for Curve Interpolation with Variable Control Point Approximation)

Adobe Systems, Inc. (1985a). POSTSCRIPT™ *Language Reference Manual*, ISBN 0-201-10174-2. Addison-Wesley, Reading, MA (I.9 Scanline Coherent Shape Algebra)

Adobe Systems, Inc. (1985b). POSTSCRIPT™ *Language Tutorial and Cookbook*, ISBN 0-201-10179-3. Addison-Wesley, Reading, MA (I.9 Scanline Coherent Shape Algebra)

Airey, John M., Rohlf, John H., and Brooks, Frederick P. (1990). "Towards Image Realism with Interactive Update Rates in Complex Virtual Building Environments," *Computer Graphics ACM Workshop on Interactive Graphics Proceedings* **24**(1), 41–50. (VI.4 Radiosity via Ray Tracing)

Amanatides, John, and Mitchell, Don P. (1990). "Antialiasing of Interlaced Video Animation," *Computer Graphics* **4**(24), 77–85. (III.6 Television Color Encoding and "Hot" Broadcast Colors)

Amanatides, J. and Woo, A. (1987). "A Fast Voxel Traversal Algorithm for Ray Tracing," *EuroGraphics '87.* (V.7 Avoiding Incorrect Shadow Intersections for Ray Tracing)

Anderberg, M. R. (1973). *Cluster Analysis for Applications.* Academic Press, New York. (III.2 Efficient Statistic Computations for Optimal Color Quantization)

Apple Computer (1988). *Inside Macintosh, Volume V*, Chapter 6. Addison-Wesley, Reading, MA. (III.1 Efficient Inverse Color Map Computation)

Arnaldi, Bruno, Priol, Thierry, and Bouatouch, Kadi (1987). "A New Space Subdivision Method for Ray Tracing CSG Modelled Scenes," *The Visual Computer*, **3**(3), 98–108. (V.4 Improved Ray Tagging for Voxel-Based Ray Tracing; V.5 Efficiency Improvements for Hierarchy Traversal in Ray Tracing; V.7 Avoiding Incorrect Shadow Intersections for Ray Tracing)

Atkinson, William D. (Nov. 11, 1986). Method and Apparatus for Image Compression and Manipulation, United States Patent number 4,622,545. (I.9 Scanline Coherent Shape Algebra)

Ball, W. W. R. (1939). *Mathematical Recreations & Essays.* McMillan, London. (IV.3 Exact Dihedral Metrics for Common Polyhedra)

Barry, Phillip J., and Goldman, Ronald N. (1988). "A Recursive Evaluation Algorithm for a Class of Catmull–Rom Splines," *Computer Graphics* **22**(4), 199–204. (VIII.4 Using Geometric Constructions to Interpolate Orientation with Quaternions)

Baum, Daniel R., Rushmeier, Holly E., and Winget, James M., "Improving Radiosity Solutions through the Use of Analytically Determined Form-Factors," *Computer Graphics (SIGGRAPH'89 Proceedings)*, **23**, (3), pp. 325–334. (VI.1 Implementing Progressive Radiosity with User-Provided Polygon Display Routines)

Baumgart, B. G. (1975). "A Polyhedron Representation for Computer Vision," *Proc. NCC*. (IV.6 Maintaining Winged–Edge Models)

Baumgart, B. G. (1974). "Geometric Modeling for Computer Vision," Stanford AI Project memo 249. (IV.6 Maintaining Winged–Edge Models)

Beeler, M., Gosper, R. W., and Schroeppel, R. (1972). *HAKMEM, Massachusetts Institute of Technology Artificial Intelligence Laboratory Report AIM-239*. (VII.3 Of Integers, Fields, and Bit Counting)

Behnke, H., Bachmann, F., Fladt, K., and Suss, W. (1983). *Fundamentals of Mathematics, Vol. III, Analysis*. MIT Press, Cambridge, MA, 191–195. (I.6 Appolonius's 10th Problem)

Bieri, H., and Nef, W. (1984). "Algorithms for the Euler Characteristic and Related Additive Functionals of Digital Objects," *Computer Vision, Graphics, and Image Processing* **28**, 166–175. (II.12 Computing the Area, the Circumference, and Genus of a Binary Digital Image)

Boehm, W. (1984). "Efficient Evaluation of Splines," *Computing* **33**, 171–177. (X.4 Symmetric Evaluation of Polynomials)

Booth, Kellogg (1989). *Graphics Interface '89 (London)*, private conversation. (VIII.3 Of Integers, Fields, and Bit Counting)

Born, M., and Wolf, E. (1975). *Principles of Optics, 5th ed.* Pergamon Press, Oxford. (V.8 A Body Color Model: Absorption of Light through Translucent Media; V.9 More Shadow Attenuation for Ray Tracing Transparent or Translucent Objects)

Bouknight, W. I. (1970). "A Procedure for the Generation of 3D Halftoned Computer Graphics Presentations," *Comm. ACM* **13**(9), 527–536. (IV.9 InterPhong Shading)

Brainard, David H. (1989). "Calibration of a Computer Controlled Color Monitor," *Color Research and Application* **14**, 23–34. (III.7 An Inexpensive Method of Setting the Monitor White Point)

Bresenham, J. E. (1977). "A Linear Algorithm for Incremental Digital Display of Circular Arcs," *Comm. ACM* **20**(2), 750–752. (IX.9 Fast Anti-Aliased Circle Generation)

Burrus, C. S., and Parks, T. W. (1985). *DFT/FFT and Convolution Algorithms*. Wiley and Sons, New York. (VIII.2 Faster Fourier Transform)

Butz, Arthur R. (1971). "Alternative Algorithm for Hilbert's Space-Filling Curve," *IEEE Transactions on Computers*, **C-20**, 424–426. (I.7 A Peano Curve Generation Algorithm)

Carling, Richard (1990). "Matrix Inversion," *Graphics Gems* (Andrew S. Glassner, ed.). Academic Press, Boston, 470–471. (VII.5 Fast Matrix Inversion)

Cashwell, E. D., and Everett, C. J. (1969). *Intersection of a Ray with a Surface of Third or Fourth Degree*, Los Alamos Scientific Laboratory Report LA-4299 UC-32 Mathematics and Computers TID-4500, Los Alamos, New Mexico. (V.2 Intercepting a Ray with an Elliptical Torus)

Catmull, Edwin (1979). "A Tutorial on Compensation Tables," *Computer Graphics* **13**, 1–7. (III.8 Some Tips for Making Color Hardcopy)

Cohen, Michael F., Chen, Shenchang Eric, Wallace, John R., and Greenberg, Donald P. (1988). "A Progressive Refinement Approach to Fast Radiosity Image Generation," *Computer Graphics (SIGGRAPH '88 Proceedings)* **22**(4) 75–84. (VI.1 Implementing Progressive Radiosity with User-Provided Polygon Display Routines; VI.4 Radiosity via Ray Tracing)

Cohen, Michael F., and Greenberg, Donald P. (1985). "The Hemi-Cube: A Radiosity Solution for Complex Environments," *Computer Graphics (SIGGRAPH '85 Proceedings)* **19**(3), 31–40. (VI.1 Implementing Progressive Radiosity with User-Provided Polygon Display Routines; VI.2 A Cubic Tetrahedral Adaptation of the Hemi-Cube Algorithm; VI.4 Radiosity via Ray Tracing)

Cook, R. L. (1982). "A Reflection Model for Realistic Image Synthesis," Master's Thesis, Cornell University, Ithaca, New York. (V.9 More Shadow Attenuation for Ray Tracing Transparent or Translucent Objects)

Cook, R. L., and Torrance, K. (1982). "A Reflectance Model for Computer Graphics" *ACM Transactions on Graphics* **1**(1), 7–24. (V.9 More Shadow Attenuation for Ray Tracing Transparent or Translucent Objects)

Cowan, William B. (1987). "Colorimetric Properties of Video Monitors," *Notes for OSA Short Course*. (III.7 An Inexpensive Method of Setting the Monitor White Point)

Cowan, William B. (1983). "An Inexpensive Scheme for Calibration of a Colour Monitor in Terms of CIE Standard Coordinates," *Computer Graphics* **17**, 315–321. (III.7 An Inexpensive Method of Setting the Monitor White Point)

Cowan, William B., and Rowell, Nelson (1986). "On the Gun Independence and Phosphor Constancy of Colour Video Monitors," *Color Research and Application* **11**, S34–S38. (III.7 An Inexpensive Method of Setting the Monitor White Point)

Coxeter, H. S. M. (1948). *Convex Polytopes*. Methuen, London. (IV.3 Exact Dihedral Metrics for Common Polyhedra)

de Boor, C. (1987). "*B*-form basics," *Geometric Modeling: Algorithms and New Trends* (G. Farin, ed.). SIAM, 131–148. (IX.1 Least-Squares Approximations to Bézier Curves and Surfaces; IX.2 Beyond Bézier Curves)

de Boor, Carl (1972). "On Calculating with *B*-Splines," *Journal of Approximation Theory* **6**, 50–62. (VIII.4 Geometric Constructions to Interpolate Orientation with Quaternions)

Ditchburn, R. W. (1976). *Light, Third Ed*. Academic Press, London. (V.9 More Shadow Attenuation for Ray Tracing Transparent or Translucent Objects)

Donato, Nola, and Rocchetti, Robert (1988). "Techniques for Manipulating Arbitrary Regions," unpublished. Sun Microsystems, Inc. (I.9 Scanline Coherent Shape Algebra)

Dörre, Heinrich (1965). "The Loxodrome Problem," (76 and 77), *100 Great Problems of Elementary Mathematics* (translated from German). Dover, London. (IX.8 Great Circle Plotting)

Duff, Tom (1984). "Families of Local Matrix Splines," *The Mathematics of Computer Graphics* (SIGGRAPH 1984 Course Notes #15). (IX.3 A Simple Formulation for Curve Interpolation with Variable Control Point Approximation)

Duff, T. (1979). "Smoothly Shaded Renderings of Polyhedral Objects on Raster Displays," *Computer Graphics SIGGRAPH '79 Proc.* **13**(2), 270–275. (IV.9 InterPhong Shading)

Dyer, C. R., Rosenfeld, A., and Samet, H. (1980). "Region Representation: Boundary Codes from Quadtrees," *Comm. ACM* **23**(3), 171–179. (IV.7 Quadtree/Octree-to-Boundary Conversion)

Euclid, *Elements, Book III, Proposition 20.* (VIII.5 A Half-Angle Identity for Digital Computation: The Joys of the Halved Tangent)

Evans, David M. W. (1987). "An Improved Digit-Reversal Permutation Algorithm for the Fast Fourier and Hartley Transforms," *IEEE Trans. ASSP.* (VIII.2 Faster Fourier Transform)

Farin, G. (1988). *Curves and Surfaces for Computer Aided Geometric Design: A Practical Guide.* Academic Press, New York. (IX.1 Least-Squares Approximations to Bézier Curves and Surfaces)

Faux, I. D., and Pratt, M. J. (1979). *Computational Geometry for Design and Manufacture.* Ellis Horwood Ltd., Chichester, England 73. (IV.2 Getting Around on a Sphere)

Floyd, R. W., and Steinberg, L. (1975). "An Adaptive Algorithm for Spatial Gray Scale," *International Symposium Digest of Technical Papers*, Society for Information Displays, 36. (II.2 A Comparison of Digital Halftoning Techniques; II.3 Color Dithering)

Foley, James D., and van Dam, Andries (1982). *Fundamentals of Interactive Computer Graphics.* Addison-Wesley, Reading, MA. (VII.5 Fast Matrix Inversion)

Foley, James D., van Dam, Andries, Feiner, Steven K., and Hughes, John F. (1990). *Computer Graphics Principles and Practice.* Addison Wesley, Reading, MA. (I.9 Scanline Coherent Shape Algebra; II.3 Color Dithering; IV.8 Three-Dimensional Homogeneous Clipping of Triangle Strips; VI.4 Radiosity via Ray Tracing)

Freeman, H. (1974). "Computer Processing of Line-Drawing Images," *ACM Computer Surveys* **6**, 57–97. (IV.7 Quadtree/Octree-to-Boundary Conversion)

Gargantini, I. (1982a). "An Effective Way to Represent Quadtrees," *Comm. ACM* **25**(12), 905–910. (IV.7 Quadtree/Octree-to-Boundary Conversion)

Gargantini, I. (1982b). "Linear Octrees for Fast Processing of Three-Dimensional Objects," *Computer Graphics and Image Processing* **20**(4), 365–374. (IV.7 Quadtree/Octree-to-Boundary Conversion)

Gargantini, I., and Henrici, P. (1972). "Circular Arithmetic and the Determination of Polynomial Zeros," *Numerische Mathematik* **18**, 305–320. (I.6 Appolonius's 10th Problem)

Gervautz, Michael, and Purgathofer, Werner (1990). "A Simple Method for Color Quantization: Octree Quantization," *Graphics Gems* (A. Glassner, ed.). Academic Press, Boston. (III.1 Efficient Inverse Color Map Computation; III.2 Efficient Statistic Computations for Optimal Color Quantization; III.5 Mapping RGB Triples onto 16 Distinct Values)

Gilbert, William J. (1976). *Modern Algebra with Applications*. John Wiley and Sons, New York. (VII.5 Fast Matrix Inversion)

Glassner, Andrew S. (1990a). "Useful Trigonometry," *Graphics Gems* (A. Glassner, ed.). Academic Press, Boston, 13–17. (VIII.5 A Half-Angle Identity for Digital Computation: The Joys of the Halved Tangent)

Glassner, Andrew S. (1990b). "Useful 2D Geometry," *Graphics Gems* (Andrew S. Glassner, ed.). Academic Press, Boston, 3–11. (I.6 Appolonius's 10th Problem)

Glassner, A. S., *et al.* (1989). *An Introduction to Ray Tracing*. Academic Press, London, 92–93. (V.2 Intercepting a Ray with an Elliptical Torus); 121–160 (V.9 More Shadow Attenuation for Ray Tracing Transparent or Translucent Objects)

Goldman, Ronald (1990a). "Matrices and Transformations," *Graphics Gems* (Andrew S. Glassner, ed.). Academic Press, Boston. (VII.2 Recovering the Data from the Transformation Matrix; VII.3 Transformations as Exponentials)

Goldman, Ronald (1990b). "Triangles," *Graphics Gems* (Andrew S. Glassner, ed.). Academic Press, Boston, 20–23. (I.1 The Area of a Simple Polygon)

Goldsmith, Jeffrey, and Salmon, John (1987). "Automatic Creation of Object Hierarchies for Ray Tracing," *IEEE Computer Graphics and Applications* **7**(5), 14–20. (V.5 Efficiency Improvements for Hierarchy Traversal in Ray Tracing)

Gonzalez, Rafael C., and Wintz, Paul (1987). *Digital Image Processing, Second Edition*. Addison-Wesley, Reading, MA. (II.1 Image Smoothing and Sharpening by Discrete Convolution)

Goral, Cindy M., Torrance, Kenneth E., Greenberg, Donald P., and Battaile, Bennett (1984). "Modeling the Interaction of Light Between Diffuse Surfaces," *Computer Graphics (SIGGRAPH '84 Proceedings)* **18**(3), 213–222. (VI.1 Implementing Progressive Radiosity with User-Provided Polygon Display Routines; VI.4 Radiosity via Ray Tracing)

Gosling, James (1986). "Curves Made Trivial," unpublished. (I.9 Scanline Coherent Shape Algebra)

Gouraud, H. (1971). "Continuous Shading of Curved Surfaces," *IEEE Transactions on Computers* **C-20**(6), 623–629. (IV.9 InterPhong Shading; VI.1 Implementing Progressive Radiosity with User-Provided Polygon Display Routines)

Graham, R. L. (1972). "An Efficient Algorithm for Determining the Convex Hull of a Planar Set," *Information Processing Letters* **1**, 132–133. (VIII.7 Fast Approximation to the Arctangent)

Grassmann, E., and Rokne, J. (1979). "The Range of Values of a Circular Complex Polynomial over a Circular Complex Interval," *Computing* **23**, 139–169. (I.4 An Easy Bounding Circle)

Gubareff, G., Janssen, J., and Torborg, R. (1960). *Thermal Radiation Properties Survey: A Review of the Literature*. Honeywell Research Center, Minneapolis. (V.8 A Body Color Model: Absorption of Light through Translucent Media)

Guibas, Leo, and Stolfi, Jorge (1982). "A Language for Bitmap Manipulation," *ACM Transactions on Graphics* **1**(3), 191–214. (VIII.5 A Half-Angle Identity for Digital Computation: The Joys of the Halved Tangent)

Haines, Eric A., and Greenberg, Donald P. (1986). "The Light Buffer: A Ray Tracer Shadow Testing Accelerator," *IEEE Computer Graphics and Applications* **6**(9), 6–16. (V.5 Efficiency Improvements for Hierarchy Traversal in Ray Tracing; V.6 A Recursive Shadow Voxel Cache for Ray Tracing)

Hall, E. L., *et al.* (1971). "A Survey of Preprocessing and Feature Extraction Techniques for Radiographic Images," *IEEE Trans. Comp.* **20**(9), 1033. (II.9 Image File Compression Made Easy)

Hall, R. (1990). *Illumination and Color in Computer Generated Imagery*. Springer-Verlag, New York. (II.3 Color Dithering; III.6 Television Color Encoding and "Hot" Broadcast Colors)

Hall, R. (1986). "A Characterization of Illumination Models and Shading Techniques," *The Visual Computer* **2**(5), 268–277. (IV.9 InterPhong Shading)

Hall, R. A. (1983). "A Methodology for Realistic Image Synthesis," Master's Thesis, Cornell University, Ithaca, New York. (V.8 A Body Color Model: Absorption of Light through Translucent Media; V.9 More Shadow Attenuation for Ray Tracing Transparent or Translucent Objects)

Hall, R. A., and Greenberg, D. P. (1983). "A Testbed for Realistic Image Synthesis," *IEEE Computer Graphics and Applications* **3**(10), 10–20. (V.8 A Body Color Model: Absorption of Light through Translucent Media; V.9 More Shadow Attenuation for Ray Tracing Transparent or Translucent Objects)

Hanrahan, P. (1982). "Creating Volume Models From Edge–Vertex Graphs," *SIGGRAPH '82*, 77–84. (IV.6 Maintaining Winged–Edge Models)

Hawley, Stephen (1990). "Ordered Dithering," *Graphics Gems* (Andrew S. Glassner, ed.). Academic Press, Boston, 176–178. (II.2 A Comparison of Digital Halftoning Techniques; II.3 Color Dithering)

Heckbert, Paul S. (1990). "Adaptive Radiosity Textures for Bidirectional Ray Tracing," *Computer Graphics* SIGGRAPH '90 Proceedings **24**(4), 145–154. (III.5 Detection of Shadow Boundaries for Adaptive Meshing in Radiosity)

Heckbert, P. (1982). "Color Image Quantization for Frame Buffer Display," *Computer Graphics* **16**(3), 297–307. (III.1 Efficient Inverse Color Map Computation; III.2 Efficient Statistic Computations for Optimal Color Quantization)

Hong, M. T., Magnenat Thalmann, N., and Thalmann, D. (1988). "A General Algorithm For 3D Shape Interpolation in a Facet-Based Representation," *Graphics Interface Proc. '88*, Edmonton, Canada. (IV.9 InterPhong Shading)

REFERENCES

Jarvis, J. F., Judice, N., and Ninke, N. H. (1976). "A Survey of Techniques for the Display of Continuous Tone Pictures on Bilevel Displays," *Computer Graphics and Image Processing* **5**(1), 13–40. (II.2 A Comparison of Digital Halftoning Techniques)

Jenkins, F., and White, H. (1937). *Fundamentals of Physical Optics*. McGraw-Hill, New York. (V.8 A Body Color Model: Absorption of Light through Translucent Media; V.9 More Shadow Attenuation for Ray Tracing Transparent or Translucent Objects)

Johnson, N. W. (1966). "Convex Polyhedra with Regular Faces," *Canadian Journal of Mathematics* **18**(1), 169–200. (IV.3 Exact Dihedral Metrics for Common Polyhedra)

Kailath, Thomas (1980). *Linear Systems*. Prentice-Hall, Englewood Cliffs, NJ. (VII.5 Fast Matrix Inversion)

Kay, D. S., and Greenberg, D. P. (1979). "Transparency for Computer Synthesized Images," *ACM Computer Graphics (SIGGRAPH '79)* **13**(2), 158–164. (V.8 A Body Color Model: Absorption of Light through Translucent Media)

Kay, Timothy L., and Kajiya, James T. (1986). "Ray Tracing Complex Scenes," *Computer Graphics* **20**(4), 269–278. (V.1 Fast Ray–Convex Polyhedron Intersection; V.5 Efficiency Improvements for Hierarchy Traversal in Ray Tracing)

Kirk, David, and Arvo, James (1988). "The Ray Tracing Kernel," *Proceedings of Ausgraph 88, Melbourne, Australia*. (V.4 Improved Ray Tagging for Voxel-Based Ray Tracing)

Kochanek, Doris, and Bartels, Richard H. (1984). "Interpolating Splines with Local Tension, Continuity, and Bias Control," *Computer Graphics* **18**(3), 33–41. (IX.3 A Simple Formulation for Curve Interpolation with Variable Control Point Approximation)

Lasseter, John (1987). "Principles of Traditional Animation Applied to 3D Computer Animation," *Computer Graphics* **21**(4), 35–44. (IX.3 A Simple Formulation for Curve Interpolation with Variable Control Point Approximation)

Lawson, C. L., and Hanson, R. J. (1974). *Solving Least Squares Problems (Prentice-Hall Series in Automatic Computation)*. Prentice-Hall. (IX.1 Least-Squares Approximations to Bézier Curves and Surfaces)

Lee, D. T., and Preparata, Franco (1984). "Computational Geometry—A Survey," *IEEE Transactions on Computers* **C-33**(12), 1072–1101. (VIII.7 Fast Approximation to the Arctangent)

Lee, M. E. (1986). "Development of a Ray Tracing Model for Realistic Image Synthesis," Master's Thesis, University of Tulsa, Tulsa, Oklahoma. (V.9 More Shadow Attenuation for Ray Tracing Transparent or Translucent Objects)

Lee, M. E., Redner, R. A., and Uselton, S. P. (1985). "Statistically Optimized Sampling for Distributed Ray Tracing," *Computer Graphics* **19**(3), 61–67. (V.9 More Shadow Attenuation for Ray Tracing Transparent or Translucent Objects)

Linsternik, L. A. (1963). *Convex Figures and Polyhedra* (translated from Russian). Dover, New York. (IV.3 Exact Dihedral Metrics for Common Polyhedra)

Liu, C. L. (1968). *Introduction to Combinatorial Mathematics*. McGraw-Hill, New York. (III.2 Efficient Statistic Computations for Optimal Color Quantization)

Loop, Charles, and DeRose, Tony (1990). "Generalized B-Spline Surfaces of Arbitrary Topology," *ACM, SIGGRAPH '90* **24**(4), 347–356. (IX.2 Beyond Bézier Curves)

Loop, Charles, and DeRose, Tony (1989). "A Multisided Generalization of Bézier Surfaces," *ACM Transactions on Graphics* **8**(3), 204–234. (IX.2 Beyond Bézier Curves)

Lorig, G. (1986). *Advanced Image Synthesis: Shading* (G. Enderle, M. Grave, and F. Lillegen, eds.). Springer-Verlag. (IV.9 InterPhong Shading)

Lucassen, Marcel P., and Walraven, Jan (1990). "Evaluation of a Simple Method for Color Monitor Recalibration," *Color Research and Application* **15**, 321–326. (III.7 An Inexpensive Method of Setting the Monitor White Point)

Magnenat Thalmann, N., and Thalmann, D. (1987a). *Image Synthesis: Theory and Practice*, Springer–Verlag, Tokyo. (IV.9 InterPhong Shading)

Magnenat Thalmann, N., and Thalmann, D. (1987b). "The Direction of Synthetic Actors in the Film *Rendez-Vous à Montréal*," *IEEE Computer Graphics and Application* **7**(12), 9–19. (IV.9 InterPhong Shading)

Maillot, Patrick-Gilles (1986). "Contribution à l'Étude des Systèmes Graphiques: Architectures Logicielle et Matérielle," Ph.D. Thesis, University Claude Bernard, Lyon I, Lyon, France. (IV.8 Three-Dimensional Homogeneous Clipping of Triangle Strips)

Maling, D. H. (1973). *Coordinate Systems and Map Projections*, London, George Philip and Son, (Describing the Equidistant Cylindrical Plate Carrée of Anaximander, *circa* 550 B.C.) (IX.8 Great Circle Plotting)

Malley, Thomas J. V. (1988). "A Shading Method for Computer Generated Images," Master's Thesis, University of Utah. (VI.4 Radiosity via Ray Tracing)

Meyer, Gary W. (1990). "The Importance of Gun Balancing in Monitor Calibration," *Perceiving, Measuring, and Using Color* (Michael H. Brill, ed.). *Proc. SPIE* **1250**, 69–79. (III.7 An Inexpensive Method of Setting the Monitor White Point)

Meyer, Gary W. (1986). "Color Calculations for and Perceptual Assessment of Computer Graphic Images," Ph.D. dissertation, Cornell University. (III.7 An Inexpensive Method of Setting the Monitor White Point)

Meyer, Gary W., and Greenberg, Donald P. (1987). "Perceptual Color Spaces for Computer Graphics," *Color and the Computer* (H. John Durett, ed.). Academic Press, Boston, 83–100. (III.7 An Inexpensive Method of Setting the Monitor White Point)

Montani, C. (1984). "Region Representation: Parallel Connected Stripes," *Computer Vision, Graphics and Image Processing* **28**, 139–165. (IV.7 Quadtree/Octree-to-Boundary Conversion)

Morton, M. (1990). "A Digital 'Dissolve' Effect," *Graphics Gems* (A. Glassner, ed.). Academic Press, Boston. (III.1 Efficient Inverse Color Map Computation)

Newman, William M., and Sproull, Robert F. (1979). *Principles of Interactive Computer Graphics*. McGraw-Hill, New York. (VII.5 Fast Matrix Inversion; VIII.5 A Half-Angle Identity for Digital Computation: The Joys of the Halved Tangent)

Paeth, Alan W. (1990a). "A Fast Algorithm for General Raster Rotation," *Graphics Gems* (A. Glassner, ed.). Academic Press, Boston, 189. (VIII.3 Of Integers, Fields, and Bit Counting; VIII.5 A Half-Angle Identity for Digital Computation: The Joys of the Halved Tangent)

Paeth, Alan W. (1990b). "A Fast Approximation to the Hypotenuse," *Graphics Gems* (Andrew S. Glassner, ed.). Academic Press, Boston, 427–431. (III.6 Television Color Encoding and "Hot" Broadcast Colors)

Paeth, Alan W. (1990c). "Circles of Integral Radius on Integer Lattices," *Graphics Gems* (A. Glassner, ed.). Academic Press, Boston, 57–60. (VIII.5 A Half-Angle Identity for Digital Computation: The Joys of the Halved Tangent)

Paeth, Alan W. (1990d). "Digital Cartography for Computer Graphics," *Graphics Gems* (A. Glassner, ed.). Academic Press, Boston, 307–320. (VIII.5 A Half-Angle Identity for Digital Computation: The Joys of the Halved Tangent; IX.8 Great Circle Plotting)

Paeth, Alan W. (1990e). "Mapping RGB Triples onto Four Bits," *Graphics Gems* (A. Glassner, ed.). Academic Press, Boston, 233–245. (III.5 Mapping RGB Triples onto 16 Distinct Values; IV.3 Exact Dihedral Metrics for Common Polyhedra)

Paeth, Alan W. (1990f). "Proper Treatment of Pixels as Integers," *Graphics Gems* (A. Glassner, ed.). Academic Press, Boston, 249–256. (III.5 Mapping RGB Triples onto 16 Distinct Values)

Paeth, Alan W. (1990g). "Trigonometric Functions at Select Points," *Graphics Gems* (A. Glassner, ed.). Academic Press, Boston, 18–19. (IV.3 Exact Dihedral Metrics for Common Polyhedra; IX.8 Great Circle Plotting)

Paeth, A. W. (1987). *The IM Raster Toolkit—Design, Implementation and Use*. Institute for Computer Research Report UW/ICR 87-03. (II.9 Image File Compression Made Easy)

Paeth, A. W. (1986). *The IM Raster Toolkit—Design, Implementation and Use*. University of Waterloo, Technical Report CS-86-65. (II.9 Image File Compression Made Easy)

Papoulis, Athanasios (1965). *Probability, Random Variables, and Stochastic Processes*. McGraw-Hill, 195. (II.11 Noise Thresholding in Edge Images)

Peano, G. (1980). *Selected Works of Guiseppe Peano*. Allen and Unwin, Winchester, MA. (I.7 A Peano Curve Generation Algorithm)

Pearce, A. (1990). "Shadow Attenuation for Ray Tracing Transparent Objects," *Graphics Gems*. Academic Press, Boston, 397–399. (V.9 More Shadow Attenuation for Ray Tracing Transparent or Translucent Objects)

Pearce, A. (1987). "An Implementation of Ray Tracing Using Multiprocessing and Spatial Subdivision," Master's Thesis, University of Calgary, Dept. of Computer Science. (V.7 Avoiding Incorrect Shadow Intersections for Ray Tracing)

Perlin, K. (1985). "An Image Synthesizer," *Computer Graphics* 19(3), pp. 287–296. (VIII.10 A Recursive Implementation of the Perlin Noise Function)

Phong, Bui-Tuong (1975). "Illumination for Computer-Generated Pictures," *Comm. ACM* 18(6), 311–317. (IV.9 InterPhong Shading)

Polya, George (1962). *Mathematical Discovery*. John Wiley and Sons, 104–105. (VIII.5 A Half-Angle Identity for Digital Computation: The Joys of the Halved Tangent)

Post, David L., and Calhoun, Christopher S. (1989). "An Evaluation of Methods for Producing Desired Colors on CRT Monitors," *Color Research and Application* **14**, 172–186. (III.7 An Inexpensive Method of Setting the Monitor White Point)

Pratt, William K. (1978). *Digital Image Processing*. John Wiley and Sons, New York, NY. (II.1 Image Smoothing and Sharpening by Discrete Convolution)

Preparata, F. P., and Shamos, M. I. (1985). *Computational Geometry*. Springer-Verlag, New York. (III.1 Efficient Inverse Color Map Computation)

Press, William H., Flannery, Brian P., Teukolsky, Saul A., and Vetterling, William T. (1988). *Numerical Recipes in C*. Cambridge University Press, Cambridge, England. (VII.5 Fast Matrix Inversion; VIII.2 Faster Fourier Transform)

Purdue University (1970a). *Thermophysical Properties of Matter, Vol. 7: Thermal Radiative Properties of Metals*. Plenum, New York. (V.8 A Body Color Model: Absorption of Light through Translucent Media)

Purdue University (1970b). *Thermophysical Properties of Matter, Vol. 8: Thermal Radiative Properties of Nonmetallic Solids*. Plenum, New York. (V.8 A Body Color Model: Absorption of Light through Translucent Media)

Purdue University (1970c). *Thermophysical Properties of Matter, Vol. 9: Thermal Radiative Properties of Coatings*. Plenum, New York. (V.8 A Body Color Model: Absorption of Light through Translucent Media)

Rademacher, H., and Toeplitz, O. (1957). *The Enjoyment of Mathematics*. Princeton University Press, Princeton, NJ. (I.4 An Easy Bounding Circle)

Ramshaw, Lyle (1978). "On the Gap Structure of Sequences of Points on a Circle," *Proceedings of the Koninklijke Nederlandse Akademie van Wetenschappen, Amsterdam, Series A* **81**(4), 527–541. (VIII.9 Interval Sampling)

Ritter, Jack (1990). "An Efficient Bounding Sphere," *Graphics Gems* (Andrew S. Glassner, ed.). Academic Press, Boston, 301–303. (I.4 An Easy Bounding Circle)

Rogers, D. F. (1985). *Procedural Elements for Computer Graphics*, McGraw-Hill, New York. (IV.9 InterPhong Shading)

Roth, Scott D. (1982). "Ray Casting for Modeling Solids," *Computer Graphics and Image Processing* **18**(2), 109–144. (V.1 Fast Ray–Convex Polyhedron Intersection)

Rubin, Steven M., and Whitted, Turner (1980). "A 3-Dimensional Representation for Fast Rendering of Complex Scenes," *Computer Graphics (SIGGRAPH '80 Proceedings)* **14**(3), 110–116. (V.5 Efficiency Improvements for Hierarchy Traversal in Ray Tracing)

Samet, Hanan (1990b). *Applications of Spatial Data Structures*, ISBN 0-201-50300-X. Addison-Wesley, Reading, MA. (I.9 Scanline Coherent Shape Algebra; IV.7 Quadtree/Octree-to-Boundary Conversion)

Samet, Hanan (1990a). *The Design and Analysis of Spatial Data Structures*. ISBN 0-201-50255-0. Addison-Wesley, Reading, MA. (I.9 Scanline Coherent Shape Algebra)

Samet, H., and Webber, R. E. (1988). "Hierarchical Data Structures and Algorithms for Computer Graphics—Part I: Fundamentals," *IEEE Computer Graphics and Applications*, 48–68. (IV.7 Quadtree/Octree-to-Boundary Conversion)

Samet, H. (1982). "Neighbor Finding in Images Represented by Quadtrees," *Computer Graphics and Image Processing* **19**, 37–57. (IV.7 Quadtree/Octree-to-Boundary Conversion)

Schumacher, D. (1990). "Useful 1-to-1 Pixel Transforms," *Graphics Gems* (A. Glassner, ed.). Academic Press, Boston. (II.3 Color Dithering)

Shoemake, Ken (1990). "Bit Patterns for Encoding Angles," *Graphics Gems* (A. Glassner, ed.). Academic Press, Boston, 442. (VIII.5 A Half-Angle Identity for Digital Computation: The Joys of the Halved Tangent)

Shoemake, Ken (1985). "Animating Rotation with Quaternion Curves," *Computer Graphics* **19**(3), 245–254. (VII.6 Quaternions and 4×4 Matrices; VIII.4 Using Geometric Constructions to Interpolate Orientation with Quaternions)

Shoemake, Ken (1989). "Quaternion Calculus for Animation," *SIGGRAPH Course Notes*, **23**, Math for SIGGRAPH. (VII.6 Quaternions and 4×4 Matrices)

Siegel, Robert, and Howell, John R. (1981). *Thermal Radiation Heat Transfer*. McGraw-Hill, New York. (VI.4 Radiosity via Ray Tracing)

Sillion, François, and Puech, Claude (1989). "A General Two-Pass Method Integrating Specular and Diffuse Reflection," *Computer Graphics ACM, SIGGRAPH '89 Proceedings* **23**(3), 335–344. (VI.4 Radiosity via Ray Tracing)

SMPTE* (1990b). "Proposed American National Standard—Three-Channel Parallel Component Analog Video Interface," *SMPTE Journal* **253**, 699–702. (III.6 Television Color Encoding and "Hot" Broadcast Colors)

SMPTE (1988). "SMPTE Standard: Signal Parameters—1125/60 High-Definition Production System," *SMPTE*. Also SMPTE (1990a). *SMPTE Journal* **240M**, 723–725. (III.6 Television Color Encoding and "Hot" Broadcast Colors)

SMPTE (1987). "SMPTE Recommended Practice: Color Monitor Colorimetry," *SMPTE* **RP-145**. (III.6 Television Color Encoding and "Hot" Broadcast Colors)

SMPTE (1984). "SMPTE Recommended Practice: Bit-Parallel Digital Interface for Component Video Signals," *SMPTE* **RP-125**. (III.6 Television Color Encoding and "Hot" Broadcast Colors)

*SMPTE document note: The SMPTE is the Society for Motion Picture and Television Engineers. It publishes a series of *Standards, Recommended Practices, and Guidelines* covering various topics in television and film engineering. Individual copies of these documents may be obtained from SMPTE headquarters at 595 West Hartsdale Avenue, White Plains, NH 10607. These documents also are published in the *SMPTE Journal*, and copies of this may be easier to find in a library. The data of appearances in the *Journal* is noted if known. In addition, unapproved standards are published in the *Journal* for comment.

SMPTE (1977). "SMPTE Recommended Practice: Setting Chromaticity and Luminance of White for Color Television Monitors Using Shadow–Mask Picture Tubes," *SMPTE* **RP-71**. (III.7 An Inexpensive Method of Setting the Monitor White Point)

SMPTE (1969). "SMPTE Recommended Practice: Color Temperature for Color Television Studio Monitors," *SMPTE* **RP-37**. (III.6 Television Color Encoding and "Hot" Broadcast Colors)

Sparrow, E., and Cess, R. (1970). *Radiation Heat Transfer*. Brooks/Cole, Belmont, CA, 63–64. (V.9 More Shadow Attenuation for Ray Tracing Transparent or Translucent Objects)

Steiner, Jakob (1971). *Jakob Steiner's Gesammelte Werke*. Chelsea, Bronx, NY. (III.5 Mapping RGB Triples onto 16 Distinct Values)

Steinhart, Jonathan E. *et al.* (1990). Introduction To Window Management, SIGGRAPH '90, Course #11 Notes. (I.9 Scanline Coherent Shape Algebra)

Steinhart, Jonathan E. *et al.* (1989). Introduction To Window Management, SIGGRAPH '90, Course #11 Notes. (I.9 Scanline Coherent Shape Algebra)

Stevens, R. J., Lehar, A. F., and Preston, F. H. (1983). "Manipulation and Presentation of Multidimensional Image Data Using the Peano Scan," *IEEE Transactions on Pattern Analysis and Machine Intelligence*, **PAMI-5**(5), 520–526. (I.7 A Peano Curve Generation Algorithm)

Stone, Maureen C., Cowan, William B., and Beatty, John C. (1988). "Color Gamut Mapping and the Printing of Digital Color Images," *ACM Transactions on Graphics* **7**(4), 249–292. (III.8 Some Tips for Making Color Hardcopy)

Stone, M. G. (1986). "A Mnemonic for the Area of Polygons," *Amer. Math. Monthly* **93**, 479–480. (I.1 The Area of a Simple Polygon)

Stucki, P. (1981). "MECCA—a multiple-error correcting computation algorithm for bilevel image hardcopy reproduction," *Research Report RZ1060*, IBM Research Laboratory, Zurich, Switzerland. (II.2 A Comparison of Digital Halftoning Techniques)

Sutherland, I. E., and Hodgman, G. W. (1974). "Reentrant Polygon Clipping," *CACM* **17**(1), 32–42. (IV.8 Three-Dimensional Homogeneous Clipping of Triangle Strips)

Thompson, Kevin (1990). "Area of Intersection: Two Circles," *Graphics Gems* (Andrew S. Glassner, ed.). Academic Press, Boston, 43–46. (I.5 The Smallest Circle Containing the Intersection of Two Circles)

Thompson, Kelvin (1990). "Fast Matrix Multiplication," *Graphics Gems* (Andrew S. Glassner, ed.). Academic Press, Boston, 460–461. (VII.5 Fast Matrix Inversion)

Turkowski, Ken (1990). "Fixed-Point Trigonometry with Cordic Iterations," *Graphics Gems* (A. Glassner, ed.). Academic Press, Boston, 494–497. (VIII.5 A Half-Angle Identity for Digital Computation: The Joys of the Halved Tangent)

Turkowski, Ken (1990). "Properties of Surface-Normal Transformations," *Graphics Gems* (Andrew S. Glassner, ed.). Academic Press, Boston, 539–547. (VII.5 Fast Matrix Inversion)

Ulichney, R. (1988). *Digital Halftoning*. MIT Press, Cambridge, MA. (II.3 Color Dithering)

Wallace, John R., Elmquist, Kells A., and Haines, Eric A. (1989). "A Ray Tracing Algorithm For Progressive Radiosity," *Computer Graphics (SIGGRAPH '89 Proceedings)* **23**(3), 335–344. (VI.1 Implementing Progressive Radiosity with User-Provided Polygon Display Routines; VI.4 Radiosity via Ray Tracing; VI.5 Detection of Shadow Boundaries for Adaptive Meshing in Radiosity)

Wan, S., Wong, S., and Prusinkiewicz, P. (1968). "An Algorithm for Multidimensional Data Clustering," *ACM Trans. on Math. Software* **14**(2), 153–162. (III.2 Efficient Statistic Computations for Optimal Color Quantization)

Watson, Andrew B., Nielson, Kenneth R. K., Poirson, Allen, Fizthugh, Andrew, Bilson, Amjyo, Nguyen, Khan, and Ahmuda, Albert J. Jr. (1986). "Use of a Raster Frame Buffer in Vision Research," *Journal of Behavior Research Methods, Instruments, and Computers* **18**(6), 587–594. (III.8 Some Tips for Making Color Hardcopy)

Weghorst, Hank, Hooper, Gary, and Greenberg, Donald P. (1984). "Improved Computational Methods for Ray Tracing," *ACM Transactions on Graphics* **3**(1), 52–69. (V.5 Efficiency Improvements for Hierarchy Traversal in Ray Tracing)

Welch, Terry A. (1984). "A Technique for High-Performance Data Compression," *IEEE Computer* **6**(17), 8–20. (II.9 Image File Compression Made Easy)

Whitted, Turner (1980). "An Improved Illumination Model for Shaded Display," *Comm. ACM,* **23**(6), p. 343–349. (V. Introduction: Ray Tracing)

Whitten, I. H., and Neal, R. M. (1982). "Using Peano Curves for Bilevel Display of Continuous-Tone Images," *IEEE Computer Graphics and Applications,* **82**(3), 47–52. (I.7 A Peano Curve Generation Algorithm)

Wiebelt, J. A. (1966). *Engineering Radiation Heat Transfer.* Holt, Rinehart and Winston, New York, 19–22. (V.9 More Shadow Attenuation for Ray Tracing Transparent or Translucent Objects)

Winkler, Dean M. (1990). "Video Technology for Computer Graphics," Course Notes #22 at *SIGGRAPH '90.* (III.6 Television Color Encoding and "Hot" Broadcast Colors)

Wu, X., and Witten, I. (1985). "A Fast *k*-Means Type Clustering Algorithm," *Research Report No. 85/197/10,* Dept. of Computer Science, Univ. of Calgary. (III.2 Efficient Statistic Computations for Optimal Color Quantization)

Zavada, Roland J. (1988). "Challenges to the Development of a Standardized Professional Studio Color-Picture Monitor," *SMPTE Journal,* 703–710. (III.6 Television Color Encoding and "Hot" Broadcast Colors)

INDEX

GRAPHICS GEMS II

Cover
and interior
designed by Camille
Pecoul. Chapter opening graphics
drawn by Andrew S. Glassner. Composed
by Science Typographers Incorporated in Century
Schoolbook, Tegra Humanist 521. Printed
and bound by the Maple Vail
Book Manufacturing
Group.